Baedeker's
AUSTRIA

Cover picture: Ebensee, on the Traunsee

158 colour photographs
56 maps and plans
1 large road map

Text:
Rosemarie Arnold (History)
Walter R. Arnold (Music)
Prof. Dr Hans Bobek (Geography, etc.)
Rolf Lohberg (Austria from A to Z)
Gerald Sawade (Climate)
Christine Wessely (Art)

Editorial work and further material:
Baedeker Stuttgart
English language: Alec Court

Cartography:
Ingenieurbüro für Kartographie
Huber & Oberländer, Munich

Design and layout:
H. F. Ottman,
Atelier für Buchgestaltung und Grafik-Design,
Leonberg

Conception and general direction:
Dr Peter Baumgarten,
Baedeker Stuttgart

3rd Edition

English translation:
James Hogarth

© Baedeker Stuttgart
Original German edition

© Prentice-Hall Inc.
US & Canada

© The Automobile Association 57299
United Kingdom and Ireland

© Jarrold and Sons Ltd
English language edition worldwide

Licensed user:
Mairs Geographischer Verlag GmbH & Co.,
Ostfildern-Kemnat bei Stuttgart

Reproductions:
Gölz Repro-Service GmbH,
Ludwigsburg

The name *Baedeker* is a registered trademark. In a time of rapid change it is difficult to ensure that all the information given is entirely accurate and up to date, and the possibility of error can never be entirely eliminated. Although the publishers can accept no responsibility for inaccuracies and omissions, they are always grateful for corrections and suggestions for improvement.

Printed in Italy By Sagdos, Milan

ISBN 0 86145 146 5 UK
    0-13-056127-4 US & Canada
    3-87504-202-6 Germany

Source of illustrations:

Most of the illustrations were provided by the Austrian National Tourist Office in Vienna or by local, municipal, regional and provincial tourist information offices, etc., throughout Austria.

Others:
Hans Baedeker (p. 136; p. 143; p. 226)
Allianz-Archiv (p. 256)
Zentrale Farbbild Agentur GmbH, Düsseldorf (p. 257)

How to Use this Guide

The principal towns and areas of tourist interest are described in alphabetical order. The names of other places referred to under these general headings can be found in the very full Index.

Following the tradition established by Karl Baedeker in 1844, sights of particular interest and hotels and restaurants of particular quality are distinguished by either one or two asterisks.

In the lists of hotels b. = beds, SB = indoor swimming bath and SP = outdoor swimming pool. Where the word "inn" appears in brackets after the name of a mountain hut this means that food and drink are available, though not necessarily all the normal amenities of an inn.

The symbol ⓘ at the beginning of an entry or on a town plan indicates the local tourist office or other organisation from which further information can be obtained. The post-horn symbol on a town plan indicates a post office.

Only a selection of hotels and restaurants can be given: no reflection is implied, therefore, on establishments not included.

A Glossary of common German topographical terms and elements in place-names is given on pp. 264–66.

This guidebook forms part of a completely new series of the world-famous Baedeker Guides to Europe.

The English editions are now published for the first time in this country. Each volume is the result of long and careful preparation and, true to the traditions of Baedeker, is designed in every respect to meet the needs and expectations of the modern traveller and holiday-maker.

The name of Baedeker has long been identified in the field of guidebooks with reliable, comprehensive and up-to-date information, prepared by expert writers who work from detailed, first-hand knowledge of the country concerned. Following a tradition that goes back over 150 years to the date when Karl Baedeker published the first of his handbooks for travellers, these guides have been planned to give the tourist all the essential information about the country and its inhabitants: where to go, how to get there and what to see. Baedeker's account of a country was always based on his personal observation and experience during his travels in that country. This tradition of writing a guidebook in the field rather than at an office desk has been maintained by Baedeker ever since.

Lavishly illustrated with superb colour photographs and numerous specially drawn maps and street plans of the major towns, the new Baedeker-AA Guides concentrate on making available to the modern traveller all the information he needs in a format that is both attractive and easy to follow. For every place that appears in the gazetteer, the principal features of architectural, artistic and historic interest are described, as are the main scenic beauty-spots in the locality. Selected hotels and restaurants are also included. Features of exceptional merit are indicated by either one or two asterisks.

A special section at the end of each book contains practical information to ensure a pleasant and safe journey, details of leisure activities and useful addresses. The separate road map will prove an invaluable aid to planning your route and your travel within the country.

Contents

Introduction
to Austria

Land (Province)	Area in sq. km (sq. miles)	Population 1981	1984	Capital
Burgenland	3,966 (1,531)	270,100	268,100	Eisenstadt
Kärnten (Carinthia)	9,533 (3,681)	537,100	538,900	Klagenfurt
Niederösterreich (Lower Austria)	19,171 (7,402)	1,431,400	1,422,000	St Pölten
Oberösterreich (Upper Austria)	11,979 (4,625)	1,276,800	1,280,000	Linz
Salzburg	7,154 (2,762)	447,000	452,700	Salzburg
Steiermark (Styria)	16,387 (6,327)	1,188,900	1,183,300	Graz
Tirol	12,647 (4,883)	591,100	597,900	Innsbruck
Vorarlberg	2,601 (1,004)	307,200	307,900	Bregenz
Wien (Vienna)	415 (160)	1,524,500	1,501,700	Vienna
Republik Österreich (Republic of Austria)	88,853 (34,306)	7,574,100	7,552,600	Vienna

The **Republic of Austria** (Republik Österreich) is one of the smaller European states, lying between Portugal and Ireland in terms of area and between Sweden and Switzerland in terms of population. The population of Austria has a density of just over 90 to the sq. kilometre (233 to the sq. mile): a low figure which reflects the predominantly mountainous character of the country and its situation off the main axes along which the great concentrations of population in Europe have developed.

98% of the population is of Germanic stock, the remainder being made up of small Croat, Magyar, Slovene and Czech minorities. Almost 85% profess the Roman Catholic faith; some 6% are Protestants, concentrated mainly in Burgenland and Carinthia; while other religious minorities (including some 7000 Jews) are found mainly in the large towns.

In spite of its strictly maintained political neutrality Austria unequivocally belongs, socially and economically, to the Western world. A federal republic based on Parliamentary and demo-cratic principles, it is divided into nine **federal provinces** (Bundesländer), each electing its own provincial assembly (Landtag) and head of government (Landeshauptmann); Vienna, capital of the Republic and itself a province, has a Municipal Council which is also the provincial assembly and a Mayor (Bürgermeister) who acts also as Landeshauptmann and is chairman of the city's executive, the Municipal Senate (Stadtsenat).

The Austrian Federal Assembly or Parliament (Bundesversammlung) consists of two houses, the Federal Council (Bundesrat), the members of which are appointed by the provincial assemblies and the Vienna municipal council, and the National Council (Nationalrat), which is elected by the population as a whole.

The head of state is the directly elected Federal President (Bundespräsident), who appoints the federal government, presided over by the Federal Chancellor (Bundeskanzler).

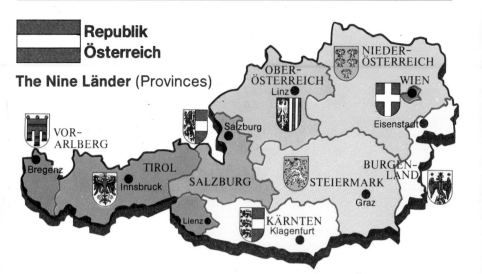

Republik Österreich

The Nine Länder (Provinces)

VOR-ARLBERG
Bregenz
TIROL
Innsbruck
SALZBURG
Salzburg
OBER-ÖSTERREICH
Linz
NIEDER-ÖSTERREICH
WIEN
Eisenstadt
BURGEN-LAND
STEIERMARK
Graz
Lienz
KÄRNTEN
Klagenfurt

Austria is one of the most popular holiday and tourist countries in Europe, drawing large numbers of visitors not only in summer and in winter – which in the mountain regions is almost as busy a season as summer – but also in the in-between seasons. For most visitors, perhaps, the attraction of Austria lies in the beauty of its mountains and its countryside; but its towns and cities have also much to offer, and two of them – the historic capital of Vienna, with its treasures of art and architecture, and the fascinating town of Salzburg – rank among the great tourist areas of the world.

Austria is an integral part of Central Europe – however one may choose to define that term – and down the centuries, in different circumstances and different contexts, it has played an important role within Central Europe and at times far beyond it. This has given its people and its whole cultural pattern a particular stamp which differentiates them from the rest of the German-speaking world. Central to this development has been Austria's situation in an area of transition between the "Atlantic" and "Danubian" territories of Central Europe – though in the course of the country's thousand years of history its relative situation has more than once been fundamentally changed. From a frontier region on the south-eastern fringes of the West in its early days it became a central component in the Habsburg empire, and in the divided Europe of our day is now once again a frontier territory.

The ORIGINS of Austria lay in the narrow funnel-shaped Danube corridor, at the point where it opens

out into the Vienna basin, the prelude to the great Pannonian and Carpathian plain and an area of major European significance, situated at the meeting-place of important traffic routes. The territory, established as a defensive Eastern March against the restless Hungarians and first referred to as "Ostarrîchi" in 996, was soon extended by the Babenbergs to include the greater part of the Vienna basin, reaching as far as the Leitha-March-Thaya line (1043). From this position, constantly disputed by the neighbouring peoples but with some extension to the W, further expansion at first took place towards the S (Styria 1192, Carinthia and Carniola 1335, Duino 1335, Trieste 1382) under the Habsburgs, who sought to establish a link with their hereditary domains in Switzerland and SW Germany, but also towards the W (Tirol 1363, territory in Vorarlberg and SW Germany 15th c.). From this strong position, controlling both important Alpine passes and the Vienna basin, the Habsburgs were able to build up their great empire by dynastic marriage and inheritance. Two late acquisitions were the Innviertel (from Bavaria, 1779) and the ecclesiastical principality of Salzburg (1805).

Present-day Austria is very different from this historical complex of territories. The Republic established in 1919 was, broadly, what was left over after the aspirations of the country's hostile neighbours – Italy, Yugoslavia and Czechoslovakia – had been satisfied. Austria now lost its access to the sea, together with large parts of Tirol and Styria and smaller areas in Carinthia and Lower Austria; against this, however, it gained Burgenland (previously Hungarian) with its German-speaking population. Within its 1919 boundaries Austria extends from W to E for some 560 km/350 miles (roughly as far as from Bregenz to Paris or from Basle to Amsterdam), with a maximum width from N to S of only some 280 km/175 miles. The western third of the country is a narrow corridor no more than 40–60 km/25–40 miles wide separating the two EEC (and NATO) countries of Germany and Italy and reaching westward to Switzerland. In consequence Austria has a very long frontier of some 2650 km/1650 miles, which it shares with six other countries (or seven if Liechtenstein is included): 800 km/500 miles with Germany, 430 km/265 miles with Italy, 550 km/340 miles with Czechoslovakia, 366 km/225 miles with Hungary, 312 km/195 miles with Yugoslavia and 200 km/125 miles with Switzerland and Liechtenstein.

Even the population of the first Austrian republic doubted its viability; and after severe economic and political crises, with internal conflicts amounting almost to civil war, it was incorporated in Hitler's German Reich in 1938. After Germany's collapse at the end of the Second World War it became a separate entity again, but was at first divided into four occupation zones. Then in 1955, under the Staatsvertrag ("State Treaty") signed in that year, it recovered its independence as a country pledged to neutrality.

Austria is a country of richly varied topography, bringing together within a relatively small area the combination of plain, upland and mountain territory which is frequently thought of as characteristic of Central Europe as a whole. Almost two-thirds of its total area are occupied by the Austrian section of the Eastern Alps: the very core of the country, where the

glacier-crowned main ridge of the Alps advances into Austria from the SW, flanked on both sides by broad upland regions. Only a little more than a quarter of the country consists of flat or rolling terrain favourable to human settlement, in the form of a strip of territory of varying width along the Danube, in the Vienna basin and on the eastern fringes of the Alps: the whole of the western part of the country is given up to mountains. Finally a tenth of the area of Austria is occupied by the southern reaches of the Bohemian Forest, a plateau-like upland region of granitic formations which at several points extends S over the Danube.

The main concentrations of population are, naturally, in the lower parts of the country, and are accordingly peripheral; and this is true particularly of the capital, Vienna. That present-day Austria can hold together as a coherent state is due to the relative ease of passage through the Eastern Alps, mainly as a result of the marked division into geological zones – the flysch zone, the northern Calcareous Alps, the greywacke zone, the Central Alps, the Drau zone and the southern Calcareous Alps – which has led to the formation of long longitudinal valley chains facilitating movement between E and W: to the N the Arlberg, Inn, Salzach and Enns valleys, in the middle the Murtal, Mürztal

Landscape Forms

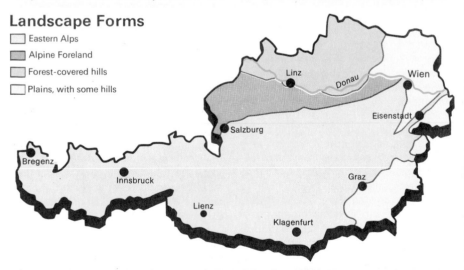

- Eastern Alps
- Alpine Foreland
- Forest-covered hills
- Plains, with some hills

| Austria presents an enormous variety of landscape forms between the low plains in the E and the high Alpine peaks in the W: few countries in the world present such topographical diversity within a relatively small area. | The areas classified as plains consist of land not more than 250 m/820 ft above the Adriatic. Above these are areas of hilly country. Then, above 1500 m/4920 ft, come the upland regions **(Mittelgebirge)**. The high mountains **(Hochgebirge)** begin at altitudes of 2000 m/6560 ft. |

and Semmering, to the S the Pustertal and Drautal. There are also a series of transverse tectonic depressions and valleys, creating a kind of grid pattern of natural traffic routes of varying convenience or difficulty which were used in successive periods according to the needs and the technological capacity of the time. In addition the opening-out of the Alps to the E, as in the Klagenfurt basin, made possible the development of independent political entities. At the other end of the country, in Tirol, the local barons built up their authority in smaller valley basins on both sides of the important Brenner and Reschen (Resia) passes, in southern Tirol (now in Italy) and the middle Inn valley.

The CLIMATE, PLANT LIFE and SOIL show a wide range of variation between the eastern part of the country, under continental influence, and the western part, where Atlantic influences make themselves felt – between the plain around the Neusiedler See (alt. 115 m/375 ft) on the one hand and the high peaks and glaciers of the Alps on the other.

The general downward slope of the land from W to E accentuates the contrasts, producing particularly striking relief patterns at certain points. Thus the eastern slopes of the gneiss plateau at Krems, the Manhartsberg, the Wienerwald and the Bucklige Welt form the clearly marked western boundary of the climatic region – under Pannonian influence and thus dry and hot in summer – which embraces the Weinviertel, the Vienna basin and northern Burgenland. Here we find the same black earth as in southern Russia, while elsewhere in the plains brown earth predominates and on the hills, except in limestone areas, podzols (an infertile, ash-like soil) come to the fore. The rest of Burgenland and the Graz basin show an Illyrian pattern (with sweet chestnuts, hop-hornbeam, etc.). In the northern Alpine foreland the transition to the S German climatic type takes place very gradually. Intimations of a sub-Mediterranean rainfall pattern reach Austria only in the Carnic Alps, on the frontier with Italy.

There is also a clearly marked zoning of the forest according to altitude, blurred though it frequently is by the predominant forestation with conifers. The boundaries of the zones are lower on the weather side of the Alps to the N than in the more continental climate of the interior, the beech-fir level on the northern flanks corresponding to a mixture of oak and pine on the warm dry slopes to the S. Characteristic of the Alpine valleys are the sudden changes of temperature which are familiar to every skier.

The fall in the height of the peaks from about 3500 m/11,500 ft in the W to some 1800 m/5900 ft in the E is accompanied by a corresponding fall in the upper limits of the forest, human settlement and the various forms of land use. Thus the tree-line in the inner Ötztal lies at about 2100 m/6900 ft, while along the northern and eastern edges it lies at 1700–1800 m/5600–5900 ft; the upper limit of settlement at 1900 m/6250 ft in the W, 1000 m/3300 ft in the N and E; the (former) limit of wheat-growing at 1700 m/5600 ft in the W, at 1000 m/3300 ft in the N and E.

In the late Middle Ages and early modern period human settlement and land use had advanced to the extreme limits of what was ecologically possible. This had been achieved through the development of mining and communications and increasing over-population. In some areas, indeed, settlement had gone beyond these limits. Later there was a withdrawal, and this retreat took on major proportions in the industrial age. The main contributory factors were the decline in the small-scale ironworks, using charcoal for smelting, around the Styrian and the Carinthian Erzberg ("Ore Mountain"), accompanied by a drift of population to the new industrial towns, and the efforts of landowners to round off their large forest estates and hunting grounds. Further impetus has been given to the drift of population by current efforts to reorganise agriculture.

POPULATION. – With the exception of Vorarlberg the population of Austria is basically of Bavarian stock – although only Upper Austria, in the old core of the country, can be classed as purely Bavarian.
In Tirol and Salzburg, and also in Vorarlberg, an earlier Raeto-Romanic (a Romansh dialect) population had already been overlaid and gradually absorbed in pre-Carolingian times, although in many valleys (e.g. in the Montafon and the highest reaches of the Inn valley) it long survived, as it still does in the Swiss Engadine to the W. In the E, particularly in Carinthia and Styria, the Bavarians settling the area in Carolingian times came up against an earlier Slav population, which itself had encountered remains of the previous Celto-Roman population. The Slovenes of Carinthia, a minority of mixed Slav and German descent and language are known as *Windische* and are a last remnant of these Slavs who have survived the melting-pot of the centuries.
Lower Austria which (like eastern Styria and Burgenland) had been almost completely laid waste by centuries of fighting with nomadic horsemen from the East (most recently the Magyars), was populated systematically by German settlers – also predominantly of Bavarian origin – only from the mid 10th c. onwards. Population losses in these areas resulting from later Turkish or Hungarian incursions were made good mainly by the settlement of Croat refugees, while in Burgenland some Magyar frontier settlements of an earlier period survived. More recent infusions of Hungarian population have mostly disappeared. The Croat minority, like the Slovenes, is estimated at about 35,000, the Magyars amount to only a few thousand.

SETTLEMENT PATTERNS. – In the regions settled in Carolingian or earlier times and in the old territorial nucleus of Austria settlement takes the form of irregularly shaped villages and fields (hamlets and scattered villages with fields of block or strip form, usually of small size), while the areas settled in later (early medieval) times in the eastern plains have regularly planned villages laid out along a street or around a green, with fields of considerable size. The upland regions, settled in several phases, have isolated farmsteads, with summer shielings (pasture with a hut for shelter) at higher altitudes, particularly in Tirol and Salzburg province.

The TOWNS show a certain continuity of settlement since Roman times only in the Alpine Foreland (e.g. *Iuvavum*= Salzburg, *Ovilava*=Wels, *Lentia*=Linz, *Cetium*=St Pölten, *Vindobona*=Vienna, *Brigantium*=Bregenz); in the interior of the Alps there is no such continuity. Most of the towns were later foundations, established either by ruling princes to maintain control over their domains or by lay or ecclesiastical rulers or landowners on trading routes or in mining areas. Many of them are dominated by old castles and are simply markets which have grown up along a single street. Others show a development towards a regular layout.

The Austrian capital, Vienna – focus of the wide-ranging political interests of the Habsburgs and, from the end of the 16th c., of the Counter-Reformation which they promoted – became a magnet for incomers from all over Europe, officers and officials, churchmen, artists and adventurers. In the service of the dynasty, profiting by the overthrow of the old order, they soon formed a new upper social class. Later, with the beginnings of industrialisation, they were followed by entrepreneurs from western Europe and Jewish businessmen and intellectuals. Finally the economic boom of the "Gründerzeit" (the years of industrial expansion after 1871) brought large numbers of Sudeten Germans and non-German-speaking (particularly Czech) workers, craftsmen and servants to settle in the outlying districts and suburbs of the city, which by 1910 had a population of 2 million. All this led to the development of a distinctively Viennese character and way of life, cosmopolitan and strongly influenced by the court and the nobility, which was diffused into the provinces by the army and officialdom.

Thus in language and habits, in attitudes and way of life – indeed even in physical appearance – the various Austrian stocks are very different from one another. The Viennese type is the youngest of them all, but in foreign eyes it is seen as characteristically Austrian; although any claim by the Viennese to be *the* Austrians, based though it might be on a long metropolitan tradition, would no longer be admitted without question by other Austrians.

The social gulf between town and country goes extremely deep in Austria, given the enormous differences between Vienna, with its population of over a million and a half, at one end of the spectrum, and the numerous tiny rural communes at the other. In the country, particularly in the mountain regions, many old customs still survive and the traditional local costumes are still worn on Sundays and on religious or secular festivals.

FOLK TRADITIONS are fostered by many local associations in the most popular tourist and holiday areas; and although they are now mainly geared to the entertainment of visitors this does at least ensure their preservation and continuance.

The existence of the separate Austrian provinces – all of them, apart from Vorarlberg, old-established units with centuries of tradition behind them – has done much to promote and strengthen these distinctive regional characteristics. In spite of the losses of territory and population which some of them suffered after the First World War they are well-defined geographical units of notable internal stability and, notwithstanding their considerable variation in size, provide a firm foundation for the Austrian federal system. This is true also of the province of Vienna, established in 1922, since the separation of the over-mighty old Imperial capital from the province of Lower Austria was seen as serving the best interests of both parties. Since then regret has sometimes been felt in Lower Austria at being thus deprived of a capital of its own; but the idea which has been voiced of establishing a separate Lower Austrian capital outside Vienna has so far remained no more than an idea. Vienna, too, has its problems, since the 1922 boundaries (largely restored in 1945 after a considerable extension of the city limits during the Nazi period) have become steadily more cramping. There has for some time been a plan to set up a planning region covering both Vienna and Lower Austria.

In the **lowlands of Lower Austria and northern Burgenland** are the rolling loess-soiled country of the Weinviertel and the only plains of any size in Austria – the Tullnerfeld, the Marchfeld, the Heidboden and Seewinkel, the southern part of the Vienna basin. A broad swathe of wooded meadowland borders the *Danube*, which forces its way through the last foothills of the Alps at the Wiener Pforte (Vienna Gate) and through the S end of the Lesser Carpathians at the Hainburger Pforte (Hainburg Gate). Here, in the Pannonian climatic zone, lies Austria's granary and its principal sugarbeet-, wine-, fruit- and vegetable-growing region. The intensively cultivated arable land is interrupted only in a few places by fields of sand-dunes, as in the Marchfeld, or sterile expanses of gravel, as in the Steinfeld ("Field of Stones") near Wiener Neustadt, long since planted with Austrian pine.

Beyond the reed-fringed *Neusiedler See,* always shallow and occasionally, for a brief period, completely dried up, extends an area which had all the character of the Hungarian puszta (prairie land) but has now largely been brought under cultivation. The strange, almost uncanny, beauty of the country around the lake (itself a noted bird sanctuary), the pleasant bathing it offers and its situation within easy reach of the capital – it is called the "Viennese sea" – have led to a considerable development of tourism in this area – (Lake Festival, Mörbisch).

Between large expanses of fields, which in Burgenland have been reduced by constant subdivision into narrow strips, complicating the process of land reform, are populous villages, either of linear type or built around a green, and nearby, carefully sited away from the villages, are imposing Baroque country houses, some of them now restored, set in large parks – relics of the days when the land was owned by noble families.

Along the fringes of the hills and in the *Wachau* are numerous large vine-growing villages and old-world little market towns, while along the "Thermenlinie" ("Hot Springs Line") to the S of Vienna are a series of spas. Notable among these spas is Baden bei Wien, an attractive little town occupying the site of a Roman settlement which became fashionable and prosperous during the Biedermeier period and in the closing years of the monarchy.

Other towns, sometimes succeeding earlier Roman settlements, grew up along the *Danube,* some thriving in medieval times on the busy trade which passed along the river (Kremms, Tulln, Klosterneuburg), others founded as strong points to defend the frontier (Wiener Neustadt, Bruck an der Leitha, Zistersdorf, Laa an der Thaya). In some of these little towns and market villages an old Gothic or even Romanesque building can still be found amid the otherwise predominant Baroque. The large numbers of castles and country houses, churches and convents built or remodelled in Baroque style reflect the influence of the metropolis during the great days of the House of Austria; and at the same time a certain falling-off in the prosperity of the townspeople and a fall in the standard of living of the peasants, if not a decline into downright poverty, can be detected in this area. In the *Marchfeld* and in parts of the Weinviertel and Burgenland, where many centuries of serfdom left their mark, old-established towns are almost wholly absent.

Since the thirties of this century the landscape of the Marchfeld and of the eastern *Weinviertel* has been transformed by the erection of numerous derricks to drill for natural gas and oil (refined in the large refinery at Schwechat). Apart from this, and from a number of factories processing agricultural produce (sugar refineries at Hohenau, Dürnkrut and Leopoldsdorf; Bruck an der Leitha; Siegendorf, Burgenland) there has so far been little development of industry either in the Weinviertel and the Marchfeld, in the Wiener Boden or in northern Burgenland.

In the southern part of the **Vienna basin,** on the other hand, industries established themselves at an early date, thanks to the excellent communications and the proximity of a large market in Vienna. Here there grew up the most varied concentration of industry in Austria, extending in an almost continuous built-up area along the Südbahn railway line – at first to Mödling, later by way of Baden-Traiskirchen, Wiener Neustadt and Ternitz-Wimpassing to Gloggnitz. In addition to a number of very large enterprises there are numerous small and medium-sized firms, mainly engaged in metalworking and textiles but also producing paper, timber products and building materials. By addition to Vienna *Wiener Neustadt* plays an important part as the hub of the southern part of this industrial area.

The position of **Vienna** can be understood only in its wider historical context. Excellently situated on the western edge of the Vienna basin, at the point where the *Danube* enters the basin and at the intersection of important traffic routes, it was both a base for the expansion of Habsburg power in the middle Danube region and the principal beneficiary of that expansion. With the collapse of that power Vienna was cut off from more than one of its roots. The Baroque and later splendours of the Imperial capital would now seem no more than museum pieces were it not that the city has contrived, at the cost of some sacrifice, to adapt itself to the changed circumstances.

Vienna: view towards St. Stephen's Cathedral

The townscape of Vienna, with the grand radial layout which developed organically over the years, is dominated in its older parts by the buildings erected by the court, the church and the nobility – some of them now occupied by government and other offices – and by those other buildings of the country's former (and present-day) economic metropolis, the banks, offices, department stores and specialised shops, these last still reflecting a more cultivated taste than the larger stores. In comparison with these buildings the middle-class residential blocks and industrial premises in the side streets and quieter corners of the city fall into the background. Only on the Ring, magnificently laid out on the glacis (gently sloping bank) outside the old fortifications, does the architecture of the 19th c. *grande bougeoisie* assert itself more vigorously alongside the buildings of the court and the nobility.

Contrasting with this splendour are the grey blocks of rental apartments which cover the semicircle of hills to the S of the river and have swallowed up the old vine-growing villages. Still drearier are the haphazardly developed quarters beyond the river where some industry has also established itself, as it has to the S of the city. Most of this industry takes the form of countless small and medium-sized firms in the streets and back courts of the outer districts and suburbs both inside and outside the outer ring road known as the Gürtel. Other distinctive Vienna landmarks are the huge apartment developments built by the municipality, sometimes merely filling gap sites but elsewhere forming large housing estates and satellite towns.

The **Upper and Lower Austrian Alpine Foreland** lies between the northern edge of the Alps and the Danube, here flowing far to the N and cutting through the foothills of the Bohemian Forest in various narrow canyons. It rises in broad terraces and wooded round-topped hills towards the Alps, from which there flow a series of mountain streams bringing down quantities of gravel. The moist W winds make the region unsuitable for wine growing but, as in the neighbouring Flachgau (Salzburg province), favour arable and pastoral farming. This is rich agricultural land, efficiently farmed by highly mechanised holdings geared to the production of dairy products and beef cattle (large cattle markets at

Ried and Wels). Handsome four-square farmsteads stand by themselves or grouped in small hamlets, always surrounded by fruit-trees, which produce the *Most* (unfermented apple or pear juice) popular with many families. In this area of early settlement there are numbers of large villages, interspersed with little country towns which provide shopping facilities for the rural population.

Here and there are great abbeys and other religious houses founded in Bavarian or Frankish times, with famous schools which for many centuries trained the elite of the region.

In recent times the aspect of the Upper Austrian foreland region along the axis of the Westbahn railway line has changed considerably. Between *Linz* – which was deliberately developed during the Nazi period as an area of heavy industry and later expanded still further – and Wels and in the Schwanenstadt-Vöcklabruck-Lenzing area there is now a large and efficient industrial concentration, based mainly on expanding branches of industry, which has brought with it a considerable increase in population and a corresponding growth in housing accommodation. The resettlement of refugees here after the last war brought not only a valuable increase in the labour force but also led to the development of new industries, including the jewelry industry transferred from Gablonz (Jablonec) in Czechoslovakia.

Power for industry is provided by a number of power stations, either harnessing the rivers, particularly the Enns and the Inn (Ranshofen aluminium plant), or using lignite from the Hausruck and Salzach fields (Timelkam). Drilling for oil and natural gas in the Upper Austrian foreland area has also yielded excellent results.

Important older industrial areas are the picturesque old ironworking town of *Steyr* and the Lower Austrian town of *St. Pölten.*

Along the Danube are the steep wooded slopes of the Waldviertel and Mühlviertel hills, the summits of which (1000–1380 m/ 3280–4530 ft) are still covered with dark forests. Human settlement was fairly late in coming to this harsh and windy granite plateau, whose thin soils yield only meagre returns. Only the lower eastern part of the Waldviertel and the Horner Bucht offer more favourable conditions for agriculture. From an early stage the population of these areas, with large families to support, found a subsidiary source of income in cottage industry, which later developed into a regular textile industry. The glass-blowing which was formerly a traditional craft here has now almost completely disappeared. There are also granite quarries which supplied Vienna with its street paving and some kaolin and graphite workings.

Population pressure in the *Waldviertel,* an area of small peasant holdings, led in the mid 19th c. to a heavy exodus of younger people to the capital. This trend, which still continues, has led to a substantial aging of the population.

With the development of Linz the *Mühl-viertel* has become a popular com-muting area. Castles perched on steeply scarped slopes above turns in the river, little towns built for defence and ancient abbeys are scattered about this region of passage into Bohemia and Moravia, which now lies off the main traffic routes and is little known to foreign visitors. The modest domestic holiday trade does little to augment the incomes of the predominantly agricultural popula-tion.

In the **hilly country of Styria and southern Burgenland,** to the SE of the Alps, the warmth of the south can already be felt. Here the long flat-topped ridges between valleys and the rounded hills are covered with an attractive patchwork of meadow and forest, vineyards and arable fields. The villages, churches and chapels are found on the high ground, as are the oldest roads. Maize flourishes here, and there is a superabundance of fruit. The people are of milder disposition and their dialect is more resonant than elsewhere in Austria. The stout old castles on the vine-clad volcanic hills, however, are a reminder that this was once a frontier region exposed to all the hazards of war.

There are few towns in this region, which has only become easily accessible since the development of bus transport, and such towns as there are have remained small, since there is only a sporadic scatter of industry. This has led to some agricultural over-population and a certain backwardness, particularly in southern Burgenland. Only on the western fringes of the region, in the Köflach coalfield, has there been a modest concentration of industry; and there has also been a considerable spread of industry, of the most varied kind, around Graz, reaching up and down the Mur valley.

The Styrian capital, **Graz,** lies in an attrac-tive green setting at the point where the Mur emerges from the hills, with many fine old buildings to recall its importance in earlier centuries as an outpost of Austria and an armoury against the Turks. Thanks to its situation on the important railway line to Trieste and its nearness to supplies of coal and iron ore, it has developed important industries and is now Austria's second largest city, while still preserving its ancient cultural traditions (university and technical college, theatre, opera; congresses; trade fairs).

The characteristics of the Alpine regions of Austria are largely determined by the nature of the rock and the pattern of mountain formation. The *Northern Calcareous Alps* ("calcareous" means "formed of limestone") rear up from the foreland region into massive chains in the W and mighty rock masses in the E, their sheer rock faces and rugged plateaux offering little foothold for any form of life. Only the forests – sometimes only a few stunted trees – cling to the steep mountainsides, defying the avalanches; and even the valleys, with their covering of loose stones and gravel, are not favour-able to agriculture. The climate is cool, with heavy rainfall, and the snow lasts far into spring. Were it not for a few transverse valleys, often no more than gorges, and some more open stretches of valley and saddles in the argillaceous rocks, the mountains would be even more of an obstacle to traffic than they are.

The *Inn valley,* which runs between the limestone mountains and the gentler schist hills, is the main area of settlement of **Tirol.** Its flat detrital fans and extensive low terraces are dotted with trim villages and covered with arable fields on which, under the influence of the föhn (a warm, dry wind), maize flourishes, while the valley floor is occupied mainly by meadowland.

The old towns of the Inn valley, places full of character, grew up at traffic junctions or on passages through the mountains (Innsbruck, Kufstein, Landeck) or near deposits of minerals such as salt (Hall in Tirol), silver (Schwaz, Rattenberg) or copper (Kitzbühel). In our own day there has been a considerable development of industry, of the most varied type, and of tourism in the Inn valley, and also in the Ausserfern area (Plansee hydroelectric scheme, Reutte).

Innsbruck, capital of Tirol, situated at the intersection of traffic routes between E and W and from N to S over the Brenner, has developed into the only large Austrian town within the Alps. Its handsome old buildings recall the days when it was an imperial residence. It is now primarily concerned with tourism and is a focus of culture whose influence extends throughout Tirol and has significantly improved the standard of living of its population.

Salzburg lies on the N side of the Alps, on the important traffic route over the Tauern passes into the mountains. In a magnificent setting, it is one of the most beautiful towns in Europe, with a splendid array of buildings reflecting its history as a great religious focal point and capital of an independent principality, the residence of art-loving Prince-Bishops. All this, combined with its attraction as a festival city, has made Salzburg one of the busiest tourist meccas of Austria. After the Second World War fresh stimulus was given to the town's development by the transfer of industry from eastern Austria and the establishment of subsidiaries of German firms. In consequence an almost continuous built-up area, industrial and residential, extends up the Salzach valley towards Hallein.

Another very popular tourist and holiday area is the *Salzkammergut* with its numerous lakes, lying partly in Salzburg province and partly in Upper Austria (Gmunden, Bad Ischl) and Styria (Bad

Salzburg: view from the Mirabellgarten

Aussee). A favourite resort of the citizens of Vienna from the first half of the 19th c. onwards, this area is now mainly patronised by foreign visitors, mostly from Germany.

The **high plateaux of the Calcareous Alps,** which in the *Dachstein* group (2995 m/9827 ft) still bear glaciers, lose height gradually towards the E, ending in the *Rax* and *Schneeberg* (2076 m/6811 ft) near Vienna, which fall away to the Vienna basin. In the valleys of the Upper and Lower Austrian Pre-Alpine zone a busy small-scale ironworking industry developed at an early stage, thanks to the proximity of the iron-mines in the area of the Erzberg and the abundance of timber and of water power; but in the latter part of the 19th c. this declined, following the establishment of large modern industries in the foreland region, particularly in the old ironworking regions of Steyr and Waidhofen an der Ybbs but also in Traisen, St. Pölten and Ternitz.

The **western Central Alps** of Tirol, Salzburg province and Upper Carinthia rear up into the region of permanent ice. Their great massifs and ridges of crystalline rock are broken up by deep valleys gouged out by the ice. There are few areas favourable to human settlement in the valley bottoms and only narrow strips of forest along the steep valley sides, but great expanses of stony Alpine meadows and desolate wastes. Only where the lower and gentler schist hills become wider is there room for more numerous human settlement. The *Hohe Tauern* mountains (Grossglockner, 3797 m/12,458 ft) were made more accessible to visitors by the construction of the Tauernbahn railway (with the international resorts of Badgastein and Hofgastein) and the Grossglockner Road, running up into the world of the glaciers. More recently the Felber Tauern Road has opened up a new N–S connection. The "stepped" structure of the valleys and the abundance of water in the mountains have made possible the development of large hydroelectric projects (Kaunertal-Prutz, Kaprun, Gerlos, Reisseck).

The **eastern Central Alps** are lower, with larger expanses of forest and, in the Austrian heartland, more broken up into separate ranges, between which are wide valleys and basins with deposits of lignite

(Fohnsdorf, St. Stefan im Lavanttal, etc.). The abundance of iron ore in the grey-wacke (a conglomerate or grit rock) zone extending eastward to the *Semmering* pass made this a region of great industrial activity and importance. Old foundries and forges are still to be seen in this area, and the handsome houses in the smaller cities and market towns (Leoben, Bruck, Mürz-zuschlag, Judenburg) bear witness to the wealth of the old ironmasters and the active trade with Italy which passed up and down the roads through the mountains and introduced strong Renaissance in-fluences. In contrast to Carinthia, *Upper Styria*, thanks to its Erzberg ("Ore Mountain"), was able to retain and develop its old established ironworking industry (Leoben-Donawitz), so that steelworks and housing areas now extend almost continuously along the banks of the Mur and the Mürz.

In striking contrast to this busy activity are the surrounding uplands, in which only a few scattered villages and areas of Alpine pasture interrupt the mantle of forest. There is little water power available for harnessing in this area. In the *Nock area* and in the higher parts of the Central Alpine valleys there are still magnificent stands of arolla pines. Timber-working and stock-farming are the main sources of income, with only a limited additional revenue from the tourist and holiday trade, still relatively undeveloped in this area.

Between the Central Alps and the limestone walls of the Southern Alps lies the **Klagenfurt basin,** the largest such basin within the Eastern Alps. This Carinthian heartland has become more easily accessible by the com-pletion of the Tauern motorway (Salzburg–Klagenfurt).

Between the forest-covered ranges of hills and the Sassnitz plateau lie numerous *lakes*, large and small, with warm water which makes them popular bathing re-sorts in summer. The main holiday centre, now predominantly patronised by foreign visitors as well as by the Viennese, is the Wörther See, with the well-known resorts of Velden and Pörtschach.

Favourable climatic and soil conditions have led to the development of a varied pattern of agriculture and stock-farming. The agriculture of this area, particularly the fertile Krappfeld, is well organised and productive, with large specialised farms. The extensive forests in the surrounding area supply a large and important wood-working industry.

Of the old established towns in the Klagen-furt basin two have prospered particularly, the traffic junction point of *Villach* and the provincial capital, *Klagenfurt.*

The **Southern Calcareous Alps,** boun-ding Carinthia on the S with the great ramparts of the *Karawanken,* resemble the Northern Calcareous Alps in their variety of form but differ from them in their milder climate and richer vegetation. Timber-working, stock-farming and the tourist and holiday trade are the main sources of revenue, with mining in certain areas (Bleiberg); there has so far been little industrial development. There are still pockets of Slovene population in the Drau valley and the Karawanken.

Finally there is **Vorarlberg**, a little world on its own but one of astonishing variety, extending over the broad Rhine valley, the molasse and flysch zones (geological formations) and the limestone Pre-Alps and Alps. The huge hydroelectric schemes which have been developed here supply power to wide areas, ex-tending as far as the Ruhr in Western Germany.

In the *Bregenzer Wald* the main source of income, in addition to the old craft of embroidery, now using machines, is the highly developed dairy-farming industry. The old-established textile industry of the *Rhine valley,* largely geared to export, was given fresh stimulus by an influx of popula-tion after the Second World War and was supplemented by the establishment of new industries producing consumption goods. These developments led to con-siderable building activity, so that an almost continuous ribbon of housing now extends along the foot of the hills from Bregenz to Feldkirch.

The tourist and holiday trade is con-centrated in the customs-free zone in the Kleinwalsertal, the skiing areas on the *Arlberg* and the Hochtannberg, the *Montafon* valley and the provincial capital, *Bregenz* (Lake Festival). *Dornbirn,* the largest town in Vorarlberg, attracts many visitors to its Textile Fair.

This little province (the "Ländle") shares the dialect and the building styles of the wider Lake Constance area. Its economy and communications, too, link it almost more firmly with Switzerland and Germany than with the rest of Austria.

Climate

The climate of Austria is determined by the predominantly mountainous nature of the country and its situation on the SE borders of Central Europe. *In the W* Atlantic influences (W winds) predominate, with moderately warm summers, winters which are not unduly cold and rainfall throughout the year, but particularly in the summer months. *In the E* continental influences are predominant, with hot summers and severe winters; rainfall, particularly in the Wachau, the Vienna basin, Burgenland and southern Styria, is distinctly lower than in the W. Particularly extreme climatic conditions are found in basins, such as the Klagenfurt basin, and in closed valleys like the Enns and Salzach valleys and the highest reaches of the Mur valley (Lungau).

Temperatures. – The Atlantic influences, with their moderate extreme temperatures, become progressively weaker from W to E and from the northern fringes of the Alps to the valleys in the interior. Temperatures are of course influenced by altitude, and in the examples of temperatures at various places which are given below the altitudes are also indicated. Averaged over the year, temperatures fall by approximately ·5°C/·9°F for every 100 m/330 ft of height. In winter the fall is between ·3°C/·54°F and ·6°C/1·08°F, in summer between ·6°C/1·08°F and ·7°C/1·26°F for every 100 m. – The gradual transition from an oceanic to a continental climate is shown in the following figures, which also indicate the increase in the moderating maritime influences with increasing altitude: Bregenz (412 m/1352 ft) annual average 8·6°C/47°F, January −1·4°C/29°F, July 16·5°C/62°F; Ebnit (1100 m/3610 ft, high above the Rhine valley) annual 6·5°C/44°F, January −2°C/28°F, July 14°C/57°F; Landeck (813 m/2667 ft, in the Inn valley) annual 8·2°C/47°F, January −2·6°C/27°F, July 17°C/63°F; Innsbruck (582 m/1910 ft) annual 8·5°C/47°F, January −3·3°C/26°F, July 17·5°C/64°F; Zell am See (754 m/2474 ft, in a basin) annual 6·4°C/44°F, January −6°C/21°F, July 16·5°C/62°F; Salzburg (428 m/1404 ft, on fringe of mountains) annual 8·5°C/47°F, January −1·5°C/29°F, July 17·5°C/64°F; Bischofshofen (545 m/1788 ft, in the narrow Salzach valley) and Admont (641 m/2103 ft, in the Enns valley) annual 6·9°C/44°F and 6·3°C/43°F, January both −5°C/23°F, July 15·5°C/60°F; Klagenfurt (448 m/1470 ft, in a basin) annual 8·2°C/47°F, January −5°C/23°F, July 18°C/64°F; Graz (365 m/1198 ft) annual 9°C/48°F, January −2·3°C/28°F, July 18°C/64°F; Vienna (Hohe Warte, 203 m/666 ft) annual 9·5°C/49°F, January −1·7°C/29°F, July 19°C/68°F. – The increase in the maritime influence with increasing height is shown by the following examples: Obergurgl (1927 m/6322 ft) annual 2·8°C/37°F, January −4·5°C/24°F, July 11·3°C/52°F; Zugspitze (2962 m/9718 ft, on edge of mountains) annual −5°C/23°F, January −11·7°C/11°F, July 2°C/36°F, average winter minimum −13·8°C/7°F, absolute winter minimum −34·6°C/−30°F; Sonnblick (3106 m/10,191 ft, in Hohe Tauern) annual −6·4°C/20°F, February −13·5°C/8°F, July 1·5°C/35°F.

The annual **precipitation** (rainfall and snow) decrease, in general, from W to E, as can be seen by comparing the figures for a number of places lying between 200 m/656 ft and 500 m/1640 ft: Bregenz 1428 mm/56 in., Kufstein 1313 mm/52 in., Salzburg 1336 mm/53 in., Gmunden am Traunsee 1234 mm/49 in., Steyr 980 mm/39 in., St. Pölten 735 mm/29 in., Vienna 685 mm/27 in. With increasing altitude the figures increase considerably, particularly on the weather side of the hills:

Ebnit (1100 m/3609 ft, high above the Rhine) 2122 mm/84 in., Hallstatt-Salzberg (1012 m/3320 ft) 2118 mm/83 in., Feuerkogel (1587 m/5207 ft, above the Traunsee) 2556 mm/101 in., Nassfelder Hütte (1513 m/4964 ft, in the Carnic Alps) 2803 mm/110 in. At still greater heights the figures usually fall: Hafelekar (2293 m/7523 ft) 1688 mm/66 in., Sonnblick (3106 m/10,191 ft) 1466 mm/58 in., Zugspitze (2962 m/9718 ft) 1350 mm/53 in. On the lee side of the mountains (in the rain shadow) and in the innermost valleys of the Central Alps precipitation is relatively low: Landeck (813 m/2667 ft) 721 mm/28 in., Innsbruck (582 m/1910 ft) 855 mm/34 in., Leoben an der Mur (540 m/1772 ft) 765 mm/30 in., Vent (1892 m/6208 ft, in the innermost reaches of the Ötztal) 706 mm/28 in., Ferleiten (1147 m/3763 ft, on the N side of the Tauern ridge) 1285 mm/51 in., Heiligenblut (1378 m/4521 ft, on the S side of the Tauern ridge) 859 mm/34 in. Outside the Alps, too, precipitation remains low: Linz (260 m/853 ft) 844 mm/33 in., Oberschützen (350 m/1148 ft, in southern Burgenland) 698 mm/27 in., Graz (365 m/1198 ft) 873 mm/34 in. Krems, at the sheltered eastern end of the Wachau, has a particularly low rainfall (521 mm/21 in.). – Almost everywhere in Austria the lowest precipitation is in February and March; in some places it is in January (Krems January and March each 21 mm/0·8 in.; Altaussee in the Salzkammergut, March 130 mm/5·1 in., October and November each 135 mm/5·3 in.), the highest in July (Krems 74 mm/2·9 in., Altaussee 270 mm/10·6 in.). Only in the Karawanken are there spring and autumn maxima (May, October), on the Mediterranean pattern. – At heights of over 3000 m/9800 ft the precipitation falls as snow. In the central Alps the *snow-line* lies between 2800 m/9200 ft and 3100 m/10,200 ft, in the outer chains around 2500−2600 m/8200−8500 ft. In a snowy winter there can be a depth of over 5 m/16 ft of snow. Some of the glaciers reach down almost to the tree-line.

In the evening and during the night the air, which has been cooled and become heavier, flows down the valley slopes, and during the day, having warmed up, blows up again into the mountains. On summer afternoons clouds frequently form; the best visibility, therefore, is early in the morning. In winter the peaks often rise through the clouds into warm sunshine, while in calm weather cold air collects in the valleys, producing a curious temperature reversal. When there is an area of low pressure on the N side of the Alps air is sucked up from the S, rises over the main ridge, with clouds and heavy rain, and then falls down into the valleys as the warm, dry *föhn*, increasing in temperature by 1°C/1·8°F for every 100 m/330 ft. It is this warm wind that is said to "eat up" the snow in spring.

Plant life

Austria belongs to the Central European province of the Euro-Siberian and Boreo-American floral region; but its variety of landscape forms, soils and climatic influences gives its plant life much greater diversity than in neighbouring countries, with Baltic elements in the N, Atlantic features in the upland regions and Pannonian and Mediterranean/Illyrian species in the E and SE. The Alps provide a home for many survivals from earlier periods and endemic species (plants found nowhere else). And all over Austria there is a constant alternation between forest and rock, moorland and steppe.

The predominant form of vegetation is **forest**, which covers more than a third of the country's area. Its natural habitat extends from the meadowland of the Danube valley right up into the mountains, with the tree-line running at about 2000 m/6560 ft in the Central Alps and 1700 m/5580 ft in the Northern and Southern Alps. In the Waldviertel and Muhlviertel forests of spruce, beech and fir predominate, with Scots pine and birch also well represented; in the Pannonian regions oak and hornbeam forests (Weinviertel) and oak and beech (southern Burgenland, eastern Styria, Leithagebirge, Wienerwald). Other species which do well are the Turkey oak, Austrian pine, downy oak, sweet chestnut, lime, Tartar maple, dwarf medlar and Savoy medlar. The Illyrian black pine has its most northerly habitat at Vienna.

On the warm, dry sandy soils of the Marchfeld, the Hundsheimer Berge near Hainburg and northern Burgenland these various species of trees combine with other characteristic plants to form areas of wooded steppe.

Along the rivers Danube, March and Leitha are lush meadows which support a mixed woodland of willows, poplars, ashes and elms, with areas of marshland overgrown with alders.

In the western Wienerwald (Vienna Woods), the Alpine foreland region, the Calcareous Alps of Lower Austria and Styria, the Salzkammergut and the Bregenzer Wald there are fine tracts of sub-Alpine mixed forest of beech and fir, with an admixture of wych elm, yew, maple and other species. Large areas, however, are now being replanted with spruce.

At higher levels and farther W the larch begins to occur more frequently, producing a mixed forest of spruce, beech and larch which usually also includes Scots pine. On damp hillsides above 1350 m/4400 ft the spruce predominates, on drier slopes the Scots pine. They are almost always associated with heaths, maples and junipers (as at Ahornboden in the Karwendel). Just below the tree-line are found spruce and maple, in the Tauern and in Tirol frequently the arolla or stone pine (a high Alpine species), on the limestone plateaux the green alder.

The variety of undergrowth to be found in, say, a beech forest can be appreciated only by visiting a number of different tracts of forest. Holly and yew are found almost exclusively in the W of Austria, the Christmas rose, box and butcher's broom in the E. These are probably relics of the neoglacial warm period. From the Mediterranean area comes the hop hornbeam, found for example near Graz and Innsbruck.

A plant of extreme rarity is **Wulfenia carinthiaca,** found only at Hermagor in Carinthia and on the Albanian-Yugoslav frontier.

In addition to these special cases numerous other plants grow under trees, including – to mention only a selection – herb Paris, daphne, wood sorrel, toothwort, fumitory, many species of violets, dead nettle, Turk's cap lily, foxglove, valerian, bilberry, ericas and numerous orchids, including the bird's nest orchid, the twayblade, the lizard orchid, the fragrant orchid, the marsh orchid, the helleborine and the famous lady's slipper, now unfortunately much rarer than it used to be.

Biologically the most interesting of the orchids is the inconspicuous wasp orchid, which has the odour of the sexual organs of the female digger wasp. The male wasps

The rare Wulfenia (Nassfeld, Carinthia)

take it, therefore, for a female and perform their mating dance on it, thus pollinating the flowers.

Large tracts of forest were cleared in the Middle Ages to provide pasture for cattle stock, and these areas are now covered by lush *Alpine meadows* which in summer are gay with flowers. In addition to a variety of *grasses* the flowers include clover, dandelions, daisies, orchids, bellflowers, meadow saffron, sorrel, speedwell, white campion, wild pink, yellow rattle, cranesbill, common storksbill, knotgrass, plantain, yarrow, scabious, hogweed, hemlock and many other **meadow plants.** The meadows around Mariazell and Lunz are particularly beautiful when the daffodils are in flower.

Of a very different character is the *dry grassland* found in the Wachau, on the Bisamberg, in the Leiser Berge, around Mödling, in the Hundsheimer Berge and in northern Burgenland. In addition to various grasses the flora consists mainly of pheasant's eye, pasque flower, milkvetch, Cheddar pink, rock rose, dwarf iris, grape hyacinth, anemones, bellflowers, cinquefoils, cypress spurge, swallowwort, bloody cranesbill, various wild roses, blackthorn, whitethorn and dwarf medlar.

On *sandy soils* (e.g. the travelling dunes near Oberweiden in the Marchfeld) *annuals* predominate – mostly small and inconspicuous plants which germinate, bloom, bear their seeds and die within the space of a few weeks in spring. Characteristic examples are yellow whitlow grass and umbellate chickweed.

Most striking of all are the silvery *feather-grass meadows,* the strongly perfumed sand pink, the red lanterns of the ground cherry and the birthwort, an insect-trapping plant with heart-shaped leaves and tubular flowers.
The *salt steppe* of the Seewinkel area in Burgenland (Illmitz, Apetlon, Podersdorf) has all the air of a desert. When the salt lakes dry up in summer the ground is covered with a white coating of salt crystals. The annual rainfall in this area is only a twentieth of the Salzburg figure, and more water is lost by evaporation than falls in the form of rain. Only plants which have adapted to these extreme conditions survive the hot summers – among them salt cress, hog's bean, a species of rush and

various goosefoots *(Salicornia, Sueda)* with succulent stems or leaves, which give a reddish tint to the ground in autumn.

In contrast to the steppe areas are the marshes and water meadows. The *meadow woodlands* are overgrown with impenetrable undergrowth, the predominant species in which are privet, elder, spindleberry and various *lianas* (traveller's joy, etc.). In the Lobau it is possible, with luck, to find the wild form of the cultivated vine *(Vita silvestris,* also a liana). Among *other plants* stinging nettles, celandine, violets, wild garlic, snowdrops and arum predominate.

On the banks of the rivers, from the Rhine to the March, and in areas of *level moorland* (seen most typically at Ebergassing and Gramatneusiedl in Lower Austria) a very characteristic plant community is found, with numerous *orchids* and *irises,* including the yellow iris and the light blue Siberian lily, the red marsh gladiolus and various sedges, rushes and bulrushes. In the wettest places are numerous kinds of willow, mostly natural crosses between two or more species. On the very edge of the water are *reeds,* intermixed with reed-mace, bur-reed and water plantain.

In the water itself are *water-lilies,* hornwort, milfoil, water soldier, a variety of pondweeds, arrowhead, the flowering rush with its 3 feet high purple umbels and many more. A very common water plant is the *bladderwort,* with thread-like leaves and small bladders which catch tiny water creatures to nourish the plant. – The surface of stagnant water is often completely covered with *duckweed.*
No account is taken here of two large groups, the algae and the mushrooms and toadstools.

A very characteristic landscape pattern is that of the **high moorland** areas. Although these are gradually disappearing as a result of drainage operations, they can still be encountered in the Waldviertel and the Enns and Mur valleys and on many Alpine terraces. A moor comes into being through the long-continued growth of peat mosses, which with their sponge-like consistency can raise water above the level of the surrounding area; the lower layers of moss then die, and in time turn into *peat.* Typical plants of this biotope are cotton grass, heather, certain sedges, the dwarf birch and the insect-eating *sundew* with its mobile tentacles.

The best-known representatives of Austrian plant life comes from the mountains, and there is surely no more colourful and varied **Alpine plant life** in Europe than that of Austria. The Alpine species are also among the toughest forms of plant life, engaged in a continual struggle with natural forces – ultraviolet light in massive doses, long cold winters, perpetual storms. Unstable areas of scree and gravel, minute crevices in the rocks and rushing mountain streams demand very specialised adaptation.

Above the tree-line extends a zone of *Alpine meadows.* The higher the altitude, the shorter is the grass; and when the livestock leave only the poisonous, bitter or prickly plants this produces a very marginal form of pasture. During the spring an Alpine meadow which has not degenerated in this way is a glorious show of colour, with a wide range of species – Alpine aster, Alpine flax, Alpine poppy, Alpine pink, soldanella, arnica, all species of *gentian,* black vanilla orchid, lousewort, bird's eye primrose and other *primulas,* mountain avens, false helleborine, globe-flower, the "viviparous" Alpine meadow-grass and many more.

Another typical Alpine formation is the *heath,* with heather, bilberries, cranberries, crowberries, reindeer moss, Icelandic moss and above all *rhododendrons,* which clothe the hillsides in fiery red. As with many plants (e.g. the gentian), there are different forms for different soils: the hairy rhododendron *(Rhododendron hirsutum)* grows on limestone, the rust-leaved rhododendron *(Rhododendron ferrugineum)* on volcanic rock.

Distinctive plants are also found on *rocks*

and in rock crevices. Among plants which grow in these conditions are the *edelweiss* and the *auricula* (both protected plants which must not be picked). .– At altitudes from 2000 m/6560 ft to over 4000 m/13,000 ft is found the highest European flowering plant, the glacier crowfoot.

Plants growing on scree and rock detritus have also to cope with mechanical problems. Among such plants are the green alder and the dwarf willow, which have enormously large root systems providing a natural defence against avalanches. Certain grasses and sedges knit together the smaller stones, forming numerous terraces on which other plants can secure a foothold. In the rocky regions wafer-thin *crustaceous lichens* cover every square inch of rock; where even this is not possible they live under the surface of the stone.

Animals

Austrian animal life comprises, in addition to several thousand invertebrates, some 20,000 different species of insects and some 260 vertebrate species.

All Austrian *waters,* particularly the abandoned arms of rivers with their abundant food supply and the lowland lakes, are inhabited by microscopic protozoa. In stagnant water are found the small lumps or crusts that are fresh-water sponges.

In the same habitat live the fresh-water polyps (hydras), up to 2 cm/·8 in. in size, which catch small water creatures with their stinging tentacles.

In the mud on the bottom live a great variety of turbellarians (flatworms), nematodes (roundworms) and rotifers (wheel animalcules). The annelids are represented by the leech.

Molluscs are also found – pulmonate snails (amber snail, mud snail, plate snail, bowl snail), prosobranch snails such as *Paludina vivipara,* and bivalves (fresh-water mussels, including the river mussel, which grows to a length of 8 cm/3 in.).

The *arthropods* are abundantly represented in rivers and lakes. In addition to the crayfish there are numerous smaller species such as the water-flea, which provides an excellent food supply for fish,

Gentian

as well as water spiders, water-mites, etc. – Numerous insects spend their larval period in the water (midges, the predatory dragonfly larva).

The most familiar aquatic creatures are, of course, the **fish,** and there is excellent angling to be had in the large lakes of Carinthia and the Salzkammergut, Lake Constance, the many mountain streams and the Danube. Of more than 80 native Austrian fish species 60 are found (some only found) in the Danube. In the Alpine regions the commonest species are trout, char, grayling, tench and whitefish, in the Danube perch, catfish, the Danube salmon and eels. Carp are found mainly in the small lakes of the Waldviertel.
All the Austrian *amphibians* are statutorily protected species.
The lakes are inhabited by the smooth newt, the warty newt and the Alpine salamander as well as the edible frog. The fire-bellied toad is found on the shores of lakes in the lowland areas, the yellow-bellied toad in the uplands. In addition the larvae of many terrestrial newts and frogs live in small pools or near the shores of lakes, where tadpoles may be found.

The lakes are also frequented by numerous **marsh and water birds.** The fringe of reeds around the Neusiedler See in particular is an internationally famous bird sanctuary, with many rare species, some of which occur nowhere else in Europe – bearded reedling, penduline tit, bee-eater, kingfisher, common tern, spoonbill, various species of heron, bittern, warblers, avocet, snipe, mallard, sandpiper, spotted crake, water-rail, hoopoe, wild duck, wild geese. Storks nest on the roofs of villages near the lakes and in trees on the water-meadows of the River March.

Bird sanctuary, Neusiedler See

Among the handsomest birds to be seen on the Austrian lakes is the mute swan.

The *soil* is inhabited by an enormous variety of *worms,* wood-lice, centipedes and millipedes, spiders and insect larvae (cockchafers, etc.), which improve the quality of the soil as well as provide food for many other creatures. A great variety of *snails* are found in the soil of forests and on the plants – the edible snail (which can be collected only with a permit from the provincial government), the striped wood snail, brown, red and black slugs, a "loner" such as *Isognomostoma* with its hairy shell, and many others with shells of varying size and shape, blunt or pointed, large or small. In spring a patient observer can watch a fascinating sight – the mating behaviour of the hermaphroditic snails, which culminates in the discharge of a "love-dart".

In numbers of species the **insects** amount to half of the whole animal world, and in total numbers they far exceed all the rest. They are also the most highly developed living creatures (bees, ants, termites, etc.) after the vertebrates. Species particularly characteristic of the Alps are the Apollo butterfly and the snow flea, of the Pannonian region the cicada and the praying mantis.
Among the *butterflies and moths* the festoon, one of the most brilliantly coloured butterflies, scarcely strays out of the Marchfeld, while the gamma moth travels long distances like the migratory birds: night after night in spring countless millions of gammas fly N over the Alpine passes, returning S in autumn.
Many insects are under strict statutory protection, including the Alpine sawyer, the stag and rhinoceros beetles, the swallowtail butterfly, the death's head moth, the Camberwell beauty, the cynthia moth, the Viennese peacock moth (the largest Austrian butterfly or moth) and many others. – Many insects, on the other hand, are dangerous pests, among them the *Tineidae* (clothes moths, etc.), cabbage white butterfly, nun moth and greenfly.

Most visitors, however, are more likely to be interested in the vertebrates, which are also well represented in Austria. Walking through the woods after rain, they may come across the yellow and black checked *fire salamander,* looking like some prehistoric animal; in the mountains this gives place to the Alpine salamander. – The croaking of the tree frog can be heard in the Alpine foreland region; the brown marsh frog, agile frog and moor frog are found only in the lowlands. The common toad occurs all over the country, while the green toad is not uncommon in the E of the country.

Almost all Austrian *reptiles* are under statutory protection. In spite of this the European mud tortoise has almost died out, though it is said to have been sighted occasionally in the Lobau. *Lizards* can be seen darting about on warm rocks and walls; particularly notable is the brilliantly coloured green lizard, common in eastern Austria, which can reach a length of 40 cm/16 in.

Although **snakes** have a bad name they are wholly useful creatures. Particularly common in the vicinity of water is the grass snake, easily recognisable by its white collar; the dice snake, also a great water-lover, is one of the rarer inhabitants of warm valleys. Warmth also appeals to Austria's largest snake, the Aesculapian snake, an adept climber which may be as much as 2 m/6½ ft long. – The venomous snakes are all smaller (not more than 90 cm/3 ft long), viviparous, and recognisable by their short, blunt tail and their cat-like eyes with vertical pupils. The commonest venomous snake, the *adder,* is found on moorland and in mountain country; it is totally absent from the Vienna region. A species peculiar to the Neusiedler See is Orsini's viper. The nose-horned viper is found in heaps of stones and walls in Carinthia and southern Styria.

The characteristic **Alpine birds** can be seen only in remote valleys and among the peaks. Golden eagles, lammergeiers, Alpine swifts, ravens, rock partridges, finches, Alpine wall creepers and all game birds (except sparrows and pigeons) are statutorily protected. Austrian game birds include capercaillies, pheasants, partridges and wild duck. Each biotope has its own particular species – cuckoos and screech owls in woodland, larks and nightingales in open country, swallows and kestrels in villages.

Many Austrian *mammals* are under statutory protection, including all bats and insect-eaters (hedgehogs, moles, shrews). Among the commonest and most active mammals are the **rodents.** Mice and rats are found everywhere; forest and woodlands are inhabited by dormice and squirrels; hamsters and ground-squirrels live on the sandy soils of the Pannonian region; and the mountains provide the right habitat for the *marmot,* which only feels at home between 1300 m/4250 ft and 2700 m/8850 ft. Among the commonest predators are foxes, badgers and martens; more rarely found are the polecat, the ermine and the weasel; and the wild cat, wolf and otter seem doomed to extinction. Among the commonest game shot by sportsmen are hares and rabbits. The *blue hare* is found in the Alps at heights of over 1300 m/4250 ft.

Game. – The *wild pig,* once confined to the Leithagebirge, has spread since the last war to the Ernstbrunner Wald, the Ellender Wald and some parts of the Wienerwald. The *chamois,* that characteristic denizen of the Alps, has also considerably increased its numbers in recent years; and it has even been possible to re-establish the ibex. Although the elk and bison are now extinct in Austria wild sheep (moufflons) and fallow deer still survive in captivity (Lainzer Tiergarten, Sparbach), and large numbers of roe-deer roam over fields and forests. The *red deer* can occasionally be encountered in the forests of the mountain regions.

Ibex

History

Prehistoric and early historical times. – During the *Palaeolithic period* (*c.* 600,000–10,000 B.C.) men live by hunting, food-gathering and fishing, first in the Alpine foreland regions, then reaching higher altitudes during the interglacial periods. Their implements and weapons are made from stone, wood and bone and they live in tents, huts or caves.

8000–1800   Transition to the establishment of permanent settlements (timber huts, pile-dwellings on the Pre-Alpine lakes) and to farming and stock-rearing; beginnings of trade. Bandkeramik culture.

1800–750   *Bronze Age* in Central Europe. Implements and ornaments made of bronze, amber and gold; copper mining in the Alps. Tumulus culture.

About 1000   Beginning of *Iron Age* in Europe.

800–400   **Hallstatt culture** (named after a cemetery at Hallstatt, Upper Austria) of *Illyrians* and *Celts*. Increasing prosperity through ironworking, salt-working and the salt trade; fortified strongholds, the residences of chieftains.

400 B.C. to about the beginning of the Christian era   Continuance of Hallstatt culture in the Eastern Alps; **La Tène culture** (potter's wheel, building of towns, coining of money) in S and NW. The Romans call the tribes in the western part of the Eastern Alps *Raetii*, in the eastern part *Taurisci*.

113 B.C.   The *Cimbri* defeat the Romans at Noreia (Carinthia) and move on to the W.

15–9 B.C.   The **Romans** establish the provinces of *Noricum* (W of the Zillertal), *Raetia* (extending E to the rivers Mürz and Mur) and *Pannonia* (on the eastern edge of the Alps). – Thereafter Roman authority is secured and consolidated by the construction of roads, the LIMES (system of frontier defences) in Upper Germany and Raetia and numerous forts and settlements, such as *Brigantium* (Bregenz), *Aguntum* (near Lienz, Eastern Tirol), *Virunum* (in the Zollfeld near Klagenfurt) and *Vindobona* (Vienna).

From A.D. 260   During the *great migrations* the **Huns** press into Pannonia and conscript into their army the Germanic tribes which had established themselves in the Danube region.

A.D. 453   Death of *Attila;* end of Hun rule. (This is the historical core of the story of the Nibelungs in the "Nibelungenlied").

493–536   The Ostrogothic empire is extended from Italy as far as the northern fringe of the Alps.

About 500   The last Romans withdraw from the three provinces.

From the establishment of the Ostmark (Eastern March) to the assertion of Austrian predominance in the German empire (6th–14th c.) – Austrian history begins with the establishment of Bavarian rule in the Danube region and the Alps. The **Ostmark** (Eastern March) and later *Austria* defend the frontiers against Bohemian and Hungarian attack, and at the same time promote the settlement and Christianisation of the territories to the E. After gaining the German crown the *Habsburgs* regard their Austrian domains as dynastic possessions, which they seek continually to increase.

500–700   The western Alpine foreland region is settled by **Alamanni,** the Eastern Alps (to the E of the Lech) by the **Bajuwari** (Bavarians).

From 550   The Bavarians are loosely attached to the kingdom of the **Franks.**

700–800   Under their hereditary dukes, the *Agilolfings,* the Bavarians bring under cultivation territory extending as far E as the Wienerwald and reaching up into higher levels in the Eastern Alps. Repulse of the Slovenes, pressing in from the SE. Foundation of religious houses in Salzburg by St Rupert (696) and of the monasteries of Innichen (769), Kremsmünster (777), Mattsee (*c.* 777), etc. by Duke *Tassilo III.*

788   **Charlemagne** deposes Tassilo III. Austrian territories incorporated in the Carolingian empire.

791–796   Charlemagne's campaigns against the **Avars,** who had advanced as far as the Eastern Alps. Establishment of the Bavarian Ostmark (Eastern March), between the rivers Enns, Raab and Drau, to protect the newly won territories. Further settlement in Styria and Carinthia. – The territories are Christianised by missionaries from Salzburg, Passau and Aquileia.

From 900   Incursions by the **Magyars** (Hungarians) into the German empire almost every year. Disintegration of the Ostmark; strengthening of the authority of the old Bavarian duchy.

Development of Austria

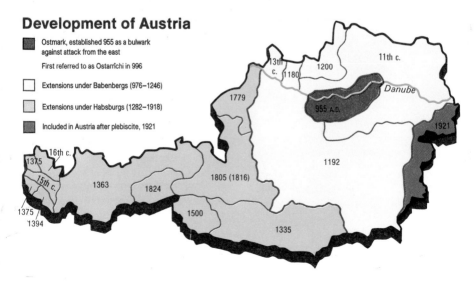

■ Ostmark, established 955 as a bulwark against attack from the east

   First referred to as Ostarrîchi in 996

□ Extensions under Babenbergs (976–1246)

▨ Extensions under Habsburgs (1282–1918)

■ Included in Austria after plebiscite, 1921

955 *Otto I, the Great*, defeats the Hungarians in the battle of Augsburg. The Bavarian Ostmark (referred to as *Ostarrîchi* for the first time in 996) is re-established, bounded by the Enns and Traisen.

976 The **Babenbergs** become Margraves of the Ostmark; Carinthia becomes an independent duchy.

1000–1100 Main period of bringing the eastern part of the Eastern Alps under cultivation; building of castles and foundation of religious houses – Melk (*c.* 985), Göttweig (1072), Lilienfeld (1202), etc.

1096 After the passage of the Crusaders Vienna becomes a focal point of trade with the East.

1142–1286 The *Counts of Tirol* become rulers of the area N and S of the Brenner.

1156 Under the Babenbergs the Ostmark becomes an independent hereditary duchy with Vienna as its capital. – The minnesinger *Walther von der Vogelweide* stays at the ducal court.

1180 Styria becomes a duchy, ruled from 1192 by the Babenbergs.

1246 After the death of the last Babenberg Austria and Styria become Imperial fiefs.

1251–78 King *Ottokar II* of Bohemia becomes ruler of Austria after the Babenberg male line dies out.

1278 Death of Ottokar in the battle of the Marchfeld against **Rudolf of Habsburg,** who founds the *Habsburg dynasty* (King Rudolf I).

1282 Rudolf's sons are granted the fiefs of Austria and Styria; Carinthia and Carniola are granted to relatives.

1335 Duke *Albrecht II* of Austria is granted the fiefs of Carinthia and Carniola.

1363 *Margarethe Maultasch*, last ruler of Tirol, hands it over to Austria. – Duke *Rudolf IV* forges a charter *(Privilegium maius)* granting large privileges to Austria.

1363–1523 Various lordships in Vorarlberg fall to Austria by purchase.

1365 Foundation of Vienna University.

1377–1445 *Oswald von Wolkenstein*, the last of the knightly poets of the Middle Ages, lives in Tirol.

1382 Trieste falls to the Habsburgs.

1406 First meeting of the Austrian Estates (nobility, church, towns), the *Landtag*, in Vienna.

1438–39 Duke *Albrecht V* becomes Emperor as Albrecht II. – Until 1806 the Habsburgs retain the German Imperial crown with only a brief interruption (1742 – 45), and are also kings of Bohemia and Hungary.

1453 The Emperor *Frederick III* makes Austria an *archduchy*.

1469 Foundation of the diocese of Vienna (diocese of Wiener Neustadt in 1477).

1477 Archduke *Maximilian* acquires the Low Countries and Burgundy by marrying Mary of Burgundy; strengthening of the Habsburg dynastic power.

1477–90 Frederick III makes war against King *Matthias Corvinus* of Hungary, who occupies Lower Austria and resides in Vienna from 1485 to 1490.

1491 The Habsburgs establish a hereditary right to the crowns of Bohemia and Hungary; union of all their Austrian hereditary dominions.

1493–1519 The Emperor *Maximilian I*, the "last of the knights", reforms the administration of the hereditary territories (civil service, postal system), extends Habsburg dynastic authority by marriage and succession contracts (marriage of his son Philip with the heiress to Spain and its associated territories, including Naples and the new colonies in America) and thus lays the foundations of the *Habsburg world empire.*

From the Reformation to the Congress of Vienna (beginning of the 16th c. to 1815). – The 16th c. is dominated by the struggle between the Habsburgs and the nobility, which favours Protestantism. Together with the Wittelsbachs of Bavaria the Habsburgs assume the *leadership* of the *Counter-Reformation* in the German Empire. Through its successes in the East and its close association with the Holy Roman Empire the state which has developed out of the hereditary Habsburg possessions becomes a European great power.

1521 *Martin Luther* is outlawed at the Diet of Worms. Rapid spread of the *Reformation* in the Habsburg hereditary lands.

1521–22 The Emperor *Charles V* hands over the Austrian hereditary territories to his younger brother *Ferdinand I.*

1526 The **Turks** attack Hungary. Defeat and death of King *Lewis II* of Hungary and Bohemia in the battle of Mohács; his lands pass to Ferdinand I. – Hungary falls temporarily under Turkish rule.

1529 First (unsuccessful) siege of Vienna by the Turks.

1541 The physician and natural scientist *Paracelsus* dies in Salzburg.

1556 Abdication of the Emperor Charles V; his brother Ferdinand becomes Emperor. – The main political concern of Ferdinand I and his successors is the defence of the Empire against France in the W and against the Turks in the E.

1571 The Emperor grants religious freedom in Austria. Only about an eighth of the population remain Roman Catholic: this is the high point of the spread of Protestantism in Austria.

1576 Under the Emperor *Rudolf II* the **Counter-Reformation** begins in Austria, with the help of the Jesuits. The conflict between Catholics and Protestants becomes more acute. – Between now and 1650 the Habsburg possessions are restored to the Catholic faith by various measures of compulsion (Protestants expelled from Styria, Carinthia and Carniola).

1586 Opening of Graz University under Jesuit direction.

1618–48 **Thirty Years War.** Among its causes are the conflicts between Catholics and Protestants, the struggle by the Estates to achieve greater power, the efforts of the Habsburg Emperor to secure the religious and political unity of the Empire and the rivalries between European states (conflict between France and the Habsburgs, attempts by Sweden to achieve dominance in the Baltic, etc.). The immediate occasion of the war is the rebellion by the Protestant nobility in Bohemia against the Emperor ("Defenestration of Prague"). The conflict develops into a European war through the intervention of King *Christian IV* of Denmark, King *Gustavus Adolphus* of Sweden and the French under Cardinal *Richelieu.*

From 1645 Swedish armies fighting on Austrian soil.

1648 Treaty of Westphalia: Austrian sovereignty in

Alsace ceded to France; weakening of the Empire; Protestants denied equal rights with Catholics in Austria; victory of *absolutism* over the Estates in the Habsburg hereditary dominions.

1663–99 Turkish wars. Turkish incursions into the Christian West are repelled under the leadership of Austria; the Turks are driven out of Europe.

1664 An Imperial army commanded by Count *Montecuccoli* defeats the Turks in the battle of St. Gotthard, on the eastern boundary of Styria.

1683 Second Turkish siege of Vienna. The siege is raised after an Imperial army commanded by Duke *Charles of Lorraine* defeats the Turks in a battle on the Kahlenberg.

1677 Foundation of Innsbruck University.

1683–1736 *Prince Eugene of Savoy* in the Imperial service as general and statesman. War with Turks and French.

1699 Conquest of Hungary, Transsylvania and most of Slovenia and Croatia. Eastern territories populated by German settlers. The Habsburgs gain the hereditary right (in the male line) to the Hungarian throne; establishment of the **Dual Monarchy** of Austria and Hungary. – Vienna becomes the political, economic and cultural centre of the monarchy.

1701–14 *War of the Spanish Succession.* After the death of the Habsburg king *Charles II* Austria and France fight for the succession to the Spanish throne. In spite of Prince Eugene's victories Austria, under Charles VI, gains only most of the subsidiary Spanish possessions (the Low Countries, Milan, Naples).

1708 The duchy of Mantua falls to Austria.

1713 The Pragmatic Sanction, which secures the right of female succession to the throne on the basis of treaties with the Empire, Spain, Prussia, Britain and France. (This makes possible the succession of Maria Theresa.)

1720 Austria acquires Sicily.

1735 Austria cedes Naples and Sicily to the Spanish Bourbons, receiving Parma and Piacenza in return.

1740–80 Maria Theresa, Queen of Bohemia and Hungary, Archduchess of Austria, from 1745 Empress; married to *Francis Stephen of Lorraine.* She fights in the *War of the Austrian Succession* (1740–48) for recognition of her right to the Austrian throne. In the Silesian Wars and the Seven Years War (1756–63) she loses Silesia to *Frederick the Great* of Prussia.

1742–80 Reforms during the reign of Maria Theresa: creation of a modern state and civil service; financial and army reform; establishment of a public educational system; maintenance of an independent peasantry in German territories. – Further settlement of land within the Empire ("internal colonisation"), e.g. of Swabians in the SE.
The capital of the Empire, Vienna, becomes a great focal point of classical music *(Gluck, Haydn, Mozart, Beethoven).* Foundation of the Burgtheater (1741).

1763 Peace of Hubertusburg between Austria, Prussia and Saxony. Beginning of the rivalry between Prussia and Austria.

1772 In the first partition of Poland Austria receives Eastern Galicia and Lodomeria. – Brenner road opened 1772, Arlberg road 1785.

1781–90 *Joseph II,* Maria Theresa's son (joint ruler from 1765), the most characteristic representative of enlightened absolutism: toleration for Protestants (1781); abolition of serfdom (1781–85); dissolution of superfluous religious houses (some 700 out of 2000: 1782–86); German the sole official language (1784). – There is bitter opposition to Joseph's over-hasty reforms, and at the end of his reign (1790) he is obliged to withdraw many of his measures.

1795 In the third partition of Poland Austria receives Western Galicia, with Cracow and other territories.

1792–1805 The Emperor *Francis II* (German Emperor 1792–1806, Emperor of Austria 1804–35) takes part in three coalition wars against France.

1797 Napoleon advances over the Alps from Italy as far as Leoben in Styria. Austria cedes Belgium to France and receives in return the Republic of Venice.

1804 Francis II assumes the title of **Emperor of Austria** as **Francis I.**

1805 The French army occupies Vienna. Napoleon wins a decisive victory at Austerlitz in Moravia. Venice ceded to the kingdom of Italy, Tirol and Vorarlberg to Bavaria; Austria receives Salzburg.

1805 *Dissolution of the Holy Roman Empire:* under pressure from Napoleon, Francis II gives up the title of German Emperor.

1809 War between Austria and France. Unsuccessful struggle by the Tirolese, under the leadership of *Andreas Hofer* (shot in Mantua in 1810), to free themselves from Bavarian rule. – After being defeated by Archduke *Charles* at Aspern, Napoleon wins a decisive victory at Wagram. Peace signed in Vienna: cession of Austrian territory to Bavaria, Russia and Italy (under French rule).

1810 Rapprochement between Austria and France through Napoleon's marriage to the Emperor's daughter, *Marie Louise.*

1813–15 *Wars of Liberation* after the destruction of Napoleon's army in Russia (1812). Austria allies itself with Prussia and Russia against Napoleon, who is defeated in the Battle of the Nations at Leipzig (1813); final defeat of Napoleon at Waterloo (1815).

1814–15 Congress of Vienna, under the chairmanship of Prince *Metternich* (Austrian Foreign Minister): Austria cedes Belgium to Holland and the district of Breisgau to Baden and Württemberg but recovers Tirol, Vorarlberg, Carinthia, Carniola, Trieste, Galicia, Milan, Venice, Salzburg and the Innviertel.
Austria assumes the presidency of the **German Confederation** (39 states – 35 principalities and 4 free cities). (The Bundestag or Federal Diet meets in Frankfurt am Main.)
From the Restoration to the end of the First World War (1815 to 1918–19). – During the Restoration Austria's external and internal policies are aimed at the *maintenance of the established order in Europe,* and are thus irreconcilably opposed to liberalism and to all revolutionary or nationalist movements. After 1850, until the First World War, the *problem of reconciling the interests of the different nationalities* in this multinational state can never be lost sight of.

1814 *Madersberger* constructs the first sewing machine.

1819 Carlsbad Decrees, instigated by Metternich and Prussia: introduction of censorship, universities under State supervision, political agitation to be suppressed, strict control by police.

1826 *Ressel* invents the screw propeller.

1848 March Revolution in Austria, reflecting liberal and nationalist aspirations; dismissal of Metternich. The October rising is quashed by military force.

The Emperor Ferdinand I abdicates and is succeeded by his nephew **Francis Joseph I** (b. 1830), who reigns until 1916.

1849 Austria is granted a constitution. Equal status for all national languages.

1848–49 Rising in Hungary led by *Kossuth*; repressed by the Austrians with Russian help.

1848–66 Risings in northern Italy against Austrian rule. After initial military successes Austria gives up its Italian territories.

1850 Re-establishment of the German Confederation under Austrian leadership.

1854–1909 Construction of mountain railways – Semmering 1854, Brenner 1867, Arlberg 1884, Tauern 1909.

From 1860 Increasing interest in climbing in the Alps; opening up of the Eastern Alps for tourists.

1862 Foundation of the Austrian Alpine Club. The first mountain hut in the Eastern Alps, the Stüdlhütte, is built in 1868.

1864 Austria and Prussia go to *war with Denmark* over Schleswig-Holstein. – First typewriter constructed by *Mitterhofer*, first car running on gasoline by *Marcus*.

1866 *Austro-Prussian War* for predominance in the German-speaking countries. The Austrians are defeated at Königgrätz (Hradec Králové). Peace of Prague: the German Confederation is dissolved; Austria opts out of the move towards a German national state.

1867 Agreement with Hungary (the *Ausgleich*, "Compromise"): Hungary (with Croatia and Transsylvania) is recognised as an autonomous part of the Empire with its own government and parliament; **Austria** and **Hungary** joined in a *personal union.* – The problem of the different nationalities becomes steadily more acute in the Austrian part of the Empire until the First World War.

1873 "Three Emperors' League" between Austria, Russia and Germany.

1877 Free-flying model aircraft by *Kress*.

1878 Austria occupies the Turkish provinces of Bosnia and Herzegovina.

1879 Dual Alliance between Austro-Hungary and Germany. The Austrian-Russian conflict of interests in the Balkans becomes more acute.

1882 Triple Alliance between Austro-Hungary, Germany and Italy.

1885–1903 *Auer von Welsbach* invents the gas mantle (1885), the osmium filament lamp (1898) and Auer's metal (used in cigarette lighters, etc.: 1903).

From 1902 The Hungarian parliament opposes the use of German as the sole language of command in the army, and thus in effect opposes the idea of a common army.

1906 Introduction of equal and universal suffrage in the Austrian part of the Empire.

1908 Austria annexes Bosnia and Herzegovina. Violent opposition by Serbia, supported by Russia.

1914–18 **First World War.** The immediate occasion is the murder of the heir to the Austrian throne and his wife by Serbian nationalists at Sarajevo (28 June); the causes are rivalry between the European states, commitments to military and political alliances, the armaments race, the difficulties of the Austro-Hun-

garian multi-national state, Russia's Balkan policies, excessive nationalism among the smaller peoples of the eastern Mediterranean and over-hasty mobilisation and ultimatums. On 28 July 1914 Austro-Hungary declares war on Serbia; Germany declares war on Russia on 1 August and on France on 3 August; Britain declares war on Germany on 4 August. – Fighting in western, southern and eastern Europe and in the Near East. The Central Powers win initial successes against Serbia and Russia on the eastern front.

1915 Italy declares war on Austro-Hungary on 23 May, Romania on 27 August. Fighting on the Isonzo line, in Carinthia and in Tirol.

1916 Death of the Emperor *Francis Joseph I.* His grand-nephew and successor *Karl* tries, unsuccessfully, to secure a separate peace in order to preserve the multi-national state.

1917 The United States come into the war on the side of the Allies. – Crisis situation in Austro-Hungary: efforts by the nationalities to achieve autonomy.

1918 Peace treaty between the Central Powers and Russia signed at Brest-Litovsk. *Revolution in Vienna* (21 October); armistice between Austro-Hungary and the Allies (3 November); abdication of the Emperor Karl (11 November); proclamation of the **Republic of German Austria** (*Republik Deutsch-Österreich:* 12 November).

1919 Peace treaty between the Allies and Austria signed at St-Germain-en-Laye (10 September): dissolution of the Austro-Hungarian monarchy; southern Tirol, Istria, Trieste and some areas in Dalmatia, Carinthia and Carniola to Italy; recognition by Austria of the independent states of Czechoslovakia, Poland, Hungary and Yugoslavia; union with Germany prohibited; abandonment of the style "German Austria".

Republic of Austria (1919 to the present day). – The period after the First World War is marked by *economic difficulties* and *internal political conflicts* (risings against the government by both the "left" and the "right"). In 1938 Austria is incorporated in Hitler's German Reich (the *Anschluss*), and in the following year is involved along with Germany in the Second World War. After the war, unlike Germany, it preserves its unity as a state and secures the recognition by the occupying powers of the central government in Vienna.

1918–20 Carinthia fights for its freedom against the Slovenes.

1920 New constitution in force (10 November): Austria becomes a *federal state.* – Austria joins the League of Nations.

1921 Plebiscites in Tirol, Salzburg province and Burgenland show majorities in favour of union with Austria.

1919–24 Severe economic crisis and *inflation.* – International credits granted to Austria under League of Nations guarantee (1922).

1927 Socialists riot in Vienna; general strike. – In subsequent years Austrian domestic policies are increasingly influenced by socialist and nationalist defence leagues.

1929 Constitutional reform: the parliamentary republic becomes a *presidential republic.*

1930 Cancellation of Austrian reparations obligations (January). Treaty of friendship with Italy (February). Fascist influence increases in domestic politics.

1931 Proposals for a German-Austrian customs

union are frustrated by French resistance (March). Severe financial crisis and high unemployment as a result of the *world economic depression* (failure of large banks).

1933   **Coup d'état** by the Federal Chancellor, *Dollfuss*, in order to prevent the growth of the National Socialist movement (March). The parliamentary constitution is abrogated and an authoritarian régime instituted ("Austro-Fascism"). The National Socialist party is banned (June).

1934   Street fighting in Vienna and other towns. The Socialist party and all other parties, except the "Fatherland Front", are banned (February). – Rapprochement with Italy and Hungary for the purpose of political and economic cooperation ("Rome Protocols", March). – Unsuccessful *National Socialist putsch* (July). Murder of Dollfuss, who is succeeded by *Schuschnigg*. The threat of military action by Italy under *Mussolini* prevents German intervention in Austria.

1936   Introduction of general conscription.

1938   Under pressure from *Hitler* Schuschnigg agrees to amnesty Austrian National Socialists and to include them in the government; *Seyss-Inquart* becomes Minister of the Interior. National Socialist disturbances in Graz and other towns (March).
After an ultimatum and the resignation of Schuschnigg *German troops* march *into Austria* (11 March). The **Anschluss** (incorporation of Austria in the German Reich) is proclaimed (13 March) and ratified by a national plebiscite (April). Territorial reorganisation: Austria is divided into gaus *(Gaue)*, with Seyss-Inquart as Reichsstatthalter (Governor) until 1940. The National Socialist party is given wide powers; many non-Austrians in important political posts.

1939–45   **Second World War**, in which Austrians fight in the German army in all theatres of war.

From 1943   Allied air attacks on Austria, causing heavy damage in the larger towns, particularly Vienna. – At the Moscow Conference the Allies declare that after the war Austria will be restored within its 1937 frontiers.

1944–45   Germans flee to Austria to escape Soviet troops and partisans.

1945–46   Expulsion of almost all Germans from former German territory in the E, Czechoslovakia (Sudetenland) and Hungary.

1945   Vienna is occupied by the Soviet army (13 April). Provisional government under *Renner*, leader of the Socialist party and a former Federal Chancellor (27 April). Austria is divided into four *occupation zones* (4 July). The Soviet zone comprises Lower Austria, Upper Austria N of the Danube and Burgenland; the American zone Upper Austria S of the Danube and Salzburg province; the British zone Styria, Carinthia and Eastern Tirol; and the French zone Northern Tirol and Vorarlberg. Vienna, divided into four sectors, becomes the headquarters of the Allied Control Council.
General election (25 November). The National Council elects Renner as Federal President (20 December). *Figl* becomes Federal Chancellor and forms a coalition government from members of the Austrian People's Party, the Socialist Party and the Communist Party.

1945–53   Economic difficulties. *Currency reforms* in 1945, 1947 and 1953.

1946   Agreement between Austria and Italy, negotiated by Gruber and de Gasperi, providing for the cultural and administrative autonomy of the German-speaking territory, formerly southern Tirol, transferred to Italy.

1946–47   Nationalisation of almost all the country's primary industry and other key industries.

1947–54   Austria receives Marshall Aid.

1955   The **Staatsvertrag** (State Treaty) between the four great powers and Austria is signed on 15 May: full sovereignty restored to Austria; prohibition of political or economic union with Germany; all occupation troops to be withdrawn; restrictions on Austrian armaments. The National Council declares Austria's perpetual *neutrality* (October). Austria is admitted to the United Nations (December).
The former Southern Tirol remains a major foreign policy problem. Negotiations with Italy are broken off on several occasions. Bomb attacks on Italian installations.

1956   Austria becomes a member of the Council of Europe.

1960   Austria joins the European Free Trade Association (EFTA).

1966   The Austrian People's Party secures an absolute majority in elections to the National Council.

1969   The National Council approves the *"Southern Tirol package"*: increased autonomy for Southern Tirol; German language given equal status with Italian.

1971   The Socialist Party secures an absolute majority; new government under *Kreisky*. The economic laws (e.g. on price regulation) designed to check inflation introduced in 1962 are continued in force. The schilling is revalued upwards by 11·59%.

1972   Free trade treaty between Austria and the EEC: reduction of duties on industrial products.
Austria establishes diplomatic relations with the German Democratic Republic – one of the first Western states to do so. – Count *Waldheim*, a former Austrian Foreign Minister, becomes Secretary-General of the United Nations.

From 1974   Sharp increases in oil prices lead to a world-wide *energy crisis* and *economic recession;* fall in export orders, increasing costs of energy production.

1975   The Socialist Party win an absolute majority in elections to the National Council (October). – Attack on meeting of OPEC ministers in Vienna by Palestinian terrorists (December).

1976   Plan for stimulating the economy (January). – Difficulties with the Slovenian minority in Carinthia, which complains of discrimination against Slovenes. "1000 years of Carinthia" celebrated in Klagenfurt (26 June).
The close alignment of the schilling with the European "currency snake" is abandoned (July). – Collapse of the Reichsbrücke in Vienna (1 August).

1977   Demonstrations calling for the closing of the only Austrian nuclear power station (Zwentendorf, Lower Austria) and for the abandonment of plans to build any further nuclear power stations (March). Measures to stabilise the economy and balance the national budget (June). Ratification by the National Council of the Council of Europe's Anti-Terrorist Convention (August).

1978   Tension between Austria and the United Nations over the employment of Austrian UN troops in Southern Lebanon. The Federal Chancellor pays a state visit to East Berlin (March). A national referendum shows a majority against bringing the Zwentendorf nuclear power station into operation (November). The passing of a law forbidding the use of atomic power for the provision of energy in Austria.

1979 In elections for the National Council the SPÖ secured an absolute majority (May). – On 5 June Federal Chancellor Kreisky swears in his 4th cabinet. An agreement is signed (September) for a programme of cultural and scientific co-operation with East Germany.

1980 Federal Chancellor Kreisky visits Yugoslavia (April). – In May leading politicians from the East and the West meet in Vienna in connection with the 25th anniversary of the agreement on Austrian sovereignty. Rudolf Kirchschläger, President of the Austrian Parliament since 1974, is re-elected for a further 6 years (May). – The East German leader Erich Honecker visits Austria (November).

1981 Vice-Chancellor and Finance Minister Androsch resigns (January); Reorganisation of the government. – Federal Chancellor Kreisky visits Egypt (February). – Death of the leading actor Paul Hörbiger in Vienna (March). The conductor Karl Böhm dies in Salzburg (August). – Federal President Kirchschläger visits Switzerland (September).

1982 Libyan Head of State Gaddafi visits Austria (March).

The National Assembly passes a new law controlling arms exports.

1983 UN conference in Vienna on Human Rights. In parliamentary elections the SPÖ (Austrian Socialist Party) loses its absolute majority. Chancellor Bruno Kreisky resigns; the new chancellor is Fred Sinowatz, SPÖ. Formation of a SPÖ–FPÖ coalition government (May). Pope John Paul II visits Austria for the Catholic Congress (September). – Chancellor Sinowatz becomes leader of the SPÖ (October). – Austria and Poland sign a cultural and economic agreement.

1984 Chancellor Sinowatz visits Yugoslavia (January). Reorganisation of the government. Leopold Gratz becomes the new Foreign Minister (September). – Chancellor Sinowatz visits the USSR (November).

1985 Austria introduces strict controls on exhaust emission for vehicles. – Foreign Ministers of East and West meet on the 30th anniversary of the signing of the Austrian Treaty (May). – The Finnish President Koivisto visits Austria (October).

Art

Any account of Austrian art is faced with the problem of the country's changing boundaries over the centuries (see above, under History). The following survey is concerned essentially with the territory of present-day Austria; but it must be borne in mind that there were always intensive contacts with the countries to the west, north, east and south, based in the first place on political but necessarily also intellectual and artistic relationships. In general it can be said that artistic influences from other countries tended to affect Austria only with a certain time-lag, sometimes amounting to as much as a century and a half; and accordingly the dates of the Romanesque, Gothic and Baroque periods in Austria are considerably later than in Germany, France and Italy.

Austria is believed to have been first settled by man during the last interglacial period (about 150,000 B.C.,) but the earliest artistic object of any significance found on Austrian soil dates from a much later period. This is the famous "Venus of Willendorf" (Natural History Museum, Vienna), a cult statuette 10 cm/4 in. high of a generously proportioned female figure which was found at Willendorf in Lower Austria in 1908. It is though to be about 25,000 years old – i.e. to date from the *Palaeolithic* period.

The next period of artistic interest is again much later: the **Hallstatt** period (Early Iron Age, 800–400 B.C.), named after the type site at Hallstatt in Upper Austria. Important material of this period can be seen in the museum at Hallstatt and in

the prehistoric collection of the Natural History Museum in Vienna.

The second half of the 1st millennium B.C. saw the flowering of the Celtic culture of the *Late Iron Age* and the coming of Roman influence. A notable example of Roman art is the "Magdalensberg Youth", a Roman copy of a Greek statue which was found at St. Veit an der Glan (Carinthia) in 1502 and is now in the Museum of Art in Vienna.

In 16 B.C. Raetia and the kingdom of Noricum were occupied by Rome, and Austria thus became Roman territory. Interesting material of the *Roman period* can be seen at Carnuntum (now Petronell) and in the Museum Carnuntinum at Bad Deutsch-Altenburg (both in Lower Austria).

After the withdrawal of the Romans (c. A.D. 400), during the period of the *great migrations*, successive waves of Germanic peoples – Huns, Avars, Slavs and finally Bajuwari (Bavarians) passed through Austria and sometimes settled there. The history of this period is still obscure, but some evidence of artistic and architectural achievement can be identified. In Salzburg St Rupert founded the monasteries of St. Peter and Nonnberg in 690 and about 700, and in the 8th c. other religious houses were established at Mondsee (748) and Kremsmünster (777). One of the treasures of Kremsmünster Abbey is the Tassilo Chalice, a masterpiece of early medieval art presented by Duke Tassilo III when the abbey was founded.

A first great flowering of art came with the consolidation of the political and economic power of the Babenbergs. At the court of Duke Leopold VI, the Glorious, there was a "Court of the Muses" to which such leading *minnesingers* as Walther von der Vogelweide, Neidhart von Reuenthal and Ulrich von Liechtenstein belonged, and it was in Austria that the great national epics, the "Gudrunlied" and the "Nibelungenlied", received their final form about 1200.

The Crusades, and no doubt also the numerous Babenberg marriages with Byzantine princesses, brought in influences from the East. During the **Romanesque** period Austrian art, like all medieval art, was devoted to the service of the Church and the Christian faith. The beginnings of a continuous process of artistic development in Austria can thus be set in the 12th c., except in Salzburg, which was already a considerable artistic place in the Ottonian period. The Salzburg illuminated manuscripts of the 11th c. are works of consummate artistic perfection; and here, too, Byzantine influence is clearly detectable in the 12th c.

There was also a flowering of monumental art in the form of magnificently conceived frescoes, remains of which have been preserved in the Nonnberg church (Salzburg) and St. John's Chapel at Pürgg in the Ennstal. One of the outstanding works of this period is the Verdun Altar (1180) at Klosterneuburg (Lower Austria), with champlevé enamel panels of Old and New Testament scenes.

Few major examples of Romanesque sculpture have survived. Not to be missed, however, are the sculptural decoration on the outer wall of the apse of Schöngräbern parish church (Lower Austria) and the sculpture on the Riesentor (Giant's Doorway) of St. Stephen's Cathedral, Vienna. In western Austria the architecture of the 12th c. was mainly the work of the Benedictines (abbeys of St. Peter, Nonnberg, Mondsee, Lambach, Kremsmünster), in the E mainly of the Cistercians, who from 1135 onwards built a series of abbeys which rank among the finest works of Romanesque architecture in Austria (Heiligenkreuz, Zwettl, Lilienfeld). From this early period date the splendid nave of the church at Heiligenkreuz and the chapterhouse at Zwettl. The supreme achievement of Romanesque architecture in Austria is Gurk Cathedral (Carinthia), a massive three-aisled pillared basilica (consecrated 1174) with a crypt containing a hundred columns of marble; a notable feature is the cycle of late

Romanesque frescoes (*c.* 1260) on the W gallery.

The first Gothic influences were brought in by the Cistercians. In the richly decorated cloisters at Zwettl, Heiligenkreuz and Lilienfeld, built in the early 13th c., Gothic elements can already be detected, and the church at Lilienfeld (completed 1263), a three-aisled pillared basilica with an ambulatory, incorporates features which are pure Burgundian early Gothic. But although local Austrian architects were susceptible to influences of this kind, most of the buildings of the late Babenberg period have a sturdiness and a massiveness which is still entirely Romanesque (charnel-houses at Tulln and Mödling; nave of the Franciscan Church, Salzburg).

Gothic art became fully established in Austria only towards the end of the 13th c. The Gothic art and architecture of the 14th c. were closely bound up with the House of Habsburg, which came to power in 1278 with the accession of Rudolf I. Since there were active contacts between the courts in Vienna and Prague (which was an Imperial residence for some time), French, Italian and German influences reached Vienna and the rest of Austria by way of Bohemia.

In Lower Austria the Cistercians continued to promote lively artistic activity (choir and fountain-house at Heiligenkreuz, in pure Gothic style). Notable landmarks of 14th c. Gothic architecture are the Leechkirche in Graz and the Augustinian Church in Vienna.

The 14th c. also produced some major works of Gothic sculpture (figures on the Singertor, St. Stephen's Cathedral, Vienna; Madonna of Klosterneuburg) and stained glass (choir of Viktring parish church, Carinthia; fountain-house, Heiligenkreuz), as well as the first panel painting.

The 15th c. saw a great flowering of late Gothic architecture. The masons' guild of St. Stephen's in Vienna now made a particular mark, the most impressive proof of their skill being St. Stephen's Cathedral itself with its mighty S tower, which took only 25 years to build. In contrast to the delicately articulated Viennese late Gothic, as exemplified by St. Stephen's, the church of Maria am Gestade with its charming openwork steeple and the

"Spinnerin am Kreuze" column on the Wienerberg, is the type of large hall-church which was preferred elsewhere in Austria (choir of the Franciscan Church, Salzburg). Here, too, mention must be made of the finest Gothic burgher's house in Austria, the Kornmesserhaus in Bruck an der Mur (Styria), built about 1500.

There was also a flowering of painting and sculpture in the late Gothic period, when local schools with distinctive styles of their own grew up not only in Vienna and Salzburg but also in more remote parts of the country. The sculpture of this period found expression both in stone (sometimes in realistic style, sometimes in the gently rounded "soft" style) and in wood, notably in winged altars of consummate craftsmanship (Kefermarkt, before 1500; St. Wolfgang, by Michael Pacher, 1481; both in Upper Austria). The central panel and the wings of such altars may be either carved or painted. Notable painters of this period are the anonymous masters known as the Albrechtsmeister (Klosterneuburg) and the Schottenmeister ("Flight into Egypt", 1469, with the earliest view of Vienna), Konrad Laib (Graz, Vienna, Salzburg) and Rueland Frueauf the Elder, perhaps the finest talent of the period (Passau, Salzburg). During this period, too, Jörg Kölderer was working in Innsbruck on the Goldenes Dachl and other buildings, showing a harmony and balance which already points towards a new age.

The medieval world picture now gives way to new conceptions. The development of a money economy had transformed the economic structure of Europe, and the old cultural structure was likewise ripe for renewal. The ideas of the **Renaissance** now spread from Italy all over Europe, and this "rebirth of antiquity" set man in the middle of the stage, in conscious reaction against the medieval withdrawal from the world and concern with the life beyond. In Austria this restless time of transition found its incarnation in the figure of the Emperor Maximilian I. Although his attachment to the past earned him the name "last of the knights", he was receptive to new ideas, attracted new and progressive artists to his court and promoted craftsmanship and learning. Among the most interesting works of art of this period is the magnificent tomb in the Hofkirche at Innsbruck which the Emperor commissioned for himself (although in the event he was buried in Wiener Neustadt and not in Innsbruck) but which remained unfinished, with 28 over-lifesize bronze statues (some of them to the design of Dürer and Peter Vischer).

Late Gothic art, firmly established in the Alpine regions, was slow to give way to the new spirit; but local boundaries now became increasingly blurred, and with the removal of territorial barriers (Carinthia became part of Austria in 1335, Tirol in 1363) new trends were able to make headway.

At the turn of the 15th c. there developed in the Danube region a new style of painting, the *Danube school,* Which sought to achieve an intimate harmony between the content and action of a picture and its setting (brightly illuminated interiors, landscapes). Among the leading members of this school were Lukas Cranach the Elder, Albrecht Altdorfer of Regensburg and Wolf Huber (a native of Vorarlberg) with his delicate landscapes.

That the art and architecture of the Renaissance are less well represented in Austria than Gothic and Baroque is due to the bitter struggle with the Turks which began in the time of Maximilian and continued for the next two centuries. Although this was mostly fought out in the Balkans there was also frequent fighting on Austrian soil. In 1529 and 1683 the Turks laid siege to Vienna, and although they were repulsed they devastated the surrounding country and repeatedly ravaged Carinthia and Styria. The whole strength of the country was devoted to the Turkish wars, and little energy was left over for art. The defensive line against the Turks was reinforced, and Klagenfurt, Graz and Vienna were protected by powerful *fortifications.* In Graz the military engineer Domenico d'Allio also built the main block of the Landhaus with its beautiful arcaded courtyard (1557–65), and in Vienna the Amalientrakt of the Hofburg, with the Schweizertor, was built. Other examples of the building activity of this period are the Riegersburg in Styria, Burg Hochosterwitz in Carinthia and many castles in Burgenland. Among the finest buildings of the period are the Schallaburg in Lower Austria with its magnificent terracotta-decorated courtyard and Schloss Porcia at Spittal an der Drau (Carinthia). Most of the buildings erected in this period were the work of Italian military architects, who left their mark on the architecture not only of the Renaissance but of the early Baroque.

In addition to the Turkish wars there were also peasant wars in Upper Austria and Salzburg province, and the Thirty Years War brought the Swedish army almost to the gates of Vienna in 1648. Under the Emperor Rudolf II, whose main residence was in Prague, Mannerism made its entry into Austrian art. To this period belong the Imperial crown (1602) in the Treasury in the Hofburg and the great works of Mannerist painting in the Museum of Art in Vienna (among them the extraordinary compositions of G. Arcimboldo). In Salzburg, under the patronage of the Archbishops, there developed a purely Italian Mannerist and early Baroque style, exemplified in the Cathedral (1624–28), by Santino Solari, who also built Schloss Hellbrunn.

Only after the final elimination of the Turkish danger by the great generals Charles of Lorraine, Prince Eugene of Savoy and G. von Laudon was the Austrian (Habsburg) state firmly established; and this "heroic age" of Austria also saw the triumphant establishment of the **Baroque** style which was to give Austria its most brilliant flowering of art and architecture. The consolidation of the absolutist state was accompanied by a resurgence of strength in the Roman Catholic Church after the trauma of the Reformation and the victory of the Counter-Reformation, due largely to the work of the Jesuits. The result was a great burst of building activity during which numbers of palaces and religious houses and churches were erected and sculpture and painting also flourished.

As we have seen, the early stages of Baroque were the work of Italian architects (the d'Allio family; G. P. de Pomis, who began Ferdinand II's mausoleum in Graz in 1614; S. Solari). After this preliminary phase Austrian architecture achieved its finest consummation in the splendour and magnificence of High Baroque. The sumptuous buildings of this period were mostly commissioned by the Imperial House, the high nobility and the Church. After the troubles of the Turkish wars Vienna enjoyed a period of brilliance which made it a worthy Imperial capital, and numerous palaces and noble mansions were built, particularly in the outlying districts which had been devastated during the wars.

The outstanding figures of this period in the field of architecture are Lukas von Hildebrandt (Schloss Belvedere, Vienna, built for Prince Eugene, 1721 onwards; rebuilding of Schloss Mirabell, Salzburg; Piarist Church, Vienna; Göttweig Abbey, 1719 onwards; Schloss Schlosshof and Schloss Halbthurn in the Marchfeld), Johann Bernhard Fischer von Erlach and his son (Karlskirche, National Library, Bohemian Court Chancery, Palais Trautson, Prince Eugene's Stadtpalais and the Plague Column in the Graben, Vienna; Kollegienkirche, Salzburg), Jakob Prandtauer (Melk Abbey, 1702–26) and Josef Munggenast (church, Dürnstein, Lower Austria). Fine work was also done by Italian architects: Carlo Antonio Carlone built the fish-ponds at Kremsmünster and drew up the plans for St. Florian (built by J. Prandtauer), and Donato Felice d'Allio began in 1730 the rebuilding of Klosterneuburg Abbey, modelled on the Escorial near Madrid, but of which only a small part was completed.

This vigorous building activity was accompanied by an equally lively output of sculpture and painting. Among the most notable sculptors of the period were Matthias Steinl or Steindl, Meinrad Guggenbichler, Balthasar Permoser ("Apotheosis of Prince Eugene", 1721, in the Baroque Museum, Lower Belvedere, Vienna), Balthasar Moll (sarcophagus of Maria Theresa and Francis I in the Kapuzinergruft, Vienna), Georg Raphael Donner (fountain in the Neuer Markt, Vienna; Pietà in Gurk Cathedral) and the extraordinary Franz Xaver Messerschmidt (grotesque sculpture in the Historical Museum, Vienna).

The leading Baroque painters, mainly producing altarpieces and large cycles of frescoes, were Johann Michael Rottmayr, Daniel Gran, Bartolomeo Altomonte, Paul Troger, Martin Johann Schmidt ("Kremser Schmidt") and Anton Maulpertsch. Some of these artists were active in the second half of the 18th c., which is usually regarded as the Rococo period; but since Baroque art continued into the second half of the century in full strength and vigour and then quite suddenly came to an end, as if exhausted, Rococo art did not achieve any great development in

Austria (basilica at Wilten in Tirol; interior of Schönbrunn Palace, Vienna).

The Napoleonic wars which followed the French Revolution again engaged the whole energies of the nation, and it was only after the Congress of Vienna (1815) that a new era began. The Holy Roman Empire was dissolved in 1806, two years after Austria had become an independent empire. Francis II had the Imperial crown jewels transferred to Vienna to save them from the French, and they can now be seen in the Treasury in the Hofburg (the finest item being the 10th c. German Imperial crown).

The international *neo-classical style* (main works in Vienna: the Gloriette in Schönbrunn park, by F. von Hohenberg, 1775; a pyramid-shaped tomb in the Augustinian Church, by A. Canova, 1805; Burgtor, by P. von Nobile, 1824) soon gave way to a local and more intimate style, the Austrian **Biedermeier**. The leading architect of this period was Josef Kornhäusel (rebuilding of Baden bei Wien after a fire, 1812; Husarentempel on the Anninger, Mödling, 1813).

In the painting of this period three main groups can be distinguished. Heinrich Füger and Johann Peter Krafft adhere to the neo-classical school. The romantic school is represented by Ludwig Ferdinand Schnorr von Carolsfeld, an East Prussian working in Vienna, and Joseph von Führich, whose pictures show the influence of the Nazarenes. Like Führich, Moritz von Schwind and Leopold Kupelwieser carried over romantic features into the later "Historicism" of the Ringstrasse era. The real Biedermeier painting, however, was concerned with scenes from middle-class life, showing great delicacy and subtlety in the delineation of the figures; but it also devoted loving care to the depiction of nature and the human environment. Leading representatives of this school were Moritz Michael Daffinger, Josef Kriehuber, Josef Danhauser, Friedrich von Amerling, Friedrich Gauermann, Peter Fendi and Karl Schindler. Another painter of the period whom it is difficult to assign to any particular school was Ferdinand Waldmüller, an incomparable portrayer of nature.

But the Biedermeier period was above all a great age of *music*, for Beethoven and Schubert, both working in Vienna, had succeeded Haydn and Mozart. The Viennese classical period is one of the undisputed high points of Western music, and the musical culture of Vienna, mainly supported by the interest and enthusiasm of the middle classes, remained active and vital throughout the whole of the 19th c. and into the beginnings of the modern period after the turn of the century (Schönberg, Webern).

After the 1848 Revolution and the shattering of the comfortable and apparently secure Biedermeier world it seemed as if the Austro-Hungarian dual monarchy, now heading towards its final decline, sought to pour all its strength into an autumnal flowering of art. In the expansion of Vienna which began in 1859 the development of the Ring on the line of the old fortifications offered a unique opportunity to give durable expression to the theories of **Historicism** in a magnificent new ensemble planned as a whole. The principal architects concerned with the Ringstrasse development were Theophil von Hansen (Academy of Fine Art, Parliament, Stock Exchange), Heinrich von Ferstel (Museum of Applied Art, Votivkirche, University), Friedrich Schmidt (Rathaus), August Siccard von Siccardsburg and Eduard van der Nüll (Opera House) and Gottfried Semper and Karl von Hasenauer (Burgtheater, Neue Hofburg, the Museums in Maria-Theresien-Platz). Leading painters of the Historicist school were Emil Jacob Schindler, August von Pettenkofen and above all Hans Makart, who evolved his neo-Baroque "Makart style". The paintings of Anton Romako, which already show elements of Naturalism and Expressionism, look forward to a new age.

The pictures of Gustav Klimt and his cartoons for frescoes reflect the transition to the art of the 20th c., combining a romantic and almost sentimental closeness to nature with symbolic and abstract ornament. Klimt became the leader of the *Secession,* a group allied to **Jugendstil** (Art Nouveau) which was founded in 1897; other prominent members of the group were the painter Kolo Moser, the architect Joseph Maria Olbrich (who designed the Secession building, 1897–98) and the set-designer Alfred Roller. In the spirit of Art Nouveau, there was a great upsurge of activity in the arts and crafts, reflected in the foundation of the *Wiener Werkstätte* (Vienna Workshop) by the architect Josef Hoffmann in 1903, where well-known artists and large numbers of craftsmen created a variety of craft products – glass, porcelain, wooden articles, leather, jewelry, textiles, etc.

Other leading architects of this period were Adolf Loos, whose epoch-making building in the Michaelerplatz in Vienna (1910) gave rise to a furore, and Otto Wagner, who designed the Stadtbahn buildings, the Post Office Savings Bank (1904–06) and other buildings in Vienna. A painter who stood apart from the Secession group was the Tirolese Albin Egger-Lienz, an Expressionist of trenchant and monumental vitality. Egon Schiele, who died young, became a leading representative of early **Expressionism** in Austria with his often harrowing representations of people and his delicate and vulnerable depictions of nature. The towering figure of Oskar Kokoschka already belongs to our own day. A contemporary who must also be mentioned is Alfred Kubin, whose drawings are masterly delineations of a dark dream world.

After the collapse of the Danube monarchy at the end of the First World War the arts showed a falling off in creative power, with only a few exceptions such as the painter Herbert Boeckl, the sculptors Anton Hanak and Fritz Wotruba (with his archaic repertoire of forms a classic of modern sculpture) and the architect Clemens Holzmeister.

Soon after the Second World War the painter and writer Albert Paris Gütersloh (real name A. C. Kiehtreiber) gave stimulus and inspiration to the Viennese school of *Fantastic Realism,* the leading representatives of which were Erich (Arik) Brauer, Rudolf Hausner, Wolfgang Hutter, Anton Lehmden and Ernst Fuchs. Other important contemporary artists are the painters Friedensreich Hundertwasser (real name Friedrich Stowasser) and Arnulf Rainer, the sculptor and graphic artist Alfred Hrdlička and the sculptors Joannis Avramidis and Rudolf Hoflehner, both pupils of Wotruba.

Music

Austria's geographical situation and historical development, combined with a variety of outside influences (from Germanic, Romance, Magyar, Slav and other sources), make it difficult, until the 17th c., to identify any specifically Austrian music distinct from the music of the neighbouring nations.

For the prehistoric, Hallstatt and Roman periods there is some evidence of the practice of music in the form of the remains of whistles and instruments and in figural representations of music-making. The Christianisation of Austrian territory and its occupation by Germanic peoples (Bajuwari, Alamanni) laid the foundations for the development of a musical culture in the Middle Ages and later. The earliest focal points of Austrian music were Salzburg and Vienna, which through all the vicissitudes of the centuries have maintained their importance as musical towns down to the present day.
Under Archbishop Arno of Salzburg (785–821) the *cantus romanus* on the pattern of the Carolingian reform (with

elements taken over from late antiquity and Early Christian and Byzantine features) became widely practised.

Until the 10th c. the monasteries were the main areas for liturgical singing ("Codex Millenarius Minor", Kremsmünster; Gospel Book, Mondsee). Perhaps the most important document of the choral tradition of the 12th c. is the Gradual of Seckau (Styria). Hymns were composed for the celebration of Easter, and Klosterneuburg preserves the complete text and melody of one such hymn, "Christ is risen", dating from 1325.

Among leading representatives of the art of *Minnesang,* which reached a high pitch of perfection at the Babenberg court in Vienna, were *Walther von der Vogelweide* (c. 1170-c. 1230), who learned his craft in Austria, *Neidhart von Reuenthal* (c. 1240) and *Oswald von Wolkenstein* (c. 1377–1445). – *Meistergesang,* the art of the mastersingers, on the other hand, is attested only at one or two places (Schwaz, Steyr, Wels).
In the 15th c. *part-song* had a rapid rise in popularity, and practitioners from the Low Countries (H. Isaac, J. de Cleve, A. v.

Bruck, C. Hollander, etc.) were summoned to the Habsburg court chapels at Vienna, Innsbruck and Graz. German influence on the religious and secular music of the period is evidenced by the presence of *Ludwig Senftle, Heinrich Fink, Paul Hofhaimer, Hans Judenkünig* (*c.* 1450–1526), *H. Edlerauer* (choirmaster of St Stephen's Cathedral and the earliest known polyphonist in Vienna) and others.

In Vienna a musicians' guild was established in the form of the Brotherhood of St. Nicholas, the earliest institution of its kind in the German-speaking countries (1280–1782). Between the 15th and 17th c. associations of musicians were founded in other towns (Graz, Innsbruck, Salzburg, etc.), but their privileges were abolished by the Emperor Francis II.

During the 17th c. Italian influence, coming particularly from Venice, became increasingly strong, as a result both of territorial proximity and later of the Counter-Reformation. Leading Italian musicians were now summoned to the courts of Vienna and Salzburg (T. Massanini, S. Bernardi, O. Benevoli). When Ferdinand II became Emperor in 1619 another Italian, *G. Priuli,* became director of the court orchestra and initiated the age of *Baroque* music (1600–1750), the showy and festive character of which found expression mainly in opera. One notable and brilliant occasion during this period was the performance of an opera by the Italian composer *Antonio Cestis,* "Il pomo d'oro" ("The Golden Apple"), on the occasion of Leopold I's marriage to Margaret of Spain (1666).

The *oratorio* now came into vogue, along with its specialised form the *sepolcro.* This period also saw the beginnings of *ballet* and of most forms of *instrumental music* – the sonata, the concerto, the concerto grosso, the fugue, the suite, the toccata, the passacaglia, etc. Opera was also brought to the general public by performances in the Kärntnertor theatre in Vienna and by visiting Italian troupes (e.g. P. and A. Mingotti).
Austrian music was also influenced by an English and a French composer, *Henry Purcell* (1659–95; "Dido and Aeneas") and *J. B. Lully* (1632–87; "Tragédies lyriques"). Nevertheless a distinctive Viennese style developed, its leading representatives in the 17th and 18th c.

being *Johann Jakob Froberger* (1616–67), *Gottlieb Muffat* (1653–1704) and *Johann Joseph Fux* (1660–1741).

The monastic culture which enjoyed a revival in the 18th c. at the hands of the Jesuits and Benedictines, together with the Church's involvement in education, led to the introduction of *popular elements* into serious music. During the transition from Baroque to the classical period these influenced the content and the themes of the instrumental music of *Matthias Georg Monn, Georg Christoph Wagenseil, Leopold Mozart* and other pre-classical composers in Vienna, Salzburg and elsewhere. This period also saw the first new-style operas of *Christoph Willibald Gluck* (1714–87; "Orpheus and Eurydice", "Alceste"). One specific form influenced by the popular theatre was the *Viennese singspiel* (from 1778), the basis from which Mozart's German operas developed ("Il Seraglio", "Magic Flute").

Inherited traditions and the ready acceptance of elements from related musical cultures provided the basis for the emergence of the *Viennese classical school*, the principal representatives of which were *Joseph* **Haydn** (1732–1809; 104 symphonies, 24 operas, etc.), *Wolfgang Amadeus* **Mozart** (1756–91; 45 symphonies, "Marriage of Figaro", "Don Giovanni", "Così Fan Tutte", "Clemenza di Tito") and *Ludwig van* **Beethoven** (1770–1827; 9 symphonies, "Fidelio"). Instrumental music, opera, the Mass and the oratorio now reached a summit of excellence, and Vienna became the capital of the European musical world.

In the 19th c. Vienna's musical predominance was consolidated by *Franz* **Schubert** (1797–1828; "Die Winterreise", "Die schöne Müllerin"), who brought the *lied* to a high pitch of perfection, and also by *Anton Bruckner* (1824–96), *Franz Liszt* (1811–86), *Johannes Brahms* (1833–97), *Hugo Wolf* (1860–1903) and *Gustav Mahler* (1860–1911).

The famous *Viennese waltz* and *Viennese operetta* developed out of a variety of elements – folk music (the Ländler, a country dance), the Bouffes Parisiennes (Jacques Offenbach, 1819–80) and the older local singspiel. Celebrated representatives of these genres were *Josef Lanner* (1801–43), *Johann Strauss the*

Elder (1804–49; "Radetzky March") and *Johann Strauss the Younger* (1825–99; "Fledermaus", "Gipsy Baron"). The tradition was carried on into the 20th c. by *Carl Michael Ziehrer, Franz von Suppé, Karl Millöcker, Oscar Straus, Franz Lehár* (1870–1948; "Merry Widow", "Land of Smiles"), as well as *Emerich Kálmán* and *Nico Dostal.*

Also popular in the 19th c. was the *Viennese Posse* ("farce"), the principal representatives of which were *Ferdinand Raimund* (1790–1836) and *Johann* **Nestroy** (1801–62). – The brothers *Johann* and *Josef Schrammel* founded a famous trio in 1877, and their *Schrammelmusik* is still the inevitable background to an evening's wine-drinking in one of Vienna's *Heurigenschänken* (see p. 204).

In the 20th c. the *twelve-tone (dodecaphonic) music* pioneered by *Josef Matthias Hauer* (1883–1959) and developed by *Arnold* **Schönberg** (1874–1951) and his pupils *Alban Berg* (1885–1935; "Wozzeck", "Lulu") and *Anton von Webern* (1883–1945) has been internationally recognised as a major contribution to modern music.

Contemporary operatic composers are *Wilhelm Kienzl* (1857–1941; "Der Evangelimann"), *Franz Schrecker* (1878–1934), *Erich Wolfgang Korngold* (1897–1957; "The Dead City") and *Ernst Křenek* (b. 1900; "Charles V"), who developed the twelve-tone technique in a very personal fashion from 1938 onwards. Other dodecaphonic composers are *Hans-Erich Apostel* (b. 1901) and *Hans Jelinek* (b. 1901).

Other contemporary composers are the *neo-romantics Franz Schmidt* (1874–1939), *Josef Marx* (1882–1964), *Karl Schiske* (b. 1916) and *Anton Heiller* (b. 1923), and the *neo-classicists Johann Nepomuk David* (b. 1895) and *Gottfried von Einem* (b. 1918; "Dantons Tod", "Der Zerrissene"). – *Serial music* is composed by *Friedrich Cerha.*

Salzburg, with its Festival (founded by Hugo von Hofmannsthal, Richard Strauss and Max Reinhardt), and Vienna with its Opera House are still focal points of both Austrian and international musical life, with reputations extending far beyond the bounds of Austria.

Literature

The history of literature in Austria can be dated back more than 1800 years, to the time when the Emperor *Marcus Aurelius* wrote his "Meditations" in the Roman Vindobona, predecessor of Vienna. – During the Middle Ages there was a rich flowering of literature in Austria – epic poetry, lyrics, drama – bearing witness to a vigorous intellectual life.

The two most famous medieval *epics* were composed in Austria in the 13th c. – the "Nibelungenlied" and the "Gudrunlied". The **"Nibelungenlied"**, which gives a masterly characterisation of the hero and is written in a language of the highest literary quality, is preserved in thirty manuscripts, some of them incomplete. This celebration of male loyalty has a worthy counterpart in the **"Gudrunlied"**, which celebrates a woman's fidelity; it is preserved in the Ambras Manuscript, written for the Emperor Maximilian in the 16th c.

The first poetess writing in German was *Frau Ava*, the Lady Ava, who wrote on the life of Christ, on Antichrist and on the Last Judgment and died in 1127, much revered, as a nun in Melk Abbey.

The songs written between 1150 and 1170 by the poet known as the *Kürnberger* are the earliest examples of Austrian *minnesong*. Although he uses the "Nibelungenlied" verse form it is not certain whether he is to be identified with the author of the "Nibelungenlied". *Dietmar von Aist* (b. before 1171) wrote poems in both popular and cultivated style. The poems of *Reinmar the Elder* (b. 1160) mark the beginning of the great age of courtly poetry – which takes religion, delight in arms and the service of love as its principal themes and strives after beauty and perfection of form – and the lyrical *minnesong*. Reinmar lived for a time at the court of Leopold V in Vienna and had as his pupil **Walther von der Vogelweide** (c. 1170–1230,), the greatest and most versatile of the German minnesingers. The courtly romance by *Ulrich von Liechtenstein* (c. 1200–c. 1275) entitled "Service of Women" is important for the light it throws on the life of the period and its autobiographical account of the life of a travelling minstrel in the Middle Ages.

Heinrich von Melk, the first Austrian satirical writer, was the author of a poem in which he castigated the sins of the nobility and clergy. *Rudolf von Ems (c.* 1200–1252) wrote verse romances modelled on those of the great German poets of the 12th c., Hartmann von Aue and Gottfried von Strassburg, turning his attention to the middle classes of society. *Wernher the Gardener,* a monk in the Innviertel, wrote his well-known verse tale "Meier Helmbrecht" (the story of a peasant who wants to become a knight and ends up as the leader of a gang of robbers) at some time after 1250. *Peter Suchenwirt,* who is recorded in Vienna in 1386, wrote *Sprüche* (a form of gnomic verse). Between 1350 and 1377 *Heinrich der Teichner* wrote many hundred *Reimreden* (poems in rhyming couplets). **Oswald von Wolkenstein** (*c.* 1377–1445), a Tirolese knight who led an adventurous life which took him from Lithuania to Palestine, was the greatest song-writer of the late medieval period, on the threshold between the minnesong and humanism. *Hugo von Montfort* (1357–1423), a great nobleman of Bregenz who became governor of Styria in 1413 and was a delegate to the Council of Constance in 1414, wrote allegorical poems portraying the manners of the period; although still a practitioner of minnesong, he was also the first Austrian representative of the *Meistergesang,* the art of the mastersingers.

The *Emperor Maximilian* (1459–1519) wrote quasi-autobiographical works on his own life ("Theuerdank") and that of his father Frederick II ("Weisskunig"). *Abraham a Sancta Clara* (born Ulrich Megerle, 1644–1709) was a fiery preacher who sought to rouse the people of Vienna during the miseries of the plague and the Turkish wars and did not flinch from criticising the court.

During the Napoleonic wars and the Biedermeier period *Karoline Pichler* (1769–1843) wrote historical novels and dramas. In her memoirs ("Denkwürdigkeiten aus meinem Leben") she gives a vivid picture of middle-class Vienna, in which her salon was a fount of cultural life.

The *Austrian classical writer Franz* **Grillparzer** (1791–1872) began life as a civil servant but turned to literature as a result of his friendship with the playwright Joseph Schreyvogl. His first dramas, "Die Ahnfrau" and "Sappho" (1817), achieved immediate success, but his fiery spirit was distressed by the censorship restrictions of the "Vormärz" period (the years before the March Revolution of 1848).

After the tragic death of his mother Grillparzer went to Italy in 1819, and this journey provided the inspiration for his great cycle of plays, "Das goldene Vlies" (1821). The relative failure of these plays, combined with disappointments in his official career, discouraged his creative urge for a time, but soon, with the sympathetic support of Count Stadion, he turned to historical themes. But even his patriotic drama "König Ottokars Glück und Ende" displeased the censorship authorities, and it was only through the personal intervention of the Empress that the play received its first performance after being held up for two years.

After a visit to Germany in 1826, when he was flatteringly received by Goethe in Weimar, Grillparzer wrote "Ein treuer Diener seines Herrn" (1826), "Des Meeres und der Liebe Wellen" and "Der Traum, ein Leben" (1831); but these works too suffered from petty bureaucratic criticism. After the failure of his comedy "Weh dem, der lügt" (1838) Grillparzer withdrew, embittered. It was only on his 80th birthday that he was accorded full public recognition. His great dramas still hold the stage, thanks to the authentic problems they depict and their pregnant dramatic language.

If Grillparzer is the great Austrian classical dramatist, the great master of the novel is *Adalbert* **Stifter** (1805–68). Born in the Bohemian Forest, he made Upper Austria his second home, where he earned his living as tutor in noble houses. His novels are written in a lucid style which depicts his characters and their background in loving detail, returning again and again to celebrate the beauties of nature. His principal works are "Die Mappe meines Urgrossvaters" (1840), "Der Hochwald" (1841), "Bergkristall" (1845), "Bunte Steine" (1853) and "Nachsommer" (1857). Thrown by the 1866 war into a severe depression, he committed suicide in 1868.

The leading exponent of the Viennese *Volksstück* (farce) was *Ferdinand* **Raimund** (1790–1836), whose fairytale and magic plays combine sensuous romantic feeling with delightful humour. With their genuine humanity and wisdom they still retain their naturalness and interest.

Raimund, originally a confectioner's apprentice and later a popular actor, wrote his first play ("Der Barometermacher auf der Zauberinsel", 1823) simply because his theatre needed one, but its success encouraged him to become a professional dramatist. The best known of his plays are "Der Bauer als Millionär" (1826) and "Der Verschwender" (1834). In spite of his humour Raimund was at heart a melancholy man, and after being bitten by a dog, fearing that he had contracted hydrophobia, he shot himself.

Like Raimund, *Johann* **Nestroy** (1801–62) acted in his own plays. He began to write plays at the age of 21, when he was an actor in the Kärntnertor theatre and had played in Graz, Brün (Brno) and Amsterdam as a member of a touring company. Altogether he wrote more than sixty plays – farces, romantic comedies and satires on life in the Vormärz period and the 1848 Revolution. Nestroy is master of a colourful language which depicts in a cross-fire of witty dialogue the human failings of his characters. His "Lumpazivagabundus" (1833) and "Einen Jux will er sich machen" (1842) are still frequently performed.
Friedrich Halm (real name Freiherr von Münch-Bellinghausen, 1806–71), director until 1870 of the two court theatres, was a popular dramatist in his day, but his plays are now forgotten.

The greatest lyric poet of the Vormärz period was *Nikolaus* **Lenau** (pseudonym of Nikolaus Franz Niembsch, Edler von Strehlenau, 1802–50), the poet of *Weltschmerz*. His restless life (he studied philosophy, law, agriculture and medicine, emigrated to America but returned in disappointment) is reflected in his poems, which range between a delicate perception of nature and haunting musical rhythms on the one hand to profound melancholy and despair on the other. Lenau died insane.
Anastasius Grün (pseudonym of Anton Graf Auersperg, 1806–76) enjoyed an ephemeral success as the writer of political lyrics during the Vormärz period. – The ballads of *Johann Nepomuk Vogl* (1802–66), like those of *Johann Gabriel Seidl* (1804–75), author of the old Austrian national anthem "Gott erhalte . . ." (music by Joseph Haydn), are remembered only because they were set to music by Carl Loewe. – *Eduard von Bauernfeld* (1802–90), a friend of Schubert and the painter Moritz von Schwind and, like Anastasius Grün, a liberal, was a master of the light comedy of manners. Like *Robert Hamerling* (1830–99), he continued to be popular during the second half of the 19th c.

The beginnings of industrialisation brought a trend towards writing which was closer to ordinary life and reality. This period produced a number of great *popular writers,* who found new literary themes in the realistic portrayal of peasant life, either in narrative or in dramatic form, exploiting the resources of dialect.
Peter **Rosegger** (1843–1918), son of a Styrian farmer who started life as a tailor's apprentice, published his first dialect poems in 1869 with the support of Robert Hamerling. His first major work, "Die Schriften des Waldschulmeisters", was published in 1875. In 1876 he founded a periodical in Graz, "Heimgarten", in which his poems were published. His simple, sentimental tales and novels depicting the life of his native Styria make him the greatest Austrian *Volksdichter* (popular writer, folk writer), vividly portraying the joys and sorrows of peasant life. His best-known work is probably "Als ich noch der Waldbauernbub war" (1902).
Ludwig **Anzengruber** (1839–89) wrote his first successful play, "Der Pfarrer von Kirchfeld" (1870), after years of hardship as an actor in a travelling troupe. His plays, ranging from comedies of village life to peasant tragedies, reflect the emergence of *Naturalism* in their realistic presentation and their concern with social problems. His most notable dramatic works were "Der Meineidbauer" (1871), "Der G'wissenswurm" (1874) and "Das Vierte Gebot" (1877). He also wrote novels ("Der Schandfleck", 1876; "Der Sternsteinhof", 1883).
The leading dialect writer of Upper Austria was *Franz Stelzhamer* (1802–74), who led a restless and poverty-stricken life, reciting his poems to the public.
Ferdinand **von** **Saar** (1833–1906) abandoned his career as an officer in 1856 in order to devote himself to writing. He

wrote lyric poetry, including the "Wiener Elegien' (1893), in varied and sometimes melancholy mood, but his finest works were his *Novellen*, the specifically German form of short story ("Novellen aus Österreich", 1897; "Hermann und Dorothea", 1902). The other great Novelle-writer of the period was *Marie* **Von Ebner-Eschenbach** (b. Countess Dubsky, 1830–1916), whose works faithfully reflect the life of the nobility and countryfolk, studying the psychology of social relationships, and are written in vivid language, with delicate humour. Her best known tale is "Krambambuli", the gripping story of a dog.

The late 19th c. produced such an abundance of major poets, novelists and dramatists that it can fairly be classed as the third great period of Austrian literature. The first great name to be mentioned is that of *Rainer Maria* **Rilke** (1875–1926), the poet of *Sehnsucht* (longing), to which he gives delicately romantic expression without excessive emotionalism. Born in Prague, he travelled widely, became private secretary to the French sculptor Auguste Rodin and served in the ranks in the First World War, and his experiences are reflected in the often mystical tone of his poetry. Among his most famous works are "Die Weise von Liebe und Tod des Cornets Christoph Rilke" (1899), "Das Buch der Bilder" (1902), "Das Stundenbuch" (1905) and the "Duineser Elegien" (1922).

At the turn of the century the school known as *Viennese Impressionism* came to the fore, its most prominent representatives being Hugo von Hofmannsthal, Arthur Schnitzler, Stefan Zweig, Peter Altenberg, Hermann Bahr, Richard von Schaukal and Felix Braun. In every field of literature the aim is now to anatomise the soul; life and death, waking and dreaming are never far apart; and all the phenomena of human existence are contemplated with weary scepticism and accompanied by the melancholy smile of the man who has seen it all. The psychoanalysis of *Sigmund Freud* (1856–1939) was the medical and philosophical counterpart of this approach to literature.

Richard von Schaukal (1874–1942) was a lyric poet and essayist whose uprightness, genuine sensibility and deep love of his native soil are reflected in all his work. *Georg* **Trakl** (1887–1914), a native of Salzburg, was a major lyric poet whose prophetic poems, seeking the new order which should emerge from chaos, were appreciated at their true worth only in a later period. *Ottokar Kernstock* (1848–1928), choirmaster at Vorau Abbey in Styria and author of the Republic's first national anthem (until 1938), re-creates in his poems something of the spirit of medieval lyric poetry. The lyric poet *Heinrich Suso Waldeck* (1873–1944) was also an ecclesiastic. – *Alfons Petzold* (1882–1923) was a poet of working-class origin and poor circumstances who achieved an austere lyricism. *Josef Luitpold* (pseudonym of J. L. Stern, 1886–1966) wrote poems and ballads of social concern giving expression to his longing for freedom.

The turn of the century was marked by the work of three outstanding dramatists – Arthur Schnitzler, Hermann Bahr and Hugo von Hofmannsthal.
Arthur **Schnitzler** (1862–1931), a doctor before he became a writer, was the much fêted darling of the Viennese salons. His plays combine dramatic emotional expression with passionate vitality and an air of melancholy resignation, and in his subtle psychological studies he is constantly concerned with the theme of love and brilliantly satirises the society of his day ("Anatol", 1893; "Liebelei", 1895; "Professor Bernhardi", 1905).
Hermann **Bahr** (1863–1934) likewise displays a profound understanding of human psychology, both in his light comedies of manners and in his topical, and often satirical, novels and plays. Bahr, a native of Germany who became a fervent Austrian patriot, was a dramatic critic as well as a dramatist, and his essays and diaries are an interesting reflection of the life and thought of his day.
Hugo **von Hofmannsthal** (1874–1929) stood at the opposite extreme from Naturalism with works which ranged between delicate aesthetic sensibility and a kind of daemonic possession. After a group of plays concerned with death ("Der Tod des Tizian", 1892; "Der Tor und der Tod", 1893; "Alkestis", 1894) he returned to the pattern of the medieval mystery play with his "Kleines Welttheater" (1897) and the famous "Jedermann" ("Everyman", 1911). He also wrote the texts of Richard Strauss's operas "Der Rosenkavalier" (1911), "Ariadne auf Naxos"

(1912) and "Die Frau ohne Schatten" (1919).

Like Anzengruber, the doctor and dramatist *Karl Schönherr* (1867–1943) was a master of the naturalistic *Volksstück* and the peasant drama.
Among the great storytellers of the first half of the 20th c. was *Enrica Handel-Mazzetti* (1871–1955), whose historical novels were mostly set in the period of the Reformation and Counter-Reformation. Another important novelist, though dealing with a very different subject-matter, was *Karl Heinrich* **Waggerl** (1897–1973), who settled in Wagrain (Salzburg province) after the First World War and wrote novels reflecting the happiness of the simple life in the country. – Other regional writers are the Styrians *Paula Grogger* (b. 1892), *Hans Kloepfer* (1867–1944) and *Paul Anton Keller* (b. 1907), *Gertrud Fussenegger* (b. 1912), a native of Pilsen, and *Franz Tumler* (b. 1912), from southern Tirol (now in Italy).

Three writers with a military background – officers in the Austrian Imperial army – were *Franz Karl Ginzkey* (1871–1963), a sensitive portrayer of the traditional Austrian way of life, *Roda Roda* (actually Sandor Friedrich Rosenfeld, 1872–1945), who portrayed the Austrian Imperial Monarchy principally in anecdotes and short stories, and *Rudolf Jeremias Kreuz* (1876–1949), who castigated the society of the day in his shrewd satires.

A great master of language – in his striking aphorisms, his brilliant satires and also in his bitter scorn and cynicism – was *Karl* **Kraus** (1874–1936), editor of a famous periodical, "Die Fackel" ("The Torch"), in which he attacked anything that seemed to him bad or wrong and described the intellectual and moral decline of the age.
Peter Altenberg (pseudonym of Richard Engländer, 1862–1919) wrote witty accounts of the life and manners of the day and critical aphorisms. His posthumous works were published in 1925 by *Alfred Polgar* (1875–1955), himself a vigorous and trenchant writer.

Three powerful and consummately skilful writers of the earlier part of the 20th c. were Franz Kafka and Franz Werfel, both natives of Prague, and Stefan Zweig. *Franz* **Kafka** (1883–1924), an Expressionist

and a forerunner of Surrealism, combines realism with a feeling of the sinister ("Der Prozess", 1925; "Das Schloss", 1927). *Franz* **Werfel** (1890–1945) emigrated in 1938 to France and in 1940 to America; a representative of the Austrian Expressionist school, he spoke out for the oppressed ("Juarez und Maximilian", 1925; "Jacobowsky und der Oberst", 1944) and later went in for religious themes. *Stefan* **Zweig** (1881–1942) also had to emigrate; his great novels are masterpieces of style ("Sternstunden der Menschheit", 1928; "Ungeduld des Herzens", 1938).

Robert Edler von **Musil** (1880–1942) resembled Kafka in his metaphysical realism and wrote works with a psychoanalytical approach ("Die Verwirrung des Zöglings Törless", 1906). His great novel "Der Mann ohne Eigenschaften" ("The Man without Qualities", 1930–42) remained unfinished. – *Egon Friedell* (1878–1938) was an actor, a cultural historian and a writer of ironically philosophical essays. *Joseph Roth* (1894–1939) was a fine novelist and essayist of the "Vienna school". *Anton Wildgans* (1881–1932) wrote a "Rede an Österreich" ("Address to Austria") declaring his loyalty to the smaller Austria of the post-war period, and his poems and plays similarly reflected, with simple naturalness, his love for Austria and its people. *Josef Weinheber* (1892–1945) was another poet who wrote of the life of the ordinary people; he wrote lovingly, in Viennese dialect, of the life and environment of the city, whose most characteristic representative he was.
Paula von Preradović (1887–1951) celebrated in her novels and sensitive lyric poetry the beauty of the old Austrian heartland; she also wrote the words of the new Austrian national anthem.

Contemporary Austrian literature has continued to produce a rich flowering, from the works of established writers of the older generation to the promising new work by younger writers since the Second World War.
Egon Cäsar Conte Corti alle Catene (1886–1953) made a name for himself with his historically authentic biographies. *Mirko Jelusich* (1886–1969) also dealt with historical subjects but moulded them in accordance with his personal views. – *Bruno Brehm* (1897–1974), long under a cloud for his Nazi affiliations, wrote a

trilogy – his greatest work – devoted to the fall of the Austro-Hungarian monarchy. – *Erwin Rainalter* (1892–1960) took the themes of his novels both from the present and the past. As a lyric poet *Alexander Lernet-Holenia* (A. von Hollenia, 1897–1972) was influenced by Rilke. In his dramas and in the novel, to which he mainly devoted himself, he displays a penetrating spirit of satire and dazzling narrative skill. – *Felix Braun* (1885–1973) was a writer of great subtlety. *Ernst Lothar* (pseudonym of E. L. Müller, 1890–1974), the novelist of longing and resignation, carried on the inheritance of Schnitzler.

Franz Theodor Czokor (1885–1969) was a dramatist who dealt with historical subjects in the spirit of the present and even when treating mystical themes remained a realist. *Max Mell* (1882–1971) dressed up old legends in dramatic form, and the action of his plays has all the inevitability of fate. The third great dramatist of the postwar period is *Fritz Hochwälder* (b. 1911), who has lived in Switzerland since 1938.

Hermann Broch (1886–1951), who emigrated to the United States in 1938, seeks in his novels to portray the collapse of human values ("Der Tod des Virgil", 1945). *Max Brod* (1884–1968), a poet, dramatist and novelist, emigrated to Palestine in 1939.

Friedrich Schreyvogl (1899–1976), great-grandnephew of Joseph Schreyvogl, the 19th c. director of the Burgtheater, was a successful dramatist and the author of passionate and pregnantly characterised novels. – *Rudolf Henz* (b. 1897), whose Roman Catholic faith invests his poems and novels, has his counterpart at the other end of the spectrum in *Rudolf Brunngraber* (1901–60), a ruthless critic of greed and exploitation in modern society. *Adalbert Muhr* (b. 1896) gives expression in his novels to the magical relationship between man's destiny and the landscape ("Der Sohn des Stromes", 1946). *Franz Nabl* (1883–1974), with his thoughtful, slightly sceptical, novels and short stories, can be regarded as a follower of Ferdinand von Saar. – *Ernst Scheibelreiter* (b. 1897) has written lyric poetry, novels and dramas, as well as children's books.

Heimito von Doderer (1896–1966), a great-grandnephew of Nikolaus Lenau, grained a considerable reputation with his novels, "Die Strudlhofstiege" and "Die erleuchteten Fenster oder die Menschwerdung des Amtsrates Zihal" (1951). – *Erika Mitterer* (b. 1906) shows profound social understanding. *Johannes Urzidil* (1896–1970), a lyric poet, writer of short stories and translator, emigrated to Britain in 1939 and to New York in 1941. A native of Prague, he pictures life in his Bohemian homeland, describes the life of émigrés in America and draws droll character sketches.

The various provinces of Austria have, of course, produced distinguished writers who devote themselves to the life, landscape and problems of their own particular region. In Tirol there are *Rudolf Greinz* (1866–1942) and *Josef Georg Oberkofler* (1889–1962); in Carinthia the versatile *Josef Friedrich Perkönig* (1890–1959); in Styria the sensitive writer *Rudolf Bartsch* (1873–1953); in Lower Austria *Friedrich Sacher* (b. 1899), novelist reminiscent of Stifter; in Upper Austria the dramatist *Richard Billinger* (1890–1965) and the novelist *Ferdinand Kögl* (b. 1890); in Salzburg province *Georg Rendl* (b. 1903), a working-man and beekeeper, and *Franz Braumann* (b. 1910), once a farm-boy.

Among younger writers there are many promising names, some of them known beyond the borders of Austria, including *Christine Busta* (pseudonym of Christine Dimt, b. 1915), *Christine Lavant* (pseudonym of Christine Habernig, 1915–73), *Ilse Aichinger* (b. 1921) and *Ingeborg* **Bachmann** (1926–73; "Das dreissigste Jahr", 1961), who died under tragic circumstances in Rome. *Hans Carl Laertes Artmann* (b. 1921) writes experimental lyric poetry. The works of *Hermann Schreiber* (b. 1920) are brilliantly observed; those of *Herbert Zand* (1923–70) are succinctly and economically written. *Fritz Habeck* (b. 1916) is a master of vivid and gripping historical writing. *Harald Zusanek* (b. 1922) and *Raimund Berger* (1917–54), a native of Tirol, are dramatists. *Herbert Eisenreich* (b. 1925) has made a name for himself as the author of short stories and radio plays.

The Bulgarian-born novelist *Elias Canetti* (b. 1905) emigrated in 1938 to Paris and later settled in London. His most important work is "Masse und Macht" (1960). – The essayist and dramatic critic *Friedrich Torberg* (pseudonym of F. Kantor-Berg, 1908–79) published the posthumous works of *Franz von Herzmanovsky-Orlando* (1877–1954; novels, short stories). – *Jean Améry* (pseudonym of Hans Mayer, 1912–78), a writer influenced by the neo-Positivist "Viennese school", emigrated to Belgium in 1938, was held in a concentration camp from 1943 to 1945 and lived after the war in Brussels, where he committed suicide.

One great author of post-war bestsellers has been *Johannes Mario Simmel* (b. 1924). He has written novels ("Es muss nicht immer Kaviar sein", 1960; "Lieb Vaterland, magst ruhig sein", 1965; "Und Jimmy ging zum Regenbogen", 1969), children's books and television plays. – The Budapest-born journalist *Hans Habe* (pseudonym of H. Békessy, 1911–77) wrote entertaining and topical novels.

The Carinthian writer *Peter* **Handke** (b. 1942) has gained an international reputa-

tion, first with his *Sprechstücke* (plays without a plot) and subsequently with novels ("Die Hornissen", 1966; "Der Hausierer", 1967), short stories ("Die Angst des Tormanns beim Elfmeter", 1970) and dramas ("Das Mündel will Vormund sein", 1969; "Der Ritt über den Bodensee", 1971; "Die Unvernünftigen sterben aus", 1973), usually concerned with the alienation between man and his environment. After spending some time in Düsseldorf, West Berlin and Paris Handke now lives in Salzburg.

Other notable contemporary writers include *Paul Celan* (pseudonym of P. Antschel, 1920–70), *Friederike Mayröcker* (b. 1924), *Ernst Jandl* (b. 1925), *Andreas Okopenko* (b. 1930) and *Gerhard Rühm* (b. 1930), one of the founders of the "Vienna Group", who together with *Friedrich Achleitner* (b. 1930), *Konrad Bayer* (1932–64) and *Oswald Wiener* (b. 1935) founded a literary review, "das literarische cabaret", in 1958–59. Among other more recent writers are *Alois Brandstetter* (b. 1938), *Helmut Eisendle* (b. 1939), *Gerhard Roth* (b. 1942), *Franz Innerhofer* (b. 1944) and *Peter Rosei* (b. 1946).

Economy

Austria's economy is well adapted to the circumstances of the country, with its limited mineral and other natural resources, relatively small labour force and small domestic market. In spite of the much greater economic strength of its neighbours Germany and Italy, it has successfully established its own economic base.

In the thirties of this century the economy of Austria was still dependent on a balance between industry and agriculture. Industry was then concentrated in the east of the country, mainly in Vienna and the Vienna basin, where in the course of the 19th c., thanks to the excellent communications of the area, the availability in the early days of adequate water power and the proximity of the capital, the largest and most diverse industrial zone in modern Austria had developed, growing out of the older small-scale industrial activity in this area. The second main element was the old iron-working industry, which in the latter part of the 19th c. had moved out of the mountain

regions to new locations on the railway – in the valley of the Mur and Mürz, on the fringes of the Alps to the N (Steyr, Waidhofen/Ybbs, Traisen), E (Vienna basin) and S (Graz).

The rest of Austria had little in the way of old-established industries – small-scale foodstuffs industries in the larger towns, here and there textiles, developed out of earlier domestic craft production (Waldviertel, western Mühlviertel, upper Inn valley), woodworking and papermaking. In addition there were some industries associated with mining (upper Inn valley, Hallein, Salzkammergut) and various factories in rural areas processing the local produce (sugar refineries, mills). An exceptional case was the Rhine valley in Vorarlberg, where an active textile industry had grown up during the 19th c. – an offshoot from neighbouring Switzerland.

This industrial pattern inherited from the days of the monarchy, and the distribution of population to which it gave rise, were altered by the second great wave of industrialisation which began when Austria was incorporated in Hitler's

Greater German Reich. This brought a large increase in energy supply and promoted the development not only of existing industrial areas but also of the relatively un-industrialised western part of Austria through the move to these areas of important armaments industries. Upper Austria in particular gained a series of large industrial establishments (steel-works and nitrogen plant at Linz, aluminium plant at Ranshofen, rayon factory at Lenzing).

After the Second World War this industrialisation was vigorously continued in those parts of Austria which were occupied by the Western Allies, partly with the help of Marshall Aid, partly by the transfer of factories from the Soviet-occupied zone. In the Soviet zone industry was crippled by the dismantling and expropriation of many factories as "German property", and began to recover only after the end of the occupation (1955). Western Austria thus now possesses mainly young and expanding branches of industry, whereas in the eastern part of the country, with the exception of the Vienna basin, the industry is mostly aging, insufficiently diversified and in need of far-reaching rationalisation.

Austria's economic development as a whole is still in process of transition from an agrarian economy to an industrial society. The proportion of the population engaged in agriculture and forestry has fallen from something like a third in 1910 to some 15% today, while industry, which before the Second World War was concentrated in eastern Austria, to the S of Vienna, is now distributed over the whole country. The principal industrial towns are Vienna, Linz and Graz, the hubs of the iron and steel industry Steyr, Judenburg and Knittelfeld. The opencast iron mine on the Erzberg at Eisenerz represents a major element in the mining industry of the Austrian Alpine regions, where iron, salt, copper and precious metals have been worked for many centuries and in some areas are still major sources of income.

Since the 1930s deposits of oil and natural gas have been discovered and worked in Austria, particularly in the Weinviertel to the N of the Danube. A large oil refinery at Schwechat and smaller refineries in other oilfields on the fringes of the Alps now supply a third of the domestic consumption of gasoline and mineral oils, and in addition various plants producing petrochemicals and other chemicals have been established. The last Austrian coal-mines were closed down some years ago, but substantial quantities of lignite (brown coal) are still mined in various parts of Austria, particularly in Styria and Upper Austria. Other major industries, mostly run by firms of medium size, include paper-making, the manufacture of machinery and electrical appliances, the production and processing of foodstuffs and the manufacture of aluminium and copper products. Vorarlberg has a considerable textile industry. Austria has no car industry of its own, but produces motorcycles and specialised cross-country vehicles. Something like a third of the population works in industry.

In addition to coal, oil and natural gas, an important contribution to Austria's energy supplies is made by the production of electricity. Hydroelectric stations on the Danube and its tributaries and other stations fed by huge artificial lakes in the mountains, where the great drops in height yield an abundant supply of power, have made power production a major branch of the economy. The power stations are mostly State-run, and the continually increasing demand for energy calls for steady expansion in this field. The first Austrian nuclear power station was built at Zwentendorf, but following a national referendum in 1978 it has not been brought into operation.

During the inter-war period Austrian agriculture and forestry were still largely on the lines of a traditional peasant economy designed to meet local needs. Since the last war, however, the steadily increasing exodus of agricultural workers into industry and the service trades has led to a rapid process of mechanisation and rationalisation. In the Pannonian region, particularly in the Vienna basin and the Marchfeld, many family-run farms were compelled by labour shortage to give up stock-farming and concentrate on highly mechanised arable farming (wheat, barley, sugar-beet), while the vine-growers of the Weinviertel, for the same reason, rapidly adopted the labour-saving method of growing their vines on tall supports in widely spaced rows. South-eastern Styria and southern Burgenland, however – both ecologically favoured regions but with little non-agricultural employment –

have become agricultural problem areas, since the small size of the holdings and the relative over-population have hampered the process of modernisation.

Stock-farming, based since time immemorial in the mountains and the rainy Alpine foreland regions, has increasingly tended, in face of the over-production of milk and butter, to go over to the fattening of beef cattle, even outside the traditional beef-production areas; and shortage of labour has led to a decline in the old *Almwirtschaft* (dairy farming, with summer grazing on the Alpine pastures).

The people of the mountain regions have long abandoned the practice of growing food for their own needs, and much poor land has been planted with trees. The area under forest has thus increased considerably, in some cases at the expense of Alpine meadowland.

In the upland farming regions, which contain a third of Austria's farms and produce much of the country's breeding stock, half of its beef cattle and half of its milk, the population can often maintain a reasonable standard of living only with the help of subsidiary earnings from non-agricultural work. In the higher parts of the Mühlviertel and Waldviertel, on the eastern fringes of the Alps and in the Niedere Tauern there is only limited scope for such work (road-building, forestry). The consequence has been a continuing drift of population from the upland regions. In the mountain regions to the W, however, the tourist and holiday trade has provided substantial employment and halted the population decline.

In spite of their continued decline, however, agriculture and forestry are still highly important elements in the Austrian economy. More than a third of the country's area is covered with forest, and almost half its usable area is devoted to agriculture. Cereals, potatoes, fruit, wine and animal produce are mainly produced on small and medium-sized farms; the larger units in some areas in eastern Austria are almost exclusively engaged in forestry rather than farming. More than 80% of domestic requirements are met by home-produced food, and in the case of certain products (wine, beef, butter, cheese) Austria produces more than it can consume.

Tourism, which has grown by leaps and bounds in the post-war period, is of great economic importance to Austria, since its large earnings of foreign currency make good most of the country's permanent deficit on its balance of trade, with more than 20 million bed-nights, had surpassed the peak level of the inter-war years (1930–31); by 1960 this figure had been doubled, and by 1974 the 100 million mark had been passed (1984 about 114·6 million). Austria is thus more heavily dependent than most other countries on the tourist trade, which is particularly valuable in providing work, directly or indirectly, in the mountain regions which have few other sources of revenue.

Apart from Vienna and Salzburg the main tourist and holiday regions are the western provinces of Vorarlberg, Tirol, Salzburg and Carinthia. The principal tourist attractions have developed in the mountain areas, which have two seasons, a summer holiday season and a winter sports season. Among these are Kitzbühel, Seefeld, Zell am See, the Kleinwalsertal, the Montafon valley and the resorts on the Arlberg, in the upper Ötztal and in the Zillertal. Also busy throughout the year the resorts of Badgastein and Bad Hofgastein in the Gasteiner Tal, which claims one of the highest number of bed-nights after Vienna. Also popular with visitors are spas such as Bad Ischl, Bad Aussee, Bad Hall, Bad Kleinkirchheim, Bad Schallerbach, Baden bei Wien, Bad Tatzmannsdorf and Bad Gleichenberg. In summer the Salzkammergut with its lakes and the lakes of Carinthia, with their warm water and pleasant bathing, are among the busiest holiday areas. Skiing enthusiasts are attracted by the summer skiing facilities (lifts, etc.) on some of the glaciers; while those who want a quiet and relaxing holiday or prefer to discover for themselves the less frequented parts of the country will find what they want in northern and eastern Austria.

The stimulating effect of tourism on the local economy is very evident in the areas concerned; and the small size of most of the hotels, etc., combined with the large numbers of private lettings, ensures that the revenue is widely spread. The winter season is becoming increasingly important, and in many places is already busier than the summer: a trend which has been promoted by the increasing numbers of cableways and lifts, well-maintained downhill runs and cross-country ski trails.

Austria
A to Z

Achensee

Land: Tirol (T).
Altitude: 929 m/3048 ft.
ⓘ **Fremdenverkehrsverband Achenkirch,**
6213 Pertisau;
tel. (0 52 43) 5363.

ACCOMMODATION. – IN MAURACH/EBEN: *Alpenrose,* A, 100 b., SP, sauna; *Huber-Hochland,* A, 70 b., SB, sauna; *Edelweiss,* B, 100 b., sauna; *Buchau,* B, 100 b.; *Hanslwirt,* B, 68 b., SB; *Rotspitz,* B, 60 b.; *Alpenblick,* B, 60 b., SP; *Vierjahreszeiten,* B, 55 b. – IN PERTISAU: *Rieser,* A, 158 b.; SB, sauna; *Strandhotel,* A, 150 b., SB, SP, sauna; *Fürstenhaus,* A, 120 b., SB, SP, sauna; *Pfandler,* A, 100 b., SB, sauna; *Kristall,* A, 85 b., SP, sauna; *Post,* B, 140 b., SP, sauna; *Tyrol,* B, 45 b., sauna. – IN ACHENKIRCH: *Post,* A, 211 b., SP, SB, sauna; *Windegg,* B, 90 b., SB, sauna; *Achentalerhof,* B, 62 b., SP; *Tiroler Adler,* C, 40 b. – IN ACHENSEE: *Imhof,* B, 50 b., sauna. – CAMPING SITES.

WATER SPORTS. – Open-air swimming baths; water skiing; sailing and windsurfing schools; fishing.

RECREATION and SPORTS. – Walking; climbing; golf course (9 holes); tennis; riding; winter sports.

The light green *Achensee, surrounded by dark coniferous forests, is the largest and most beautiful of the Tirolean lakes (9 km/5½ miles long, 1 km/¾ mile wide, 133 m/436 ft deep). To the W are the imposing peaks of the Karwendelgebirge, to the E the Rofangebirge or Sonnwendgebirge. The lake offers excellent facilities for water sports, and Maurach, Pertisau and Achenkirch are popular winter sports resorts.

The road from the Inn valley climbs, with many turns and magnificent views, to **Maurach** (alt. 960 m/3150 ft, pop. 1600), at the S end of the lake, with a Baroque parish church; herb garden. 750 m/½ mile S in the village of *Eben* stands the sumptuous Baroque pilgrimage church of St Notburga (15th–18th c.). 5 km/3 miles NW of Maurach, on the W side of the lake, is the popular resort of **Pertisau** (alt. 930 m/3050 ft), with a parish church designed by Clemens Holzmeister (1969). – The impressively engineered *road runs N near the eastern shore through tunnels, and affords beautiful glimpses of the lake. On the other side the Seekarspitze (2053 m/6736 ft) slopes steeply down to the water. At the N end of the lake, a little off the road, is the village of *Achensee* (alt. 924 m/3032 ft), and 3 km/2 miles beyond this is *Achenkirch* (930 m/3052 ft, pop. 1910) with a parish church of 1748; toboggan-run in summer. – In another 9 km/6 miles, just before the *Achen pass* (941 m/3087 ft) the road reaches the German frontier.

SURROUNDINGS. – From Maurach the Rofan cableway (2246 m/7369 ft long) runs up to the *Erfurter Hütte* (1834 m/4541 ft; inn), on the *Mauritzköpfl.* From here there are magnificent views and good walking and climbing – up the **Hochiss** (2299 m/7543 ft; 1½ hours), the **Rofanspitze** (2260 m/7415 ft; 1¾ hours) and the **Vorderes Sonnwendjoch** (2224 m/7297 ft; 2½–3 hours), a superb viewpoint. – From Pertisau a chair-lift ascends the **Zwölferkopf** (1483 m/4866 ft).

Achenkirch, between the lake and the Achenpass, has a chair-lift and is the starting-point for climbs up the *Adlerhorst* (1230 m/4037 ft) and *Hinterunutz* (2007 m/6585 ft). From a point half-way between the village and the lake there is a beautiful view of an isolated chapel and the mountains around the lake.

Admont

Land: Styria (Stm).
Altitude: 641 m/2103 ft. – Population: 3400.
Post code: A-8911. – Telephone code: 0 36 13.
ⓘ **Fremdenverkehrsbüro,** Rathaus;
tel. 21 64.
Reisebüro Lubensky, Rathausplatz 46;
tel. 23 39.

ACCOMMODATION. – *Post,* A, 55 b., sauna; *Traube,* B, 29 b., *Felsenkeller,* C, 16 b.; *Mafalda,* C, 15 b. – YOUTH HOSTEL: *Schloss Röthelstein.*

RECREATION and SPORTS. – Hunting and fishing; tennis; canoeing and kayaking; open-air swimming bath.

Admont is a Styrian market town in an open stretch of the Enns valley, near the Gesäuse, which attracts many visitors to the famous Benedictine abbey. It is also a popular summer resort and winter sports complex.

The **Benedictine abbey,** founded in 1074, was burned down in 1865, only the valuable

View over the Achensee towards Pertisau

library being saved from the flames, and was rebuilt later in the 19th c. The *church*, with twin towers 70 m/230 ft high, contains a carved Nativity group ("crib") of 1755. The Baroque **Library* (72 m/236 ft long, 14 m/ 46 ft across), in the E wing of the abbey, contains some 150,000 volumes, including 1100 manuscripts and 900 early printed books. The *Natural History Museum* has, among much else, a large collection of insects. There are also a *Museum of Art* and a *Heimatmuseum* (local museum).

SURROUNDINGS. – 3 km/2 miles S, on a wooded hillside, is *Schloss Röthelstein*, with a two-storey arcaded courtyard and a Baroque chapel. – 6 km/4 miles W is the *pilgrimage church of Frauenberg*, originally in late Gothic style but remodelled in Baroque style in the 17th c. – 7·5 km/4½ miles E is the *Gesäuse, a wooded gorge 16 km/10 miles long through which the River Enns surges down between the rugged limestone crags of the Ennstal Alps, falling 154 m/505 ft in its passage through the gorge. The boldly engineered road and railway line cling to the steep hillsides, frequently crossing the river. On both sides are imposing peaks including the Himberstein; 1218 m/3996 ft), Grosser Buchstein (2223 m/7294 ft), Planspitze (2120 m/6956 ft), Hochtor (2372 m/7783 ft) and Tamischbachturm (2034 m/6674 ft).

20 km/12½ miles W is **Liezen** (alt. 659 m/2162 ft; pop. 6500; Hotel Karow, B, 60 b.), an industrial town and the chief place in the Styrian part of the Enns valley. The parish church has pictures by Schmidt of Krems. Liezen is a good base for climbs in the Warscheneck group, e.g. *Hochmölbing* (2331 m/7648 ft; 6½ hours), which commands far-ranging views.

From Liezen a road crosses the *Pyhrn pass* (945 m/ 3101 ft) to the resort of Spital *am Pyhrn* (647 m/2123 ft; pop. 2500), 16 km/10 miles NE, with a fine Baroque church. On a crag above the little town is the late Gothic church of St Leonard. From here it is a 1½ hours' walk to the beautiful *Dr.-Vogelsang-Klamm* (gorge) and another 2¾ hours to the *Rohrauer Haus* (1348 m/4423 ft; overnight accommodation), from which it is a 4½ hours' climb

to the summit of the *Grosser Pyhrgas* (2244 m/7363 ft). – 4 km/2½ miles SW of Spital is the lower station (806 m/ 2644 ft) of the cableway to the *Wurzeralm* (1426 m/ 4679 ft), popular both with summer visitors and winter sports enthusiasts.

Altenburg

Land: Lower Austria (NÖ).
Altitude: 387 m/1270 ft. – Population: 700.
Post code: A-3591. – Telephone code: 0 29 82.
ⓘ **Gemeindeamt**, Nr. 40;
tel. 27 65.

ACCOMMODATION. – *Friedrich Papst*, C. 10 b.

The **Benedictine abbey of Altenburg, founded in 1144, preserves a Romanesque window and part of a Gothic cloister, but in its present form is a masterpiece of Rococo architecture 1729–42), the finest work of Joseph Munggenast. The abbey church was also rebuilt (1730–33). Notable

Altenburg Abbey

Admont

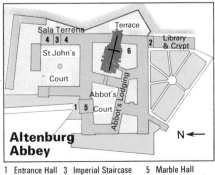

1 Entrance Hall	3 Imperial Staircase	5 Marble Hall
2 Staircase	4 Imperial Apartments	6 Medieval remains

features of the abbey are the magnificent stucco decoration, mural paintings by P. Troger and a very impressive *Library, under which lies an unusual crypt.

SURROUNDINGS. – 5 km /3 miles SE is the *Rosenburg, a richly articulated structure laid out around a fine tiltyard (an area use for tilting; conducted tour; fine views; restaurant in castle).

7 km/4½ miles NW of Altenburg is Schloss Greillenstein (16th–17th c.), with a fine interior and a museum of criminal law.

6 km/4 miles NE is the ancient little town of Horn (alt. 309 m/1014 ft; pop. 8000; Hotel Heidinger, B/C, 55 b.), with a Schloss of the 16th and 18th c. (now occupied by the tax office), the Höbarth Museum (Wiener Strasse 4: prehistoric and local material, pictures; closed Mon.) and a museum in the Stadtturm (closed Mon.) devoted to an early 19th c. bandit leader named Grasel. – 3 km/2 miles NE of Horn is the Renaissance Schloss Breiteneich (restored). – 5 km/3 miles SE of Horn stands the pilgrimage church of Maria-Dreieichen, a fine late Baroque building of 1750.

13 km/8 miles E of Horn, in the upper Schmida Valley, is the pretty little town of Eggenburg (alt. 325 m/1066 ft; pop. 4000), with a Gothic parish church (1482–1537; Romanesque towers), the Krahuletz Museum (early history) and a motor cycle and technical museum. 8 km/5 miles N is Pulkau (alt. 280 m/919 ft, pop. 1500), with the Gothic Heiligenblutkirche (large winged altarpiece of c. 1520); 14th c. charnel-house.

Arlberg

Länder: Tirol (T) and Vorarlberg (V).
ⓘ Verkehrsamt Lech, Postfach 54, A-6764 Lech; tel. (0 55 83) 21 61 0.
  Fremdenverkehrsverband St Anton, Postfach 40, A-6580 St Anton; tel. (0 54 46) 2 26 90 and 2 46 30.
  Verkehrsamt Zürs, Posthaus, A-6763 Zürs; tel. (055 83) 22 45.

ACCOMMODATION. – IN ST ANTON: *Alberg-Hospitz, A1 178 b, SB, sauna; Bellevue, A, 151 b., SB, sauna; Arlberg, A, 120 b; Tannenhof, B, 40 b. – IN LECH: *Arlberg, A1, 79 b., SB, sauna; Post, A1, 75 b., SB, sauna; Berghof, A, 89 b. – YOUTH HOSTEL. – IN ZÜRS (open in winter only): *Zürserhof, A1, 180 b., sauna; Alpenrose-Post, A, 137 b., SB, sauna; Edelweiss-Central-Sporthotel, A, 112 b., sauna; Flexen, B, 60 b., sauna. – IN STUBEN: Mondschein, A, 70 b., SB, sauna; Hubertushof, A, 60, SB; Post, A, 45 b., sauna; Berghaus, B, 34 b. – IN LANGEN: Arlbergerhof, C, 35 b.

RECREATION and SPORTS. – Hang-gliding school at Lech; climbing school at St Anton. Indoor golf in two hotels in Zürs (winter); tennis, riding, fishing; winter sports.

The *Arlberg, the boundary between two quite different peoples, the Tirolese and the Vorarlbergers, is the highest mountain massif in the Lechtal Alps, forming the watershed between the Rhine and the Danube and also marking a meteorological divide. In consequence there are regularly heavy falls of snow in winter, and this has led to the development of such well-known winter sports resorts as St Anton, Lech, Zürs, Stuben and Klösterle. The massif is now served by numerous mountain railways and hundreds of ski-tows and ski-lifts; many of these are used in summer to take walkers and climbers up the various peaks – chief among them the mighty Valluga (2811 m/9223 ft).

Two pass roads traverse the Arlberg. The Arlbergstrasse (Arlberg Road) runs from W to E from the Rhine valley through the *Klostertal, which begins at Bludenz, to the Inn, reaching a height of some 1800 m/5900 ft at the Arlberg pass. A road tunnel 14 km/9 miles long between Langen and St Anton, opened in December 1978, now permits safe passage on this route eveh in winter. The *Flexenstrasse (Flexen Road) branches off this road E of Stuben and runs N over the Flexen pass (1784 m/5853 ft) into the Lechtal. It is scenically more impressive, affording superb views of the Verwall group and skirting the rugged rock walls of the Stubenbach gorge in tremendous turns. Numerous galleries provide protection against avalanches for the road, which whenever possible is kept open during the winter; the northern approach road, however, is frequently closed in winter between Warth and Lech.

From the old-established winter sports resort of St Anton am Arlberg (1287 m/4223 ft) there are cableways up Valluga (2811 m/9223 ft) and Galzig (2185 m/7169 ft) and to the Brandkreuz (2100 m/

Lech am Arlberg in winter

6890 ft) and *Kapall* (2333 m/7655 ft). Here Hannes Schneider developed the Arlberg style of ski-jumping and Stefan Kruckenhauser the technique of wedeling: ski museum. – The parish church of Maria Hilf (1691–98) was enlarged by Clemens Holzmeister in 1932.

Lech *am Arlberg* (alt. 1447 m/4748 ft), chief place of the Tannberg area, lies on the N side of the Arlberg in an open stretch of valley at the confluence of the Lech and the Zürser Bach. It has a fine parish church with a massive tower (14th–15th c., enlarged in Baroque style in 18th c.). *Oberlech* (alt. 1705 m/5594 ft) is a summer and winter sports resort with numerous ski-lifts and cableways. To the NW is the *Braunarlspitze* (2651 m/8698 ft), the highest peak in the Bregenzer Wald. Cableway up the *Rüfikopf* (2348 m/7704 ft); several mountain excursions.

Zürs (1720 m/5643 ft), on the Flexenstrasse, is a mountain village which has developed into a world-famed winter sports resort, the barrier effect of the Arlberg giving it an abundance of snow. In summer it is an excellent base for walks and climbs. There are chair-lifts up the surrounding peaks – the *Seekopf* (2208 m/7244 ft), *Nördlicher Trittkopf* (2581 m/8468 ft) and *Krabachjoch* (2305 m/7563 ft).

Stuben *am Arlberg* (1409 m/4623 ft), finely situated, is both a summer and a winter sports resort. Chair-lift up *Albona* (2364 m/7756 ft). The Flexenstrasse branches off at the *Alpe Rauz* (1628 m/5341 ft; chair-lift to 2280 m/7478 ft).

To the W of Stuben are the villages of **Langen** *am Arlberg* (1228 m/4030 ft), a good base for walkers, and *Klösterle* (1069 m/3507 ft).

Attersee

Land: Upper Austria (OÖ).
Altitude: 494 m/1621 ft.
ⓘ **Fremdenverkehrsverband Attersee,**
Nussdorfer Strasse 15, A-4864 Attersee;
tel. (0 76 66) 2 19.
Fremdenverkehrsverband Nussdorf, Postfach,
A-4865 Nussdorf; tel. (0 76 66) 80 64.
Fremdenverkehrsverband Weyregg,
Gemeindeamt, Postfach 4, A-4852 Weyregg;
tel. (076 64) 2 36.

ACCOMMODATION. – IN ATTERSEE: *Oberndorfer*, A, 40 b., sauna; *Traschwandtner*, C, 73 b.; *Lindenhof*, C. 39 b. – IN NUSSDORF: *Ragginger*, B, 56 b.; *Bräugasthof*, B, 40 b., SP. – Three CAMPING SITES. – IN WEYREGG:

Staudinger, C, 76 b.; *Post*, C, 59 b., SP, sauna; *Födinger*, C, 48 b. – IN UNTERACH: *Georgshof*, A, 48 b., SB, sauna. – One CAMPING SITE.

RECREATION and SPORTS. – Sailing schools at Attersee and Weyregg, yachting school at Kammer, diving instruction; fishing; tennis, riding, indoor swimming bath.

The *Attersee (alt. 467 m/1532 ft) is the largest Alpine lake in Austria (20 km/12½ miles long, 2–3 km/1–2 miles across), extending from the limestone walls of the Höllengebirge (1862 m/6109 ft) in the SE to the low hills of the Alpine foreland. There is a series of pretty little holiday resorts around the bluish-green waters of the lake – Seewalchen and Kammer at the E end, Weyregg, Steinbach and Weissenbach on the E side.

A road follows the whole circumference of the lake. From the W side there are impressive glimpses of the *Höllengebirge*, and there are beautiful views of the lake from the parking place between Attersee and Buchberg and the hill between Buchberg and Seewalchen. – From the S end of the lake, W of Burgau, a footpath leads in 10 minutes to the **Burggrabenklamm* (gorge), with a waterfall.

SURROUNDINGS. – From Weissenbach a delightful road (SP Bad Ischl) runs SE through wooded country to the *Weissenbacher Sattel*, a pass at 585 m/1919 ft (chapel). From the adjoining plateau there is a fine view into the *Weissenbachklamm* (gorge) below.

The Attersee

Bad Aussee

Land: Styria (Stm).
Altitude: 657 m/2156 ft. – Population: 5500.
Post code: A-8990. – Telephone code: 0 61 52.
ⓘ **Kurverwaltung,** Postfach 45;
tel. 23 23.

ACCOMMODATION. – *Post*, A, 376 b.; *Erzherzog Johann*, A, 140 b.; *Paradies*, A, 39 b.; *Kristina*, A, 21 b.; *Alpenhof*, A, 16 b.; *Wasnerin*, B, 58 b.; *Sonne*, B, 45 b.; *Stadt Wien*, B, 30 b.; *Blaue Traube*, C, 22 b. – YOUTH HOSTEL. – CAMPING SITE at Reith.

RECREATION and SPORTS. – Walking; climbing school in Altaussee, riding, tennis, fishing, swimming, diving, surfing, sailing.

This old market town lies in the Traun valley between the Totes Gebirge and the Dachstein. A health resort and salt-water spa (Kneipp treatment), it is also a popular winter sports area.

In the little *Spitalkirche* are four Gothic wooden panels (15th c.). Opposite the church is the *birthplace of Anna Plochl* (1804–85), the postmaster's daughter who became the wife of Archduke Johann. The old Kamerhof now houses the *Heimatmuseum* (local museum).

The surrounding area is famous for the myriads of narcissi which flower from mid-May to mid-June (Festival of narcissi).

SURROUNDINGS. – 5 km/3 miles N is the *Altausseer See, in a magnificent setting between the SW faces of the Totes Gebirge. It is 3 km/2 miles long by 1 km/¾ mile across (open-air pool; hire of rowing boats). On the shores of the lake is the little spa town of **Altaussee** (alt. 723 m/ 2372 ft; pump-room; Hotels: Seevilla, Tyrol, Am See), also noted as a winter sports resort. From here the *Aussee salt-mine*, 3·5 km/2 miles NW, can be visited (alt. 948 m/ 3110 ft; conducted tour, about 1½ hours). A panoramic road (toll) runs N from Altaussee by way of the *Loserhütte* (1564 m/5131 ft; inn) to the *Augstsee* (10 km/6 miles). From the car park at the Loserhütte is an hour's climb to the summit of the *Loser* (1838 m/6030 ft), from which there are superb views; skiing area.

5 km/3 miles NE of Bad Aussee is the *Grundlsee* (alt. 709 m/2326 ft), in a beautiful setting at the foot of the Totes Gebirge, amid the green forest-framed valley of the Wiesental. The lake is 6 km/4 miles long by 1 km/¾ mile across and is up to 64 m/210 ft deep (open-air pool). The village of *Grundlsee* (Hotel Riegler, B, 25 b.) straggles along the shores of the lake. The village of *Gössl*, at the E end of the lake, is the starting-point of the "three lakes tour", taking in the Grundlsee, the *Toplitzsee* and the little *Kammersee*; the excursion, which lasts some 2 hours, is by motorboat (no vehicles carried).

Baden bei Wien

Land: Lower Austria (NÖ).
Altitude: 234 m/768 ft. – Population: 25,000.
Post code: A-2500. – Telephone code: 0 22 52.
ⓘ **Kurdirektion**, Hauptplatz 2;
   tel. 8 68 00/310.

ACCOMMODATION. – *Parkhotel*, A1, 175 b., SB, sauna; *Gutenbrunn*, A1, 169 b., SB, sauna; *Sauerhof zu Rauhenstein*, A1, 160 b., SB, sauna; *Club-hotel Baden*, A1, 148 b., SB, sauna; *Herzoghof*, A1, 118 b., SB, sauna; *Schlosshotel*, A, 77 b.; *Eden*, A, 50 b.; *Johannesbad*, C, 79 b. – IN HELENENTAL: *Krainerhütte*, A1, 210 b., SB, sauna.

RESTAURANTS. – In most hotels; also *Stadtkeller*; *Batzenhäusl*; restaurant in the Congress Building.

CASINO. – In Kurpark (roulette, baccarat, blackjack; daily from 4 p.m.).

RECREATION AND SPORT. – 18-hole golf course in Enzesfeld, riding, tennis, thermal baths.

EVENTS. – International trotting races (mid-June to August); concerts in the Kurhaus.

Baden, the principal Austrian spa with sulphurous water, lies 30 km/18 miles S of Vienna on the eastern edge of the Wienerwald (Vienna Woods), where the River Schwechat, in the Helenental, emerges. The water of Baden was already being used for curative purposes in Roman times, when the town was known as Aquae, but the spa owes its reputation to the regular summer visits of the Hapsburg Court between 1803 and 1834, when the town became the rendezvous of Viennese society and leading personalities. The sulphur springs, at a temperature of 39 °C (97 °F), have a daily flow of 6·5 million litres (1·4 million gallons).

SIGHTS. – In the Hauptplatz is a *Trinity Column* (1714). Here, too, are the *Rathaus* (1815) and, at No. 17, the *Kaiserhaus* (1792), which was Francis I's summer residence from 1813 to 1834. In Frauengasse, which runs S to Josefsplatz, is the Baroque *Frauenkirche* (interior remodelled in neo-classical style in 1812). NE of the Hauptplatz are the *Municipal Theatre* (Stadttheater: 1909) and the *parish church of St Stephen* (15th c.), a hall-church with a Baroque helm-roofed tower (many monuments, including a commemorative plaque for Mozart, who composed his "Ave Verum" for the choirmaster of this church).

To the W of the Hauptplatz by way of Rathausgasse (at No. 10 of which Beethoven lived in 1821–23) is the fruit and vegetable market. Farther W still are the **Kurmittelhaus** (treatment centre), *thermal bath* (Hallenbad), *mineral swimming pool* (Mineralschwimmbad) and Hotel Gutenbrunn.

To the N, on the southern slopes of the *Badener Berg*, is the **Kurpark**, containing the *Kongresshaus*, the *Casino* and the *Arena*, an open-air theatre. Close by, in a rock basin, is the Römerquelle (Roman Springs). Here, too, are monuments to distinguished visitors to the spa – a temple (1927) for Beethoven, a smaller temple with a bronze bust (1961) for Mozart, busts of the playwright Grillparzer

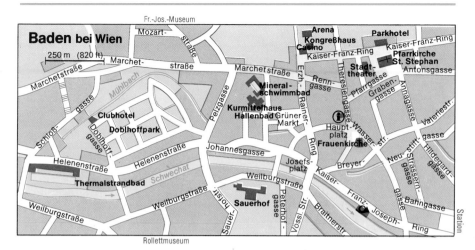

Baden bei Wien

250 m (820 ft)

Map labels: Fr.-Jos.-Museum · Mozart-straße · Marchet-straße · Marchetstraße · Marchetstraße · Mühlbach · gasse · Clubhotel · Doblhoffpark · Pelzgasse · Mineral-schwimmbad · Kurmittelhaus · Hallenbad · Grüner Markt · Arena · KongreßHaus · Casino · Kaiser-Franz-Ring · Parkhotel · Kaiser-Franz-Ring · Pfarrkirche · St. Stephan · Antonsgasse · Stadt-theater · Renngasse · Renn-Rainer-Str. · Pfarrgasse · Graben-gasse · Haupt-platz · Frauenkirche · Wasser-gasse · Annagasse · Valeriestr. · Helenenstraße · Helenenstraße · Johannesgasse · Josefs-platz · Breyer-gasse · Neu-stift-gasse · Strassen-gasse · Hildegard-gasse · Schloß-gasse · Doblhoff-gasse · Thermalstrandbad · Schwechat · Weilburgstraße · Kaiser-Franz-Joseph-Ring · Bahngasse · Weilburgstraße · Weilburgstraße · Sauerhof · hofstr. · Sauer- · Peterhof-gasse · Vöslr. Str. · Braitnerstr. · Station · Rollettmuseum

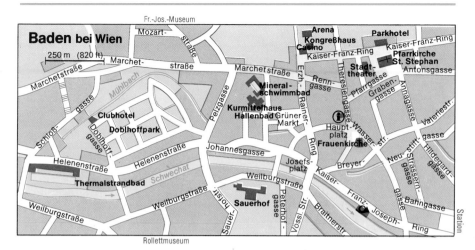
Schloss Doblhoff (Clubhotel), Baden

(1874) and the Emperor Joseph II (1894) and a bronze group (1912) commemorating the composers Lanner and Strauss, who often played here. The unusual *Undine Fountain*, with numerous figures, was erected in 1903. – There are concerts in the park throughout the year.

To the W of the town is the *Doblhoffpark*, a natural park with a lake (hire of boats), a garden restaurant and a rose-garden. Still farther W, on the banks of the Schwechat, is the large **thermal complex** (Thermal-strandbad), with four pools (24–33 °C/ 75–93 °F), a sandy beach and a restaurant.

S of the Schwechat, the *Rollett Museum* (Weikersdorfer Platz 1; open 1 May to 15 October, Wed. and Sat. 3–6 p.m., Sun. 9 a.m.–12 noon), houses a rich collection of local material and a collection of skulls which belonged to the anatomist Josef Gall (1758–1828), founder of the science of phrenology.

SURROUNDINGS. – To the N of the Kurpark are many footpaths with fine viewpoints (Theresienwarte, 416 m/ 1365 ft, ½ hour's walk). – To the W of the park by way of Andreas-Hofer-Zeile is the *Kaiser-Franz-Josef-Museum*, with displays of the folk art and crafts of Lower Austria and material of the prehistoric and early historical periods (Hochstrasse 51: ½ hour's walk).

To the N are the **Pfaffstättner Kogel** (541 m/1775 ft, 1¾ hours: view) and *Anninger* (674 m/2111 ft, 2¾ hours), to the W the **Hoher Lindkogel** (834 m/2736 ft; refreshments) with magnificent views in all directions from the look-out tower.

13 km/8 miles and 15 km/9 miles NW of Baden are the Cistercian *Heiligenkreuz Monastry** (founded 1135; monastic buildings rebuilt in 17th and 18th c.; church 12th–13th c., stalls of 1707, fine stained glass, 13th c. cloister) and the Carmelite nunnery of *Mayerling*, on the site of the hunting lodge in which Crown Prince Rudolf of Austria killed himself in 1889. – The road to Heiligenkreuz and Mayerling runs through the forest-fringed **Helenental**, the valley of the River Schwechat. To the left, on the other bank, are the imposing remains of **Burg Rauheneck** (12th–13th c.). To the right stands the *parish church of St Helena* (originally Gothic) which gave its name to the valley; it contains the "Potters' Altar" (*c.* 1500) which was removed from St Stephen's Cathedral in Vienna in 1745 because Pope Benedict XIV had forbidden any representation of the Trinity in human form. On the hill above the church are the extensive ruins of *Burg Rauhenstein* (alt. 336 m/1102 ft; 12th and 17th c.).

5 km/3 miles S of Baden is **Bad Vöslau** (alt. 270 m/ 886 ft; pop. 11,000; Hotel Witzmann, 127 b.), with a thermal spring (24 °C/75 °F), gushing out of the rockface, which supplies a large open-air swimming pool. SW of the pool is a Schloss (17th–18th c.).

12 km/7½ miles N of Baden is **Mödling** (alt. 240 m/787 ft; pop. 19,000; Hotel Babenbergerhof, 36 b.), a favourite resort of the people of Vienna. Beethoven lived at Hauptstrasse 79 from 1818 to 1820, Arnold Schönberg at Bernhardgasse 6 from 1918 to 1925. Mödling has a Renaissance Rathaus (Town Hall) (1548); and the church of St Othmar (late Gothic), with a late Roman-esque charnel-house (frescoes). Above the town (20 minutes' walk) are *Schloss Liechtenstein* (1820–22) and *Burg Liechtenstein*, with a Romanesque chapel (12th c.).

Bludenz

Land: Vorarlberg (V).
Altitude: 588 m/1929 ft. – Population: 13,000.
Post code: A-6700. – Telephone code: 0 55 52.
ⓘ **Verkehrsamt**, Werdenbergerstrasse 42;
tel. 6 21 70.

ACCOMMODATION. – *Schlosshotel*, A, 50 b.; *Altdeutsche Stuben*, B, 34 b.; *Herzog Friedrich*, B, 25 b.; *Einhorn*, C, 72 b.; *Alfenz*, C, 52 b.

Bludenz, chief town of a Bezirk (district) of Vorarlberg, lies at the intersection of five valleys – the Montafon, the Walgau and the Brandnertal, Klostertal and Grosswalzertal. The ancient part of the town has an attractive old-world air with narrow streets and tightly packed houses.

SIGHTS. – The parish *church of St Lawrence* (16th–17th c.) rises above the old town, with a war memorial in a round tower on the cemetery wall. Nearby is *Schloss Gayenhofen* (*c.* 1746), now occupied by the district authorities. At the SE end of the town stands the *Heiligkreuzkirche*, a handsome modern church on a central plan (1932–34); pedestrian zone.

SURROUNDINGS. – To the N of the town is the **Muttersberg** (1412 m/4633 ft; cableway).

To the SW is the *Brandner Tal, a valley extending for some 12 km/7½ miles to Brand. It is a popular health and winter sports area, with a number of small hamlets. There is a cableway to the summit of *Tschengla (1250 m/4100 ft), covered with Alpine meadows. – **Brand** (alt. 1037 m/3402 ft; pop. 650; Schesaplana-Hotel, A, 134 b., SP, SB; Colrosa, A, 75 b., SB; Walliserhof, A, 65 b., SB) is a mountain village at the mouth of the Zalimtal. The choir of the church contains old frescoes; the nave is a tent-like timber structure built in 1964. Brand is the main tourist attraction of the Rätikon area, a health resort (open-air swimming pool) and winter sports complex. There is a chair-lift up the *Eggen* (1271 m/4170 ft), continuing to the *Niggenkopf* (1596 m/5236 ft), from which it is a 25 minutes' walk to the *Palüd-Hütte* (1720 m/5643 ft; inn).

A beautiful *road (6·5 km/4 miles: gradients up to 12%) climbs from Brand via *Innertal* (chair-lift up to Melkboden, 1611 m/5286 ft) and the *Schattenlagant-Alpe* to the lower station of the *Lünerseebahn* (1565 m/5135 ft). The upper station is at the *Neue Douglass-Hütte* (1979 m/6494 ft; inn in summer) on the *Lüner See* (1970 m/6464 ft). The lake, 1·5 km/1 mile long, stores water for the Illwerke (hydroelectric installations in the Ill valley). A scenic footpath encircles the lake (1½ hours). From here it is a 3–3½ hours' climb to the summit of the *Schesaplana (2697 m/9735 ft), the highest peak in the Rätikon, with superb views. The summit can also be reached direct from Brand, but the climb, by way of the *Oberzalimhütte*

In the Brandner Tal

(1930 m/6332 ft; inn in summer) and *Mannheimer Hütte* (2700 m/8859 ft; inn in summer), is fairly strenuous (6 hours).

6·5 km/4 miles NW of Bludenz is *Ludesch*, with an early Baroque church containing an altarpiece of 1640. Above the village (1 km/¾ mile SE) stands the beautiful Gothic *church of St Martin*, the oldest parish church in the Walgau (begun *c.* 800); it has a free-standing belfry. From Ludesch there is a road (10 km/6 miles) via Raggal to the mountain village of *Ludescherberg* (1087 m/3566 ft), on the Hoher Frassen (1979 m/6493 ft), from which there are splendid views.

Braunau am Inn

Land: Upper Austria (OÖ).
Altitude: 352 m/1155 ft. – Population: 18,000.
Post code: A-5280. – Telephone code: 0 77 22.
ⓘ **Fremdenverkehrsamt,** Stadtplatz 9;
   tel. 27 18 and 26 44.

ACCOMMODATION. – *Post*, A, 55 b., sauna; *Mayr Bräu*, B, 48 b.; *Gann*, C, 60 b. – YOUTH HOSTEL. – CAMPING SITE.

The old Upper Austrian town of Braunau lies on the right bank of the Inn opposite the Bavarian town of Simbach, to which it is linked by a bridge. It has many handsome burghers' houses of the 16th and 17th c. and remains of its medieval walls.

SIGHTS. – In the Stadtplatz is one of the old town gates, the *Salzburger Torturm* (carillon). In Johann-Fischer-Gasse, which runs W from the Stadtplatz, is the *Glockengiesserhaus* ("Bellfounder's House": No. 18), now containing a local museum. There are also interesting historical and cultural exhibits in the Bezirksmuseum in the former *Herzogsburg*. To the S, the **parish church of St Stephen** (1439–66) has a tower 95 m/312 ft high. The church contains 15th and 16th c. tombs and, in the fifth chapel to the left of the choir, the spectacular 16th c. "Bakers' Altar". S of the parish church is the former *St Martin's Church* (1497), with a war memorial chapel in the lower church.

SE of the Stadtplatz is the 15th c. *Spitalkirche* and opposite this the *Palmpark*, named after the Nürnberg bookseller Johannes Palm (b. 1766: bronze statue), who was shot by the French in 1806 for distributing patriotic literature. On a house at Salzburger Strasse 19 (in the Salzburger suburb to the S of the old town gate) is a tablet commemorating his execution. In Palmweg, which branches off at this house, is a memorial stone, and Palm is buried in the local cemetery. – Braunau was the birthplace of Adolf Hitler (1889–1945).

SURROUNDINGS. – Immediately below the town are two artificial lakes on the Inn, 10 km/6 miles long and 1 km/¾ mile wide. 3 km/2 miles upstream is another lake, 9 km/5½ miles long and up to 2 km/1¼ miles wide, with facilities for bathing and boating.

4 km/2½ miles S is *Ranshofen* which has an Augustinian monastery founded in 1125, rebuilt between 1624 and 1651 and dissolved in 1811 and also a Baroque church (16th c.), with an elaborately decorated altar. – 4·5 km/ 3 miles E of Braunau, at *St Peter am Hart*, there is a Gothic parish church containing a fine high altar by Thomas Schwanthaler (1680).

8 km/5 miles SE *St Georgen an der Mattig* possesses a little church containing three fine carved altars (*c.* 1650).

19 km/12 miles S lies **Pischelsdorf**, where the church, built between 1392 and 1419, is probably an early work by Hans Stethaimer. In the funerary chapel is a wall painting of about 1400.

Bregenz

Land: Vorarlberg (V).
Altitude: 398 m/1306 ft. – Population: 27,000.
Post code: A-6900. – Telephone code: 0 55 74.
ⓘ **Fremdenverkehrsamt,** Inselstrasse 15;
tel. 2 33 91–92.
Landesverkehrsamt Vorarlberg,
Römerstrasse 7;
tel. 2 25 25.

ACCOMMODATION. – *Mercure*, Platz der Wiener Symphoniker, A, 170 b.; *Messmer*, Kornmarktstr. 16, A, 129 b., sauna; *Schwärzler*, Landstr. 9, A, 148 b., SB, sauna; *Weisses Kreuz* (no rest.), Römerstr. 5, A, 80 b.; *Germania*, A, Steinenbach 9, B, 33 b.; *Fröhlich*, Heldendankstr. 6c, C, 16 b. – YOUTH HOSTEL: Belruptstr. 16a. – several CAMPING SITES.

RESTAURANTS. – *Burgrestaurant Gebhardsberg; Messmer* (see above); *Berghaus Pfänder, Gourmet-Restaurant Zoll.* – CAFÉS: *Theatercafé; Rosett.*

CASINO. – (roulette, baccarat, blackjack: daily from 4 p.m.), on the lakeside, next to the Festival House.

RECREATION and SPORTS. – Boat trips on Lake Constance, sailing, hire of boats; fishing, water-skiing, tennis, riding; footpaths and cycle paths; skiing on Pfänder.

EVENTS. – **Bregenz Festival** (performances on floating stage in lake: July–Aug.); *Spring Festival* (mid May); *sailing regattas* (June–Aug.).

Bregenz, the old capital of Vorarlberg, lies on the shores of Lake Constance at the foot of the Pfänder. The upper town, with some well-restored old buildings, has preserved its old-world character, while the newer districts on the lake are modern and well equipped with tourist facilities – an open-air pool, the covered baths, the Stadium, tennis courts, the lakeside gardens (bandstand, mini-golf), the floating stage with its stand for 4300 spectators

and the **Festspielhaus (for festivals and conferences).**

SIGHTS. – The *****Vorarlberg Provincial Museum** (*Vorarlberger Landesmuseum*) in the Kornmarkt has a collection of cultural and artistic interest and a theatre; to the S stands the *Rathaus* (1685) adjoining which is the *Lake Chapel of St George* (Seekapelle: 1698). To the S of the Römerstrasse the new **Landhaus** (1982) accommodates the provincial council and the provincial government (Landtag and Landesregierung). At the W end of the lake promenade is the **Festival and Congress Building** (*Festspiel und Kongresshaus*) (1980) with the lakeside theatre in front of it. In the Upper Town, which occupies the site of a Celtic settlement and of the Roman military camp of "Brigantium", rises the massive **St Martin's Tower** (*Martinsturm*), a relic of the medieval fortifications (onion-dome of 1602); on the upper floor is the *Heimatmuseum* (local museum), on the lower floor *St Martin's Chapel* (Martinskapelle) founded in 1363 with fine 14th c. wall paintings. The *Old Rathaus* is a half-timbered building of 1662. To the S, above the Upper Town, stands the *Parish Church of St Gallus* (14th/15th c.; restored in 1738) with an impressive interior.

SURROUNDINGS. – To the W of the town, near Lake Constance, is the Cistercian *monastery of Mehrerau*, founded at the end of the 11th c., with a neo-Romanesque church of 1859 (remodelled in modern style in 1961–64). – 3 km/2 miles S of Bregenz is the **Gebhardsberg** (597 m/1959 ft), on which are the ruins of *Burg Hohenbregenz* (destroyed by the Swedes in 1647), and a pilgrimage chapel of 1791. From the Burgrestaurant and the terrace there are magnificent views of the town and the lake. – An attractive lakeside road runs 3 km/2 miles N from the lakeside gardens (*Seeanlagen*) to *Lochau*.

St Martin's Tower, Bregenz

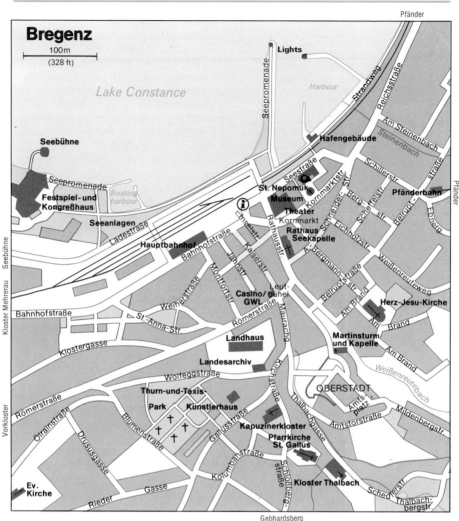

Immediately E of Bregenz is the *Pfänder (1604 m/ 3491 ft). A cableway 2 km/1¼ miles long, the lower station of which is some 500 m/550 yards E of the Kornmarkt, ascends to the summit in 6 minutes. From Lochau (3 km/ 2 miles N of Bregenz) there is a road (7 km/4½ miles) to the *Schwedenschanze Inn*, and there is also a fairly steep footpath from Bregenz via *Hintermoos* (2 hours).

At the upper station of the cableway are a look-out terrace and the *Berghaus Pfänder* (restaurant). 5 minutes' walk below this is the *Gasthof Pfänderdohle* (open only in winter), near which is an Alpine zoo. From the cableway station it is a 5 minutes' climb to the summit, from which there is a breathtaking **view of the Alps. – A tunnel under Pfänder, opened in 1980 (6·7 km/4 miles long) provides a link between the German motorway network and the Austrian motorway in the Rhine valley; the new road bypasses Bregenz.

Bregenzer Wald

Land: Vorarlberg (V).

ⓘ **Verkehrsverband Bregenzerwald,**
A-6883 Egg;
tel. (0 55 12) 23 65.

ACCOMMODATION. – IN EGG: *Post,* B, 50 b.; *Hubertus,* C, 50 b., SP, sauna. – IN BEZAU: *Post,* A, 73 b., SB, sauna; *Gams,* A, 64 b., SP, sauna; *Sonne,* B, 52 b., sauna. – IN MELLAU: *Kreuz,* A, 96 b., SB, sauna; *Engel,* B, 86 b., SB, sauna; *Sonne,* B, 72 b., SB, SP, sauna. – IN AU: *Krone,* A, 139 b., SB, sauna; *Alpenrose,* B, 36 b. – IN SCHOPPERNAU: *Krone,* A, 72 b., SB, sauna; *Hirschen,* B, 66 b., sauna. – IN SCHRÖCKEN: *Tannberg,* B, 51 b., sauna. – CAMPING SITES.

The *Bregenzer Wald (Bregenz Forest), the northern part of the Vorarlberg Alps, rises from Lake Constance to the Arlberg. The lower parts consist of rounded hills, partly forest-covered; higher up it is dominated by rugged peaks. The deeply slashed valley of the Bregenzer Ache descends from the Hochtannberg to Lake Constance, into which the river flows at Bregenz, and through this valley runs a federal highway which gives easy access to the holiday areas and the fine walking country. In spite of its name there is relatively little forest left in the

Bregenzer Wald, large areas having
been cleared in past centuries to win
grazing land.

The meadow-covered slopes of the hills are
increasingly being developed for skiing and
equipped with ski-lifts and other facilities.
The barrier effect of the Alps brings down
heavy falls of snow, though at this com-
paratively low altitude (between 500 and
2000 m/1500 and 6500 ft) it frequently
disappears again quite quickly. In the 1950s
the old mountain path from the E end of the
Ache valley over the Hochtannberg pass
(1679 m/5509 ft) was replaced by an
excellent motor road.

The *Bödele (1156 m/3794 ft), between
the Rhine valley and the valley of the Ache, is
a favourite recreation area, with panoramic
views extending from Säntis in the W to the
Mädelegabel, Trettach and Braunarlspitze in
the E. – 4 km/2½ miles E of *Alberschwende*
(721 m/2366 ft) an attractive side road
branches off and crosses the *Lingenau
bridge* (88 m/298 ft high) into the tributary
valley of *Hittisau* (800 m/2626 ft). *Egg*
(565 m/1854 ft) and *Bezau* (651 m/2136 ft)
are good starting-points for walks and ski
treks. From Bezau there is a cableway to the
Baumgartenhöhe (1631 m/5351 ft). Other
resorts in the valley are *Mellau* (700 m/
2297 ft) and *Au* (796 m/2612 ft), under the
sheer rock walls of *Kanisfluh* (2050 m/
6728 ft), where a road (11 km/7 miles:
gradients up to 10%) goes off for *Damüls*
(1431 m/4695 ft; winter sports; many
hotels). – From *Schoppernau* (860 m/
2823 ft) there is a chair-lift up the *Diedams-
kopf* (2090 m/6859 ft), from which there
are unobstructed panoramic views. –
Schröcken (1260 m/4135 ft) is the starting-
point of the *Hochtannbergstrasse*, which is

flanked by the Hochkünzelspitze (2397 m/
7865 ft), Braunarlspitze (2649 m/8691 ft)
and Widderstein (2533 m/8311 ft). Beyond
the pass (1679 m/5509 ft) the road runs
down to *Warth* (1494 m/4902 ft), where the
Flexenstrasse branches into the Arlberg.

Brenner Road

Land: Tirol (T).

ⓘ **Tiroler Fremdenverkehrswerbung,**
Bozner Platz 6, A-6020 Innsbruck;
tel. (0 52 22) 2 07 77.

ACCOMMODATION. – IN MATREI: *Krone*, B, 100 b., – IN
STEINACH: *Steinacherhof*, A, 110 b., SB, sauna; *Weisses
Rössl*, A, 80 b., SB, sauna; *Post*, B, 70 b. – IN GRIES:
Humler, C, 44 b.

**The Brenner, the lowest pass (1374 m/
4508 ft) over the main chain of the Alps,
is one of the oldest passages through
this mountain barrier, already in use in
Roman times. In our own day a railway
line, a federal highway and a motorway
(toll) run from Innsbruck through the
Wipptal, the valley of the Sill, to the
pass, which since 1918 has marked the
frontier between Austria and Italy.**

The *Brenner motorway* runs S from Innsbruck, passing under the Patscherkofel, and
crosses the 815 m/890 yds long *Europabrücke* (Europe Bridge), which spans the
Sill valley at a height of 190 m/625 ft. The
Stubaital branches off to the SW. – **Matrei
am Brenner** (alt. 922 m/3255 ft; pop. 3000),
the Roman *Matreium*, is a popular resort in
both summer and winter. In the old town are
attractive old peasants' houses and the parish
church, with a Baroque interior and ceiling
paintings of 1500. – 5 km/3 miles beyond

Schnepfau, Bregenzer Wald

The Europabrücke, on the Brenner motorway

this is **Steinach** (alt. 1048 m/3438 ft; pop. 2700), at the mouth of the Gschnitztal. The neo-Romanesque parish church has frescoes by G. Mader in the manner of the early 19th c. group known as the Nazarenes and an altarpiece by M. Knoller. – Just before the pass, at the foot of the *Padauner Kogel* (2068 m/6785 ft), is **Gries** (alt. 1163 m/3816 ft; pop. 1500), a popular resort in both summer and winter. – The road continues past the *Brennersee* (Brenner Lake) and in 5 km/3 miles reaches the frontier.

SURROUNDINGS. – 2 hours' drive W from Matrei is the former Servite priory of *Maria Waldrast* (1636 m/5368 ft), with a pilgrimage church, under the *Serles massif (*Waldrastspitze*, 2719 m/8921 ft), which can be climbed in just over 3 hours (extensive views).

From Steinach a chair-lift ascends by way of the *Bergeralm* (1600 m/5250 ft) to the *Nösslachjoch (2223 m/7323 ft), from which there are far-ranging views.

The *Gschnitztal, which joins the Silltal at Steinach, is served by a road which runs via *Trins* (1233 m/4045 ft), with a church (remodelled in Baroque style) and a handsome schloss, to *Gschnitz* (1242 m/4075 ft). The late Gothic *chapel of St Magdalene*, 1¼ hours E, has old frescoes.

At Gries is the lower station of a chair-lift to the *Sattelalm* (1652 m/5420 ft; inn), from which it is a 1½ hours' climb to the summit of the *Sattelberg* (2113 m/6933 ft), with magnificent views extending well into Italy.

From the Brennersee there is a rewarding climb (about 5½ hours) by way of the *Landshuter Hütte* (2693 m/8836 ft; inn) to the summit of **Kraxentrager** (2998 m/9836 ft), on the frontier with Italy.

worth seeing are the arcaded courtyards of the Apothekerhaus and the Town Hall (1530; local museum). Above the Hauptplatz rears the Gothic *parish church* (15th c.). From the square Rosegger-Strasse leads to the former Minorite *church of Maria im Walde* (13th c.), with remains of old wall paintings and an early Gothic cloister. The conventual buildings now house the *Heimatmuseum* (local museum). A stepped footpath leads up in 5 minutes to the scanty remains of *Burg Landskron*, with its clocktower; the climb is well worth while for the sake of the beautiful view of the town.

SURROUNDINGS. – To the S, 2½ hours' walk away, is the *Hochanger* (1282 m/4206 ft; inn), with a look-out tower. From here it is possible to walk along the ridge to the *Hochalpe* (1643 m/5391 ft; 2½ hours), from which there are beautiful views. – E of Bruck (3½ hours) is the *Rennfeld* (1269 m/5346 ft; inn), a skiing area.

26 km/16 miles NW of Bruck is **Trägoss-Oberort** (780 m/2560 ft; pop. 1200; Hotel Brückenwirt, C, 15 b.), beneath the S face of the Hochschwab group, with a Gothic church (12th c.). To the NW (¾ hour) is the *Grüner See* (Green Lake: 757 m/2484 ft; inn), which disappears in winter. 3½ hours' walk away is the *Sonnschien-Alm* (1515 m/4971 ft; inn), a good base from which to explore the western Hochschwab area: there is, for example an easy walk (2 hours) NW to the summit of *Ebenstein* (2124 m/6969 ft), with rewarding views, and another easy but rather longer walk (5 hours) E by way of the *Häusl-Alm* (1514 m/4967 ft; inn) to the summit of the *Hochschwab (2278 m/7474 ft).

16 km/10 miles SE of Bruck is *Mixnitz*, the starting-point of a walk (4½ hours) through the wild *Bärnschützklamm* (gorge) to the summit of *Hochlantsch (1720 m/5643 ft), from which there are sweeping views.

Bruck an der Mur

Land: Styria (Stm).
Altitude: 487 m/1598 ft. – Population: 17,000.
Post code: A-8600. – Telephone code: 0 38 62.
ⓘ **Städtisches Reisebüro,**
Koloman-Wallisch-Platz 25;
tel. 5 18 11.

ACCOMMODATION. – *Bahnhof*, A, 100 b.; *Bayer*, A, 60 b., sauna; *Bauer*, B, 88 b. – YOUTH HOSTEL. – CAMPING SITE at Oberaich.

Bruck is a busy Styrian town at the junction of the rivers Mürz and Mur, an important focal point of regional communications and an industrial town (steel and paper works).

SIGHTS. – In the old-world Hauptplatz (charming wrought-iron fountain of the Renaissance period, 1626) is the handsome Gothic *Kornmesserhaus* (1494–1510), with arcades and a magnificent loggia. Also

Burgenland

Land: Burgenland (B). – Capital: Eisenstadt.
Area: 3966 sq. km/1531 sq. miles.
Population: 268,100.
ⓘ **Amt der Burgenländischen Landesreglierung,**
Fremdenverkehrsabteilung, Freiheitsplatz 1,
A-7000 Eisenstadt;
tel. (0 26 82) 60 00.
Landesfremdenverkehrsverband,
Schloss Esterházy, A-7000 Eisenstadt;
tel. (0 26 82) 33 84.

Burgenland ("land of castles"), the most easterly of the Austrian *Länder*, is made up of two quite different territories. To the E are the great plains of the puszta, extending over the Hungarian frontier to the Carpathians; in this area is Europe's only steppe lake, the Neusiedler See. The southern part of Burgenland is a region of

wooded hills, the eastern outliers of the Alps, with many castles – built here in what was for centuries a frontier area, occupied by the Romans and later exposed to attack successively by the Huns and the Turks. It is now a region of pastureland, fruit orchards and vineyards.

Burgenland is a relatively narrow strip of territory along the Austro-Hungarian frontier, extending from the Danube in the N to the Yugoslav frontier in the S, occupying the eastern slopes of the Leithagebirge around the Neusiedler See and the intricately patterned upland region which extends S and SE from the foothills of the Wechsel range and the hills of eastern Styria.

The most northerly part of Burgenland lies E of the Leithagebirge, on both sides of the River Wulka, and is bounded on the S by the Mattersburg hills. Here, too, is the extensive plain between the Danube and the N end of the Neusiedler See, interrupted by gently rolling hills and watered by the River Leitha. On the slopes of the Leithagebirge, which forms the border with Lower Austria for part of the way, are large vineyards.

The flat shores of the Neusiedler See where many aquatic birds can be seen, are overgrown with reeds for miles on end, and, from the villages dotted along the road, damp water meadows extend into the lake. At Eisenstadt this area merges into the Wulka plain, with a broad ridge of hills between the town and the lake, an area which produces the best wine grapes in Burgenland, the Rust grapes. S of Eisenstadt the "bay" of Ödenburg (Hungarian Sopron) reaches far into a gently rolling area which continues without any obvious boundary to near Wiener

Neustadt. This hilly area is bounded on the W by the Rosaliengebirge and on the S by the Ödenburg hills, which separate it from central Burgenland.

The Neusiedler See, two-thirds of which lie in Austria, with the remaining third in Hungary, occupies much of northern Burgenland, exerting a predominant influence on its landscape and climate.

Central Burgenland is a hilly and wooded region which falls towards the E and gives place to wide rolling country. It is separated from southern Burgenland by the Günser Gebirge, extending eastward from the Wechsel range.

Southern Burgenland is a region of long ranges of hills enclosing broad valleys and sloping down towards the E to form large plains around Rechnitz and Eberau which continue into Hungary. In between are the vine-covered hills of Eisenberg and Burg. To the S is the wide Raab valley, reaching towards Hungary, while the most southerly part of the province is occupied by wooded and fairly steeply scarped hills, sharply marked off from the flatter territory in the adjoining regions of Hungary and Yugoslavia.

HISTORY. – The history of Burgenland, reflected in the pattern of its castles and towns, was conditioned by its situation between two different worlds. Culturally a part of western Europe, it was constantly exposed to pressures from the east.

In the time of the *Romans* this was the heart of the province of Pannonia, occupied by *Illyrians, Celts*, Roman settlers and later *Ostrogoths* and *Slavs*. About 800, German settlers came to this region but were exposed to fierce onslaughts from the Avars and later the Hungarians. After the battle of Augsburg in 955, settlers from Central Europe pressed ever farther E, occupying Burgenland and building a great many castles of which so many still survive.

During the 15th c. the *Hungarians* several times conquered the region; in 1459 Burgenland became part of *Austria*, but after the Treaty of Ödenburg (1462) King Matthias Corvinus united it with Hungary again; after his death King Maximilian won it back for Austria; but in 1647 the Emperor Ferdinand III gave it up to Hungary without a blow being struck.

When the Austro-Hungarian monarchy collapsed in 1918 the people of Burgenland sought union with Austria, and this was provided for in the treaties of Saint-Germain (1919) and Trianon (1920). The allegiance of the Ödenburg (Sopron) area was to be determined by a plebiscite, in which a majority voted for union with Hungary. The province of Burgenland was given its present name in 1920 – derived from the common element in the names of the former counties of western Hungary (Ödenburg, Pressburg, Wieselburg, Eisenburg). – Since the end of the Second World War the federal province (*Bundesland*) of Burgenland has shared the destinies of the re-established Republic of Austria.

Farmhouse, Mörbisch (Neusiedler See)

ART. – The architecture of Burgenland cannot rival the magnificent buildings to be seen in other provinces of Austria: in the vicissitudes of its history too much has been destroyed. Some *palaces* and *castles* have been preserved, including the splendid Esterházy palace in Eisenstadt, Kittsee, some charming houses in Rust, the imposing Burg Forchtenstein and the fine castles and palaces of Rotenturm and Kohfidisch, Eberau and Bernstein, Stadtschlaining, Lockenhaus and Güssing. Among ecclesiastical buildings the most impressive are to be seen at Eisenstadt, Frauenkirchen, Mariasdorf and Rust. It is noteworthy that Burgenland can claim no major monastic establishment and only a few churches of artistic merit, although it has large numbers of castles and castle ruins, so that any study of its architectural history is almost exclusively confined to this field. The buildings of this type are all based on medieval foundations, preserving many Romanesque features in the substructures and in certain parts of the main structure, particularly the keep. In the 14th and 15th c. many castles were remodelled in Gothic style. The 16th c. was a period of intense building activity, when a number of castles were either rebuilt or replacd by new buildings.

The people of Burgenland have *music* in their blood, and Franz Liszt was born in this region. The famous actor Josef Kainz was also a native of Burgenland. – Among local *crafts* are embroidery and the working of serpentine.

Scenically Burgenland offers attractive contrasts, with wooded and often steeply scarped hills, narrow wooded valleys, wide fertile depressions, the rich vineyards of the lower uplands and extensive plains all contributing to give the province its own distinctive character.

From the hills on the edge of the Pannonian steppe there are striking views, both to E and W, of the Alps of Styria and Lower Austria. Burgenland also displays features characteristic of the S, and the sunny slopes of its hills yield almonds and chestnuts, peaches, apricots, sweet grapes and, in sheltered situations, figs.

Landscape and buildings characteristic of the puszta can be seen at their most typical in *Bruck an der Leitha*, with its straggling farmhouses and oriel-windowed houses. **Eisenstadt** (see p. 72) still breathes the spirit of Prince Esterházy, who rebuilt several older castles to give them the aspect which we see today.

Of the numerous castles and castle ruins which are worth a visit, only a selection can be mentioned.

On a high crag near *Mattersburg* is the mighty ***Burg Forchtenstein** (alt. 504 m/ 1654 ft), one of the finest castles in Austria. Originally founded in the early 14th c., it was rebuilt by the Esterházys between 1635 and 1652 as a powerfully fortified stronghold. A series of gates and courtyards lead into the interior, the most notable features of which are the rich collection of arms and armour, the Hunting Hall, the Armoury and the collection of carriages. The well, 142 m/ 466 ft deep, was dug by Turkish prisoners; it has a famous echo. A Grillparzer Festival is held in the castle in summer, with performances of his plays. 3 km/2 miles SW, on the highest point in the Rosaliengebirge (746 m/2448 ft), is the *Rosalienkapelle* (chapel), from which there are far-ranging views.

NE of the little town of *Kirchschlag* are the ruins of ***Burg Landsee** (13th and 15th–17th c.), an extensive range of buildings with a massive keep, surrounded by four rings of walls; it was destroyed in 1772. To the E, in *Raiding*, is the house where Franz Liszt (1811–1886) was born; it is now a museum.

Above the little market town of **Lockenhaus** (alt. 333 m/1093 ft) the imposing Burg Lockenhaus (13th c.) has a fine vaulted

Burg Forchtenstein

Burg Güssing

Knights' Hall. In the town itself are a Baroque parish church (1669) and a mansion which belonged to the Esterházys, now housing a natural history museum.

Schloss Bernstein, above the village of the same name (alt. 619 m/2031 ft; pop. 2500), is a handsome building of the 14th and 17th c., with a fine Knights' Hall (Renaissance and Baroque). Part of the castle is now a hotel.

The little town of *Stadtschlaining* (406 m/ 1332 ft), surrounded by remains of its walls, has a 13th c. castle, altered in later periods (keep, walls; folk museum, picture gallery).

Burg Güssing (12th c.), above the town of Güssing (alt. 229 m/751 ft; pop. 3700; airfield for light aircraft), was once a Benedictine monastery. The Romanesque church tower was originally a keep. In the Gothic chapel is a 17th c. chest organ. Museum.

*Neusiedler See: see p. 143.

Carinthia (Kärnten)

Land: Kärnten (K). – Capital: Klagenfurt.
Area: 9533 sq. km/3680 sq. miles.
Population: 538,900.
(i) **Landesfremdenverkehrsamt,**
Kaufmanngasse 13, A-9010 Klagenfurt;
tel. (0 42 22) 55 48 80.

Carinthia (Kärnten), Austria's most southerly province, lies in a basin entirely surrounded by mountains and watered throughout almost its whole length by the Drau, of which most of the other streams are tributaries. Its mild climate, which at times seems almost southerly, is due to its situation S of the main chain of the Alps, which keeps off the cold air masses from the N. In addition to this, areas of high pressure over Italy also usually extend into Carinthia, so that the number of days of sunshine is much above the Austrian average. In consequence the Carinthian lakes frequently have a water temperature between 24 and 27 °C (75 and 81 °F). The largest of these lakes – numbering more than a hundred in all – are the Wörther See, Ossiacher See, Millstätter See, Weissensee and Faaker See.

The province is sheltered on the N by the Hohe Tauern range, rising well above 3000 m/10,000 ft, with its highest peak the Grossglockner (3797 m/12,458 ft), at the foot of which is the Pasterze glacier, the largest in the Eastern Alps.

To the E the mountains fall away: the Gurktal Alps barely reach the 2500 m/8200 ft mark, and the adjoining Nockberge are gently rounded heights. The eastern boundary of Carinthia is formed by the Saualpe and Koralpe ranges, between which the Lavant valley runs N–S.

To the S are the Karawanken, with the Austro-Yugoslav frontier running along the crests, and farther W are the Carnic Alps. The western boundary of the province is formed by the Lienz Dolomites; and beyond the "Tiroler Pforte" (Tirolese Gate), where the Drau has carved a passage, the ring of mountains is closed by the Schober group.

The interior of the province also has its mountains, including the Villach Alps, the Gerlitzen, the Magdalensberg and the Ulrichsberg, between which lie the valleys and basins which are the main areas of human settlement and the lakes which attract so many visitors. Many of the upland areas have become popular winter sports regions.

Carinthia has a wide variety of plants. More than half its territory is covered with forest, and it preserves relics of the flora of the Ice Ages, such as *Linnaea borealis* and *Wulfenia* (a member of the Scrophulariaceae family), found in the Nassfeld.

The province also has a distinctive population structure, with a considerable Slovene minority, particularly in the southern areas, dating back to the Slav immigration in the 6th c. A.D.

HISTORY. – Lying remote within its ring of mountains, Carinthia was settled by man much later than the territories beyond this mountain barrier. The first traces of human occupation date only from the Neolithic; but the archaeological evidence becomes more abundant in the Bronze Age, when the area was inhabited by an Illyrian people, the *Veneti*, and the Iron Age which followed it. – About 400 B.C. the *Celts* began to move in, bringing with them a highly developed culture and systematically establishing new settlements – notable among them Teurnia (at Spittal an der Drau), Virunum (on the edge of the Zollfeld plain) and Juenna (in the Jaun valley).

Shortly before the beginnig of the Christian era the *Romans* began to occupy the territory, protecting the important trade routes from Italy to northern Europe by the establishment of forts and garrisons and founding civilian settlements. In 476, with the fall of the Western Empire, the Roman occupation came to an end. The period of the great migrations brought in *Slav peoples*, driven westward by the advancing Avars. In 750 the Slovene leader Boruth sought help against the Avars from Tassilo III of Bavaria, leading to an alliance between the two countries which lasted until 976, when the Emperor Otto II separated them and made Carinthia a duchy on its own to which the territories of Istria and Verona belonged.

In the 8th and 9th c. *Franks, Bajuwari* (Bavarians) and *Saxons* moved into Carinthia, forming an upper class which dominated the *Slovenes* and founding churches and religious houses (St Georgen, St Paul, Millstatt, etc.). In subsequent centuries the country was ruled by a number of ducal families, among them the Eppensteiners (until 1122) and the Sponheimers (until 1269). Then it was controlled by King Ottokar of Bohemia (1269–76) and King Rudolf I (1276–86); and in 1335 it passed to the *Habsburgs*.

Towards the end of the 15th c. *Hungarians* and *Turks* pressed into Carinthia, and evidence of these troubled times is still provided by the numerous fortified churches. Soon afterwards Carinthia was combined with neighbouring territories to form the province of Inner Austria.

Until the beginning of the modern period the chief town of Carinthia was St Veit an der Glan. Then in 1518 the Emperor Maximilian I presented to the Estates of Carinthia, at their request, the market town of Klagenfurt, which became the capital of the province. – The *Reformation* found fertile territory among the people and nobility of Carinthia; but the Counter-Reformation of the 17th c. restored the status quo without great difficulty or disturbance. – The Thirty Years War did not directly affect Carinthia, but had indirect effects on its economy. After the Peace of Westphalia economic life was slow to recover, until Maria Theresa and the Emperor Joseph II set out to promote the development of industry – most notably mining, metalworking and the Ferlach arms manufactory.

Carinthia was exposed to further troubles during the occupation by *Napoleon*, which was preceded by a number of battles between French and Austrian forces. Until 1849 much of the province was incorporated in the "Illyrian kingdom", with its capital at Ljubljana (Laibach); thereafter it again became directly subordinate to the Austrian crown.

After the First World War Yugoslav troops occupied part of Lower Carinthia but were driven out; then in October 1920 a plebiscite produced a decisive vote in favour of remaining part of Austria. – During the Nazi period the Eastern Tirol and, from 1942, large parts of Krajina (Krain) in Yugoslavia were attached to Carinthia, but after 1945 the old provincial boundaries were restored. Since then Carinthia has shared the destinies of the re-established Republic of Austria.

ART. – The earliest works of art produced in Carinthia were the lead figures of horsemen, dating from the *Bronze Age* and the *Hallstatt* period (Iron Age), which are named after the place where they were found (Frögg, in the Rosental) as "Frögger Reiter". – The *Roman Period* is represented by numerous works of art found in Carinthia, including one of the finest pieces of sculpture dicsovered N of the Alps, the bronze statue of a youth from Virunum (Magdalensberg) which was admired by Dürer. Many pieces of relief carving have been found, often reused in the masonry of later buildings.

A number of Romano-Celtic temples have also been excavated, for example at Wabelsdorf, Hohenstein and in the Lavant valley. As the Roman period neared its end Celtic features again increasigly came to the fore.

The development of a distinctive local style can be detected even in the *Early Christian period* (e.g. in the mosaic pavement of the basilica at Teurnia). The Carolingian period is represented by parts of the church at Karnburg, a number of pieces of ornamental stonework and the Ducal Throne in the Zollfeld (see under Maria Saal).

There was a rich flowering of *Romanesque* architecture in Carinthia, a famous example being the cathedral at Gurk (crypt *c.* 1170, the church a little later). From this period, too, date the monastic churches of Millstatt and St Paul and numbers of small village churches. The art of wall painting also flourished in Carithia.

Gothic architecture likewise achieved a distinctive Carinthian form, avoiding the over-elaborate decoration sometimes found elsewhere. A characteristic feature is the *charnel-house* to be seen all over the province – richly decorated with frescoes, as were the interiors of the churches. Also covered with imagery were the windows of the churches (Magdalene

The Weissensee, with Techendorf

Window from Weitensfeld, now in Klagenfurt; windows at Viktring) and the characteristically Carinthian "Lenten veils" with which the altars are covered during Lent (the largest being the one in Gurk Cathedral). – In addition to the churches increasing numbers of secular buildings were now erected, including the castles of Hochfeistritz, Diex, Grades and Frauenstien (St Veit).

The trend towards secular building was still more marked at the *Renaissance*, which came into Carinthia from the N. The finest building of this period is Schloss Porcia at Spittal an der Drau; other examples of Renaissance work are the Landhaus in Klagenfurt, Burg Hochosterwitz and, in the field of sculpture, the Dragon Fountain in Klagenfurt.

During the Baroque period building activity in Carinthia declined, the only notable Baroque building being Klagenfurt Cathedral.

Sculpture is represented only by a few altars and figures of saints. Josef Ferdinand Fromiller produced a number of altarpieces. – Little of consequence was produced in Carinthia in the Empire period and during the rest of the 19th c. In recent years *painting* has begun to flourish.

The large valleys of Carinthia meet in the **Klagenfurt Basin**, making this area the geographical as well as the administrative and economic hub of the province.

In addition to the numerous **lakes**, with facilities for bathing, the tourist attractions of Carinthia include the river valleys and the beautiful walking country in the eastern part of the region. From the Grossglockner massif the *Möll valley* at first runs S and then turns E, to enter the Drau valley at Möllbrücke. At Döllach the Zirknitz valley joins the Möll valley, with a beautiful waterfall and a cave. Above *Rangersdorf* is a Gothic church which forms a conspicuous landmark. From Obervellach there is a rewarding climb up *Polinik*, from which there are far-ranging views. At the foot of the Reisseck group lies the village of Kolbnitz (power station).

The Carinthian section of the *Drau valley* begins at Oberdrauburg, to the N of which is *Zwickenberg*, with a Gothic church (frescoes).

The late Gothic church at *Gerlamoos* also had fine frescoes. Then follow **Spittal** an der *Drau*, Fresach and **Villach**, after which the Drau flows under the S face of the Sattnitz group and into the *Völkermarkter Stausee* (artificial lake).

The most southerly part of the province is the *Lesach valley*, running parallel to the Italian frontier, which is continued by the *Gail valley* and which joins the Drau valley at Villach. *Maria Luggau*, near the boundary of Tirol, has a beautiful pilgrimage church. At Kötschach-Mauthen a road

goes off to the *Plöcken pass* to the S, and before Hermagor a road leads into the **Nassfeld**, a favourite skiing area. Shortly before Villach the Gail flows below the S side of the *Villacher Alpe* and joins the Drau at Maria Gail.

The *Malta valley*, N of Spittal an der Drau, is worth seeing not only for its scenery but for a great technological achievement, the large hydroelectric station fed by several artificial lakes. NE of Spittal is the **Nock district**, which affords excellent walking, climbing and winter sports. Also popular with climbers and skiers are the *Saualpe*, to the N of Völkermarkt, and the *Koralpe*, beyond the Lavant valley.

Carnic Alps
(Karnische Alpen)

Land: Carinthia (K).
Altitude: Highest point: Hohe Warte (2780 m/9121 ft).
ⓘ Österreichischer Alpenverein *Section*
Hermagor, c/o Dr. Zimek, A-9620 Hermagor.

The long straggling chain of the Carnic Alps, which, half-way along the range, begins to increase in height and wildness from W to E, extends to the S of the Gail valley, its crest forming the frontier with Italy. Like the Gailtal Alps (Lienz Dolomites), it is part of the Southern Alps.

Although this region of varied mountain scenery has good roads and is well provided with mountain huts, it is still not overcrowded by holiday visitors. The least frequented part of the range is its western end – the area around the little *Füllhornsee* (Sillian), the *Obstanser See* (Kartitsch) and St Lorenzen in the Lesach valley.

The best-known part of the region lies around the *Wolayer See*, which contains finest peaks in the whole group. In this area are the massive dark peak of the **Hohe Warte** (2780 m/9121 ft), the highest point in the Carnic Alps, the austere *Biegengebirge* with its two great buttresses, the *Wolayer Kopf* (2470 m/8104 ft) and the *Seekopf* (2554 m/8380 ft), and the *Kellerwand* (2769 m/9085 ft), rearing its sheer ice-covered rock-faces above the Valentin valley. Most of these peaks, however, are for experienced climbers only.

From the beautiful **Plöcken pass** (1360 m/ 4462 ft), which carries the steep road from Kötschach-Mauthen into Italy, fit and experienced walkers can follow the whole chain westward (numerous mountain huts) to the *Helm* (2433 m/7983 ft).

There are also many fine mountains E of the Plöcken pass, fairly easily reached from the Gail valley, among them the *Gailtaler Polinik* (2331 m/7648 ft), near Mauthen, the massive *Trogkofel* (2279 m/7477 ft) and the jagged and botanically interesting *Gartner-kofel* (2195 m/7202 ft), the latter two accessible from the Sonnenalpe Nassfeld by way of the *Nassfeld hut* (1513 m/4964 ft), which is also much frequented by skiers.

The gentler eastern part of the Carnic Alps has also much to offer climbers and skiers. *Poludnig* (2000 m/6560 ft) is a particularly fine peak. Few of the better known skiing areas can offer such a fine long descent as the run from *Oisternig* (2052 m/6733 ft) down to Feistritz in the Gail valley.

There is a good ridge walk, the Karnischer Höhenweg, from the Nassfeld to St Andrä in the Gailitz valley.

Dachstein

Länder: Salzburg (S), Upper Austria (OÖ) and Styria (Stm).
Altitude: Highest point: Hoher Dachstein (2955 m/ 9826 ft).
(i) **Österreichischer Alpenverein,** *Sektion Hallstatt,* Gosaumühlstr. 79, A-4830 Hallstatt.

The *Dachstein, in the Salzkammergut, is perhaps the most varied mountain group in the Northern Alps. The gigantic massif, with a steeply scarped N face, consists of a series of mighty peaks, sharply profiled, with large glaciers between them.

To the S the mountains fall sharply in a long wall some 1000 m/3300 ft high to the green Alpine foreland of the *Ramsau*, which extends in a large garden-like terrace between the Dachstein and the deeply slashed Enns valley.

The N face encloses within steep rock walls two magnificent mountain lakes, the fjord-like *Hallstätter See** and the *Gosausee.*

There are good paths up to the two main huts in the glacier region, the Simony hut

(2203 m/7228 ft) and the Adamek hut (2196 m/7205 ft) near Gosau, from which the **Hoher Dachstein** (2995 m/9830 ft) can be climbed, on ice and fairly difficult rock; there are superb views from the top. – The Dachstein in general offers plenty of scope for testing rock-climbs.

Climbers who want something more than the relatively easy ascent to the glacier plateau can tackle the difficult S faces (Torstein, Dirndl, Koppenkarstein).

Also popular with climbers is the jagged *Gosaukamm*, a rugged chain of Dolomitic type which branches NW off the main massif and gives the Gosau valley its characteristic aspect. Below the highest peak, the *Bischofsmütze* (2459 m/8068 ft), is the Hofpürgl hut (1703 m/5588 ft), from which there is a path of moderate difficulty, the Linzer Steig, to Adamek hut. The path continues along the whole Gosau ridge to the Gablonzer Haus (1550 m/5085 ft), on the Zweiselalm near Gosau – one of the most beautiful areas of Alpine meadow in the Salzkammergut.

Abutting the main mountain massif on the E is the much eroded plateau known as *Auf dem Stein*, with numerous swallow-holes, on the N face of which, above the Hallstätter See and the Traun valley, are the two huge **Dachstein Caves** (*Dachsteinhöhlen*), the *Giant Ice Cave* (Rieseneishöhle) and the *Mammoth Cave*

The Gosausee and Dachstein

(Mammuthhöhle; up to 1174 m/3853 ft deep). They can be reached by way of the Dachsteinhöhlen-Haus (1345 m/4413 ft) or from the Schönbergalpe, to which there is a cableway from Obertraun (see page 88).

Both the glacier area and the plateau of Auf dem Stein offer good Alpine skiing, and for fit and experienced climbers there are fine mountain treks to be made, both in summer and in winter, over the plateau to the Guttenberg-Haus (2145 m/7038 ft) on the S rim or farther to the **Kammergebirge** and the Brünner Hütte (1747 m/5732 ft), on *Stoderzinken* (extensive views) near Gröbming in the Enns valley.

The most easterly outlier of the Dachstein is **Grimming** (2351 m/7714 ft), which is separated from the Kammergebirge by the deeply slashed Salza valley. This great mass of rock, the principal landmark of the middle Ennstal, is one of the most imposing peaks in Styria.

Danube Valley

Länder: Upper Austria (OÖ) and Lower Austria (NÖ).
(i) **Landesfremdenverkehrsverband Oberösterreich**, Schillerstrasse 50, A-4020 Linz; tel. (07 32) 66 30 21.
Niederösterreichisches Landesreisebüro, Heidenschuss 32, A-1014 Wien; tel. (02 22) 6 34 77 30.
Werbegemeinschaft "Die Donauländer", Margaretenstrasse 1, A-1040 Wien; tel. (02 22) 56 16 66-0.

The Danube is Austria's principal river and the longest in Europe after the Volga. Although barely more than 300 km/185 miles of the river's total course of some 2900 km/1800 miles – from its source in South Germany to its outflow into the Black Sea in Romania – lie within Austria, the names of Austria and the Danube are so closely linked that it is difficult to think of the one without the other.

As the only major European waterway flowing from W to E the Danube has for millennia played an important part in the history of the many peoples through whose territory it flows. It marked out the route of the great military highway which ran from the Rhine to the Black Sea; the Romans built a series of fortified camps such as Vindobona and Carnuntum along the valley; the legendary Nibelungs passed this way; and here,

too, passed the Celts, Charlemagne's Franks, Frederick Barbarossa's Crusaders and finally Napoleon.

In the opposite direction, going upstream, Attila led his Huns towards France and the Avars and Hungarians pressed into western Europe. Great battles which decided the fate of Europe have been fought on the banks of the Danube: twice the West withstood Turkish assaults at Vienna, and at Aspern (now within the city limits of Vienna) Napoleon suffered his first defeat.

Between the German frontier at Passau and the Upper Austrian town of Linz the Danube describes a series of great loops in the forest-fringed valley between the *Mühlviertel* to the N and the *Innviertel* to the S. Below Linz is the **Studengau**, a wooded defile between Ardagger and Ybbs, and beyond this, extending to Melk, is the **Nibelungengau**, with the conspicuous pilgrimage church of Maria Taferl.

The best-known stretch is perhaps the *Wachau, famous for its wine, with a series of ancient little towns between Melk and Krems. Just beyond this is Vienna, and the low-lying area which extends E to Hainburg and Bratislava (Czechoslovakia) begins to take on the aspect of the Hungarian puszta.

SAILING DOWN THE DANUBE – Between Passau and Vienna the Danube – now harnessed to supply hydroelectric power by a number of dams – flows through varied scenery, passing some 40 castles, palaces and ruins, a dozen celebrated Baroque buildings and numerous other historic sites. With all this, and three capital cities on the route, a trip along the Danube valley is one of the most memorable journeys in Europe.

In this section we describe a boat trip down the Danube. The road and railway accompany the river for considerable stretches, frequently taking short cuts when the hills along the banks compel it to take a wide turn but always – particularly at the most beautiful parts of the valley – returning to run close to it again.

PASSENGER SERVICES between Passau and Vienna, continuing to Budapest, Belgrade and through the Iron Gates to the Black Sea.
(i) **Erste Donau-Dampfschiffahrtsgesellschaft** (*DDSG*), Handelskai 265, A-1020 **Wien**; tel. (02 22) 26 65 36.
Stadthafen, A-4010 **Linz**; tel. (07 32) 27 00 11.
Im Ort 14a, D-8390 **Passau**; tel. (08 51) 3 30 35.

As the boat leaves **Passau**, a town of almost southern aspect, there is a view of the graceful silhouette of the old town, built on a tongue of land at the confluence of the Inn and the Ilz with the Danube and almost seeming to float on the water. – Then follows a winding stretch of wooded valley to *Obernzell*, the last Bavarian town on the left bank. The first castle on the (Upper) Austrian side is *Krempelstein*. On the right, high above the river, is *Schloss Vichtenstein*. Then comes the *Jochenstein hydroelectric station*.

After *Engelhartszell* (on the right), with the Rococo church of *Engelszell Abbey* (Trappist Monastery), *Schloss Rannariedl* and *Schloss Marsbach* are seen on the ridges of hills on the left. – The valley now becomes still narrower, with little human habitation.

Then, after the great loop known as the **Schlögener Schlinge**, the picture changes, and the boat sails past a series of friendly little holiday villages such as *Obermühl* and *Neuhaus* (with an old castle looming over it, a conspicuous landmark). – At the straggling little town of *Aschach*, with a row of Baroque houses, the hills draw away from the river and open up a view of the chain of the Alps. A little way S is the little town of **Eferding** (mentioned in the "Nibelungenlied"), with several old churches and a Schloss (15th and 18th c.). *Schloss Ottensheim*, on the left bank, lies obliquely across from **Wilhering Abbey** (see under Linz –

Surroundings), a large complex of buildings with a church, externally plain, which has one of the most exquisite Rococo interiors in Austria.

To the N of the Danube, rather off the main traffic routes, is the *Mühlviertel* (see p. 141), the foreland of the Bohemian Forest. This is the tranquil countryside described by the 19th c. novelist Adalbert Stifter, with great expanses of dark forest, sleepy little villages and lonely ruins. Here, too, are many remains of the past, great religious houses containing notable works of art.

Beyond Wilhering comes a narrower stretch of valley. On the right is the *Kürnberger Wald*, with an old pagan place of assembly and a later Saxon castle. On the left is the little tower of *Schloss Puchenau* and behind it, on the *Pöstlingberg*, an imposing Baroque church. – Then, after another wide turn, the boat arrives at the Upper Austrian capital of **Linz** (p. 124). Its beautiful setting can be appreciated much more easily from the river than from road or railway. To the left is the Pöstlingberg (537 m/1762 ft), a popular viewpoint from which in clear weather there is a superb prospect of the Alps; there is an electric mountain railway to the top.

As the vessel continues on its way there is a fine view, looking backwards, of Linz in its setting of hills. – Beyond the inflow of the Traun and opposite that of the Enns is

The Schlögener Schlinge

the old customs post of **Mauthausen**, with *Schloss Pragstein* (15th c.; Heimatmuseum) projecting into the river. In the Romanesque St Barbara's Chapel in the late Gothic parish church are well-preserved 14th c. wall paintings. Mauthausen has the largest granite quarries in Austria. 3 km/2 miles NW is the site of the notorious Nazi concentration camp (memorial).

Some 5km/3 miles up the Enns, on the site of the Roman fort of *Lauriacum*, is the town of **Enns** (pop. 10,000). Under the Gothic church of St Lawrence (13th c.) were found remains of the Roman Capitol, an Early Christian basilica and a Carolingian church. In the main square are the Stadtturm (1564–68), 59 m/194 ft high, the old Rathaus (1547), now housing the Municipal Museum, and, to the N, Schloss Ennsegg (16th–17th c.). The parish church of St Mary (12th and 15th c.) has a Gothic cloister. – 7·5 km/4½ miles W of Enns is *St Florian* with its magnificent Augustinian abbey (see p. 173).

Beyond Mauthausen, on the right, are the Habsburg *Schloss Wallsee* and, at the mouth of the **Strudengau**, the little market town of *Ardagger*. 2·5 km/1½ miles SE is **Ardagger Abbey**, originally a college of secular canons (1049–1784); it has a late Romanesque pillared basilican church with late Gothic, Baroque and neo-classical furnishings, and in the choir the "St Margaret window" of *c.* 1240.

Next, on the left bank, comes the picturesque little town of **Grein**, the life of which is closely associated with shipping. Above the town to the W is an imposing castle, the *Greinburg*, which now houses the Austrian Shipping Museum. The castle (15th c.) has a charming 17th c. arcaded courtyard. In the Stadtplatz is an unusual little Rococo

theatre (1791), with seating for only 163. – The boat now enters a reach which was formerly a very dangerous stretch of rapids, the Greiner Strudel. The rocks were blasted away in the second half of the 19th c. to make the passage easier. – Off the little market town of *Struden* (on left), with the ruined castle of *Werfenstein*, is the wooded island of *Wörth*. Beyond this is another charming stretch, with the picturesque little town of *St Nikola* and *Sarmingstein*, where the Danube enters Lower Austria. Above Sarmingstein-Waldhausen are the ruined castles of *Säbnich* and *Freyenstein*. – The Strudengau now gradually opens out.

Above **Persenbeug** (on left) stands *Schloss Persenbeug*, on a crag overhanging the river. First established in the 9th c., it dates in its present form from 1617–21. Karl I, the last Austrian Emperor (1887–1922), was born here. – Below this is the large *Ybbs-Persenbeug power station* (conducted tours).

A road bridge links Persenbeug with **Ybbs**, the Roman *Ad Pontem Isidis*, on the right bank. This marks the beginning of the **Nibelungengau**. – The Danube now rounds a projecting tongue of land, the Gottsdorfer Scheibe, in a great loop known as the *Böse Beuge* ("Wicked Bend"), and the River Ybbs comes in on the right. At *Sarling* the railway line from Linz to Vienna comes close to the river on the right. Beyond this is the ruined castle of *Säusenstein*.

High up on a hill to the left is the pilgrimage church of **Maria Taferl** (landing-stage at Marbach). – Then, on the right, comes **Pöchlarn**, Roman *Arelape* and the *Bechelaren* of the "Nibelungenlied", residence of Margrave Rüdiger. – Opposite are *Klein-Pöchlarn* and, behind it, *Schloss Artstetten*, with the tombs of Archduke Franz Ferdinand of Austria and his wife, whose murder at Sarajevo in 1914 led to the First World War.

On the left bank is the market town of *Weitenegg*; then the splendid Baroque buildings of **Melk Abbey** (p. 136) come into view on the right.

Beyond Melk begins what is perhaps the most beautiful section of the Danube trip, the stretch through the **Wachau* (p. 235). In the woods on the left bank can be seen the late Gothic church of *Emmersdorf*. – The valley, wooded on both sides, narrows at

Lock at Ybbs-Persenbeug

Schönbühel, a beautifully situated little market town, with its castle perched on a crag 40 m/130 ft above the river. Beyond this, on the right, is a small Servite monastery. Then, also on the right bank, comes *Aggsbach Dorf*, from which an excursion can be made up the Aggsbach valley to the monastery of *Maria Langegg*. On the left bank is **Aggsbach Markt**, first mentioned in the records in 830, from which the pilgrimage church of *Maria Laach* can be visited.

Dominating the scene, at the narrowest point in the Wachau, is the historic old castle of **Aggstein**, perched on a crag (320 m/ 1050 ft) which falls steeply down on three sides. This was once a stronghold of the Kuenringer, a family of robber knights who plundered boats on the river and merchants' wagons passing along the road. The castle was destroyed in 1296, rebuilt by a later robber knight named Jörg Scheck vom

Walde in 1429 and again devastated by the Turks a century later.

Opposite Burg Aggstein is *Willendorf*, where the famous "Venus of Willendorf", one of the oldest works of art known, was found in 1909. – Along the banks of the river the forest now increasingly gives way to vineyards, on laboriously constructed terraces on the sunny hillsides.

To the left is the attractive village of *Schwallenbach*, to the right the little church of *St Johann*. – The Teufelsmauer ("Devil's Wall"), a curious spur of rock, projects into the river on the left. Then follow the ruined castle of *Hinterhaus* and below it the market town of **Spitz**, the chief place of the inner Wachau, magnificently situated around the isolated vine-clad hill known as the *Tausendeimerberg* ("Thousand Bucket Hill") because in good years it yields enough

The Danube at St Nikola in the Strudengau

grapes for that quantity of excellent wine. A popular excursion is to the summit of the *Jauerling* (959 m/3146 ft), the highest point in the Wachau, commanding extensive views (telecommunications tower).

On the right bank the little village of *Arnsdorf* nestles amid vines and the lighter green of fruit trees (particularly apricots). On the left bank is the late Gothic fortified church of St Michael. – Then comes *Weissenkirchen*, with another old fortified church. – In the background are the smaller hills of *Seiberer* and *Sandl* (also popular viewpoints) and the large ruined castle of *Hartenstein* (not visible from river).

The Danube now describes a large turn to the right, opening up a view, beyond the prominent Vogelsberg on the left bank, of the picturesque little town of **Dürnstein**, the pearl of the Wachau, famous for its wine.

Opposite it is the pleasant little market town of *Rossatz*. – As the boat sails on there is a beautiful view to the rear, until Dürnstein disappears behind the luxuriant vineyards and orchards of *Loiben*. Most visitors are more interested in this little town as the source of one of the best wines of the Wachau than as the scene of a bloody battle with the French in 1805 (commemorated by a round tower, tapering towards the top, which is popularly known as the Franzosenmanndl, "Frenchman").

The Danube now veers left in another wide turn. On the right, some distance away from the river on a dark green hill, can be seen the façade of **Göttweig Abbey**, a Benedictine monastery which is one of the most impressive in Austria.

The road to Göttweig goes over the road bridge linking the three towns of Mautern, Stein and Krems, under which the boat now sails. *Mautern*, on the right bank, is the oldest of the three: it was the Roman *Castrum Favianis*, the favourite residence of St Severinus (d. 482), and appears in the "Nibelungenlied" as *Mutaren*.

On the left bank are the towns of *Stein* and **Krems** (see p. 114), together forming the largest and most important complex in the Wachau, which ends here. Picturesquely huddled on the steep hillside, from the old houses on the banks of the river to the lanes, towers and churches higher up, it is enclosed by the dark bluish-green of the surrounding vineyards.

Beyond Krems, an important hub of communications and a good base from which to explore the Wachau, the Waldviertel and the *Dunkelsteiner Wald* on the opposite bank, the scenery is less attractive. The valley opens out, with the lowland area known as the *Tullner Feld* extending along the S bank. A series of small islands appear in the river. – On the right is *Hollenburg*, with the little church of *Wetterkreuz* on the ridge above it. – On the left is *Altenwörth*, where Charlemagne defeated the Avars in 791. – Beyond *Zwentendorf*, on the right bank, with Austria's only nuclear power station (not in operation), is **Tulln**, to which King Etzel (Attila in the "Nibelungenlied") travelled to meet his bride Kriemhild; it was the Roman settlement of *Comegena*.

The **Wienerwald** now comes steadily closer to the S bank of the Danube. – Beyond *Langenlebarn*, *Muckendorf* and *Zeiselmauer* is *Greifenstein* (right bank), with its castle high above the river; on the left *Burg Kreuzenstein* comes into view some distance away. At *Höflein* the Danube flows past the last foothills of the Wienerwald and turns SE.

On the left bank is **Korneuburg**, an attractive old town which preserves part of its circuit of walls; opposite it is *Kritzendorf*, and soon after this **Klosterneuburg**, with a famous Augustinian abbey. – On the left is the *Bisamberg*, and opposite it, on the bank of the river, the *Leopoldsberg*, with a twin-towered church built about 1100 on the site of the castle of Leopold the Saint, which was known as the "cradle of Austria".

Soon afterwards the boat comes in sight of **Vienna** (p. 202).

Dornbirn

Land: Vorarlberg (V).
Altitude: 437 m/1434 ft. – Population: 40,000.
Post code: A-6850. – Telephone code: 0 55 72.
ⓘ **Verkehrsverein**, Altes Rathaus;
tel. 6 21 88.

ACCOMMODATION. – *Bischof*, A, 78 b., sauna; *Parkhotel*, A, 60 b.; *Verwalter* (no rest.), A, 64 b.; *Hirschen*, B, 74 b.; *Katharinenhof*, B, 26 b.; sauna. – *Sporthotel Rickatschwende*, A, 88 b.; SB, sauna, 6 km/4 miles SE. – CAMPING SITE.

RECREATION and SPORTS. – Riding; tennis; flying (Hohenems airfield); cycle paths.

EVENTS. – **Dornbirn Fair** (July–Aug.).

Dornbirn, the largest town in Vorarlberg (larger than the provincial capital, Bregenz), is spaciously laid out at the foot of the Bregenzerwald on the edge of the wide valley of the Rhine. It is an industrial town (textiles, engineering).

SIGHTS. – In the Marktplatz stands the handsome neo-classical *parish church* (1840), with a separate Gothic belfry (1453). Adjoining is the **Rotes Haus**, a handsome half-timbered building of 1639 (restaurant). Nearby, at Marktstrasse 33, is an interesting natural history museum, the *Vorarlberger Naturschau* (plant and animal life of Vorarlberg and patterns of settlement).

SURROUNDINGS. – 2·5 km/1½ miles S is the **Karren** (975 m/3199 ft; inn), with fine views; cableway to the top (5 minutes), on foot 1½ hours. 10 minutes' walk from the upper station of the cableway stands the *Alpe Kühberg* mountain inn. There is a pleasant walk down (1½–2 hours) by way of the *Staufenalpe* to *Gütle*, 4 km/2½ miles SE of Dornbirn, with a pleasant garden café. From here it

The Rappenlochschlucht, near Dornbirn

is 10 minutes' walk to the *Rappenlochschluct*, a magnificent gorge through which the turbulent Ache flows. A track leads from here to the *Staufensee* reservoir (20 minutes), from which it is 10 minutes' climb to the picturesque *Alplochschlucht*, with a waterfall 120 m/395 ft high. – From Gütle it is 7 km/4½ miles SW to *Ebnit* (1075 m/3527 ft), and another 3 hours' climb to the summit of the **Hohe Kugel** (1645 m/5397 ft; views).

10 km/6 miles E of Dornbirn is the *Bödele*. The road with numerous turns climbs to the Alpenhotel Rickatschwende (850 m/2789 ft) and continues through the forest and a tunnel and over the outflow from a small lake. The Bödele itself (1148 m/3767 ft) is a charming rounded hill, covered with Alpine pasture and surrounded by pine forests; it draws many visitors as a health and winter sports resort. From a viewpoint NW of the hotel there is a magnificent prospect of Lake Constance. From the Bödele it is an hour's walk S to the *Hochäpele* (1467 m/4813 ft;

inn), which also commands fine views. – 5·5 km/3½ miles from the Bödele, lower down, is **Schwarzenberg**, a beautifully situated village with a parish church (*c.* 1760) containing an altarpiece by the woman painter Angelica Kauffmann (1741–1807) and a marble bust of the artist.

6 km/4 miles SW of Dornbirn is **Hohenems** (alt. 432 m/ 1417 ft; pop. 13,000; Gasthof Schiffle, A, 80 b.), a popular summer resort with a large parish church (1797) and Schloss Hohenems (1560; conducted tour), belonging to the Counts of Waldburg-Zeil, in which two manuscripts of the "Nibelungenlied" were found in 1755 and 1778. From the Schloss a footpath leads up in 40 minutes to the ruined 12th c. castle of *Alt-Ems* (alt. 713 m/2339 ft).

Eastern Tirol

Land: Tirol (T).
Altitude: Area: 2020 sq. km/780 sq. miles.
Population: 42,000.

ⓘ **Verkehrsverein Osttirol,**
Albin-Egger-Strasse 17,
A-9900 Lienz/Osttirol;
tel. (0 48 52) 31 27.

The mountainous region of Eastern Tirol, within the administrative district of Lienz, takes in the uppermost reaches of the Drau valley, the Isel valley and its side valleys, and the area round the source of the River Gail. It is ringed by a series of lofty peaks – to the N the Hohe Tauern, with the Grossglockner and the Grossvenediger, to the E the Schober group, to the W the Rieserferner group and to the S the Carnic Alps and Lienz Dolomites.

Cut off from Innsbruck, the traditional capital of Tirol, by the area in southern Tirol which since 1919 has been Italian, Eastern Tirol is closely linked, in terms of communications and the tourist trade, with the neighbouring province of Carinthia.

The upper **Drau**, which rises in Italy, flows through narrow gorges between Sillian (at the mouth of the Villgratental, a valley still little frequented by holiday visitors) and Lienz and then continues E towards Carinthia through the wide and sunny Lienz basin, in which is the Tristacher See. Apart from the Drau valley the principal traffic route of Eastern Tirol is the pleasant **Isel valley**, with its various side valleys (the *Virgental*, the *Tauerntal*, the *Kalser Tal* and the *Deféreggental*).

To the S, between the Drau valley and the upper Gail valley, are the rugged ridges of the *Lienz Dolomites (see under Lienz – Surroundings), with picturesque short valleys, high corries of Alpine pasture and beautiful lakes.

HISTORY. – The remains at *Aguntum* (5 km/3 miles E of Lienz) bear witness to the Roman occupation of this area. In the early medieval period the eastern Tirol was settled by Slavs. Thereafter it became part of Carinthia, and was long attached to the county of Görz (Gorizia), with which it passed to Austria in 1500. In 1805 it became Bavarian, and from 1809 to 1814 it was French. The cession of the southern Tirol to Italy in 1919 separated the eastern from the northern part of the province. During the Nazi period it was incorporated in Carinthia, and between 1945 and 1955 it was in the British occupation zone of Austria. Since then, as part of the *Land* of Tirol, it has shared the destinies of the rest of Austria.

ART. – In the much ramified Alpine valleys of Eastern Tirol, particularly in the Defereggental and Virgental, the craft of *woodcarving* has been practised for many centuries. – Among the artists of Eastern Tirol two painters have established a reputation extending beyond the boundaries of the province – *Franz von Defregger* (1835–1921), who painted charming pictures of peasant and popular life, and *Albin Egger-Lienz* (1868–1926), who portrayed sturdy peasant figures in a very different style. – In the field of folk art, Eastern Tirol has maintained the old tradition of *folk plays.*

The chief town of Eastern Tirol, **Lienz** (see p. 122), is reached from the N (Mittersill) on the *Felber-Tauern-Strasse*, which from the province of Salzburg passes under the mountains, into Eastern Tirol, through the *Felber-Tauern Tunnel*, more than 5 km/3 miles long. Another approach, practicable in summer, is by way of the tremendous **Grossglockner Road** and the *Iselberg* (between the Möll and Drau valleys), along the summit of which runs the boundary between Eastern Tirol and Carinthia.

There are also roads to Lienz from the Val Pusteria (Pustertal) in Italy, the Plöcken pass and the Gailberg saddle.

Restful holiday places in imposing mountain scenery are to be found in the Defereggental, Virgental and Kalser Tal, which run up to the southern foothills of the two glacier-clad giants, the Grossglockner and Grossvenediger.

For skiers who prefer the simple life the remote *Villgratental* can be recommended. With ample snow in winter, it also has the abundant sunshine of the southern slopes of the Alps.

Eisenerz

Land: Styria (Stm).
Altitude: 745 m/2444 ft.
Population: 10,070.
Post code: A-8790.
Telephone code: 0 38 48.

(i) **Verkehrsbüro Eisenerz,**
Hieflauer Strasse 19;
tel. 37 00.

ACCOMMODATION. – *Eisenerzer Hof,* C, 30 b.; *Hirschen,* C, 25 b.; *Volkskeller,* C, 20 b.; *Pichlerhof,* C, 20 b.; *Post,* C, 15b.

RECREATION and SPORTS. – Water sports (Leopold-steinersee); wild-water trips on the Salza; indoor and open-air swimming pools; tennis; mountaineering school; winter sports.

The old Styrian mining town of Eisenerz ("iron ore") is beautifully situated in the wooded valley of the Erzbach, surrounded by mountains about 2000 m/6564 ft high, among them the Pfaffenstein (1871 m/6139 ft) and the Kaiserschild (2083 m/6834 ft).

SIGHTS. – On a hill to the E of the town stands the Gothic *parish church of St Oswald* (1279–1517), with well-preserved defensive walls. To the W of the town is the *Schichtturm* ("Shift Tower"; look-out terrace), with a bell (1581) which used to be rung to mark the change-over of shifts in the mines.

The main feature of interest in Eisenerz, however, is the *Erzberg ("Ore Mountain",* 1466 m/4810 ft), the largest deposit of spathic iron in Europe. There are both step-like opencast and underground workings. Iron has been mined here since ancient times, and the present annual output is about 3·5 million tons of spathic iron ore (siderite) with a 33% iron content. There are good general views of the workings from the

Opencast mine-workings on the Erzberg

Schichtturm, from the viewpoint at the Krumpental railway halt and from the Polster (1911 m/6270 ft; chair-lift from Präbichl). There are conducted tours of the workings twice daily from May to October, starting from the lower station of the old mine cableway.

SURROUNDINGS.– 7 km/4½ miles SE of Eisenerz is the *Präbichl, a pass (1227 m/4026 ft) with fine views and facilities for winter sports. Nearby is the lower station of a chair-lift to the *Polster* (1911 m/6270 ft). From the Präbichl a footpath ascends (2 hours) to the *Eisenerzer Reichenstein* (2166 m/7107 ft).

NE of Eisenerz (2¾ hours' walk) is an interesting cave, the *Frauenmauerhöhle* (W entrance 1435 m/4708 ft); a guide and warm clothing are necessary. The main cave tunnels right through the mountain for 640 m/700 yds, with numerous side passages. Just beyond the entrance, on the left, is the Eiskammer (Ice Chamber), with numerous pillars of ice. It takes between 30 and 45 minutes to reach the E entrance (1560 m/5118 ft), from which there is a magnificent view of the Hochschwab group. From the E entrance it is 2½ hours' walk down to *Tragöss-Oberort*, or 1¾ hours to the *Sonnschien-Alm*.

Eisenstadt

Land: Burgenland (B).
Altitude: 181 m/594 ft. – Population: 10,100.
Post code: A-7000. – Telephone code: 0 26 82.
ⓘ **Fremdenverkehrsbüro**, Rathaus,
Hauptstrasse 35;
tel. 27 10.

ACCOMMODATION. – *Burgenland*, A, 200 b., SB, sauna; *Parkhotel*, A, 60 b.; *Mayr*, C, 77 b.; *Goldener Adler*, C, 43 b.; *Ohr*, C, 24 b.

EVENTS. – *Burgenland Wine Week* (end Aug. to beginning Sept.); *Haydn Memorial Concerts* (May–June).

Eisenstadt, capital of the province of Burgenland, on the southern fringes of the Leithagebirge, has aristocratic traditions. **In the 17th and 18th c. this was the principal seat of the great Esterházy family, who left a distinctive imprint on the town. Josef Haydn (1732–1809) was Kapellmeister here for thirty years: his house can be visited, and he is buried in the Bergkirche above the town. Eistenstadt is important in the wine trade of this region.**

HISTORY. – Eisenstadt is mentioned in a chronicle of 1118 and in a document of 1264. It was granted a municipal charter in 1373. From 1445 to 1648 it was in pledge to the Habsburgs; thereafter it became a royal free city within Hungary and the residence of the Esterházys. In 1921 it was reunited with Austria, and in 1925 became capital of Burgenland – the smallest of the Austrian provincial capitals. It became the see of a bishop in 1960.

SIGHTS.– The town is dominated by **Schloss Esterházy**, the palace of the Princes Esterházy. Originally a medieval stronghold with four corner towers and an inner courtyard, it was rebuilt in Baroque style in 1663–72. The rear façade, looking on to the extensive gardens, was remodelled in neo-classical style between 1797 and 1805. Visitors can see the Haydn Room, in which

Schloss Esterházy, Eisenstadt

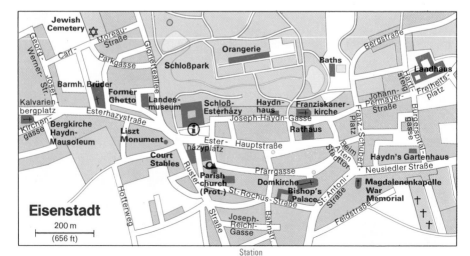

the composer performed many of his works; it is still occasionally used for concerts. Other rooms in the palace house periodic special exhibitions by the Provincial Art Gallery. Facing the palace are the *Court Stables* (Hofstallungen, 1793), and nearby (in front of the National Bank) is a monument to Franz Liszt (1936).

To the E of Esterházyplatz extends the *Old Town*, traversed by three streets which open off the square (Hauptstrasse, Pfarrgasse, Haydngasse). In the broad Hauptstrasse are a *Trinity Column* (1713), the *St Florian Fountain* (Florianibrunnen, 1628) and the *Rathaus* (1650). In Pfarrgasse stands the **Cathedral** (*Domkirche*), a Gothic hall-church (end of 15th c.) with a Baroque pulpit (1775) and organ (1778). In Haydngasse are the **Haydnhaus** (now a museum) and the *Franciscan Church* (Franziskanerkirche, 1630), with the Esterházy family vault in the conventual buildings.

NW of Esterházyplatz the **Burgenland Provincial Museum** (Burgenländisches Landesmuseum), houses a fine collection illustrating the history, folk art and natural history of the province. There is an interesting display of the bird life of the Neusiedler See. Also of interest is the section devoted to the history of the local Jews, who still lived in a ghetto on this site in the earlier part of the 20th c. In the house on the corner of Wertheimergasse is a Jewish Museum.

Esterházystrasse leads up to the *Kalvarienberg* (Calvary Hill), with a chapel (1701–07), and the **Bergkirche**, within which (to left of entrance) is the mausoleum of Josef Haydn.

SURROUNDINGS. – 10 km/6 miles N at *Loretto* is a pilgrimage church (1654–59) notable particularly for its frescoes (1680). – 15 km/9 miles S of Eisenstadt lies *Drassburg* (*Schlosshotel, A, 62 b., SB, SP, sauna, tennis, riding), near the Hungarian frontier, beyond which is the town of Sopron.

Ennstal Alps (Gesäuse)

Land: Styria (Stm).
Altitude: Highest point: Hochtor (2372 m/7783 ft).
ⓘ **Österreichischer Alpenverein,**
  Sektion Admont,
  Aigen 48, A-8911 Admont.

The most imposing part of the Ennstal Alps is the *Gesäuse, among the wildest mountain groups in the Alps, with one of their grandest defiles. Here the brawling waters of the Enns have carved a gorge 15 km/9 miles long through the mighty limestone massif between Admont and Hieflau – an unforgettable spectacle, both for travellers who look up to the fearsome rock walls of the gorge from their train or car and for climbers seeking a way up the face.

The mountains are at their highest and most impressive in the ridge which runs from the *Planspitze* (2120 m/7783 ft), to the massive *Grosser Ödstein* (2355 m/7727 ft) and then falls sheer down to the gorge in a long N face up to 1000 m/3300 ft high. To the right are the three rugged peaks of *Admonter-Reichenstein* (2247 m/7372 ft), and beyond the Enns, on its N bank, rises the *Grosser Buchstein* (2223 m/7294 ft), which is linked by a long ridge with the gentler **Tamischbachturm* (2034 m/6674 ft). The ascent of all these peaks calls for fitness, experience and sure-footedness, and the more difficult faces are for tried and tested rock-climbers only.

In marked contrast to the massive solidity of the Gesäuse massif is the openness of the **Haller Mauern** to the NW; but these mountains, too, along the N of a wide stretch of the Enns valley, have great areas of rock, and the long ridge which runs from *Natterriegel* (2066 m/6779 ft) – easily reached by way of the Admonter Haus (1725 m/5660 ft) near Admont – to the **Grosser Pyhrgas* (2244 m/7363 ft), the highest peak, has many jagged crags and sheer rock faces.

Hieflau, in the Gesäuse

The **Eisenerz Alps** to the SE of the Gesäuse are quieter and tamer, with a green covering of vegetation at many places on their steeply scarped ridges. The highest peak, the *Eisenerzer Reichenstein* (2166 m/7107 ft), attracts many climbers for the sake of the view it affords. – One mountain in the group is of more importance from the economic than from the tourist point of view – the *Erzberg* (see under Einsenerz), the location of one of the richest iron ore deposits in the world, its reddish-brown workings hewn out of the hillside like a gigantic staircase.

Feldkirch

Land: Vorarlberg (V).
Altitude: 459 m/1506 ft. – Population: 25,000.
Post code: A-6800. – Telephone code: 0 55 22.
ⓘ **Verkehrsverein**, Postfach 4, Herrengasse;
tel. 2 34 67.

ACCOMMODATION. – *Illpark Hotel*, A, 184 b., SB, sauna; *Weisses Kreuz*, A, 70 b.; *Bären*, A, 52 b.; *Büchel*, B, 87 b., sauna; *Altdeutsche Stuben*, B, 53 b. – YOUTH HOSTEL in Levis. – CAMPING SITE.

EVENTS. – *Concerts* in Schattenburg and Schloss Liechtenstein.

This old district capital in Vorarlberg lies at a road and rail junction on the route from Lake Constance to the Arlberg up the valley of the Ill, which here carves a way through a rocky gorge from the Walgau into the Rhine valley. Feldkirch is an important educational base, with many schools, including the Jesuit Stella Matutina College, founded in 1855. Since 1968 it has been the see of a bishop.

SIGHTS.– This old-world little town still preserves some of its old walls, with two gates and four towers. The two principal streets, the *Markt* and *Neustadt*, are lined with handsome old arcaded houses. – In the Domplatz is the late Gothic *Cathedral of St Nicholas* (*Dom*, completed 1478), with a fine interior (on the right-hand altar a "Lamentation" by Wolf Huber of Feldkirch, 1521; charming wrought-iron tabernacle, converted into a pulpit, 1540; modern stained glass). On the S side of the square stands the *Rathaus*, with a handsome Council Chamber. The former church of St John serves as the Museum of Ecclesiastical Art. On a rocky hill to the E of the town (now pierced by a road tunnel) is the 12th c. **Schattenburg**, housing the Heimatmuseum (local museum), with a beautiful courtyard and a restaurant.

SURROUNDINGS. – There are pleasant walks NW (20 minutes) to the *Ardetzenberg* (629 m/2064 ft), with a deer-park; NE (30 minutes) to *Schloss Amberg* (1502; privately owned), with fine views; and SE (1 hour) to the *pilgrimage chapel of Maria Ebene*, with a beautiful view of the Walgau. – 2 km/1¼ miles W is the ruined *Burg Tosters* (13th c.).

7·5 km/4½ miles NE is **Rankweil** (alt. 463 m/1519 ft; pop. 10,000; Hotel Hoher Freschen, B, 72 b.), a beautifully situated little town at the mouth of the Laternser Tal. In the lower town is the 13th c. St Peter's Church, with a seated figure of the Virgin (1350). On a crag in the middle of the town, the Liebfrauenberg (515 m/1690 ft), are the ruins of a medieval castle, with the pilgrimage church of Mariä Heimsuchung (the Visitation; 15th and 17th c.), which contains a wooden crucifix of 1450 and a 15th c. figure of the Virgin. The old castle walls now enclose the churchyard, from which there are superb views. – A steep road runs 6 km/4 miles SE to the beautifully situated village of *Übersaxen* (900 m/2950 ft), with a church of 1383 which contains a statue of the Virgin of 1460 and a processional cross of about 1250.

Rankweil lies at the mouth of the winding **Laternser Tal**, in which are a series of attractive villages – *Batschuns* (570 m/1870 ft), with a modern church (1923), the little Schloss Weissenberg (*c.* 1400) and a large house of retreat built in 1964; *Laterns*, the chief place in the valley; *Innerlaterns* and *Bad Innerlaterns*.

Feldkirch

Marktplatz, Feldkirch

From Laterns there is a footpath (2 hours) through the "Üble Schlucht" ("Evil Gorge") to Rankweil. 1 hour's walk N of Laterns is the *Alpe Furx* (1100 m/3610 ft), a popular health resort and winter sports area, with magnificent views. From here it is 3½ hours' climb via the *Alpwegkopf* (1430 m/4692 ft) and the *Untere Saluveralm* (1609 m/5279 ft) to the *Freschenhaus* (1846 m/6057 ft), and another half-hour from there to the summit of the *Hoher Freschen (2006 m/6582 ft), with fine views in all directions.

From Feldkirch an excursion can be made into the **PRINCIPALITY OF LIECHTENSTEIN** (15 km/9 miles to Vaduz). – This tiny sovereign state, with an area of only 157 sq. km/61 sq. miles and a population of 25,000, at present ruled by Prince Franz Josef II, was formed in 1712 out of the two lordships of Vaduz and Schellenberg, which had been purchased by the old Austrian house of Liechtenstein. Economically it is attached to Switzerland (Swiss currency, customs and postal administration, but with its own stamps). The national colours are blue and red, with a red and gold coat of arms. – Administration is concentrated in the capital **Vaduz** (pop. 5000). On the E side of the main street, called Städtle, are the neo-Gothic parish church (1869–73), the government offices (1903–05), the Historical Museum (material of the early historical period, religious art, a remarkable relief model of the principality on the scale of 1:10,000) and the "Engländerbau" ("Englishmen's Building", No. 18), which houses the Tourist Information Office and a permanent collection of pictures from the important Liechtenstein Gallery (Rubens, Frans Hals, van Dyck, Brueghel, etc.), together with the Natural History Museum and the Postal Museum (sale of stamps). On the W side of the street is the Landesbank, and at the N end the Rathaus and Post Office. Above the town, to the E, stands Schloss Vaduz (alt. 570 m/1870 ft), which has belonged to the Princes of Liechtenstein since 1712; it was rebuilt between 1904 and 1910 in the style of the 16th c. As the residence of the princely family it is not open to visitors.

Friesach

Land: Carinthia (K).
Altitude: 634 m/2080 ft. – Population: 7100.
Post code: A-9360. – Telephone code: 0 42 68.
ⓘ **Fremdenverkehrsbüro**, Stadtgemeindeamt, Postfach 18; tel. 22 13.

ACCOMMODATION. – *Metnitztaler Hof*, B, 65 b.; *Zum lustigen Bauer*, B, 11 b.; *Pötscher*, C, 40 b.; *Weisser Wolf*, B, 25 b.

EVENTS. – Summer festival in the Dominican courtyard (June–Aug.).

The ancient little town of Friesach, which first appears in the records in 860, belonged to the Archbishops of Salzburg until 1803. Its situation in the wide Metnitz valley, at an important point on the trade route between Vienna and Venice, made it a place of some consequence in earlier days.

SIGHTS. – The town still preserves remains of its medieval defences – a stretch of the *town walls* (built 1131), a *moat* 800 m/

875 yds long on the valley side of the town and two *castles* on the upper side. – A little way N of the main square (Hauptplatz), in Wiener Strasse, is the **Stadtpfarrkirche** (town parish church), originally Romanesque, with beautiful 13th c. stained glass in the choir. Farther N, at Fürstenhofgasse 115 (just off Fürstenhofplatz), is the well-stocked *Municipal Museum*. Farther N again, beyond the moat (on right), is the *Dominican Monastery* (rebuilt 1673), with a church dating from 1217–64 (14th c. crucifix; stone figure of the Virgin, *c.* 1300). – S of the Hauptplatz is the *Heiligblutkirche* (Church of the Holy Blood, 13th–14th c.).

To the W of the town – a steep and narrow road (1·5 km/1 mile) or a footpath from the upper end of the Hauptplatz (10 minutes) leads to the **Petersberg**, with the little *St Peter's Church*, which dates from before 927 (picture of 1525), and the imposing remains of a *castle* which belonged to the Archbishops of Salzburg.

The 16th c. Commandant's Lodging (Bürgerhauptmannschaft; restaurant) has a three-storey arcaded front. In the keep (1130) is St Rupert's Chapel, with 12th c. wall paintings. In an open-air theatre in the Oberhof the Burghofspiele are performed.

On the *Geiersberg* to the N of the town (1·5 km/1 mile) stands another castle (12th c.; partly restored). – To the NE, below the Petersberg, are the ruins of the 16th c. *Burg Lavant*. – S of Friesach on the *Virgilienberg* are remains of the Propstei-kirche (Gothic), which was burned down in 1816.

SURROUNDINGS. – 13 km/8 miles W is the loftily situated village of **Grades** (863 m/2832 ft), with a

Stadtpfarrkirche, Friesach

Schloss (16th and 17th c.) which belonged to the Bishops of Gurk, a Romanesque parish church with 13th c. frescoes and St Wolfgang's Church (1465–75), surrounded by a defensive wall, which has a fine 15th c. carved altar. – 4 km/2½ miles farther W **Metnitz** (867 m/ 2845 ft) has a fortified church (Gothic) containing thirteen life-sized late Baroque wooden figures of the Apostles. Adjoining the cemetery is an octagonal *charnel-house, originally decorated externally with a painted Dance of Death (c. 1500) which is now kept inside the church. – Farther up the Metnitz valley, 37 km/ 23 miles from Friesach, lies the mountain resort and winter sports area of **Flattnitz** (alt. 1390 m/4561 ft; Hotels: Winterhalerhof, A, 70 b.; Ladinig, B, 40 b.), with a *round church (Gothic, c. 1330; originally Romanesque, consecrated 1173).

SE, on the frontier, is *Poludnig*, 2000 m/6560 ft high. From this road it is possible also to see the *Garnitzenklamm*, a gorge through which flows a tumbling mountain stream. – 7 km/4½ miles W of Hermagor a good road branches off on the left and runs S through the *Trögelbach valley* to the **Sonnenalpe Nassfeld** (1552 m/5092 ft; Alpenhotel Wulfenia, Sonnenalpe, A, 100/110 b.), a saddle (extensive views) on the summit ridge of the Carnic Alps (Italian frontier). From this recently developed summer and winter resort area there is a chair-lift to the foot of the *Gartnerkofel* (2195 m/7202 ft; upper station 1885 m/6185 ft), on which *Wulfenia carinthiaca* blooms – a plant unique in Europe and which has survived from the Ice Age. To the SW is the *Rosskofel* (2239 m/7346 ft), which commands wide views; the climb takes about 3 hours. – 5 km/3 miles E of Hermagor is the *Pressegger See*, 1 km/¾ mile long.

Gailtal
(Gail Valley)

Land: Carinthia (K).

ⓘ **Fremdenverkehrsverein Kötschach-Mauthen-Plöckenpass,** Rathaus, A-9640 Kötschach 390; tel. (0 47 15) 2 68. **Verkehrsamt Hermagor,** Rathaus, A-9620 Hermagor; tel. (0 42 82) 20 43.

ACCOMMODATION. – IN KÖTSCHACH-MAUTHEN: *Kürschner*, A, 95 b.; SP, sauna; *Gailtalerhof*, B, 33 b.; *Erlenhof*, B, 24 b. – IN NASSFELD: *Sonnenalpe*, A, 110 b., SB, sauna; *Wulfenia*, A, 100 b., SB, sauna; *Gartnerkofel*, A, 90 b., sauna; *Krieber*, B, 40 b., sauna. – IN HERMAGOR: *Gasser*, B, 27 b.; *Rieder*, B, 11 b. – several CAMPING SITES.

The Gailtal runs from E to W, parallel to the Drau Valley, between the Gailtal Alps and the Carnic Alps. An excellent road runs down the valley to the junction of the Gail with the Drau at Villach.

Kötschach-Mauthen (706 m/2316 ft), the chief place in the upper Gailtal, with a church of Our Lady (1518–27) which is known as the "cathedral of the Gailtal", is an important junction on the road over the Plöcken pass (1360 m/4462 ft) into Italy. The road climbs the 650 m/2135 ft to the pass in only 13·5 km/8½ miles, with gradients of 14% and several hairpin turns. The name Mauthen recalls the toll (*Maut*) which was once levied here.

Hermagor (590 m/1936 ft; pop. 7000), in the heart of the Gailtal, is a good base for walks and climbs in the surrounding hills. The 15th c. parish church has a small winged altar.

SURROUNDINGS. – of Hermagor. – From *Möderndorf*, S of the Gail, a narrow road of great scenic beauty (10 km/ 6 miles) climbs steeply up into the **Carnic Alps**, coming to an end at 1500 m/4900 ft, near the Italian frontier. To the

Gasteiner Tal
(Gastein Valley)

Land: Salzburg (S).

ⓘ **Kurverwaltung, Haus Austria,** A-5640 Badgastein; tel. (0 64 34) 25 31–38. **Kurverwaltung Bad Hofgastein,** Kurplatz 1, tel. (0 64 32) 64 81–0. **Verkehrsverein Dorfgastein,** Haus Nr. 8, A-5632 Dorfgastein; tel. (0 64 33) 2 77.

ACCOMMODATION. – IN BADGASTEIN: *Elisabethpark*, A1, 180 b., SB, sauna; *Parkhotel Bellevue*, A1, 162 b., SB; *Grand Hotel de l'Europe*, 160 b., SP, sauna; *Kaiserhof*, A1, 100 b., SB, sauna; *Miramonte*, A1, 60 b., sauna; *Eurotel*, A, 310 b., SB, sauna; *Salzburgerhof*, A, 138 b., SB, sauna; *Weismayer*, A, 137 b.; *Grüner Baum*, A, 103 b., SB, SP, sauna; *Germania*, A, 100 b., SB; *Savoy*, A, 100 b., SB; *Sanotel*, A, 76 b., SB, sauna; *Alpenhof Bellevue*, A, 50 b.,

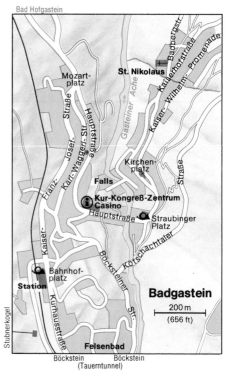

Bad Hofgastein

Badgastein

200 m
(656 ft)

SB, SP; *Söntgen*, B, 120 b.; *Mozart*, B, 116 b. – YOUTH HOSTEL. – Two CAMPING SITES. – IN BAD HOFGASTEIN: *Palace Gastein*, A1, 300 b., SB, sauna; *Norica*, A1, 140 b., SB, sauna; *Grand Parkhotel*, A1, 132 b., SB, sauna; *Alpina*, A, 103 b., SB, sauna; *Germania*, A, 104 b., sauna; *Kärnten*, A, 100 b., SB, SP, sauna; *Moser*, A, 85 b.; *Sendlhof*, A, 87 b., SB, sauna; *Tirol*, A, 85 b., SB, sauna; *Österreichischerhof*, A, 83 b., SB, sauna; *Astoria*, A, 76 b., SB, sauna; *Carinthia*, A, 60 b., SB, sauna; *Kurparkhotel*, B, 97 b.; *Berglift*, B, 40 b. – IN DORFGASTEIN: *Römerhof*, B, 70 b.; *Steindlwirt*, B, 48 b. – IN BÖCKSTEIN: *Gallent*, A, 48 b.; *Haas*, B, 58 b.; *Alpenhaus*, B, 48 b.

CASINO. – (roulette, baccarat, blackjack; daily from 5 p.m.) in the Grand Hotel de l'Europe.

RECREATION and SPORTS. – Riding, tennis, golf in Badgastein (9 holes; winter school in Hotel de l'Europe); artificial ice rink in Bad Hofgastein; winter sports.

The Gasteiner Tal (alt. 831–1137 m/ 2727–3730 ft) climbs in two "steps" through the wildly romantic Gasteiner Klamm (gorge), heading S towards the Hohe Tauern. Large numbers of visitors are drawn to the valley by the radon mineral springs of Badgastein and the beautiful scenery. In addition to the world-famous spa of Badgastein there are the modern health resort of Bad Hofgastein, the quiet little country resort of Dorfgastein and the village of Böckstein at the head of the valley. In recent years the extensive skiing area of Sportgastein has been developed as a further attraction.

The valley is traversed by a federal highway and the Tauernbahn (railway), which cuts through the main ridge of the Tauern in a tunnel 8·5 km/5¼ miles long and was for many years, until the opening of the Felber-Tauern Tunnel, the quickest route into Carinthia (carrying cars between Böckstein and Mallnitz).

To the S of the *Gasteiner Klamm*, through which the *Gasteiner Ache* surges tumultuously down between almost vertical rock walls, is **Dorfgastein** (alt. 836 m/2743 ft;

pop. 1400), on the lowest "step" of the valley. (The road bypasses the gorge in a tunnel.) This is a quiet little summer and winter sports resort with an open-air swimming pool heated by solar energy (32 °C/90 °F).

The 14th c. parish church is partly remodelled in Baroque style. – There is a chair-lift to the *Brandalm* (1500 m/4923 ft).

Bad Hofgastein (870 m/2854 ft; pop. 6000), long the chief place in the valley, is an old-established spa and winter sports resort. In the 16th c., thanks to its gold-mines, it was, after Salzburg, the richest town in the province. The Weitermoserschlössl (15th c.; now a restaurant) was the home of the Weitmosers, a wealthy mining family.

The late Gothic parish church (1498–1507) has a fine Baroque altar. The various sanatoria and treatment establishments and the modern Alpenthermalbad (Alpine Thermal Baths) are supplied with water from the radioactive springs at Badgastein, and there is a large Kurzentrum (Treatment Complex) and Kurpark.
A footpath affording extensive views leads past the Café Gamskar to Badgastein (2¼ hours).

Badgastein (alt. 840–1100 m/2757–3610 ft; pop. 6000) was already famous for its medicinal waters in the Middle Ages, and in the 19th c. it became world-famous when it attracted the patronage of royalty and prominent figures from many countries.

The radioactive mineral water is used in both bathing and drinking cures for nervous complaints, rheumatism, gout, circulatory disturbances and geriatric ailments.

Among the many treatment facilities available is the Felsenbad, blasted from the rock, with both indoor and outdoor baths. By the upper falls on the Ache, which flows through the town, is the modern Treatment and Conference Complex (Kur- und Konggresszentrum), with a museum. To the N is the late Gothic St Nicholas's Church. – Footpath to Böckstein (1 hour).

At the head of the valley is the old village of **Böckstein** (1131 m/3711 ft), with the parish church high up above the village. – To the S is the *Radhausberg*, with gold-mines which were worked from time immemorial (most recently in 1910–27 and 1938–44). A shaft 2·4 km/1½ miles

Treatment and Conference Complex, Badgastein

long driven through the hill in 1940 was converted after the war into a new form of treatment facility, using the warm (up to 41·6 °C/106·9 °F), humid and radioactive air in the tunnel.

At the entrance is the Stollenkurhaus, and patients are conveyed by electric railway to the treatment rooms in the tunnel (*Stolle*).

SURROUNDINGS. – The hills round all three resorts are brought within easy reach by various chair-lifts and cableways. – The best views are from the *Stubnerkogel (2246 m/7369 ft; cableways from Badgastein station to 2231 m/7320 ft). The *Graukogel* (2419 m/7937 ft) can be reached from the upper station on the *Reicheben-Alm* (1983 m/6506 ft) by way of the *Hüttenkogel* (2331 m/7648 ft) in an easy walk or 1½–2 hours. – From Bad Hofgastein there are cableways to the *Schlossalm* (1965 m/6447 ft) and the *Hohe Scharte* (2300 m/ 7550 ft). – There are cableways up the *Kreuzkogel* (2686 m/8813 ft) from Sportgastein. – There is also a rewarding climb from Hofgastein by way of the *Rastötzen-Alm* (1727 m/5666 ft; refreshments) to the summit of the *Gamskarkogel* (2465 m/8088 ft; inn in summer).

SW of Böckstein is the *Nassfelder Tal, a favourite skiing and walking area, watered by the Ache. A toll road from Böckstein leads past a series of waterfalls – the *Kesselfall*, the *Schleierfall* (100 m/330 ft high) and the *Bärenfall* – to the *Nassfeld* (1588 m/5210 ft), with the new winter sports resort of **Sportgastein** (cableways, ski-lifts). There are pleasant climbs up the Kreuzkogel and the *Silberpfennig* (2600 m/8530 ft).

Gmünd

Land: Carinthia (K).
Altitude: 749 m/2457 ft. – Population: 2600.
Post code: A-9853. – Telephone code: 0 47 32.
ⓘ **Fremdenverkehrsamt,**
    Rathaus, Hauptplatz 20;
    tel. 21 97.

ACCOMMODATION. – IN GMÜND: *Kohlmayr*, B, 45 b.; *Mentebauer*, B, 35 b.; *Platzer*, B, 35 b.; *Post*, C, 34 b. – IN MALTA: *Malteinerhof*, A, 42 b.; *Hubertus*, C, 36 b. – CAMPING SITE.

The little town of Gmünd is beautifully situated in the lower valley of the Lieser, at the mouth of the charming Malta valley, on the busy road from the Katschberg pass to the Millstätter See and the Drau valley. It is both a staging point on the way from Salzburg to Carinthia and a good base from which to explore the Nock district.

SIGHTS. – The *Old Town* is still surrounded by a circuit of 16th c. walls, with four gates. The massive *Altes Schloss*, largely in ruins, dates from the 15th–17th c., the *Neues Schloss* in the Hauptplatz, a much plainer building, from 1651–54. The Gothic *parish*

church of Mariä Himmelfahrt (the Assumption) has a Baroque high altar of 1742. The 16th c. Stadtturm houses the *Heimatmuseum* (local museum). The Porsche works were in Gmünd from 1944 to 1950, and there is a monument to Ferdinand Porsche in the park (museum).

Gmünd

SURROUNDINGS. – The *Malta valley, which runs NW from Gmünd, is one of the most beautiful valleys in Austria, with a number of waterfalls on the Malta and its tributary streams. The village of *Malta* has a church of the 14th–15th c. The public road ends at the *Falleralm*, 14 km/ 8½ miles from Gmünd, from which a road and footpaths continue up the valley for 18 km/11 miles by way of the *Gmünder Hütte* (1185 m/3888 ft) to the new artificial lakes in the Ankogel group. The *Malta Valley Nature Reserve* contains a rich selection of mountain animal life. In *Trebesing* excursions can be made into the former gold mining tunnels.

SE of Gmünd is the **Nock district**, much frequented by climbers and winter sports enthusiasts. From the top of *Tschiernock* (2082 m/6831 ft; 4 hours) there are extensive views. – To the W is the **Reisseck group**, with peaks of up to 3000 m/9900 ft and numerous small mountain lakes, which can be reached in walks lasting between 5 and 10 hours.

Graz

Land: Styria (Stm).
Altitude: 365 m/1189 ft. – Population: 243,000.
Post code: A-8010. – Telephone code: 03 16.
ⓘ **Fremdenverkehrsbüro der Stadt Graz,**
    Kaiserfeldgasse 25;
    tel. 7 65 91.
    Amt der Steiermärkischen Landesregierung,
    Landesfremdenverkehrsabteilung,
    Landhaus, Herrengasse 16/1;
    tel. 8 31–22 87.

ACCOMMODATION. – *Steirerhof*, Jakominiplatz 12, A1, 150 b.; *Weitzer-Goldener Ochs*, Griesgasse 15–17, A, 330 b.; *Daniel*, Europlatz 1, A, 189 b.; *Erzherzog Johann*, Sackstr. 3–5, A, 110 b.; *Alba-Hotel Wiesler*, Grieskai 4–6, 110 b.; *Parkhotel*, Leonhardstr. 8, A, 100 b.; *Mariahilf*, Mariahilfer Str. 9, A, 85 b.; *Gollner*, Schlögelgasse 14–16, A, 80 b.; *Drei Raben*, Annenstr. 43, B, 100 b. – YOUTH HOSTEL, Idlhofgasse 74. – CAMPING SITES.

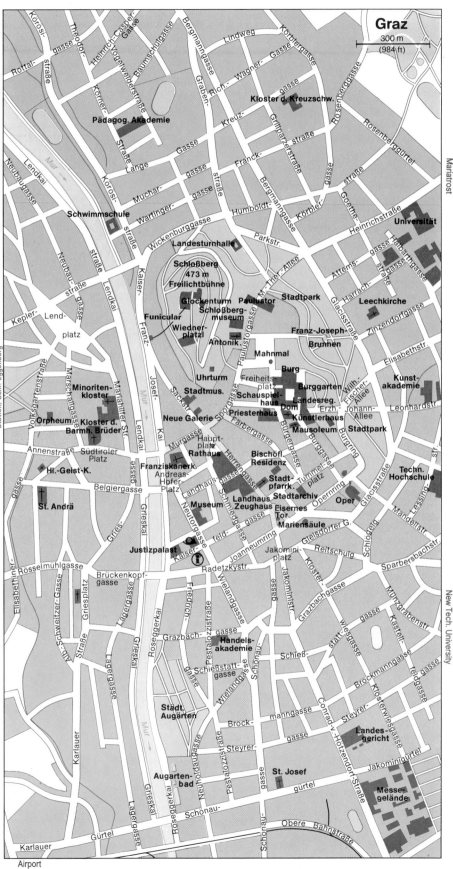

Graz

RESTAURANTS. – In most hotels; also *Krebsenkeller,* Sackstrasse 12; *Schlossberg-Höhenrestaurant; Gambrinuskeller,* Färbergasse 6–8.

CASINO. – (roulette, baccarat, blackjack; daily from 4 p.m.), in the Congress House, Landhausgasse.

RECREATION and SPORTS. – Riding school; tennis; climbing school.

EVENTS. – *Steirischer Herbst* ("Styrian Autumn", Oct.–Nov.); *concerts* in Schloss Eggenberg, the Minoritensaal and a number of churches; *Spring* and *Autumn Fairs.* – Open-air theatre on Schlossberg.

The old capital of Styria and Austria's second largest town, Graz is the economic and commercial focus of the whole region. It lies on the River Mur, which here emerges from a narrow defile to enter the fertile basin known as the Grazer Feld. Above the town rears a prominent hill, the Schlossberg. Graz, the seat of the provincial government and a major industrial town, has the Karl-Franzens University, a Technical University, various institutes and an Academy of Music and Dramatic Art. Its tourist attractions include many historic old buildings; these and the old town with numerous Baroque façades are of great interest.

HISTORY. – Excavation has shown that there were settlements here as early as A.D. 800, but the town is first mentioned in the records in 1128. The name comes from the Slavonic *gradec* (small castle). Graz was of some consequence in trading under the Traungau family and later under the Babenbergs. In 1233 it passed into the hands of the Habsburgs, and in 1281 King Rudolf I granted the town special privileges.

From 1379 to 1619 Graz was the residence of the Leopoldine branch of the Habsburgs. As a stronghold of the Habsburg empire against attack from the East, the town was strongly fortified in the 15th–17th c. and several times withstood sieges by the Turks.

The architecture of the town was influenced by Italian models, among the fine buildings erected during this period being the sumptuous palace of Prince Hanns Ulrich von Eggenberg. In the 19th c. Graz became an important cultural magnet. The Habsburg period came to an end in 1918. In 1938 the city reached its present extent with the incorporation of a number of adjoining communes. It suffered considerable damage during the last war but this was made good after the war.

SIGHTS. – In the middle of the **Old Town** on the left bank of the Mur is the *Hauptplatz,* with a statue of the popular Archduke Johann (1782–1859). On the S side of the square stands the **Rathaus** (1888–93), and at the N end, on the corner of Sporgasse, the 17th c. *Haus am Luegg,* with an arcaded and stucco-decorated façade. To the W of the square is the Gothic *Franciscan Church* (Franziskanerkirche), with a tower of 1643. At Sackstrasse 16 is the *Neue Galerie* (19th and 20th c. pictures), and at No. 18 the *Municipal Museum* (Stadtmuseum) with the *Apothecary's Museum* and the *Robert Stolz Museum.* In *Herrengasse* (pedestrian precinct), which runs SE from the Hauptplatz, are many handsome old mansions. At No. 3 is the *Painted House* (Gemaltes Haus), with frescoes of 1742. On the right-hand side (No. 16) is the Renaissance *Landhaus (by Domenico dell'Allio, 1557–65), meeting-place of the old Styrian Estates; arcaded courtyard with Renaissance fountain, Knights' Hall with a splendid stucco ceiling of 1746.

In the Arsenal, Graz

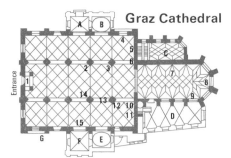

Graz Cathedral

A	St Francis Xavier's Chapel
B	Plague Chapel
C	St Barbara's Chapel
	(Diocesan Museum on first floor)

D	New Sacristy
E	Dolorosa Chapel
F	Chapel of the Cross
G	Landplagenbild (1480)

1	Organ (1772)
2	Tomb of Caspar, Count Cobenzl (1741)
3	St John Nepomuk Altar (1744)
4	Tomb of Sigismund von Trauttmansdorff (1619)
5	Altar of the Sacrament (1767)
6	Reliquary (before 1477)
7	Court Oratory (1733)
8	High altar (1730–33)

9	Herberstein epitaph (1572) and Archducal votive image (1591)
10	Reliquary (before 1477)
11	Altar of St Ignatius (1766)
12	Tomb of Caspar, Freiherr von Breuner (1570)
13	Altar of St Aloysius (1745)
14	Pulpit (1710)
15	Fresco of St Christopher (before 1500)

Adjoining the Landhaus is the **Landeszeughaus** (Provincial Arsenal, 1642–44), with a unique store, completely preserved, of 17th c. arms and armour for 28,000 mercenaries. Opposite this is the Gothic *Stadtpfarrkirche* (town parish church), built in 1519, with a Baroque façade added in 1742.

To the right, in a street named after the great Baroque architect Fischer von Erlach (1656–1723), is his birthplace.

Herrengasse ends at the *Platz am Eisernen Tor*, with a column bearing a figure of the Virgin (*Mariensäule*, 1665–71). To the S is the spacious *Jakominiplatz*, where the newer part of the town begins.

To the W of the Platz am Eisernen Tor in Neutorgasse is the *Museum Joanneum, a complex of buildings housing natural history collections, applied art, the Alte Galerie (Old Gallery) and the Provincial Library.

The **Stadtpark** (Municipal Park), at the E end of the Opernring (Opera House), was laid out in 1869 on the site of the old fortifications. In the park are the *Emperor Francis Joseph Fountain* and numerous monuments, including a marble statue (by Kundmann, 1887) of the writer Anastasius Grün (1806–76), a bust (by Pirker, 1965) of the astronomer Johannes Kepler (1571–1630), a marble statue (by Hellmer, 1900) of Mayor Moritz von Franck (1814–95), a marble statue (by Kundmann, 1904) of the writer Robert Hamerling (1830–98) and a marble bust (by Gasser, 1859) of the great German dramatist Friedrich Schiller (1759–1805). – E of the park, beyond Glacisstrasse, is the twin-towered *Leechkirche*, the oldest church in Graz (founded 1202), afterwards a church of the Teutonic Order; the choir windows have the earliest *stained glass in Graz (14th c.).

NE of the Hauptplatz is the **Burg**, originally a massive 15th c. Imperial stronghold but much altered in later centuries and now preserving only a few of the remains of the original structure. Notable features are the grand courtyard, with a double spiral staircase of 1499, and a smaller courtyard with portrait busts of eminent Styrians (the "Styrian Gallery of Honour").

S of the Burg stands the late Gothic *Cathedral (*Dom*, 1438–62), on the site of an earlier church dedicated to St Giles,

which is first referred to in 1174. In 1564 it became the court church, and in 1786 the seat of the Bishops of Seckau. Particularly fine is the main doorway, decorated with coats of arms. On the S external wall, facing on to a small square, are the remains of a late Gothic fresco (1485), the "Landplagenbild", depicting Graz threatened by pestilence, the Turks and a plague of locusts. – The interior of this hall-church is impressive. The wide nave is separated from the choir by a narrow triumphal arch, flanking which are two fine reliquaries of 1477.

The choir is dominated by the high altar of coloured marble (1730). Notable also is the pulpit (1710). Fine monuments in the aisles.

To the S of the Cathedral is the sumptuous Baroque **Mausoleum** of the Emperor Ferdinand II (d. 1637), partly designed by J. B. Fischer von Erlach. It consists of the domed St Catherine's Church and a burial vault, also domed, below the church.

NE of the Burg is the *Karmeliterplatz*, a charming square laid out after 1578 as the central feature of an extension to the town and named after the former Carmelite convent which was secularised in 1784 and now houses the police headquarters. On the E side of the square is a memorial to those who fell in the Second World War. On the S side stands the *Palais Galler* (*c.* 1690), with a *Trinity Column* (1680) in front of it.

Above the old town rears the *Schlossberg** (473 m/1552 ft), which can be ascended by funicular (3 minutes) or on foot (20–25 minutes). On the hill is the great

Clock Tower, Graz

landmark of Graz, the 28 m/92 ft high **Clock Tower** (*Uhrturm*, 1561; clock 1712). The nearby *Turkish Well* (Türkenbrunnen) is 94 m/308 ft deep. The *Belfry* (Glockenturm, 1588) on top of the hill is 35 m/115 ft high and contains a heavy bell (4 tons) popularly known as Liesl; it now houses the *Schlossmuseum.*

The fortifications on the Schlossberg were blown up in 1809 and converted into a park. An *open-air theatre* was constructed in 1949, with boxes in the old castle walls. In a tunnel used during the last war as an air-raid shelter there now runs a miniature railway 600 m/ 650 yds long, the *Märchengrottenbahn* ("Fairytale Grotto Line").

NE of the Stadtpark is the *University*, to the SE the *Technical University* (Technische Universität).

On the right bank of the Mur are the *Convent of the Brothers of Mercy* (Kloster der Barmherzigen Brüder), with a church of 1769, and the *Minorite Friary* (Minoritenkloster), with the Mariahilfkirche (1607–11), containing an image of the Virgin, the "Madonna of Graz", painted by the architect, Giovanni Pietro de Pomis.

SURROUNDINGS. – It is 45 minutes' walk N to the *Rosenberg* (479 m/1572 ft; inn), from which it is another hour to the *Rainerkogel* (501 m/1644 ft) or 1¼ hours to the *Platte* (651 m/2136 ft; look-out tower).

2 km/1¼ miles W of Graz station is *Schloss Eggenberg* (1625–35), with four towers, fine state apartments, a Hunting Museum, collections of prehistoric and early historical material, a deer park and a lapidarium (Roman remains) in its extensive grounds.

At *Stübing*, on the right bank of the Mur, 15 km/9 miles N of Graz by way of the north-western suburb of *Gösting* (18th c. Schloss), we find the very interesting *Austrian Open-Air Museum* (Österreichisches Freilichtmuseum), with old peasant houses, barns and mills from the various Austrian provinces. It can be reached from Graz by bus. Plan opposite.

10 km/6 miles farther N, at *Peggau*, is the *Lurgrotte*, a stalactitic cave through which flows a small stream (conducted tours; restaurant).

18 km/11 miles NE of Graz is the health resort of *St Radegund* (714 m/2343 ft; medicinal springs). From here there is a cableway to the summit of *Schöckl* (1446 m/ 4744 ft; inn), from which there are extensive views.

35 km/22 miles W of Graz, the little mining and industrial town of *Voitsberg* (394 m/1293 ft; pop. 10,000) has a ruined castle; to the NW of the town is the beautiful *Kainach valley*. – 6 km/4 miles farther W is *Köflach* (449 m/1473 ft; pop. 13,000).

3·5 km/2 miles NE of the town is the *Piber Stud Farm*, where the famous Lipizzaner horses are bred for the Spanish Riding School in Vienna (two conducted tours daily in summer). The horses originally came from Spain and were later bred at Lipica in Slovenia: hence their name. The Schloss (1696–1728) has a beautiful arcaded courtyard. The adjoining Romanesque church is first mentioned in the records in 1066.

40 km/25 miles SW of Graz, the little town of **Deutschlandsberg** (372 m/1221 ft), is dominated by a castle (517 m/1696 ft). This is a good base for the fine walking and skiing area of the *Koralpe (Grosser Speikkogel, 2141 m/7025 ft), to the W of the town.

The road to Deutschlandsberg runs through the little market village of *Stainz*, noted for its red wine; on a hill to the N is a former Augustinian monastery (1229–1785), with a handsome church of 1724. – 5 km/3 miles S of Deutschlandsberg is *Schloss Hollenegg* (sumptuous state apartments, armoury; park), to the E of which lies the wine-producing village of *Kitzeck* (museum of viticulture).

Grossglockner Road

Länder: Salzburg (S) and Carinthia (K).

(i) **Grossglockner-Hochalpenstrassen AG**, Rainerstrasse 2, A-5020 Salzburg; tel. (0 62 22) 7 36 73.

ACCOMMODATION. – IN BRUCK: *Höllern*, B, 85 b.; *Post*, C, 50 b.; *Glocknerhof*, C, 45 b.; *Lukashansl*, C, 160 b. – IN FUSCH: *Römerhof*, B, 100 b.; *Post*, B, 65 b., *Lampenhäusl*, B, 70 b.; *Wallackhaus*, B, 45 b. – ON FRANZ-JOSEPHS-HÖHE: *Alpenhotel Kaiser-Franz-Josephs-Haus*, A/B, 100 b. – IN HEILIGENBLUT: *Glocknerhof*, A, 120 b., SB, sauna; *Post*, A, 100 b., SB, sauna; *Kärntnerhof*, A, 70 b., SB, SP. – YOUTH HOSTEL. – several CAMPING SITES.

RECREATION and SPORTS. – Climbing school; riding; tennis; water and winter sports.

The **Grossglockner Road (Grossglockner-Hochalpenstrasse) from Bruck in the Pinzgau to Heiligenblut was constructed between 1930 and 1935 and has been steadily improved and developed since then. It is one of the most magnificent mountain roads in Europe; and although its importance as a N–S route through the Alps has declined since the opening of the Felber-Tauern Road and the Tauern motorway, both of which are practicable in winter (tunnels), it is still a splendid highway through Austria's highest mountain massif and one of the country's outstanding tourist attractions.

Although this route through the Alps was used by the Romans it was thereafter forgotten for many centuries, and it was only in the 20th c., when the automobile came into its own, that the decision was made to build a modern panoramic road.

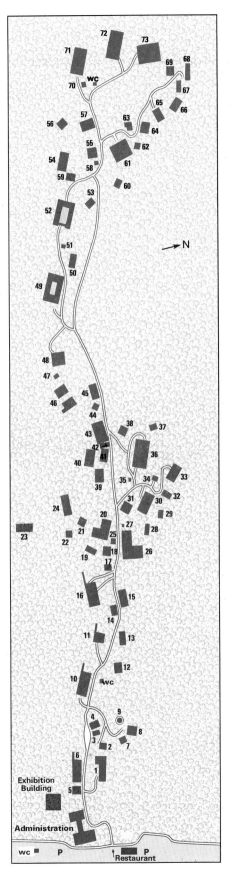

Austrian Open-Air Museum Stübing

1 Peasant house ("Berglerhaus"), Neustift, near Güssing (B)
2 Belfry, Schallendorf, near St Michael (B)
3 Storehouse (1771), Unterschützen (B)
4 Barn, St Nikolaus, near Güssing (B)
5 Dovecote, Blumau (Stm)
6 Stamping mill, Winkl-Boden, near Pöllau (Stm)
7 Charcoal-burner's hut, St Jakob im Walde (Stm)
8 Woodman's hut, Bärenschützklamm, near Mixnitz (Stm)
9 Charcoal pile (planned)
10 Sawmill, Kindthalgraben, Mürztal (Stm)
11 Corn-mill, Feistritz, near Birkfeld (Stm)
12 Corn-mill (1745), Badendorf, near St Georgen an der Stiefing (Stm)
13 Flax-worker's hut, Baierdorf, near Anger (Stm)
14 Cart-shed, Semriach (Stm)
15 Smithy (1703), Feistritz, near Birkfeld (Stm)
16 Hammer mill, Krakauhintermühlen, near Murau (Stm)
17 W Styrian farmhouse "Niggas" with mixed farming, Mooskirchen (Stm)
18 Barn, Geistthal (Stm)
19 Pigsty, Kalchberg, near St Bartholomä (Stm)
20 Smoking hut (16th c.), Eggartsberg, near Geistthal (Stm)
21 Cellar (1822), Kalchberg, near St Bartholomä (Stm)
22 Pressing house, Geistthal (Stm)
23 Smoking hut, Gams near Frohnleiten (Stm)
24 Vintner's house (recorded 1564), Tieschen, near Radkersburg (Stm)
25 Drying kiln, Kornberg, near Stiwoll (Stm)
26 Barn, Naintsch, near Heilbrunn, Birkfeld (Stm)
27 Field cross, Prätis, near Pöllau (Stm)
28 Cattle-trough, Feistritz, near Birkfeld (Stm)
29 Beehive, Fischbach (Stm)
30 Smoking hut (originally 1409), Sallegg, near Birkfeld (Stm)
31 Corn-bin (1836), Wenigzell (Stm)
32 Chapel, Brandlucken, near Birkfeld (Stm)
33 School (originally a flax-worker's hut), Prätis, near Pöllau (Stm)
34 Corn-bin, Schlag, near St Lorenzen am Wechsel (Stm)
35 Wayside shrine, Fischbach (Stm)
36 Farm building, Einach an der Mur (Stm)
37 Hay-shed, Einach an der Mur (Stm)
38 Corn-bin, Oberzeiring (Stm)
39 Stable, Öblarn (Stm)
40 Barn, St Nikolai im Sölktal (Stm)
41 Cottage (17th c.), St Nikolai im Sölktal (Stm)
42 Chapel, Lassing, Ennstal (Stm)
43 Smoking hut (17th c.), St Nikolai im Sölktal (Stm)
44 Corn-bin, St Nikolai im Sölktal (Stm)
45 Drying frame, Dellach, Gailtal (K)
46 Log barn, Winkl, Reichenau (K)
47 Corn-bin (1716), Saureggen, Reichenau (K)
48 Smoking hut (early 18th c.), Saureggen, Reichenau (K)
49 Farm building, St Ulrich, near Steyr (OÖ)
50 Barn (1812), Tarsdorf, Innviertel (OÖ)
51 Baking oven, Rammelhof, near Arbesbach (NÖ)
52 Farmhouse, Rammelhof, near Arbesbach (NÖ)
53 Corn-mill (1733), Schnals (southern Tirol)
54 Thatched barn, Vöran (southern Tirol)
55 Farmhouse (renovated 1811), St Walburg im Ultental (southern Tirol)
56 Post barn, St Anton, Jaufental (southern Tirol)
57 Barn, St Walburg im Ultental (southern Tirol)
58 Pigsty (1845), St Walburg im Ultental (southern Tirol)
59 Field cross, Kuppelwies, Ultental (southern Tirol)
60 Corn-bin (c. 1620), Hintertux (T)
61 Farmhouse (17th c.), Alpbach (T)
62 Bath-house, Alpbach (T)
63 Baking oven, Alpbach (T)
64 Feeding stall (1769), Alpbach (T)
65 Alpine dairy hut, Durlassboden, Gerlos (T/S)
66 Alpine hut, Limmeralm, Johnsbach (Stm)
67 Alpine Hut, Sattental, Ennstal (Stm)
68 Alpine stable, Gstatterboden, Ennstal (Stm)
69 Pigsty, Gstatterboden, Ennstal (Stm)
70 Mill, Lamm im Lungau (S)
71 Smoking hut (recorded 1631), Siezenheim (S)
72 Peasant house of Bregenzer Wald type, Schwarzenberg (V)
73 Alpine farm (1641), Mittelargenalpe, near Au, Bregenzer Wald (V)

Constructed by Fritz Wallack (1887–1966), it runs for 22 km/13½ miles through the mountains at an altitude of over 2000 m/ 6500 ft. A long succession of turns lead up to the summit tunnel on the Hochtor (2506 m/ 8222 ft) and down into the valley on the far side. The total distance from Bruck to Heiligenblut is 48 km/30 miles, with a maximum gradient of 12%. A toll road, it is normally open throughout its entire length during the summer months, continuing into October (the period varying according to snow conditions).

From the southern approaches, coming from the Möll valley or Drau valley over the saddle on the *Iselsberg* (1204 m/3950 ft; a popular summer and winter holiday area), there are superb views of the Grossglockner.

From the car park (Parkplatz II) at the **Fuscher Törl** (2428 m/7966 ft) there is a magnificent *prospect of the mountains and a view down into the upper Fuscher Tal. – The road runs under the summit of the pass (the Hochtor) in the **Hochtor Tunnel** (311 m/ 340 yds long) at an altitude of some 2500 m/ 8200 ft (highest point 2506 m/8222 ft), passing in the process from the province of Salzburg into Carinthia.

Two attractive side roads branch off the main road to magnificent look-out points. – Some 6 km/4 miles short of the tunnel on the N side, below the *Dr-Franz-Rehrl-Haus*, the *Edelweisstrasse (2 km/1¼ miles) goes off on the E and climbs, with gradients of 14%, to the car park at the *Edelweissspitze* (2571 m/8435 ft). From the look-out tower at the Edelweiss hut (inn; accommodation) there is a splendid panoramic *view of 37 peaks over 3000 metres (9800 ft). – 7 km/4½ miles below the tunnel on the S side, at the *Posthaus Guttal* (1859 m/6099 ft), the *Gletscherstrasse (Glacier Road, 9 km/5½ miles) branches off on the W. If the weather is clear this is a detour which should on no account be omitted.

The excellently engineered road runs up, passing a number of parking places and the *Margaritze* artificial lake below the road (2000 m/6560 ft), to the *Freiwandeck* (2369 m/7773 ft; parking garage; souvenir shops; refreshments), on the **Franz-Josephs-Höhe** (Alpenhotel at 2422 m/7947 ft). From here there is one of the grandest views in Europe: immediately opposite is the **Grossglockner** (3797 m/12,458 ft; nature reserve), Austria's highest peak; to the left, on the Adlersruhe (3454 m/11,333 ft), the Erzherzog-Johann-Hütte; farther left the Schwerteck and the Leiterköpfe; to the right the Glocknerwand, the Teufelskamp, the Romariswandkopf, the three rocky peaks of the Burgstall and the perpetually snow-capped pyramid of the Johannisberg to the rear. Below the look-out platform, reached by a steep path or by funicular (212 m/696 ft), is the *Pasterze, the largest glacier in the Eastern Alps, over 9 km/5½ miles long and up to 1·6 km/1 mile wide (care necessary).

Heiligenblut (alt. 1301 m/4270 ft; pop. 2870) is a popular summer and winter resort, magnificently set on the steep

On the Grossglockner Road

meadow-covered slopes of the Möll valley. Its Gothic parish church (15th c.), with a characteristic pointed steeple, contains a beautiful little tabernacle (1496) with a phial of what is believed to be the blood of Christ (said to have been brought from Constantinople in 914), a carved high altar of 1520 and a number of fine paintings. – Chair-lift to the *Schareck* (2604 m/8544 ft; ski-lift to the Glockner Road); easy climbs to the *Kalvarienberg* ($\frac{1}{2}$ hour), *Wirtsbauer-Alm*

Parish church, Heiligenblut

(1$\frac{1}{2}$ hours) and the *Leiterfall*, a 130 m/430 ft high waterfall (2 hours); and ample scope for high Alpine climbs by experienced climbers.

Gurk

Land: Carinthia (K).
Altitude: 662 m/2172 ft. – Population: 1428.
Post code: A-9342. – Telephone code: 0 42 66.
ⓘ **Marktgemeideamt**, Dr-Schnerich-Strasse 12; tel. 81 25.

ACCOMMODATION. – *Alte Post*, C, 16 b, SP.

The little market town of Gurk, N of Klagenfurt, became the see of a bishop in 1072, having previously been the site of a nunnery. In 1787 the see was transferred to Klagenfurt, and since 1858 it has embraced the whole of Carinthia.

SIGHTS. – The ***Cathedral** (*Dom*), a three-aisled pillared basilica with a transept and three apses built between 1140 and 1200, is one of the finest Romanesque churches in Austria. The exterior is plain, with twin W towers 41 m/135 ft high (onion domes added in 1682), a richly ornamented S

doorway and relief decoration on the central apse. The *porch*, with a doorway of 1200, has been enclosed since the Gothic period, when it was richly decorated with wall paintings and stained glass (1348). The *interior* has 16th c. reticulated vaulting. The pulpit and Kreuzaltar at the end of the nave, both dating from about 1740, are luxuriant Rococo creations, with lead reliefs and a "Pietà" by the Viennese sculptor G. R. Donner. The Samson Doorway, to the left, dates from 1200. Between the choir and the transept is a Rococo screen of 1740. Fine wall paintings: St Christopher (*c.* 1250), Saul's downfall (*c.* 1380), death and assumption of the Virgin (*c.* 1390). Six painted wooden reliefs depict the legend of St Hemma, foundress of the convent. The Baroque high altar (1626–38) has 72 statues and 82 angels' heads; during Holy Week it is covered by a Lenten veil (1458) with 99 Old and New Testament scenes.

Gurk Cathedral

Gurk Cathedral

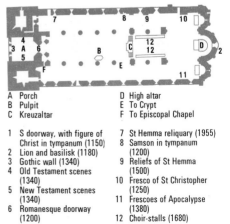

A Porch	D High altar
B Pulpit	E To Crypt
C Kreuzaltar	F To Episcopal Chapel

1 S doorway, with figure of Christ in tympanum (1150)	7 St Hemma reliquary (1955)
2 Lion and basilisk (1180)	8 Samson in tympanum (1200)
3 Gothic wall (1340)	9 Reliefs of St Hemma (1500)
4 Old Testament scenes (1340)	10 Fresco of St Christopher (1250)
5 New Testament scenes (1340)	11 Frescoes of Apocalypse (1380)
6 Romanesque doorway (1200)	12 Choir-stalls (1680)

Two features of the church which can be seen only on a conducted tour are the **Episcopal Chapel** in the W gallery, with exceptionally well-preserved frescoes of Paradise and the Heavenly Jerusalem (c. 1220), and the *Crypt* ("Hemmagruft"; 1174), with a hundred columns, containing the sarcophagus of St Hemma (d. 1045), under an altar of c. 1720. – The *conventual buildings* (1637–64) have been occupied since 1932 by Salvatorians.

SURROUNDINGS. – 4 km/2¼ miles E lies **Strassburg** (alt. 658 m/2159 ft; pop. 3000), a little walled town of medieval aspect. The Gothic parish church has a Baroque organ (1743) and tombstones of Bishops of Gurk. On the W side of the town is a round church, the Heilig-Geist-Spital-Kirche (13th–16th c.), with beautiful frescoes. High above the town rises the Schloss (built 1147 and enlarged in later centuries), which was until 1780 the residence of the Prince-Bishops of Gurk; it now houses a local and diocesan museum. – 15 minutes W of Strassburg is *Leiding*, a picturesque little place with a richly furnished Gothic church.

Hainburg

Land: Lower Austria (NÖ).
Altitude: 161 m/528 ft. – Population: 5700.
Post code: A-2410. – Telephone code: 0 21 65.
ⓘ **Gemeindeamt,** Hauptplatz 23;
tel. 21 11.

ACCOMMODATON. – *Goldene Krone,* B, 47 b.

RECREATION and SPORTS. – Bergbad (swimming pool), with mini-golf and tennis; golf-course (9 holes), 5 minutes from the middle of town.

Hainburg, beautifully situated between two hills on the Danube E of Vienna, was in the early medieval period a fortified town on the eastern frontier of the Holy Roman Empire, and it still preserves an old-world aspect. The town lies just short of the Czechoslovak frontier.

SIGHTS. – The town is surrounded by well-preserved 13th c. walls, with 12 towers, and above it rear the ruins of a massive 11th c. castle. It has many handsome burghers' houses of the Gothic, Renaissance and Baroque periods. – At the W entrance to the town is the *Wiener Tor* (Vienna Gate), over 20 m/65 ft high, which was begun about 1244; the upper part was rebuilt in the 15th c. It now houses the *Heimatmuseum* (local museum). The two figures on the gate are popularly known as Etzel (Attila) and Kriemhilde (who, according to the "Nibelungenlied", spent a night here). In the *Marktplatz* are a fountain commemorating Haydn, who went to school here in 1737–40,

Mariensäule, Hainburg

and a *Mariensäule* (column with a figure of the Virgin), an ornate Rococo creation (1749). The graceful "lantern of the dead" outside the Romanesque charnel-house dates from the 15th c. On the E side of the town towers the massive 13th c. *Ungartor* (Hungarian Gate).

SURROUNDINGS. – A road (2·5 km/1½ miles) runs NE up the *Braunsberg* (344 m/1129 ft), from which there are extensive views. – To the SE is the *Hundsheimer Berg* (476 m/1562 ft; nature reserve), with a large limestone quarry. – *Petronell* and Roman *Carnuntum*: see p. 150.

Hallein

Land: Salzburg (S).
Altitude: 469 m/1539 ft. – Population: 16,000.
Post code: A-5400. – Telephone code: 0 62 45.
ⓘ **Verkehrsverein,** Schöndorferplatz 14;
tel. 25 14–169.

ACCOMMODATION. – IN HALLEIN: *Bockwirt,* C, 54 b.; *Brückenwirt,* B, 42 b.; *Stern* (no rest.), C, 65 b.; *Haffner,* C, 60 b.; *Scheicher,* C, 52 b.; *Auwirt,* C, 21 b. – YOUTH HOSTEL in Schloss Wispach. – IN BAD DÜRRNBERG: *Kranzbichlhof,* B, 52 b., sauna.

This old Celtic town lies S of Salzburg on the River Salbach, which here emerges from the mountains into the Alpine foreland. It is the regional capital of the Tennengau, an educational

centre (wood and stone craft, fashion, etc.) as well as a thriving industrial town.

SIGHTS. – In the picturesque old town, opposite the *parish church* (Gothic choir), is the house of the organist Franz Xaver Gruber (1787–1863: bust), composer of "Silent Night"; in front of the house is his grave. In the old *Orphanage* (1654) is the municipal **Keltenmuseum* (Celtic museum containing pre-historic material, including finds from the Latène era 500–15 B.C.; salt-mining, history of the town, original score of "Silent Night").

SURROUNDINGS. – The **Salt-Mine* at *Dürrnberg*, S of Hallein, can be reached by cableway in a few minutes or on foot in an hour. The conducted tour (summer only) takes 1½ hours, during which visitors toboggan downhill on polished tree-trunks, see huge underground salt chambers, cross a salt lake on rafts and finally travel on miners' trucks through long galleries to the exit. – On the Dürrnberg visitors can see a Celtic village (reconstruction of a Celtic trading settlement with the tomb of a prince). Mining museum. – *Dürrnberg-Zinkenkogel* winter sports area (1330 m/4365 ft; fine views).

12 km/7½ miles S of Hallein, at *Golling*, the **Golling Falls* (*Gollinger Wasserfall*) tumble down 62 m/205 ft over a rock wall (admission charge). From Golling a road leads E through the beautiful *Lammertal* to *Abtenau*, a summer and winter resort in the **Tennengebirge**. Half-way between Golling and Abtenau a footpath goes off the *Lammeröfen*, a narrow gorge hewn by the Lammer through the mountains (narow footpath along the gorge: admission charge). – *Abtenau* (alt. 715 m/2346 ft: 14th–15th c. parish church) is a good base for walks and climbs in the Tennengebirge: e.g. (7 hours, with guide) by way of the *Laufener Hütte* (1726 m/5663 ft) to the *Bleikogel* (2412 m/7914 ft). There is a chair-lift from Abtenau to the *Karkogel* (1200 m/3940 ft).

Golling Falls

Hallstatt

Land: Upper Austria (OÖ).
Altitude: 511 m/1677 ft. – Population: 1200.

Post code: A-4839. – Telephone code: 0 61 34.
ⓘ **Fremdenverkehrsverband,** Seestrasse 56; tel. 2 08.

ACCOMMODATION. – IN HALLSTATT: *Seehotel Grüner Baum*, B, 60 b.; *Bergfried*, B, 83 b.; *Seewirt*, C, 25 b.; *Sarstein*, C, 25 b.; *Hirlatz*, C, 20 b. – YOUTH HOSTELS in Lahn and Hallstatt-Markt. – CAMPING SITE. – IN GOSAU: *Sommerhof*, B, 70 b., sauna; *Koller*, B, 40 b., SP; *Gosauschmied*, C, 82 b.; *Kirchenwirt*, C, 60 b. – YOUTH HOSTEL.

RECREATION and SPORTS. – Climbing school at the Simony hut; diving school; water sports; tennis.

EVENTS. – *Lake Procession* (Corpus Christi); lake festival and concerts.

This little market town, one of the most attractive places in the Salzkammergut, is picturesquely set on the SW side of the Hallstätter See below the mighty Dachstein massif, its houses crowded together on a narrow tract of alluvial land deposited by the Mühlbach (waterfall) and climbing up the steep hillside. It takes its name (*hall*, "salt") from the salt-mine here which has been worked since prehistoric times.

The first phase of the European Iron Age (8th–4th c. B.C.) is known as the Hallstatt period, characterised by the grave goods in the numerous tombs found on the Salzberg (see below). – The **Hallstätter See*, enclosed by steeply sloping wooded shores, is 8 km/5 miles long, 1–2 km/¾–1¼ miles wide and some 125 m/401 ft deep.

SIGHTS. – Near the landing-stage is the Gothic *parish church*, with a beautiful carved altar (*c.* 1520). In the charnel-house behind the church are old skulls. The *Prehistoric Museum* (Seestrasse 56) contains material from the Hallstatt excavations. The *Heimatmuseum* (local museum) occupies the oldest secular building in Hallstatt-Markt (14th c.).

SURROUNDINGS. – Above Hallstatt, to the NW, is the **Salzberg** ("Salt Mountain", 1030 m/3379 ft), with the salt-mine (conducted tour, 1 hour). It can be reached by taking the funicular from Lahn and continuing on foot (15–25 minutes), or by walking all the way on the Salzbergweg (fine views), via the *Rudolfsturm* (850 m/2789 ft: restaurant and look-out terrace) and the Iron Age cemetery (1¼ hours). – To the W there is an attractive walk (1¼ hours) through the *Echerntal* to the **Waldbachstrub** at the head of the valley (beautiful waterfalls). – To the SW there is a climb (not difficult, 3 hours) to the *Tiergartenhütte* (1457 m/4570 ft: inn, open in summer), from which it is another 1¼ hours to the *Wiesberghaus* (1883 m/6178 ft: inn); then 1¾ hours to the *Simony-Hütte* (2206 m/7235 ft; inn, open in summer), magnificently situated below the Hallstatt glacier.

From the Simony hut the *Hoher Dachstein* (2995 m/ 9827 ft), the highest peak in the *Dachstein group, can be climbed in 3 hours. The massif is steepest on its S side; its higher western section, with small glaciers, is broken up into precipitous ridges, separated from the jagged Gosaukamm by the valley containing the Gosau lakes. The eastern part consists of the fissured plateau called *Auf dem Stein*, an excellent skiing area which can be reached by cableway from Obertraun (several ski-lifts). On the S side there is a toll road up to the *Türlwandhütte* (1715 m/5627 ft).

To the Dachstein Caves. – Take the road to *Obertraun* (514 m/1686 ft) and in 4 km/2½ miles turn right into a side road which in 2·5 km/1½ miles reaches the lower

In the Giant Ice Cave on the Dachstein

station (608 m/1995 ft) of a cableway. This runs up in a few minutes to an intermediate station (1350 m/4430 ft) on the *Schönbergalm*, with the *Schönberghaus*. From here it is 15 minutes' walk to the **Dachstein Caves** (up to 1174 m/3853 ft deep), on the northern rim of the Dachstein plateau, which rank with the Eisriesenwelt at Werfen as the most impressive caves in the Eastern Alps. They are open only from May to October. The *Giant Ice Cave* (Rieseneishöhle), with a temperature in summer of −1°C/30°F, has great caverns with magnificent frozen waterfalls and other features. The *Mammoth Cave* (Mammuthöhle) consists of huge pipe-shaped galleries formed by an ancient underground river. The conducted tours take 1½ and 1¼ hours respectively. – From the Schönbergalm station the cableway continues to the upper station (2079 m/6821 ft; Berghaus Krippenstein) on the *Hoher Krippenstein* (2109 m/6920 ft). 15 minutes' climb above the cableway station is a chapel (1959), with a bell commemorating 13 students and teachers from Heilbronn in Germany who were killed in the Dachstein area in 1954. From the Krippenstein another cableway descends to the *Gjaidalm* (1795 m/ 5889 ft). – The ascent of the Krippenstein from Obertraun by way of the Gjaidalm (4 hours: also army cableway) takes 5¾ hours.

10 km/6 miles W of the Hallstätter See, before the *Gschütt pass* (964 m/3163 ft: 17% gradient), straggles the village of *Gosau* (779 m/2556 ft; pop. 1800). From here a road runs S (7 km/4½ miles) to the *Vorderer Gosausee* (933 m/3061 ft), a mountain lake enclosed by sheer rock walls, with a beautiful view across the water to the Dachstein and the Gosau glacier. A cabin cableway goes up to the *Gablonzer Hütte* (1587 m/ 5207 ft; refreshments) on the *Zwieselalm*, a popular skiing area with a view extending to the Hohe Tauern. From here it is 2¼ hours' climb to the summit of the *Grosser Donnerkogel*. A road (closed to cars) along the lake, past the *Holzmeisteralm* (973 m/3192 ft), leads to the *Hinterer Gosausee* (1154 m/3786 ft: 1¾ hours), in a magnificent valley basin. From here it is 3 hours' climb to the *Adamekhütte* (2196 m/9205 ft; inn); then another 3 hours' rock-climbing (with guide) to the summit of the Hoher Dachstein.

Hallstatt, on the Hallstätter See

Heiligenkreuz

Land: Lower Austria (NÖ).
Altitude: 317 m/1040 ft. – Population: 1105.
Post code: A-2352. – Telephone code: 0 22 58.
ⓘ **Gemeindeamt,** Haus Nr. 15;
    tel. 22 86.

ACCOMMODATION. – *Krainerhütte,* A, 105 b., SB,
sauna; *Helenenstüberl,* in Schwechatbach, B, 39 b.

Heiligenkreuz in the Wienerwald, Austria's oldest Cistercian abbey, was founded in 1133, taking its name from a relic of the True Cross which was presented to the abbey by an Austrian duke. The conventual buildings were rebuilt in the 17th and 18th c., when a new courtyard with two-storey arcades and a gatehouse tower were added. The church dates from the 12th and 13th c.

SIGHTS. – The Romanesque nave of the *Abbey Church is in sharp contrast to the light Gothic choir, which has stained glass of about 1300. The neo-classical stalls date from the first half of the 18th c. The *Cloister,* with 300 red marble columns, is in a style transitional between Romanesque and Gothic (1220–50). In the courtyard are a richly decorated *Trinity Column* and the Josefsbrunnen (Baroque). The abbey has a large *Library* (visit by application) with valuable manuscripts of the 11th–13th c., some of them written in the abbey itself.

SURROUNDINGS. – 6 km/4 miles SW is the Carmelite convent of **Mayerling,** on the site of an earlier hunting lodge belonging to Crown Prince Rudolf of Austria, where in 1889 the Crown Prince and his mistress Maria Vetsera took their own lives, in circumstances that have never been fully explained.

Heiligenkreuz Abbey

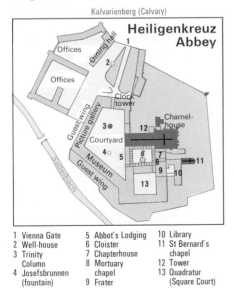

Kalvarienberg (Calvary)

Heiligenkreuz Abbey

1	Vienna Gate
2	Well-house
3	Trinity Column
4	Josefsbrunnen (fountain)
5	Abbot's Lodging
6	Cloister
7	Chapterhouse
8	Mortuary chapel
9	Frater
10	Library
11	St Bernard's chapel
12	Tower
13	Quadratur (Square Court)

Hochkönig

Land: Salzburg (S).
Altitude: Highest point: Hochkönig (2941 m/9649 ft).
ⓘ **Österreichischer Alpenverein,**
    Sektion Bischofshofen, Südtiroler Strasse 26,
    A-5500 Bischofshofen.

The *Hochkönig group, one of the finest mountain massifs of the Northern Alps in the province of Salzburg, adjoins the Steinernes Meer on the SE. Its massive bulk, falling away in precipitous rock faces, is crowned by a gently rounded icefield, from which the summit of the Hochkönig (2941 m/ 9649 ft) projects only a short way.

The view from the summit of the massif is particularly far-ranging and grand. The ascent from the Arthur-Haus (1503 m/ 4931 ft) at Mühlbach is relatively easy, and the alternative approach from Werfen by way of the Ostpreussen-Hütte (1630 m/5348 ft) presents no particular difficulty. Both routes are also popular ski-runs, reckoned among the finest in the Alps, with a drop of 2400 m/ 7900 ft. The ascents from Hintertal by way of the *Teufelslöcher* ("Devil's Holes") and from the Torscharte on the mighty *Hochseiler* (2793 m/9164 ft) are for more experienced climbers only. Rock-climbers favour particularly the towers and pinnacles of the *Manndlwand,* on the rugged and jagged ridge which runs E from the Hochkönig towards the Mitterfeldalm.

To the S of the Hochkönig are the **Dientener Berge**, a typical range of Alpine schist hills. In summer its long green ridges are excellent walking country, with fine views, while in winter they offer good skiing. The highest point in the range is the *Hundstein* (2116 m/6943 ft), at Thumersbach near the Zeller See; on the summit is the Statzer Haus.

Hohe Tauern

Länder: Salzburg (S), Tirol (T) and Carinthia (K).
Altitude: Highest points: Grossglockner (3797 m/12,458 ft) and Grossvenediger (3674 m/12,054 ft).

ⓘ **Österreichischer Alpenverein,**
    Sektion Oberpinzgau, Gasthaus Braüruep,
    A-5730 Mittelsill.
    Sektion Zell am See, Fuchslehenstrasse 4,
    A-5700 Zell am See.
    Sektion Badgastein, c/o Ing. Walter Rud,
    A-5640 Badgastein.
    Sektion Bad Hofgastein, Griesgasse 8,
    A-5630 Bad Hofgastein.
    Sektion Matrei/Osttirol, Lienzer Strasse 11,
    A-9971 Matrei in Osttirol.
    Sektion Lienz, c/o Dipl.-Ing. G. Platzer,
    Bedawebergasse 19, A-9900 Lienz.
    Sektion Mallnitz, c/o Mathias Sieder,
    A-9822 Mallnitz.

The massive mountain range of the *Hohe Tauern extends from W to E along the S side of the Pinzgau and its eastward continuation the Pongau – that is, to the S of the long valley of the Salzach – forming the boundary between the province of Salzburg and its neighbours to the S, Eastern Tirol and Carinthia. Here the Central Alps are seen in all their magnificence before they gradually fall away to the E. Great expanses of névé (permanent snow), much fissured hanging glaciers, precipitous pinnacles of rock girdled by ice, dazzlingly white slopes and cornices of snow: all this contributes to the magnificent scenery offered by the long main ridge of the Hohe Tauern, extending from the Birnlücke to the Murtörl.

The short and deeply slashed valleys on the N side of the range, descending in a succession of steep steps, flow as regularly as the teeth of a comb into the Salzach valley, which runs parallel to the mountains from W to E. The streams flowing down from the glaciers, known as *Achen,* tumble down the valleys in great waterfalls (Krimmler Fälle, Kesselfall, Gasteiner Fall) or carve out deep gorges (Siegmund-Thun-Klamm, Kitzlochklamm, Liechtensteinklamm).

On the S side, however, a series of subsidiary ridges, some of them with peaks of considerable height, run down from the main massif towards the Drau valley. Here the side valleys – the Iseltal in Eastern Tirol and the Mölltal in Carinthia – extend far into the main range between these outliers. Wider, friendlier and relatively densely populated – thus better equipped to cater for visitors – these southern valleys form a striking contrast with the austere grandeur of most of the valleys on the Salzburg side of the range.

The **Venediger group**, the most westerly part of the Hohe Tauern, has the largest area of glaciers in the Austrian Alps after the mountains of the Ötztal. Its main peak, the *Grossvenediger (3674 m/12,054 ft), is the second highest in the Tauern. Its magnificent névé-covered pyramid, surrounded on all sides by ice, presents no great difficulty to experienced glacier-walkers, and is frequented not only by large numbers of climbers in summer but also by skiers, particularly for the splendid descent on the *Obersulzbachkees.*

The Venediger group is easily reached from the N on the Pinzgautalbahn, which runs up through the upper Salzach valley from Zell am See, accompanied by the road from Salzburg via Hallein, Bischofshofen, St Johann im Pongau and Bruck (where the Grossglockner Road branches) to the Gerloss pass. From Hollersbach, Habachtal, Rosental-Grossvenediger and Krimml it is a relatively short climb up the various parallel valleys to the Fürther Hütte (2200 m/7220 ft) on the *Kratzenbergsee* (2154 m/7067 ft), the Thüringer Hütte

Tauern valley near Matrei, with Grossvenediger

(2300 m/7545 ft) on the *Hohe Fürleg* (3244 m/10,644 ft), the Kürsingerhütte (2258 m/7408 ft), magnificently situated under the *Grosser Geiger* (3365 m/11,041 ft), and the Warnsdorfer Hütte (2430 m/7975 ft) on the rugged *Krimmler Kees*, under the sheer rock walls of the beautiful **Dreiherrnspitze** (3499 m/11,480 ft), on the Austrian–Italian frontier.

The approaches from the S are not quite so easy. The best base is the Neue Prager Hütte (2796 m/9174 ft), which is accessible from Matrei. The highest mountain hut in the area, the Defreggerhaus (2962 m/9718 ft), is reached from Hinterbichl in the Virgental by way of the Johannis-Hütte (2121 m/6959 ft). – The most south-easterly outlier of the Venediger group, **Eichham** (3371 m/11,060 ft), can be climbed from Virgen by way of the Bonn-Matreier-Hütte (2750 m/9025 ft).

The narrow ridge of the *Granatspitze group* links the Grossvenediger with the Grossglockner. Its highest peak is not the *Granatspitze* itself (3086 m/10,125 ft) but the **Grosser Muntanitz** (3232 m/10,604 ft), to the S. A difficult route but one affording extensive views, the St Pöltner Weg, runs from the Neue Prager Hütte via the St Pöltner Hütte (2481 m/8140 ft) on the Felber Tauern and along the whole ridge to the Rudolfs-Hütte (2250 m/7380 ft; alpine centre) on the *Weissee*. This is a magnificent setting at the head of the Stubach valley, which climbs up between the Granatspitze group and the Grossglockner group from Uttendorf to the Enzingerboden.

The Felber Tal and the Stubachtal, which form important routes into the Matreier Tal and Kalser Tal, are noted for their beautiful lakes (Hintersee, Grünsee, Weissee, Tauernmoossee) and their fine forests (nature reserve).

The mountains of the Hohe Tauern are seen at their highest and grandest in the **Grossglockner group.** Here, within a relatively small area, is a great world of wild glaciers and mighty peaks of overwhelming splendour. The largest glacier in the Eastern Alps, the **Pasterze** (10 km/6¼ miles long), lies in a great circle under the sheer walls of the *Grossglockner (3797 m/12,458 ft), flanked by fissured ice slopes – a scene of grandeur scarcely equalled anywhere else in the whole of the Alps.

The high mountain world of the Grossglockner group is easily reached in summer by the **Grossglockner Road** (see p. 82), a magnificently engineered highway which runs from Zell am See (province of Salzburg) through the *Fuscher Törl* in the Fuscher Tal up to the commanding *Edelweisspitze* (2571 m/8435 ft), goes over the main ridge of the Central Alps at the **Hochtor(** 2506 m/8222 ft) and then descends to the famous little Carinthian mountain village of *Heiligenblut* (1301 m/4269 ft) in the Möll valley.

A panoramic road which branches off the Grossglockner Road to the S of the pass leads by way of the *Glockner-Haus* (2131 m/6992 ft) to the most beautiful spot in the whole area, the *Franz-Josefs-Höhe (2422 m/7947 ft), on the edge of the Pasterze glacier. – From here it is no great distance, by way of the much fissured *Hoffmann glacier*, to the Erzherzog-Johann-Hütte on the imposing *Adlersruhe* (3454 m/11,333 ft), the highest mountain hut in the Austrian Alps. – The Oberwalder Hütte (2793 m/9754 ft), on an island of rock in the upper reaches of the Pasterze glacier, can also be quickly reached from the Grossglockner Road.

On the gentler S side, the Grossglockner area can be reached from Heiligenblut by way of the Salm-Hütte (2638 m/8655 ft) or from Kals by way of the Stüdl-Hütte (2802 m/9193 ft).

The *Tauernhöhenweg* (Tauern Ridgeway) runs from the valley of the Krimmler Ache past the Grossvenediger and Grossglockner, then by way of the Franz-Josefs-Höhe and Heiligenblut and through the Ankogel group to the Tauern pass.

Höllental

Land: Lower Austria (NÖ).

ⓘ **Fremdenverkehrsamt Gloggnitz,** Wiener Strasse 85, A-2640 Gloggnitz; tel. (0 26 62) 24 01–4.

ACCOMMODATION. – IN GLOGGNITZ: *Neue Welt*, B/C, 28 b.; *Stuppacher Hof*, C, 9 b.; *Maurer*, C, 9 b.

NW of Gloggnitz, beyond Hirschwang, is the wildly romantic gorge known as the *Höllental ("Hell Valley"), which the River Schwarza has cut through the limestone rock between the Raxalpe (2007 m/6585 ft) to the S and the Schneeberg (2075 m/6808 ft) to the N. For some 12 km/7½ miles the rocks are often so close

together that there is barely room for the road. Parallel with the road runs a pipe carrying water to Vienna.

Gloggnitz (alt. 442 m/1450 ft; pop. 6300), in the *Schwarza valley* NE of the Semmering pass, is a popular summer resort, the starting-point of the road and railway over the Semmering and a good base for exploring the Raxalpe and Wechsel area. On the Schlossberg are the 18th c. buildings of a former *Benedictine abbey* (c. 1084 to 1803), with remains of defensive walls (16th c.) and a church, originally Gothic, which was re-modelled in Baroque style in the 18th c. There is a modern church designed by Clemens Holzmeister, the *Christkönigkirche* (Christ the King, 1933).

SURROUNDINGS – of Gloggnitz. – To the N is the *Wiener Schneeberg (2075 m/6808 ft; extensive views), the highest point in Lower Austria; there is a rack railway from Puchberg. – From *Hirschwang* (494 m/ 1621 ft), 12 km/7½ miles NW of Gloggnitz at the mouth of the Höllental, the Raxbahn, a cabin cableway more than 2 km/1¼ miles long, ascends to the *Raxalpe (upper station 1545 m/5069 ft). The Raxalpe (Heukuppe, 2007 m/6585 ft) is a plateau much frequented both by summer visitors and by winter sports enthusiasts (several mountain huts). It is well provided with footpaths (walks of between 2 and 6 hours).

7 km/4½ miles SE of Gloggnitz is *Kranichberg* (620 m/ 2034 ft), with a 16th c. Schloss (rebuilt in 18th c.; old keep). From here there is a road over the *Ramssattel* (818 m/2684 ft; inn) to the *Hermannshöhle*, a cave with many-coloured stalactites N of *Kirchberg am Wechsel* (577 m/1893 ft; Baroque parish church of 1755).

Innsbruck

Land: Tirol (T).
Altitude: 574 m/1883 ft.
Population: 117,300.
Post code: A-6020.
Telephone code: 0 52 22.
(i) **Städtisches Verkehrsbüro**, Burggragen 3; tel. 2 57 15.
Informationsstelle (Information Bureau), Südtiroler Platz (in station); tel. 2 37 66.
United Kingdom: Salurner Strasse 15/IV, tel. 2 83 20.

ACCOMMODATION. – *Holiday Inn, Salerner Str. 15, A1, 388 b., SB, sauna; *Europa-Tyrol, Süd Tiroler Platz 2, A1, 223 b.; *Innsbruck, Innrain 3, A1, 140 b., SB, sauna; *Austrotel*, Bernard-Höflstr. 16, A, 274 b., sauna; *Grauer Bär*, Universitätsstr. 5–7, A, 240 b.; *Maria-Theresia*, Maria-Theresien Str. 31, A, 200 b.; *Central*, Gilmstr. 5, A, 150 b.; *Sailer*, Adamgasse 6–10, A, 150 b.; *Greif*, Leopoldstr. 3, A, 130 b.; *Neue Post*, Maximilianstr. 15, A, 120 b.; *Roter Adler*, Seilergasse 4–6, A, 100 b.; *Schwarzer Adler*, Kaiserjägerstr. 2, A, 50 b., SB, SP; *Atrium*, Technikerstr. 7, B, 230 b.; *Ibis*, Schützenstr. 43, B, 196 b.; *Panorama*, Fürstenweg 176, B, 170 b.; *Bellevue*, Hungerburg, Höhenstr. 141, B, 135 b., SB; *Union*, Adamgasse 22, B, 117 b. – YOUTH HOSTELS. – CAMPING SITES.

RESTAURANTS – in most hotels, in particular the *Goldener Adler* (with Goethestube), the *Greif* (Greifkeller) and the *Grauer Bär*; also *Belle Epoque*, Zeughausgasse; *Goldenes Dachl*, Hofgasse 1 (old town); *Basco* Anichstrasse 12, kitchen on show; *Churrasco*, Innrain 2 (Italian cuisine); *Orangerie*, Maria-Theresien-Strasse 10; *Alt Innsbrugg*, Maria-Theresien-Strasse 16, *Weinhaus Jörgele*, Herzog-Friedrich-Strasse 13 (old town); *Weinhaus Happ*, Herzog-Friedrich-Strasse 14 (old town); *Weisses Kreuz*, Herzog-Friedrich-Strasse 31 (old town); *Moby Dick*, Adamgasse 3–5, kitchen on show (fish a speciality); *s'Bratwürstl*, Hofgasse 1 (old town). – Several BEER-HOUSES.

CAFÉS. – *Central*, Erlerstrasse 11; *Katzung*, Seilergasse 2; *Lamprechter*, Herzog-Friedrich-Strasse 28; etc.

RECREATION and SPORTS. – Olympic Ice Stadium; riding; tennis; several climbing schools; two golf courses (9 and 18 holes).

EVENTS. – *Tirolean Summer* (July–Aug.); *Festival of Old Music* (Aug.); *Costume Festivals* (summer); *Innsbruck Fair* (Sept.); *Alpine Folk Music Competition* (Oct.).

The old provincial capital of Tirol lies in the wide Inn valley at the intersection of two important traffic routes, between Germany and Italy and between Vienna and Switzerland. From all over the city there are vistas of the ring of mountains which rear up above the gentler terraces of lower ground on which it lies. To the N are the jagged peaks of the Nordkette (North Chain), in the Karwendel range; to the S, above the wooded Bergisel ridge, the Saile and the Serles group; to the SE, above the Lanser Köpfe, the rounded summit of the Patscherkofel.

Innsbruck still preserves its medieval core, the historic old town with its narrow and irregular streets and its tall houses in late Gothic style, many of them with handsome oriel windows and fine doorways. The newer parts of the town lie outside this central nucleus, particularly to the E and N.

Goldenes Dachl, Innsbruck

New sports facilities were built for the 1964 and 1976 Winter Olympic Games, and these are now the scene every year of national and international sporting contests. Innsbruck is a university town and the see of a bishop, but it also has a variety of industry and holds regular trade fairs. It has a mild climate, thanks to the mountains which shelter it from N winds, and is a major tourist attraction.

HISTORY. – Bronze Age remains found here point to the establishment of human settlement on the site at a very early stage. Evidence has also been found of later occupation by the Illyrians and the Romans. Soon after the beginning of the Christian era a small Roman fort (*Veldidena*) was established in the plain bordering the river, but this was later destroyed. The site was occupied in the 12th c. by a monastery of Premonstratensian Canons, which took over the Roman name in the form Wilten. The real foundation of the town dates from 1180, when the Count of Andechs established a market settlement at a bridge over the river (*Innspruke*, "Inn bridge"). In 1239 Innsbruck was granted the status of a town, and thereafter it was surrounded by walls and towers. In 1363 the town passed to a junior branch of the Habsburgs, and from 1420 to 1665 was a ducal residence. Under the Emperor Maximilian I (1490–1519) it became an administrative capital and a focal point for art and culture. At the first count of its population in 1567 it numbered 5050 citizens. The University was founded in 1669. In 1703 the Bavarians tried, unsuccessfuly, to take Innsbruck and the whole of Tirol, but under pressure from Napoleon Tirol was ceded to Bavaria in 1806. Later, in spite of a successful war of liberation and victories in battles on the Bergisel (1809, under the leadership of Andreas Hofer), Tirol was again returned to Bavaria. The Congress of Vienna (1814–15), however, assigned it to Austria, and Innsbruck now became a capital of the province of Tirol. The construction of the Brenner railway (1867) marked the beginning of a period of industrialisation and steady growth.

SIGHTS. – In the late Gothic **Old Town**, with its narrow house-fronts, handsome doorways and oriel windows, there are many examples of old Tirolese architecture, in which southern influence is detectable (for example in the arcaded house fronts); and Innsbruck's past importance as a ducal residence is reflected in its many sumptuous Renaissance, Baroque and Rococo buildings.

The picturesque quarter (well restored) enclosed by the ring of streets known as the *Graben* ("Moat") is now a pedestrian zone. The arcaded *Herzog-Friedrich-Strasse*, lined with handsome burghers' houses, enters the quarter from the S, making straight for the famous ***Goldenes Dachl**, the "Golden Roof" which is every tourist's first objective. This magnificent late Gothic oriel window roofed with gilded copper tiles was built in 1494–96 to commemorate Maximilian I's marriage to Bianca Maria Sforza and served as a box from which the court watched civic festivities in the square below.

The house behind (Olympia Museum), completely rebuilt in 1822, was previously a ducal palace (the Neuer Hof), formed by the conversion, at some time after 1420, of two earlier burghers' houses. The lower balustrade is decorated with coats of arms, the open balcony above with ten figural reliefs. – Opposite the Goldenes Dachl is the *Helblinghaus (originally late Gothic, remodelled in Baroque style *c.* 1730).

Nearby is the *Goldener Adler* ("Golden Eagle"), one of the oldest inns in Innsbruck (16th c.), in which Goethe stayed twice and from which Andreas Hofer (the Tirolese patriot) addressed the people in 1809. On the E side of Herzog-Friedrich-Strasse rises the 57 m/187 ft high **Stadtturm**, originally

Innsbruck, against the backdrop of the Stubai Alps

built in the 14th c., together with the adjoining *Old Rathaus*, as a watch-tower but altered at a later date; from the sentry-walk 33 m/108 ft above the street there are good views in all directions. At the W end of the street, on the banks of the Inn, is the *Ottoburg*, a residential tower of 1495 with four oriel windows (restaurant). In front of it is a monument to the 1809 rising erected in 1909.

At Herzog-Friedrich-Strasse 22 is the *Trautsonhaus* (1541), a fine old house which shows the transition from Gothic to Renaissance architecture. – In Hofgasse, which runs E from the Goldenes Dachl, are the *House of the Teutonic Order* (Deutschordenshaus: No. 3), built in 1532, and the *Burgriesenhaus* (Castle Giant's House: No. 12), built by Duke Siegmund the Wealthy in 1490 for his court giant, Niklas Haidl.

Pfarrgasse, to the right of the Goldenes Dachl, runs N to the Domplatz, in which is the **Cathedral** (*Dom*; the town parish church of St James), with an imposing twin-towered W front and a high dome over the choir. It was built in 1717–22 to the design of the Baroque architect Johann Jakob Herkommer (d. 1717); restored after the last war, after suffering heavy damage in 1944. The interior has ceiling paintings and stucco-work by the Asam brothers; High Baroque marble altars (1726–32), with famous image of the Virgin ("Maria Hilf") by Lukas Cranach the Elder (*c.* 1530) on the high altar; richly carved pulpit (*c.* 1725). In the N aisle is the sumptuous *monument (1620) of Archduke Maximilian II, Grand Master of the Teutonic Order (d. 1618).

The busy *Maria-Theresien-Strasse*, lined with handsome 17th and 18th c. houses and numerous shops, affords a magnificent *vista of the mountains to the N, towering up to more than 2300 m/7500 ft. The northern part of the street opens out almost into the proportions of a square. In the middle of the street, in front of the *Rathaus* (1849), stands the **Annasäule** (St Anne's Column), erected in 1706 to commemorate the withdrawal of Bavarian troops on St Anne's Day in 1703.

At the corner of Meraner Strasse is the **Altes Landhaus**, a monumental Baroque palace (1725–28) with a sumptuous and elaborately articulated façade which now houses the Provincial Assembly and Provincial Government (*Landesregierung*). In the courtyard between the two wings of the building is a chapel. Adjoining it on the E, with its main front on Wilhelm-Greil-Strasse, stands the *Neues Landhaus*, built in 1938–40 in the style of the period. To the S, in the spacious Landshausplatz, is a 14 m/46 ft high *Memorial* to the year 1945, with an inscription commemorating the dead.

Obliquely across from the Altes Landhaus is the *Servite Church* (built 1615, with later alterations). At the S end of the street, against the backdrop of the jagged summits of the Serles group, towers the *Triumphpforte* (Triumphal Gateway), erected by Maria Theresa in 1765 on what was then the boundary of the city to mark the marriage of her son Leopold (later Emperor Leopold II) with the Spanish Infanta Maria Ludovica; the gateway was built with stone from the earlier St George's Gate, pulled down to make way for the new one. The marble reliefs (1774) on the S side depict the wedding, and on the N side lament the sudden death of the Emperor Francis I during the festivities.

To the E of the old town are two streets, the *Burggraben* ("Moat") and the *Rennweg*, in which are some of the city's principal public buildings – the Imperial Castle (Hofburg), Court Church, Museum of Folk Art, Theatre and Conference Complex.

The **Hofburg**, a palace in Viennese late Rococo style, with four wings, was originally built in the 15th and 16th c. but was remodelled in Baroque and Rococo style in the 18th c. Visitors are shown a number of sumptuous state apartments on the second floor, with period furniture and pictures, and the Riesensaal (Giant Hall), a grand hall two storeys high, decorated in white and gold, with portraits of the Imperial family and three large ceiling paintings (1775).

To the S of the Hofburg is the *Adliges Damenstift* (18th c.), a religious house for noble ladies, with two handsome Baroque doorways. – Above the Franziskanerbogen (Franciscan Arch), through which the Burggraben leads into the Rennweg, is the *Silver Chapel* (Silberne Kapelle: entrance from Hofkirche), built in 1578–87 as the burial chapel of Archduke Ferdinand II.

The chapel takes its name from a silver image of the Virgin and the embossed silver reliefs on the altar symbolising the Lauretanian (Loreto) Litany. In recesses in the wall are the tombs of the Archduke (d. 1595) and his wife Philippine Welser (d. 1580), both by Alexander Colin. There is a fine 16th c. organ.

The ***Hofkirche** (Court Church), built in 1553–63 in the local late Gothic style, is a three-aisled hall-church with a narrow chancel, a tower set to one side and a beautiful Renaissance porch. The furnishings date from the time of construction, with the exception of the high altar (1758), side altars (1775) and choir screen (17th c.).

To the left of the entrance is the *monument* (1834) of *Andreas Hofer* (b. St Leonhard in Südtirol 1767, shot in Mantua 1810), whose remains were deposited here in 1823. On either side are his comrades in arms Josef Speckbacher (1767–1820) and the Capuchin friar Joachim Haspinger (1776–1858). In the middle of the nave is the **Tomb of the Emperor Maximilian I* (d. 1519, buried in Wiener Neustadt), the finest work of German Renaissance sculpture, conceived as a glorification of the Holy Roman Empire.

The central feature of the monument is the massive black marble sarcophagus with a bronze figure of the Emperor (by Alexander Colin, 1584). The wrought-iron screen was the work of the Prague craftsman G. Schmiedhammer (1573).

Around the sarcophagus are 28 over-lifesize *bronze statues (1508–50) of the Emperor's ancestors and contemporaries. The finest of these are on the right-hand side – Count Albrecht IV of Habsburg (after a design by Dürer) and King Theodoric of the Ostrogoths and King Arthur of England (regarded as the

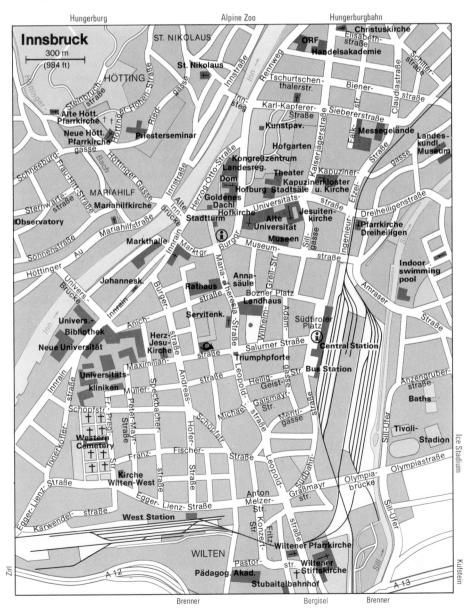

finest statue of a knight in Renaissance art), both the latter being designed by Dürer and cast by Peter Vischer of Nürnberg in 1513. Along the sides are 24 marble reliefs of events in the Emperor's life (1562–66, mostly by Colin). In the N gallery of the church are other pieces of sculpture from the tomb – 23 bronze statuettes of saints (1508–20) and 20 bronze busts of Roman emperors (c. 1530).

Adjoining the Hofkirche on the E, in the *Neues Stift* (New Abbey) or Theresianum (16th and 18th c.) is the *Tirolese Museum of Folk Art (Tiroler Volkskunstmuseum).* The museum's extensive collections, excellently displayed on three floors, include more than 20 old Tirolese rooms, ranging in style from Gothic to Rococo, and a rich store of traditional costumes, furniture and folk art both religious and secular. There is also a collection of Christmas cribs (Nativity groups) from the 18th c. to the present day. In the cloister on the W side of the building is the tomb of the Innsbruck sculptor Alexander Colin (d. 1612), by Colin himself.

On the E side of the Rennweg are the *Stadtsäle* (Municipal Rooms), with the *Provincial Theatre* (Landestheater, 1846). To the N is the **Hofgarten**, with fine trees and an Art and Concert Pavilion (Kunstpavilion). On the W side of the street (Nos. 3–5) is the **Tirolese Conference Complex** (*Kongresszentrum*, 1973), a multi-purpose building with a number of halls and a restaurant.

In the Universitätsstrasse, which runs E from the Hofkirche, are the *Old University* (Alte Universität), built in 1562 as a Jesuit college and rebuilt in 1673, and the *University Library* (rebuilt 1722). Between them, set back a little, is the *Jesuit Church* (Jesuitenkirche), a cruciform building on a central plan with a mighty 60 m/200 ft high dome (1627–40). Farther NE, in Kaiserjägerstrasse (on right), is the *Capuchin Convent* (Kapuzinerkloster, 1593). The side chapel on the left in the church has an altar with a painting of the Virgin by Lukas Cranach the Elder (1528).

In Museumstrasse, which branches off the Burggraben, is the *Tirolese Provincial Museum (Tiroler Landesmuseum Ferdinandeum)*, with rich collections on the history and art of Tirol and a gallery of Dutch and Flemish masters. The originals of the sculpture on the Goldenes Dach are displayed here.

To the E of the Hofgarten are the *Exhibition Grounds* (Messegelände), where trade fairs and other shows are held.

Still farther E, on the banks of the Sill, is the old *Arsenal* (Altes Zeughaus), now occupied by the *Tirol Regional Museum*, a museum of cultural and natural history covering a very wide field (mineralogy, mining, coining, cartography, hunting, technology, clocks and musical instruments, etc.).

To the S of the Alte Innbrücke (Old Inn Bridge), on the Innrain, is the *Market*, a scene of lively activity in summer.

In the middle of the Innrain, here much widened, is the striking **St John's Church** (*Johanneskirche*), a lovely High Baroque building with a twin-towered gabled front (1735); it contains ceiling paintings of 1794.

To the S are the *University Library* (Universitätsbibliothek) and the **New University** (*Neue Universität*, 1914–23), with various clinics and institutes.

The Alte Innbrücke leads into the **Mariahilf** district, with the Baroque *Mariahilfkirche* (1649; frescoes of 1689) and the *Botanic Garden* (Observatory). To the N is the district of **Hötting**, with the tower of the *old parish church* (Alte Pfarrkirche: originally late Gothic, enlarged c. 1750) rising above the new parish church (1911).

At Höttinger Gasse 15 is a tablet commemorating *Peter Mitterhofer* (1822–93) of Partschins in the southern Tirol, inventor of the typewriter. From the church the Höttinger Höhenstrasse (Hötting Ridgeway) runs NW, reaching after 5 km/3 miles the upper station of the Hungerburg funicular and the lower station of the Nordkettenbahn (cableway). Downstream is the district of **St Nikolaus**, with a neo-Gothic church.

1 km/$\frac{3}{4}$ mile farther N are the 15th c. *Schloss Weiherburg* and the popular *Alpine Zoo*.

On high ground above the Inn, downstream, is the villa suburb of **Mühlau**, with a Baroque parish church (1748). In the new cemetery, in front of the chapel, is the tomb of the poet *Georg Trakl* (1887–1914).

In the southern district of **Wilten** stands one of the finest Rococo churches in northern Tirol, the twin-towered *parish church* (1751–55). Ceiling frescoes by Matthäus Günther and stucco-work by

Franz Xaver Feichtmayr; on the high altar a 14th c. sandstone figure of "Mary under the four Pillars". Opposite the parish church is the large complex of buildings (remodelled in Baroque style between 1670 and 1695) of *Stift Witlen*, a Premonstratensian abbey founded in 1138. The church (1651–65) has in the porch a large Gothic wooden figure of the giant Haymon, to whom legend attributes a share in the foundation of the monastery.

SURROUNDINGS. – S of Innsbruck is the hill (under which the Brenner railway and motorway pass in tunnels) of *Bergisel (750m/2460 ft: 15 minutes' walk from Wilten), with the high *Olympic ski-jump*, from which there are magnificent views. The hill owes its fame to the heroic battles of 1809, when the Tirolese peasants, led by Andreas Hofer, three times freed their capital from the French and Bavarian occupying forces. On the N side of the hill, below the ski-jump, stands a memorial to all the Tirolese who fought for their country's freedom. The central feature of this is the *Andreas Hofer Monument* (1893); adjoining this is a *memorial chapel* (1909), to the rear of which is the *Tomb of the Tirolese Kaiserjäger* (Imperial Riflemen). Here, too, is the *Tiroler-Kaiserjäger-Museum*, with many relics and mementoes of the struggle for liberation and the history of the Kaiserjäger down to the First World War; from the *Hall of Honour, which contains 1954 volumes with the names of all the Tirolese who fell between 1796 and 1945, there is a tremendous view of Innsbruck and the mountains to the N.

To the N of Innsbruck, on an upland terrace (900 m/ 2950 ft: wide views), is the outlying villa suburb of **Hungerburg**, which can be reached either by the Hungerburgbahn, a funicular which runs up from the *Mühlauer Brücke* (at a circular building with the Bergisel Panorama, which depicts the battle of 1809), or on the Höttinger Höhenstrasse.

From Hungerburg the *Nordkettenbahn, a cableway 3·5 km/2 miles long, goes up via the intermediate station of *Seegrube* (1905 m/6250 ft) to *Hafelekar (2334 m/ 7658 ft), from which there are superb views; terrace café at the upper station, 10 minutes' climb below the summit.

3·5 km/2 miles SE of the town, beyond the Inn valley motorway, is **Schloss Ambras** or *Amras*, a residence of Archduke Ferdinand from 1563 to 1595. In the Unterschloss (Lower Castle) are two rooms containing arms and armour; on the first floor of the Kornschüttgebäude is a valuable art collection (sculpture, applied art); the splendid Spanish Hall is one of the earliest Renaissance interiors in Germany (1570–71). In the Hochschloss (Upper Castle) is the bathroom of Philippine Welser, Ferdinand's wife; on the first and second floors are paintings and sculpture. The park is open to the public.

12 km/7½ miles W of Innsbruck, on the N bank of the Inn, is *Zirl* (622 m/2041 ft), from which a road runs N by way of the *Zirler Berg* to Seefeld and Mittenwald. The road, now with some of the sharpest turns removed (with a rise of some 400 m/1300 ft in 3 km/2 miles), affords beautiful views of the Inn valley to the rear.

5 km/3 miles S of Innsbruck lies the health and winter sports resort of **Igls** (870–900 m/2850–2950 ft) (*Sport-hotel, *Parkhotel, *Schlosshotel). From here a cableway 3·7 km/2¼ miles long ascends the **Patscherkofel** (2247 m/7372 ft). From the upper station (1951 m/ 6400 ft: hotel) the summit can be reached in an hour's climb or by chair-lift. There are splendid panoramic views. This is a good skiing area, with long downhill runs.

18 km/11 miles SW of Innsbruck, above the village of *Axams* (878 m/2881 ft), is a well-known winter sports area, the **Axamer Lizum** (*Lizum-Alpe*, 1633 m/5358 ft), with skiing slopes which were used in the Winter Olympics. Numerous cableways and lifts, including a funicular and a chair-lift up the *Hoadl* (2340 m/7678 ft) and a chair-lift up the *Birgitzköpfl* (upper station 2044 m/ 6706 ft).

10 km/6 miles W of Innsbruck, at *Kematen*, is the mouth of the beautiful **Sellrain Valley**, which attracts many visitors both in summer and for winter sports. From the chief place in the valley, **Sellrain** (909 m/2982 ft), there are a number of attractive walks and climbs – for example, W by way of the little late-Gothic mountain church of *St Quirin* (1243 m/4078 ft) to the *Rosskogel* (2649 m/ 8691 ft: 5 hours, not difficult), or S to the *Potsdamer Hütte* (2020 m/6628 ft; good skiing), above which, to the W, is the peak of *Sömen* (2797 m/9177 ft).

From **Gries** (1238 m/4062 ft) a road runs S up the *Linsenser Tal*. The Sellraintal Road continues W from Gries over the *Kühtaisattel* (2016 m/6641 ft) to **Kühtal** (1967 m/6454 ft; several hotels; covered tennis courts), a health and winter sports resort (cableways and ski-lifts). Good climbing and walking; many small mountain lakes.

Schloss Ambras, near Innsbruck

Inn Valley (Inntal)

Land: Tirol (T).

(i) **Tiroler Fremdenverkehrswerbung,** Bozner Platz 6, A-6010 Innsbruck; tel. (0 52 22) 2 07 77.

The River Inn flows through the province of Tirol from SW to NE for a distance of 230 km/145 miles, from the Swiss frontier at the Finstermünz gorge to the German frontier at Kufstein. On either side rear up the great mountain massifs of the Samnaun group and the Ötztal Alps, the Lechtal

and Stubai Alps, the Karwendel and the Kitzbühel Alps. The deeply slashed valley has been a traffic route for more than two thousand years. The Tirolese capital, Innsbruck, lies at the junction of the Sill and the Inn.

To the S of the *Finstermünz defile* (1006 m/ 3301 ft) is **Nauders** (1365 m/4479 ft; Hotel Tirolerhof, A, 140 b., SB; Edelweiss, A, 66 b., SB; Almhof, 80 b., SB; Schwarzer Adler, A, 60 b.), a popular health and winter sports resort. Skiing areas *Bergkastel* (2600 m/ 8533 ft) and *Tscheyeck* (2700 m/8861 ft); ski-lifts. The late Gothic parish church has two carved altars of the 15th–16th c.; the Romanesque St Leonard's Chapel has old wall paintings. – Schloss Naudersberg (café-restaurant).

Between Nauders and *Landeck* (see p. 119), high above the W bank of the river, is the old mountain village and pilgrimage focal point of **Serfaus** (1427 m/4683 ft; *Hotel Cervosa, A, 130 b., SB; Löwen, A, 130 b. SB; Alpenhotel, A, 100 b.; Furgler, A, 80 b.), now a popular summer and winter resort, with two medieval churches (1332 and *c.* 1500). Cars are not permitted in the village and there is an underground hover-railway which is harmless to the environment. Cableways to the *Komperdellalm* (2000 m/6560 ft), good skiing (lifts to 2500 m/8205 ft). To the SW is the *Hexenkopf* (3038 m/9968 ft), the highest peak in the Samnaun group. – N of Serfaus are the health and winter sports resorts of *Ladis* (1190 m/3904 ft) and *Obladis* (1386 m/4547 ft), both with sulphur springs.

Imst (828 m/2717 ft; pop. 6000; Hotel Post, A, 77 b.; Eggerbrau, B, 138 b., three camping sites), an ancient little town, beautifully situated on a terrace above the Inn at the mouth of the Gurgl valley, is an important road junction on the Innsbruck–Landeck route and a good base for the Ötztal and Pitztal. The "Schemenlaufen", a picturesque Shrovetide festival, is held every 3–5 years (next probably in 1988). – In the old-world Unterstadt (Lower Town) is the *Rathaus*, in the Oberstadt (Upper Town) the handsome *parish church* (15th c., external frescoes of 15th–18th c.). There is an interesting *Heimat-museum* (local museum).

SURROUNDINGS. – Chair-lift through the Rosengartl gorge to *Alploch* (2050 m/6725 ft), S of the *Muttekopf-hütte* (1934 m/6345 ft) below the SE side of the **Muttekopf** (2777 m/9111 ft), which commands extensive views. – 13 km/8 miles N E of Imst, in a wider part of the valley at the foot of the Miemingergebirge, is the summer and winter sports resort of **Nassereith** (843 m/ 2766 ft; Hotel Post, B, 71 b.), where every two or three years the "Schellerlaufen", a Carnival procession in which old masks are worn, is held on the Sunday before Shrovetide. A well-engineered panoramic road crosses the Mieming plateau to Telfs, and to the N the road continues over the *Fernpass* (1209 m/3967 ft) to Ehrwald and Garmisch-Partenkirchen in Germany.

Stams (670 m/2199 ft; Hotel Hirschen, C, 55 b.) is a trim little town on high ground a little way S of the Inn, with a large *Cistercian abbey* (rebuilt *c.* 1700 in Baroque style, with 180 rooms; conducted tours). The abbey was founded in 1273 by the mother of Conradin, the last of the Hohenstaufens (executed in Naples in 1268), in memory of her son. The church (13th c., remodelled in Baroque style in 17th–18th c.), the burial-place of the Dukes of Tirol, has a high altar of 1613, a fine pulpit of *c.* 1740 and 18th c. wrought-iron screens. In the Heiligblut-kapelle (Chapel of the Holy Blood, 1716), on the S side of the church, is the beautiful Rosengitter (Rose Screen). – To the W is the *parish church* (1313–18; interior, Baroque, 1755).

Telfs (630 m/2068 ft; Hotel Tirolerhof, B, 74 b.) is a little market town of some 8500 inhabitants, beautifully situated at the foot of the Miemingergebirge. To the N is the *Hohe Munde* (2661 m/8731 ft). The "Schleicher-laufen", an old Shrovetide custom, takes place here every five years.

Solbad Hall (574 m/1883 ft; pop. 13,000; Hotel Tyrol, B, 75 b.; Maria-Theresia, B, 50 b.; camping site) lies 10 km/6 miles E of Innsbruck at the foot of the precipitous Bettelwurf chain (2725 m/8940 ft). It has been a place of some consequence for centuries thanks to its salt-mines, which have been worked since the 13th c., and it is also frequented as a spa.

Stams Abbey

SIGHTS. – In the *Unterstadt* (Lower Town), to the S of the Unterer Stadtplatz, is *Burg Hasegg* (c. 1280), in which from 1566 to 1809 coins were minted from the silver mined at Schwaz. The *Münzerturm* (Coiner's Tower) is the town's principal landmark. The *Münzertor* (gate) dates from 1480.

In the middle of the picturesque *Old Town*, higher up, is the Oberer Stadtplatz. Here is the medieval *Rathaus*, with a fine Council Chamber (1477) and the Municipal Museum. In Fürstengasse, to the S of the Square, the *Mining Museum* has displays illustrating the old methods of salt-working (conducted tours). The **parish church**, standing on a terrace, is basically late Gothic, with a Rococo interior (1752). In the N aisle, enclosed by a fine screen, the Waldauf Chapel houses a remarkable collection of relics. Built on to the outside of the choir are two chapels – the Magdalene Chapel (15th and 16th c. wall paintings), now a war memorial chapel, and the Baroque St Joseph's Chapel, adjoining which are some remains of the old arcades in the churchyard. – In the eastern part of the old town is the harmonious little Stiftsplatz, in which are the *Jesuit Church* and Jesuit College (17th c.) and the *Damenstift*, a religious house founded in 1566 by the Emperor Ferdinand's daughter and reoccupied as a nunnery in 1912; the church has an elegant Baroque tower. – To the N, in a park, is the **Spa Establishment** (events).

SURROUNDINGS. – 2 km/1¼ miles N the old village of *Absam* (632 m/2074 ft) possesses a much frequented pilgrimage church (originally late Gothic, remodelled c. 1780). The old salt road runs N past the *Bettelwurfbrünnl* (spring) and climbs some 6 km/4 miles to the *Herrenhäuser* (1485 m/4866 ft), on the **Haller Salzberg**, with the old salt-workings (closed 1968). – A pleasant excursion from Hall is to the **Gnadenwald** (to the NE), a beautiful upland terrace 15 km/9 miles long and up to 3 km/2 miles wide below the Bettelwurf range. The hamlet of *St Martin* was the birthplace of Andreas Hofer's companion in arms Josef Speckbacher. – 7 km/4½ miles E of Hall, on the S bank of the Inn, is **Wattens**, with a fine open-air swimming pool. (Manufacture of paste diamonds and optical apparatus.) SW of the village are excavations of an old Raetian settlement of the 3rd–4th c. A.D.

Schwaz (535 m/1755 ft; pop. 10,900; Hotel Goldener Löwe, B, 65 b.) lies 28 km/17 miles NE of Innsbruck, mainly on the S bank of the Inn. From the 15th to the 17th c. the town flourished thanks to its productive silver- and copper-mines; now only mercury is worked. The town is a tourist attraction.

SIGHTS. – In the Stadtplatz, near the bridge, is the late Gothic *Fuggerhaus* (turrets with oriel windows, arcaded courtyard), a relic of the days when the great merchant family of the Fuggers played the leading role in the mining and precious metals trade of Schwaz. – To the E, higher up, is the *Franciscan Church*, a Gothic hall-church (no tower) of 1515, with Rococo ornament in the vaulting, pulpit and altars (1736) and modern stained glass in the choir. In the cloister (decorated with coats of arms) is a striking series of 22 *wall paintings of the Passion (1512–26; restored 1937–44). – Above this again is the *Altes Pfleggericht*, a picturesque 16th c. building now occupied by a religious house. The *parish church (second half of 15th c.) is the largest Gothic hall-church in Tirol, roofed with 15,000 plates of beaten copper. Opposite the tall tower is a two-storey mortuary chapel with carved decoration (1506). The interior of the church is Baroque (1728–30), with four aisles (reticulated vaulting) and two choirs; the N half was

for the townspeople, the S half for the miners. In the left-hand choir is the Gothic high altar; the right-hand one has three vividly coloured stained-glass windows of 1962. The Baroque St Anne's Altar in the S aisle has a beautiful 16th c. group of the Virgin and Child with St Anne. In the gallery is a tripartite organ.

SURROUNDINGS. – Above Schwarz to the SE is **Burg Freundsberg** (707 m/2320 ft), the ancestral castle of the Frundsberg family, to which the famous mercenary leader Georg von Frundsberg (1473–1528) belonged. The castle is first recorded about 1100. The keep now houses a local museum. – SE of Schwarz is the *Kellerjoch (2344 m/7691 ft); cableway to the *Arbeser* (1880 m/6168 ft), then an hour's climb to the ridge. – On the N bank of the Inn, beyond the motorway, is the Benedictine abbey of **Fiecht**, moved here from the St Georgenberg in 1706. From Fiecht a steep and narrow road climbs 5 km/3 miles to the *St Georgenberg* (895 m/2936 ft), with a pilgrimage church of 1733 picturesquely situated above the Stallental. 2 km/1¼ miles S of the abbey, on the banks of the Inn, is the village of *Vomp*, with Schloss Sigmundslust (15th c.).

Innsbruck (see entry).

Jenbach (531 m/1742 ft; pop. 6000; Hotel Toleranz, B, 70 b.) is a trim little resort on the N bank of the Inn, from which a cog railway runs up to the Achensee. – On a hillside 3 km/2 miles W is *Schloss Tratzberg*, rebuilt in the 16th c. after a fire at the end of the 15th c. It contains a mural painting 46 m/150 ft long depicting 148 members of the Habsburg family. Conducted tours. View of Inn valley.

4 km/2½ miles E of Jenbach, on the S bank of the Inn, is **Strass**, from which a road runs up the Zillertal.

Brixlegg (524 m/1719 ft; pop. 2600), situated below the Rofangebirge (3000 m/9800 ft), is a former mining town now a popular summer and winter resort. In the charming surroundings are five castles, including Lichtenwerth (13th c.) and the *Matzen Nature Park*. The town, which has a late-Gothic parish church (16th c.) is a good

Burg Matzen, near Brixlegg

base for walking in the lower Inn valley. – To the S of Brixlegg is the *Alpbach valley*. A road leads 10 km/6 miles up the valley to the chief place, *Alpbach* (973 m/3192 ft; *Hotel Böglerhof, A, 110 b., SB), on an upland terrace commanding fine views. Several cableways. To the S is the *Grosser Galtenberg* (2425 m/7956 ft).

Rattenburg (513 m/1683 ft), a little town of under 1000 inhabitants, still preserves an entirely medieval appearance with its handsome oriel-windowed burghers' houses of the 15th and 16th c. The *parish church*, originally late Gothic (15th c.), was remodelled internally in Baroque style in 1735.

The *Servite Church* (1709) has fine stuccowork and frescoes. On a projecting spur are the ruins of the *castle* (view; open-air dramatic performances in summer), massively fortified from 1505 onwards. Here the Chancellor of Tirol, Wilhelm Biener, was beheaded in 1651 on a false charge.

SURROUNDINGS. – Opposite Rattenberg on the N bank of the Inn (bridge) is the summer and winter resort of **Kramsach** (519 m/1703 ft), with the 17th c. castle of the Counts of Taxis and a glass-working school. To the NE are the *Buchsee*, the *Krummsee* and the *Reintaler See* (restaurant; hire of rowing boats). From Mariatal there is a chair-lift up the *Rosskopf* (1788 m/5866 ft). – There is a rewarding walk (6 hours) N from Kramsach through the gorge-like *Brandenberger Tal* to the *Erzherzog-Johann-Klause* (defile: 824 m/2704 ft).

Wörgl (511 m/1677 ft; pop. 8000; Hotel Linde, A/B, 100 b., sauna; Alte Post, A/B, 65 b.; Hotel Schachtner, B, 100 b.; Morandell, B, 100 b.) nestled in the broad lower Inn valley, at the point where the Brixenthaler Ache flows into the Inn from the SE, is a road and railway junction some 15 km/9 miles SW of Kufstein. There is a fine figure of the Virgin (*c.* 1500) in the *parish church*.

SURROUNDINGS. – 8 km/5 miles N of Wörgl is the beautiful village of *Mariastein* (563 m/1847 ft), with a pilgrimage chapel and a 14th c. castle. – S of Wörgl is the high valley (Alpine meadows) of **Wildschönau**, a popular skiing area, with the scattered commune of the same name. Chair- and ski-lifts up the surrounding heights. In *Oberau* is a small local museum. 15 km/9 miles farther up the valley is *Auffach* (875 m/2871 ft); cableway to the Schatzberg (1900 m/3282 ft). – A scenic road, accompanied by the railway, runs SW to Kitzbühel (30 km/19 miles). 10 km/6 miles from Wörgl is the little holiday resort of **Hopfgarten**, with a handsome twin-towered Rococo church (1758–64). From here a chair-lift (3 sections) ascends to the **Hohe Salve** (1829 m/6001 ft; skiing; extensive views), with a 17th c. chapel and an inn. 10 km/6 miles E of Hopfgarten is **Brixen** *im Thale* (794 m/2605 ft), with a church of 1795. Good walking country all around; winter sports resort of *Hochbrixen*.

Innviertel

Land: Upper Austria (OÖ).

ⓘ **Holiday region Innviertel – Hausruckwald,** Schärdinger Tor 3, 4910 Ried; tel. (0 77 52) 46 11.

ACCOMMODATION. – IN RIED: *Motel Ried*, B, 42 b. – IN OBERNBERG: *Goldenes Kreuz*, C, 56 b. – IN SCHÄRDING: *Schärdingerhof*, B, 85 b. – YOUTH HOSTEL. – IN FRANKENBURG: *Redltalerhof*, A, 24 b., SB, sauna. – IN AMPFLWANG: *Sporthotel Parcours*, A, 100 b., SB, SP, sauna; *Hausruckhof*, B, 105 b., sauna.

The Innviertel is an upland region of fertile and well-cultivated land lying to the S of a line from Passau to Linz, bounded on the N by the Danube, on the W by the rivers Inn and Salzach and on the S by the Hausruckwald. The area is studded with small villages and hamlets, farms and churches, in a style reminiscent of Bavaria; and in fact the Innviertel was part of Bavaria until 1779.

Ried *im Innkreis* (450 m/1476 ft; pop. 11,000), the centrally situated chief place of the Innviertel, is a busy little industrial and market town.

At Schwanthalergasse 11 is a house which belonged to the well-known 17th c. family of sculptors, the Schwanthalers, who were responsible for two altars in the parish church. Heimatmuseum (local museum) in the Innerviertler Volkskundehaus in Kirchenplatz. – 6 km/4 miles N of Ried is *Aurolzmünster*, with a Schloss built by Zuccali (1691–1711).

Obernberg *am Inn* (365 m/1198 ft) lies on the Inn (here dammed) 15 km/9 miles NW of Ried. The quiet market place with its 18th c. gabled houses recalls the time when

Marktplatz, Schärding

the little town was a staging point for the salt trade on the river.

Schärding (317 m/1040 ft; pop. 6000), situated high above the Inn 17 km/10½ miles S of Passau, has remains of its old town walls, gates, towers and Baroque houses.

The Roman Catholic parish church, originally Gothic, was remodelled in Baroque style in 1720–27. The Burgtor (1583) now houses the Municipal Museum.

In the southern part of the *Hausruckwald* (Göbelsberg, 800 m/2625 ft), to the S of Ried, is **Frankenburg** (515 m/1690 ft). The "Frankenburger Würfelspiele", performed in an open-air theatre, recall the peasant wars. The parish church is 15th c. – To the E is the village of **Ampflwang** (560 m/1837 ft), well known for riding (races, coach-drives, etc.), which is an increasingly popular resort.

In the SW of the Innviertel, 5 km/3 miles SE of *Moosdorf* is the massive Benedictine **Michaelbeuern Abbey**, dominating the village of Michaelbeuern. The abbey has a history going back more than a thousand years; Romanesque church with a famous high altar (17th c.).

To the S of the Hausruckwald, some 10 km/ 6 miles N of the Mondsee, is **Irrsdorf**, which has a Gothic church with fine carved doors of 1408.

Bad Ischl

Land: Upper Austria (OÖ).
Altitude: 469 m/1539 ft. – Population: 13,000.
Post code: A-4820.
Telephone code: 0 61 32.
ⓘ **Kurdirektion**, Bahnhofstrasse 6;
   tel. 35 20, 69 09.

ACCOMMODATION. – *Kurhotel*, A, 185 b., SB, sauna; *Goldenes Schiff*, A, 77 b.; *Schenner*, B, 58 b.; *Goldener Ochs*, B, 55 b.; *Goldenes Hufeisen*, B, 55 b.; *Stadt Salzburg*, B, 47 b. – YOUTH HOSTEL.

RECREATION and SPORTS. – Indoor swimming pool, bathing beach, golf-course (9 holes); tennis; riding; fishing.

EVENTS. – IN BAD ISCHL: *Operetta Festival* (July–Aug.). – IN BAD GOISERN: *Gamsbart-Olympiade* (at Assumption in alternate years).

The little spa of Bad Ischl, in the heart of the Salzkammergut, lies on a peninsula between the River Traun and its tributary the Ischl, surrounded by wooded hills. It was for many years the summer residence of the Emperor Francis Joseph, and much of the town shows the architectural style of the old Austro-Hungarian monarchy, when it became the rendezvous of the fashionable world of the day. Bad Ischl, a town of trim gardens and handsome villas, still attracts many visitors as a brine spa and health resort.

SIGHTS. – In the middle of the town lies Ferdinand-Auböck-Platz, with the *parish church* (Pfarrkirche, 1753). Pfarrgasse, an elegant shopping street, leads to the famous *Esplanade*, with villas dating from the Imperial period. On the opposite bank of the Traun is the *Lehár Villa*, in which Franz Lehár, composer of "The Merry Widow" and other operettas, lived from 1912 until his death in 1948 (Lehár Museum).

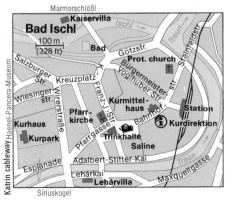

Bad Ischl, with the Imperial Villa

Katrin cableway Haenel-Pancera-Museum

To the W of the old town is the large *Kurpark*, with the *Kurhaus*. The *Treatment Complex* (Kurmittelhaus), *Brine Bath* and *Spa Administration* (Kurdirektion) are in the NE of the town. To the W of the Kurpark, at Concordiastrasse 3, is the *Haenel-Pancera Museum* (furniture, pictures, porcelain, autograph scores, etc.). On the N bank of the Ischl stands the *Imperial Villa* (Kaiservilla), the summer residence of Kaiser Franz-Josef I (visits possible), and higher up is the Marmorschlössl in which the Empress Elisabeth lived.

SURROUNDINGS. – Immediately above the town to the S is the *Siriuskogel (598 m/1962 ft), with a look-out tower; reached by chair-lift, or ¾ hour on foot. – A cableway runs up to the *Katrinalm* (upper station 1419 m/4656 ft), also to the S, from which *Hainzen* ((1639 m/5378 ft) can be climbed. – ½ hour S of Bad Ischl is the **Salt-Mine** (conducted tour, fully an hour). From here there is a good walk (1¾ hours) to the *Hütteneckalm* (1240 m/4068 ft; inn), from which experienced climbers can ascend the *Sandling* (1717 m/5633 ft: 3½ hours).

10 km/6 miles S of Bad Ischl, in the Traun valley, is **Bad Goisern** (500 m/1640 ft; Alpenhotel Muhlkogel, A, 280 b.; Kurhotel, A, 113 b.), with a sulphorous spring containing iodine. This trim little resort is popular in summer and for winter sports. Recommended climbs: *Hochkalmberg* (1833 m/6014 ft: 4 hours), *Predigtstuhl* (1278 m/4193 ft: 2¼ hours). There is also a chair-lift.

Judenburg

Land: Styria (Stm).
Altitude: 778 m/2553 ft. – Population: 11,000.
Post code: A-8750. – Telephone code: 0 35 72.
ⓘ **Fremdenverkehrsverein,**
   c/o Rasthaus F. Schaffer, Burggasse 132;
   tel. 31 41, 24 37.

ACCOMMODATION: –*Judenburger-Hütte*, B, 38 b., SB, sauna; *Reichsthaler*, B, 46 b.; *Grünhübl*, B, 32 b.

Judenburg, situated on a terrace above the right bank of the Mur, is an old Styrian hill town with a legacy of fine old buildings from its long history. The earliest record of the town dates from the 11th c. It is a good base for exploring the Seetal Alps.

SIGHTS.– In the Hauptplatz is the *Römerturm* ("Roman Tower", 1449–1509), 73 m/ 240 ft high; visitors can climb to the top. The emblem of the town is a stone Jew's head, 500 years old, on the oriel window of the Post Hotel. The town **parish church** of St Nicholas (*c*. 1500, altered in 17th and 19th c.) has two interesting figures of the Virgin, one of sandstone (*c*. 1420) in the Lady Chapel, the other of wood (16th c.).

The 14th c. *Magdalene Church* has wall paintings and beautiful stained glass of the same period.

SURROUNDINGS. – ¾ hour above the town to the E are the ruins of *Burg Liechtenstein* (12th c.), ancestral seat of the minnesinger Ulrich von Liechtenstein (d. about 1275). – From Judenburg a mountain road leads 18 km/11 miles SW up to the *Sabathy hut* (1616 m/5302 ft; refreshments), from which it is a 2 hours' climb to the summit of the *Zirbitzkogel (2397 m/7865 ft; Zirbitzkogelhaus a little way below the top). From this peak, the highest in the *Seetal Alps*, there is an extensive prospect of the whole of the Eastern Alps. 10 km/6 miles E of Judenburg, on the N bank of the Mur, lies the little industrial town of **Zeltweg** (670 m/2198 ft; steelworks). 3 km/2 miles N of the town is the *Österreichring*, a Formula One motor-racing circuit 6 km/4 miles long. – 5 km/3 miles E of Zeltweg the industrial town of **Knittelfeld** (626 m/2054 ft; pop. 15,000) has Austrian Railways workshops and a large enamel factory.

10 km/6 miles N of Knittelfeld via the village of *Kobenz* is the Benedictine *Seckau Abbey, outside the little market town of Seckau. This famous abbey, enclosed within its walls, was founded by Augustinian Canons between 1140 and 1142, dissolved in 1782 and reoccupied by Benedictines from Benediktbeuern in 1883. The present buildings mostly date from the 17th c. Beautiful arcaded courtyard; interior with rich stucco decoration; boarding school. The *Cathedral, originally Romanesque (consecrated 1164), was roofed with Gothic vaulting between 1480 and 1510 and was further altered in the 19th and 20th c. In the N aisle is the Renaissance mausoleum (1587–99) of Archduke Karl II; the choir contains a Crucifixion of the 12th–13th c. (restored in 20th c.); in the Angels' Chapel is a cycle of modern frescoes (by H. Böckl, 1952–60) depicting the Apocalypse. The abbey guestrooms have preserved their original furnishings. – There is a rewarding climb from Seckau to the summit of the *Seckauer Zinken* (2398 m/7868 ft: 5½ hours), to the N of the town, the highest point in the Seckau Alps (magnificent views).

Kaisergebirge

Land: Tirol (T).
Altitude: Highest point: Ellmauer Halt (2344 m/7691 ft).
ⓘ **Österreichischer Alpenverein,**
   Sektion Wilder Kaiser, Kaiserstrasse 26,
   A-6380 St Johann in Tirol.

The *Kaisergebirge (nature reserve), familiarly known merely as the "Kaiser", rears its mighty and precipitous walls and towers directly out of the extensive foreland region. It is covered with forest and Alpine meadows, to the N of the Kitzbühel Alps and E of the Inn, which turns N at Kufstein towards Bavaria. The towering peaks with their majestic silhouettes, separated by gloomy gorges, are of incomparable force and beauty. This wild and rugged massif is a paradise for climbers and rock-climbers.

View of the Wilder Kaiser from St Johann in Tirol

The deep *Kaisertal*, which joins the Inn valley at Kufstein, separates the **Zahmer Kaiser** ("Tame Emperor") or *Hinterer Kaiser* (*c.* 2000 m/6560 ft), with the *Vorderer Kesselschneid* and the magnificent *Pyramidenspitze*, from the **Wilder Kaiser** ("Wild Emperor") or *Vorderer Kaiser*, the highest point of which, the *Ellmauer Halt* (2344 m/ 7691 ft), with its three jagged peaks, can be climbed either from the Anton-Karg-Haus at Hinterbärenbad in the Kaisertal or from the S by way of the Grutten-Hütte (1620 m/ 5315 ft) at Ellmau. Keen rock-climbers will make their base at the Stripsenjoch hut (1580 m/5184 ft), immediately below the N face of the difficult *Totenkirchl* (2193 m/ 7195 ft). From here the route descends through the dark Steinerne to the Gaudeamus hut (1270 m/4167 ft) near Ellmau.

The **Walchsee**, with the village of the same name, in an open landscape of forest and Alpine meadows, is one of Tirol's larger lakes. Smaller, but of rare beauty, is the *Hintersteiner See* (892 m/2927 ft), under the SW face of the Wilder Kaiser, which mirrors in its clear water the rock walls of the *Scheffauer* (2113 m/6933 ft).

Kaprun

Land: Salzburg (S).
Altitude: 786 m/2579 ft. – Population: 2600.
Post code: A-5710. – Telephone code: 0 65 47.
(i) **Verkehrsverein**, Salzburger Platz;
tel. 86 43 and 86 44.

ACCOMMODATION. – *Sporthotel*, A, 108 b., sauna; *Kapruner Hof*, A, 45 b., sauna; *Tauernhof*, A/B, 100 b.; *Zur Mühle*, A/B, 64 b., SB, sauna; *Burgruine*, A/B, 50 b., SB, sauna; *Hubertus*, A/B, 43 b., sauna; *Orgler*, B, 50 b., sauna; *Glatscherblick*, B, 28 b., sauna. – YOUTH HOSTEL. – CAMPING SITE.

RECREATION and SPORT. – Winter and water-sports; tennis; riding; flying; golf (18 holes).

The mountain village of Kaprun, now a summer and winter sports resort, lies SW of Salzburg at the mouth of the Kapruner Tal in the Hohe Tauern. Together with Saalbach and Zell am See it is part of the so-called "Europa-Sport-Region", a good centre for mountain walks and climbs, with ample scope for skiers, including summer skiing on the Kitzsteinhorn. Kaprun developed into a place of some consequence only after the construction of the impressive hydroelectric scheme, the Tauernkraftwerk Glockner-Kaprun, from 1939 onwards.

The *Kapruner Tal* (Kaprun valley). – The beautiful *Kesselstrasse* (maximum gradient 12%) along the right bank of the *Kapruner Ache*, passes the works village and the large *Kaprun-Hauptstufe power station*, which harnesses the water power of the extensive glacier areas of the Hohe Tauern. On the mountainside can be seen the massive pipes bringing down the water under pressure from the Maiskogel. The road then winds its way up the slopes of the Bürgkogel (950 m/ 3117 ft), which blocks the valley. – 2 km/ 1¼ miles from Kaprun, on the right, is the lower station (832 m/2730 ft) of the cableway up the **Maiskogel** (1552 m/5092 ft; Naturfreunde hut), from which there is a superb view, extending as far as the Grossglockner. – The road continues up a high valley, passing the small *Klamm reservoir*. Ahead can be seen the huge wall of the Limberg dam. – 6·5 km/ 4 miles from Kaprun the road comes to the large car parks of *Kaprun-Thörl*, with the lower stations of a cableway and a funicular. The cableway, *Gletscherbahn Kaprun 1* (928 m/3045 ft), runs up SW in three stages, via the Salzburger Hütte (1897 m/6224 ft) and the Alpincenter (2452 m/8045 ft; hotel; ski-lifts; cableway to the Schmiedinger Grat (2755 m/9039 ft), near the Krefelder Hütte (2294 m/7527 ft), to the *Kitzsteinhorn* (3202 m/10,506 ft). The upper station, on the Nordwestgrat (3029 m/9938 ft), has a self-service restaurant; viewing tunnel in the Schmiedinger Gletscher; skiing all year round, with several ski-lifts; safeguarded footpath to the summit (1½ hours). The funicular, *Gletscherbahn Kaprun 2* (911 m/ 2989 ft), 4 km/2½ miles long (600 m/650 yds on a steel bridge, 3·3 km/2 miles in a tunnel), goes up to the Alpincenter near the Krefelder Hütte. – 1·5 km/1 mile farther on is the *Limbergstollen car park* (983 m/3225 ft), from which a lift in an inclined shaft, the Limbergstollen (3 km/2 miles long), gives access to the Limberg dam. Here application can be made to visit the dam installations and the power stations. – The road continues steeply uphill, with many windings and to hairpin turns, to the **Kesselfall-Alpenhaus** (1068 m/3504 ft), beautifully set in a wooded defile; below, to the right, are the *Kessel falls*. To the SW (7–8 hours) is the Kitzsteinhorn (cableway: see above). – The *Lärchwandstrasse* which continues from here (mail buses only: shuttle service) runs through forest, then comes out into the open and continues uphill in sharp turns and through a tunnel to the end of the road

(1210 m/3970 ft), 10 km/6 miles from Kaprun. From here a lift goes up by way of an intermediate station on the *Königstuhl* (1560 m/5118 ft), where a road goes off (1·5 km/1 mile) to the *Limberg power station* (1573 m/5161 ft), to the upper station on the Lärchwand (1641 m/5384 ft). The *Mooserbodenstrasse* (maximum gradient 12%: works bus) leads up from here, passes through two tunnels and comes in 1 km/¾ mile to the Limberg dam (120 m/395 ft high), at the N end of the *Wasserfallboden* **reservoir** (1672 m/5486 ft; magnificent views), which has a capacity of 84·5 million cubic metres/18,587 million gallons. The road continues for another 5 km/3 miles, at first running along the W side of the reservoir (fine view of the head of the valley) and then climbing in two sharp turns to the "*Heidnische Kirche*" ("Pagan Church", 2051 m/6729 ft). This was a secret meeting-place for Protestants during the Counter-Reformation. Here the road comes to an end, with a fine view to the rear over the reservoir towards the Steinernes Meer.

The *Mooserboden reservoir* (2036 m/ 6680 ft), formed by the *Mooser* and *Drossen dams*, has a capacity of 85·4 million cubic metres/18,785 million gallons and is linked with the Margaritze reservoir on the Glockner Road by a tunnel 11·5 km/7 miles long. From the *Höhenburg* (2108 m/6916 ft), between the two dams, there is a superb panoramic *view of the surrounding mountains and glaciers, with the tremendous rock wall of the *Karlinger Kees* in the middle ground; Berghaus Mooserboden (2044 m/6706 ft; Alpine climbing school). There is a good climb – for experienced climbers only, with guide – by way of the Heinrich-Schwaiger-Haus (2082 m/6831 ft; accommodation) to the summit of the *Gross Wiesbachhorn* (3564 m/11,693 ft: 5–5½ hours), which commands magnificent distant views.

The Mooserboden reservoir, near Kaprun

Karawanken

Land: Carinthia (K).
ⓘ **Landesfremdenverkehrsamt,**
Kaufmanngasse 13, A-9010 Klagenfurt;
tel. (0 42 22) 55 48 80.

The rocky Karawanken range, with numerous separate peaks, continues the line of the Carnic Alps eastward, and since 1919 has formed the frontier between Austria and Yugoslavia. This

long ridge extending between the valleys of the Drau (Drava) and Save lacks the rugged conformation of the Carnic Alps, but consists of a series of finely shaped mountains falling steeply away on the N side. Most of the principal peaks are relatively easy to climb and command magnificent views of the Carinthian lake basin; and there are a number of ridge walks which enable several peaks to be climbed without losing too much height. The highest point in the Karawanken is the Hochstuhl (2238 m/7343 ft).

There are several important *routes through the Alps* in the Karawanken range. The road from Klagenfurt to Ljubljana in Yugoslavia runs under the Loibl pass (1369 m/4492 ft) in the *Loibl Tunnel*; at the W end of the range the *Wurzen pass* (1073 m/3521 ft) carries the road from the Gailtal into the Valley of the Sava Dolinka (Yugoslavia), and at the E end the *Seeberg saddle* (1218 m/3916 ft) links Eastern Carinthia with Slovenia. The railway runs under the Rosenbach saddle in the 8 km/6 mile long *Karawanken Tunnel* between Rosenbach and Jesenice in Yugoslavia; a road tunnel is under construction.

From *Ferlach* (446 m/1529 ft), on the northern approach to the Loibl pass, a steep and narrow road climbs 15 km/9 miles S (toll payable beyond Zell) to a point near the main ridge of the Karawanken, ending at the *Koschutahaus* (1279 m/4196 ft; inn), with tremendous *views of the surrounding limestone peaks and crags. A climbing school is based here.

6 km/4 miles before the summit tunnel on the Loibl Road is the *Kleiner Loibl* (759 m/2490 ft), with the St Christopher or

Magdalene Chapel. – A side road runs W by way of Windisch Bleiberg into the beautiful *Bodental*.

Beyond this, near the entrance to the Loibl Tunnel, the road crosses the wild and romantic *Tscheppaschlucht* (gorge). A 5 minutes' climb from here leads up to the *Tschaukofall* (30 m/100 ft high).

The Loibl pass (1369 m/4492 ft) can be easily reached, and is a magnificent viewpoint; but since the opening of the road tunnel in 1964 there has been no frontier crossing point on the pass. The **Loibl Tunnel**, 1·6 km/1 mile long, runs under the pass at a height of 1070 m/3511 ft.

A succession of constantly changing views of the whole range can be enjoyed from the *Karawanken Panoramic Highway* (Karawanken-Aussichtsstrasse), which branches off the road from Klagenfurt to the Loibl pass at Viktring and runs SW along the Drau to Velden on the Wörther See.

Standing high above the Drau near *Maria Rain* (Baroque pilgrimage church) is *Schloss Hollenburg*, a stud farm noted for its Haflinger horses.

A popular base for walks and climbs in the Karawanken is *Feistritz im Rosental* (545 m/1788 ft; pop. 3000), at the mouth of the 6·5 km/4 mile long *Bärental*, through which a road climbs up, with many turns, to *Bärental* village (950 m/3117 ft) at the head of the valley. The *Klagenfurter Hütte* (1663 m/5456 ft; inn) can be reached in 2 hours; the highest peak in the Karawanken, the **Hochstyhl** (Slovenian *Veliki Stol*, 2238 m/7343 ft), on the Yugoslav side, in another 2½ hours.

Karwendel

Land: Tirol (T).
(i) **Österreichischer Alpenverein,**
   Sektion Innsbruck, AV-Haus,
   Wilhelm-Greil-Strasse 15, A-6020 Innsbruck;
   tel. (0 52 22) 2 78 28.

The *Karwendel range, part of the Calcareous Alps of Tirol and Bavaria, lies between the Seefeld saddle, the Isar valley, the Achensee and the Inn valley. Once noted for its abundant wildlife and now a nature reserve, it is a region of massive rock walls and high corries. The highest peak is the

An Alpine meadow in the Bodental, below the Karawanken

Birkkarspitze (2749 m/9019 ft), the only permanent settlement the hamlet of Hinteriss, which is accessible only from the N (Bavaria).

The Karwendel is made up of four parallel and much indented mountain chains with deeply slashed longitudinal and transverse valleys. Many of the peaks can be climbed fairly easily on good paths, but some have stretches graded as difficult and very difficult.

The most southerly of the four chains, the Solsteinkette, rises directly above the Inn valley, overlooking Innsbruck. Every visitor to Innsbruck is familiar with the famous view from Maria-Theresien-Strasse of the snow-capped mountains of the "Nordkette" (North Chain) which give the city its characteristic backdrop. The Innsbruck Nordkettenbahn (cableway) runs up by way of the Seegrube intermediate station (1900 m/6235 ft) to the summit of *Hafelekar* (2334 m/7658 ft; wide views). The highest and most westerly peak in the Solsteinkette is the *Solstein* (2633 m/8639 ft), with the legendary Martinswand falling vertically down to the Inn valley. – The most notable peak in the second chain is the mighty *Grosse Bettelwurfspitze* (2725 m/8941 ft), one of the finest viewpoints in Tirol. – In the third chain, the Hintere Karwendel-kette, are the regularly shaped pyramid of the *Birkkarspitze* (2749 m/9019 ft), above the Karwendelhaus (1790 m/5873 ft), and the magnificent *Lamsenspitze* (2501 m/8206 ft), which in spite of its imposing appearance is easy to climb. – The principal peaks in the fourth chain, the Vordere Karwendelkette, are the *Östliche Karwendel-spitze* (2539 m/8330 ft) and the *Westliche Karwendelspitze* (2385 m/7825 ft), which present no difficulties to experienced climbers.

From Hinterriss a toll road runs up to the *Grosser Ahornboden (1216 m/3990 ft), in the heart of the Karwendel, an area of Alpine meadows which attracts many visitors (mountain hut).

From Mittenwald in Bavaria there is a cabin cableway to the *Westliche Karwendel-spitze (2385 m/7825 ft).

At the W end of the Karwendel range, on the pass road from Mittenwald to the Zirler Berg, is the well-known summer and winter sports resort of **Seefeld** (see p. 177) and the less fashionable resort of *Scharnitz* (964 m/3163 ft), a good base for walkers and climbers. A road (closed to cars) runs NE to the *Karwendelhaus* (1765 m/5971 ft; inn), which can also be reached on foot in 5 hours; and from there the *Birkkarspitze (2749 m/9019 ft) can be climbed in 3½ hours. – To the E there is a 5 hours' walk through the Hinterau valley to the *Hallerangerhaus* (1768 m/5801 ft; inn), near which is the source of the *River Isar*. From there the *Speckkarspitze* (2621 m/8600 ft) can be climbed in 3 hours, the **Grosse Bettel-wurfspitze** (2725 m/8941 ft) in 5 hours.

Among the lakes in the Karwendel is the little *Wildsee*, in a beautiful open setting at Seefeld on the Mittenwaldbahn cableway. A short distance away is the tiny *Möserer See*. The **Achensee**, below the E end of the Kar-wendel range, is Tirol's largest and most beautiful lake, attracting many visitors to the well-known summer resorts – including Pertisau, Maurach, Eben and Scholastika – set round its turquoise-blue waters.

To the E of the Achensee is the **Sonnen-wendgebirge** (*Rofan group*), which reaches its highest point in *Hochiss* (2299 m/7543 ft). On the eastern slopes of the meadow-covered *Rofanspitze* (2260 m/7415 ft) lies the lonely little *Zireiner See*.

Kauner Tal

Land: Tirol (T).

ⓘ **Gemeindeamt Prutz,** A-6522 Prutz; tel. (0 54 72) 62 67.

ACCOMMODATION. – IN PRUTZ: *Post*, D, 56 b.

The Kauner Tal is a lateral valley, 28 km/17 miles long, on the right bank of the upper Inn, traversed by the Faggenbach. There is a road (maximum

Scharnitz, in the Karwendel range

gradient 14%) up the valley from Prutz, open to ordinary traffic as far as the Gepatsch reservoir.

Prutz (866 m/2841 ft; pop. 1300) is a little summer resort on the upper Inn, with a hydroelectric station using water which is piped down from the Gepatsch reservoir 13 km/8 miles away. – 3 km/2 miles and 10 km/6 miles W of Prutz, on a terrace above the Inn, are the mountain resorts of *Ladis* (1190 m/3904 ft) and *Obladis* (1386 m/4547 ft), both with sulphurous mineral springs.

From Prutz the road runs past the village of *Kauns* and continues up the valley, passing the ruins of the 13th c. *Burg Berneck*, above the road on the left, and soon afterwards Grimstein, with the *church of Mariä Himmel-fahrt* (the Assumption). – 8 km/5 miles beyond the village of *Feichten* (1289 m/4230 ft) the dam of the Gepatsch reservoir is reached. From here a toll-road about 15 km/9 miles long leads to the summer ski area on the Weisseeferner (lifts).

The **Gepatsch reservoir** (dam 630 m/670 yds long and 130 m/430 ft high) is 6 km/4 miles long and has a capacity of 140 million cubic metres/30,795 million gallons. A narrow road 8·6 km/5 miles long skirts the lake to the *Gepatsch-Alm* (2000 m/6560 ft) at the head of the valley. To the S is the *Gepatschferner*, some 10 km/6 miles long, the second largest glacier in the Eastern Alps. From the *Gepatschhaus* (1928 m/6326 ft; accommodation) the *Weisseespitze* (3526 m/11,569 ft), on the Italian frontier, can be climbed (road to the Weisseeferner; guides).

CASINO. – in Goldener Greif Hotel (roulette, baccarat, blackjack: daily from 7 p.m.).

EVENTS. – *International races on the Hahnenkamm* (third weekend in Jan.); *Koasa run* (beginning Feb.); *Kitzbühel Fair* and *Kitzbühel Head Cup* (beginning Aug.); *International mountain road run on the Kitzbühler Horn* and *International golf tournament* (end Aug.).

RECREATION and SPORTS. – Riding; indoor swimming pool; golf-course (9 holes); tennis; winter sports; climbing school.

Kitzbühel is one of the largest and best known winter sports resorts in Austria. Chief town of a district, with a long history, it lies in a wide basin in the valley of the Kitzbüheler Ache, on the busy road from St Johann to the Thurn pass. Kitzbühel rose to prosperity in the 16th and 17th c. thanks to its copper- and silver-mines: it is now a

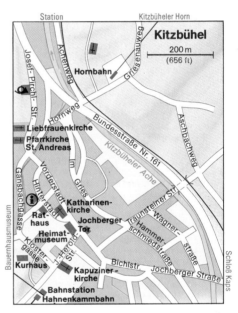

Kitzbühel

Land: Tirol (T).
Altitude: 763 m/2053 ft. – Population: 8000.
Post code: A-6370. – Telephone code: 0 53 56.
ⓘ **Fremdenverkehrsverband,** Hinterstadt 18; tel. 21 55.

ACCOMMODATION. – *Schloss Lebenberg*, A1, 200 b., SB, sauna; *Tiefenbrunner*, A1, 120 b., SB, sauna; *Tennerhof*, A1, 75 b., SB, sauna; *Goldener Greif*, A1, 100 b., sauna; *Parkhotel*, A, 180 b., SP, sauna; *Erika*, A, 74 b., SB, sauna; *Seebichl*, A/B, 80 b.; *Montana*, A/B, 80 b., SB, sauna; *Schweizerhof*, A/B, 62 b.; *Strasshofer*, B, 45 b., sauna; *Hofer*, B, 43 b., sauna; *Hahnenhof*, B, 34 b.; *Alpina*, B/C, 48 b.; *Christopherus* (no rest.), B/C, 40 b. – *Ehrenbachhöhe*, A1, 90 b., SB, sauna, on the Ehrenbachhöhe (1085 m/5922 ft), chair-lift from the upper station of the Hahnerkamm cableway. – CAMPING SITE.

Kitzbühel, looking south

fashionable resort ("Kitz") catering for an international public.

SIGHTS. – The old core of the town, built on a long ridge of hills, consists of two streets of handsome old gabled houses, *Vorderstadt* and *Hinterstadt*. Between the two streets is *St Catherine's Church* (Katharinenkirche, 14th c.), with a winged altarpiece of 1520. At the S end of the old town are the 16th c. *Pfleghof* (of which a corner tower and a staircase tower are preserved), the *Jochberger Tor*, a 15th c. town gate, and a *Heimatmuseum* (local museum). At the N end stands the **parish church** (*Pfarrkirche St Andreas*), with 15th c. frescoes in the choir; on the S side of the choir is the *Rosakapelle*. Just N of this is the small two-storey *Liebfrauenkirche* (lower church built 1373; in the upper church are ceiling paintings by the Kitzbühel artist Simon Benedikt Faistenberger, 1739). – To the SE of the town is the 17th c. *Schloss Kaps*, to the NW the 16th c. *Schloss Lebenberg* (hotel).

SURROUNDINGS. – The town lies between the Hahnenkamm to the SW and the Kitzbüheler Horn to the NE, both accessible throughout the year by cableway and both affording magnificent views.

The *Hahnenkamm (1655 m/5430 ft, 900 m/2950 ft above Kitzbühel; cableway, numerous ski-lifts) offers the attractions of its mountain air, its beautiful walking country and its excellent skiing terrain. Chapel designed by Clemens Holzmeister (1959). On the N side is the *Seidl-Alm* (1206 m/3957 ft; inn; 1¼ hours' climb from Kitzbühel), from which the summit ridge can be reached in 1½ hours. There is also an attractive walk (½ hour) from the upper station of the cableway to the *Ehrenbachhöhe* (1805 m/ 5922 ft), with panoramic views. From here it is another ½ hour to the *Steinbergkogel* (1960 m/6431 ft; restaurant; also reached by chair-lift from the Ehrenbachgraben), or 1½ hours to the *Pengelstein* (1940 m/6365 ft; inn).

The **Kitzbüheler Horn, NE of Kitzbühel (1998 m/ 6555 ft; Gipfelhaus, chapel, restaurant, radio mast), can be reached by cableway via the *Pletzeralm* (1273 m/ 4177 ft) or can be climbed from Kitzbühel in 4–5 hours. From the summit there are glorious views – to the S from the Radstädter Tauern to the Ötztal Alps, to the N the nearby Kaisergebirge, away in the W the Lechtal Alps, to the E the Hochkönig. To the S of the Kitzbüheler Horn is the *Hornköpfli* (1772 m/5814 ft), also reached by cableway.

With numerous cableways and ski-lifts, the Kitzbühel area is a Mecca for skiers in winter, the whole complex of facilities being known as the "Kitzbüheler Skizirkus". Linked with the Kitzbühel "ski circus" are the cableways, ski-lifts and pistes of Aschau, Aurach, Jochberg, Pass Thurn and Kirchberg, from which the extensive skiing areas on the Hahnenkamm and Kitzbüheler Horn can also be reached.

2 km/1¼ miles NW of Kitzbühel is the *Schwarzsee* (799 m/ 2622 ft; bathing), and 1·5 km/1 mile beyond this is the 15th c. *Schloss Münichau* (hotel).

10 km/6 miles N of Kitzbühel is **St Johann** *in Tirol* (660 m/2165 ft; pop. 6000; Hotel Goldener Löwe, A,

200 b.; Sporthotel Austria, A, 100 b., SB, sauna; Crystal, A, 82 b., sauna; Fischer, A, 72 b., sauna; Moser, B, 78 b.; Dorfschmiede, B, 60 b.; Europa, B, 50 b.), a popular summer and winter sports resort, with picturesque old peasant houses, and an important road junction. The *parish church of Maria Himmelfahrt* (the Assumption; 1723–28) has fine stucco-work and a ceiling painting by Simon Benedikt Faistenberger; *St Anthony's Chapel* has a fresco in the dome by Josef Schöpf (1803). W of the town is the *Spitalkirche in der Weitau*, with a Rococo interior of 1740 and fine 15th c. stained glass. St Johann has a large leisure complex with an open-air swimming pool and sports facilities; funicular and chair-lift up the Kitzbüheler Horn, to the S.

11 km/7 miles SE of St Johann, in the valley of the *Pillersee-Ache*, is the spa and winter sports resort of **Fieberbrunn** (800 m/2626 ft; Schlosshotel Rosenegg, A, 150 b.; Alte Post, B, 120 b.). Chair-lift up the *Lärchfilzkogel* (1660 m/5446 ft). Rewarding climb (4¼ hours) to the S, via the *Lärchfilz-Hochalm* (1364 m/4475 ft; Touristenhaus), to the *Wildseeloder* (2119 m/6952 ft), with magnificent panoramic views. – 10 km/6 miles N of Fieberbrunn on the road to Waidring is the beautiful *Pillersee* (834 m/2736 ft).

Kitzbühel Alps

Länder: Tirol (T) and Salzburg (S).
Altitude: Highest point: Kreuzjoch (2558 m/8393 ft).

ⓘ **Österreichischer Alpenverein,**
Sektion Kitzbühel, Sonnental 18,
A-6380 St Johann in Tirol.

The *Kitzbühel Alps lie to the N of the Pinzgautal, the valley of the River Salzach, which separates them from the Hohe Tauern. They are the largest range of schist mountains in Austria, extending in a series of gently rounded ridges for some 100 km/65 miles, with treeless or sparsely wooded Alpine meadows sloping down from the summits into the numerous longitudinal and transverse valleys. This conformation has made the Kitzbühel Alps one of the largest and most popular skiing areas in Austria, and indeed in Europe.

Although the mountains are lower here than in other parts of the Alps there are numerous peaks affording superb far-ranging views which attract many summer visitors. The highest summits and the most strikingly formed massifs are to be found at the western end of the range, in the ridge which runs E from the **Kreuzjoch** (2558 m/8393 ft), near Gerlos, and round a desolate lake-filled hollow to the *Torhelm* (2495 m/8186 ft), and then bears N by way of various lesser peaks to the *Grosser Galtenberg (2425 m/7956 ft) near Alpbach, and in the **Salzachgeier** (2470 m/8104 ft).

The most striking peak in the Kitzbühel Alps is the *Grosser Rettenstein (2363 m/7753 ft), which can be climbed from the Oberland hut (1041 m/3417 ft) near Aschau. From its summit there is a fine ridge walk S to the Wildkogel-Haus (2007 m/6585 ft) near Neukirchen on the Grossvenediger.

During the skiing season the mountains in the immediate vicinity of Kitzbühel are thronged with skiers from all over the world, who are catered for by numerous cableways and ski-lifts on the slopes of the **Kitzbüheler Horn (1998 m/6555 ft), above St Johann to the NE, and the *Hahnenkamm (1655 m/5430 ft) and the Steinbergkogel (1970 m/6464 ft) to the SW.

A good viewpoint in the eastern Kitzbühel Alps is the Wildseeloder (2117 m/6946 ft), which can be reached from Fieberbrunn by way of the Wildseeloder-Haus on the little Wildsee. – Famous for its extensive panoramic views is the **Schmittenhöhe (1965 m/6447 ft), in the SE of the range, which can be reached by cableway from Zell am See. From there fit walkers can do the "Pinzgau walk" (Pinzgauer Spaziergang) westward to the *Geisstein (2363 m/7753 ft), taking in twelve peaks and following the ridge above the S side of the magnificent Saalbach skiing area.

In the Kitzbühel Alps

The valleys of the Kitzbühel Alps contain two very beautiful lakes – the little Schwarzsee (779 m/2556 ft), enchantingly situated below the cliffs of the Kaisergebirge, and the *Zeller See (750 m/2460 ft), one of the most beautiful lakes in the Salzburg Alps, with the glaciers of the Hohe Tauern mirrored in its waters.

Klagenfurt

Land: Carinthia (K).
Altitude: 445 m/1460 ft.
Population: 87,300.
Post code: A-9020.
Telephone code: 0 42 22.
ⓘ Fremdenverkehrsamt, Rathaus;
tel. 537–223, 224.
Europapark Tourist Complex (May–Sept.);
tel. 2 36 51.

ACCOMMODATION. – *Musil, 10-Oktober-Str. 14, A1, 29 b., SB, sauna; Moser-Verdino, Domgasse 2, A, 140 b., sauna; Dermuth, Kohldorferstr. 52, 80 b., SB, sauna; Porcia, Neuer Platz 13, A, 80 b.; Sandwirt, Pernhartgasse 9, A, 80 b.; Europapark, Villacher Str. 222, A, 60 b.; Goldener Brunnen, Karfreistr. 14, A, 38 b.; Carinthia, 8-Mai-Str. 41, A, 54 b.; Wörthersee, Villacher-Str. 338, B, 60 b., sauna; Hopf, Waidmannsdorferstr. 57, B, 50 b.; Blumenstöckl, 10-Oktober-Str. 11, B, 27 b. – YOUTH HOSTEL, Kumpfgasse 20. – CAMPING SITES.

RESTAURANTS. – In most hotels; also Ascot, Kramergasse; Maria Loretto, Loretta Peninsula; Volkskeller, Bahnhofstr.; Schweizerhaus, Kreuzbergl.

RECREATION and SPORTS. – Several open-air pools on Wörther See (naturist area in Loretto); fishing; watersports (sailing school); leisure complex in Europapark; artificial ice rink; tennis; riding.

EVENTS. Gastronomy and Tourism Trade Fair (March); Trade Fair for the Leisure Industry (Apr.); Klagenfurt Fair – Austrian Timber and Woodworking Fair (Aug.); lake festivals, sailing regattas, excursions on the Wörther See.

Klagenfurt, capital of Carinthia, lies on the edge of the wide Klagenfurt basin, which is bounded on the S by the wooded ridge of the Sassnitz range, with the Karawanken rearing up behind. Although Klagenfurt is an important traffic junction and a busy industrial and commercial town, it has an attractive old quarter with picturesque little lanes and historic old buildings. It is also a university town.

HISTORY. – Klagenfurt was founded about 1161 as a market village and was granted a municipal charter in 1252. The old town was destroyed by fire in 1514, whereupon the provincial Estates of Carinthia petitioned the Emperor Maximilian I to grant them possession of the now impoverished little town. It was duly transferred to their ownership in 1518, and Klagenfurt then displaced St Veit an der Glau as capital of the province and began to expand. Between 1527 and 1558 a canal was constructed to supply water for the moat surrounding the town, and this still links Klagenfurt with the Wörther See. The line of the old fortification is marked by a circuit of streets, the Ring, round the old part of the town.

SIGHTS. – In the middle of the oldest part of the town is a long street known as the *Alter Platz*, with a Trinity Column (1681) and many handsome Baroque buildings. Among these are the 17th c. *Altes Rathaus* (Old Town Hall), with a picturesque three-storey arcaded courtyard, and the *Haus zur Goldenen Gans* (Golden Goose: *c.* 1500).

To the N is the **parish church** of St Egyd or Giles (*Stadtpfarrkirche*), a handsome but rather gloomy building of the 17th–18th c., with many gravestones on the external walls. From the 91 m/300 ft high tower with its onion dome there are extensive views. The church has a trompe-l'œil ceiling painting. Between the Alter Platz and the Heiligen-geistplatz stands Klagenfurt's most imposing secular building, the **Landhaus**, built in 1574–90 on the site of an earlier moated ducal castle, with two onion-domed stair-case towers and a two-storey arcaded courtyard. The fine Heraldic Hall (Grosser Wappensaal) was built in 1739–40 after a fire; on the walls are 665 coats of arms belonging to members of the Carinthian

Estates; trompe-l'œil ceiling painting. There are 298 more coats of arms in the Lesser Heraldic Hall (Kleiner Wappensaal). In the garden are Roman stones with inscriptions.

The central feature of the newer part of the town is the spacious *Neuer Platz*, with the massive ***Dragon Fountain*** (*Lindwurm-brunnen*), the heraldic emblem of Klagenfurt. This huge piece of sculpture was carved by Ulrich Vogelsang about 1590 out of a single block of chloritic schist. Legend has it that the town was built on a swamp inhabited by a dragon, which was slain. The model for the dragon's head was the skull of a woolly-haired rhinoceros found near the town (now in the Provincial Museum). The figure of Hercules and the iron railings were added in 1636. – On the W side of the square is the former Palais Rosenberg (mid 17th c.), now the *Rathaus*. In front of it stands a bronze statue of the Empress Maria Theresa (1873).

At Burggasse 8 (once the residence of the governor of the castle) is the *Provincial Art Gallery* (Landesgalerie), with a collection of pictures and sculpture.

SE of the Neuer Platz is the **Cathedral** (*Domkirche*), built by the Protestant Estates of Carinthia in 1578–91. It was handed over to the Jesuits in 1604, and from 1787 was the cathedral of the Prince-Bishop

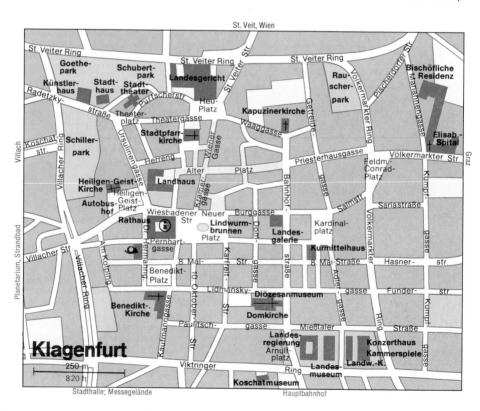

of Gurk, who resided in Klagenfurt. The interior has rich stucco decoration and wall and ceiling paintings (18th c.); pulpit of 1726; painting on high altar by Daniel Gran (1752). – In the Domplatz is the *Gurk Diocesan museum* (vestments, religious art, altarpieces, stained glass).

SE of the middle of the town lies Arnulfplatz, on the E side of which is the handsome building occupied by the Provincial Government (*Landesregierung*). Immediately E of this is the ***Provincial Museum** (*Landesmuseum*), built in 1879–84, with rich collections of material on the natural history, art and life of Carinthia, and also on the history of the town (including a model of Klagenfurt as it was about 1800). Particularly notable among the medieval items are the "Fürstenstein" (Prince's Stone) from Karnburg, on which until 1414 the duke elected by the peasantry was enthroned, and the ceremonial sword of the Knights of St George from Millstatt (1499). Items of interest in the natural history section include the rhinoceros skull which provided the model for the Dragon Fountain and relief models of the Grossglockner, the Villach Alps and the Eastern Karawanken. In the garden are Roman gravestones and votive stones from *Virunum* in the Zollfeld and other sites.

To the E of the Museum is the *Concert Hall* (Konzerthaus), which also houses the Little Theatre (Kammerspiele).

S of Arnulfplatz, on the far side of the Viktringer Ring, the *Koschat Museum* houses relics and mementoes of the Klagenfurt composer Thomas Koschat (1845–1914), author of many lieder.

Dragon Fountain, Klagenfurt

NW of the central area of the town, on the edge of a group of parks, are the *Municipal Theatre* (Stadttheater: opera, operettas, plays), the *Stadthaus* and the *Artists' House* (Künstlerhaus: exhibitions). To the NE is the *Bishop's Palace* (Bischöfliche Residenz), built at the end of the 18th c. as a palace for the Emperor Joseph II's sister.

To the S of the town are the *Stadthalle*, the *Messegelände* (Exhibition Grounds) and the *railway station*.

SURROUNDINGS. – The **Kreuzbergl** (515 m/1690 ft), NW of the town, is a recreation area with numerous footpaths. At the foot of the hill can be found the interesting *Botanic Garden*, which specialises in the plants, rocks and minerals of Carinthia. Here, too, is a *Mining Museum*. On the hill is a look-out tower housing a *"People's Observatory"*.

4 km/2½ miles W of the town, on the Wörther See, is the outlying district of Klagenfurt-See, with a water-skiing school and boat landing-stages. In the *Europapark* are a mini-golf course, many works of modern sculpture and ***Minimundus**, a miniature town with models of well-known buildings reduced to $\frac{1}{25}$ of their size and railway and port installations on the same scale, as well as a space-flight planetarium and a reptile zoo.

5 km/3 miles SE of Klagenfurt, on the Glan, is *Ebenthal* (427 m/1401 ft), with an 18th c. Schloss and parish church. To the SW is the *Predigerstuhl* (713 m/2339 ft; 1¼ hours' climb).

6 km/4 miles SW of the town is **Viktring** (454 m/1490 ft), now part of Klagenfurt, with a Cistercian abbey founded in 1142 and dissolved in 1786. Two beautiful arcaded courtyards; early Gothic church with Burgundian pointed vaulting; fine stained glass of about 1400 in the choir.

Kleinwalsertal

Land: Vorarlberg (V).

Verkehrsamt Kleinwalsertal,
Walserstrasse 54,
A-6991/D-8984 Riezlern;
tel. from Austria (0 55 17) 51 15,
from Germany (0 83 29) 51 15.

ACCOMMODATION. – IN RIEZLERN: *Sporthotel,* A, 132 apartments with about 400 b., SB, sauna; *Erlebach,* A, 100 b., SB, sauna; *Stern,* A, 73 b., SP, sauna; *Almhof Rupp,* A, 49 b., SB, sauna; *Riezlerhof,* B, 46 b.; *Traube,* B, 43 b.; *Post,* B, 41 b.; *Alpin Appartmenthaus,* C, 52 b. – Many CAMPING SITES. – IN HIRSCHEGG: **Ifenhotel,* A1, 120 b., SB, sauna; *Walserhof,* A, 60 b., SB, sauna; *Adler,* B, 43 b.; *Schuster,* B, 31 b.; *Haus Tanneneck,* B, 27 b., SB. – IN MITTELBERG: *Alte Krone,* A, 55 b., SB, sauna; IBG *Apart Hotel,* B, 609 b., SB, sauna; *Rosenhof* (apartments), B, 90 b., SB, sauna; *Alpenrose,* B, 76 b.; *Neue Krone,* B, 52 b.; *Alpinum,* B, 40 b., SB, sauna; *Pühringer,* in Baad, B, 52 b., sauna; *Haus Höft* (no rest.) in Baad, B, 36 b., SB, sauna. – CAMPING SITE.

CASINO. – In Riezlern (roulette, baccarat, blackjack: open daily from 5 p.m.).

RECREATION and SPORTS. – Tennis; riding; walking; climbing school in Mittelberg; winter sports.

The *Kleinwalsertal (Little Walser Valley) – to be distinguished from the Grosswalsertal (Great Walser Valley) N of Bludenz beyond the Bregenzer Wald – is in Vorarlberg province but has no road connections with the rest of the province, being cut off by the surrounding mountains. It thus lies within the German customs and economic area and uses German currency. The people of the valley came here about 1300 from the Swiss canton of Valais and have preserved many distinctive characteristics down to the present day.

This wide valley, watered by the *Breitach*, with rugged limestone peaks rearing above the valley sides with their sparse covering of forest, is one of the best known and most attractive of Austria's mountain valleys, and its widely scattered villages attract many visitors, who come in summer for the healthy mountain air and in winter for the snow

Mittelberg, in the Kleinwalsertal

which can always be relied upon here. The commune, made up of four separate parts (Riezlern, Hirschegg, Mittelberg and Baad), has a population of some 5000.

The starting-point of a visit to the Kleinwalsertal is Oberstdorf. – 6 km/4 miles up the valley, at the Walser Schanz Inn, is the German-Austrian frontier. Beyond this there are fine views of the Hoher Ifen and the Gottesackerwände, with the Widderstein (2533 m/7720 ft) in the background.

The first place of any size is Riezlern; then follow Hirschegg and Mittelberg; and at the head of the valley, 14 km/8½ miles beyond the frontier, is Baad.

Near the frontier, at the Walser Schanz (991 m/3251 ft), is the upper entrance to the *Breitachklamm* (gorge). A footpath, with numerous bridges and galleries, runs between rock walls up to 100 m/330 ft high and past a waterfall to the mouth of the gorge, in German territory (restaurant, car park).

Riezlern (1100 m/3610 ft), the largest village in the valley, lies at the mouth of the Schwarzwassertal, which descends from the Hoher Ifen. In addition to a local museum and a casino it has a variety of leisure facilities (heated open-air swimming pool, indoor pool, tennis courts).

To the S a cableway, the Kanzelwandbahn, runs up to 2000 m/6560 ft), where there is an extensive area of good walking and skiing country.

To the N is the Fellhorn (2039 m/6690 ft), reached by a cabin cableway on the German side.

A little mountain road runs SW from Riezlern (4 km/2½ miles) to the Auenhütte (1250 m/4100 ft), from which a chair-lift runs up to the Ifenhütte (1595 m/5233 ft). From here it is a 2½ hours' climb to the Hoher Ifen (2232 m/7323 ft), to the NW, a limestone plateau with steeply scarped sides from which there are magnificent views.

Hirschegg (1124 m/3688 ft) is a long straggling village which is a popular base for walkers and skiers. Function centre; enclosed swimming pool. Chair-lift up the Heuberg (upper station 1373 m/4505 ft).

Mittelberg (1218 m/3996 ft) has a parish church partly dating from the 14th c. and a local museum (in Bödmen); tennis, heated open-air swimming pool. A cabin cableway runs up to the Walmendinger Horn (1993 m/6539 ft; restaurant), to the W, a chair-lift to the Zaferna-Alpe (upper station 1419 m/4656 ft).

Baad (1251 m/4105 ft) is a hamlet at the head of the valley with the Widderstein (2533 m/8311 ft) rearing above it to the S.

In summer it is possible to cross the Hochalppass (1921 m/6303 ft) to join the Bregenzer Wald Road at the Hochtannberg pass.

Klopeiner See

Land: Carinthia (K).

ⓘ **Gemeindeamt St Kanzian,**
Gemeindehaus, A-9122 St Kanzian;
tel. (0 42 39) 22 24–12.

ACCOMMODATION. – IN ST KANZIAN: *Sonne*, A, 140 b.,
SP, sauna; *Marolt*, B, 300 b., SB, SP, sauna; *Florianihof*, B,
154 b., SP, sauna; *Wank*, B, 100 b., SP; *Seewirt*, B, 60 b.,
SB, SP. – CAMPING SITES. – IN KLOPEIN: *Amerika*, A,
69 b., SP; *Birkenhof*, B, 95 b., SP; *Kärntnerhof*, B, 65 b.,
SP.

RECREATION and SPORTS. – Riding; tennis; sailing;
surfing school.

**The Klopeiner See (alt. 446 m/1463 ft),
lying S of Völkermarkt in a wooded
setting, claims to be the warmest lake
in Carinthia, with temperatures of up
to 28 °C/82 °F. Motorboats are not
permitted on the lake, which is 1900 m/
$1\frac{1}{4}$ miles long by up to 800 m/$\frac{1}{2}$ mile
wide. During the summer it attracts
large numbers of holidaymakers and
bathers.**

The Klopeiner See

The resorts around the lake – *Klopein,
Seelach* and *Unterburg* – belong to the
commune of **St Kanzian,** which has a parish
church of about 1100 and a modern
observatory. Immediately W of the Klopeiner
See is the *Kleinsee*; 2 km/$1\frac{1}{4}$ miles S is the
Turner See.

SURROUNDINGS. – 5 km /3 miles SE of the Klopeiner
See, beneath the S side of a low wooded hill, *Kulm*
(627 m/2057 ft), is the resort of **Eberndorf** (477 m/
1565 ft; pop. 4500), with a former Augustinian monastery
above the town. The monastery, founded about 1150,
was fortified during the Turkish wars of the 15th c.; from
1603 to 1783 it was held by the Jesuits; and in 1809 the
property was made over to the abbey of St Paul. The
church has a separate belfry (15th c.); Gothic ceiling
paintings in choir; crypt of *c.* 1380; imposing red marble
tomb of Christoph Ungnad von Sonnegg, victor over the
Turks (d. 1490). – 7 km/$4\frac{1}{2}$ miles beyond Eberndorf is the
village of *Globasnitz*, which has a Romanesque charnel-
house with 16th c. frescoes. 2 km/$1\frac{1}{4}$ miles W of the village
is the *Hemmaberg (841 m/2759 ft; view), crowned by
a late Gothic church (1498–1519).

12 km/$7\frac{1}{2}$ miles SW of the Klopeiner See, to the S of
Wildenstein, are the **Wildenstein Falls** (20 minutes'
walk), where the water tumbles down 52 m/170 ft from a
cleft in the rock.

Klosterneuburg

Land: Lower Austria (NÖ).
Altitude: 192 m/630 ft.
Population: 25,000.
Post code: A-3400.
Telephone code: 0 22 43.

ⓘ **Fremdenverkehrsverein,** Niedermarkt 19;
tel. 20 38.

ACCOMMODATION. – *Schlosshotel Martinschloss,* A,
94 b., SB, sauna; *Buschenreiter,* B, 76 b., SB, sauna;
Anker, B, 57 b.; *Alte Mühle,* C, 30 b. – YOUTH HOSTEL in
Gugging.

RECREATION and SPORTS. – Leisure complex; riding.

**12 km/$7\frac{1}{2}$ miles N of Vienna, below the
S side of the Wienerwald, is Klosterneuberg, separated from the Danube
by a broad belt of meadowland, with a
famous Augustinian abbey founded
in 1108 by the Babenberg Margrave
Leopold III, the Saint. The town has
a Federal college of wine-making.**

SIGHTS. – On the E side of the upper town
is the *Augustinian Abbey, originally

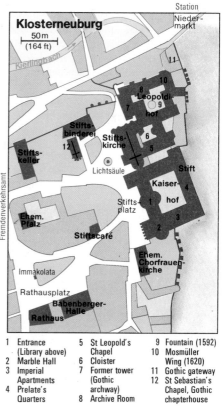

1	Entrance (Library above)	5	St Leopold's Chapel	9	Fountain (1592)
2	Marble Hall	6	Cloister	10	Mosmüller Wing (1620)
3	Imperial Apartments	7	Former tower (Gothic archway)	11	Gothic gateway
4	Prelate's Quarters	8	Archive Room	12	St Sebastian's Chapel, Gothic chapterhouse

established in 1108 on the site of a Roman fort and considerably enlarged and developed in the 15th–19th c. (conducted tours).

The Romanesque **church** was built between 1114 and 1136; the towers were begun respectively in 1394 and 1638, but received their neo-Gothic spires only in 1887–92. The interior in its present form dates from the mid 17th c.

The decoration and furnishings were renewed in Baroque style in the 17th and 18th c. The high altar dates from 1728, the organ from 1632. A flight of steps leads down to the 12th c. *St Leopold's Chapel* (originally the chapterhouse), in which, behind a richly wrought screen, is the famous ****Verdun Altar**. Perhaps the finest existing example of medieval enamel work, this consists of 51 panels of champlevé work on gilded copper depicting Bibilical scenes by Nicholas of Verdun (1181), originally on the ambo (reading pulpit) of the Romanesque church. After a fire in 1329 the panels were put together to form the present winged altarpiece. The remains of the founder are contained in a gilded silver reliquary. Four painted panels, the oldest in Austria (Vienna, before 1329), formerly on the rear face of the altarpiece, are new in the museum. Note also the beautiful 14th and 15th c. stained glass in the chapel.

From the beautiful Gothic *Cloister* we enter the Freisinger or *Wehinger Kapelle* (1384) and the Refectory, now housing a *Lapidarium* with a collection of sculpture, including the marble "Madonna of Klosterneuberg" (*c.* 1310). – SW of the church is the old *Cooper's Shop* (Stiftsbinderei), with the Tausendeimerfass, a cask (1704) holding 560 hectolitres/12,300 gallons; on St Leopold's Day (15 November) *Fasslrutschen* (sliding down the cask) is a popular amusement.

The **New Buildings** (Neues Stiftsgebäude) or Residenztrakt are a magnificent Baroque complex (1730–55), although they represent only a quarter of the buildings originally planned by the Emperor Charles VI. The two domes on the E side bear copper representations of the German Imperial

Verdun Altar, Klosterneuburg

crown and the archducal cap of Lower Austria. Above the entrance hall is the *Library*, with a large collection which is open only to students. Among the apartments shown to visitors are the *Marble Hall*, the *Imperial Apartments* and the *Tapestry Hall* (Brussels tapestries). On the second and third floors is the *Museum.* – In the Stiftsplatz is a *lantern of the dead* (Lichtsäule) of 1381. The large *Stiftskeller* (Cellar) of 1670 is now a restaurant.

SW of the monastery lies the Rathausplatz with the *Rathaus* on its south side. Adjoining the latter is the *Babenberger-Halle* (1969: multi-purpose hall). Nearby is the *Rostockvilla* (museum). Also of interest are the archaeological museum in *St Martin's Church* and the *Kafka Memorial* in Kierling.

SURROUNDINGS. – 25 km/15 miles W, on the right bank of the Danube (bridge), is Tulln (177 m/581 ft; pop. 11,000), one of the oldest towns in Austria, the Roman naval base of *Comagena* and the *Tulne* of the "Nibelungenlied" where King Etzel (Attila) received Kriemhild. The Gothic parish church of St Stephen has preserved a beautiful Romanesque doorway with figures of the Apostles. Adjoining the church is the eleven-sided Chapel of the Three Kings (1160). The charnel-house has a magnificent doorway. – 12 km/7½ miles W of Tulln is Zwentendorf (182 m/597 ft; pop. 3000), with a parish church remodelled in Baroque style and a Schloss of 1750. 1 km/¾ mile beyond Zwenterdorf is the site of the *Roman fort of Piro Torto* (1st c. A.D.), excavated from 1952 onwards. Near the town is the first Austrian nuclear power station (completed 1978), never brought into operation as a result of a national referendum.

Krems an der Donau

Land: Lower Austria (NÖ).
Altitude: 202 m/663 ft. – Population: 32,000.
Post code: A-3500. – Telephone code: 0 27 32.
ⓘ **Fremdenverkehrsamt,**
Künstlerhaus, Wichnerstrasse 8;
tel. 26 76.

ACCOMMODATION. – *Parkhotel*, A, 140 b.; *Alte Post*, B, 42 b.; *Jell*, B, 14 b., SP; *Goldenes Kreuz*, C, 52 b.; *Karpischek*, C, 30 b. – YOUTH HOSTEL. – IN STEIN: *Am Förthof*, A, 44 b.

RECREATION and SPORTS. – Swimming pools; artificial ice rink; tennis.

Krems, chief town of its district, situated at the E end of the very beautiful Wachau, is the oldest town in Lower Austria. The *old town with its handsome burghers' houses, first recorded as an Imperial stronghold in 995, is built on higher ground at the mouth of the Kremstal, with the

newer districts on the banks of the
Danube. It is now a busy industrial and
commercial town (river port, wine
trade, engineering, school of wine and
fruit growing).

SIGHTS. – The main E–W axis of the Old
Town, which still preserves many buildings
of the Gothic period, is formed by the *Obere*
and *Untere Landstrasse*. At its W end stands
the **Steiner Tor** (Stein Gate) of 1480, the
principal landmark and emblem of Krems,
with a tall Baroque tower (1765) between
two stubby medieval towers with pointed
roofs. In the Obere Landstrasse is the *Rathaus*
(1548), with a beautiful oriel window.
Opposite it, to the S, the *Bürgerspitalkirche*
(1470) has a charming little tabernacle. At
the corner "Zum täglichen Markt" is the
Göglhaus (12th and 15th c.), with an oriel
window containing a chapel. From here a
narrow lane runs N to the Pfarrplatz, on the W
side of which is the *Pfarrhof* (Presbytery), a
relic of the old Passauerhof which was
demolished in 1878–82.

The **parish church** (*Pfarrkirche St Veit*),
built by C. Biasino between 1616 and 1630,
is one of the earliest Baroque churches in
Austria. The ceiling paintings (1787) and the
paintings on the side altars were the work
of Martin Johann Schmidt (1718–1801), a
very productive Baroque artist who lived in
Krems and is generally known as *Kremser
Schmidt*, Schmidt of Krems. The high altar,
pulpit and choir-stalls were the work of J. M.
Götz (1733–35).

From here Margaretengasse goes up to the
Hoher Markt, passing the *Sgraffitohaus* at
No. 5 (*c.* 1560), so called because of the
paintings on its walls. On the S side of the
Hoher Markt is the **Gozzoburg**, built in
1260–70 by a municipal judge Gozzo, with
a fine loggia and an arcaded courtyard
decorated with coats of arms. – Piaristengasse runs up to the Piaristenkirche (Piarist
Church), a handsome late Gothic building
(1475–1520). Most of the altarpieces are by
Kremser Schmidt; choir-stalls of 1600. From
here a covered lane, the Piaristenstiege,
returns to the Pfarrplatz.

W of the Pfarrplatz is the former *Dominican
Church* (1236), a late Romanesque and

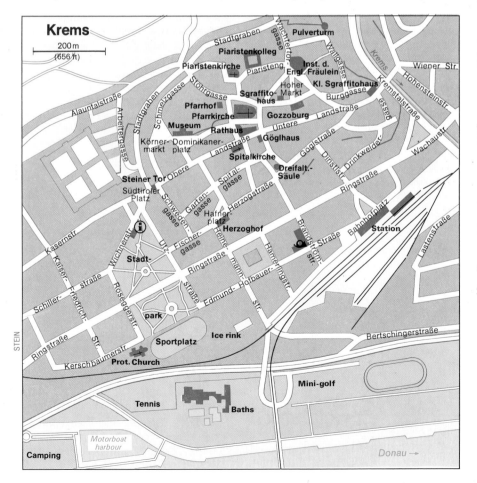

early Gothic building which was restored in 1968–71 and together with the cloister, chapterhouse and refectory of the old Dominican priory now forms a richly stocked **Historical Museum** and a **Wine Museum**. The church is also used for concerts.

From the Steiner Tor we can go down through the district of **Und** (hence the joke "Krems Und Stein sind drei Städte", "Krems And Stein are three towns") to the **Stein** district on the banks of the river (200 m/ 655 ft), which has also preserved its old-world aspect. Beyond the Kremser Tor, a little way off to the right, is the former *Minorite Church* of St Ulrich (1264; 14th and 17th c. frescoes). – Farther on is the *parish church of St Nicholas*, a Gothic hall-church with two Baroque altarpieces by Kremser Schmidt. From the choir of this church a flight of steps leads up to the former *Frauenbergkirche* (14th c.), with a massive tower, which since 1966 has been a memorial to the dead of both world wars. In the Steiner Landstrasse there are many old houses, among them the *Kleiner* and *Grosser Passauerhof* (Nos. 72 and 76; *c.* 1530). In front of the Linzer Tor, on the right, is the house once occupied by the painter Schmidt of Krems.

SURROUNDINGS. – On the S bank of the Danube is the ancient little town of **Mautern** (195 m/640 ft), a toll-collecting point at the bridge over the Danube, the *Mutaren* of the "Nibelungenlied". Remains of town walls. Early Gothic parish church, with pictures by Kremser Schmidt. Roman museum in the Margarethenkapelle, with finds from the Roman station of *Castrum Favianis*, which occupied this site.

10 km/6 miles S of Krems, prominently situated on a wooded hill 260 m/850 ft above the Danube, stands the Benedictine *Göttweig Abbey, originally founded in 1074 by Bishop Altmann of Passau. The present buildings were begun in 1719 to the design of the Baroque architect Lukas von Hildebrandt, and work continued until 1783, leaving the plan unfinished. The parts completed were the

E and N fronts, with the Kaiserstiege (1738), one of the finest staircases of the Baroque period. At the entrance can be seen some remains of the medieval castle which previously occupied the site. The church has an imposing Baroque façade with two towers (1750–65), a light 17th c. nave and a Gothic choir (15th–16th c.). The interior decoration and furnishings are early Baroque. In the crypt is a painted stone figure of Abbot Altmann (*c.* 1540). Notable features of the conventual buildings are the four Imperial Apartments, the Altmann Room (grand hall, 1731), with ceiling paintings and pictures, and the well-stocked Library, with stucco decoration by Franz Amon. From the balcony and the garden terrace (restaurant) there are superb views.

Krems is also a good base from which to explore the *Wachau (see p. 235), which extends westward along the Danube to Melk.

Kremsmünster

Land: Upper Austria (OÖ).
Altitude: 345 m/1132 ft. – Population: 6000.
Post code: A-4550. – Telephone code: 0 75 83.
ⓘ **Fremdenverkehrsverband**, Rathausplatz 1;
tel. 72 12.

ACCOMMODATION. – *Schlair*, B, 53 b.; *Haugeneder*, C, 56 b.; *Schmidthaler*, C, 32 b.

Kremsmünster, 35 km/22 miles SW of Linz in the Krems valley, is famous for its Benedictine abbey, founded in 777, which had a scriptorium celebrated in the Middle Ages. The church, originally 13th c., was remodelled in Baroque style about 1700. The present monastic buildings date from the 17th and 18th c.

Kremsmünster
150 m
(492 ft)

A Oberer Meierhof   E Konvikthof
B Äusserer Stiftshof   F Küchenhof
C Unterer Meierhof   G Portnerhof
D Prälatenhof   H Kreuzhof

1 Eichentor (Oak Gate)   10 Chapterhouse
2 Fish-ponds   11 Imperial Hall
3 Bridge Tower   12 Refectory (Library above)
4 Guest wing   13 Lady Chapel
5 Seminarists' Refectory 14 Conventual Range
6 Seminary wing   15 Clerical Range
7 Academic Chapel   16 School (Gymnasium)
8 Treasury   17 Observatory
9 Art Collections   18 "Mosque"

Göttweig Abbey

projected completion

1 Porter's Lodge   5 Wing of cloister   9 Grand Hotel
   (from earlier   6 Treasury   10 Imperial
   castle)   7 Imperial   Apartments
2 Erentrudiskapelle   Staircase   11 St Cecilia's
3 W gatehouse   8 Imperial   Hall
4 Obelisk (fountain)   Apartments   12 Library

SIGHTS. – The principal feature of the abbey is the **Treasury**, with the valuable *Tassilo Chalice* (Tassilo-Kelch) of about 780 (photograph, p. 29) and the *Tassilo

Candlesticks. The *Imperial Hall* (Kaisersaal) dates from 1685. The magnificently appointed *Library* (1675) contains among other treasures the Codex Millenarius, a valuable 8th c. manuscript of the Gospels. Also worth seeing is the *Parish Church* (1709–31; rebuilt in Baroque style). The *Observatory* (1748–59), 50 m/165 ft high, contains natural history collections. Also of interest is a group of five fish-ponds (1691), surrounded by arcades, with mythological decoration. School (1549), in which the novelist Adalbert Stifter was a pupil from 1818 to 1826.

SURROUNDINGS. – 1½ km/1 mile E of Kremsmünster is the Kremsegg Castle with an old-timer museum, and 10 km/6 miles SE the spa of **Bad Hall** (388 m/1273 ft; pop. 5000), with a brine spring containing iodine; the water is among the strongest of the kind in Central Europe (treatment complex, indoor thermal pool).

16 km/10 miles S of Kremsmünster, off the main road, the village of **Schlierbach** (407 m/1335 ft; pop. 2500) has a Cistercian abbey founded in 1355. The church was rebuilt by P. F. and C. A. Carlone in the late 17th c. in splendid Baroque style, with a sumptuous interior. To the N of Kremsmünster extends the beautiful and interesting **Krems valley**. – At *Kematen* is *Schloss Weyer* (13th–14th c.). – *Neuhofen* was the birthplace in 1606 of Georg von Derfflinger, a peasant's son who rose to become a field-marshal in the Brandenburg service. Neuhofen is now popular for holidays. – W of the road, near the motorway, is **Pucking**, with *St Leonard's Church* (15th–16th and 18th c.), which has fine old frescoes.

Krimml Falls (Krimmler Wasserfälle)

Land: Salzburg (S).

ⓘ **Verkehrsverein Krimml,** A-5743 Krimml; tel. (0 65 64) 2 39.

ACCOMMODATION. – IN KRIMML: *Klockerhaus,* B, 92 b.; *Zur Post,* B, 82 b., sauna.

To the S of the Gerlos pass, which links the Ziller valley in Tirol with the Salzach valley in Salzburg, the Krimmler Ache, flowing through a narrow wooded valley, plunges down 380 m/1250 ft in three tremendous steps. The excursion to see these falls, the grandest in the Eastern Alps, takes 3 hours. The nearby village of Krimml is a popular holiday resort, and in winter there is excellent skiing on the Gerlosplatte.

The starting-point for a visit to the ****Krimml Falls** is the village of *Krimml* (1076 m/ 3530 ft), magnificently situated high above the Salzachtal in the wooded valley of the Krimmler Ache, between the Hohe Tauern and the Kitzbühel Alps. From the car park at the S end of the village it is half an hour's walk to the 1st viewpoint, overlooking the Lower Falls; from there it is 10 minutes' walk to the 2nd viewpoint, the Regenkanzel, and another 5 minutes to the 3rd. All these viewpoints are always shrouded in spray. The path then leads up by way of the 4th and 5th viewpoints (the Riemannkanzel) to the *Middle Falls* (6th and 7th viewpoints), and comes in another 20 minutes, passing the *Schönangerl* (1285 m/4216 ft; inn), to the *Bergerblick*, with the finest view of the falls; total time 1½ hours. From here it is another 15 minutes up to the *Schettbrücke* (1463 m/ 4800 ft), at the *Upper Falls* (140 m/460 ft high). Over the bridge is the Tauernweg, which runs down the right bank into the valley.

SURROUNDINGS. – There is a rewarding climb of 4 hours, starting from Krimml, going up past the falls to the Schettbrücke (1¾ hours) and continuing (2¼ hours) to the *Krimmler Tauernhaus* (1622 m/5322 ft; inn). From there expert climbers can scale the *Glockenkarkopf (2913 m/9558 ft; 4½ hours), on the Italian frontier, and other peaks in the Zillertal Alps. The climb from the Tauernhaus to the *Krimmler Tauern* pass (2633 m/ 8639 ft) takes 3½ hours.

The splendidly engineered ***Gerlos Road** (toll; max. gradient 9%; several bridges) runs NW from Krimml. From the *Filzsteinalpe car park* (1628 m/5341 ft) there is a road (1 km/¾ mile) to the *Filzstein* (1643 m/5391 ft; inn), from which there is a *view to the rear into the valley of the Krimmler Ache. 11 km/7 miles from Krimml a road branches off to the **Gerlosplatte**, a high plateau (c. 1700 m/5600 ft) noted for its excellent snow, with hotels and winter sports facilities. To the S is the *Plattenkogel* (2040 m/6693 ft), an hour's climb; chair-lift to top of slope in winter. The old pass (1504 m/4935 ft) is a little off the road, which now enters the province of Tirol.

The village of **Gerlos** (1246 m/4088 ft; Hotel Gerloserhof, B, 50 b.; Glockenstuhl, B, 50 b.), a summer and winter sports resort, has a parish church (1730–35) with an interior in rustic Baroque style.

Krimml Falls

Enclosed swimming pool. – To the E is the *Durlass-boden reservoir* (1376 m/4515 ft), where the beautiful *Wildgerlostal* turns S. It is 2½ hours' walk to the *Alpengasthof Finkau*, from which it is another 3½ hours to the *Zittauer Hütte* (2329 m/7641 ft; inn), on the *Unterer Gerlossee*, in a magnificent setting at the head of the valley.

Kufstein

Land: Tirol (T).
Altitude: 499 m/1637 ft.
Population: 13,000.
Post code: A-6330.
Telephone code: 0 53 72.
ⓘ Verkehrsbüro, Münchner Strasse 2;
tel. 22 07.

ACCOMMODATION. – *Tourotel-Kufsteinerhof*, A/B, 90 b.; *Goldener Löwe*, A/B, 70 b.; *Alpenrose*, A/B, 36 b.; *Tirolerhof*, A/B, 25 b.; *Andreas Hofer*, B, 130 b. – YOUTH HOSTEL. – CAMPING SITE.

RECREATION and SPORTS. – Tennis; riding; fishing; climbing school; hobby courses; winter sports.

Kufstein is an old Tirolese frontier town in the lower Inn valley, situated at the point where the river cuts its way through the Alps between the Kaisergebirge and the truncated cone of Pendling. Possession of the town was much disputed during the Middle Ages, and the imposing stronghold of Feste Kufstein was built here. Kufstein is now a popular holiday resort, with attractive lake scenery in the surrounding area and good walking and climbing in the Kaisergebirge. It plays an important part in trade and traffic between Bavaria and Tirol.

SIGHTS. – Unlike the town, the castle which rears above it on a precipitous crag, *Feste Kufstein,* has survived the storms of the centuries relatively unscathed. It can be reached by a covered stepped lane to the right of the *parish church* or by a lift from the Römerhofgasse. First recorded in 1205, the fortress was considerably enlarged and strengthened after the Emperor Maximilian I captured it from the Bavarians in 1504. The 90 m/295 ft high Kaiserturm (Emperor's Tower) was built in 1518–22. It has a famous *Heroes' Organ* (Heldenorgel) in the Bürgerturm (open to visitors), with 4307 pipes and 46 stops. The organ is played daily at 12 noon (in summer also at 6 p.m.) in memory of those who died in the two world wars; it can be heard 13 km/8 miles away. The castle also contains a *Heimatmuseum* with material illustrating the history of the town.

SURROUNDINGS. – From the Oberer Stadtplatz it is 10 minutes' walk to the *Kalvarienberg*, with an Andreas Hofer Monument (1926); fine view of the town. – SE of the town is the Kaiserlift, which runs up the **Stadtberg** (upper station 1140 m/3740 ft), with extensive views of the mountains. – The *Duxer Köpfl* (715 m/2346 ft), to the NE, can be reached either by lift or by car. – Round Kufstein are a number of small lakes (bathing, hire of boats). Particularly beautiful are the *Stimmersee*, in a forest setting 3 km/2 miles SW, and the *Hechtsee*, to the N. – SW of Kufstein is the fine viewpoint hill of *Pendling* (1565 m/5135 ft; Kufsteiner Haus; inn open in summer), which can be climbed in 3½–4 hours.

To the E of Kufstein is the *Kaisergebirge* (nature reserve), a rugged bastion of rock rising steeply above gently rounded foothills, with the Kaisertal and Kaiserbachtal separating the **Wilder Kaiser** (2344 m/7691 ft) to the S – one of the most popular Alpine rock-climbing areas – from the **Zahmer Kaiser** (2002 m/6569 ft) to the N. The *Kaisertal* (closed to cars) runs E through the range. It is a 2¾ hours' walk up the valley to *Hinterbärendad* (831 m/2727 ft) in magnificent surroundings, the main base for exploring the Kaisergebirge. From here experienced climbers can scale the highest peaks in the range – to the S the *Ellmauer Halt* (2344 m/7691 ft; 5 hours) and the *Sonneck* (2260 m/7415 ft; 4½ hours), to the N a 2 hours' climb to the *Stripsenjoch* (1580 m/5184 ft), and an easy climb (¾ hour) from there up the *Stripsenkopf* (1810 m/5939 ft).

A road runs SE through the valley of the *Weissache*, below the S face of the Wilder Kaiser, to St Johann in Tirol (30 km/19 miles). From this road there is a rewarding walk on a footpath known as the Steinerne Stiege (1 hour) to the beautiful *Hintersteiner See* (892 m/2927 ft), which can also be reached on a minor road from *Scheffau* (4 km/2½ miles).

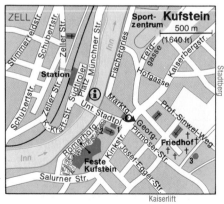

1 Rathaus   2 Parish church   3 Andreas Hofer Monument

Lambach

Land: Upper Austria (OÖ).
Altitude: 366 m/1201 ft.
Population: 3800.
Post code: A-4650.
Telephone code: 0 72 45.
ⓘ Gemeindeamt des Marktes Lambach,
Marktplatz 8;
tel. 83 55 and 24 16.

ACCOMMODATION. – *Weisses Lamm*, C, 22 b.; *Grüner Baum*, C, 20 b.; *Harrer*, C, 20 b.

This old Upper Austrian market town lies in the Alpine foreland region 25 km/ 15 miles N of the Traunsee, on the left bank of the River Traun.

Gateway, Lambach Abbey.

SIGHTS. – In the Marktplatz is the Benedictine **Abbey**, founded in 1056, with a magnificent Baroque façade. A marble gateway (1693) leads into the first courtyard, and we then pass through the cloister to enter the *church* (1652–56), which has a high altar ascribed to J. B. Fischer von Erlach. From the first courtyard a staircase leads up to the *Theatre* (1746–70), Austria's only surviving monastic theatre. Another staircase leads to the "Läuthaus" (ringing chamber), with fine 11th c. frescoes which are among the earliest Romanesque wall paintings in Austria; the colours are unusually well preserved. The *Refectory* (18th c.) and *Library* are sumptuously decorated. The *Picture Gallery* contains works by Kremser Schmidt, Altomonte and Maulpertsch. – It is 10 minutes' walk to the chapel (1720) on the *Kalvarienberg* (fine views).

SURROUNDINGS. – On the S bank of the Traun is **Stadl-Paura**, with a conspicuous pilgrimage church dedicated to the Trinity, a handsome Baroque building (Johann Michael Prunner, 1714–17) on a triangular plan with three towers; sumptuous interior. There is also an interesting Boatmen's Museum.
5 km/3 miles SE of Lambach the beautifully situated spa of **Bad Wimsbach-Neydharting** boasts a Kurhaus, mud baths, the Paracelsushaus (Mud Baths Museum) and the Stiftungshaus (Mud Baths Research Institute).

20 km/12½ miles SW of Lambach is the attractive little town of **Vöcklabruck** (435 m/1427 ft; pop. 11,000; Hotel Auerhahn, A, 120 b.; Schillerhof, B, 80 b.; Lindner,

C, 60 b.), with old gate towers and remains of town walls. On a low hill to the S stands the Gothic church of *Schöndorf* (1481).

Landeck

Land: Tirol (T).
Altitude: 816 m/2677 ft. – Population: 7500.
Post code: A-6500. – Telephone code: 0 54 42.
ⓘ **Fremdenverkehrsverband Landeck und Umgebung,** Stadtplatz;
tel. 23 44.

ACCOMMODATION. – *Post*, A, 180 b., sauna; *Mozart*, A, 50 b., SB, sauna; *Schrofenstein*, B, 100 b.; *Schwarzer Adler*, B, 70 b.; *Tramserhof*, B, 60 b.; *Kaifenau*, B, 58 b. – Two CAMPING SITES.

Landeck lies S of the Lechtal Alps in the upper Inn valley, at the junction of the Sanna with the Inn. The roads from the Arlberg and the Reschen (Resia) pass meet here, and the approaches to both passes were thus commanded by the castle which dominates the town.

SIGHTS. – The most notable feature of the *parish church* (1471) is the late Gothic winged altar (16th c.). On the hill above the town is the 13th c. **Burg Landeck** (with later alterations), which now houses the District Museum; fine views from the tower. Perfuchs, the quarter on the left bank of the Inn, has a small *Plague Chapel* (Pestkapelle, 1656).

SURROUNDINGS. – Above Landeck to the N, on the N bank of the Sanna, is the old village of *Stanz* (1035 m/ 3396 ft), birthplace of the Baroque architect Jakob Prandtauer (1660–1726), which has a late Gothic church. Higher up, to the NE, are the ruins of *Burg Schrofenstein* (first recorded 1196). – 3 km/2 miles NE, on the S bank of the Inn, is *Zams* (775 m/2543 ft), to the N of which is the *Zammer Loch*, a gorge on the Lochbach, with the *Lötzer Wasserfall*. From Zams the Venet cableway runs SE up the *Krahberg* (2208 m/ 7244 ft; panoramic views), with Landeck's main skiing area. To the E is the **Venetberg** (2513 m/8245 ft), an easy 1½ hours' climb.

Lavant Valley (Lavanttal)

Land: Carinthia (K).
ⓘ **Fremdenverkehrsamt Wolfsberg,** Bamberger Strasse 100, A-9400 Wolfsberg;
tel. (0 43 52) 33 40.

The Lavant valley extends from the Obdacher Sattel, on the Styrian-Carinthian border S of Judenberg, to

Lavamünd on the Yugoslav frontier, linking the Mur valley to the N with the Drau valley to the S. To the W are the Seetal Alps, reaching their highest point in the Zirbitzkogel (2397 m/ 7865 ft), and the Saualpe (over 2000 m/ 6560 ft), to the E the Packalpe (almost 2200 m/7200 ft) and the Koralpe (2141 m/7025 ft).

10 km/6 miles S of the *Obdacher Sattel* (945 m/3101 ft), in the upper Lavant valley, is the ancient little town, now a summer resort, of **Bad St Leonhard** (721 m/2366 ft; Moselbauer, B, 70 b., SB, sauna; Schöllerhof, B, 56 b., SP, sauna), a spa with a sulphurous mineral spring. Above the town are Burg Ehrenfels and the ruined Burg Leonhard. On a hill stands the beautiful Gothic church of St Leonard (14th–15th c.), with fine stained glass. – 8 km/5 miles S, at *Twimberg* (604 m/ 1982 ft), the **Packstrasse* branches off and runs up through beautiful scenery to the *Packsattel* (summit at the Vier Tore, 1166 m/ 3826 ft).

The chief place in the valley is the little industrial town of **Wolfsberg** (462 m/ 1516 ft; pop. 29,000; Hotel Torwirt, B, 100 b.), which is also a summer and winter sports resort. The twin-towered Romanesque parish church dates from the time when the town was in the diocese of Bamberg (until 1759). The old episcopal castle, which had already undergone alteration in the 16th c., was rebuilt in neo-Gothic style after passing into the hands of the Silesian Count von Henckel-Donnersmarck in 1846.

St Andrä (433 m/1421 ft) was the seat of the Prince-Bishops of Lavant from 1225 to 1859, when the see was transferred to Marburg, now Maribor in Yugoslavia, and their palace became a Jesuit college. The former cathedral (Gothic), now the parish church, has remains of 15th c. wall paintings and numerous gravestones bearing coats of arms. The twin-towered Baroque Jesuit church of Maria-Loreto (1697) originally belonged to a convent of Dominican nuns which was dissolved in 1792.

St Paul (378 m/1240 ft) is a charmingly situated market town and summer resort. The Benedictine **Abbey*, on a rocky hill 70 m/230 ft high, was founded in 1091 and has been occupied since 1809 by Benedictines from St Blasien in the Black Forest (SW Germany). The twin-towered *church* (consecrated 1264) is the finest Roman-

esque church in Carinthia apart from Gurk Cathedral. Notable features of the exterior are the choir and the S doorway. The interior has Gothic vaulting and wall paintings of 1470, but the furnishings, including the fine pulpit, are Baroque. The tomb of fourteen members of the Habsburg family of the 13th and 14th c., with coats of arms, was brought here from St Blasien. The abbey has a valuable art collection, including vestments, liturgical utensils, glass, coins, a Carolingian ivory carving and numerous manuscripts. It also runs a school, one of the largest in Austria, at which the composer Hugo Wolf (1860–1903) was once a pupil. – On the hills around the town are three pilgrimage churches.

Laxenburg

Land: Lower Austria (NÖ).
Altitude: 174 m/571 ft. – Population: 1900.
Post code: A-2361. – Telephone code: 0 22 36.
ⓘ **Marktgemeindeamt**, Schlossplatz 8; tel. 7 11 01.

ACCOMMODATION. – IN MÖDLING (6 km/4 miles W): *Babenbergerhof*, B, 36 b. – CAMPING SITE.

This little market town, 15 km/9 miles S of Vienna amid the meadows bordering the Schwechat in the Vienna basin, is noted for its fine 18th c. Imperial summer palace, set in a beautiful park in the old hunting grounds of the Dukes of Austria.

SIGHTS. – On the W side of the Schlossplatz stands the Baroque *Hofkirche* (Court Church: 1693–1726). Opposite it is the **Neues Schloss** or *Blaue Hof*, an Imperial

The Franzensburg in the Schlosspark, Laxenburg

summer palace with extensive outbuildings which was begun about 1752. In the reign of Maria Theresa and during the Congress of Vienna it was a busy focus of court life; and in 1917 the last Austrian Emperor, Karl, received his brother-in-law Prince Sixtus of Bourbon-Parma here to discuss possible peace terms. The *park, laid out 1780–90, has many features characteristic of the landscape gardening of the Romantic period; a walk round it takes 1½ hours.

The medieval **Altes Schloss** now houses the Austrian Film Archives and is also used for exhibitions. On an island in the Grosser Teich (Great Pond) is the neo-Gothic *Franzensburg* (1798–1836), modelled on the castle of Habsburg in Switzerland, and which now houses a museum.

In the courtyard are 37 busts of members of the Habsburg family; and notable features of the interior (conducted tour) are the Habsburger Saal (Habsburg Hall), Lothringer Saal (Lorraine Hall) and Cappella Speciosa. Café on the island. At the W end of the park is a leisure and recreation area.

Lechtal Alps

Land: Tirol (T).
Altitude: Highest point: Parseierspitze (3036 m/9961 ft).
ⓘ **Österreichischer Alpenverein,**
Sektion Landeck,
Ulrichstr. 39, A-6500 Landeck.
Sektion Reutte,
Untermarkt 24, A-6600 Reutte.

The long range of the Lechtal Alps, one of the mightiest chains in the Northern Alps, extends from the Arlberg to the Fernpass, bounded on the S by the Stanz valley and its continuation the Inn valley and on the N by the Lech valley which gives the range its name.

The principal peak in the Lechtal Alps is the **Parseierspitze** (3036 m/9961 ft), which claims the title of "Queen of the Northern Calcereous Alps". Among other major peaks are the *Wetterspitze* (2895 m/9498 ft), the interesting and relatively easy *Muttekopf* (2777 m/9111 ft), the long rocky ridge of the *Heiterwand* and the mighty *Valluga* (2809 m/9216 ft), much favoured by winter visitors to the Arlberg.

The numerous mountain huts in the Lechtal Alps are easily reached from the Stanz valley and Inn valley. They are linked by a magnificent ridge path leading from the Ulmer Hütte (2280 m/7481 ft) near St Anton am Arlberg or from the Stuttgarter Hütte (2303 m/7556 ft) near Zürs am Arlberg by way of the Leutkircher Hütte (2250 m/7382 ft) and the Kaiserjoch-Hütte (2300 m/7545 ft) to the Ansbacher Hütte (2380 m/7810 ft), and from there by way of the difficult Augsburger Höhenweg to the Augsburger Hütte (2345 m/7694 ft), then on via the Memminger Hütte (2242 m/7356 ft) on the *Unterer Seewisee*, the Württemberger Haus (2200 m/7220 ft), the Hanauer Hütte (1920 m/6300 ft) and the Anhalter Hütte (2040 m/6695 ft) to the **Fernpass** (1210 m/3970 ft).

The whole of the Lechtal Alps area offers endless scope for walks and climbs in summer, while the western end, around the Arlberg and Flexen passes – usually known simply as the **Arlberg* – is, thanks to its magnificent terrain and abundance of snow, one of the most famous skiing areas in the world. Names like St Anton, St Christoph, Zürs and Lech am Arlberg are familiar to skiing enthusiasts everywhere.

Of the many lakes in these mountains the largest is the **Spullersee** (1825 m/5990 ft) at Danöfen, on the Arlbergbahn, which is noted for its large hydroelectric station. The little *Zürser See* (2149 m/7050 ft) disappears in winter under a deep covering of snow, and there are numbers of other tiny lakes.

In the area where the eastern outliers of the Lechtal Alps fall down to the wide furrow of the Fernpass are a number of quiet lakes in magnificent forest settings – the *Fernsteinsee*, the *Blindsee*, the *Weissensee* and the *Mittersee*.

NE of the Lechtal Alps, separated from them by the Hintertorental, is the double basin of the **Plansee** and the **Heiterwanger See** (997 m/3206 ft). It can be reached from Reutte, close to which are two other charming lakes, the *Urisee* and the *Frauensee*.

Leoben

Land: Styria (Stm).
Altitude: 540 m/1772 ft.
Population: 40,000.
Post code: A-8700.
Telephone code: 0 38 42.
ⓘ **Verkehrsbüro,** Hauptplatz 12;
tel. 4 40 18.

ACCOMMODATION. – *Baumann*, A, 140 b., sauna; *Brücklwirt*, A, 130 b., SB, sauna; *Kindler* (Krempl), B, 93 b.; *Sebinger*, C, 64 b. – CAMPING SITE.

RECREATION and SPORTS. – Riding; artificial ice rink; tennis; open-air and covered swimming pools; winter sports.

EVENTS. – *Gösser Kirchweih* (Göss Fair, second Thursday in October); *Upper Styrian Fair* (Sept).

Leoben, on a loop of the River Mur, is the headquarters of the ironworking and lignite-mining region of Upper Styria, with a Mining College.

SIGHTS. – In the Hauptplatz are the *Hacklhaus* (No. 9), with a Baroque façade of about 1680, and the *Altes Rathaus* (Old Town Hall) of 1568, adorned with coats of arms. To the W is the twin-towered *parish church* (Pfarrkirche) of 1660–65, and beyond it, in a former Jesuit college (17th c.), the well-stocked *Municipal Museum*. The *Mautturm* (Toll Tower), popularly known as the Schwammerlturm ("Mushroom Tower") dates from 1615, the *Municipal Theatre* from 1790. On the Stadtkai, on the right bank of the Mur, stands the *Neues Rathaus* (New Town Hall). To the S of the bridge over the Mur is the *church of Maria am Waasen*

(14th–15th c.) with fine stained glass in the choir. In the district of *Göss* (2 km/1¼ miles S of the town) is the brewery which produces the famous Gösser beer; it is housed in a former nunnery founded before 1020 and dissolved in 1782 (late Gothic church).

SURROUNDINGS. – 10 km/6 miles SW of Leoben the *Liesingtal* goes off to the NW in the direction of the *Schober pass* (843 m/2766 ft; skiing area), which leads into the Ennstal. The chief place in the valley is **Mautern** (713 m/2339 ft; Hotel Liesingtalerhof, B, 58 b.), from which a chair-lift runs up to the *Wildpark Steiermark-Mautern* (wildlife park; 1250 m/4100 ft). The park, with an area of some 50 hectares/125 acres, has a large enclosure for deer. Two climbs from Mautern (each about 5 hours) which afford fine views of the Eisenerz Alps, are up the *Wildfeld* (2046 m/6713 ft) and the *Reiting* (2215 m/7267 ft).

Lienz

Land: Tirol (T).
Altitude: 673 m/2208 ft. – Population: 13,000.
Post code: A-9900. – Telephone code: 0 48 52.
ⓘ **Fremdenverkehrsverband Lienzer Dolomiten,**
    Albin-Egger-Lienz-Strasse 17;
    tel. 47 47.
    Hauptplatz; tel. 28 80.

ACCOMMODATION. – *Sonne*, A, 110 b., sauna; *Traube*, A, 100 b., SB, sauna; *Post*, A, 53 b.; *Stocker*, A, 48 b.; *Glöcklturm*, B, 77 b.; *Sporthotel*, B, 69 b.; *Haidenhof*, B, 52 b.; *Sun Valley*, B, 48 b. – YOUTH HOSTEL. – Three CAMPING SITES.

RECREATION and SPORTS. – Climbing school; covered tennis courts; open-air and covered swimming baths.

Lienz, main town of a district in Eastern Tirol, lies in a wide basin in the valley of the Drau, which is joined here by its much larger tributary the Isel. To the S rear up the rugged Lienz Dolomites. Thanks to its location on the road from

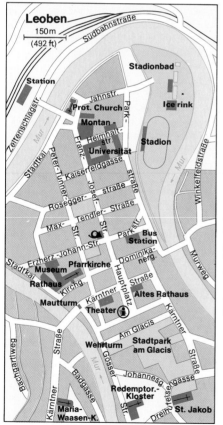

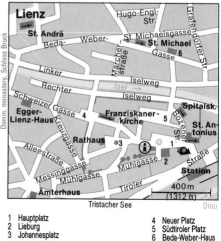

1 Hauptplatz	4 Neuer Platz
2 Lieburg	5 Südtiroler Platz
3 Johannesplatz	6 Beda-Weber-Haus

the **Glockner to Carinthia and the Italian Dolomites and as the gateway to the valleys on the S side of the Tauern the town is busy with tourists.**

SIGHTS. – In the middle of the old town which extends along the banks of the Isel is the *Hauptplatz*, with a bronze statue of St Florian (1956). The square is dominated by the *Lieburg*, a 16th c. mansion with two towers which houses local government offices. At the E end of the square is the old *Mortuary Chapel* (Friedhofskapelle;

Hauptplatz, Lienz

originally 16th c.), a small building preceded by a round tower. In Muchargasse, which leads from Johannesplatz to the Neuer Platz, is the *Franciscan Church* (Franziskaner-kirche), an aisleless church (altered in 15th c.) with a Gothic "Pietà" and medieval wall paintings; cloister with 18th c. wall paintings.

From the Neuer Platz, Schweizergasse continues W to the *Klösterlekirche* (partly 13th c.) belonging to the Dominican monastery (rebuilt). Opposite the church is the *Klösterleschmiede* (smithy), now part of an open-air museum.

On the N bank of the Isel, on higher ground, is the ***parish church** of St Andrä, the finest Gothic building in Eastern Tirol (consecrated 1457); the choir was altered in the 18th c. By the organ gallery are the tombs, both of red Adnet marble, of burgraves belonging to the Görz-Tirol and Wolkenstein families. The beautiful organ-loft dates from 1616; the winged altars were the work of Friedrich Pacher (end of 15th c.); wooden crucifix of 1500. The whole churchyard is surrounded

by arcades with wall paintings containing tombs. The *Memorial Chapel (by Clemens Holzmeister, 1925) commemorating citizens of Lienz who died during the First World War contains four fine murals by Albin Egger-Lienz (1868–1928), whose bronze tomb-slab is set into the floor.

On a wooded hill W of the town (1·5 km/ 1 mile from the Hauptplatz) is ***Schloss Bruck** (724 m/2375 ft; restaurant), built in the 13th c., with a massive keep, and enlarged in the 16th c. It was the seat of the Counts of Görz (Gorizia), from whom it passed to the Habsburgs in 1500. Since 1943 it has housed the *Heimatmuseum of Eastern Tirol*, with works by local artists, in particular pictures by the genre painter Franz Defregger (1835–1921) and Albin Egger-Lienz, and folk and natural history collections. The two-storey *chapel* is completely covered with wall paintings (1485).

The imposing *keep* contains flags and weapons; from the top there is a view of the town.

SURROUNDINGS. From the Schlossberg a chair-lift runs up to the *Venedigerwarte* (1017 m/3337 ft; on foot 1 hour) and the *Leisacher Alm* (1511 m/4958 ft), from which it is a 1½–2 hours' climb to the summit of the **Hochstein** (2023 m/6637 ft; Hochsteinhütte; inn in summer). – To the N of the town is the skiing area of **Zettersfeld** (1800–2200 m/5900–7200 ft), which can be reached by a cabin cableway from Grafendorf (several chair- and ski-lifts).

5 km/3 miles E of Lienz, beyond the road to the Iselsberg, are the excavated remains of the *Roman town of Aguntum*, the oldest Roman valley settlement in Austria (1st–2nd c. A.D.; museum). – The **Iselsberg** (1200 m/ 3940 ft) is a saddle, commanding extensive views, between the Möll and Drau valleys, on the boundary between Eastern Tirol and Carinthia. It attracts many visitors with its fine mountain air and is also a popular winter sports area (ski-lifts, toboggan runs).

5 km/3 miles S of Lienz is the **Tristacher See** (826 m/ 2710 ft; hotel; bathing), a good base for walks and climbs in the Lienz Dolomites. To the S is the Rauchkofel (1911 m/6270 ft), and farther S still the *Lienzer-Dolomiten-Hütte* (1620 m/5315 ft), reached by a mountain road from Bad Jungbrunn.

To the S of Lienz, between the Drau and Gail valleys, rise the ***Lienz Dolomites**, the north-western part of the Gailtal Alps. Their imposing peaks, among the finest in the Austrian Alps, offer ample scope for climbers, scramblers and rock-climbers, with great walls of rock rising straight up from the Drau valley. Behind the *Laserzwand* (2614 m/ 8577 ft) rears up the **Grosse Sandspitze** (2772 m/ 9095 ft), the highest peak in the whole range. To the E is the massive **Hochstadel** (2680 m/8793 ft), with a N face 1500 m/4900 ft high. To the W of the Grosse Sandspitze are the *Spitzkofel* (2718 m/8919 ft) and *Kreuzkofel* (2694 m/8839 ft). There are many well-located mountain huts. Some 5 hours' climb from Lienz is the *Kersch-baumeralm-Schutzhaus* (1902 m/6240 ft; inn in summer; accommodation), from which the Spitzkofel can be climbed (3½ hours; not difficult for experienced climbers). To the E is the *Karlsbader Hütte* (2260 m/7415 ft; inn in summer; accommodation), in a mighty rock cirque containing two lakes, the *Laserzseen*; from here it is an easy climb (1 hour) to the Laserzwand, with impressive downward views.

N of Lienz, lying to the S of the Grossglockner area, is the **Schober group**, a massif over 3200 m/10,500 ft high between the Isel and Möll valleys (*Petzeck*, 3283 m/ 10,772 ft; *Roter Knopf*, 3281 m/10,765 ft; *Hochschober*, 3240 m/10,630 ft), with jagged peaks, finely shaped corries, many small lakes and numerous névé (permanent snow) glaciers. – In the middle of a network of paths is the **Lienzer Hütte** (1977 m/6487 ft; inn in summer; accommodation), some 5 hours N of Lienz on the Debantbach. From here there is an easy climb (2½ hours) to the *Wangenitzsee* (2508 m/8229 ft; hut), to the N of which, on the Wiener Höhenweg, are the *Adolf-Nossberger-Hütte* (2488 m/8163 ft) and the *Elberfelder Hütte* (2346 m/7697 ft), both with inn facilities in summer.

Other attractive excursions from Lienz are to the *Grossglockner* area (see p. 82), to *Matrei* (p. 135) in the *Isel valley*, through the *Pustertal* (Val Pusteria) into Italy and through the *Lesachtal*, running parallel to the Italian frontier, and down the Gailtal to Villach.

Linz

Land: Upper Austria (OÖ).
Altitude: 260 m/853 ft. – Population: 200,000.
Post code: A-4020. – Telephone code: 07 32.
ⓘ **Städtisches Fremdenverkehrsbüro,**
Altstadt 17; tel. 23 93/13 78–13 82.
Tourist Information,
Hauptbahnhof; tel. 5 40 00.

ACCOMMODATION. – *Schillerpark*, Rainerstr. 2–4, A1, 218 b., sauna; *Tourotel Linz*, Untere Donaulände 9, A, 352 b., SB, sauna; *Novotel Linz*, Wankmüllerhofstr. 37, A, 230 b., SP; *Mercure*, Wankmüllerhofstr. 39, A, 210 b.; *Spitz-Hotel*, Karl Fiedler Str. 6, A, 108 b.; *Domhotel*, Baumbachstr. 17, A, 97 b., sauna; *City Hotel*, Schillerstr. 52, A, 84 b.; *Schwarzer Bär*, Herrenstr. 9–11, B, 60 b.;

Prielmayerhof, Weissenwolffstr. 33, B, 64 b.; *Nibelungenhof*, Scharitzerstr. 7, B, 70 b.; *Drei Mohren*, Promenade 17, B, 67 b. – YOUTH HOSTEL, *Jugendgästehaus*. – CAMPING SITE.

RESTAURANTS. – In most hotels; also *Allegro; Donautal; Freiseder; Klosterhof; Landhof; Theater-Casino; Ursulinenhof.*

CASINO. – Hotel Schillerpark, Rainerstr. 2–4 (roulette, baccarat, blackjack), daily from 4 p.m.

RECREATION and SPORTS. – Tennis; riding; water-sports (water-skiing school); artificial ice rink; 18-hole golf course in Tillysburg, near St Florian.

EVENTS. – *Bruckner Festival* (Sept.); *Urfahr Market* (spring/autumn).

Linz, capital of Upper Austria, is Austria's third largest city (after Vienna and Graz). It is attractively situated on both banks of the Danube, here 230 m/ 250 yds wide after emerging from its narrow passage through the outliers of the Bohemian Forest into the Linz basin.

Linz first appears in the records as the Roman fortified camp of *Lentia* in the 2nd c. A.D. In 1497 the town was granted permission to build the first bridge over the Danube between Passau and Krems. It became the see of a bishop in 1785. In 1832 a horse-drawn railway began to run between Linz and Budweis (České Budějovice in Czechoslovakia). Among those who lived and worked in Linz were the novelist Adalbert Stifter, Mozart, Kepler and Anton Bruckner.

The town, now busy with industry and commerce, has extensive port installations. The main part of the city lies on the right bank of the Danube, backed on the W by the

Linz: general view

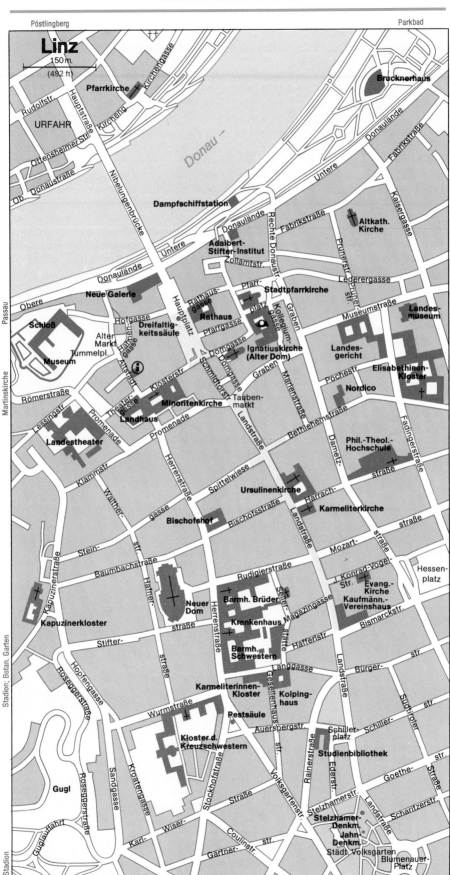

Freinberg (336 m/1102 ft). On the left bank is the district of *Urfahr*, with the *Pöstlingberg* (537 m/1762 ft) rising above it to the NW. Among the principal industrial establishments in Linz are the VÖEST-Alpine-Montan iron and steel works and Chemie Linz (chemicals). The city has a University of Social and Economic Sciences, established in 1966.

SIGHTS. – In the middle of the old town is the *Hauptplatz*, the original market square (220 m/240 yds long, 60 m/65 yds wide), surrounded by handsome Baroque buildings. On the E side of the square is the 17th c. *Rathaus*, opposite which, in the middle of the square, is the *Trinity Column* (Dreifaltigkeitssäule), a 20 m/66 ft high column of Untersberg marble erected in 1723 in thanksgiving for the town's preservation from plague and war. Obliquely across from the Rathaus (No. 18) is the *Feichtingerhaus*, with a beautiful arcaded courtyard. At the far end of the square in the direction of the Danube (on left) the **Neue Galerie** Gurlitt Museum has 19th and 20th c. pictures, a Kubin-Kabinett, devoted to the work of the 20th c. graphic artist of that name and periodic special exhibitions.

Downstream from the bridge at the end of the Hauptplatz is the *Boat Station* (Schiffstation). On the Untere Donaulände (No. 6) is the house in which *Adelbert Stifter* lived from 1848 until his death in 1868. From 1850 to 1865 he was Inspector of Schools for Upper Austria; he is buried in the town cemetery.

Farther downstream is the **Brucknerhaus** (by H. Siren, 1969–73), a multi-purpose building which serves cultural and conference purposes and hosts a variety of events and social occasions. About 200 m/220 yds away is the *Parkbad*.

In the Pfarrplatz, to the E of the Hauptplatz, is the **parish church** (*Stadtpfarrkirche*), originally Gothic but remodelled in Baroque style in 1648 (frecoes by B. Altomonte); it received its characteristic helm roof in 1818. Anton Bruckner was organist here, and also in the Old Cathedral, from 1856 to 1868. Behind a red marble slab on the right of the high altar (1772) is buried the heart of the Emperor Frederick III, who resided in Linz in 1489–93; his body is in St Stephen's Cathedral in Vienna. In the S aisle is St John Nepomuk's Chapel, with a view of Linz in the year 1694 on St Florian's altar. – Nearby, to the S, is the twin-towered Jesuit *Church of St*

Ignatius (Ignatiuskirche), until 1909 the Cathedral (*Alter Dom*, Old Cathedral), an aisless church in Jesuit Baroque style, richly decorated by Italian artists (1669–78); high altar of 1683, pulpit of 1678, richly carved choir-stalls of 1633.

To the E, at Museumstrasse 14, is the *Upper Austrian Provincial Museum* (Landesmuseum), with natural history collections and a permanent exhibition, "The Soil of Linz" (principal exhibits now in the Schloss). At Bethlehemstrasse 7 is the *Municipal Museum* (Stadtmuseum), in a well restored Baroque building of 1607 known as *Nordico* (recalling the time when boys from northern Europe were given a Catholic education here).

SW of the Hauptplatz is the *Landhaus* (seat of the provincial government of Upper Austria), built in 1564–71 on the site of an earlier Minorite convent and rebuilt after a fire in the early 19th c. The magnificent doorway bears the coats of arms of the original Austrian provinces. In the fine arcaded courtyard, in which serenade concerts are given, is the octagonal Planet Fountain (1582). The astronomer Kepler taught from 1612 to 1626 in the college which then occupied the building. The little **Minorite Church* (*Minoritenkirche*), a charming Rococo building (1758) has a massive high altar and three red marble side altars (pictures by M. J. Schmidt). – In the street which runs N from here, known as the *Altstadt*, are the finest old houses in Linz. To the W of the Landhaus is the *Theatre*, built in 1803 and remodelled by Clemens Holzmeister in 1957–58.

High above the Danube stands the handsome **Schloss**, built in the 15th c. as the residence of the Emperor Frederick III, enlarged in the 16th c. and rebuilt after a fire in 1800. Of the original building only the W gate (1481) survives. The interior was remodelled in 1960–63, and the building now houses the ***Schlossmuseum**, with the artistic and historical collections of the Provincial Museum (prehistoric, early historical, Roman and medieval periods; pictures, sculpture, arms and armour, etc.), a Railway Museum, and occasional special exhibitions. – Below the Schloss to the W, in Römerstrasse, is the little ***St Martin's Church** (*Martinskirche*), the oldest church in Austria preserved in its original form. Built on the remains of Roman walls and first recorded in 788, it is a characteristic example of Carolingian architecture. The frescoes in the interior date from the 15th c.

The N–S axis of Linz is the *Landstrasse*, 1200 m/$\frac{3}{4}$ mile long, which runs from the Promenade towards the station. On the E side are the *Ursuline Church* (Ursulinenkirche, 1732–72) and the *Carmelite Church* (Karmeliterkirche, 1674–1726).

To the E, in Harrachstrasse, is the *Seminary Church* (Seminarkirche), a small round church built in 1717–25 for the Teutonic Order, which has a fine interior.

Parallel to the Landstrasse on the W is *Herrenstrasse*, on the W side of which stands the **New Cathedral** (*Neue Dom*), a three-aisled neo-Gothic pillared basilica of yellow sandstone, with an ambulatory surrounded by a ring of chapels. This massive building, built between 1862 and 1924 to the plans of the Cologne architect Vinzenz Statz, covers a rather larger area than St Stephen's Cathedral in Vienna and has a tower 135 m/445 ft high. The large organ was built in 1968. NE of the Cathedral, in Herrenstrasse, is the *Bishop's Palace* (Bischofshof; 1721–26).

Some 300 m/325 yds W of the Cathedral is the *Capuchin Church* (Kapuzinerkirche; 1660–62). Here, marked by an epitaph, is buried the heart of Count Montecuccoli, victor over the Turks in the battle of Mogersdorf (1664) and who died at Linz in 1680.

To the W of the town is the *Freinberg* (336 m/1102 ft), on the eastern slopes of which are the *Botanic Garden* and the *Stadium*. Higher up, in Freinberger Strasse, are the Linz *radio transmitter* and a *Jesuit convent*, with a massive round tower which formed part of the town's 1835 defences.

The district of **Urfahr**, on the left bank of the Danube, was a separate commune until 1919. To the right, beyond the bridge, is the *parish church* (Pfarrkirche; 1690–1702).

Above Urfahr to the NW is a prominent hill, the *****Pöstlingberg** (537 m/1762 ft), which can be reached either by one of the steepest mountain railways or by road (5·5 km/3$\frac{1}{2}$ miles). The *Pilgrimage church* (1738–48) has an 18th c. Pietà of carved wood which is the object of great veneration.

An old defensive tower has been converted into a *Fairytale Grotto* (Märchengrotte), with fairytale figures. The view from the hill is finest in the evening, with the Mühlviertel and the foothills of the Bohemian Forest to the N and the chain of the Calcareous Alps, from the

Wiener Schneeberg to the Schafberg, to the S.

SURROUNDINGS. – Trips on the Danube from the Nibelungenbrücke. – 9 km/5½ miles W of Linz is **Wilhering** (269 m/883 ft), on the S bank of the Danube, with a Cistercian *Abbey* founded in 1146 and rebuilt from 1733 to 1751 after a fire (Rococo *interior, frescoes by B. Altomonte, notable choir stalls). – 6 km/4 miles S of Linz on the S bank of the Traum stands Schloss Ebelsberg (originally 13th c.; museum of military history). – 15 km/9 miles SE of Linz is the abbey of **St Florian (see p. 173).

Lower Austria (Niederösterreich)

Bundesland: Niederösterreich (NÖ).
Administrative capital: St Pölten (previously Vienna).
Area: 19,172 sq. km/7400 sq. miles.
Population: 1,422,000.

(i) **Office of the Niederösterreichische Landesregierung,**
Fremdenverkehrsabteilung, Strauchgasse 1,
A-1014 Wien;
tel. (02 22) 6 35 71 10.
Niederösterreichische Fremdenverkehrswerbung,
Paulanergasse 11, A-1041 Wien;
tel. (02 22) 5 65 51 80.

Lower Austria is the largest of the nine Austrian provinces, including within its area the Federal capital, Vienna (itself a separate province), where the provincial government has its headquarters. Lower Austria is bounded on the N and E by Czechoslovakia, on the SE by the province of Burgenland, on the S by Styria and on the W by Upper Austria. Lying as it does in the area where the Eastern Alps fall away to the Hungarian plain, the province has a very varied topography, with a wide range of scenic beauty of many different types, from lofty mountains by way of the gentle wooded hills of the Alpine foreland to the Danube with its vine-clad loess terraces, from the granite plateau of the Waldviertel – geologically part of the Bohemian land mass – to the borders of Burgenland, where the landscape begins to show the distinctive characteristics of the Pannonian steppe.

The Danube flows through the province from W to E, dividing it into two roughly equal parts. To the N of the river, the terrain, at first flat, then becoming increasingly hilly towards the Czechoslovak frontier, comprises the Waldviertel and to the E of this the Weinviertel. S of the Danube the land rises gradually into wooded ranges of hills, including the well-known Wienerwald (Vienna Woods), and then into peaks of the Calcareous Alps, reaching heights of over 2000 m/6560 ft in the Schneeberg and the Rax, holiday regions much favoured by the people of Vienna.

Rarely has a river as strongly influenced the destinies of a country as the Danube has influenced those of Lower Austria. The political and cultural forces of the continent have met and mingled and fertilised one another on the Danube: a continuing process reflected equally in the meagre finds of potsherds of the prehistoric and early historical periods, in the abundant material of the Roman period (*Carnuntum*), in the castles and fortified churches of the Romanesque and Gothic periods and in the great monasteries (Melk, Göttweig, Zwettl, Altenburg, Klosterneuburg) and pilgrimage churches (Maria Taferl, Maria Laach) of the Baroque age.

The principal tributaries of the Danube in Lower Austria are the March and the Thaya, which form the frontier with Czechoslovakia to just NE of Vienna. The Leitha runs close to the Danube on the S but flows into it only in Hungary.

Of central importance within Lower Austria is the Vienna basin surrounding the capital, where many traffic routes intersect. This is approached from the W by the motorway from Linz, for the most part following the Danube, and the federal highway which runs through the Strudengau and the Nibelungengau, the Wachau and the Tullner Feld.

Old-established trade routes link the Vienna basin with Prague, Brno and Budapest; and to the SW roads cross the Semmering and Wechsel passes into Styria and beyond this to Zagreb and Ljubljana.

This central situation with its excellent communications promoted the development of a varied range of industries in the Vienna basin, now the largest industrial area in Austria.

Fossil sources of energy, such as coal and oil, are also worked here.

Lower Austria's well-developed and efficient agriculture also makes a major contribution to its economy. A particularly important part is played by wine production, with large areas of vineyards around Krems (particularly in the Wachau), S of Vienna and in the Weinviertel NE of the capital.

Since the 19th c., too, the tourist trade has been a steadily increasing source of revenue, the Wachau, the Wienerwald and the country around Semmering, with the Schneeberg and the Rax, being particularly popular areas.

HISTORY. – Lower Austria, a favoured area of settlement from prehistoric times onwards, is the heartland of Austria. After the indigenous population had been displaced by Illyrian immigrants these in turn were followed by *Celts*, bring the Hallstatt culture into Lower Austria. Further cultural influences resulted from the situation of the province at the intersection of the two great trade routes along the Danube and from the Baltic to Italy. – The *Romans* advanced from the S as far as the natural frontier on the Danube, establishing *Carnuntum* and other fortified camps to defend it. The territory N of the river remained thinly populated. The great migrations brought the end of Roman rule, and in subsequent centuries Lower Austria was frequently the scene of fighting with migrating peoples. In the 6th c. the Bajuwari (Bavarians) sought to establish themselves in this area but were frustrated by the invading *Avars* and *Slavs*. Charlemagne finally succeeded, after many years of fighting (791–797), in subduing these peoples and establishing his authority over the territory. The March (frontier territory) which he founded was the basis of the whole of Austria's later development.

The area was still, however, exposed to a major threat from the East, now represented by a Ural-Altaic tribe of horsemen, the *Hungarians*. In the 9th and 10th c. they advanced several times far into the lands on the western Danube, but in 955 suffered an annihilating defeat at the hands of Otto the Great in the battle of Augsburg. Otto II continued his father's efforts to win back the Danube territories, and his Margrave ("Count of the March") Leopold reached (*c.* 996) the Leitha, still in places the boundary between Lower Austria and Burgenland. About the same time the name of *Ostarrîche* – the origin of the modern Österreich, Austria – began to be applied to this area, which Frederick Barbarossa elevated into a hereditary duchy in 1156. The first duke was a scion of the Babenberg family, Henry II Jasomirgott. In 1192 the Babenbergs also inherited Styria, which long remained part of Lower Austria.

The early 13th c. saw several armed conflicts between local nobles and a continuing threat from the Hungarians on the eastern frontier. In 1251–52, however, King Ottokar of Bohemia gained control of the territory, ending the interregnum which existed since the death of Duke Frederick II, and thereafter he managed to establish a large measure of security on the eastern frontier, settle the internecine quarrels of the nobility and bring a degree of prosperity to the country.

The election of Rudolf of Habsburg as German Emperor brought a critical stage in the development of Lower Austria. The Babenberg possessions were declared Imperial fiefs, and Ottokar of Bohemia lost the ducal title. The final decision came in 1278 with the battle of the Marchfeld, in which Ottokar was killed. The Habsburgs now gained possession of the duchy, which was to become the most important of the hereditary Habsburg territories, and built numerous castles to defend it against the Hungarians.

After the division of the hereditary territories in 1379 the province was beset by conflicts between the heirs of Duke Albrecht II, which continued well into the 15th c. The NW part of Lower Austria was also much involved in the Hussite wars. Much more serious, however, were the ravages caused by the Hungarian invasions of 1479–90 under King Matthias Corvinus, during which almost the whole territory of Lower Austria was overrun. Only after Corvinus's death was the future Emperor Maximilian I able to re-establish Habsburg rule.

In the 16th c. a new enemy, long to remain a threat to the Habsburg empire, came to the fore. In 1529 the *Turks* advanced to Vienna, devastating the low-lying country and threatening the territory as far W as the Enns. Nevertheless it was during this period – the time of the great overseas discoveries – that the region's economy and trade developed and flourished.

The *Reformation* saw a rapid spread of Protestantism in Austria, particularly in the towns and among the minor country nobility. The Catholic princes, however, were opposed to this development, and the *Counter-Reformation* of the early 17th c. culminated in 1629–30, during the reign of Ferdinand II, with the expulsion of the Protestants.

Meanwhile the *Thirty Years War*, which was to bring Europe to the verge of total destruction, had broken out. In the earlier years of the war the northern parts of Lower Austria were ravaged by plundering and destructive hordes, while in its closing stages (1645) the *Swedes* occupied almost the whole territory N of the Danube.

The slow recovery which began after the Treaty of Westphalia in 1648 was hampered by two factors – the plague of 1679 in which many thousands died, particularly in and around Vienna, and the reappearance of the Turks at the gates of Vienna in 1683. On 12 September in that year, however, the besieging Turkish army suffered an annihilating defeat at the hands of a combined German and Polish force. The danger which had threatened Austria for 150 years was now finally removed, and the way was clear for a new cultural and economic upsurge, on which even further Hungarian risings and a further outbreak of plague in the early 18th c. had no lasting effect. There was a vigorous burst of building activity, both sacred and secular, the evidence of which is to be seen all over the country, and an equally vigorous development of industry.

This period of prosperity continued until the French wars (1805 and 1809) brought further devastation to Lower Austria. The subsequent trend towards political centralisation in Austria cut across the independence of this as of the other Austrian provinces; and it was not until 1848, with the establishment of a constitutional monarchy in place of the previous absolutist regime, that a modest degree of self-government was restored.

After the collapse of the Austro-Hungarian monarchy at the end of the First World War, Lower Austria became a province in the new federal state of Austria. In 1920 Vienna was made a separate province, and Lower Austria became the only part of the Republic without a capital of its own, its political institutions and administration being based in the Federal capital, Vienna.

The Second World War, like the First, brought further trials to Lower Austria. Indeed it suffered even more severely in the Second, with almost a third of the war damage in the whole country. Reconstruction after the war was hampered by the Soviet occupation, which continued until the conclusion of the Staatsvertrag of 1955. Since then Lower Austria has shared the destinies of the rest of Austria.

ART. – The earliest evidence of artistic activity in Lower Austria dates back to the *prehistoric period*. The best-known find of this period is the 25,000-year-old limestone statuette known as the "Venus of Willendorf", thought to be a fertility symbol. This, the earliest Austrian work of art, was found near the village of Willendorf in the Wachau together with a figurine carved from a mammoth's tusk. To a later period belong items excavated in the Leiser Berge which are assigned to the *La Tène* culture, the successor (*c.* 400 B.C.) to the Hallstatt culture.

There are numerous remains of the *Roman period*, particularly those excavated at Carnuntum, a frontier stronghold and a flourishing Roman town. The remains of temples and baths, mosaic pavements, cult statues, jewelry and much else besides bear witness to the high standard of culture and civilisation reached in this outlying province under the late Empire. A military base of about the same period has been excavated near Zwentendorf.

After the fall of the Roman Empire there was a great flowering of art in the **Romanesque** period. Although many buildings of this period were remodelled in the Gothic and to an even greater extent in the Baroque period, there are still examples of Romanesque architecture to be seen all over the province. The Romanesque style reached Lower Austria along the Danube from the W or on the "amber road" from Italy, achieving its first flowering in the great monastic buildings which the Babenbergs did so much to promote. The Cistercians were particularly active in this respect.

The abbey of Heiligenkreuz, founded in 1133, has a church with a Romanesque nave but a Gothic choir and Gothic vaulting; and the architectural influence of this mother house can be seen in the Cistercian abbeys of Lilienfeld and Zwettl. Lilienfeld Abbey, founded in 1202, has a church built in that year which already shows the transition to Gothic. The originally Romanesque abbey of Zwettl (founded 1159), however, was drastically remodelled in the Baroque period and has preserved little of the original structure – the chapterhouse (1159–80), the chapel (1218) and the cloister (1180–1240), which shows forms transitional to Gothic. Lower Austria has preserved numbers of *charnel-houses* (*Karner:* bone-houses, with a chapel for worship), dating from both the Romanesque and the Gothic periods. There are many secular buildings of Romanesque origin, including a number of ruined castles. The art of the period is also represented by many smaller works of art, the most splendid item being the Verdun Altar in Klosterneuburg with its 51 panels of champlevé enamel. Much fine stained glass and book illumination was also produced.

Gothic made headway in Lower Austria relatively late, about 1250, and its later development also showed a certain time-lag. It reached its full flowering only in the 15th c. and continued into the 16th c., when the rest of Europe was already in the throes of the Renaissance. In its earlier phase the Gothic style was still frequently combined with Romanesque elements, producing a mixed or transitional style, with many variants, which can be observed in some monastic buildings and churches, for example at Heiligenkreuz, Lilienfeld and Zwettl. The cloister at Heiligenkreuz, built between 1220 and 1250, shows in its successive phases a steady increase in Gothic stylistic elements, and the cloister at Zwettl (1180–1240) similarly shows a mingling of Romanesque and Gothic; the E end of the church at Zwettl (1343–83) is in *High Gothic* style (the rest is Baroque). The cloister at Lilienfeld (*c.* 1350), the largest of its kind in Austria, is stylistically uniform and wholly Gothic. – The architecture of the area was strongly influenced by St Stephen's Cathedral in Vienna, then reckoned to rank with Cologne and Strassburg as the finest cathedral of its day. The church at Eggenburg, in *late Gothic* style, was modelled on St Stephen's.

During this period sculpture began to throw off its earlier predominantly ornamental and archaic character. The figures of the Virgin and of saints which were now produced took on individual features and lost their former rigidity. This development can be observed in many winged altarpieces, particularly in the Waldviertel and the Wachau. – Panel painting also gained increased refinement. Among the oldest examples of this art form are the four paintings from the rear face of the Verdun Altar at Klosterneuburg, now in the abbey museum.

Simultaneously with the Reformation the **Renaissance** came to Lower Austria, bringing with it not only a new style of art but a change in human consciousness and patterns of thought which marked the beginning of the modern age. While hitherto the main artistic influences had come from the W, there now came a wave of influence, at least equally strong, from Italy. There was an increasing development of secular building, and the 16th c. saw the construction of the first aristocratic residences not primarily planned with military considerations in mind. At the same time the rapid development of firearms required a new approach to the techniques of fortification. Italian architects were the leading practitioners in this field, and they found a rich field of activity after the destructions of the Hungarian and Turkish wars. – The Counter-Reformation gave a fresh impetus to church building, which continued into the Baroque period.

The finest example of Renaissance architecture in Lower Austria is the Schallaburg near Melk, a remodelling (*c.* 1572) of a medieval fortified castle, with an arcaded courtyard of the kind which now came into fashion. –

Schloss Sierndorf (rebuilt 1516), also near Melk, has a chapel containing early Renaissance sculpture. A new form of decoration, used mainly on the façades of buildings, was the sgraffito technique, fine examples of which are to be seen at Krems, Horn and elsewhere.

Sculpture and panel painting now flourished, in both the religious field (altars) and the secular. The carved altar of Mauer, near Melk, shows the transition from Gothic to Renaissance.

The zenith of Lower Austrian architecture was reached in the **Baroque** period. The international situation was stable after the defeat of the Turks, and the economy prospered. Situated as it was on the old-established trade route along the Danube, Lower Austria benefited particularly from the busy trading activity of the period. During the *Early Baroque* period sumptuous monasteries and palaces were built and the art of fortification was still further perfected, as can be seen at Wiener Neustadt, Retz, Eggenburg and Drosendorf. The new architectural style was not, however, confined to palatial religious and secular buildings but also influenced more modest burghers' and peasants' houses.

Older churches were now increasingly remodelled in the fashionable style, the interiors being decorated with frescoes and later with stucco-work. The 18th c. also saw the building or rebuilding of many monastic complexes, promoted particularly by the Emperor Charles VI. Magnificent buildings of this period are to be seen at Melk, Göttweig, Klosterneuburg and Dürnstein. The structure of the building was now increasingly concealed under a riot of ornamental forms. Among architects principally active in Lower Austria were Jakob Prandtauer, Josef Munggenast and Lukas von Hildebrandt.

A leading representative of the sculpture of this period

Schloss Lichtenfels, on the Ottenstein reservoir (Waldviertel)

– often displayed in "plague columns" or "Turkish columns" commemorating a town's preservation from these dangers – was Georg Raphael Donner. The best-known Lower Austrian painter of the period was Martin Johann Schmidt, known as Kremser Schmidt, who was responsible for many altarpieces.

The Baroque period ended in the gay decorative forms of *Rococo*. – The only considerable buildings of the *Empire* period are to be seen at Baden, S of Vienna.

During the subsequent period no great architectural showpieces were built, but with the increasing development of technology attention was concentrated on works of engineering serving a functional need. The growth of travel and tourism also led to the building of large hotels and other buildings which still dominate the townscape of many resorts.

In every field of art there was now an increasing concentration on Vienna, with a consequent impoverishment of artistic activity in other parts of the country. Movements such as Art Nouveau, Expressionism, etc., made little headway in the provinces.

In recent times, too, the emphasis has been on buildings serving some technological function, including the large hydroelectric station at Ybbs-Persenbeug on the Danube or the nuclear power station at Zwentendorf, which a national referendum decided should not be brought into operation.

The **Waldviertel** (see p. 237) occupies the north-western part of Lower Austria. Where it approaches the Danube it merges into the romantic wine-producing **Wachau** (p. 235). Between the Waldviertel and Austria's eastern frontier on the rivers March and Thaya is the **Weinviertel** (p. 239).

N of the Danube, between Vienna and the March, stretches the **Marchfeld**, the largest plain in Lower Austria, which over the last two thousand years has seen bitter fighting between Romans and Germanic peoples, long-continued frontier warfare with Hungarians and Turks and the battles of the Napoleonic wars. – The Marchfeld is now the granary of Austria, and the fertile loess soil, constantly exposed though it is to the danger of degenerating into steppe, produces abundant crops of wheat and sugar-beet, with areas of pine forest and moorland here and there. In an area of this kind near Gänserndorf is Austria's only *safari park*.

Prince Eugene of Savoy, victor over the Turks, built his splendid hunting lodges around Hainburg, at the E end of the Marchfeld, and his example was followed by many other great nobles. One such mansion, *Schloss Marchegg*, now houses the large Lower Austrian Hunting Museum. The nearby *Schloss Orth*, a massive moated castle in the wide Danube meadowland, contains an interesting Fishery Museum.

S of the Marchfeld is the **Donauland** ("Danube Land"). – *Bad Deutsch-Alten-burg*, on the right bank of the Danube near the site of Roman *Carnuntum* (open-air museum; see p. 151), has a strong sulphur spring which was already being used for medicinal purposes in Roman times and still attracts visitors to the spa. A short distance S is *Rohrau*, the birthplace of Haydn, and the Schloss of the Harrach family, with one of the richest private collections of paintings in Austria.

To the S of the Danube the land rises into the **Alpine foreland** of Lower Austria, with the Ötscher and the Gemeindealpe, the Gippel and the Göller, the Hochkar and the Dürrenstein. Excellent roads ascend the valleys of the Ybbs, Erlauf, Pielach and Traisen into this beautiful region, which can also be reached from the E by way of the Triesting or Piesting valleys.

The *Ybbs* formerly powered many hammer-mills – the forerunners of the present-day heavy industry of Traisen and Böhlerwerk – and the ruins of some of these early industrial establishments can still be seen. The Ybbs valley is now also a popular holiday area, with little medieval towns and romantic narrow-gauge railways to add to the attractions of the countryside with its abundance of wildlife, and the river itself, well stocked with fish. In the area around its source is an expanse of unspoiled primeval forest.

The valleys of the *Grosse* and *Kleine Erlauf* were originally opened up by Carthusian monks from Gaming, providing access for the charcoal-burners and workers in the hammer-mills. The *Erlaufsee*, on the border with Styria near the source of the Erlauf, is the largest Alpine lake in Lower Austria. Farther down the valley the stream has cut a wildly romantic gorge through the limestone rocks.

The River *Pielach* (from the Slav *biela*, "white") is formed by the junction of two smaller streams, the Schwarzenbacher Pielach and the Nattersbach, near the massive ruins of the Weissenburg. The narrow-gauge Mariazellerbahn follows the windings of this quiet valley. Near Franken-fels, on the Nattersbach, is the *Nixhöhle*, one of the largest cave systems in the Alpine foreland region of Lower Austria.

The road through the *Traisen* valley has been used since the early Middle Ages by pilgrims making their way to *Lilienfeld Abbey* and *Mariazell*. The former wood-cutters' and miners' settlements are now trim summer holiday resorts, the mountains popular skiing areas.

The **Wienerwald**, which forms a wide arc round the NW and SW sides of Vienna, is at the north-east outer rim of the Alps, composed of limestones and sandstone. The Kahlenberg and Leopoldsberg in particular are popular resorts with the people of Vienna and visitors to the city.

Lungau

Land: Salzburg (S).

(i) **Verkehrsverein Tamsweg**, Rathaus, A-5580 Tamsweg; tel. (0 64 74) 4 16.

ACCOMMODATION. – IN TAMSWEG: *Knappenwirt*, B, 47 b.; *Grössingbräu*, B, 33 b.; *Weinstüberl*, B, 32 b.; *Weber*, B, 25 b., sauna. – CAMPING SITE. – IN MARIAPFARR: *Berghotel*, A, 36 b., SB, sauna; *Haus Carinth*, B, 65 b.; *Post*, B, 39 b.; *Neuwirt*, C, 25 b. – IN MAUTERNDORF: *Elisabeth*, A, 36 b., SB, sauna; *Neuwirt*, B, 60 b.; *Post*, B, 50 b., *Salzburger Land*, B, 41 b.; *Weitgasser*, B, 41 b. – CAMPING SITE. – IN ST ANDRAX: *Passager*, B, 37 b.; *Andlwirt*, C, 32 b. – IN ST MICHAEL: *Wastlwirt*, B, 107 b., SB, sauna; *Eggerwirt*, B, 72 b., sauna; *Urban*, B, 52 b., SB, sauna; *Bacher*, C, 70 b. – CAMPING SITE. – IN ZEDER-HAUS: *Kirchenwirt*, B, 38 b.

RECREATION and SPORTS. – Walking; old-time steam railway from Tamsweg to Mauterndorf; winter sports.

EVENTS. – *Samson Parades* throughout the Lungau, with figures up to 6 m/20 ft high (first Sunday in August); at Zederhaus and Muhr, procession (24 or 29 June) with flower-decked poles 6 m/20 ft long.

The Lungau, in the SE of Salzburg province, is a wide forest-covered basin (alt. 1000–1200 m/3300–3900 ft) watered by the tributary streams which form the River Mur, lying between the Schladminger Tauern (part of the Niedere Tauern) to the N and the Gurktal Alps to the S. Open only to

Schloss Moosham (Lungau)

the E, it is cut in two by the long flat-topped ridge of the Mitterberg (1581 m/5187 ft). In winter it is one of the coldest areas in Austria. Many old customs have been preserved in this remote high valley.

Until 1975 the Lungau could be reached from the N only by the Tauernpass Road (pass 1739 m/5706 ft), from the S only by way of the Katschberg (1641 m/5384 ft). Now, however, the Tauern motorway (toll), passing through the Tauern Tunnel (6·5 km/ 4 miles) to the N and the Katschberg Tunnel (5 km/3 miles) to the S, has opened up this sunny valley, with its fine walking country and its new winter sports facilities.

The main town in the valley is **Tamsweg** (1024 m/3360 ft; enclosed and open-air swimming pools), an attractive little town with a Rathaus of 1570 and a Baroque parish church of 1741. On a hill outside the town is the *Pilgrimage Church of St Leonard*, enclosed within defensive walls (1424–33), with fine stained glass (1430–50), Gothic panel paintings (*c.* 1460) and old frescoes.

SURROUNDINGS. – 9·5 km/6 miles NE is the *Prebersee* (1492 m/4895 ft), with good skiing in the area. From here it is 3½ hours' climb to the summit of the **Preber** (2741 m/ 8993 ft), to the N, from which there are magnificent views of the Lungau. – 10 km/6 miles SW is **Schloss Moosham**, with the interesting Lungau Museum.

A rewarding day trip from Tamsweg is up the Göriach valley (to the N) to the **Hochgolling** (2863 m/9394 ft), the highest peak in the Schladminger Tauern.

Mariapfarr (1120 m/3675 ft) has a pilgrimage church with 13th–14th c. wall paintings and a beautiful late Gothic winged altar. The town is also a skiing resort, with numerous ski-lifts.

Mauterndorf (1122 m/3681 ft; enclosed and open-air swimming pools), on the road which runs NW to the Tauern pass, is a summer holiday and winter sports resort. Above the handsome market square is an old *castle* (restored) built on the foundations of a Roman fort; the chapel has Gothic frescoes and a winged altar of 1452. The Romanesque cemetery church of St George has a beautifully carved gallery balustrade (1513).

A cableway runs up to the *Speiereckhütte* (2074 m/6805 ft), to the W, from which the *Speiereck* (2411 m/7910 ft) can be climbed. – 6 km/4 miles S is Schloss Moosham (see above).

St Michael (1068 m/3504 ft), on the road

to the Katschberg pass, is an old market village with a Gothic parish church (13th and 14th c. frescoes).

SURROUNDINGS. – To the W of St Michael the *Zederhaus valley*, through which the highway runs to Salzburg, joins the Mur valley. – A road leads W through the Mur valley to *Muhr* (1124 m/3688 ft) and *Rotgülden*, from which it is a 4–5-hour climb by way of the *Unterer Rotgüldensee* (1702 m/5584 ft; mountain hut) and the *Oberer Rotgüldensee* (1710 m/5611 ft) to the summit of the **Grosser Hafner** (3076 m/10,092 ft).

The pass over the **Katschberghöhe** (1641 m/5386 ft; Hotel: *Salzburger Hof, A1, 76 b., SB, sauna; Club Robinson) once dreaded for its steepness, maximum 29% (and still 16% after reconstruction of a short stretch) is little used now since the completion of the motorway tunnel. On the high slopes where snow is always to be found, lifts and pistes have been constructed. The Kareckhaus (1884 m/6052 ft) to the W, can be reached on foot in about an hour.

Maria Saal

Land: Carinthia (K).
Altitude: 505 m/1657 ft. – Population: 3450.
Post code: A-9063. – Telephone code: 0 42 23.
(i) **Marktgemeindeamt**, Am Platzl 7;
tel. 2 14 and 2 19.

ACCOMMODATION. – *Plieschnegger*, C, 33 b.; *Krassnig*, C, 19 b., SP; *Fleissner*, D, 14 b.

EVENTS. – *Vierbergewallfahrt* ("Four Hills Pilgrimage") in April.

The pilgrimage church of Maria Saal, on a hill above the Zollfeld some 10 km/ 6 miles N of Klagenfurt, is one of the leading places of pilgrimage in Carinthia. Here about the year 750 Bishop Modestus consecrated a church dedicated to the Virgin, from which the surrounding area was Christianised. In 1480 the Hungarians besieged the present fortified church but were unable to take it.

Carinthian Ducal Throne, Maria Saal

SIGHTS. – The twin-towered *church dates from the first half of the 15th c. The church and cemetery are surrounded by a defensive wall. On the S wall of the church are some fine old gravestones, including Gothic stones of red Adnet marble; there is also a Roman relief depicting a post wagon (probably 3rd c. A.D.). In front of the S doorway is a late Gothic *"lantern of the dead"*.

There is a fine octagonal Romanesque *charnel-house*, surrounded by a frescoed arcade of about 1500. Notable features in the interior of the church, a three-aisled hall-church, are a Tree of Jesse (1490) in the panels of the vaulting; in the second chapel on the left a pre-Romanesque altar table, under which is a Roman sarcophagus containing the remains of St Modestus (d. 763); and on the high altar (1714) a much venerated image of the Virgin (1425).

SURROUNDINGS. – N of the town is the *Carinthian Open-Air Museum*, with old peasant houses from all over Carinthia. – 2 km/1¼ miles W is *Karnburg* (508 m/1667 ft), with a parish church, originally the chapel of a Carolingian palace, which is the oldest church in Carinthia (9th c.). From here there is a road (6 km/4 miles) to the **Ulrichsberg** (1015 m/3330 ft), known to the Romans as *Mons Carantanus* (which gave its name to Carinthia), the site of a Noric sanctuary. This site was later occupied by a Gothic church, now in ruins; and it is now a memorial to the 1920 plebiscite and the dead of both world wars. Extensive views. – 1·5 km/1 mile N of Maria Saal, on the right of the road, is the ancient *Carinthian Ducal Throne* (*Kärntner Herzogstuhl*), surrounded by an iron railing. This double throne, on which the Dukes of Carinthia granted fiefs, is crudely constructed of old Roman stones. To the N extends the **Zollfeld**, a wide expanse of meadowland in which much material has been recovered from the site of Roman *Virunum*.

From *Willensdorf* there is a road (6 km/4 miles) to the *Magdalensberg* (1060 m/3478 ft), an ancient site which attracts many visitors. Here have been excavated the remains of a Celto-Roman settlement of the 1st c. B.C. and A.D., the oldest Roman settlement N of the Alps. The remains include the foundations of a temple, a law court, an imposing public building and a villa with baths and mosaic decoration. The Museum contains among much else a copy of the bronze figure of a youth which was found here in 1502. On the highest point of the hill is the Gothic *Magdalenenkirche*, with Roman blocks of dressed marble built into its walls. This is the starting-point of the "Four Hills Pilgrimage" held annually in April. Far-ranging views.

Maria Taferl

Land: Lower Austria (NÖ).
Altitude: 440 m/1444 ft. – Population: 800.
Post code: A-3672. – Telephone code: 0 74 13.
(i) **Marktgemeinde- und Fremdenverkehrsamt**, Haus Nr. 35; tel. 3 02.

ACCOMMODATION. – *Krone*, A, 100 b., SB, sauna; *Kaiserhof*, A, 40 b., SB, SP, sauna.

High above the Danube at the finest viewpoint in the Nibelungengau, as the section of the river between Ybbs and Melk is known, is the handsome early Baroque pilgrimage church of Maria Taferl. The church is said to have been built on the site of an oak tree on which was an image of the Virgin.

SIGHTS. – The twin-towered *pilgrimage church, in front of which is a Celtic sacrificial stone, was built between 1661 and 1711 by Jakob Prandtauer. It has a gilded pulpit with a multitude of figures and an organ-loft with rich gold decoration, both of the 18th c. From the hill on which the church stands there is a magnificent view over the Danube valley to the chain of the Alps, extending from the Wiener Schneeberg to the Traunstein, on the Traunsee.

SURROUNDINGS. – 5 km/3 miles downstream, on the S side of the Danube, is the old-world little town of **Pöchlarn** (213 m/699 ft; Hotel Moser, B, 66 b.), with a 15th c. tower and walls. The late Gothic church,

remodelled in the Baroque period, has altarpieces by Kremser Schmidt. In the Welserturm is a local museum, with finds from the Roman Danube port of *Arelapus*. In the "Nibelungenlied" *Bechelaren* is the seat of Margrave Rüdiger. The painter Oskar Kokoschka was born in the town in 1886 (memorial in his birthlace). – 5 km/3 miles N of Klein-Pöchlarn, on the left bank of the Danube, stands *Schloss Artstetten* (360 m/1180 ft), with a Baroque chapel in which Archduke Franz Ferdinand and his wife, murdered at Sarajevo in 1914, are buried.

Mariazell

Land: Styria (Stm).
Altitude: 870 m/2854 ft.
Population: 1900.
Post code: A-8630.
Telephone code: 0 38 82.
ⓘ **Fremdenverkehrsverein**, Hauptplatz 13; tel. 23 66.

ACCOMMODATION. – *Feichtegger*, A, 120 b.; *Mariazellerhof*, A, 30 b.; *Schwarzer Adler*, A/B, 65 b.; *Drei Hasen*, B, 130 b.; *Goldenes Kreuz*, B, 770 b.; *Rohrbacherhof*, B, 57 b.; *Goldene Krone*, B, 45 b. – YOUTH HOSTEL. – IN ST SEBASTIAN: *Marienwasserfall*, A, 30 b.; *Alpenhof*, B, 40 b. – CAMPING SITE.

RESTAURANTS. – *Jägerwirt*, Hauptplatz; *Altes Brauhaus*, Wiener Str.; *Goldene Krone*, Grazer Str.

Mariazell, Austria's most famous place of pilgrimage, founded by Abbot Otker in 1157, is also a mountain and winter sports resort. The church with its three towers looms over the town.

SIGHTS. – The **pilgrimage church** of the Nativity of the Virgin was built in Romanesque style about 1200. The Gothic choir was added in 1380–96, and the central tower at the W end is also largely Gothic; it is flanked by two Baroque towers with

Maria Taferl, above the Danube

Mariazell in winter

onion domes, and the whole church was remodelled in Baroque style in the 17th c. The great Baroque architects Fischer von Erlach the Elder and Younger played a major part in this reconstruction, and were also responsible for several altars. The treasury contains valuable votive offerings accumulated over six centuries.

Inside the basilica can be seen the tomb of the Hungarian Cardinal Mindszenty.

SURROUNDINGS. – There are superb panoramic views from the Bürgeralpe (1267 m/4157 ft; hotel) which can be reached by cableway. The descent on foot by way of the Hohlenstein (with a small cave) takes 1¾ hours. – 3·5 km/ 2 miles NW is the beautiful Erlaufsee. 2 km/1¼ miles N is the lower station of the chair-lift to the Gemeindealpe (1626 m/5335 ft), from which there are extensive views. – 16 km/10 miles N is the winter and summer resort of Wienerbruck (795 m/2608 ft), from which the *Ötscher (1892 m/6208 ft) can be climbed (6½ hours) by way of the Ötschergräben. The caves on the SE face are of interest for their ice formations. There is a chair-lift up to the Ötscherhaus (1420 m/4659 ft; inn); the lower station is in the village of Lackenhof (810 m/2658 ft), on the W side, which can be reached from Mariazell on a mountain road (30 km/19 miles) running NE through beautiful scenery.

A narrow but very beautiful road runs 13 km/8 miles S from Mariazell to the *Niederalplpass (1229 m/4032 ft; gradients up to 12%), which links the valley with the parallel valley of the Mürz. From the pass there are views of the Raxalpe and the Schneeberg. From the hamlet of Niederalpl (648 m/2126 ft) the Hohe Veitsch (1982 m/ 6503 ft) can be climbed in 2½–3 hours.

The road to Bruck continues climbing to the *Seeberg-pass (1254 m/4114 ft), a meadow-covered saddle surrounded by forest below the E face of the Hochschwab group. From the holiday resort of Seewiesen (986 m/ 3235 ft), to the S of the pass, the Hochschwab (2277 m/ 7471 ft; wide views; skiing) can be climbed in 5¼ hours. – From Aflenz (765 m/2510 ft) there are cableways to the Bürgeralm (1506 m/4941 ft; inn) and from there to the summit of the Windgrube (1818 m/5965 ft), from which there are magnificent panoramic views.

Matrei in Osttirol

Land: Tirol (T).
Altitude: 1000 m/3282 ft.
Population: 4300.
Post code: A-9971.
Telephone code: 0 48 75.

ⓘ Fremdenverkehrsverband, Rauterplatz;
tel. 65 27.

ACCOMMODATION. – Rauter, A, 120 b., SB, sauna; Goldried, A, 120 b., SB, sauna; Panzlwirt, B, 110 b.; Hinteregger, B, 45 b. – CAMPING SITE.

The little market town of Matrei in Ost-tirol, a popular health and tourist resort, nestles delightfully below the S face of the Hohe Tauern in a wide valley basin.

The town has been easily accessible from the N since the opening of the Felbertauern Tunnel (5200 m/5700 yds long) in 1967. It is a good base for walks and climbs in the surrounding valleys and mountains.

SIGHTS. – The imposing late Baroque parish church (c. 1780) has a 14th c. Gothic tower on the W front and St Nicholas' Church has frescoes dating from the 12th c. – On a limestone crag above the Matrei is Schloss Weissenstein (1029 m/3376 ft; privately owned).

SURROUNDINGS. – To the W of the town is the mouth of the Virgental. A road runs up the valley to Hinterbichl (17 km/11 miles), passing through gorges and several tunnels, opening up a *view of the head of the valley, with the Dreiherrenspitze (3499 m/11,480 ft).

From Prägraten (1310 m/4298 ft) it is 6½ hours' climb to the Defreggerhaus (2962 m/9718 ft; inn in summer), from which it is another 2½ hours to the summit of the *Grossvenediger (3674 m/12,054 ft; experienced climbers only, with guide). From Hinterbichl (1331 m/ 4367 ft) there is a pleasant walk up the Dorfer Tal past a number of waterfalls, including the almost subterranean *Gumpbachfall.

16 km/10 miles N of Matrei is the Matreier Tauernhaus (1512 m/4961 ft), at the entrance to the tunnel, from which a bridle-path leads up (3 hours) to the St Pöltner Hütte on the Felbertauern pass (2481 m/8140 ft).

8·5 km/5 miles S of Matrei two deep side valleys, one on either side, run into the Iseltal. To the W is the wild and romantic Defereggental, which has a good road (22 km/14 miles) up to St Jakob (1398 m/4587 ft). From the villages of Hopfgarten (with the Defereggen "rock garden"), St Jakob and Erlsbach (1555 m/5102 ft; 28 km/17 miles), the last settlement in the valley, there are good climbs on the peaks of the Defereggen group.

The Rotspitze (2956 m/9699 ft) can be climbed in 5½ hours, the Weissspitze (2963 m/9722 ft) in 7. At the head of the valley a road (closed to traffic) runs up from Erlsbach to the Patscherhaus (1667 m/5469 ft; inn), from which it is 3 hours' climb to the Barmer Hütte (2521 m/8271 ft), a base for climbs in the Rieserferner group. The valley is being increasingly developed as a winter sports resort.

The other side valley is the Kaiser Tal, which goes to the village of Kals (1325 m/4347 ft), 13 km/8 miles from the Felbertauern road. The slopes above the village on the *Glocknerblick have been developed as a skiing area (lifts). In summer the Goldried mountain railways can be taken as the start of walks along the *Panoramaweg Matrei-Kals, with 63 peaks above 3000 m/9846 ft in view. The Panoramaweg leads to the *Kals-Matreier-Törl (2207 m/7241 ft; inn in summer; 1–1¼ hours), from which the *Rotenkogel (2762 m/9062 ft) can be climbed (2¼ hours).

8 km/5 miles NE of Kals (toll road) is the Lucknerhaus (1848 m/6063 ft; inn), the starting-point of a 7-hour climb to the summit of the **Grossglockner (3797 m/ 12,458 ft). Between Kals and Lienz (see p. 124) is the Schober group, the highest peak in which is the Hoch-schober (3240 m/10,630 ft), best climbed from St Johann im Walde (749' m/2457 ft) by way of the Hochschoberhütte (2322 m/7618 ft); the climb to the hut takes 4½ hours, to the peak another 2½ hours.

Melk Abbey

Melk

Land: Lower Austria (NÖ).
Altitude: 228 m/748 ft. – Population: 6000.
Post code: A-3390. – Telephone code: 0 27 52.
ⓘ **Fremdenverkehrsstelle**, Rathausplatz 11;
tel. 23 07.

ACCOMMODATION. – *Stadt Melk*, A, 31 b., sauna;
Goldener Ochs, B, 70 b., sauna; *Fürst*, B, 20 b.; *Goldener
Stern*, C, 25 b.; *Stoll*, C, 22 b. – CAMPING SITE.

**At the point where the Danube enters
the celebrated wine-producing region
of the Wachau is the little town of
Melk, dominated by the massive bulk
of its Benedictine abbey, one of the
best-known and most splendid monastic houses in Austria. The abbey is
perched on a hill which slopes steeply
down to the Danube and is accessible
only from the E.**

HISTORY. – Melk was originally a Roman fortified post
(*Namare*). The hill was occupied by a Babenberg castle
which was made over in 1089 to the Benedictines. The
magnificent Baroque abbey was built by Jakob Prandtauer and Joseph Munggenast between 1702 and 1738.

SIGHTS. – The buildings of **Melk Abbey**
are laid out around seven courtyards. The
most prominent part of the complex, which
has a total length of 325 m/1065 ft, is the W
end, with the twin-towered church rising
above a semicircular terrace range. The
conducted tour takes about an hour. Visitors
are shown the *Prälatenhof* (Prelates' Court),
with a fountain; the 195 m/640 ft long
Kaisergang (Imperial Corridor), with portraits
of Austrian rulers; the *Marmorsaal* (Marble
Hall), with fine ceiling paintings by Paul

Troger; and the *Western Terrace*, from which
there are views both of the imposing façade
of the church and the Danube valley.

The high point of the visit is the interior of the
church, which ranks as the finest Baroque
church N of the Alps and has an intricately
carved pulpit. In the N wing is the *Library*,
with bookcases on the main floor and in a
gallery, and beautiful ceiling paintings; it
contains some 90,000 volumes and 1850
manuscripts.

SURROUNDINGS. – 7 km/4½ miles S of Melk is the
Renaissance *Schloss Schallaburg, with a magnificent
two-storey arcaded courtyard and terracotta decoration,
which now houses a museum of culture (conferences;
inn). – Between Melk and Schallaburg is the *Wachberg*
(285 m/935 ft), from which there are magnificent views of
Melk Abbey and the Danube valley.

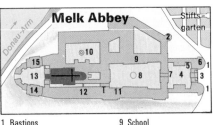

1 Bastions	9 School
2 Defensive tower	10 Konventshof (monks'
3 Entrance: to right St	quarters)
Koloman (Colman), to left	11 Kaisertreppe (Imperial
St Leopold	Staircase)
4 Forecourt	12 Kaiserzimmer (State
5 Ticket office	Apartments)
6 Kellerstüberl (restaurant)	13 Altane (Galleries)
7 Galleries (statues of Peter	14 Marmorsaal (Marble
and Paul, coat of arms,	Hall)
Melk Cross)	15 Library
8 Prälatenhof (Prelates'	T toilets
Court)	

Millstätter See

Land: Carinthia (K).

ⓘ **Kurverwaltung Millstatt,** Rathausplatz,
A-9872 Millstatt; tel. (0 47 66) 20 22.

ACCOMMODATION. – IN MILLSTATT: *Alexanderhof,* A,
120 b.; *Forelle,* A, 81 b., sauna; *Berghof,* A, 70 b.; *Seewirt*
with *Hubertusschlössl,* B, 90 b.; *Lindenhof,* B, 85 b.;
Seevilla, B, 76 b.; *Löcker,* B, 70 b. – IN SEEBODEN: *Royal
Hotel Seehof,* A, 120 b., SB, SP, sauna; *Bellevue,* A, 90 b.,
SB, sauna; *Strandhotel Koller,* A, 90 b., SB, sauna;
Seehotel Steiner, A/B, 100 b., SB, sauna; *Pichler,* B, 60 b.;
Moserhof, B, 47 b.; *Landhaus Gastein,* B, 37 b., SP. –
several CAMPING SITES. – IN DÖBRIACH: *Zanker,* A, 98 b.,
SB, SP, sauna; *Burgstallerhof,* A, 96 b., sauna; *Seefischer,*
A, 60 b., SP, sauna; *Post,* B, 72 b.; *Pucher,* B, 48 b. – several
CAMPING SITES. – IN BAD KLEINKIRCHHEIM: **Kurhotel
Ronacher,* A1, 168 b., SB, SP, sauna; **Pulverer,* A1,
150 b., SB, SP, sauna; *Alte Post,* A, 118 b., sauna;
Sporthotel, A, 95 b., sauna; *Kirchheimerhof,* A, 60 b., SB,
sauna; *Trattlerhof,* A, 50 b., sauna; *Kolmhof,* B, 80 b., SB,
SP, sauna; *Römerbad,* B, 47 b., sauna. – IN MÖLLBRÜCKE:
Kreinerhof, B, 84 b., SP, sauna. – IN SACHSENBURG:
Sonnenhof, C, 50 b.

WATER SPORTS. – Sailing, water-skiing, surfing instruction, pedalos, etc.

RECREATION ON LAND. – Guided walks (botanical
expeditions, mineral-collecting, walks on Alpine
meadows, etc.); hobby courses (woodcarving, verre
églomisé, copper-beating, etc.); art forum; exhibitions;
riding; tennis; covered thermal ozone bath.

**The *Millstätter See (alt. 588 m/
1929 ft), 12 km/7½ miles long, 1·5 km/
1 mile wide and up to 141 m/463 ft
deep, is beautifully set between the
wooded Seerücken (866 m/2841 ft) to
the S and the Nockberge to the N. The
main road runs along the N side of the
lake, with only narrow minor roads on
the S side. The lake is popular for water
sports, with water temperatures of up
to 25 °C/77 °F.**

The largest place on the lake is **Millstatt**
(pop. 1275), on a site which was occupied in

Roman times. It has a former Benedictine
abbey founded in 1070, with a High Romanesque church, a three-aisled pillared basilica
with a recessed doorway (*c.* 1170) and two
high towers. The fresco of the Last Judgment
by Urban Görtschacher (1513–19) is one of
the masterpieces of Austrian Renaissance art.
The choir and vaulting are Gothic, the altars
Baroque. The abbey museum is interesting.

SURROUNDINGS. – There are rewarding climbs, N of
Millstatt, to the **Millstätter Alpe** (2091 m/6861 ft), the
Tschiernock (2088 m/6851 ft) and the rolling country
round it. – From **Seeboden** (tennis coaching), at the W
end of the lake, there is a narrow road (10 km/6 miles) to
the *Hansbaueralm* (1718 m/5637 ft), with the lower
station of a cableway up Tschiernock.

On the E shore of the lake is **Döbriach**, from which there
is a road (12 km/7½ miles) into the Drau valley. 3·5 km/
2 miles along this road two side roads run E into the
mountains (fine views).

At **Radenthein** (746 m/2448 ft; magnesite plant), 5 km/
3 miles E of the lake on the road to the Turracher Höhe
(see p. 199), a very beautiful road branches off, running
along the shores of the **Brennsee** and the **Afritzer See**
to Villach.

12 km/7½ miles E of the lake is **Bad Kleinkirchheim**
(1073 m/3521 ft), a popular spa with thermal springs
and thermal bath. At the hot Katharinenquelle (spring)
is the pilgrimage church of St Katharina im Bade, with
famous bas-relief carvings. The winter sports area around
the little town is equipped with many cableways and lifts
going up to more than 2000 m/6560 ft. The Kaiserburg
chair-lift runs up to the *Kaiserburg* (upper station 1905 m/
6250 ft). From here the *Wöllanernock* (2145 m/7040 ft)
can be reached on foot. In the late Gothic parish church
in *St Oswald* (1319 m/4329 ft) can be seen frescoes
dating from the beginning of the 16th c. There is a chair-
lift up the *Brunachhöhe* (1910 m/6268 ft).

13 km/8 miles W of the Millstätter See are *Möllbrücke*
(558m/1831 ft; 15th c. Gothic church with carved altar)
and *Sachsenburg* (552 m/1811 ft; old town walls). Both
of these villages are good walking and climbing bases.
Between the two valleys is the **Salzkofel* (2498 m/
8196 ft), which can be climbed in 6 hours.

Sailing on the Millstätter See

Bad Mitterndorf

Land: Styria (Stm).
Altitude: 809 m/2654 ft. – Population: 2800.
Post code: A-8983. – Telephone code: 0 61 53.

ⓘ **Kurverwaltung,** Hauptplatz;
tel. 27 84 and 24 44.

ACCOMMODATION. – **Kurhotel Heilquelle Heilbrunn,*
A1, 160 b., SB, SP, sauna; *Hubertushof,* A, 48 b.; *Binder,*
A, 30 b., sauna. – IN IRDNING (17 km/11 miles SE): **Hotel
Schloss Pichlarn,* A1, 128 b., SB, sauna.

**The health resort of Bad Mitterndorf,
together with Tauplitz (891 m/2923 ft),
is a very popular summer and winter
sports resort with thermal baths. The
two places lie below the Mitterndorfer**

Seenplatte (Mitterndorf Lake Plateau; 1600–1700 m/5250–5575 ft) in the southern foothills of the Totes Gebirge. Around the Tauplitzalm is an excellent skiing area with numerous lifts.

SURROUNDINGS. – 2 km/1¼ miles S of Mitterndorf is the spa of **Bad Heilbrunn**, on the road to the *Stein pass* (gorge with a reservoir 5 km/3 miles long, formed by damming the Salza). Bad Heilbrunn has a thermal spring (28 °C/82 °F). – In *Thörl-Zauchen* a road branches off and runs N to the **Tauplitzalm** (1650 m/5414 ft), in the heart of an extensive area of good walking and skiing country. The Tauplitzalm has been developed into a modern skiing complex with numerous hotels and tourist facilities. It can be reached from *Tauplitz* by chair-lift. ½ hour's walk from the upper station of the chair-lift is the picturesque *Steyrer See* (1457 m/4780 ft); to the W a chair-lift runs up the *Lawinenstein* (1961 m/6434 ft; extensive views). – To the S of Tauplitz is the *Grimming* (2351 m/7714 ft), a 5-hour climb (with guide).

12 km/7½ miles E of Bad Mitterndorf is the village of **Pürgg** (786 m/2579 ft), with two interesting churches. The parish church of St George, originally Romanesque (1130) but later remodelled in Gothic, has fine *frescoes in the ringing chamber (12th c.). On a hill to the S is the little Romanesque chapel of St John, the whole interior of which is covered with 12th c. *frescoes. – 3 km/2 miles beyond this, in the Enns valley, stands *Trautenfels*, which has a fine castle built in the 13th c. to command the valley, with massive bastions and round towers. It contains rooms decorated with frescoes and stucco-work.

19 km/12 miles SW of Bad Mitterndorf, at the foot of the *Stoderzinken* (2047 m/7897 ft), lies the holiday and winter sports resort of **Gröbming** (776 m/2546 ft), the headquarters of Styrian horse-breeding. The parish church (1491–1500) is notable for its richly gilded *winged altar (1520) with figures of the Apostles. – The Stoderzinken, which commands extensive views, can be climbed in 3½–4 hours. There is also a toll road (12 km/7½ miles) to a car park at 1950 m/6400 ft.

Möll Valley (Mölltal)

Land: Carinthia (K).

ⓘ **Fremdenverkehrsamt Obervellach,**
Nr. 21, A-9821 Obervellach;
tel. (0 47 82) 25 10.

ACCOMMODATION. – IN DÖLLACH: *Schlosswirt*, A, 60 b., sauna; *Kahn*, B/C, 20 b.; *Pichler*, C, 34 b. – CAMPING SITE. – IN WINKLERN: *Post*, B, 90 b.; *Hasslacher*, B, 52 b. – IN OBERVELLACH: *Alpenhof*, B, 138 b.; *Post*, B, 57 b. – CAMPING SITES.

The valley of the Möll, which rises on the Grossglockner and flows into the Drau at Möllbrücke, runs rapidly down from the main Alpine chain towards the Klagenfurt basin. As a convenient

traffic route it was already of strategic importance in Roman times, and this beautiful valley is now the southern approach to the Grossglockner Road and the Tauern railway tunnel at Mallnitz.

The first place of any size on the Möll is **Heiligenblut** (see p. 84). – 10 km/6 miles S of Heiligenblut is **Döllach** (1024 m/3360 ft; pop. 1500), in the 15th and 16th c. a silver- and gold-mining area. There is an interesting local and mining museum in Schloss Grosskirchheim. There are a number of waterfalls near here, including one at the mouth of the *Zirknitz valley* and the 130 m/425 ft high *Jungfernsprung* at Pockhorn, to the N.

At **Winklern** (946 m/3104 ft; pop. 2500), which has a fine parish church and a medieval watch-tower, the Möll valley turns E. – 30 km/19 miles farther on is **Obervellach** (686 m/2251 ft; pop. 2600). Gold was discovered in this area in the Middle Ages, and there are many old mining shafts. The late Gothic parish church has a fine Dutch winged altar of 1520. Round the little town are a number of imposing medieval castles – *Oberfalkenstein* (15th c.), *Niederfalkenstein* (restored 1906), *Groppenstein* (12th and 15th c.), *Schloss Trabuschgen* (16th and 18th c.).

SURROUNDINGS. – Good climbs from Döllach; up the Gradenbach valley to the *Adolf-Nossberger-Hütte* (4¼ hours; inn) on the Gradensee (2488 m/8163 ft), from which the peaks of the **Schober group** can be climbed – e.g. by way of the *Lienzer Hütte* (1977 m/6487 ft) to the summit of the *Hochschober* (3240 m/10,630 ft). – The magnificently scenic *Wangenitzsee* (2508 m/8229 ft) can be reached from Döllach in 4¼ hours by way of the Wangenitz valley. From there it is 3 hours' climb to the summit of the *Petzeck* (3283 m/10,772 ft), the highest peak in the Schober group.

At Winklern a road branches off and runs over the pass, by way of the winter sports resort of *Iselsberg*, to the Drau valley and *Lienz* (p. 122). – *Ausserfragant* lies at the mouth of the grand *Fragant valley*, which leads to the glaciers and artificial lakes (reservoirs) of the *Goldberg group*, with peaks rising above 3000 m/9800 ft (Schareck, 3122 m/10,243 ft).

Below Burg Groppenstein, at Obervellach, are the 40 m/130 m high *Groppenstein Falls*. – 5½–6 hours SW of Obervellach is the highest peak in the Kreuzeck group, *Polinik* (2784 m/9134 ft), offering extensive views. – The road to the Tauern rail tunnel branches off and runs N. – 10 km/6 miles down the valley from Obervellach, at Kolbnitz, is the lower station of the Reisseckbahn, which ascends to the *Schoberboden* (2237 m/7340 ft; restaurant), from which the Höhenbahn, 3230 m/3530 yds long, continues to the *Reisseck plateau*, with numerous reservoirs at altitudes of about 2300 m/7550 ft. From the *Reisseckhütte* (2281 m/7484 ft) the /**Grosses Reisseck** (2959 m/9708 ft) can be climbed in 2¾ hours.

Mondsee

Land: Upper Austria (OÖ).
ⓘ **Fremdenverkehrsamt Mondsee,**
    Dr.-Franz-Möllner Strasse 5,
    A-5310 Mondsee;
    tel. (0 62 32) 22 70.

ACCOMMODATION. – IN MONDSEE: *Motel Mondsee*, A, 57 b.; *Weisses Kreuz*, A, 30 b.; *Seehotel Königsbad*, B, 65 b.; *Seehotel Lackner*, B, 32 b.; *Stabauer*, B, 32 b.; *Dachsteinblick*, C, 27 b. – several CAMPING SITES. – IN LOIBICHL: *Seehof*, A1, 50 b.

The **Mondsee* (alt. 481 m/1578 ft), 11 km/7 miles long and over 2 km/1¼ miles wide, one of the warmest lakes in the Salzkammergut, is picturesquely set against the backdrop of the sheer Drachenwand and the Schafberg. On the wooded slopes around the lake there is little human habitation – apart from the modest market town of Mondsee at the NW end and the villages of Scharfling and See at the S end only a few scattered hotels and houses. Water sports are available (bathing beaches, sailing schools).

At the NW corner of the lake is **Mondsee** (493 m/1618 ft; pop. 2000), a popular holiday resort. The church (1470–87), with a Baroque façade and an 11th c. crypt, originally belonging to a Benedictine abbey (founded in 748 and dissolved in 1791), has fine 17th c. altars. The old monastic building now houses a local museum (material from prehistoric lake dwellings). SE of the church in Hilfbergstrasse is the Mondseer Rauchhaus, an old peasant house (with furniture and furnishings), now an open-air museum.

On the SW shore of the lake the *Drachenwand* rears up vertically for almost 600 m/2000 ft. – From *Scharfling* (485 m/1591 ft) a road (partly blasted out of the rock) runs above the S side of the lake to the village of *See*, situated on a road which runs E to the Attersee. – To the S is the *Schafberg*, almost 1800 m/5900 ft high, which can be reached by cableway from St Wolfgang.

Montafon

Land: Vorarlberg (V).
ⓘ **Verkehrsverband Montafon,**
    Dorfgasse 521, A-6780 Schruns;
    tel. (0 55 56) 22 53.

ACCOMMODATION. – IN SCHRUNS: *Löwen*, A, 180 b., SB, sauna; *Kurhotel Montafon*, A, 100 b., SB, sauna; *Zimba*, A, 90 b.; *Alpenhof-Messmer*, A, 73 b., SB, sauna; *Taube-Post*, B, 56 b. – IN TSCHAGGUNS: *Verwall Alpenparkhotel*, A, 90 b.; *Cresta-Hotel*, A, 70 b., SB, sauna; *Sonne Sporthotel*, B, 72 b., SB, sauna. – IN ST GALLENKIRCH: *Adler*, B, 60 b. – IN GASCHURN: *Epple*, A, 121 b., SB, sauna; *Sonnblick*, A, 110 b., SB, sauna; *Posthotel Rössle*, A, 120 b., SB, sauna; *Verwall*, A, 70 b., SB, sauna. – IN BARTHOLOMÄBERG: *Fernblick*, B, 56 b., sauna; *Bergerhof*, B, 30 b. – IN VANDANS: *Central-Sporthotel Kaspar*, A, 60 b., SB, sauna; *Sporthotel Sonne*, B, 80 b., SB, sauna; *Brunella*, B, 60 b. – IN GARGELLEN: *Madrisa*, A, 126 b., SB, sauna; *Bachmann*, A, 70 b., SB, sauna; *Feriengut Gargellenhof*, A, 60 b.; *Heimspitze*, A, 38 b., sauna. – several CAMPING SITES.

RECREATION and SPORTS. – Montafoner Bahn, an old-time railway from Bludenz to Schruns (passengers can travel on footplate); riding, angling, etc.; climbing school in Schruns; climbing garden near Gaschurn.

The **Montafon* is a high valley some 40 km/25 miles long through which the Ill flows NW to join the Rhine. It begins S of Bludenz and runs up

Mondsee – a bird's-eye view

between the Rätikon massif in the W and the Verwall group in the E to the Bielerhöhe (2032 m/6667 ft), now traversed by the Silvretta-Hochalpenstrasse. The first settlers were Raeto-Romanic, and they have left their mark on the place-names and family names of the valley. This attractive valley and its side valleys are popular with walkers and skiers in both summer and winter.

The lower part of the Montafon is dominated by the pyramidal peak of Zimba (over 2600 m/8500 ft), whose shape has earned it the name of the "Matterhorn of Austria". The upper part of the valley lies under the peaks, the glaciers and the artificial lakes of the *Silvretta massif (Piz Buin, 3312 m/ 10,867 ft; Piz Linard, 3411 m/11,191 ft, which is in Switzerland).

At the mouth of the valley is the scattered community of Vandans (650 m/2133 ft). A road (closed to ordinary traffic) serving the Ill hydroelectric project climbs the beautiful Rellstal to the Untere Zaluandaalm (1700 m/ 5580 ft), and there is a pleasant walk (5½ hours) along this road to the *Lüner See (1970 m/6464 ft). There is a chair-lift from Vandans to Latschau, connecting with the Golmerbahn.

In a wider part of the valley, on the right bank of the Ill at the point where it is joined by the Litzbach, is the chief town in the Montafon, Schruns (690 m/2264 ft; pop. about 3500), which together with

Tschagguns (686 m/2251 ft; pop. 2400), on the left bank, forms the main tourist attraction of the valley. Schruns has an interesting local museum in a 17th c. peasant house; Tschagguns a pilgrimage church (1812–15; 14th c. choir).

SURROUNDINGS. – A cableway from Schruns serves the Kapellalpe (1855 m/6086 ft; restaurant; magnificent views), E of the town, continuing to the Sennigrat (2300 m/7550 ft), on the E side of the Hochjoch (2520 m/8268 ft). – Chair-lift from Tschagguns to Grabs (1365 m/4479 ft). – From Latschau there is a funicular up the Golm (upper station 1890 m/6200 ft). The whole area offers great scope for mountain walks and climbs.

From Schruns a road goes 5 km/3 miles NE up the Litzbach valley to Silbertal (889 m/2917 ft), where silver and copper were mined from the 14th to the 16th c. Cableway to the Kristberg (1442 m/4731 ft), with a chapel of 1407 (late Gothic carved altar).

N of Schruns is *Bartholomäberg (1085 m/3560 ft), probably the oldest settlement in the Montafon. The parish church (1732) has a carved altar of 1525, a fine late 18th c. organ and a valuable 13th c. *processional cross with Limoges enamels.

Farther up the valley is St Gallenkirch (900 m/2954 ft; pop. 2000), a picturesque and rather straggling settlement with a parish church built in 1478 and altered in 1669; harmonious Rococo interior with several altars, a pulpit and an organ. – A chair-lift runs up to the Garfreschahüsli (1850 m/6070 ft).

From here a road leads 8 km/5 miles SW up the Gargellental to the health and winter sports resort of Gargellen (1450 m/4759 ft), between the Rätikon and Silvretta massifs. Chair-lift to the Schafberg (upper station 2100 m/6890 ft; several ski-lifts). It is a climb of

Schruns, chief town of the Montafon

5–6 hours to the summit of the *Madrisaspitze* (2770 m/9088 ft) or the *Madrisahorn* (2836 m/9305 ft), which is in Switzerland.

Gaschurn (1000 m/3282 ft; pop. 1100) is the starting-point for the "Silvretta Nova" winter sports area (several ski-lifts). The Versettla chair-lift goes up, via the inter-mediate station of Rehsee (1480 m/4856 ft), to the upper station at *Burggraf* (2010 m/6596 ft; restaurant). The **Versailspitze* (2464 m/8084 ft; extensive views) can be climbed by way of the *Versailhaus* (2280 m/7481 ft; accommodation; skiing area).

At **Partenen** (1027 m/3370 ft; pop. 650) is the beginning of the magnificent **Silvretta Road (see p. 179).

Mühlviertel

Land: Upper Austria (OÖ).

(i) **Fremdenverkehrsverbände-Gemeinschaft Mühlviertel,**
Dinghoferstrasse 4, A-4020 Linz;
tel. (07 32) 7 66 16.

ACCOMMODATION. – IN FREISTADT: *Goldener Adler*, B, 51 b.; *Goldener Hirsch*, B, 50 b.; *Goldene Sense*, B, 26 b.; *Hubertus*, B, 22 b. – IN KEFERMARKT: *Horner*, C, 25 b. – IN BAD LEONFELDEN: *Kurhotel*, A, 115 b., SB; *Böhmertor*, A, 100 b., SB, sauna; *Waldschenke*, C, 30 b., SP, sauna; *Goldenes Dachl*, C, 30 b. – IN SANDL: *Braun*, A, 36 b. – IN KÖNIGSWIESEN: *Fellhofer*, C, 25 b.; *Dungerl*, C, 20 b. – IN NEUFELDEN: *Mühltalerhof*, A, 50 b., sauna. – IN AIGEN: *Almesberger*, A, 113 b., SB, sauna; *Haagerhof*, B, 52 b., SB; *Bärnsteinhof*, C, 32 b. – YOUTH HOSTEL. – two CAMPING SITES.

The **Mühlviertel in Upper Austria, to the N and NW of Linz between the Danube and the Czechoslovak frontier, is a rolling wooded plateau rising from the Danube to the Bohemian Forest, deeply slashed by the valleys of the Grosse and the Kleine Mühl. To the W it merges into the foothills of the Bavarian Forest, to the E into the Waldviertel. The highest point is the Sternstein (1125 m/3691 ft); the average altitude of the settlements is between 500 and 600 m (1640 and 1970 ft).**

This region of mainly agricultural land and forest contributes little to the national economy, and the main tourist routes pass it by. The total absence of any major industry has led to a rural exodus, princi-pally to Linz. For holiday visitors looking for quiet and relaxation, however, the

Mühlviertel offers excellent walking country and reasonably priced accommodation. Woodland alternates with pasture and arable land, here and there on higher ground can be seen a castle or the ruins of one, and there is a whole range of quiet little market towns and villages.

Freistadt (560 m/1837 ft; pop. 6700), in the NE of the area, is the chief town in the lower Mühlviertel, a fortified settlement on the old trade route into Bohemia which preserves its walls, towers and gates. In the spacious Hauptplatz is the handsome *parish church* of St Catherine (14th–15th c., remodelled in Baroque style in 1690, rebuilt in Gothic style in 1967). At the NE corner of the square is a gateway leading to the 14th c. *Schloss Freistadt*, with a 50 m/165 ft high keep which now houses the *Mühlviertler Heimathaus*, a local museum with a large collection of verre églomisé (glass decorated with a layer of engraved gold). Outside the Böhmertor (Bohemian Gate) is the little *Liebfrauenkirche* (15th c.).

11 km/7 miles S of Freistadt is **Kefermarkt** (512 m/1680 ft; pop. 1800), an old town in the valley of the Feldaist. The *parish church* of St Wolfgang (15th c.) has a superb Gothic **carved altar of limewood, with life-size figures, 13·5 m/44 ft high and 6·3 m/21 ft wide; the artist is unknown. – Above the town to the N stands the imposing *Schloss Weinberg* (17th c.; hunting trophies, pharmacy of 1680, etc.).

Kefermarkt altar: St Christopher

Waldburg (683 m/2241 ft) lies off the main road 7 km/4½ miles W of Freistadt. The *parish church* of Mary Magdalene has three fine Gothic *winged altars and old choir-stalls.

20 km/12½ miles W of Freistadt is **Bad Leonfelden** (749 m/2457 ft; pop. 3000), a spa (mud baths, Kneipp treatment) with a pilgrimage church of 1791. To the N is the Sternstein (1125 m/3691 ft; chair-lift), the highest point in the Mühlviertel, with a look-out tower. This is a popular skiing area in winter and also attracts many visitors in summer.

15 km/9 miles NE of Freistadt is **Sandl** (927 m/3041 ft), famed for its colourful verre églomisé (see p. 141). It lies below the S side of the *Viehberg* (1111 m/3645 ft; several lifts), a popular skiing area.

Königswiesen (600 m/1969 ft; pop. 3000), an old market town in the E of the Mühlviertel, now attracts summer visitors. The two-aisled *parish church* of the Assumption is a masterpiece of late Gothic architecture (fine reticulated vaulting).

Neufelden (488 m/1601 ft), another old market town (since 1217) which is now a holiday resort, lies in the valley of the Grosse Mühl, dammed here to supply water for the Partenstein hydroelectric station. It has handsome Baroque houses and a 15th c. parish church. The town has an important role in the Mühlviertel linen-weaving industry. – To the N is *Burg Pürnstein* (first recorded 1170), now largely ruined. – To the W is the *Altenfelden Wildlife Park* (birds of prey).

Aigen (596 m/1955 ft) is a pleasant old market town and holiday resort in a wooded setting in the north-western Mühlviertel. – Immediately S of Aigen is **Schlägl** (564 m/1850 ft), with a *Premonstratensian abbey* founded in 1218 and rebuilt in the 17th c. The church, originally early Gothic, was remodelled in Baroque style in the 17th c. (beautiful wrought-iron choir screen of 1684, pulpit of 1646–47, choir-stalls of 1735). Picture gallery (1898); library.

SURROUNDINGS. – From Aigen a road climbs N to the *Panyhaus* (946 m/3104 ft), from which it is a half-hour walk through beautiful forest country to the *Bärenstein* (1076 m/3530 ft), or an hour to the *Moldaublick* (1046 m/3432 ft; look-out tower 26 m/85 ft high; also reached by road from Ulrichsberg). From both of these heights there are good views of the 42 km/26 mile long Lippener-Moldau reservoir, in Czechoslovakia. – A road

runs NW from Aigen to **Ulrichsberg** (626 m/2054 ft), from which there is a continuation to the winter sports complex, 10 km/6 miles N, of *Holzschlag-Hochficht* (restaurant; several lifts, including one up the Hochficht, 1338 m/4390 ft).

Haslach (531 m/1742 ft), 12 km/7½ miles SE of Aigen, is a linen-weaving town. Weaving Museum in the old school; local museum in an old gate tower; late Gothic parish church of St Nicholas.

Murau

Land: Styria (Stm).
Altitude: 832 m/2730 ft. – Population: 2500.
Post code: A-8850. – Telephone code: 0 35 32.
ⓘ **Verkehrsverein,** At the station;
tel. 27 20.

ACCOMMODATION. – *Lercher,* A, 43 b., sauna; *Brauhaus,* B, 43 b., sauna; *Bärenwirt,* C, 26 b.

RECREATION and SPORTS. – Excursions by steam train on the **Murtalbahn.** Covered and open-air swimming baths; tennis; riding; water-sports.

The old town of Murau lies amid extensive forests in the upper valley of Styria's principal river, the Mur, below the Stolzalpe, which rises to over 1800 m/5900 ft. In summer Murau is a good base for excursions, walks and climbs in the surrounding valleys; in winter the Frauenalpe (2004 m/ 6577 ft) and the Kreischberg (2050 m/ 6728 ft) offer good skiing.

SIGHTS. – Above the left bank of the Mur rises the early Gothic *parish church of St Matthew* (13th c.; 14th c. frescoes; Gothic Crucifixion group). In front of the church is a "lantern of the dead", a fine example of late Gothic sculpture. Higher up is the handsome *Schloss Obermurau* (Renaissance, with a beautiful arcaded courtyard), seat of the

The Murtalbahn, Murau

Schwarzenberg family. To the E are the 14th c. *cemetery chapel of St Anne*, with late Gothic stained glass, and the *church of St Giles* (St Ägidius), the oldest church in the town (Romanesque, with 14th c. frescoes). – S of the Mur is the *Kalvarienberg* (Calvary), with the prominent *St Leonard's Church* (15th c.) and the ruined *Burg Grünfels*.

SURROUNDINGS. – To the S of the town is the *Frauenalpe* (2004 m/6575 ft), which can be climbed in 4–5 hours. The route runs through the Bürgerwald. – To W and E extends the **Mur valley**, in a still largely unspoiled upland region of pasture and woodland, with ample scope for walkers. The Mur rises at the Murtörl, E of Badgastein in the province of Salzburg, flows through the Lungau and enters Styria at Predlitz. It then continues E between the Niedere Tauern to the N and the Gurktal Alps to the S, cuts through the hills S of Bruck, flows through Graz and finally joins the Drau (Drava) in Yugoslavia.

20 km/12½ miles NW of Murau is *Krakaudorf* (1172 m/3845 ft), which has a parish church (15th and 18th c.) with a painted coffered ceiling of the 16th c. – 12 km/7½ miles N of Murau is the resort of *Schöder* (898 m/2946 ft), with a late Gothic church (frescoes) and the impressive Günsten Falls. From here a toll road crosses the *Sölker-Tauern pass* (1790 m/5873 ft) into the Enns valley.

15 km/8 miles SE of Murau is the market village of **St Lambrecht** (1036 m/3399 ft), with a large Benedictine abbey founded in the 11th c., probably by monks from St Blasien in the Black Forest. The church, with twin onion-domed towers, dates from the 14th–15th c., the other buildings from the 17th–18th c. The abbey has a small art collection and a large collection of Austrian birds. There is an abbey school. – The parish church of St Peter (1424) has fine carved winged altars.

Neusiedler See

Land: Burgenland (B).

ⓘ **Burgenland-Tours**, Untere Hauptstrasse 12, A-7100 Neusiedl;
tel. (0 21 67) 81 41.

ACCOMMODATION. – IN NEUSIEDL: *Wende*, A, 202 b., SB, sauna; *Haus am Tabor*, B, 63 b.; *Mauth*, B, 30 b.; *Leiner*, C, 27 b. – YOUTH HOSTEL. – IN PURBACH: *Am Spitz*, A, 34 b. – CAMPING SITE. – IN RUST: *Seehotel Rust*, A, 180 b., SB, sauna; *Arkadenhof*, C, 32 b. – YOUTH HOSTEL. – CAMPING SITE. – IN PODERSDORF: *Haus Attila*, A, 42 b.; *Martinshof*, B, 49 b.; *Seewirt*, B, 30 b. – CAMPING SITE. – AT PAMHAGEN: *Pannonia Holiday Village* (hotel and bungalows), A, total of 778 b.

WATER SPORTS. – Swimming, fishing, sailing, motor-boat trips; best facilities at Podersdorf.

RECREATION ON LAND. – Walking; trips in horse-drawn gypsy caravans; pony-trekking, particularly from Illmitz to the Lacken (nature-watching).

EVENTS. – Annual *Operetta Festival* on the floating stage at Mörbisch; *Passion Play* in the old quarry at St Margarethen.

The **Neusiedler See* (alt. 115 m/377 ft) is one of Europe's most unusual lakes. The only steppe lake on the continent, it is 35 km/22 miles long and between 5 and 15 km/3 and 9 miles wide. It is, however, extremely shallow – 1–1·8 m/40–72 in. deep. The shallow water, slightly saline, thus warms up very quickly in summer to a temperature of over 25 °C/77 °F. The water level varies according to the rate of evaporation: between 1866 and 1869 the lake dried up completely. With practically no inflow of water and no outflow, the lake is fringed round almost its whole circumference with a girdle of reeds up to 5 km/3 miles wide. The only reed-free area is on the E side of the lake around Podersdorf, where there are a number of beautiful beaches.

Puszta landscape on the Neusiedler See

The reeds provide a home for more than 250 different species of birds (birdwatching station), and there are many rare water plants. Most of the plant and animal life is under statutory protection. Visitors may not catch or alarm any of the wildlife, nor may they damage, remove or buy any plants or parts of plants.

The nature wardens responsible for ensuring that these regulations are observed are entitled to search visitors for this purpose. The reeds are cut commercially and used in stucco-work. – A huge reservoir of mineral water has been located under the lake by geologists.

To the E the land merges into the steppe-like puszta, which is covered with a luxuriant growth of vegetation in spring but in late summer becomes withered and dusty. In the Seewinkel area, towards the Hungarian frontier, there are numerous small lakes and ponds, the "Lacken", also fringed by reeds. These lakes, the most interesting of which is the Lange Lacke, can be reached on foot or on horseback (rental of horses).

Above the N of the lake is the little town of **Neusiedl** (133 m/436 ft; pop. 4000), with a Lake Museum which gives a comprehensive view of the animal and plant life of the area. The Gothic parish church has a Baroque "ship" pulpit of 1780. Above the town is a massive medieval tower. Large vineyards in the surrounding area.

A causeway 1·5 km/1 mile long runs through the belt of reeds to the bathing and other facilities on the open water (swimming pool, mud baths, restaurant, motorboat landing-stage, rental of rowing boats and dinghies, sailing school).

ON the NW side of the lake, on the "Neusiedler Lake Wine Highway" which runs from Neusiedl to Eisenstadt, is *Breitenbrunn* (140 m/460 ft), with a tall watchtower (museum) of the Turkish period in the main square. The parish church, in front of which are the Kreuzkapelle (Chapel of the Cross, 1706) and a Gothic "lantern of the dead" is surrounded by a defensive wall with loopholes. From here a road (4 km/2½ miles) and a boat canal descend to the lake (bathing beach, restaurant, rental of boats).

To the SW is **Purbach** (124 m/407 ft), a vine-growing town and holiday resort with a well-preserved circuit of walls (four massive gates), dating from the time of the Turkish raids (16th–17th c.) and old houses.

On the W side of the lake is **Rust** (121 m/397 ft), a well-known wine town and tourist resort with excellent facilities for water sports. Thanks to its wine (Ruster Ausbruch), resembling Tokay, it was given the status of a royal Hungarian free city. It has many well-preserved burghers' houses of the Renaissance and Baroque periods; many of the houses have storks' nests on their roofs.

The *Fischerkirche* (Fishermen's Church), first recorded in 1493, lost its tower in 1879; it has 15th c. wall paintings (New Testament scenes) discovered in 1953, a beautiful Gothic altar and a Gothic tabernacle, and is still surrounded by a defensive wall. In the main street is a house, known as "Zum Auge Gottes", with a fine 18th c. oriel wndow. The Seetor (late Gate) dates from 1715.

From Rust a causeway 1 km/¾ mile long runs through the reeds to the swimming area (restaurant). – On the road from Rust to *St Margarethen* (4 km/2½ miles), some 300 m/330 yds to the N, is an old *quarry of Leitha limestone which was already being worked

in Roman times. Stone from this quarry was used in the construction of St Stephen's Cathedral and other buildings in Vienna.

During the summer artists of different nationalities work here, producing works of monumental sculpture, usually abstract in form, many examples of which (some of them painted) are scattered about the quarry. Every summer a Passion Play is performed here, as it has been for the last 40 years.

In the St Margarethen quarry

5·5 km/3½ miles S of Rust, near the Hungarian frontier, is **Mörbisch** (118 m/387 ft), an attractive little town of traditional Burgenland type, with gaily decorated arcaded houses and long narrow lanes. Mineral spring (drilled in 1959); large vineyards in surrounding area.

A causeway 1·7 km/1 mile long leads to the bathing beach, with an island offshore. Here there are excellent facilities for various water sports (sailing school) and a floating stage on which performances of operettas are given in August.

On the E side of the lake, 15 km/9 miles S of Neusiedl on the "Seewinkel Wine Highway", is the bathing resort of **Podersdorf** (122 m/400 ft), with a reed-free beach (motorboat station, many wine-shops). Here, too, there are many storks' nests on the reed-thatched houses. The parish church dates from 1791.

8 km/5 miles E is **Frauenkirchen**, named after its magnificent pilgrimage church (1695–1702), which contains a much venerated Gothic image of the Virgin taken from the church's medieval predecessor; unusual Stations of the Cross (Kalvarienberg).

S of Podersdorf, between the lake and the Hungarian frontier, is the **Seewinkel**, an area of salt steppe country dotted with small lakes and ponds (the *Lacken*), with interesting plants and wildlife (many species of birds). To the W is **Illmitz** (117 m/384 ft), a typical puszta village at the foot of the vine-clad Illmitzer Höhe, with a mineral spring and a Biological Station. A causeway 5 km/3 miles long runs SW between reedy "Lacken" to the bathing beach on the Neusiedler See. E of Illmitz is the *Lange Lacke*, a well-known bird sanctuary with many rare plants.

St Andrä (123 m/404 ft), the chief town in the Seewinkel area, has a picturesque main square and reed-thatched houses. The *Zicksee*, to the W, a lake with a high sodium carbonate content, has a beach of fine sand.

SURROUNDINGS of Neusiedl. – 13 km/8 miles SE is the market village of **Halbturn** (128 m/420 ft), with many maize barns. The Imperial hunting lodge here, built by Lukas von Hildebrandt in 1710, is one of the finest Baroque buildings in Austria. The great hall has ceiling paintings by Anton Maulpertsch, commissioned by Empress Maria Theresa. There is a large and beautiful park.

12 km/7½ miles N of Neusiedl lies the old town of **Bruck** *an der Leitha* (180 m/590 ft; pop. 7000; Pension Eder, C, 86 b.), at the passage of the Leitha through the chain of hills between Burgenland and the Vienna basin. Parts of the town walls have been preserved. Schloss Prugg, originally a moated castle, dates in its present form from the 18th and 19th c.; beautiful park. The parish church in the main square was built between 1696 and 1740.

8 km/5 miles NE of Bruck is *Rohrau*, where Haydn was born in 1732, son of the local smith; the thatched house in which he was born is now a museum. The Schloss of the Harrach family (17th–18th c.), in which Haydn's mother was a cook, contains an important collection of pictures.

23 km/14 miles W of Neusiedl is **Mannersdorf** (216 m/709 ft), which in the mid 18th c. was a fashionable spa (sulphur spring). The magnificent Baroque Schloss, originally a 17th c. house, was completely rebuilt for Maria Theresa in 1754–55.

Niedere Tauern

Länder: Salzburg (S) and Styria (Stm).
Altitude: Highest point: Hochgolling (2863 m/9394 ft).
ⓘ **Österreichischer Alpenverein,**
Sektion Radstadt,
A-5550 Radstadt 467.
Sektion Schladming,
Ramsauerstr. 129, A-8970 Schladming.
Sektion Trieben,
ÖAV-Heim, A-8784, Trieben 1.
Sektion Judenburg,
Kaserngasse 9, A-8750 Judenburg.
Sektion Murau,
Erzherzog Johann Siedlung 3, A-8850 Murau.

The Hohe Tauern range is continued, E of the Murtörl, by the Niedere Tauern, with the Enns, Palten and Liesing valleys to the N and the Mur valley to the S. Many densely wooded and thinly populated valleys cut into the range on either side, but there are few low passes between the two sides. There are many small mountain lakes in the high valleys and hollows.

The higher peaks in the main range are not easy to climb, usually demanding good rock-climbing experience, but there are also many easier peaks commanding magnificent views. The Niedere Tauern also offer some of the most varied skiing terrain in Salzburg and Styria.

The western end of the Niedere Tauern is formed by the **Radstädter Tauern**, extending from the Murtörl to the Radstädter Tauern pass, with boldly shaped peaks such as the **Hohes Weisseck** (2712 m/8898 ft) and **Mosermandl** (2680 m/8793 ft). Both of these command extensive views and are relatively easy to climb, but they are so far from any of the larger places in the valleys that they attract few climbers.

The Radstädter Tauern, particularly the hills N of the main range, are a popular skiing area. The best skiing slopes are to be found in the Wagrain winter sports area, with the Wagrainer Haus and the "Wagrainer Walk" (taking in six peaks), the wide expanse of country around the *Trappenkarsee*, in the largest high mountain hollow in the Salzburg Alps, and the area round the *Radstädter Tauern pass* (1738 m/5702 ft).

E of the pass are the **Schladminger Tauern**, with what is probably the best walking country for the summer visitor in the whole of the Niedere Tauern.

The highest peaks in this part of the range, the *Hochgolling (2863 m/9394 ft) with its mighty N face and the massive pyramid of the **Hochwildstelle** (2747 m/9013 ft), can be climbed from Schladming, in the Enns valley, either by way of the Golling-Hütte (1630 m/5348 ft) or the Preintaler Hütte (1656 m/5433 ft); either way the ascent is relatively short and is accordingly very popular with climbers.

The central ridge is less suitable for skiing, but there is excellent skiing to be had on the northern outliers, including the **Planai**, with the Schadminger Hütte (1830 m/ 6004 ft), and the *Hauser Kaibling*, with the Krummholz-Hütte (1850 m/6070 ft).

The high valleys are extraordinarily rich in lakes, such as the *Giglachseen* near Schladming, the *Riesachsee* (1333 m/ 4374 ft) on the way to the Preintaler Hütte, the beautiful lakes near Aich in the Seewig valley, the *Bodensee* and *Hüttensee*, and the lonely *Schwarzensee* near Kleinsölk. The lakes are particularly numerous in the high hollows S of the Preintaler Hütte.

The main ridge of the **Wölzer Tauern**, to the E of the Schladminger Tauern, is remote from human settlements of any size. Its peaks, grass-covered for much of their height – the *Greim* (2474 m/8117 ft), the *Oberwölzer Schoberspitze* (2423 m/7950 ft), etc. – are for the most part easy to climb from the Neunkirchner Hütte (1525 m/5004 ft) near Oberwölz. The lateral ranges on the N side are among the easiest skiing areas in the Austrian Alps, the most popular slopes being on the Planneralpe (*c.* 1600 m/5250 ft). – In the Enns valley, to the N of the Wölzer Tauern, is the warm *Putterer See* (650 m/2133 ft), near Aigen, a popular lake for swimming.

The last part of the Niedere Tauern range is the **Rottenmanner Tauern**. The sharp-edged *Grosser Pölsenstein* (2449 m/ 8035 ft) can be climbed from Trieben by way of the Edelraute-Hütte (1725 m/ 5660 ft) on the *Kleiner Scheiblsee*; the **Hochreichart** (2417 m/7930 ft) from Kallwang or from the quiet Ingeringgraben (Ingeringsee), near Knittelfeld, to the S.

These and many other mountains, particu-larly around the village of Hohentauern, on the pass, draw more visitors for winter sports than in summer.

Ossiacher See

Land: Carinthia (K).

Gemeindeamt Ossiach, Nr. 8, A-9570 Ossiach; tel. (0 42 43) 4 97.

ACCOMMODATION. – IN OSSIACH: *Strandhotel Prinz*, B, 64 b.; *Elisabeth*, B, 61 b.; *Post*, B, 60 b.; *Neuhof*, 42 b. – IN BODENSDORF: *Bierpeter*, A, 52 b.; *Alpenhotel*, B, 78 b., SP, SB; *Urbaniwirt*, B, 75 b. – IN ANNENHEIM: *Kanzelhof*, B, 60 b., SP; *Villa Koch*, B, 45 b., SP, sauna; *Jäger*, B, 36 b.; *Marienheim*, B, 25 b., SP; *Lindenhof*, C, 24 b. – several CAMPING SITES, on the lake, especially on the S bank.

RECREATION and SPORTS. – Rowing, water-skiing, sailing (schools at St Andrä and Bodensdorf); walking.

EVENT. – "*Carinthian Summer*" (musical festival, July–Aug.) at Ossiach.

The *Ossiacher See, the third largest lake in Carinthia, is 11 km/7 miles long, 1 km/¾ mile wide and up to 47 m/155 ft deep, coming after the Wörther See and the Millstätter See. Surrounded by wooded hillsides and peaks affording extensive views, with a water temperature in summer of up to 26°C/79°F, the lake has become a popular holiday area and the lakeside villages draw large numbers of visitors with their facilities for water sports and other attractions.

On the S side of the lake is its largest village, *Ossiach* (pop. 600), with a Benedictine abbey founded in the 11th c., rebuilt in the 16th c. and dissolved in 1783.

Annenheim, on the Ossiacher See

The church has a fine Baroque interior and the convent buildings are decorated with 18th c. frescoes and stucco-work. – Opposite Ossiach on the N side of the lake is the resort of *Bodensdorf*, with the Gerlitzen rearing above it (reached by a beautiful toll road).

At the NE end of the lake is the pretty little resort of *Steindorf*; to the SW, on the N side near the end of the lake, *Annenheim*; and at the extreme southern tip of the lake *St Andrä*.

SURROUNDINGS. – From Annenheim the Kanzelbahn (cableway) runs up to the **Kanzelhöhe** (1489 m/4885 ft; several hotels, look-out tower), a good skiing and walking area. From the top there are splended views over the lake and the Klagenfurt basin, extending as far as the Karawanken. To the N is the Pöllinger Hütte (1630 m/5348 ft).

From Bodensdorf a toll road (12 km/7½ miles) runs up the **Gerlitzen** (1909 m/6263 ft; hotel; observatory), a popular view-point (good skiing terrain; several lifts). – Above St Andrä, to the S (1·5 km/1 mile on a steep road, with gradients up to 22%) are the imposing ruins of the Renaissance *Schloss Landskron* (677 m/2221 ft) (restaurant), from which there are extensive views of the lake and the town of Villach to the SW.

Tiffen, on the road to Feldkirchen, has an old fortified church standing on higher ground which contains carved Roman stones and 15th c. wall paintings. – **Feldkirchen** (556 m/1824 ft; pop. 12,000; Hotel Dauke, A, 40 b.; Rainer, A, 36 b.) is a lively little town with many old houses and streets which retain something of a medieval aspect. Particularly fine are the houses in the "Old Quarter" (Altes Viertel) and the Biedermeier façades (1815–48) in the Hauptplatz.

The parish church of the Assumption is Romanesque, with a Gothic choir (fine 13th c. frescoes, late Gothic winged altar and crucifix of the early 16th c.). On the surrounding heights are a number of castles, and near the town are several small lakes (Flatschacher Teich, Urbansee, Maltschacher See).

Ötztal

Land: Tirol (T).

ⓘ **Fremdenverkehrsverband,**
A-6433 Ötz;
tel. (0 52 52) 62 80.

ACCOMMODATION. – IN ÖTZ: *Posthotel*, B, 100 b.; *Alpenhotel*, B, 90 b.; *Drei Mohren*, B, 50 b.; *Seerose*, B, 48 b., sauna. – IN HABICHEN: *Habicherhof*, A, 62 b., SP, sauna. – IN UMHAUSEN: *Falknerhof*, B, 25 b.; *Hirschberger-hof*, C, 36 b. – IN LÄNGENFELD: *Sulztalerhof*, B, 70 b., sauna; *Hirschen*, B, 53 b. – IN SÖLDEN: *Central*, A, 120 b., SP, sauna; *Alpina*, A, 75 b., sauna; *Parkhotel*, B, 80 b.; *Gurglerhof*, B, 36 b., sauna. – IN HOCHSÖLDEN: *Enzian*, B, 115 b., sauna; *Schöne Aussicht*, B, 87 b., sauna.

The *Ötztal*, through which flows the Ötztaler Ache, is the longest side valley (55 km/34 miles) on the S bank of the upper Inn, extending up into the Ötztal Alps. The mouth of the valley, at Ötz, is wide and fertile; then, half-way up, it narrows into a succession of gorges alternating with wide expanses of meadowland. The road climbs S in a series of "steps", passing many waterfalls and affording impressive views of the peaks and glaciers of the Ötztal Alps.

The villages in the Ötztal are excellent bases for walks and climbs in the surrounding mountains, and they are increasingly developing also into winter sports resorts. From the head of the valley the Timmelsjoch Road (see p. 189), which is open for only a few months in the year, crosses the pass into Italy.

5 km/3 miles S of the junction of the Ötztaler Ache with the Inn is Ötz (820 m/2690 ft), which attracts many visitors on account of its mild climate. Above the town rises the 14th c. parish church (enlarged in 17th–18th c.). – 9 km/5½ miles S is **Umhausen** (1036 m/ 3399 ft), an attractive little holiday resort at the mouth of the Hairlachbach. It is the oldest settlement in the valley, and has a Gothic parish church.

10 km/6 miles farther up the valley is **Lägenfeld** (1179 m/3868 ft), the main tourist area in the middle Ötztal and a popular health resort, situated at the mouth of the Sulztal. The parish church of St Catherine in *Oberlängenfeld* (originally late Gothic) has a tower 74 m/243 ft high. – Beyond *Huben* (1194 m/3918 ft) the valley narrows into a wild gorge, opening out again only at **Sölden** (1377 m/4518 ft), a widely scattered settlement which has developed into an internationally known summer and winter sports resort. Together with **Hochsölden** (2070 m/6792 ft), which is noted for its many hours of sunshine and has excellent ski slopes, it forms the principal tourist area of the upper Ötztal. The parish church, originally Gothic, was remodelled in Baroque style in 1752. – After passing through the narrow *Kühtreienschlucht* (gorge) the road comes to **Zwieselstein** (1472 m/4830 ft), where the Ötztal divides into the *Gurgler Tal* (to left) and the *Venter Tal* (to right).

SURROUNDINGS of the Ötztal villages. – 3 km/2 miles SW of Ötz, on a wooded terrace above the valley, is a warm lake, the **Piburger See** (915 m/3002 ft; nature reserve). 45 minutes' walk NW is the *Auerklamm* (gorge).

4 hours E is the *Bielefelder Hütte* (2112 m/6929 ft), a good climbing base. – There is a fine road by way of the Ochsengarten to the *Kühtaisattel* (2016 m/6614 ft) and from there down into the Sellrain valley.

From *Umhausen* there are a number of good climbs up the peaks to the W: for example by way of the *Erlanger*

Sölden, in the Ötztal

Hütte (2550 m/8367 ft; inn) to the *Wildgrat* (2974 m/ 9758 ft; 7 hours), or by way of the *Frischmannhütte* (2240 m/7349 ft; inn) to the *Fundusfeiler* (3080 m/ 10,105 ft; panoramic views). – SE of Umhausen (3 km/ 2 miles by road, ¼ hour on foot) are the *Stuiben Falls*, which plunge down 150 m/490 ft under a natural rock bridge.

Längenfeld is a good base for climbs of the western *Geigenkamm*, the highest peak of which, the **Hohe Geige** (3395 m/11,139 ft), rears up to the SW. – 5 km/ 3 miles E of Längenfeld is *Gries* (1573 m/5161 ft), a small holiday resort in a beautiful setting of wooded hills. From here it is 2½ hours' climb NE up the Winnebach to the **Winnebachsee-Hütte** (2372 m/7783 ft); inn, accommodation) on the *Winnebachsee*, the starting-point of many local climbs. From the hut a path runs SE up the Sulztal along the Fischbach. A 2½ hour climb will bring you to the *Amberger Hütte* (2135 m/7005 ft; inn; accommodation), magnificently located on the little *Schwefelsee* (18 °C/64 °F), with the *Schrankogel* (3496 m/ 11,470 ft), the second highest peak in the Stubai Alps, to the E. – From *Huben*, 4 km/2½ miles S of Längenfeld, there is a path (5½–6 hours) through the *Pollesklamm* (gorge) and SW up the Pollesbach to the *Pitztaler Jöchl* (3035 m/ 9958 ft), at the end of a road from Sölden.

Sölden offers many opportunities for walks and excursions in the surrounding area. Good skiing in winter and summer skiing on the *Tiefenbachferner* (parking, restaurants, lifts) and on the *Rettenbachferner*. The two glacial areas are linked by a road tunnel (2822 m/9262 ft). Two cableways run up from Sölden to **Hochsölden**. The Ötztaler Gletscherbahn runs SW from Sölden–Wohlfahrt (1369 m/4492 ft) by way of the *Gaislachalm* station (2173 m/7130 ft; restaurant; ski-lifts; on foot 2 hours) to the *Gaislacher Kogel* (3058 m/10,033 ft; panoramic restaurant; magnificent views). In winter there is a chair-lift from Sölden to *Innerwald* (upper station 1464 m/ 4803 ft). From Hochsölden a chair-lift runs up to the *Rotkogel* (upper station 2364 m/7756 ft).

To the SE there is a climb by way of the *Falknerhütte* (1977 m/6487 ft; inn in summer) and the *Brunnkogelhaus* (2737 m/8980 ft; inn in summer) to the *Brunnenkogel* (2780 m/9121 ft; extensive views); to the E through the gorge-like Windachtal by way of the *Fieglwirtshaus* (1957 m/6421 ft; accommodation) and then either in 5 hours to the *Siegerlandhütte* (2710 m/ 8892 ft; inn; accommodation), at the head of the valley, or in 5½ hours to the **Hildesheimer Hütte** (2899 m/9512 ft; inn; accommodation), on the *Pfaffenferner*, the starting-

point for ascent of the *Schaufelspitze* (3333 m/10,936 ft; 1½ hours, not difficult to experienced climbers) or the *Zuckerhütl* (3507 m/11,506 ft; 3 hours with guide).

From *Zwieselstein* a road runs 13 km/8 miles SW up the *Venter Tal* to the magnificent mountain village of **Vent** (1896 m/6621 ft; Post-Hotel, A 60 b.; Vent, B, 73 b., sauna; Similaun, B, 42 b., sauna), on the waymarked footpath (No. 902) from Obergurgl to the Inn valley. Several chair-lifts and ski-tows; weather station; glacier observatory. A steep mountain road (gradients up to 30%) leads up to *Rofenhöfe* (2014 m/6608 ft), to the W, the highest village in Austria which is occupied all year round. To the N is the *Wildspitze* (3774 m/12,382 ft), the highest peak in northern Tirol; to the S the *Thalleitspitze* (3407 m/ 11,178 ft) and to the right of this the *Kreuzspitze* (3457 m/ 11,342 ft).

At the head of the *Gurgltal*, which runs S from Zwieselstein, is **Obergurgl** (1930 m/6332 ft), the highest parish in Austria (see p. 189).

Ötztal Alps

Land: Tirol (T).
Highest point: Wildspitze (3774 m/12,382 ft).
Österreichischer Alpenverein,
Sektion Innerötztal,
Riml, A-6450 Sölden 561.

The great massif of the Ötztal Alps, between the Inn valley and the Ötztal, has more glaciers than any other group in the Austrian Alps and a series of peaks rising above 3700 m/12,000 ft. The range is slashed by three long narrow valleys running down to the Inn – the densely populated Ötztal, with its highest farms lying above 2000 m/ 6500 ft, the Pitztal and the Kauner Tal.

The Austrian-Italian frontier runs along the summit ridge, with its numerous peaks over 3000 m, the highest being the gigantic ice dome of the *Weisskugel* (3739 m/

12,268 ft). The Ötztal Alps reach their highest point, however, in the northern ridge, with the precipitous, permanently snow-covered bulk of the *Wildspitze (3774 m/12,382 ft). The broad *Gepatsch-Ferner*, with its much fissured tongues of ice reaching far down the valley to the Gepatsch-Haus in the Kauner Tal (1928 m/6326 ft), is the second largest glacier in the Austrian Alps. On an island of rock amid the ice is the Brandenburger Haus (3272 m/10,735 ft), which can be reached from Vent, in the Venter Tal, by way of the Vernagt-Hütte (Würzburger Haus, 2766 m/9075 ft) or by way of the Hochjoch-Hospiz (2423 m/7950 ft) on the long *Hintereisferner*.

There are several routes up the Wildspitze – the shortest starting from the Breslauer Hütte (2840 m/9318 ft) near Vent, the best from Mittelberg in the Pitztal, under the magnificent *Mittagskogl* (3162 m/10,375 ft); alternatively from Sölden by way of the Braunschweiger Hütte (2759 m/9052 ft) and the beautiful *Mittelbergferner*.

The brilliantly white **Similaun** (3607 m/11,835 ft) and the wild *Hintere Schwärze* (3628 m/11,903 ft) can be climbed from the Martin-Busch-Hütte (Samoar-Hütte, 2501 m/8206 ft). A popular valley-to-valley walk is from Vent by way of the Ramolhaus (3006 m/9863 ft) on the **Ramolkogl** (3551 m/11,651 ft) to Obergurgl, the highest parish in Austria (1930 m/6332 ft), at the head of the Gurgltal, which branches SE off the Venter Tal at Zwieselstein.

The peaks and glaciers of the Ötztal Alps offer endless scope for climbers. Many of the highest peaks present no particular difficulty to climbers with experience in glacier-walking. Above all, however, these mountains are a paradise for skiers, with many peaks climbable right up to the summit ridge and long and relatively easy descents.

The descent from the Wildspitze by way of Hochsölden to Sölden is one of the longest and finest in the whole of the Alps, with a fall of some 2400 m/7900 ft. There is a fine waymarked path (No. 902) from Obergurgl through the tremendous world of the glaciers to Pfunds in the Inn valley.

Three long narrow ridges run N from the main range – the Geigenkamm, the Kauner Grat and the Glockturnkamm. Although they have fewer glaciers than the main ridge they are still highly impressive, with several peaks over 3000 m/9800 ft.

The *Geigenkamm* lies between the Ötztal and the Pitztal, from either of which it can be climbed. The highest peak, the **Hohe Geige** (3395 m/11,139 ft), can be scaled without great difficulty from Plangeross in the Pitztal by way of the Neue Chemnitzer Hütte (2323 m/7622 ft). The mountain huts in this range are linked by an interesting ridge path which runs from the Erlanger Hütte (2550 m/8367 ft), near Umhausen in the Ötztal, by way of the Hauersee-Hütte (2330 m/7645 ft), on the little *Hauersee* near Längenfeld in the Ötztal, to the Chemnitzer Hütte and continues, as the "Hindenburg-Steig", to the Braunschweiger Hütte.

The most difficult peaks in the Ötztal Alps are in the rugged *Kauner Grat*, which runs N in an almost straight line between the Pitztal and the Kauner Tal. This is an area for tough and experienced climbers only, with steep-sided and ice-girdled peaks such as the *Watzespitze* (3533 m/11,592 ft) and the *Hintere Ölgrubenspitze* (3296 m/10,814 ft).

Compared with other parts of the Ötztal Alps the *Glockturmkamm*, between the Kauner Tal and the upper Inn valley, attracts fewer climbers. The highest peak, the **Glockturm** (3355 m/11,008 ft) can be climbed from the Hohenzollern-Haus (2123 m/6966 ft) near Pfunds. The *Nauderer Berge*, which project W towards the Reschen (Resia) pass, are an increasingly popular skiing area.

In the mountain hollows of the Ötztal Alps, particularly in the northern ridges, there are numerous small lakes mirroring the snow-capped peaks in their crystal-clear waters. The largest of these lakes – apart from the 6 km/4 mile long **Gepatsch-Speicher**, a man-made reservoir – is the *Riffelsee* (2232 m/7323 ft) near Mittelberg in the Pitztal. The only lake in the valleys is the dark green forest-fringed *Piburger See* (915 m/3002 ft) near Ötz (nature reserve).

Paznauntal

Land: Tirol (T).

ⓘ **Fremdenverkehrsverband Ischgl**, .Postfach 24, A-6561 Ischgl; tel. (0 54 44) 3 18.

ACCOMMODATION. – IN SEE: *Mallaun*, C, 90 b. – IN KAPPL: *Post*, B, 70 b., sauna; *Silvretta*, B, 28 b.; *Auhof*, B, 26 b.; *Edelweiss*, C, 35 b.; *Hirschen*, C, 24 b. – IN ISCHGL: *Madlein*, A, 130 b., SB, SP, sauna; *Post*, A, 130 b., SB, sauna; *Ischglerhof*, A, 100 b.; sauna; *Sonne*, B, 80 b.; sauna; *Salnerhof*, B, 63 b.; sauna; *Goldener Adler*, B, 55 b.; sauna.

The narrow **Paznauntal, 35 km/ 22 miles long, runs SW from Landeck to Galtür between the Verwall group in the N and the Samnaun group in the S,** watered by the River Trisanna. The villages in the valley are good bases for walkers and climbers, and in winter this is a relatively quiet skiing area.

The road up the valley is the eastern approach to the Silvretta-Hochalpenstrasse (see p. 179), which runs up from Galtür to the Bielerhöhe. – Beyond *Pians* the road crosses the River *Sanna*, passes below *Burg Wiesberg* (16th c.; privately owned) and then under the bold **Trisanna Viaduct* (86 m/282 ft high, 230 m/250 yds long; built 1884, rebuilt 1923 and 1964) carrying the Arlberg railway (car parks; view) to enter the Paznauntal.

The road climbs steeply through the *Gfällschlucht* (gorge) and comes to **See** (1058 m/3471 ft), the lowest village in the valley. Chair-lift to the *Medrigjoch* (1834 m/ 6017 ft); footpath through the Samnaun group to Serfaus. – We continue up the beautiful valley, with farmsteads dotted about on its meadow-covered slopes. – From *Kappl* (1170 m/3829 ft) there is a chair-lift to the *Diasalpe* (1750 m/5740 ft), from which the **Hoher Riffler** (3168 m/ 10,394 ft), to the N, can be climbed.

Ischgl (1377 m/4518 ft), the main town in the valley, is a popular summer and winter resort (numerous ski-lifts; "Silvretta-Ski-Arena"). The parish church, originally late Gothic, dates in its present form from 1757. – From Ischgl-West (1362 m/4469 ft) the Silvrettabahn (cableway) goes up to the *Idalpe* (2320 m/7612 ft), from which there is a ski-lift in winter to the *Idjoch* (2763 m/ 9065 ft). From Ischgl-Ost there is a cableway to the *Pardatschgrat* (2620 m/8596 ft). – From Ischgl it is 5 hours' climb to the *Darmstädter Hütte* (2426 m/7960 ft; inn; accommodation), in the Verwall group to the N, and from there another 3½–4½ hours to the **Küchenspitze** (3148 m/10,329 ft), the highest peak in the Verwall group.

The road continues up the valley from Ischgl to *Galtür* (1583 m/5194 ft), a winter sports resort with abundant snow at the end of the **Silvretta-Hochalpenstrasse* (see p. 179).

Petronell (Carnuntum)

Land: Lower Austria (NÖ).
Altitude: 189 m/620 ft. – Population: 1250.
Post code: A-2404. – Telephone code: 0 21 63.
ⓘ **Gemeindeamt,** Kirchengasse 57; tel. 22 28.

ACCOMMODATION. – *Marc Aurel*, C, 55 b.; *Rasthaus Carnuntum*, C, 10 b., sauna.

The Roman town of *Carnuntum, on the right bank of the Danube to the E of Vienna, rapidly developed into an important trading station and focus of communications. The extensive excavated remains and the material to be seen in the museums at Petronell and Bad Deutsch-Altenburg bear witness to the long history of the settlement.

HISTORY. – Early in the 1st c. A.D. the *legionary fortress* of **Carnuntum**, on the "amber road" to northern Europe, was founded on a site to the E of the present town of Petronell. The fort, which was also designed to serve as a base for the Roman Danube fleet, was given ever stronger defences in subsequent centuries until its abandonment about A.D. 400. – The associated Roman *civilian settlement* lay to the W of Petronell. It flourished particularly in the 2nd and 4th c. A.D., when it had a population of more than 50,000 and enjoyed a high standard of life and culture. Several Roman emperors resided in the town at various times.

SIGHTS. – The remains of the legionary fortress of **Carnuntum**, which was some 475 m/520 yds long by 335–400 m/ 370–440 yds across, have been partly excavated. Some 500 m/550 yds farther E, to the left of the road, is the **first amphitheatre**, built about A.D. 180, which had seating for 8000 spectators (occasional open-air performances).

Considerable remains of the civilian settlement have also been excavated. The buildings of a former residential, trading and craftwork quarter are partly paved with mosaic. In an open-air museum can be seen documentation on gravestones in Carnuntum. Of particular interest is a mosaic depicting Orpheus among the animals. To the S of the modern road is the **second amphitheatre** (2nd c. A.D.; seating for 13,000), the grass-covered remains of which can be seen from the road. Standing by itself some 10 minutes' walk S of this amphitheatre, beyond the railway, is the **Heidentor* ("Pagans' Gate"), the remains (14 m/46 ft high) of a Roman triumphal arch (2nd c. A.D.), originally with four gates.

The *parish church* of **Petronell** is Romanesque and Gothic, with a Baroque interior.
Beside the road is a circular Romanesque
chapel, now the burial vault of the Counts
Traun. – To the N is the imposing 17th c.
Schloss of the Traun family, originally a
moated castle. It has a magnificent staircase
in the courtyard. Near the Schloss are the
remains of a *Roman palace*, including baths
(104 m/114 yds by 143 m/156 yds).

SURROUNDINGS. – 5 km/3 miles S of Petronell is
Rohrau, where Haydn was born in 1732, son of the
local smith; there is a small museum in the house in
which he was born. The Schloss of the Harrach family
(17th–18th c.), in which Haydn's mother was a cook,
contains an important collection of pictures.

4 km/2½ miles NE of Petronell is **Bad Deutsch-
Altenburg** (168 m/551 ft; Kurthotel, A, 115 b.), with
hot springs (sulphurous, containing iodine; 28 °C/
82 °F). The *Museum Carnuntinum* contains finds from
Carnuntum, including in particular a Mithraeum, with a

carving of Mithras killing the bull and votive offerings. In
the 17th c. Schloss Ludwigstorff is an *African Museum*.
Fine Romanesque charnel-house.

Pinzgau

Land: Salzburg (S).

ⓘ **Verkehrsverein Mittersill,**
Markt 110, A-5730 Mittersill;
tel. (0 65 62) 3 69.
Verkehrsverein Bruck,
A-5671 Bruck/Glocknerstrasse;
tel. (0 65 45) 2 95.

ACCOMMODATION. – IN WALD: *Walderwirt*, B, 70 b.,
SB, sauna; *Romantik Jagdhotel Graf Recke*, B, 45 b.,
SB; *Almhof Königsleiten*, B, 44 b.; *Edelweisshaus*, C,
90 b.; *Finkenhof*, C, 58 b. – CAMPING SITE. – IN
NEUKIRCHEN: *Gassner*, B, 132 b., SB, sauna; *Neuhof*, B,
99 b.; *Kammerlander*, B, 90 b.; *Unterbrunn*, B, 55 b. – IN
BRAMBERG: *Hubertus*, B, 16 b.; *Kristall*, C, 25 b.; *Keil*, C,
25 b. – CAMPING SITE. – IN MITTERSILL: *Sporthotel
Kogler*, B, 120 b., SB, sauna; *Bräurupp*, B, 78 b.;
Hirschenwirt, B, 42 b.; *Schlosshotel*, B, 39 b., sauna;
Brennerwirt, C/D, 15 b. – CAMPING SITE in Felben. – IN
UTTENDORF: *Koch*, C, 60 b.; *Liesenwirt*, C, 43 b., sauna;
Stubacherhof, C, 30 b. – IN NIEDERNSILL: *Kehlbachwirt*,
B, 55 b.; *Hutter*, B, 38 b.; *Sudentenheim*, B, 38 b. –
IN PIESENDORF: *Schett*, B, 42 b., sauna; *Neuwirt*, C, 32 b. –
IN BRUCK: *Lukashansl*, B, 80 b., sauna; *Woferlgut*, B,
36 b.; *Post*, C, 50 b.; *Glocknerhof*, C, 45 b. – IN TAXEN-
BACH: *Taxenbacherhof*, B, 48 b.; *Sonnhof*, B, 27 b.,
sauna; *Örglwirt*, C, 36 b. – IN RAURIS: *Rauriserhof*, B,
160 b., SB, sauna; *Alpina*, B, 67 b.; *Alpenrose*, B, 52 b.;
Platzwirt, B, 38 b.; *Gewerkenghof*, B, 18 b.

Heidentor, Petronell

Haydn's birthplace, Rohrau

**The Pinzgau, through which the River
Salzach flows, extends E from the
Gerlos pass to the Gasteiner Tal,
bounded on the N by the Kitzbühel
Alps and on the S by the Hohe Tauern
(national park). Beautiful lateral valleys run up into the mountains to N
and S, carrying important traffic
routes, including the road over the
Thurn pass, the Felber-Tauern Road,
the road through the Saalach valley
and past the Zeller See to Saalfelden
and the Grossglockner Road. The Pinzgau joins the Pongau (p. 153) at the
point where the Salzach turns N beyond the mouth of the Gasteiner Tal.**

Wald *im Pinzgau* (885 m/2904 ft; pop.
900) is a summer and winter sports resort at
the junction with the old road from the
Gerlos pass. Beyond the village there are
magnificent views of the mountains and
glaciers of the Grossvenediger group. – Then
comes **Neukirchen** *am Grossvenediger*
(856 m/2809 ft; pop. 2100), a holiday and
winter sports resort with a late Gothic
church (14th c. fresco) and Schloss Hoch-
neukirchen (present building 16th c.).

Farther down the valley is *Bramberg* (824 m/ 2704 ft; pop. 3300), with a Gothic parish church (Rococo altars; Virgin of *c*. 1500), a small local museum and the ruins of the *Weyerburg*, a castle which once belonged to the Bishops of Chiemsee (Bavaria).

Mittersill (789 m/2589 ft; pop. 5000), chief town of the upper Pinzgau and a winter sports resort, is situated in the Hohe Tauern National Park. It has two Baroque churches (*c*. 1750) and Schloss Mittersill (rebuilt 1532; privately owned). To the E of the town is the church of St Nicholas (1479; sculpture of *c*. 1500, Baroque high altar). In the Felberturm is a local museum. Open-air and enclosed swimming pools; climbing school; several ski-lifts.

Farther E is *Uttendorf* (806 m/2644 ft; pop. 2700), a summer resort at the mouth of the Stubach valley, with handsome peasants' houses and a lake (swimming). – The road continues via *Niedernsill* and *Piesendorf*, passes a side road to Zell am See and reaches **Bruck** *an der Grossglocknerstrasse* (757 m/ 2484 ft; pop. 3700), a resort with a busy passing trade. Parish church of St George (19th c.; Gothic Virgin); Schloss Fischhorn. – 12 km/7½ miles beyond Bruck is *Taxenbach* (750 m/2460 ft; pop. 2800), a summer resort situated at the mouth of the Rauriser Tal in the lower Pinzgau. The parish church was renovated in 1640 (architect Santino Solari); the Frauenkirche (1710) was modelled on a pilgrimage chapel at Altötting in Bavaria.

SURROUNDINGS of the various villages. – From *Wald* an excursion (strongly recommended) can be made to the ****Krimml Falls** (p. 117). – 1 hour's walk SW of *Neukirchen*, at the mouth of the Sulzbach valley, are the **Sulzbach Falls*. A chair-lift runs N from Neukirchen up the *Wildkogel* (2227 m/7307 ft; upper station 2093 m/ 6867 ft; skiing area), from which there are superb views. Neukirchen is also a starting-point for the ascent of the **Grossvenediger* (3674 m/12,054 ft); the route runs up the *Sulzbach* valley to the *Kürsingerhütte* (2549 m/ 8363 ft; 6½ hours; accommodation), from which it is another 4½ hours (with guide) to the summit. Another good climb, to the SE, is up the *Habach* valley to the *Thüringer Hütte* (2300 m/7550 ft; 6½ hours; accommodation), near the rugged Habachkees, a good base for further climbs and mountain treks.

From *Mittersill* a road goes NW to the **Thurn pass** (1232 m/4042 ft), with fine views of the Salzach valley and the Hohe Tauern; from the pass there is a chair-lift to the *Resterhöhe* (1894 m/6214 ft). – The **Felber-Tauern Road**, constructed in the 1960s, runs 16 km/10 miles S to the **Felber-Tauern Tunnel** (5·2 km/3¼ miles long; highest point 1650 m/5415 ft), which cuts through the Tauern massif. The road (toll) provides a route, open throughout the winter, into Eastern Tirol and Carinthia. From the far end of the tunnel it is 15 km/9 miles to Matrei.

From *Uttendorf* there is a beautiful road (17 km/10½ miles) through the Stubach valley to the *Enzingerboden* (1468 m/4817 ft; power station). From here a cableway ascends over the Grünsee to the *Weißsee* (2323 m/ 7624 ft). 30 minutes' walk brings the visitor to the *Hinterer Schafbichel* (2352 m/7719 ft). The *Rudolfshütte* (2315 m/7598 ft), at the upper station of the cableway, is the training centre of the Austrian Alpine Society (mountaineering courses; hotel). The hut is the starting point for ski tours and mountain climbs.

Beyond *Piesendorf* the **Kapruner Tal* (p. 103) runs S from the Pinzgau. – From *Bruck* the ****Grossglockner Road** (p. 82) runs S to Heiligenblut.

Taxenbach, 10 km/6 miles E of Bruck, lies at the mouth of the **Rauriser Tal**, with a road running 32 km/20 miles up the valley. Shortly before flowing into the Salzach the *Rauriser Ache* flows through the grand **Kitzloch-klamm*, in which the river falls 20 m/65 ft. The gorge can be easily reached from Taxenbach (from car park 1¾ hours there and back). – 10 km/6 miles S of Taxenbach is **Rauris** (948 m/3110 ft; pop. 2600), the main settlement in the valley, once a thriving market town (gold-mining) and now a well-known holiday and winter sports resort. Local museum in old schoolhouse; parish church (16th and 18th c.). Chair-lifts to the *Jack-Hochalm* (1470 m/4823 ft) and the *Kreuzboden* (1305 m/4282 ft).

20 km/12½ miles S of Rauris is **Kolm-Saigum** (1628 m/ 5341 ft), at the head of the valley under the rugged Goldberg group (good climbing and mountain trekking; climbing school). Interesting old gold workings (with a shaft running E into the Gasteiner Tal). To the SW is the **Hoher Sonnblick* (3105 m/10,188 ft), which can be climbed (with guide) in 5½ hours; on the top are the Zittelhaus (mountain hut) and a weather station (1886).

8 km/5 miles E of Taxenbach, at the end of the lower Pinzgau, a road runs 13 km/8 miles N up the Dientenbach valley to the summer and winter resort of **Dienten** *am Hochkönig* (1078 m/3538 ft; Hotel Übergossene Alm, A, 75 b., SB, SP, sauna; Salzburgerhof, B, 70 b., SP, sauna; Hochkönig, C, 55 b., SP), an old mining town SW of the *Hochkönig* (2941 m/9652 ft).

Rauris

Pitztal

Land: Tirol (T).

ⓘ **Fremdenverkehrsverband Innerpitztal,**
A-6481 Plangeross;
tel. (0 54 13) 21 46.

ACCOMMODATION. – IN WENNS: *Pitztalerhof*, B, 85 b.;
Hubertus, C, 55 b. – IN JERZENS: *Panorama-Hotel*, B, 65 b.,
sauna; *Alpenfriede*, B, 22 b.; *Venetblick*, C, 22 b. – IN ST
LEONHARD: *Haid*, C, 44 b.; *Alte Post*, C, 24 b. – IN
MANDARFEN: *Hotel Wildspitze*, B, 100 b., sauna; *Mittags-
kogel* (no rest.), B, 46 b., sauna. – IN MITTELBERG:
Gletsherblick, C, 28 b.

**To the W of Innsbruck three valleys
run S into the Ötztal Alps – the Ötztal
to the E, the Kaunertal to the W and,
between these two, the Pitztal.** Lying
rather off the main traffic routes, it
gives access to the grand mountain
scenery of the Ötztal Alps with their
numerous waterfalls.

A road runs 39 km/24 miles up the valley –
through which flows the *Pitzbach* – branching off the Inn valley road S of Imst and
ending in the magnificent scenery at the
head of the valley, at the foot of the Mittelberg glacier. The Pitztal attracts both summer
visitors and winter sports enthusiasts (mountain trekking).

Wenns (979 m/3212 ft) is a pretty village on
a fertile terrace in the valley. 5 km/3 miles SW,
higher up, is the village of *Piller* (1349 m/
4426 ft), and 4 km/2½ miles beyond this is
the *Pillerhöhe* (1558 m/5112 ft), commanding extensive views.

Beyond Wenns the valley becomes narrower
and the scenery finer. Above the road on the
left is the old mountain village of *Jerzens*
(1104 m/3622 ft), from which a side road
climbs up to *Kaitanger* (1445 m/4741 ft).
From there a chair-lift and a little mountain
road go up to the *Hochzeigerhaus* (1876 m/
6155 ft; inn), in a good skiing area; a further
chair-lift gives access to the *Hochzeiger*
(2582 m/8472 ft).

St Leonhard (1371 m/4498 ft; pop. 1200),
the main town in the Pitztal, lies below the
Rofele-Wand (3352 m/10,998 ft; ascent
5–6 hours; magnificent view), to the SW. –
The road continues up the valley through
increasingly fine scenery, passing the villages
of *Stillebach* and *Trenkwald* (1530 m/
5020 ft).

Plangeross (1616 m/5302 ft) is a small
hamlet at the foot of the *Puikogl* (3345 m/

10,975 ft). 2 hours' climb E of Plangeross is
the *Chemnitzer Hütte* (2323 m/7622 ft;
accommodation), the starting point for
climbing the main peaks in the Geigenkamm
– the *Hohe Geige* (3395 m/11,139 ft;
3 hours, with guide), the Puikogl (4–5 hours,
with guide). 4 hours' climb W of Plangeross
is the *Kaunergrathütte* (2860 m/9384 ft;
accommodation), from which the Kauner-
grat can be climbed.

S of Plangeross is *Mandarfen* (1682 m/
5519 ft), with a chair-lift to the *Riffelsee*
(2232 m/7323 ft), which can also be reached
from Mittelberg in 1¼ hours' climb.

Mittelberg (1734 m/5689 ft), is a small
hamlet in a magnificent setting at the head
of the valley, facing the *Mittelberg-Ferner*
(glacier). The summer skiing area (several
lifts) is reached from Mittelberg through a
tunnel. From here there are a whole range
of climbs on the N side of the *Weisskamm*,
the main ridge of the *Ötztal Alps with its
extensive glaciers (see p. 148). Mittelberg is
at the end of the long-distance path (No. 5)
from Vent. – 3 hours' climb SE of Mittelberg
is the *Braunschweiger Hütte* (2759 m/
9052 ft; inn; accommodation), in a good
skiing area, with a view of the expanse of
permanent snow extending to the Wildspitze. From here it is 2½ hours' climb, with
guide, to the *Mittagskogl* (3162 m/
10,375 ft), to the W; to the SW is the
Wildspitze (3774 m/12,382 ft), a 5 hours'
climb.

Pongau

Land: Salzburg (S).

ⓘ **Verkehrsverein Bischofshofen,**
Bahnhofstrasse 3, A-5500 Bischofshofen;
tel. (0 64 62) 24 71.

ACCOMMODATION. – IN PFARRWERFEN: *Sporthotel
Eulersberghof*, B, 56 b., SB, sauna; *Quehenberger*, B,
33 b.; *Sonneck*, C, 42 b. – IN BISCHOFSHOFEN: *Alte Post*,
B, 28 b.; *Rostatt*, C, 20 b.; *Tirolerwirt*, C, 18 b. –
CAMPING SITE. – IN ST JOHANN: *Huberwirt*, B, 50 b.,
sauna; *Wielandner*, B, 36 b.; *Plankenauwirt*, B, 33 b.;
Alpenhof, C, 26 b., SP, sauna. – CAMPING SITES. –
YOUTH HOSTEL. – IN SCHWARZACH: *Post*, B, 56 b.;
Schwarzacherhof, C, 28 b. – IN GOLDEGG: *Post*, A, 70 b., SP,
sauna; *Seehof*, B, 54 b., SP, sauna; *Lärchenhof*, B, 50 b.,
SP, sauna; *Bergblick*, C, 42 b.; *Grieserwirt*, C, 31 b. – IN
WAGRAIN: *Sonne*, A/B, 56 b., sauna; *Wagrainerhof*, B,
80 b., sauna; *Moawirt*, B, 56 b.; *Enzian*, B, 55 b., sauna;
Berghof, B, 46 b., SP, sauna; *Alpengasthof Kirchboden*,
B, 44 b.

**The Pongau, the middle Salzach valley,
runs S from the gap between the**

Hagengebirge in the W and the broad limestone massif of the Tennengebirge in the E to join the Gasteiner Tal. The scenery varies between green expanses of open valley and narrow gorges in which the rock faces on either side of the valley draw close together. Some tributary streams form deeply slashed gorges, such as the Gasteiner Klamm and the Liechtensteinklamm. To the SW the Pongau runs into the Pinzgau.

The highway from Salzburg runs to the W of the *Lueg pass* (562 m/1844 ft), a defile (fortified in 1630) high above the gorge of the Salzach. Here the gorge cuts its way through between the Tennengebirge and Hagengebirge into the Pongau. The wild gorge known as the *Salzachöfen* was first traversed in a collapsible boat in 1931.

A smaller road and the railway go through **Werfen** (see p. 241), from which a detour (strongly recommended if the weather is good) can be made to the ****Eisriesenwelt** ("World of the Ice Giants") cave. – The valley now opens out. On the right bank of the Salzach is *Pfarrwerfen* (553 m/1814 ft; pop. 2000), with a Gothic parish church.

Bischofshofen (544 m/1785 ft; pop. 9000; climbing school) is a considerable market town and holiday resort at the mouth of the *Mühlbach valley* (ski-jumps, world-cup jumping). The Gothic parish church of St Maximilian has 15th and 17th c. frescoes and contains the fine marble tomb (1462) of Bishop Sylvester of Chiemsee (d. 1453). The Romanesque St George's Chapel, on higher ground, has frescoes of 1230 in the apse. The Tauern motorway turns off here towards Radstadt (Eben and Altenmarkt: see under Radstadt, below).

St Johann *im Pongau* (653 m/2142 ft; pop. 8000) is a summer and winter sports resort on a sunny terrace above the right bank of the river. The town's most prominent landmark is the parish church of St John, twin-towered, which was rebuilt in 1855–73 after a fire; its imposing presence has earned it the name of the "cathedral of the Pongau". To the E is the mouth of the Wagrainer Tal, to the S the valley of the Grossarlbach. From here an excursion (strongly recommended) can be made to the Liechtensteinklamm (see opposite).

10 km/6 miles SW of St Johann is **Schwarzach** (591 m/1939 ft; pop. 3600), a little vacation spot at the W end of the Pongau,

with Schloss Schernberg (originally 12th c., rebuilt in 15th and 16th c.; now a home) above the town. In the Rathaus is the "Salzleckertisch", a table at which the Protestant peasants formed a league in 1731, whereupon 30,000 Protestants were banished from the province of Salzburg.

On a hill 5 km/3 miles W is the summer and winter sports resort of *Goldegg* (825 m/ 2707 ft; pop. 1500), with a 14th c. castle which belonged to the Counts Galen. Small lake (peat baths); holiday courses.

SURROUNDINGS of the various villages. – 6 km/ 4 miles E of *Pfarrwerfen* is the winter sports area of *Werfenweng* (901 m/2956 ft), with several ski-lifts. A chair-lift leads up to the Bischlinghöhe (1836 m/6024 ft). From here it is 2 hours' walk through the beautiful Wengerau at the head of the valley to the magnificently situated Dr.-Heinrich-Hackel-Hütte (1531 m/5023 ft; inn). From here the surrounding peaks of the Tennengebirge can be climbed: e.g. the *Eiskogel* (2321 m/ 7615 ft; 2¼ hours), to the N, with an ice cave 4 km/ 2½ miles long, or the *Bleikogel* (2412 m/7914 ft; 3¾ hours), also to the N.

From *Bischofshofen* a minor road runs 10 km/6 miles SW up the *Mühlbach valley* to **Mühlbach** (853 m/ 2799 ft), a beautiful mountain village with a copper-mine; good skiing terrain. From there a steep mountain road (toll) climbs a further 6 km/4 miles to the *Arthur-Haus* (1503 m/4931 ft; Alpenhotel), on the *Mitterberg Alm*, a popular skiing area (many ski-lifts). From the Arthur-Haus it is an hour's climb to the summit of the *Hochkeil* (1779 m/5837 ft); to the NW (5 hours, with guide) is the *Hochkönig (2941 m/9649 ft), with the Franz-Eduard-Matras-Haus, in a grand rocky setting.

Above *St Johann*, to the E, is the *Berghotel Hahnbaum* (chair-lift; by road 3 km/2 miles), the starting-point of several ski runs; from here it is an easy 2 hours' climb to the summit of the *Hochgrundeck (1827 m/5994 ft). 8 km/5 miles E of St Johann, in the beautiful *Wagrainer Tal*, is the well-known winter sports resort of **Wagrain** (838 m/2749 ft; pop. 2600; several chair-lifts and ski-lifts to 2000 m/6560 ft). A cableway runs up to the *Griesskareck* (1991 m/6532 ft), a skiing area to the E.

In the Liechtensteinklamm

In the churchyard are the graves of the writer Karl Heinrich Waggerl (1897–1973) and Josef Mohr, once curate here, who wrote the words of "Silent Night".

4·5 km/3 miles S of St Johann is the ****Liechtenstein-klamm**, one of the most impressive gorges in the Alps, carved out by the *Grossarler Ache*. The path through the gorge, partly blasted from the rock, climbs up to a huge cauldron with rock walls 300 m/1000 ft high and through the narrowest part of the gorge, only 2–4 m/6½–13 ft wide, and a tunnel to the 60 m/200 ft high waterfall at the end of the gorge (20 minutes' walk from the entrance). The best light for seeing the gorge is in the morning. – At the S end of the *Grossarl valley* are the villages of *Grossarl* (924 m/3032 ft) and *Hüttschlag* (1020 m/3347 ft), the starting-point of a number of climbs.

Radstadt

Land: Salzburg (S).
Altitude: 862 m/2828 ft. – Population: 3500.
Post code: A-5550. – Telephone code: 0 64 52.
(i) **Verkehrsverein**, Stadtplatz;
    tel. 3 05.

ACCOMMODATION. – IN RADSTADT: *Sporthotel*, B, 70 b., SB, sauna; *Seitenalm*, B, 50 b., sauna; *Post*, B, 47 b.; *Alpenhotel Diana*, B, 43 b., sauna; *Hirschenwirt*, C, 24 b. – CAMPING SITE. – IN ALTENMARKT: *Marktewirt*, B, 65 b., sauna; *Kesselgrub*, B, 50 b., sauna; *Alpenland*, B, 35 b.; *Winterbauer*, B, 34 b. – IN OBERTAUERN: *Steiner*, A, 123 b., sauna; *Perner*, A, 123 b., SB, sauna; *Kohlmayr*, A, 85 b., SB, sauna; *Gamsleiten*, A, 58 b., sauna; *Wagner*, A, 56 b., SB, sauna; *Alpina*, B, 40 b., sauna; *Berghof*, B, 36 b., sauna.

RECREATION and SPORTS. – IN OBERTAUERN: tennis, archery, clay pigeon shooting, riding; hobby courses; winter sports; mini-golf in Altenmarkt.

Randstadt, lying between the Rad-städter Tauern to the S and the Dachstein massif to the N, has pre-served an old-world quality, with remains of its old town walls and three massive 16th c. round towers. The parish church of the Assumption dates from the 14th and 15th c., and there is a "lantern of the dead" (1513) in the churchyard. Radstadt is a good base for walks and climbs in the surround-ing mountains and is a popular winter sports resort.

SURROUNDINGS. – A narrow road (12 km/7½ miles) runs N to the **Rossbrand* (1770 m/5807 ft; Rädstädter Hütte, inn), between the Dachstein and the Tauern, with views of both massifs. – 3 km/2 miles W of Radstadt is **Altenmarkt** *im Pongau* (850 m/2789 ft; pop. 2400), with a parish church containing a 14th c. image of the Virgin. 12 km/7½ miles S is the *Zauchseealm* (1350 m/4429 ft; Gamskogelbahn to 2114 m/6936 ft; a very popular skiing area in winter. 8 km/5 miles SW of Altenmarkt in the Enns valley, on the motorway, is *Flachau* (927 m/3041 ft; pop. 1600; Hotel Tauernhof, A, 129 b., SB; Alpenhof, B, 56 b., SB, sauna; Lacknerhof, B, 86 b., sauna), from which there is a chair-lift to the *Griesskareck*

(1991 m/6532 ft; winter sports area). To the S a cableway and chair-lift go up to the *Rosskopf* which rears above the Zauchsee.

7 km/4¼ miles NW of Radstadt, on the highway, is *Eben im Pongau* (856 m/2809 ft; chair-lift to 1285 m/4216 ft). 12 km/7½ miles NE of Eben is *Filzmoos* (1055 m/3461 ft; Hotel Hanneshof, A, 84 b., SB, sauna; Unterhof, A, 76 b., SB, sauna), a popular place for winter sports and for climbing and mountain trekking in the Dachstein group; toll road to the *Hoferalm* (1298 m/4259 ft), 5 km/3 miles N.

Obertauern

Radstadt is the starting-point of the 22 km/13½ miles long *Radstädter Tauern Road* to the Tauern pass (1738 m/ 5702 ft) and the Taurachbach valley to the S. Since the opening of the highway running W through the Tauern Tunnel this road has lost its importance as a through route into Styria and Carinthia but is still the approach road from the N to the popular winter sports and holiday area on the Tauernhöhe. After passing through *Untertauern* (1008 m/3307 ft) the road comes, shortly before the pass, to **Obertauern** (1650 m/5414 ft), which has developed into a popular summer and winter resort (facilities for a variety of sports, enclosed swimming pool). Cabin cableway to the *Zehnerkar* (upper station 2192 m/7192 ft); chair-lifts to the *Grünwaldkopf* (1974 m/6477 ft; restaurant) and the *Wagnerspitze* (1980 m/6496 ft).

The *Seekarspitse* (2350 m/7710 ft), to the N, can be climbed from the Seekarhaus (1790 m/5873 ft) in 2½ hours. The hotels extend up to the ***Tauernhöhe** (1738 m/5702 ft), the meadow-covered saddle of the **Radstädter Tauern**. Near the pass, from which the road runs down into the *Lungau* (p. 132), is the *Friedhof der Namenlosen* ("Cemetery of the Nameless Ones"), in which from the 16th c. onwards the unknown victims of avalanches and other natural catastrophes were buried. There is a wide network of good footpaths in this area. From Obertauern experienced climbers can scale a number of peaks over 2000 m/6500 ft in 2–4 hours.

Rätikon

Land: Vorarlberg (V).
Altitude: Highest point: Schesaplana (2969 m/9741 ft).
(i) **Österreichischer Alpenverein**,
    Sektion Vorarlberg,
    Langgasse 64, A-6830 Rankweil.

The Rätikon range, of a very different character from the neighbouring Bregenzer Wald, is a massif with sheer rock walls and bizarrely shaped peaks lying between the Ill valley (Montafon), the Rhine and the Prättigau in Switzerland, on the southern borders of the province of Vorarlberg.

The mighty rock massif of the *Schesaplana (2969 m/9741 ft), the long *Vandanser Steinwand*, with the bold horn of the *Zimbaspitze* (2645 m/8678 ft), the massive *Drusenfluh* (2835 m/9302 ft), with the *Drei Türme* ("Three Towers") at the head of the magnificent Gauertal, the *Sulzfluh (2824 m/9266 ft) with its small glacier, and the splendid horn of the **Madrisa** (2274 m/9101 ft), the main landmark of the Gargellental, are among the most impressive mountains in Vorarlberg. There are numerous mountain huts for the benefit of climbers, the principal huts being linked by a fine ridge path which runs from the Nenzinger Himmel in the Gamperdona valley by way of the Strassburger Hütte (2700 m/8860 ft), near Brand, to the Schesaplana and then down to the Douglass-Hütte (1979 m/6493 ft) on the beautiful *Lüner See* (1970 m/6464 ft), on to the Lindauer Hütte (1764 m/5788 ft) and the Tilisuna-Hütte (2211 m/7254 ft) near the little *Tilisuna-See* (2102 m/6897 ft) – both easily reached from Tschagguns in the Montafon – and down into the Gargellental. Some of the Rätikon peaks can be climbed without great difficulty on relatively easy paths, but there are also some very difficult ascents, for experienced rock-climbers only.

There is excellent skiing terrain all over the Rätikon range. Particularly popular areas are in the Gargellental, the slopes of the Golmerjoch at Schruns-Tschagguns and the northern outliers (outlying parts separated from the main range) of the Schesaplana which flank the beautiful Brandner Tal at Bludenz. The Sulzfluh offers one of the finest descents in the Alps, with a fall of over 2100 m/6900 ft.

ACCOMMODATION. – *Garten-Pension*, C, 54 b.; *Weisser Löwe*, C, 8 b.; *Winzerhof*, D, 9 b.

The old-world little town of Retz, still surrounded by its ancient walls, lies in the wine-producing area of the Retzer Senke (Retz depression) in the NW of the Weinviertel, near the Czechoslovak frontier.

SIGHTS. – The *Marktplatz* is a fine spacious square surrounded by 16th c. houses. In the middle of the square is the 16th c. **Rathaus**, originally a chapel, with the Municipal Museum. An early fresco by Martin Schmidt of Krems can be seen in the council chamber; the Rococo chapel of 1756 is also of interest. Other notable buildings in the square are the *Sgraffitohaus* (1576), decorated with scenes from Greek mythology and the Bible, and the *Verderberhaus* (c. 1580), with picturesque crenellations and an arched passage. The **Dominican Church** (1295) is an early Gothic church with a three-aisled nave and a high vaulted roof; Baroque interior. There are a number of well-preserved towers on the *town walls*, and by reason of a privilege granted to the town in the 15th c. for the wine trade there are some 20 km/12 miles of underground wine cellars (conducted tours).

SURROUNDINGS. – 14 km/9 miles NW, in the Thaya valley close to the Czechoslovak frontier, stands **Hardegg** (308 m/1011 ft; pop. 200), with an imposing four-towered castle (originally 11th c., restored c. 1900) on a crag above the village. The castle, which still preserves some of the original structure, contains relics and mementoes of the Emperor Maximilian of Mexico. In the Knights' Hall is displayed a large collection of arms and armour. – 8·5 km/5 miles W of Hardegg is *Riegersburg*, with a fine Baroque Schloss (beautiful façade, dome-roofed pavilions) of the early 18th c., rebuilt after suffering severe damage in the Second World War. The great hall, two storeys high, contains fine Baroque and Rococo furniture.

12 km/7½ miles SW of Regersburg the Premonstratensian abbey of **Geras**, founded c. 1150 and rebuilt in the 17th and 18th c. to the design of J. Munggenast, has a church, originally Romanesque, which was remodelled in Baroque style in the 17th c. Wildlife park; hobby courses.

Retz

Land: Lower Austria (NÖ).
Altitude: 264 m/866 ft.
Population: 4300.
Post code: A-2070.
Telephone code: 0 29 42.
ⓘ **Fremdenverkehrsverein**, Lehengasse 10; tel. 23 79, 22 33.

Marktplatz, Retz

Reutte

Land: Tirol (T).
Altitude: 854 m/2802 ft. – Population: 5300.
Post code: A-6600. – Telephone code: 0 56 72.
ⓘ **Fremdenverkehrsverband,**
Untermarkt 34, Postfach 20;
tel: 23 36.

ACCOMMODATION. – IN REUTTE: *Glocke*, B, 103 b.;
Goldener Hirsch, B, 90 b.; *Tirolerhof*, B, 70 b. – IN
AMMERWALD: *Ammerwald-Hotel*, B, 200 b., SB, sauna. –
IN EHENBICHL: *Maximilian*, B, 69 b. – CAMPING SITES. –
YOUTH HOSTEL.

**Reutte, in a wide basin in the valley of
the Lech, is the chief town of the
Ausserfern district, to the N of the
Fernpass, and an important traffic
junction between Füssen and Pfronten
in Germany, the Fernpass, the upper
Lech valley (Hochtannberg pass and
Flexen Road) and the Tannheimer Tal
(Oberjoch and *Gaicht pass).**

SIGHTS. – Handsome 18th c. *burghers'
houses* with painted façades, gables and oriel
windows (e.g. the Zeillerhaus in the Untermarkt); *parish church* (1691) in the
Breitenwang district, with beautiful ceiling
painting and Baroque relief medallions of the
Dance of Death in the mortuary chapel. Local
museum.

SURROUNDINGS. – The Lech valley and its side valleys
coming down from the Lechtal Alps are popular walking
and winter sports areas. An additional attraction is
provided by a series of beautiful lakes. The *Urisee* (2 km/
1¼ miles NE) and the *Frauensee* (3 km/2 miles NW) have
facilities for boating and bathing. 6 km/4 miles E of Reutte,
enclosed by wooded hills, is the dark green **Plansee*
(976 m/3202 ft), the largest lake in Tirol after the
Achensee (p. 48), 5 km/3 miles long and 1 km/¾ mile wide.
It is linked with the *Heiterwanger See* (3 km/2 miles long
(by a short watercourse. From the Plansee a road runs
9 km/5½ miles NE to the *Ammersattel* (1118 m/3668 ft),
on the German frontier (open only from May to October).

Climbs from Reutte: 3½ hours to the double peak of the
Tauern (1814 m/5952 ft and 1864 m/6116 ft); 4 hours
NW by way of the Frauensee to the *Füssener Alm*
(1520 m/4987 ft), with the Otto-Mayr-Hütte (inn), from
which it is another 1½ hours to the summit of the **Grosse
Schlicke* (2060 m/6759 ft), a favourite viewpoint. – A
cableway runs up from Höfen to the *Höfener Alm*
(1742 m/5716 ft), on the slopes of the *Hahnenkamm*
(1940 m/6365 ft).

The road to *Lermoos* (see p. 251) and the Fernpass
traverses a narrow defile, the *Ehrenberger Klause* (946 m/
3104 ft), which was the scene of bitter fighting in the 16th
and 17th c., and after passing through *Heiterwang* comes
in 12 km/7½ miles to *Bichlbach* (1075 m/3527 ft), in a
wider part of the valley (chair-lift to the *Heiterwanger Alm*,
1622 m/5322 ft). From here a side road leads to
Berwang (1336 m/4383 ft; pop. 500; Kaiserhof, A,
138 b., SB, sauna; Singer Sporthotel, A, 93 b.; Alpenstern-
Hotel, B, 82 b., sauna), a favourite winter sports resort on
a mountain saddle; chair-lifts to the *Hochalm* (1626 m/

5335 ft), the *Hochbichl* (1392 m/4567 ft) and the
Rastkopf (1640 m/5381 ft). – From Bichlbach it is another
10 km/6 miles to Lermoos.

From Reutte into the Tannheimer Tal (28 km/
17 miles). – The road runs 8 km/5 miles up the Lech valley
to *Weissenbach* (887 m/2910 ft; pop. 1000; Bären, B,
56 b.), where the road into the Tannheimer Tal branches
off to the NW.

The *Tannheimer Tal* is a high valley with large expanses of
Alpine meadows, popular both with summer visitors and
winter sports enthusiasts; chair-lifts and ski-lifts. The old
salt road from Tirol to Lake Constance goes up the valley
and over the Gaicht pass to the Oberjoch. From Weissenbach the road, partly blasted from the rock, climbs to the
*Gaicht pass (1093 m/3586 ft), a beautifully wooded
defile. To the N is the *Gaichtspitze* (1988 m/6523 ft),
which can be climbed from the village of *Gaicht* in 3 hours.
– Beyond this is *Nesselwängle* (1147 m/3763 ft; chair-
lift), to the N of which rises the Tannheim massif, over
2000 m/6500 ft high (*Kellerspitze*, 2240 m/7349 ft,
climbed in 3½ hours by way of the Tannheimer Hütte). –
After passing the *Haldensee* (1124 m/3688 ft) the road
goes through *Grän* (1134 m/3721 ft; chair-lift to the
Füssener Jöchl, 1815 m/5955 ft) and comes to the main
town in the valley.

Tannheim (1097 m/3599 ft; pop. 700; Zum Ritter, A,
90 b.), with its handsome parish church of St Nicholas
(1722–28); chair-lift to the *Neunerköpfle* (1864 m/
6116 ft). 4 km/2½ miles S of Tannheim is the beautiful
Vilsalpsee (1168 m/3832 ft), from which there are good
climbs: W, 3–4 hours, to the *Geisshorn* (2249 m/7379 ft);
S, 2½ hours, to the *Traualpsee* (1630 m/5348 ft) and the
Landsberger Hütte (1810 m/5939 ft; accommodation),
the starting-point for the ascent (1 hour) of the
Schochenspitze (2069 m/6788 ft), a commanding
viewpoint.

The road continues to *Schattwald* (1072 m/3517 ft), a
little resort beautifully located in the upper Vilstal, and then
reaches the German frontier at the *Oberjoch pass*
(1180 m/3872 ft).

From Reutte to Warth through the Lech valley
(62 km/39 miles). – The Lech valley runs SW from Reutte
towards the Arlberg between the Allgäu Alps in the N and
the Lechtal Alps in the S. In the meadowland on the floor
of the valley are many villages popular with summer
visitors and winter sports enthusiasts. A number of side
valleys, mostly narrow and gorge-like, lead to quiet little
mountain villages which are good bases for climbers and
mountain walkers. – The road from Reutte passes through
Höfen (cableway to the Höfener Alm) to *Weissenbach*,
from which a side road runs NW into the Tannheimer Tal.
10 km/6 miles farther up the Lech valley is the summer
resort of **Stanzach** (940 m/3084 ft; Neue Post, B, 40 b.).
From here a mountain road runs 9 km/5½ miles up the

In the Tannheimer Tal

wooded Namloser Tal to *Namlos* (1263 m/4144 ft), a skiing village between the Knittelkarspitze (2378 m/7802 ft) to the N and the Namloser Wetterspitze (2551 m/8370 ft; 5 hours' climb, wide views) to the S. Another roads leads SW from Stanzach to *Vorderhornbach* (973 m/3192 ft) and *Hinterhornbach* (1101 m/3612 ft), from which the *Hochvogel* (2593 m/8508 ft), to the N, can be climbed in 6 hours.

Elmen (978 m/3209 ft) lies below the E side of the *Klimmspitze* (2465 m/8088 ft; 4½–5 hours' climb). To the NE is the *Elmer Kreuzspitze* (2482 m/8143 ft; 4 hours). To the SE extends the *Bschlaber Tal*, with a road running up to Bschlabs (1314 m/4311 ft) and *Boden* (1357 m/4452 ft). 2½ hours S of Boden is the *Hanauer Hütte* (1918 m/6293 ft; accommodation), a good base for climbs in the **Parzinn group**. The road continues from Boden over the *Hahntennjoch* (1884 m/6181 ft) to Imst in the Inn valley.

At *Häselgehr* (1003 m/3291 ft; pop. 700, Sonne, C, 30 b.) the *Gramaiser Tal* runs into the Lech valley on the S. 8 km/5 miles up this valley is *Gramais* (1328 m/4357 ft) and 6 km/4 miles beyond Häselgehr is **Elbigenalp** (1040 m/3412 ft; pop. 750; Alpenrose, A, 180 b., SB, sauna), a beautifully situated little vacation spot with the oldest parish church in the Lech valley (St Nicholas, originally 12th c., rebuilt in 17th c.). The cemetery chapel of St Martin (11th–12th c.) above the village to the W contains a Dance of Death by Anton Falger. The local museum has mementoes of the painter and lithographer Anton Falger (1791–1876), a native of the village. There is also a school of woodcarving. To the W of the village is the *Bernhardseck* (1802 m/5912 ft; accommodation; 2 hours' walk), good walking and skiing country, with far-ranging views. 3 hours' climb NW of Elbigenalp is the *Hermann-von-Barth-Hütte* (2131 m/6992 ft; accommodation), a good base for climbers. – Bach (1060 m/3478 ft; painted house façades) lies at the mouth of the gorge-like *Madau valley*. To the S of *Madau* (1310 m/4298 ft) is the *Memminger Hütte* (2242 m/7356 ft).

Holzgau (1103 m/3619 ft) also has painted houses. To the N is the *Höhenbachschlucht* (gorge), with a waterfall (¼ hour's walk). – From **Steeg** (1122 m/3681 ft; Tannenhof, B, 90 b.) a steep road runs 4 km/2½ miles S above the Kaisertal to *Kaisers* (1522 m/4994 ft), with the beautifully situated Edelweisshütte, in a good skiing area. N of Steeg is the hamlet of Ellenbogen, from which the *Hohes Licht* (2651 m/8698 ft) can be climbed.

The road continues up the wooded Lech valley, the valley becoming steadily narrower. 11 km/7 miles farther on, to the left of the road, is *Lechleiten* (1540 m/5053 ft). Beyond this is **Warth** am Arlberg (1500 m/4920 ft; Warther Hof, A, 70 b., sauna; Knitel, B, 28 b.; Biberkopf, C, 40 b.), a summer and winter sports resort on an open plateau of Alpine meadows; chair-lift to the *Steffialpe* (1950 m/6398 ft), several ski-lifts. From here the road runs S to the Arlberg; to the NW is the Hochtannberg pass.

Riegersburg

Land: Styria (Stm).
Altitude: 482 m/1581 ft. – Population: 2550.
Post code: A-8333. – Telephone code: 0 31 53.
ⓘ **Marktgemeindeamt,**
    tel. 20 40.

ACCOMMODATION. – *Zur Riegersburg*, C, 70 b.; *Knapp*, D, 36 b. – YOUTH HOSTEL.

55 km/34 miles E of Graz in the south-eastern tip of Styria, on a basalt crag between Fürstenfeld and Feldbach, stands the mighty *Riegersburg, one of the finest castles in Austria, never taken by an enemy.

HISTORY. – The castle is first recorded in the 12th c. In the 13th c. there were two castles here, to the N Burg Kronegg and to the S, lower down, Burg Leichtenegg, which was

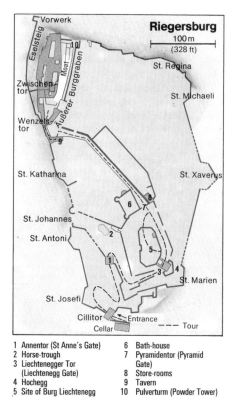

Riegersburg
100 m
(328 ft)

1 Annentor (St Anne's Gate)
2 Horse-trough
3 Liechtenegger Tor (Liechtenegg Gate)
4 Hochegg
5 Site of Burg Liechtenegg
6 Bath-house
7 Pyramidentor (Pyramid Gate)
8 Store-rooms
9 Tavern
10 Pulverturm (Powder Tower)

demolished in 1648. The owners were the Waldonier, Kuenringer and Wallseer families. In the 16th c. the main castle was enlarged by Freiherr von Stadtl, and in 1637 it passed to the Wechsler family.

Under Elisabeth von Wechsler, a legendary figure in Styrian history, the castle had its greatest days as a frontier fortress against the Turks. In 1822 the castle passed into the possession of the Princes of Liechtenstein, who restored it.

The castle is entered from the S on a rocky path defended by seven gates and numerous bastions. Between the fourth and fifth gates, on the site of Burg Lichtenegg, is the Frontier Memorial (view). On the Wenzelstor (Wenceslas Gate) are statues of Mars and Bellona.

The castle proper, with two arcaded courtyards, contains a number of handsome rooms with 16th and 17th c. furniture. Gothic chapel. Fine doorways and coffered ceilings.

Saalfelden
am Steinernen Meer

Land: Salzburg (S).
Altitude: 744 m/2441 ft. – Population: 12,400.
Post code: A-5760. – Telephone code: 0 65 82.
(i) **Verkehrsverein,**
    Bahnhofstrasse 10;
    tel. 25 13 and 31 95.

ACCOMMODATION. – IN SAALFELDEN: *Sporthotel Gut Brandof*, A, 300 b.; *Bellevue*, B, 120 b., SB, sauna; *Schörhof*, B, 75 b., SP, sauna; *Hindenburg*, B, 55 b.; *Jäger*, B, 31 b., sauna. – IN MARIA ALM: *Norica*, A, 200 b., SB, sauna; *Niederreiter*, B, 70 b., sauna; *Almerwirt*, B, 61 b., SB; *Lohningerhof*, B, 52 b. – IN LOFER: *Bräu*, A, 50 b., sauna; *Post*, B, 55 b.; *Litner*, B, 46 b.; *Dax*, B, 32 b. – CAMPING SITES.

RECREATION and SPORTS. – Recreation area on *Ritzensee*; 18-hole golf course at Sporthotel Gut Brandhof; summer toboggan-run; winter sports.

EVENT. – *International Jazz Festival* (Aug.).

The old market town of Saalfeld lies surrounded by rugged and precipitous mountains in the wide valley basin of the River Saalbach before its entry into the narrow gorges between the Steinernes Meer ("Sea of Stone") and the Leoganger and Loferer Steinberge. Situated in the middle Pinzgau, on the important highway from Bad Reichenhall to the Zeller See and the Grossglockner, Saalfelden is surrounded by a whole series of small summer and winter sports resorts in the mountains.

SIGHTS. – *Parish church* with a Gothic crypt. *Schloss Ritzen*, on a small lake to the S of the town, houses a local museum with the largest collection of Christmas cribs (Nativity groups) in Austria and a collection of minerals.

SURROUNDINGS. – A footpath (1 hour) runs NE to *Schloss Lichtenberg* (913 m/2996 ft; originally 13th c.), perched in a commanding position on the slopes of the towering Persailhorn. 10 minutes' climb above the castle is the *Palvenkapelle* (St George's, 1675; alt. 1004 m/3294 ft), with a rock-hewn pulpit and a *hermitage*. – From Kehlbach, a district on the SW side of the town, a chair-lift goes up to the *Huggenberg Alm* (1115 m/3659 ft, inn), S of Saalfelden, which can be climbed in 4 hours, the *Hundstein* (2116 m/6943 ft) in 1½ hours. From both of these summits there are fine panoramic views.

5 km/3 miles SE of Saalfelden, in the *Urslautal*, is **Maria Alm** (795 m/2608 ft; pop. 1500), a summer and winter sports resort in a beautiful setting at the foot of the Steinernes Meer. The spire of the pilgrimage church (originally Gothic; Virgin of 1480) is the highest in the province of Salzburg (84 m/275 ft). Chair-lifts and ski-lifts give access to the surrounding heights (skiing). – 9 km/5½ miles E of Maria Alm, at the head of the valley, is *Hinterthal* (1016 m/3333 ft), from which experienced

climbers can scale the *Hochkönig (2941 m/9649 ft), to the E, in 6 hours. From Hinterthal a mountain road crosses the *Filzensattel* (1292 m/4239 ft) to Dienten, on the Hochkönig (see p. 89).

Above Saalfelden to the NE is the *Steinernes Meer ("Sea of Stone"), a karstic limestone plateau (nature reserve) which is a favourite rock-climbing area. It also offers good skiing for more skilful skiers. At the western edge of the plateau, on the *Ramseider Scharte*, is the *Riemannhaus* (2177 m/7143 ft; inn; accommodation), which can be reached from either Saalfelden or Maria Alm in 4 hours. This hut is a good base for the ascent of the *Sommerstein* (2306 m/7566 ft), the *Breithorn* (2504 m/8216 ft), the *Schönfeldspitze* (2651 m/8698 ft) and the *Selborn* (2643 m/8672 ft), the highest peak in the Steinernes Meer – all climbs to be undertaken only by experienced climbers or with a guide.

A road runs W from Saalfelden to the summer and winter resort of *Leogang* (840 m/2756 ft; pop. 2500; Kirchenwirt, C, 38 b.; Wachterwirt, C, 31 b.) and the *Griessen pass* (963 m/3160 ft), continuing down to Fieberbrunn and St Johann in Tirol (see p. 108).

15 km/9 miles N of Saalfelden on the road to Lofer is **Weissbach** (666 m/2185 ft; Hotel Seisenbergklamm, B, 48 b.). NE of the village is the grand *Seisenbergklamm* (gorge); the walk through the gorge from the car park takes about an hour there and back. 2½ hours' climb SE of Weissbach is the *Diessbach reervoir* (1390 m/4561 ft) and 1 km/¾ mile beyond Weissbach on the Lofer road, on left, is the *Lamprechtsofenloch*, an interesting cavern with an underground stream (conducted tour, ½ hour). – Before reaching Lofer the road comes to the little summer resort of *St Martin* (635 m/2083 ft), above which (1·5 km/1 mile W on a toll road) is the *pilgrimage church of Maria Kirchental* (by J. B. Fischer von Erlach, 1693–1701), with a pilgrimage museum.

Lofer (625 m/2050 ft; pop. 1700), set in a wider part of the valley, is an old market town which is now a summer and winter sports resort (enclosed swimming pool, Kneipp treatment). Peasant Theatre (Bauerntheater). The parish church is Gothic, with later alteration; old Plague

Lofer, in the Saalach valley

Column, set up to commemorate the town's escape from the plague. A chair-lift runs up to Sonnegg-Loderbühel (1002 m/3288 ft) and the Loferer Alm (upper station 1400 m/4600 ft).

To the S rear up the rugged limestone walls of the **Loferer Steinberge**. A pleasant footpath (4 hours) ascends the *Loferer Hochtal* to the *Schmidt-Zabierow-Hütte* (1966 m/6450 ft; inn in summer), from which the *Hinterhorn* (2504 m/8216 ft) can be climbed in 2 hours. – NW of Lofer (road via Faistau or chair-lift) is the *Loferer Alpe* (1425 m/4675 ft; hotels), with splendid views, good walking in summer, skiing in winter.

Salzburg

Land: Salzburg (S).
Altitude: 420 m/1378 ft.
Population: 140,000.
Post code: A-5020.
Telephone code: 0 62 22.

(i) **Stadtverkehrsburö,**
Auerspergstrasse 7;
tel. 80 72–0.
Branches:
Mozartplatz 5;
tel. 80 72–34 62 or 34 63, 84 75 68.
Hauptbahnhof (Central Station), Island platform;
tel. 7 17 12 and 7 36 38.
Salzburg Mitte, Müncher Bundesstrasse 1;
tel. 3 22 28 and 3 31 10.
Salzburg Süd, Alpenstrasse 67;
tel. 2 09 66, 2 29 40.
Salzburg West, Innsbrucker Bundesstrasse 96;
tel. 85 24 51, 85 24 52 (1 Apr.–31 Oct.).
Kongressbetriebe der Stadt Salzburg,
Auerspergstrasse 7;
tel. 7 35 33 and 76 51 10.
Kurhausbetriebe der Stadt Salzburg,
Auerspergstrasse 2;
tel. 7 32 00.
Landesverkehrsamt,
Mozartplatz 1;
tel. 80 42–22 32.

ACCOMMODATION. – *Salzburg Sheraton*, Auerspergstr. 4, A1, 350 b.; *Österreichischer Hof*, Schwarzstr. 5–7, A1, 199 b.; *Bristol*, Makartplatz 4, A1, 150 b.; *Goldener Hirsch*, Getreidegasse 37, A1, 103 b.; *Kobenzl*, Gaisberg 11, A1, 55 b., SB, sauna; *Schlosshotel St Rupert*, Morzgerstr. 31, A1, 50 b.; *Fondachhof*, Gaisbergstr. 46, A1, 48 b., SP, sauna; *Schlosshotel Klessheim*, in Wals, A1, 41 b.; *Schloss Mönchstein*, Mönchsberg 26, A1, 33 b.; *Erzherzog Johann*, Egger-Lienz-Gasse 2, A1, 22 b.; *Haus Ingeborg*, Sonnleitenweg 9, A1, 22 b., SP, sauna; *Dr Wührer's Haus Gastein*, Ignaz-Rieder-Kai 25, A1, 21 b., sauna; *Maria-Theresien-Schlössl*, Morzgerstr. 87, A1, 20 b.; *Pitter*, Rainerstr. 6–8, A, 370 b.; *Cottage*, Josef-Messner-Str. 12, A, 230 b., SB, sauna; *Haus Egger-Lienz*, Egger-Lienz-Gasse 9, A, 200 b.; *Winkler*, Franz-Josef-Str. 7–9, A, 200 b.; *Humboldt*, Egger-Lienz-Gasse 3, A, 180 b.; *Europa*, Rainerstr. 31, A, 160 b.; *Stein*, at the Staatsbrücke, A, 111 b.; *Auersperg*, Auerspergstr. 61, A, 106 b.; *Kasererhof*, Alpenstr., 6, A, 100 b.; *Schaffenrath*, Alpenstr. 115, A, 100 b.; *Gablerbräu*, Linzer Gasse 9, A, 94 b.; *Stieglbräu*, Rainerstr. 14, A, 80 b.; *Hofwirt*, Schallmooser Hauptstr. 1, B, 110 b.; *Carlton*, Markus-Sittikus-Str. 3, B, 80 b.; *Grüner Wald*, Landstr. 24, C, 117 b., SP. – YOUTH HOSTELS: Aigner Str. 34, Eduard-Heinrich-Str. 2, Glockengasse 8, Haunspergstr. 27, Josef-Preis-Allee 18. – several CAMPING SITES.

RESTAURANTS. – In most hotels; also *Eulenspiegel*, Hagenauerplatz 2; *Stiftskeller St Peter*, in St Peter's Abbey courtyard; *Weisses Kreuz* (Yugoslav), Bierjodlgasse 6; *Stieglkeller*, below Hohensalzburg, with terrace (view) and garden; *Festungrestaurant*, in Hohensalzburg (during season only); *Sternbräu*, Griesgasse 23; *Höllbräu*, Judengasse 15; *Moser-Weinrestaurant*, Philharmonikergasse 3; *Don Camillo*, Gstättengasse 15; *Restaurant-Café Winkler*, on Mönchsberg, with *view of town.

CAFÉS. – *Tomaselli*, Alter Markt 9; *Bazar*, Schwarzstrasse 3; *Mozart*, Getreidegasse 22, 1st floor; *Kaffee-Häferl*, Universitätsplatz 6 (beautiful arcaded courtyard); *Glockenspiel*, Mozartplatz 2; *Konditorei Klug*, Nonntaler Hauptstrasse 24 (beautiful garden under Hohensalzburg); *Café Winkler*, on Mönchsberg.

HORSE-DRAWN CABS in Residenzplatz.

CASINO. – in Café Winkler building on Mönchsberg (roulette, baccarat, blackjack; daily from 4 p.m.).

RECREATION and SPORTS. – Riding (Reiterhof Moos, Moosstrasse 135), trotting course, shooting, tennis, golf (Klessheim) and mini-golf, flying (flying school at airport; sightseeing flights); car and motorcycle racing on Salzburg Ring.

EVENTS. – *Salzburg Festival, annually from end of July to August, with performances of the highest quality – opera (usually one première each year) in the Festspielhaus and the Felsenreitschule; drama and ballet in the Landestheater; Hofmannsthal's "Jedermann" ("Everyman") in the Domplatz; concerts in the Festspielhaus, the Felsenreitschule, the Mozarteum, and in various churches; *serenade concerts* in the courtyard of the Residenz. – *Mozart Festival Week*, end of January; *Easter Festival* (March or April); *Whitsun concerts* in Festspielhaus; *Salzburger Schlosskonzerte* in Schloss Mirabell or Residenz; *promenade concerts* on Sundays and public holidays (May–September) and *Leuchtbrunnenkonzerte* (concerts at illuminated fountain) on Wednesday evenings (May–August) in Mirabellgarten; *Salzburger Dult* (Whitsun). – *Corpus Christi procession* (June); *Street theatre* in the squares and parks (end of June to beginning of August); *Salzburger Kulturtage* (October), including traditional events. – *Arts Festival* (October). – *Puppet Theatre* (Schwarzstrasse 22; Easter to September and at Christmas and New Year); fine performances of operas (particularly Mozart), ballet and old puppet plays. – *Christkindlmarkt* ("Christ Child's Market") in Domplatz (end November to Christmas Eve). *New Year's Eve balls* in all large hotels in the town.

**Salzburg, capital of the province of Salzburg and the gateway to Austria from the NW, is one of Europe's most beautiful cities, admired equally for its buildings and for its magnificent setting. In addition it enjoys a special fame in the world of music as the birthplace of Mozart: a fame reflected and maintained in the Mozarteum and the annual Festival.

The picturesque town occupies both banks of the River Salzach, which here emerges from the Salzburg Alps into an expanse of lower land dominated by the Untersberg (1853 m/6081 ft). The**

prospect of the city, with the towers and domes of its churches and, looming over it on the Mönchsberg, the massive bulk of the Hohensalzburg, is one of unforgettable beauty.

The romantic old town, huddled on the left bank of the Salzach between the river and the Mönchsberg, is an area of narrow medieval streets, arcaded courtyards and tall narrow houses, contrasting with the town of the Prince Bishops between the Neutor and the Neugebäude, a magnificent Baroque ecclesiastical capital with handsome buildings and spacious squares. On the right bank of the Salzach are the newer districts of the town, with the Kapuzinerberg and its conspicuous Capuchin friary rising above them to the E.

HISTORY and ART. – Evidence of Neolithic settlement was found on the Rainberg. Later the site was occupied by Illyrians, whose name for the settlement, *Juvavum* ("seat of the sky god"), was taken over by the Celts and the Romans. During the Roman period (15 B.C. to A.D. 500) Salzburg had the status of a *municipium*, the chief town of a district. An important Roman road ran by way of *Cucullae* (Kuchl) and the Radstädter Tauern – where the old Roman milestones can still be seen – to *Virunum*, near Klagenfurt, and on to Rome.

The next major events in the history of Salzburg were the occupation of the surrounding territory by the Bajuwari or Bavarians, then still pagans (6th c.), and the foundation of the monastic houses of St Peter and the Nonnberg by St Rupert (*c.* 696). Under Bishop

Virgil (745–784), a native of Ireland, and his successor Arno the **bishopric**, founded in 739, became the base from which the Alpine lands and the territory in the middle Danube valley were Christianised. Virgil built the pre-Romanesque cathedral whose foundations were excavated in 1956–58. The Franciscan Church and St Michael's Church – originally the town's parish churches – also date from the 8th and early 9th c.

The Romanesque period (1000–1250) was a great era of growth and development, when the Hohensalzburg and numerous churches were built – and so well built that the German king Conrad III was moved to declare that he had never seen finer churches than those of Salzburg. The main structure of St Peter's Church dates from the 12th c. During this period, too, the Cathedral was rebuilt – with its five aisles the largest Romanesque church in the Holy Roman Empire. Remains of the frescoes which then decorated the interiors of churches have survived in the Nonnberg convent with its severe and solemn half-length figures of saints.

During the Gothic period (1250–1530) the secular power of the Archbishops suffered severe reverses in the Hungarian wars, but this was nevertheless a time of rich artistic activity. A new social class now came to the fore in the form of the well-to-do townspeople, grown wealthy through their trade with Nürnberg, Augsburg, Vienna and Venice. The energetic *Archbishop Leonhard von Keutschach* (1495–1519) rebuilt the Hohensalzburg broadly in the form in which we see it today. The Blasiuskirche (St Blaise's) was built in the 14th c., followed in the 15th c. by the magnificent choir of the Franciscan Church, the church of the Nonnberg convent and St Margaret's Chapel in St Peter's Churchyard. The sculpture of the period is represented by many pieces carved from the beautiful red Adnet marble, notable among them the magnificent monument of Archbishop Leonhard von Keutschach on the outer wall of St George's Chapel in the Hohensalzburg.

Panoramic view of Salzburg

Salzburg's third great period of artistic creation, the Baroque age, began in the reign of *Archbishop Wolf Dietrich von Raitenau* (1578–1612). A scion of the Medici on his mother's side and educated in Rome, this great prince of the Church completely transformed the aspect of the town, although most of his plans were carried to completion only in the time of his successors. The Cathedral was built up to roof level by Markus Sittikus of Hohenems (1612–19) and completed (1619–53) by Paris Count Lodron, who also enclosed the town within new and powerful fortifications (1620–44) which saved it from the horrors of the Thirty Years War.

In the reign of Archbishop Johann Ernst von Thun (1687–1709) the famous architect *Johann Bernhard Fischer von Erlach* created the magnificently harmonious ensemble of Baroque architecture to which Salzburg owes its world renown. Of the twelve buildings in and around Salzburg for which Fischer von Erlach was responsible the Kollegienkirche is particularly notable, ranking as one of the outstanding achievements of all Baroque architecture. Thun's successor, Archbishop Franz Anton von Harrach (1709–27), replaced Fischer von Erlach by his like-minded rival *Johann Lukas von Hildebrandt*, architect of the Belvedere Palace in Vienna, who was responsible for the rebuilding of the Residenz and Schloss Mirabell (particularly notable features of which are the beautiful Marble Hall and the grand staircase with delightful sculptural decoration by Raphael Donner). – Archbishop Leopold Anton von Firmian (1727–44) banished more than 20,000 Protestants from the province under an edict of 1731. – *Wolfgang Amadeus* **Mozart** was born in Salzburg in 1756.

The 19th c. saw a decline in the political importance of Salzburg. The principality was secularised in 1803, but the city remained the seat of an archbishop, who still bears the title of "Primas Germaniae", a style granted in 1660. After brief periods of French and Bavarian rule Salzburg became part of Austria in 1816, and in the second half of the 19th c. the town enjoyed a period of economical revival, after the coming of the railway linked it up with the trade and traffic of the modern world. The beauties of Salzburg and the Salzkammergut had previously been discovered and celebrated by the painters of the Romantic and realist schools – although the local artist Hans Makart tended towards an ideal of purely external splendour. In general, however, Salzburg was more notable in Makart's time and in the early decades of the 19th c. as a focus of musical life rather than of the fine arts – a development which culminated in the institution of the *Salzburg Festival*. In 1956–60 the Festival was provided with a boldly designed new theatre by Clemens Holzmeister under the rock face of the Mönchsberg, in which tradition and the requirements of modern times are happily combined.

Museums and Monuments

Dommuseum (Cathedral Museum),
in oratories on S side of Cathedral, in Domplatz.
Mid May–Oct. daily 10 a.m.–5 p.m., Sun. and public holidays 11 a.m.–5 p.m. *Cathedral excavations* in the Residenzplatz 9 a.m.–5 p.m. (Easter–Oct.).

Festspielhaus (Festival Theatre),
Entrance in Hofstallgasse.
Conducted tours May/June/Sept. Mon.–Fri. at 11 a.m. and 3 p.m., Oct.–Apr. Mon.–Fri. at 3 p.m., Sat. at 11 a.m. Easter festival Mon.–Sat. at 2 p.m.
No conducted tours in July and Aug.

Glockenspiel (Carillon),
in tower of Neugebäude, Residenzplatz.
Conducted visits daily at 10.45 a.m. and 5.45 p.m.
From Nov.–Mar. only, Mon.–Fri.

Haus der Natur (Natural History Museum),
Museumsplatz 5.
Daily 9 a.m.–5 p.m.

Hellbrunn,
6 km/4 miles S of town centre.
Schloss and fountains
Conducted tours May–Oct. 9 a.m.–4.30 or 5.30 p.m.
Folk Museum in the Monatschlösschen
Apr.–Oct. 9 a.m.–5 p.m.
Alpine Zoo
Apr.–Oct. 9 a.m.–4 or 6.30 p.m.

Hohensalzburg,
Conducted tours 9 a.m.–5 p.m. Winter 9.30 a.m.–3.30 p.m., including Burgmuseum and Rainermuseum (May–Sept.).

Johann-Michael-Haydn Gedenkstätte,
St Peter Hof.
Mid May–mid Oct. daily 10 a.m.–5 p.m.

Max-Reinhardt-Forschungs- und Gedenkstätte (Max Reinhardt Research Complex and Memorial),
Schloss Arenberg, Arenbergstrasse 8–10.
Open Mon.–Fri. 9 a.m.–noon; during the Festival daily 10 a.m.–noon and 2–5 p.m.; closed July; from 1–15 Sept. and from Christmas–New Year.

Mozart's Birthplace,
Getreidegasse 9.
Daily 9 a.m.–6 or 7 p.m.

Mozarts Wohnhaus (Mozart House),
Makartplatz 8.
Conducted tours (from Mozarteum, Schwarzstrasse 26) July and Aug. Mon.–Fri. 11 a.m.

Museum Carolino Augusteum,
Museumplatz 1 and Bürgerspitalplatz 2.
Art and cultural history.
Daily except Mon. 9 a.m.–5 p.m.

Residenz,
Residenzplatz 1.
Conducted tours of state apartments, weekdays July–Sept. 10 a.m.–2.30 p.m. every half-hour; Sat. and Sun. 10 and 11 a.m.; Oct.–June at 10 and 11 a.m., 2 and 3 p.m.
Gallery European paintings (16th–19th c.).
Daily 10 a.m.–5 p.m.

Rupertinum,
Wiener Philharmonikergasse 9.
Modern gallery. Graphic collection, sculpture and photographs.
Mon. and Tue. 10 a.m.–5 p.m.; Wed. 2–9 p.m.

Salzburger Barockmuseum (Baroque Museum),
Entrance in Mirabellgarten.
Daily except Mon. 9 a.m.–noon and 2–5 p.m., Sun. 9 a.m.–noon.

Spielzeugmuseum (Toy Museum),
Bürgerspitalplatz 2.
Daily 9 a.m.–5 p.m. Closed Mon.

Trachtenmuseum,
Griesgasse 231.
Costumes.
Daily except Sun. 10 a.m.–noon and 2–5 p.m.

Trakl-Gedenkstätte (Trakl Memorial House),
in the poet's birthplace,
Waagplatz 1 a.
Conducted tours Mon., Tue., Thu. and Fri. at 2 p.m., Sat.
at 10 a.m.

SIGHTS. – In the heart of the old town on
the left bank of the Salzach (reached by
municipal buses) is the spacious **Residenzplatz**, with the *Residenzbrunnen*, of
Unterberg marble, the largest and finest
Baroque fountain north of the Alps, the
work of an Italian sculptor (1656–61). It
stands 15 m/50 ft high, with figures of bold
horses, Atlas figures, dolphins and, crowning
the whole structure, a triton with a conch-
shell. On the S side of the square is the
Cathedral, on the W side the **Residenz**
(palace of the Prince Bishops), built between 1596 and 1619 on the site of the
medieval bishop's palace. The palace is laid
out around three courtyards; the main front
has a marble gateway of 1710. The NW
range of buildings (now the police headquarters), of little architectural merit, was
added in 1788–92.

INTERIOR (conducted tours). – The state apartments
are decorated in late Baroque and early neo-classical
style, with wall and ceiling paintings by Johann Michael
Rottmayr and Martino Altomonte, rich stucco ornament
and handsome stoves. The huge *Karabinieresaal* dates
from about 1610–1689. In the *Knights' Hall* (Rittersaal)
and *Conference Hall* (Konferenzsaal), once the scene of
court concerts, concerts are still given during the season.
The splendid *Audience Hall* (Audienzsaal) contains
Flemish tapestries (*c.* 1600) and fine Paris-made furniture.
The *Markus Sittikus* or *White Hall* has stucco ornament in
Louis XVI style (1776). In the *Imperial Hall* (Kaisersaal) are
portraits of German Emperors and Kings of the Habsburg
family from Rudolf I to Charles VI (17th and 18th c.). In the
state rooms can be seen portraits of prince-bishops.

On the 2nd floor is the **Residenzgalerie**, established in
1923, which contains works by European painters from
the 16th to the 20th c. The Czernin and Schönborn-
Buchheim collection displays works by Dutch, Flemish,
French, Italian and Spanish masters of the 16th and
17th c.

Opposite the Residenz is the **Neugebäude**
(New Building), erected in 1592–1602 as
the Archbishop's guest-house and enlarged
about 1670, which now houses provincial
government offices and the *Head Post
Office* (S end). In the tower is a *carillon*
(Glockenspiel) of 35 bells (1702), which
plays Mozart tunes twice daily (at 11 a.m.
and 6 p.m.; conducted tours begin 15
minutes before these times), to which the
"Salzburg Bull" in the Hohensalzburg (see
p. 168) responds with a chorale.

On the N side of the Residenzplatz, at the
corner of Mozartplatz, is the little *Michaels-
kirch* (St Michael's Church, 1767–76),
which was the town's parish church from
the 8th to the 12th c. In Mozartplatz is a
Mozart Monument by Ludwig Schwanthaler (1842). At No. 1 Waagplatz is the
house in which the poet *Georg Trakl*
(1887–1914) was born (memorial). The
Waagplatz is the town's oldest market
square (*c.* 1000).

The S side of the Residenzplatz is dominated
by the *Cathedral* (*Dom*, by Santino
Solari, 1614–28), built of dark grey conglomerate from the Mönchsberg; the twin
towers, 79 m/259 ft high, date from 1652–
57. This was the first deliberately Italian-
style church to be built N of the Alps. The
W front, facing the Domplatz, has four
colossal statues of light-coloured marble,
the outer ones representing SS Rupert and
Virgil, patron saints of the province (*c.* 1660),
the inner ones Peter and Paul (1697–98).
The first cathedral, built by Abbot and
Bishop Virgil in 767–74, was replaced at the
end of the 12th c. by a five-aisled Romanesque basilica, which was destroyed by fire
in 1598. The present church, the third on
the site, was severely damaged by bombs in
1944, but restoration was completed by
1959. The three massive bronze doors, with
the symbols of Faith (left), Love (middle)
and Hope (right), were the work of Toni
Schneider-Manzell, Giacomo Manzù and
Ewald Mataré (1957–58).

INTERIOR. – The Cathedral can accommodate a
congregation of more than 10,000. In the first side
chapel on the left is the font (1321), borne on 12th c.

Salzburg Cathedral

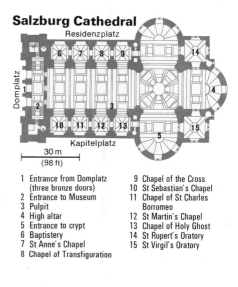

1 Entrance from Domplatz
   (three bronze doors)
2 Entrance to Museum
3 Pulpit
4 High altar
5 Entrance to crypt
6 Baptistery
7 St Anne's Chapel
8 Chapel of Transfiguration
9 Chapel of the Cross
10 St Sebastian's Chapel
11 Chapel of St Charles
   Borromeo
12 St Martin's Chapel
13 Chapel of Holy Ghost
14 St Rupert's Oratory
15 St Virgil's Oratory

figures of lions, from the Romanesque cathedral, in which Mozart was baptised. On the high altar is a "Resurrection" (1628) by Arsenio Mascagni; the frescoes in the vaulting, amid rich stucco ornament, are by Mascagni and his pupils. The bronze pulpit at the third column on the right was the work of Toni Schneider-Manzell (1959). The large organ has a prospectus of 1703. – Under the crossing, in the foundations of the medieval cathedrals, is a *crypt*, constructed in 1957–59 as a burial vault for Archbishops of Salzburg, with a number of chambers. In the antechamber is a floor mosaic showing the ground-plans of the three cathedrals. The central chamber, a chapel, has an altar set on a fragment of wall from the Carolingian cathedral, with a Romanesque crucifix of the early 13th c. The chamber to the N, which extends eastwards outside the Cathedral, was originally part of the lower church of the Romanesque cathedral and preserves the central piers, pilasters and column bases from that church. – The interesting *Cathedral Museum* (Dommuseum), which is entered from the antechamber, contains valuable liturgical objects and utensils.

To the W of the Cathedral is the *Domplatz*, linked by archways (1658–63) with the squares to N and S and thus appearing totally enclosed. In the middle of the square is a *Mariensäule* (column bearing a figure of the Virgin) of 1771. Here since 1920 Hugo von Hofmannsthal's play "Jedermann" ("Everyman") has been performed during the Salzburg Festival. The square is bounded on the S by St Peter's Abbey.

In Kapitelplatz, to the S of the Cathedral, is the *Kapitelschwemme* (1732), a magnificent horse trough of white marble with a group depicting Neptune. On the E side of the square is the *Archbishop's Palace* (Erzbischöfliches Palais), built in 1602 as the chapterhouse with the coats of arms of the 24 canons of that period under the gateway in Kapitelgasse.

On the W side of Kapitelplatz is the Benedictine **Arch-Abbey of St Peter** (*Erzabtei St Peter, St-Peter-Stift*), founded by St Rupert about 690, which was the residence of the Archbishops until 1110. The present buildings date mainly from the 17th and 18th c.

To the S, entered from Festungsgasse, is the venerable and impressive *St Peter's Churchyard* (*St-Peters-Friedhof*), surrounded on three sides by arcades (1627) containing family tombs. To the S it backs on to the sheer rock face of the Mönchsberg, in which are early Christian *catacombs* and *St Maximus's Chapel* (visit ¼ hour), hewn from the rock, probably in the 3rd c. A.D. The late Gothic *St Margaret's Chapel* (closed) in the centre of the churchyard was built in 1485–91 on the site of an earlier chapel. A passage leads from the churchyard into the outer

courtyard of the abbey, with the *Petrusbrunnen* (St Peter's Fountain) of 1673. To the left is the entrance to the *Stiftskeller St Peter* (restaurant). On the W side of the courtyard is a passage leading to the *Benedictine College* (1925–26).

*St Peter's Church (*Stiftskirche St Peter*) was built in 1130–43, altered in 1605–25 and decorated in Rococo style between 1770 and 1777. Inside the porch under the tower is the Romanesque W doorway (*c*. 1240), with sculpture in the tympanum; the Rococo door dates from 1768. The interior, in which the plan of the Romanesque basilica can still be detected, contains many monuments of great interest. In the third chapel behind the altar is the rock-cut tomb of St Rupert, with an epitaph of 1444, and in the fourth chapel are the monuments of Mozart's sister Marianne ("Nannerl"), who died in 1829 as Baroness Berchtold zu Sonnenburg, and Michael Haydn (d. 1806), brother of Joseph. By the choir-screen are two bronze candelabra of 1609. All but two of the altarpieces on the 16 marble altars were painted by Johann Martin Schmidt of Krems, "Kremser Schmidt" (1718–1801). – The *Lady Chapel* (1319) on the N side of the church (not open to the public) contains a stone figure of the Virgin dating from the same period as the chapel, early Gothic frescoes and later frescoes of 1955.

To the N of St Peter's is the **Franciscan Church* (*Franziskanerkirche*), which was the town's parish church (dedicated to the Virgin) until 1635. Notable features of the exterior are the high roof of the choir and the tower on the S side (1486–98) with its neo-Gothic helm roof of 1867. The dark late Romanesque nave (13th c.) contrasts with the high, light Gothic choir (by Hans Burghausen, 1408 to after 1450). In front of a ring of Baroque chapels (1606–1704) stands the high altar (1709; probably by J. B. Fischer von Erlach), with a carved **Madonna* by Michael Pacher (1498; the Child is 19th c.). In the central chapel behind the altar is a marble altar (1561) from the old Cathedral. – Opposite the church, to the S, is the *Franciscan Friary*.

On the S side of Max-Reinhardt-Platz and Hofstallgasse, backing on to the Mönchsberg, stands the **Festspielhaus** (Festival Theatre). It occupies the site of the old Court Stables (Hofmarstall), built in 1607 and enlarged in 1662, of which there survive three gateways in the much altered façades. The gateway in the NW façade is particularly fine (1694). Adjoining is the *Felsenreitschule* or *Sommerreitschule* (Rock Riding School, Summer Riding School) 1693, with three galleries for spectators hewn from the rock. The Karl Böhm Saal, converted from the small Winter Riding School (1662), has frescoes of 1690 (fighting with the Turks).

The Festspielhaus, 225 m/740 ft long, consists of the Altes Haus (Old House) and Neues Haus (New House), between which are the *Foyer* (frescoes by Anton Faistauer), offices, workshops and the Karl Böhm Saal. The *Old House* (*Small House*), facing on to Max-Reinhardt-Platz, was constructed in 1924–25 by the conversion of the Winter Riding School and was further altered in the following year by Clemens Holzmeister. In 1937–38 Holzmeister carried out a further drastic re-building in which the auditorium was turned 180 degrees and enlarged to a total of 1304 seats. Finally the interior was remodelled once again in 1963. The Small House is used for performances of Mozart's works.

The *New House* (*Large House*), in Hofstallgasse, was built by Holzmeister in 1956–60, with a massive stage 40 m/130 ft high cutting deep into the Mönchsberg (its construction involved the removal of more than 55,000 cu. m/71,940 cu. yds of rock). This house, which is famed for its excellent acoustics, has seating for an audience of 2170. In the entrance hall are two fountains with figures representing "Music" and "Drama", in the lower foyer a steel relief by Rudolf Hoflehner, "Homage to Anton von Webern", and in the foyer outside the first-floor boxes a tapestry designed by Oskar Kokoschka, "Amor and Psyche".

The famous *Salzburg Festival was founded in 1920 by Hugo von Hofmannsthal, Max Reinhardt, Richard Strauss and others and inaugurated with a performance of Hofmannsthal's "Jedermann" ("Everyman") in the Domplatz. Held annually in late July and August, the Festival puts on performances of the highest artistic standard with artists of international reputation and attracts large audiences from all over the world.

In Max-Reinhardt-Platz is the *Fish Fountain* (1610), and on the far side of the square the *Furtwänglerpark*, with the oldest monument to Schiller in Austria (1859). To the N of the little park is the **Kollegienkirche** (College Church), built by J. B. Fischer von Erlach (1694–1707) for the University: a cruciform church on a centralised plan in mature Baroque style, with a high central dome.

To the W is the **Paris Lodron University**, founded in 1964, occupying the buildings (Studiengebäude, 1618–52) of the former Benedictine University which was dissolved in 1810. In the central range of buildings is the Aula Academica, in early neo-classical style. There is an extensive complex of new University buildings in the district of Salzburg-Nonntal.

In Sigmundsplatz, to the W of the University is the *Pferdeschwemme* (1695), a handsome horse trough with the figure of a

"Horse-Tamer" by Michael Bernhard Mandl. Between the Festspielhaus and the Pferdeschwemme is the *Neutor*, a tunnel 123 m/134 yds long cut through the Mönchsberg in 1764–67 to the district of Riedenburg (vehicles and pedestrians; underground garage).

A short distance N of Sigmundsplatz is the little triangular *Bürgerspitalplatz*, on the W side of which, three-storey arcaded front of the Hospital, closed in 1898 (entrance at Bürgerspitalgasse 2), which now houses the study collections of the Museum Carolino Augusteum and the *Toy Museum*. At an angle to this building is the early Gothic **Blasiuskirche** (St Blaise's), consecrated in 1350 as the hospital church, which contains a carved 15th c. tabernacle.

NW of Bürgerspitalplatz by way of the *Gstättentor* (1618), on the line of the medieval town walls, and the narrow Gstättengasse (on right, at No. 4, a baker's shop of 1429) is Anton-Neumayr-Platz, with the Marienbrunnen (Fountain of the Virgin) of 1691. To the left is the *Mönchsberg lift* (1890, rebuilt 1948), in the entrance hall of which are mosaics depicting views of Salzburg in 1553 and 1818.

From Anton-Neumayr-Platz *Museumsplatz* runs N to the Franz-Josef-Kai on the banks of the Salzach, with the Haus der Natur on the left and the Museum Carolino Augusteum on the right.

The **Haus der Natur** (House of Nature, Natural History Museum; entrance at Museumsplatz 5), in a former Ursuline convent, graphically illustrates in its 80 rooms all aspects of natural history and geology, as well as the nature and use of the environment – the animals of the prehistoric world (one room devoted to models of dinosaurs); an aquarium; a coral display; a display devoted to Tibet; the landscape of the Salzburg area (minerals, geology); the animals of Europe; the animals of other continents (including skeletons); a reptile zoo; a large diorama hall, with a representation of the landing on the moon; a space city of the future; explanation of the structure of the universe and models of rockets.

The **Museum Carolino Augusteum** (Museumsplatz 1), named after the Empress Carolina Augusta, contains a wide range of material of artistic and cultural interest (carved altars of the 15th and 16th c., applied and decorative art, musical instruments, coins, Salzburg paintings from the 15th c. to the present day, a collection of graphic art, etc.). – At the far end of the Ursuline convent is the *Markuskirche* (St Mark's Church, by Fischer von Erlach, 1699–1705). A little way NW is the *Klausentor*, and old town gate of 1612.

From Universitätsplatz a number of passages (known here as "Durchhäuser") run N to the old-world *Getreidegasse* (pedestrian precinct), a busy shopping street lined with burghers' houses of the 15th–18th c. (many wrought-iron shop and inn signs, beautiful courtyards). On No. 3 is a tablet commemorating the 19th c. politician August Bebel, who worked here as an apprentice

woodturner in 1859–60. At No. 9 is *Mozart's Birthplace* (*Mozart-Geburtshaus*), in which Wolfgang Amadeus Mozart was born on 27 January 1756 (d. Vienna 5 December 1791). The rooms on the 3rd floor which were occupied by the Mozart family are now a museum (mementoes, including the young Mozart's violin, portraits, a clavichord of 1760, a pianoforte of 1780, scores, etc.). On the 2nd floor is an interesting exhibition, "Mozart in the Theatre", with illuminated miniature stages. Mozart's father Leopold, who occupied the house from 1747 to 1753, was an excellent violinist and music teacher, who from 1762 onwards took Wolfgang and his sister Nannerl, five years older, on concert tours

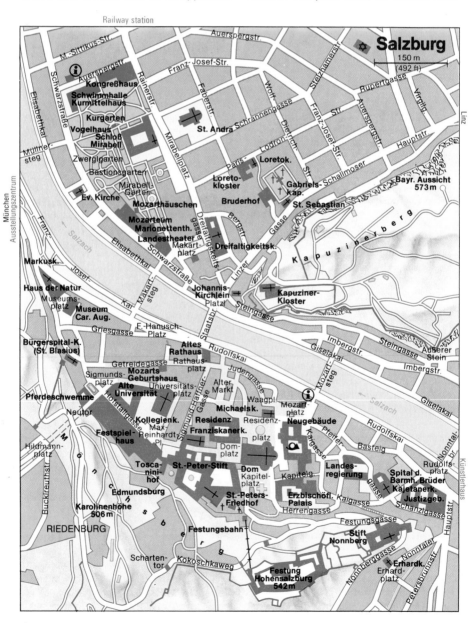

throughout Europe, when the youthful musician gained great acclaim for his virtuoso piano-playing.

At the E end of Getreidegasse is the *Kranzlmarkt*, with the **Rathaus** (Town Hall), originally built in 1407 and rebuilt in 1618 and 1775.

Around the Rathaus are many old burghers' houses, which were already reaching heights of four or five storeys in medieval times, with plain façades and a low blank wall running along the base of the roof.

The *Alter Markt*, which rises slightly towards the S, dates from the late 13th c. At No. 6 is the *Court Pharmacy* (Hofapotheke), established in 1591, with 18th c. furnishings. In front of it is the *Marktbrunnen* or *Florianibrunnen* (Market Fountain, St Florian's Fountain), with an octagonal basin (1687) and a beautiful spiral grille (Renaissance, 1583).

To the E of the Alter Markt are other narrow and twisting lanes – including the *Judengasse* leading to Mozartplatz – typical of the old town, which extends beyond Mozartplatz into the *Kaiviertel* ("Quay quarter").

In *Pfeifergasse* is a house (No. 11) occupied in 1525 by the philosopher and physician Paracelsus, who died in the neighbouring Kaigasse (No. 8). At the end of Pfeifergasse, on the right, is the **Chiemseehof**, originally built in 1305 and much altered in later periods, which was the residence of the Prince Bishops of Chiemsee until 1806 and is now the seat of the provincial government (arcaded courtyard with coats of arms). Obliquely across the street is the *Kajetanerkirche* (St Cajetan's Church), in Italian Baroque style by Gaspare Zugalli, 1685–1700), with no tower but with a massive dome; the interior has luxuriant stucco decoration of about 1730.

A little way E, at Hellbrunner Strasse 3 (beyond the Law Courts), is the *Künstlerhaus* (Artists' House), with periodic special exhibitions.

To the S of Kajetanerplatz rises the **Nonnberg** (455 m/1493 ft), the lower eastern end of the hill occupied by the Hohensalzburg, which can be reached by way of the Nonnbergstiege. On this hill is the *Stift Nonnberg*, a Benedictine nunnery founded by St Rupert about 700 – the oldest surviving nunnery in German-speaking territory. There

are magnificent views from the bastion. The late Gothic *church* was built between 1463 and 1499 on the walls of an earlier Romanesque basilica destroyed by fire in 1423, of which the doorway and frescoed porch have survived; the central window behind the carved high altar (*c.* 1515) has stained glass of 1480. In the crypt (1463) is the rock-cut tomb of St Erentrudis. The *convent museum* contains some notable art treasures, including a faldstool (a folding seat) of 1242.

Below the S side of the Nonnberg is the *Erhardkirche* (St Erhard's Church, 1685–89) the parish church of the district of NONNTALL.

The whole urban scene is dominated by the picturesque fortress of ***Hohensalzburg**, situated to the S of the old town on the southeastern summit of the Mönchsberg (542 m/ 1778 ft), 120 m/400 ft above the Salzach. It can be reached on foot (20 minutes) either from Kapitelplatz by way of Festungsgasse or from the Mönchsberg via the Schartentor, or by the funicular from Festungsgasse (in about 1½ minutes).

The castle, first built in 1077 in the reign of Archbishop Gebhard, dates in its present form mainly from about 1500, during the reign of Archbishop Leonhard von Keutschach, whose heraldic device, a turnip, is everywhere to be seen. The castle was strongly fortified in the 17th c., but was abandoned in 1861.

Getreidegasse, Salzburg

From the Festungsgasse the approach to the fortress passes through a number of arched defensive gateways under the Feuerbastei (Fire Bastion, 1681; marble coat of arms of its builder, Archbishop von Kuenburg) to the "Reisszug", a hoist (1501) for bringing up supplies, formerly powered by horses, and then through the Rossporte (Horse Gate) into the Haupthof (outer ward), with an ancient lime-tree and a cistern of 1539.

On the N side of the courtyard is the little *Georgskirche* (1501–2), on the outer wall of which is a fine red marble relief of Archbishop Leonhard (by Hans Valkenauer, 1515). The conducted tour which begins at the Gerichtsturm or Reckenturm takes in, among other

Festung Hohensalzburg

1	First Gate (Lodron Gate)	21	Bernhard von Rohr Bastion
2	Second Gate (Keutschach Gate)	22	Hasenturm (Hare Tower)
3	Third Gate (Snake Gate; Lower Trumpeter's Tower)	23	Unterer Hasengraben
		24	Pulverturm (Powder Tower)
4	Schlangenrondell (Snake Tower)	25	Restaurant
		26	Gerichts- or Reckenturm (beginning of conducted tour)
5	Lower Nonnberg Bastion		
6	Upper Nonnberg Bastion	27	Oberer Hasengraben
7	Reisszug (Hoist)	28	Schartentor
8	Schlangengang (Snake Passage)	29	Glockenturm (Bell Tower)
		30	Alter Schlosshof (well)
9	Rossporte (Horse Gate)	31	Altes Schloss (museum)
10	Höllenporte (Hell Gate)	32	Schlossbastei (Castle Bastion)
11	Zeughaus (Arsenal)		
12	Reissturm	33	Stockhaus (Prison)
13	Schmiedturm (Smith's Tower)	34	Wallmeisterhaus (Sergeant's Quarters)
14	Outer Ward (Haupthof)	35	Feuertürme (Fire Towers)
15	Cistern	36	Hungerturm (Hunger Tower)
16	Kaplanstöckl (Chaplain's Quarters)		
		37	St George's Church
17	Schüttboden (Granary)	38	"Salzburg Bull"
18	Arbeitshaus (Workshops)	39	Trompeterturm (Trumpeter's Tower)
19	Geierturm (Vulture Tower)		
20	Speisehaus (Dining Hall: tickets)	40	Feuerbastei (Fire Bastion)

features, the "Salzburg Bull" (Salzburger Stier), an organ of 1502 which is played daily after the carillon in the Neugebäude, and, on the 3rd floor, the late Gothic Prince's Apartments (beautiful tiled stove) and the Great or Golden Hall.

Adjoining the Prince's Apartments is the *Rainer Museum*, with mementoes of the old Salzburg household regiment, known as Archduke Rainer's k.u.k. 59th Infantry Regiment, which was quartered in the castle from

1871 to 1918. – On the Hoher Stock (upper floor) is the *Castle Museum*, with old documents, weapons, coats of arms, etc.

To the W of the Hohensalzburg extends the **Mönchsberg**, a ridge almost 2 km/1¾ miles long covered with deciduous forest rising to some 60 m/200 ft above the old town, with fortifications dating from the 15th–17th c. The shady paths through the trees lead to a series of fine viewpoints. On the NE side of the hill is the *Bürgerwehrsöller* (Naturfreunde, "Friends of Nature", house), a terrace from which there is a fine view of St Peter's and the Cathedral.

Above Neumayrplatz is the Café Winkler, with the Casino; magnificent view of the whole of Salzburg from the terrace. On the S side of the hill, reached from the *Schartentor* (1635) on the Oskar-Kokoschka-Weg, is the *Richterhöhe* (508 m/1667 ft), with towers belonging to the old fortifications of the town and a monument of the geographer Eduard Richter (1847–1905); superb panoramic *view of the surrounding hills.

To the N of the Café Winkler, above the Klausentor, is the *Humboldtterrasse*, a rock platform which also affords panoramic views. From here we go down through the *Monikapforte* (1623), another relic of the old fortifications, into the district of MÜLLN, with an old Augustinian monastery which was taken over by Benedictines in 1835. The church (consecrated 1453), standing on higher ground, has an early Baroque interior. The Bräustübl (Brewhouse) of the abbey, famed for its beer, has large rooms and a beautiful garden.

On the **right bank of the Salzach**, below the Kapuzinerberg, are the more recent parts of the town. The broad *Staatsbrücke* crosses the river to the *Platzl*, around which an outlying bridgehead settlement had grown up by the 12th c. In the *Linzer Gasse*, which leads from the Platzl in a north-easterly direction, is **St Sebastian's Church** (*Sebastianskirche*; on left), built 1502–12, completely remodelled in Rococo style 1749–53. A flight of steps (on the wall to the left the monument of the physician and philosopher Theophrastus Paracelsus, 1493–1541) leads up to the interesting little Friedhof St Sebastian a cemetery established in 1595–1600 on the model of an Italian campo santo. In the middle of the cemetery is *St Gabriel's Chapel (Gabrielskapelle), with ornate ceramic decoration in the interior, built 1597–1603 as a mausoleum for Archbishop

Wolf Dietrich (d. 1617). On the way to the chapel are the graves of Mozart's father Leopold (1719–87), his widow Konstanze (1763–1842) and Genoveva von Weber (d.1798), mother of the composer Maria von Weber.

To the W of the church is a passage leading to the Loreto Convent (Loretokloster) and Paris-Lodron-Strasse.

A little way NW of the Platzl is *Makartplatz*, on the E side of which is the *Trinity Church* (Dreifaltigkeitskirche), a domed Baroque structure by J. B. Fischer von Erlach (1694–1702). At No. 8 in the square is the *Mozart House* (Mozarts Wohnhaus), occupied by Leopold Mozart and his family from 1773 until his death in 1787 ("Tanzmeistersaal"; concerts of chamber music).

On the SW side of the square is the *Landestheater* (Provincial Theatre), built 1892–93, altered 1939 and 1977–78. Beyond this, in Schwarzstrasse, are (No. 22) the *Puppet Theatre* (excellent *performances, particularly of Mozart's operas) and (No. 26) the **Mozarteum**, built in 1910–14 for the College of Music and the Performing Arts, with the Academy of Music, concert halls and the Mozart Archives. In the garden is the "*Zauberflötenhäuschen*" ("Magic Flute House"), a wooden hut transferred here from the old Freihaustheater in the Nachmarkt in Vienna, in which Mozart composed "The Magic Flute" in five months in 1791.

At the N end of Dreifaltigkeitsgasse is the elongated *Mirabellplatz*, the real nucleus of the newer part of the town. Off this square to the right is Paris-Lodron-Strasse on the right of which is the little *Loreto Church* (with a sacred image known as the "*Salzburger Kindl*"), which originally belonged to a convent of Capuchin nuns.

At the end of Mirabellplatz, on right, stands the *parish church of St Andrew* (St Andrä), originally neo-Gothic (1898), with an altar commemorating those who died in the two world wars. Opposite the church is **Schloss Mirabell**, originally built by Archbishop Wolf Dietrich in 1606 for his favourite Salome Alt, sumptuously remodelled in Baroque style by J. L. von Hildebrandt (1721–27) and restored in simpler style after a fire in 1818; it now houses the burgomaster and municipal offices. In the W wing is the marble *grand staircase of the 18th c. building, with putti and statues by Georg Raphael Donner and

his pupils (1726). The Marble Hall (open to the public) is used for concerts and weddings. The Gärtnergebäude ("Gardener's Buildings") of the Orangery now houses the *Salzburg Baroque Museum*.

To the S of the Schloss is the ***Mirabellgarten** (also accessible from Makartplatz), an excellent example of Baroque landscape gardening laid out about 1690, probably by Fischer von Erlach, with terraces, marble statues and fountains. The former *Aviary* (Vogelhaus, *c.* 1700) is now used for exhibitions. At the SW corner of the gardens is a small open-air theatre. – Adjoining the Mirabellgarten to the W, on an old bastion, is the *Bastionsgarten* or *Zwerglgarten* ("Dwarfs' Garden"), with grotesque figures of dwarfs.

To the N the Mirabellgarten extends into the **Kurgarten**, on the N side of which are the *Kongresshaus* (accommodation for 2500 people, restaurant), the Hotel Sheraton and the *Paracelsusbad* (medicinal) with an enclosed swimming pool and *Kurmittelhaus* (spa treatment). – 1 km/$\frac{3}{4}$ mile N is the main *railway station* (Hauptbahnhof).

To the E is the right-bank counterpart of the Mönchsberg, the **Kapuzinerberg** (638 m/2093 ft), which is also covered with beautiful park-like woodland. On the hill is the conspicuous *Capuchin Friary* (Kapuzinerkloster), built in 1599–1602 within an old medieval fortification. Along the S side of the hill is the *Steingasse*, a well-preserved medieval street, with the *Innere Steintor*, a gate in the original town walls which was given its present form in 1634. At No. 9 is the birthplace of the local priest, Josef Mohr (1792–1848), author of the -well-known Christmas carol "Silent Night". In the eastward continuation of Steingasse, Arenbergstrasse (No. 10), is *Schloss Arenberg*, with the *Max Reinhardt Research Complex and Memorial*, commemorating the great theatre director who died in exile in 1943.

From Steingasse a stepped lane (*c.* 260 steps) leads up to the Capuchin friary, which can also be reached from the Linzer Gasse on a Way of the Cross (18th c. chapels) and through the *Felixpforte*, a gate in the 1632 town walls. From the friary it is 20 minutes' climb to the Bayrische Aussicht ("View of Bavaria", 573 m/1880 ft), and from there another 10 minutes to the Obere Stadtaussicht ("Upper View of the Town", 606 m/1989 ft), with superb views of the town, the Hohensalzburg and the mountains.

A short distance E is the *Franziskischlössl* (633 m/2078 ft), which dates from 1629.

SURROUNDINGS. – *To the N*, near the Salzburg-Mitte motorway exit, is the **Salzburg Exhibition Complex**, with twelve exhibition halls and a restaurant. – 5 km/ 3 miles N of Salzburg (tramway, then 45 minutes on foot, or by road and 30 minutes on foot), on a hill (530 m/ 1740 ft), is the conspicuous **pilgrimage church of Maria Plain**, a twin-towered Baroque church built in 1671–74, with an interior in the style of the period (painted sacred image; side altars mostly by Schwanthaler; beautiful choir screen; richly carved confessionals). Views of the town and the Alps (best in the evening).

15 km/9 miles NW of the church, on the Salzach, is the market village of **Oberndorf** (394 m/1293 ft), with a memorial chapel (1937) on the site of St Nicholas's Church (destroyed by flood-water in 1899), in which the carol "Stille Nacht" ("Silent Night") (words by the local priest Josef Mohr, music by the teacher, Franz Gruber) was sung for the first time on Christmas Eve 1818. – 15 km/9 miles NE of Salzburg is the **Wallersee** (6 km/ 4 miles long), to the N of which, between the two *Trumer Seen*, is the summer resort of *Mattsee*, with a collegiate religious house founded in 777.

The "Silent Night" Chapel, Oberndorf

To the W, some 3 km/2 miles from the middle of the town, is the district of **Maxglan**, with a late Gothic church. Farther SW is *Salzburg Airport*. – 3 km/2 miles NW of Maxglan is **Schloss Klessheim**, a Baroque palace built in 1700–9 to the design of J. B. Fischer von Erlach for the Prince-Bishop Johann Ernst von Thun; the interior was completed in 1732. The Kavalierhaus (1880) is now the Schlosshotel, with a golf-course in the park. The Schloss is used by the provincial government for receptions and other functions.

To the S, on the *Leopoldskroner Weiher* (pond: 20 minutes' walk from Salzburg-Nonntal), is **Schloss Leopoldskron**, a splendid Rococo palace (1736) of the Archbishops of Salzburg, later owned by Max Reinhardt and his heirs from 1918 to 1956. On the W side of the pond is a "Fitness Trail" almost 1 k/¾ mile long. To the W the *Moosstrasse* (Moor Road) runs in a dead straight line (4·5 km/2¾ miles) from the Riedenburg district over the *Landskroner Moos* (peat baths) to *Glanegg*. From Glanegg good climbers can reach the summit of the Geiereck (1806 m/5925 ft) and the Salzburger Hochthron (1853 m/6080 ft) in 4½ hours.

6 km/4 miles S of Salzburg, beyond *Morzg* (in the parish church, 1683, frescoes by Anton Faistauer), is *Schloss Hellbrunn, an early Baroque palace (1612–15) of the Archbishops of Salzburg, now municipal property, with gardens in German Baroque style (statues, fountains,

grottoes, trick waterworks, mechnical theatre), reconstructed 1980–84, according to an old etching. On a hill in the adjoining park is the "Monatschlössl", a hunting lodge built in 1615, so called because it was occupied for only one month in the year; since 1924 it has been occupied by the *Salzburg Folk Museum*. Behind it is the Watzmann-Aussicht (viewpoint), and nearby is the *Steinernes Theater* ("Stone Theatre"), a natural gorge, artificially widened, in which the first performance of an opera in German-speaking territory took place in 1617. On the western slopes of the hill is the **Zoo**, opened in 1960.

6 km/4 miles SW of Hellbrunn by way of *Anif* (Schloss of 1838–48, privately owned, in the middle of a lake; bathing) is *St Leonhard* (459 m/1506 ft; Schloss of 1570), with the lower station of a cableway (2800 m/ 3060 yds) up the *Salzburger Hochthron* (1856 m/ 6091 ft), the highest Austrian peak in the **Untersberg** massif (landscape reserve), the most striking hill in the Salzburg area and the only one in the Northern Calcareous Alps to rise directly out of the plain. The upper station of the cableway (1776 m/5827 ft; restaurant) lies below the summit of the Geiereck (1805 m/5924 ft), which can be reached in 8 minutes.

To the E of Salzburg, on the right bank of the Salzach 1 km/¾ mile from the Staatsbrücke, is the *Volksgarten* (Franz-Josef-Park), with a large open-air swimming pool, sports facilities, mini-golf and an ice rink. 3 km/2 miles SE is the suburb of **Algen**, with a church, originally Gothic, which was remodelled in Baroque style in 1689 and enlarged in 1909. The beautiful Schlosspark on the slopes of the Gaisberg (restaurant) is a popular resort of the people of Salzburg. – 2 km/1¼ miles NE of the Volksgarten, in the suburb of **Gnigl**, is *Schloss Neuhaus* (private property), first recorded in 1219 then rebuilt in 1424 and 1851.

The ***Gaisberg** (1288 m/4226 ft), 15 km/9 miles from the town on an attractive road, is much visited for its fine panoramic views of the surrounding area. In winter its wide expanses of Alpine meadows are a popular skiing area. On the summit are a large car park, an inn and a VHF and television relay station.

Salzburg (*Land*)

Bundesland: Salzburg (S). – Capital: Salzburg.
Area: 7155 sq. km/2762 sq. miles.
Population: 452,700.
ⓘ **Landesverkehrsamt**,
Mozartplatz 1, A-5020 Salzburg;
tel. (06 62) 80 42–22 32.

The *land* (province) is Salzburg is bounded on the NW by the Federal Republic of Germany (Bavaria), which here drives a deep wedge into Austrian territory, on the N and NE by Upper Austria, on the SE by Styria, on the S by Carinthia, Eastern Tirol and (for a short distance) Italy, and on the W by Northern Tirol. The area was named for its rich deposits of salt.

Salzburg province lies between the Upper Bavarian plain and the hilly Alpine foreland in the N, the Hohe Tauern in the S and a region of varied topography to the E. It is dominated by the Dachstein massif and watered by the river systems of the Traun, the Enns and the Mur. It extends over both sides of the Salzach valley, the principal traffic route through the region. The great turn in the river between Schwarzach and St Johann im Pongau lies roughly in the middle of the province.

Almost all the side valleys of the two principal rivers, the Salzach and the Saalach, narrow into gorges at their mouths, forming waterfalls down which their mountain streams ("Achen") tumble into the main valley.

The history and economy of the province have long been principally associated with its capital. The Bishops and later Archbishops of Salzburg, enjoying both ecclesiastical and secular authority, determined the destinies of the province and the neighbouring territories for more than a thousand years; and Salzburg is still a hub of cultural life for the whole of central Austria.

Important elements in the economy of the province are the extraction of salt (Hallein) and the hydroelectric power stations fed by large reservoirs in the mountains around Kaprun and on the Gerlos road. In addition

Entrance to the salt-mine, Hallein

there are Alpine pastoral farming and forestry, small deposits of lignite, peat and copper, and two aluminium plants. Tourism makes a major contribution to the economy throughout the whole year.

HISTORY. – During the Celtic *Hallstatt period* (early Iron Age) the region was an important focus of trade in the salt of Hallein. – The *Romans* built a road over the

Radstädter Tauern into northern Europe, and other roads extended from the Roman settlement on the site of present-day Salzburg far into the surrounding territory.

During the period of the great migrations the valleys in this region, sheltered behind high mountains, suffered less severely than the open territories of Lower and Upper Austria and Styria; and Salzburg was not totally destroyed during the troubles of the 5th c., although there is much evidence of destruction by fire to show that the town suffered heavy damage about 470. Soon afterwards the Dukes of Bavaria established bases in the region.

About 690 the abbey of St Peter was founded and granted properties which formed the basis of the later extensive possessions of the Archbishops of Salzburg. With the establishment of the bishopric of Salzburg at the beginning of the 8th c. and its erection into an archbishopric at the end of the century the foundations were laid for the creation of a great ecclesiastical domain. Thus even at this early period we can detect the beginnings of the later ecclesiastical principality, the core of which was the present-day province of Salzburg.

At the end of the 13th c. there were bitter conflicts with Duke Albrecht of Austria and Styria, and at the beginning of the 14th c. there were still fiercer wars with Bavaria. In the struggles between different branches of the Habsburgs and in the Hungarian war of the 15th c. the Archbishops of Salzburg sided with the opponents of Emperor Frederick III. The province's geographical situation protected it against attack by the Turks, but it suffered severely during the *Peasant Wars* of 1525 and 1526.

Although the Counter-Reformation of the early 17th c. caused relatively little harm, the religious problem boiled up again in 1731 with the expulsion of the Protestants.

After the secularisation of the archbishopric in 1803 Salzburg became a secular principality. In 1805 it became a duchy within Austria; in 1809 it was ceded to Bavaria; and in 1816 it was finally incorporated in Austria, with the exception of the territory around Berchtesgaden and another small area. At first administered as part of Upper Bavaria, it became a separate province in 1850.

From 1918 it was a federal province (*Bundesland*) in the Republic of Austria; and since the end of the Second World War (during which the town of Salzburg suffered several air raids) it has shared the destinies of the reestablished Republic.

ART. – Throughout the whole medieval period Salzburg was a focal pont of intellectual and artistic life. The scriptorium of St Peter's Abbey was famous for its illuminated manuscripts. *Romanesque* art is represented by the remains of frescoes in the Nonnberg convent church, Michaelbeuern Abbey and the excavated remains of the Romanesque cathedral of Salzburg.

To the *Gothic* period belong the Nonnberg church, the towers of the Hohensalzburg and St Margaret's Chapel. The Lungau is particularly rich in work of this period. Many country churches have preserved their Gothic character. In the early part of the period the great area of castle-building was the Lungau; and commanding situations were occupied by the fortresses of Hohensalzburg and Hohenwerfen. – From the 16th c. onwards many castles were built between Salzburg and Hallein, in the valley around Radstadt, in the Tamsweg basin, in the upper Pinzgau and between Zell am See and Saalfelden. – The art of the province reached its greatest flowering, however, in the **Baroque** period, when a leading role was played by the town of Salzburg.

The province of Salzburg is a region of great topographical diversity. To the N the mighty limestone massifs fall away to attractive rolling uplands and plains, while to the E the hills of the Salzkammergut, rising gradually higher, merge into the Alpine landscape of Upper Austria and extend to the borders of Styria in the Dachstein range.

At the Lueg pass, to the S of Salzburg, the massive limestone massifs of the *Tennengebirge* and *Hagengebirge* fall down in sheer rockfaces to the banks of the Salzach. Then follows the *Steinernes Meer*, a vast plateau of sublime and solitary beauty, above which rises the glittering ice of the Übergossene Alm on the *Hochkönig*, with the rugged pinnacles of the Manndlwände.

To the W the *Loferer* and *Leoganger Steinberge* mark the boundary between Salzburg and Tirol. To the S of the Leoganger Steinberge, the Steinernes Meer, the Hochkönig, the Tennengebirge and the Dachstein group the ridge of the *Pinzgauer* and *Pongauer Schieferalpen* (Schist Alps) extends into the upper Enns valley.

The *Niedere Tauern*, a chain of ancient mountains, reaches from Styria to the Murtörl, forming a transition to the Hohe Tauern. The wide hollows of the Hohe and Niedere Tauern are occupied by dark mountain lakes, and abundantly flowing mountain streams cut their way in steps and stairs through the many valleys in this rock barrier. The southern slopes of this barrier sink down into the Mur valley, where the Lungau opens out.

In a wide basin opening off the Salzach valley at Zell am See is the *Zeller See*, with the glacier on the Kitzsteinhorn overhanging it on the S and the rocky terrain of the Steinernes Meer rising out of the basin on the N.

Visitors are drawn to the province not only by the beauty of its natural scenery but by its numerous attractive towns and villages. The many summer resorts in the valleys provide a link with the uplands regions, which offer pleasant holiday accommodation and a network of footpaths; and the Salzburg region stands high among the Alpine provinces for accessibility and facilities for visitors. It also offers almost endless scope for winter sports, with excellent ski-runs until April or May in almost every part of the province. All these skiing areas on the mountain slopes, together with the heads of the high valleys, rise above the winter mists

and clouds and are bathed in sunshine; and the skiing slopes are brought within easy reach by a steadily increasing number of cableways and lifts. The best-known winter sports resorts are Zell am See, Saalbach, Badgastein and Hofgastein, the Weissee area above the Enzingerboden (where skiing is possible in summer) and Obertauern on the Radstädter Tauern pass. There are also winter resorts where non-skiers can enjoy a quiet and restful holiday and a variety of other attractions.

And on top of all this the province of Salzburg, though relatively small in comparison with neighbouring provinces, has an extensive range of sights and tourist attractions, from Mozart's city of Salzburg and the internationally renowned spa of Badgastein to the beauties of the Salzkammergut and the technological achievements of modern times, the hydroelectric power stations and their great storage reservoirs in the mountains.

The *Salzkammergut (see opposite), which extends over the provinces of Salzburg, Upper Austria and Styria, combines within a relatively small area a variety of beautiful and typically Austrian scenery – the *Wolfgangsee* with its magnificent viewpoint the Schafberg, the *Traunsee*, the oldestablished spas of *Bad Ischl* and *Bad Aussee*, the *Hallstätter See*, and the *Gosauseen* at the foot of the Dachstein, with its tremendous caves, now easily accessible by cableway.

There are many places of great attraction on the Tauern railway – the salt town of *Hallein*, the market town of *Golling* on the road to the Lueg pass, the old market town of *Werfen* below the famous Eisriesenwelt ("World of the Ice Giants"), *St Johann im Pongau* with the magnificent Liechtensteinklamm and *Bad Gastein*, the world-famed mountain spa, with the neighbouring resort of *Bad Hofgastein*. The main tourist magnet of the Pinzgau is *Zell am See*, from which there is easy access to a great range of attractions in the Tauern valleys – the *Krimml Falls*, the highest in the Alps; the massive hydroelectric installations in the *Stubachtal* and *Kapruner Tal*; and above all the *Fuscher Tal*, traversed by the superb Grossglockner Road.

The magnificent gateway to this mountain world is the provincial capital, **Salzburg (see p. 160), one of the great international tourist cities, particularly in summer during the Salzburg Festival. Here the proud fortress of Hohensalzburg looks down on the narrow streets and spacious squares of the old town and across the level basin of the Salzach to the neighbouring ring of mountains. From the town a motor road runs up to a splendid viewpoint of the Gaisberg. Another attraction within easy reach is the old summer palace of the archbishops of Hellbrunn, with its Baroque garden and fountains.

The two main traffic arteries of the province are the valleys of the Salzach and the Saalach, from which some of the busiest and grandest pass routes in the Austrian Alps branch off to the S – the Grossglockner Road, the Felber Tauern Road from Mittersill into Eastern Tirol, the approach road up the Gasteiner Tal to the Tauern Tunnel, the road over the Radstädter Tauern pass and the Katschberg.

Radstadt and the Tauern pass are the gateways to the idyllic **Lungau**, in the SE corner of Salzburg province between Carinthia and Styria. From the Taurach valley, traversed by the southern section of the Tauern pass road, numerous smaller valleys branch off, giving access to the mountains with their rushing mountain streams, their lakes and their attractive little villages.

From the Bavarian town of Lauffen visitors can reach the pleasant upland region to the E of the Salzach (which here forms the frontier between Germany and Austria), with the Salzburg "Lake District" (Wallersee, Mattsee/Obertrumer See, Niedertrumer See). From Lauffen, too, a visit can be paid to the village of *Oberndorf*, with the "Silent Night" Chapel commemorating Franz Gruber and Josef Mohr, who composed the famous Christmas carol here in 1818.

The *Salzkammergut, a much frequented tourist area of Alpine and Pre-Alpine scenery with numerous lakes, extends from Salzburg in the W to the Dachstein in the S and is bounded on the E by the Almtal. Most of it lies within Upper Austria, but it also reaches into Salzburg province (Wolfgangsee and Fuchlsee) and Styria (the Aussee area). The name originally applied only to a salt-working area around Bad Ischl where salt-water baths are available.

Schloss Ort, Gmunden (Traunsee)

The particular attraction of this mountain region lies in the sharp contrasts between its striking peaks and sheer rock faces on the one hand and its more than forty lakes, some of them of considerable size, on the other. The *Attersee, the *Mondsee and the *Wolfgangsee lie in the heart of the Salzkammergut, the best view of which is to be had from the Schafberg (reached from St Wolfgang on an old-fashioned cog railway). Everywhere visitors will find bathing beaches, camping sites and rowing and sailing boats for hire, and there are numerous popular vacation spots such as Mondsee, St Gilgen, St Wolfgang, Bad Ischl (once the favourite summer residence of the Emperor Francis Joseph) and Bad Goisern.

Salzkammergut

Länder: Upper Austria (OÖ), Salzburg (S) and Styria (Stm).

ⓘ **Salzkammergut-Verkehrsverband,** Bahnhofstrasse 6, A-4820 Bad Ischl 6; tel. (0 61 32) 69 09.
Oberösterreichisches Landesvekehrsamt, Schillerstrasse 50, A-4010 Linz; tel. (07 32) 66 30 21.
Landesverkehrsamt Salzburg, Mozartplatz 1, A-5010 Salzburg; tel. (06 62) 80 42–22 32.
Landesfremdenverkehrsamt Steiermark, Landhaus, Herrengasse 16, A-8010 Graz; tel. (03 16) 70 31–22 87.

St Florian

Land: Upper Austria (OÖ).
Altitude: 296 m/971 ft. – Population: 4500.
Post code: A-4490. – Telephone code: 0 72 24.
ⓘ **Gemeindeamt,** Thannstrasse 2; tel. 2 55 and 89 55.

ACCOMMODATION. – *Zum Goldener Pflug*, C, 44 b.; *Erzherzog Johann Ferdinand*, C, 44 b.; *Zum Märzenkeller*, C, 25 b.; *Zur Grünen Traube*, C, 20 b.

The little market town of St Florian, SE of Linz, is dominated by its famous Augustinian **Abbey, one of the most

splendid examples of Baroque architecture in Austria. The original monastery was built over the grave of St Florian, a high official in the Roman province of Noricum who became a Christian and was martyred by drowning in the River Enns about A.D. 304; he is still invoked all over Austria for protection against fire and flood. In 1071 Bishop Altmann of Passau assigned the monastery to the Augustinian Canons. – Rebuilding in Baroque style was begun in 1686 by Carlo Carlone (d. 1708), continued by Jakob Prandtauer and completed in 1751. – The abbey is still a focal point of learning and music (theological seminary; boys' choir, concerts).

SIGHTS. – The imposing **church** has twin towers 80 m/260 ft high. The interior has lavish stucco decoration; the choir-stalls and organ-loft are richly carved, with putti; and the pulpit is of black marble. In the crypt, under the main organ, is the tomb of Anton Bruckner (1824–96), who was organist here from 1848 to 1855; the great organ was his favourite instrument. – The conducted tour of the abbey buildings takes an hour. Prandtauer's masterpiece is the *grand staircase* on the W side of the main courtyard. In the E wing is the magnificent

Library, with ceiling paintings by B. Altomonte ("Marriage of Religion and Learning"), in the S wing the *Marble Hall*, with ceiling paintings depicting Prince Eugene's victories over the Turks. The *Altdorfer Gallery* in the W wing contains St Sebastian's Altar, with 14 paintings by Albrecht Altdorfer (1480–1538), The sumptuous classrooms were used by visiting Emperors and Popes. Visitors are also shown the simple *Bruckner Room* in which the composer lived. At Stiftstrasse 2 is the *Österreichische Feuerwehrmuseum* (Austrian fire-service museum).

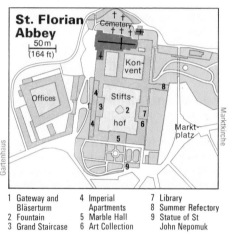

1 Gateway and Bläserturm	4 Imperial Apartments	7 Library
2 Fountain	5 Marble Hall	8 Summer Refectory
3 Grand Staircase	6 Art Collection	9 Statue of St John Nepomuk

St Florian Abbey

SURROUNDINGS. – 2 km/1¼ miles S, on the River Ipf, is **Schloss Hohenbrunn** (1725–29), a Baroque hunting lodge which now houses the Oberösterreichische Jagdmuseum (Upper Austria hunting museum). About 2 km/1¼ miles E of the market can be found the Oberösterreiches Freilichtmuseum (open-air museum) St Florian-Samesleiten with the "Sumerauer" quadrangle (peasant furniture).

St Pölten

Land: Lower Austria (NÖ).
Altitude: 265 m/869 ft. – Population: 50,000.
Post code: A-3100. – Telephone code: 0 27 42.
ⓘ **Touristik-Information,**
Am Rathausplatz 1;
tel. 25 31 (ext. 400).

ACCOMMODATION. – *Ibis*, B, 80 b.; *Seeland*, B, 51 b.; *Graf Leopold*, C, 40 b.; *Fuchs*, C, 32 b.

The busy industrial and commercial town of St Pölten, situated on the left bank of the Traisen between Vienna and Linz, on the site of the Roman Aelium Cetium, is the largest town in Lower Austria and the see of a bishop. It has recently supplanted Vienna as the capital of Lower Austria. It is notable for its Baroque architecture, architects and artists, such as Jakob Prandtauer, who lived and worked here.

SIGHTS. – In the middle of the old town, with its fine Baroque buildings, is the little *Riemerplatz*, at the meeting-place of the Wiener Strasse and the Linzer Strasse, the roads from Vienna and Linz. – A little W is the Rathausplatz, with a *Trinity Column* (1782). On the S side of the square is the **Rathaus** (originally 14th c., remodelled in Baroque style in the 18th c.). To the W of this the *Carmelite Church* (1708–12, probably by Jakob Prandtauer), with a rich Baroque

façade; the convent buildings (Prandtauer-strasse 2) now house the *Municipal Museum* and the documentation centre for modern art and literature of Lower Austria. On the N side of the square is the Rococo *Franciscan Church* (Franziskanerkirche, 1757–79), with four altarpieces by Kremser Schmidt. – In the Linzer Strasse, which runs SW from Riemerplatz, is the *Institute of the English Ladies* (Institut der Englischen Fräulein, an order of nuns founded by Mary Ward in 1609), a Baroque building of 1715–69. – From Riemerplatz the Wiener Strasse runs E. On the left of this street is the Herrenplatz, with a *Mariensäule* (column bearing a figure of the Virgin) of 1718. – Immediately N of this little square is the *Domplatz*, with the **Cathedral** (*Dom*, dedicated to the Assumption; originally Romanesque, 12th and 13th c.). Between 1715 and 1756 the interior was remodelled in Baroque style by Jakob Prandtauer (fine ceiling paintings, richly carved choir-stalls). On the N side of the Domplatz is the *Bishop's Palace* (Bischofshof, 1636–53). – To the N, at Klostergasse 15, is the house once occupied by *Jakob Prandtauer* (1660–1726). In Dr.-Karl-Renner-Promenade stands the former synagogue, now restored.

SURROUNDINGS. – 12 km/7½ miles N of St Pölten, on the left bank of the Traisen (and on the "Lower Austrian Baroque Highway"), is **Herzogenburg**, with an Augustinian monastery founded in 1112. The present monastic buildings (1714–40) were designed by Jakob Prandtauer, Josef Munggenast and J. B. Fischer von Erlach; they are now a museum and include a library. The magnificent Baroque church (1743–50) has a sumptuous interior (paintings by B. Altomonte, altarpiece by D. Gran, beautiful organ-loft); the 70 m/230 ft high tower (1767) is crowned by the Ducal cap. – *Göttweig*, with its Benedictine abbey: see under Krems.

8 km/5 miles NE of St Pölten **Pottenbrunn** has a 16th c. moated castle which contains the Austrian Museum of Tin Figures (Österreichisches Zinnfigurenmuseum: representations of battles, etc.).

23 km/14 miles S of St Pölten in the market village of **Lilienfeld** (377 m/1237 ft) stands a Cistercian abbey founded in 1202. The church (richly decorated Baroque interior) and the cloister, with a hexagonal fountain-house, date from the 13th c.; the monastic buildings (Imperial Apartments, Library) from the 17th–18th c.; beautiful park. A chair-lift runs up to the *Klosteralpe* (1112 m/3682 ft), on the slopes of the *Muckenkogel* (1311 m/4301 ft), from which there are fine views.

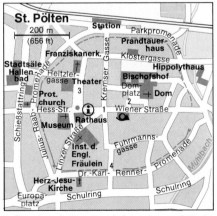

1 Riemerplatz 2 Herrenplatz 3 Rathausplatz 4 Schillerplatz

St Veit an der Glan

Land: Carinthia (K).
Altitude: 475 m/1558 ft. – Population: 13,000.
Post code: A-9300. – Telephone code: 0 42 12.
ⓘ **Fremdenverkehrsamt,** Hauptplatz 1;
tel. 23 26 13.

ACCOMMODATION. – *Mosser*, A, 25 b.; *Glantalerhof*, B, 31 b.; *Stern*, C, 31 b.

St Veit was capital of Carinthia from 1170 to 1518, when it had to relinquish this status to the more centrally located Klagenfurt. It still preserves part of its 15th c. circuit of walls (10 m/ 33 ft high).

SIGHTS. – In the elongated Hauptplatz (No. 2 has a wooden statue of the Christ child, No. 14 a stone statue of St Veit) are a *Plague Column* (1715) with numerous figures, the *Schlüsselbrunnen* ("Key Fountain"), with the figure of a miner (1566) and an antique marble basin from the Zollfeld, and another *fountain* with a bronze figure of the poet Walther von der Vogelweide (restored 1960), who lived for some time in St Veit. The **Rathaus** (1468) has a rich Baroque façade (1754), a beautiful arcaded courtyard with

sgraffito decoration and a fine council chamber (1754). The **parish church** is Romanesque, with a Gothic choir; adjoining the church is a circular *charnel-house*, now a war memorial. The former ducal castle (converted into an arsenal in 1523–29) now houses the Municipal Museum.

SURROUNDINGS. – 9·5 km/6 miles E of St Veit, on a crag rising some 160 m/525 ft above the valley, is the imposing ****Burg Hochosterwitz** (681 m/2234 ft; restaurant), built in 1571–86 by Georg von Khevenhüller as the principal stronghold in the province and never taken by an enemy. The steep access road to the castle, the *Burgweg (620 m/680 yds long), partly hewn from the rock, winds its way up through fourteen fortified gates (on the Khevenhüller Gate note the family coat of arms in white marble) to the beautiful arcaded Burghof (courtyard). At the N corner of the courtyard is a well 13 m/43 ft deep. The little *chapel has wall and ceiling paintings of 1570. The church at the SW end of the castle was rebuilt in 1586; the high altar dates from 1729. Conducted tours of the historical apartments and collections (armoury, historical paintings and other relics and documents, including a letter by the Empress Maria Theresa).

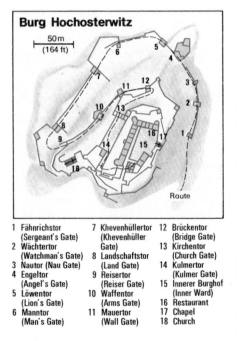

Burg Hochosterwitz

50 m
(164 ft)

Route

1 Fähnrichstor (Sergeant's Gate)	7 Khevenhüllertor (Khevenhüller Gate)	12 Brückentor (Bridge Gate)
2 Wächtertor (Watchman's Gate)	8 Landschaftstor (Land Gate)	13 Kirchentor (Church Gate)
3 Nautor (Nau Gate)	9 Reisertor (Reiser Gate)	14 Kulmertor (Kulmer Gate)
4 Engeltor (Angel's Gate)	10 Waffentor (Arms Gate)	15 Innerer Burghof (Inner Ward)
5 Löwentor (Lion's Gate)	11 Mauertor (Wall Gate)	16 Restaurant
6 Manntor (Man's Gate)		17 Chapel
		18 Church

Burg Hochosterwitz

Schladming

Land: Styria (Stm).
Altitude: 749 m/2457 ft. – Population: 4000.
Post code: A-8970. – Telephone code: 0 36 87.
ⓘ **Verkehrsverein**, Hauptplatz;
  tel. 2 22 68.

ACCOMMODATION. – *Sporthotel Royer*, A, 340 b., SB, SP, sauna; *Alte Post*, A, 75 b.; *Haus Barbara*, A, 33 b.; *Zum Stadttor*, B, 59 b.; *Rössle*, B, 46 b.; *Tritscher*, B, 27 b. – CAMPING SITE. – YOUTH HOSTEL, Coburgstrasse 253.

RECREATION and SPORTS. – Walking; climbing; winter sports.

The ancient little town of Schladming lies in the upper Enns valley, between the Dachstein in the N and the Schladminger Tauern in the S. In the Middle Ages silver and copper were mined here. The town is a good base for walks and climbs in the Ramsau area on the southern slopes of the Dachstein and in the Tauern. It is also popular for winter sports, with numerous good ski-runs in the surrounding hills.

SIGHTS. – Much of the town dates from the period when it was a mining community (old miners' houses). The 17th c. *Salzburger Tor* (Salzburg Gate) is a relic of the old fortifications. The late Gothic *parish church* (R.C.) dates from the 16th c. but has preserved a Romanesque tower; the *Protestant church* (1862) in the S of the town, the largest Protestant church in Styria, has a winged altar of the Reformation period. A memorial

stone in the Unterer Stadtplatz commemo-
rates the burning of the rebellious town
during the Peasant War (1525).

SURROUNDINGS. – To the SE of the town is an area of
good walking and skiing country under **Planai** (1894 m/
6214 ft). A cableway and a toll road (9 km/5½ miles) run
up to the *Schladminger Hütte* (1830 m/6004 ft; inn;
accommodation), from which there is a superb view of
the Dachstein massif. Near the intermediate station of
the cableway (1350 m/4430 ft) is a ski racing run for
amateurs (timing facilities). – The *Mooserboden* skiing
area (970 m/3183 ft) and the commune of *Rohrmoos-
Untertal* (900–1850 m/2950–6070 ft), SW of Schladming, can be reached on a toll road (12 km/7¼ miles)
which goes up the **Hochwurzen** (1852 m/6076 ft; hut;
extensive views).

Between the Hochwurzen and Planai the *Schladminger
Untertal* and *Obertal* (lower and upper Schladming
valley) run S into the **Schladminger Tauern**. From the
end of the road up the Untertal a footpath (2½ hours)
leads past the picturesque *Riesachsee* (1333 m/4374 ft)
and up to the *Preintalerhütte* (1656 m/5433 ft; inn;
accommodation), from which experienced climbers can
scale the **Greifenberg** (2618 m/8590 ft; 4 hours) by
way of the *Klafferkessel* with its numerous small lakes.
Another path (3 hours) runs S from the end of the road
to the *Gollinghütte* (1630 m/5348 ft; accommodation),
the starting-point of the climb (4 hours for experienced
climbers; not particularly difficult) up the **Hochgolling**
(2863 m/9394 ft), the highest peak in the Niedere
Tauern (superb panoramic views). – Another possibility
is to drive up the Obertal to *Hopfriesen* (1056 m/3465 ft),
from which a footpath (3¼–4 hours) runs SW to the
Ignaz-Mattis-Hütte (1986 m/6516 ft; accommodation),
on the NW side of the *Unterer Giglachsee*. From Hopfriesen the road continues S by way of the *Eschachalm*
(1213 m/3980 ft) to the *Neualm* (1700 m/5580 ft), from
which it is an hours' walk SW to the *Kleinprechthütte*
(1872 m/6182 ft; accommodation), another good base
for climbs in the Schladminger Tauern.

6·5 km/4 miles E of Schladming is the winter sports
resort of *Haus* (750 m/2460 ft; pop. 2300; Hotel Dobers-
berger, A, 51 b., SB; Kirchenwirt, B, 56 b.). From here a
cabin cableway ascends by way of the *Bürgerwald* to
the **Hauser Kaibling** (upper station 1838 m/6030 ft,

summit 2015 m/6611 ft), a commanding look-out point
(also reached by a mountain road from Schladming).

To the N of Schladming the **Ramsau** (1000–1200 m/
3300–3900 ft), a high plateau 18 km/11 miles long by
3 km/2 miles wide, extends from E to W below the
imposing S face of the Dachstein massif. This is a popular
walking and skiing area (observatory; lectures). A road
16 km/10 miles long (part of the way subject to toll)
runs up through *Ramsau-Kulm* (1082 m/3550 ft) and
Ramsau-Ort (1136 m/3727 ft) to a car park at the *Türlwandhütte* (1715 m/5627 ft). From here the Gletscherbahn Ramsau or Dachsteinsüdwandbahn (cableway)
climbs NE to the *Hunerkogel* (upper station 2700 m/
8860 ft), on the Schladming glacier (summer skiing); to
the E is the *Grosser Koppenkarstein* (2865 m/9400 ft).
From the Türlwandhütte it is a half-hour climb to the
Dachsteinsüdwandhütte (1871 m/6139 ft; inn; accommodation), a base of the Dachstein climbing school;
immediately opposite is the mighty S face of the
Dachstein. The *Hoher Dachstein** (3004 m/9859 ft)
can be climbed by experienced climbers in 5 hours, with
guide.

Seefeld in Tirol

Land: Tirol (T).
Altitude: 1185 m/3888 ft. – Population: 2300.
Post code: A-6100. – Telephone code: 0 52 12.
ⓘ **Verkehrsverband,** Rathausplatz;
tel. 23 13 and 23 16.

ACCOMMODATION. – *Alpenkönig Crest,* in Reith, A1,
310 b., SB, SP, sauna; *Klosterbräu,* A1, 200 b., SB,
sauna; *Schönruh,* A1, 125 b., SB, sauna; *Tümmlerhof,*
A1, 114 b., SB, SP; *Astoria,* A1, 97 b., SB, sauna;
Karwendelhof, A1, 80 b., sauna; *Tyrol,* A1, 79 b., SB,
sauna; *Eden,* A, 98 b.; *Lärchenhof,* A, 92 b., SB, sauna;
Alpina, A, 90 b., SB, sauna; *Kurhotel,* A, 85 b., SB, SP,
sauna; *Hochland,* A, 66 b., sauna; *Hocheder,* A, 60 b.;
Seespitze-Strandhotel, B, 90 b.; *Stern-Sporthotel,* B,
54 b.

CASINO. – in Hotel Karwendelhof (roulette daily from
5 p.m.; blackjack and baccarat on Saturdays).

RECREATION and SPORTS. – Tennis and golf; Olympia
Sports and Convention Complex, with a large indoor
swimming pool and a warm open-air pool; radioactive
mineral spring. – Winter sports (downhill runs, cross-
country runs, stadium at Seekirchl, ice rink).

***Seefeld lies half-way between Inns-
bruck and the German town of Mittenwald in a wide expanse of Alpine
meadows on the Seefelder Sattel,
formed by a glacier in the last Ice Age.
This health resort with its extensive
skiing areas, surrounded by forest-
covered hills and numerous higher
peaks, is one of the most popular
winter sports attractions in Tirol, and
in summer it is an equally popular base
for walkers and climbers.**

SIGHTS. – *Parish church of St Oswald*
(15th c.), with a late Gothic S doorway
(scenes depicting the miracle of the Host

On the Ramsau

and the martyrdom of St Oswald); fine paintings and sculpture in the interior. – A little way SW is the *Seekirchl*, a circular church of 1628. – At the S end of the town is the little *Wildsee* (bathing beach, two swimming pools with heated water).

SURROUNDINGS. – A funicular, operating both summer and winter, runs up to the *Rosshütte* (1784 m/5853 ft; inn), from which there are cabin cableways to the *Seefelder Joch* (2074 m/6805 ft) and the *Härmelekopf* (upper station 2041 m/6697 ft) and chair-lifts to the *Gschwandkopf* (upper station 1490 m/4889 ft) and the *Olympiaschanze* (1312 m/4305 ft). – Good climbs: S by way of the *Gschwandkopfhütte* (view) to the **Gschwandkopf** (1550 m/5086 ft; 1 hour); E by way of the Rosshütte and the Seefelder Joch to the *Seefelder Spitze** (2220 m/7285 ft; 3 hours); E by way of the **Maxhütte** (2115 m/6939 ft) and the *Nördlinger Hütte* (2242 m/7356 ft) to the *Reither Spitze** (2373 m/7786 ft; 3½–4 hours, not difficult for experienced climbers), with magnificent panoramic views from the summit.

Seefeld in winter

4 km/2½ miles SW of Seefeld (also reached on a beautiful footpath) is the quiet little hamlet of **Mösern** (1250 m/4103 ft; Inntalerhof, A, 90 b.; Hubertushof, B, 20 b.), in a magnificent *setting high above the Inn valley (views).

NW of Seefeld extends the **Leutaschtal**, one of the most beautiful mountain valleys in northern Tirol, running along under the Wettersteingebirge on the German frontier. The various villages which make up the commune of *Leutasch* (1130 m/3710 ft; pop. 1500; Quellenhof, A, 140 b., SB, sauna; Leutascherhof, A, 90 b., sauna; Kristall, A, 80 b., SB, sauna) are quiet little winter sports and summer vacation resorts. There are chair-lifts from Leutasch-Weidach to the *Katzenkopf* (1400 m/4595 ft) and from Leutasch-Moos to the *Rauthütte* (1601 m/5253 ft). Leutasch-Mühle (good restaurant), just short of the frontier, is the starting-point for the ascent of the *Grosse Arnspitze* (2195 m/7202 ft; 4½–5 hours). – Between the Wetterstein massif and the Miemingergebirge the *Gaistal*, the valley of the Leutascher Ache, runs W from Leutasch for some 15 km/9 miles. The narrow road through this valley (closed to cars) gives access to a large area of walking and climbing country.

SE of Seefeld the road descends the **Zirlerberg** into the Inn valley and Innsbruck.

Semmering

Länder: Lower Austria (NÖ) and Styria (Stm).
Altitude: 986–1050 m/3235–3445 ft.
Population: 1000.

Post code: A-2680. – Telephone code: 0 26 64.
ⓘ **Kurverwaltung,** Hochstrasse 91; tel. 3 26.

ACCOMMODATION. – *Panhans*, A1, 160 b., SB, sauna; *Stühlinger*, A, 59 b., SB, sauna; *Alpenheim*, A, 40 b., SB; *Belvedere*, A, 37 b., SB, sauna.

RECREATION and SPORTS. – Walking; skiing (several lifts). – Golf course (9 holes); mini-golf.

On the summit of the Semmering pass, which separates the Vienna basin from the Mürztal and marks the boundary between Lower Austria and Styria, is the hotel and villa colony of the same name, a popular health and winter sports resort. The scattered settlement is surrounded by forest-covered high plateaux and sunny hillsides.

Road. – There was a bridleway over the pass as early as the 12th c. The first road was constructed in 1728, during the reign of Charles VI, improved in 1839–42 and further improved and modernised in 1956–58.

Railway. – The *Semmeringbahn*, the first major mountain railway in Europe, was built between 1848 and 1854 by Karl von Ghega (1802–60). It runs through 15 tunnels and crosses 16 deep gorges on viaducts (some of them of several storeys). The maximum gradient is 1 in 40; the summit tunnel (with a parallel tunnel opened in 1952) is 1430 m/1560 yds long and reaches a height of 897 m/2943 ft.

SURROUNDINGS. – Chair-lifts run up from the summit of the pass to the *Hirschenkogel* (1324 m/4344 ft) and from Maria Schutz to the *Sonnwendstein* (1523 m/4997 ft; upper station 1481 m/4859 ft). – A toll road (6 km/4 miles; max. gradient 14%) runs SE from the pass to the *Sonnwendstein** (1523 m/4997 ft; Alpenhaus), from which there are magnificent views of the Rax and Schneeberg, the Alpine foreland and the Semmering

The Semmering Road

railway far below. From the Sonnwendstein there is a rewarding mountain walk (4½ hours) SE to the *Hochwechsel* (1743 m/5718 ft), the highest peak in the **Wechsel** massif (gneiss), which is a popular winter sports area, reached from the health resort of *Mönichkirchen* (967 m/3173 ft), on the road from Vienna to Graz.

To the N of the Semmering pass are the limestone massifs of the **Raxalpe* (2007 m/6585 ft) and the **Schneeberg* (2075 m/6808 ft), separated from one another by the Höllental. The Rax, a high plateau lying between 1500 and 2000 m/5000 and 6500 ft, is an extensive area of open Alpine meadowland, with footpaths of considerable length and several mountain huts. The highest point is the *Heukuppe* (2007 m/6585 ft), from which there are very fine views. There is a cableway from Hirschwang in the Höllental.

7 km/4½ miles SW of the pass, on the road to Mürzzuschlag, is the summer resort of **Spital** *am Semmering* (770 m/2526 ft; pop. 2500; Hotel Weinzettl, C, 20 b.), from which there is a chair-lift up the *Hühnerkogel* (1380 m/4528 ft).

To the SW is the *Stuhleck* (1782 m/5847 ft), which can also be reached from *Steinhaus am Semmering* on a road running over the *Pfaffensattel* (1368 m/4488 ft).

Mürzzuschlag (679 m/2228 ft; pop. 12,000; Hotel Zum Grünen Baum, B, 33 b.; Steinbauer, C, 14 b.), the chief settlement in the Mürztal, is a lively little town, a popular summer and winter sports resort (Winter Sports Museum), situated at the junction of the Fröschnitzbach, which flows down from the Semmering pass, with the River Mürz. There are good climbs to be had in the *Fischbach Alps* to the SE – for example up the Stuhleck (3½ hours) or *Pretul* (1653 m/5423 ft).

7 km/4½ miles N is the village of *Kapellen* (703 m/2307 ft), from which a road leads E over the Preiner-Gschied-Sattel (1070 m/3511 ft) into the Höllental.

4 km/2½ miles farther on, at the foot of the Schneealpe (1904 m/6247 ft), is **Neuberg** (732 m/2402 ft), with a former Cistercian abbey (fine 14th–15th c. church).

SW of Mürzzuschlag on the road to Bruck are the attractive summer resort of *Langenwang* (638 m/2093 ft) and **Krieglach** (614 m/2015 ft; pop. 5000), in which the Styrian writer Peter Rosegger died in 1918.

Silvretta Road

Länder: Vorarlberg (V) and Tirol (T).
ⓘ **Verkehrsverein Silvretta,**
    on the Silvretta Road, A-6974 Partenen;
    tel. (0 55 58) 83 15.

ACCOMMODATION. – IN PARTENEN: *Bierlerhöhe*, A, 67 b., SB, sauna; *Sonne*, B, 60 b., sauna; *Christopherus*, C, 25 b. – ON THE SILVRETTASEE: *Silvrettasee*, A, 80 b., SB, sauna; *Piz-Buin*, C, 80 b., sauna. – IN GALTÜR: *Ballunspitze*, A, 120 b., sauna; *Fluchthorn*, A, 95 b., sauna; *Alpenhotel Tirol*, A, 80 b., SP, sauna.

The **Silvretta Road (Silvretta-Hochalpenstrasse), completed in 1953, was built in association with the storage reservoirs supplying the power stations of the III hydroelectric scheme** (Illwerke). A toll road, open only in summer, runs from Partenen (1027 m/ 3370 ft) to Galtür (1584 m/5197 ft), linking the Montafon valley with the Paznauntal. There are a number of fine look-out points, with large car parks, from which the peaks and glaciers of the Silvretta group on the Swiss frontier appear breathtakingly close. The road climbs, with many sharp turns, to the Vermunt reservoir (1743 m/ 5719 ft) and the Gross-Vermunttal. On the highest point, the Bielerhöhe (2032 m/6667 ft) – the watershed between the Rhine and the Danube – is the large *Silvretta reservoir, which has a capacity of 38·6 million cu. m/ 8490 million gallons.**

Partenen (1027 m/3370 ft), at the head of the Montafon, is a holiday and winter sports resort, with power stations supplied by large conduits bringing down water under pressure. It is a good base for climbing and skiing in the Silvretta and Verwall groups.

There is a funicular up *Tromenir* (1730 m/ 5675 ft), from which it is a 45-minute walk (part of the way through tunnels) to the Vermunt reservoir. To the N of Partenen is the *Versalspitze* (2464 m/8084 ft).

9 km/5½ miles beyond Partenen the Silvretta Road comes to the **Vermunt reservoir** (1743 m/5719 ft; power station), with a dam 50 m/165 ft high and 273 m/300 yds long.

5 km/3 miles farther on, below the great dam of the Silvretta reservoir, a road goes off on the right to the *Madlenerhaus* (1986 m/ 6516 ft; accommodation), a good base for climbs in the Silvretta group (experienced climbers only, or with a guide) – e.g. *Vallüla*

The Silvretta Road

(2815 m/9236 ft; 4 hours), the *Grosslitzner* (3111 m/10,207 ft), the boldest peak in the Silvretta (6 hours, difficult), or the *Westliche Plattenspitze* (2880 m/9449 ft; 5 hours).

At the **Bielerhöhe** (2032 m/6667 ft), on the boundary between Vorarlberg and Tirol, is the huge *Silvretta reservoir (Silvretta-see)*, 2·5 km/1½ miles long and 0·75 km/½ mile wide. The dam is 80 m/260 ft high, 52 m/170 ft across and 430 m/470 yds long. It takes some 2 hours to walk around the lake. 2¼ hours' walk S of the lake is the *Wiesbadener Hütte* (2443 m/8015 ft; accommodation), the starting-point for the ascent of *Piz Buin* (3316m/10,880 ft), the *Schneeglocke* (3225 m/10,581 ft) and the *Dreiländerspitze* ("Three Countries Peak", 3212 m/10,539 ft), at the boundary of Vorarlberg, Tirol and Switzerland. These climbs should be undertaken only with a guide.

The road now runs down the Klein-Vermunttal. – In 5 km/3 miles the Kopserstrasse goes off on the left, running over the *Zeinisjoch* (1842 m/6044 ft), an old pass between the Montafon and the Paznaun valley, to the *Zeinisjoch-Haus* (1822 m/5978 ft; accommodation); Kops reservoir, skiing area.

Galtür (1584 m/5197 ft) is a winter sports resort in the upper Paznauntal noted for its excellent snow (numerous lifts); fine Baroque church (17th–18th c.). A road runs 5 km/3 miles S through the Jamtal to the *Scheibenalm* (1833 m/6014 ft), from which it is a 2 hours' climb to the *Jamtalhütte* (2165 m/7103 ft; accommodation), magnificently situated below the Jamtalferner (glacier). To the E of the hut is the *Fluchthorn* (3399 m/11,152 ft), the second highest peak in the Silvretta group.

Spittal an der Drau

Land: Carinthia (K).
Altitude: 554 m/1818 ft.
Population: 15,000.
Post code: A-9800.
Telephone code: 0 47 62.
(i) **Fremdenverkehrsamt**,
   Schloss Porcia, Burgplatz 1;
   tel. 34 20.

ACCOMMODATION. – *Kärnten*, A, 72 b., sauna; *Salzburg*, B, 110 b.; *Ertl*, B, 85 b.; *Alte Post*, B, 83 b.; *Simeter*, C, 50 b.; *Park Hotel*, C, 34 b. – CAMPING SITE. – YOUTH HOSTELS: at the lower station of the Goldeckbahn and in the ÖJHW Ski Club hut on the Goldeck.

EVENTS. – *Performances of comedies* in Schloss Porcia (15 July to 31 Aug.). – Lively *Carnival.* – International boat competition.

Located to the W of the Millstätter See at the junction of the Liesertal with the fertile Drau valley, Spittal is the gateway to Carinthia and has consequently developed into an important traffic and tourist junction. The name comes from a hospice founded in 1191.

SIGHTS. – The old town lies around two principal squares, the more easterly of which is closed off by an old gate, the *Liesertor.* *Schloss Porcia*, built between 1533 and 1597 on the model of an Italian palazzo, is the finest Italian Renaissance style building in Austria. The three-storeyed arcaded courtyard, decorated with fantastic figures and relief medallions, forms an attractive setting for open-air theatrical performances. The upper floors house the *Upper Carinthian Heimatmuseum.*

Attached to the palace is a beautiful park. In the Parkschlössl is the Bauernbergbau-Museum of Upper Carinthia. – The *parish church*, originally dating from the 13th–14th c., was much altered in later periods.

SURROUNDINGS. – A cableway runs SW up the **Goldeck** (2139 m/7018 ft; upper station 2059 m/6756 ft; view; skiing area). – To the E is the *Millstätter See* (p. 136). On a wooded hill 5 km/3 miles NW of Spittal on the road to the Mölltal is the village of **St Peter im Holz** (590 m/1935 ft). The village occupies the site of a Celtic settlement belonging to the Taurisci, *Teurnia*, which became the Roman *Tiburnia*, destroyed by the Slavs about A.D. 600. Excavation of the site brought to light the forum, the remains of town walls and the foundations of houses. At the foot of the hill, some 500 m/530 yds off the road, is the **Teurnia Museum**, with material recovered by excavation. Here, too, are the foundations of an early Christian basilica, with a well-preserved mosaic pavement of about A.D. 500.

The arcaded courtyard of Schloss Porcia, Spittal

35 km/22 miles N of Spittal is the *Katschberghöhe* (1641 m/5384 ft; hotels), an area of beautiful walking and skiing country surrounded by fine forests.

Steinernes Meer

Land: Salzburg (S).
Altitude: Highest point: Selbhorn (2655 m/8711 ft).
(i) **Österreichischer Alpenverein,**
   Sektion Saalfelden,
   Sonnleitenweg 10, A-5760 Saalfelden.

The *Steinernes Meer ("Sea of Stone"), a mighty high plateau (nature reserve) out of which rise a series of strikingly formed peaks, skirts the frontier between Salzburg province and the German *Land* of Bavaria. Together with the Reither Alpe to the N, the Hochkönig group to the S and the Hagengebirge to the E it encloses the wedge of German territory around Berchtesgaden which projects into Austria.

The hills on the S side of the Steinernes Meer fall steeply down to the Saalbach and Urschlaub valleys. Most of the peaks can be climbed without great difficulty, including the **Selbhorn** (2655 m/8711 ft), the pyramid-shaped *Schönfeldspitze* (2651 m/ 8689 ft), the gently scarped *Breithorn* (2496 m/8189 ft) and the *Hundstod* (2594 m/8511 ft). There are arduous but rewarding walks over the plateau, from the Reimannhaus (2170 m/7120 ft) near Saalfelden to the Ingolstädter Haus (2132 m/ 6995 ft) or to the Torscharte and on to the Hochkönig. In late winter and spring, when deep snow covers the swallowholes and boulders, there is excellent skiing on the plateau.

From the NW end of the plateau a narrow ridge extends NE to the *Hochkalter group* and the **Reither Alpe**, another small plateau. Here accommodation can be had in the Traunsteiner Hütte (1560 m/5118 ft) near Reith. The highest point in the Reither Alpe, the *Grosses Häuselhorn* (2295 m/ 7530 ft), is not difficult to climb; but some of the other peaks are for experienced rock-climbers only.

The SE end of the Steinernes Meer links up with the **Hagengebirge**, a vast and lonely high plateau on which chamois can still be encountered. Its highest peak, the *Raucheck* (2391 m/7845 ft), overlooks the Blühn-bachtal, one of the most beautiful valleys in Salzburg province.

To the N of the Hagengebirge is the *Hoher Göll* (2522 m/8275 ft: extensive views), with the Stahl-Haus (1728 m/5670 ft) near Golling, close to the German frontier; and farther N again is the *Untersberg* (1973 m/ 6473 ft), rising above the city of Salzburg.

Steyr

Land: Upper Austria (OÖ).
Altitude: 311 m/1020 ft. Population: 40,000.
Post code: A-4400. – Telephone code: 0 72 52.
(i) **Fremdenverkehrsverband,** Rathaus;
   tel. 2 32 29.

ACCOMMODATION. – *Minichmayr,* A, 94 b.; *Ibis,* B, 84 b.; *Mader,* B, 84 b.; *Motel Maria,* B, 54 b.

EVENTS. – *Town Festival* (end June); *Christkindlmarkt* (Advent).

Steyr, at the junction of the River Steyr with the Enns, is an old-established focal point of the Austrian iron and steel industry, drawing much of its supply of ore from the Erzberg at Eisenerz, 100 km/60 miles away. The *old town, on a tongue of land between the two rivers, still preserves a medieval quality.

SIGHTS. – The elongated *Stadtplatz* is surrounded by many old arcaded houses. On the E side of the square is the *Rathaus* (1765–78), with a slender tower crowned by a Baroque helm roof. Opposite it is the well-preserved Gothic *Bummerlhaus* (1497; notable courtyard). To the S of the Rathaus is the *Marienkirche* (1642–47; Gothic tabernacle in main choir). From the Stadtplatz the Grünmarkt continues S to the *Innerberger Getreidestadel* (1612), an old granary which now houses the *Municipal Museum* (history of the town; iron hammers; the "Steyrer Kripperl", a mechanical crib, operating only in December and January).

A short distance W of the Museum along Pfarrgasse stands the **parish church** (*Pfarr-kirche*, 15th–17th c.), with old gravestones, a font of 1569, a beautiful Gothic tabernacle and fine stained glass. In the nearby presbytery (Pfarrhaus) Anton Bruckner completed his last great works (1886–94). Immediately S of the parish church is the late Gothic *St Margaret's Chapel* (Margareten-kapelle).

Of the old *town walls* there survive three gates and a tower, the *Tabor* (16th c.; panoramic restaurant). The **Schloss**

(1727–31) stands on high ground at the northern tip of the old town, with a large park extending SW. – On the N bank of the River Steyr stands *St Michael's Church*, a Jesuit foundation of 1635–77. Nearby in Kirchengasse (No. 16) is the picturesque Dunkl-Hof (arcades), and in the Sierninger Strasse (No. 1) the *Lebzelterhaus* (façade of 1567).

SURROUNDINGS. – 3 km/2 miles W is the little *pilgrimage church of the Christkindl (Christ Child), by the 18th c. Baroque architects C. Carlone and J. Prandtauer. A special post office set up here at Christmas time receives letters from children all over the world. 3 km/ 2 miles N of Steyr is **Gleink**, with a fine Baroque church (originally belonging to a Benedictine abbey) built on Romanesque and Gothic foundations.

16 km/10 miles NE of Steyr is *Haag*, with a wildlife park. – 17 km/11 miles E of Steyr is the Benedictine **Seitenstetten Abbey**, founded in 1112 and rebuilt by Josef Munggenast between 1718 and 1747. Of the medieval buildings only the Knights' Chapel (Ritterkapelle) survives. The abbey contains a large collection of pictures.

6 km/4 miles farther E is *Krenstetten*, with a notable Gothic parish church (late Gothic winged altar of 1576, pulpit of 1636, 14th–16th c. stained glass in choir).

There are attractive drives from Steyr up the narrow valleys of the Steyr and Enns. At the points where the rivers force their way out of the mountains into the Alpine foreland there are impressive gorges and sheer rock faces.

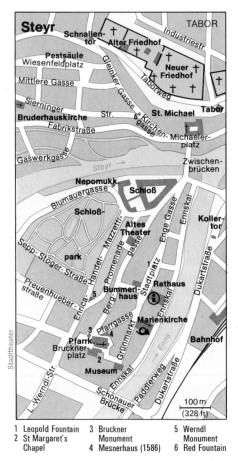

1 Leopold Fountain
2 St Margaret's Chapel
3 Bruckner Monument
4 Mesnerhaus (1586)
5 Werndl Monument
6 Red Fountain

Stodertal

Land: Upper Austria (OÖ).

ⓘ **Fremdenverkehrsverband Hinterstoder**, Mitterstoder, A-4573 Hinterstoder; tel. (0 75 64) 52 63.

ACCOMMODATION. – IN HINTERSTODER: *Berghotel*, A, 120 b., SB, sauna; *Stoderhof*, B, 58 b., SB, sauna; *Poppengut*, B, 45 b.; *Dietelgut*, B, 42 b., SB; *Post*, C, 43 b. – YOUTH HOSTEL. – IN VORDERSTODER: *Steinerwirt*, B, 57 b., SP, sauna; *Vorderramseben*, B, 40 b., sauna; *Stockerwirt*, B, 40 b., sauna. – IN WINDISCHGARSTEN: *Bischofsberg*, A, 140 b., SB, sauna; *Zur Schönen Aussicht*, A, 75 b., SB; *Seebachhof*, A, 67 b., SP.

The beautiful *Stodertal is a high mountain valley to the E of the Totes Gebirge through which flows the upper course of the River Steyr. It runs S from the road to the Pyhrn pass NW of Windischgarsten, and should not be missed by visitors passing through this part of Austria.

Schiederweiher (Stodertal)

Steyr, from the panoramic restaurant on the Tabor

From *Steyrbrücke* (bridge over the Steyr) the road ascends the left bank of the river through the narrow wooded valley. 8 km/5 miles up the valley, below the road on the right, are the *Stromboding Falls*, 24 m/80 ft high. Beyond this is *Mitterstoder*, from which a road runs E to Windischgarsten. The Stodertal road then comes to the main town in the valley, **Hinterstoder** (585 m/1919 ft; pop. 1200), a summer and winter sports resort. The village is magnificently situated between the Warscheneck group (2386 m/7828 ft) to the SE and the wooded hills of the Totes Gebirge to the NW. A chair-lift runs up S by way of the *Hutterer Böden* (1387 m/4551 ft; several ski-lifts) to the *Hutterer Höss* (1831 m/6008 ft; good walking country; fine views). From Hinterstoder the *Grosser Priel* (2523 m/8278 ft), in the Totes Gebirge, can be climbed in 7 hours. There is a waymarked educational path from Hinterstoder with information about herbs.

From Hinterstoder the road continues to the *Dietlgut* (650 m/2133 ft) and ends at the hamlet of *Baumschlagerreith*, near the source of the Steyr. There is a chair-lift from Hochhauser (660 m/2165 ft) up the *Schafferreith* (upper station 1153 m/3783 ft; ski-lifts).

The side road from Mitterstoder to Windischgarsten (16 km/10 miles) traverses wooded country to *Vorderstoder* (808 m/2650 ft), on the watershed between the Steyr and Teichl valleys. Beyond this is the little summer resort of *Rossleithen* (690 m/2264 ft), 20 minutes' walk S of which is the picturesque cave of *Piessling-Ursprung* (500 m/1640 ft).

Windischgarsten (603 m/1978 ft), a winter sports resort, is beautifully located below the S side of the Sengsen-Gebirge. A chair-lift runs E up the *Wurbauerkogl* (859 m/2818 ft; toboggan-run in summer). A narrow mountain road (6 km/4 miles) climbs SE to the *Gleinker See* (807 m/2648 ft; accommodation), below the N face of the *Seestein* (1570 m/5151 ft), from which it is 5½ hours' climb to the summit of the *Warscheneck* (2389 m/7838 ft; view), also reached from Vorderstoder on a waymarked path.

Stubai Alps

Land: Tirol (T).
Altitude: Highest point: Zuckerhütl (3507 m/11,506 ft).
ⓘ **Österreichischer Alpenverein,**
Sektion Stubai,
Schmelzhüttengasse 20,
A-6166 Fulpmes im Stubai.

The *Stubai Alps (Stubaier Alpen), an intricately patterned range slashed by numerous valleys, extend immediately NE of the Ötztal Alps. The main ridge,

between the Timmelsjoch and the wide Brenner depression, forms the Austrian-Italian frontier, as does the main range of the Ötztal Alps. The magnificent Stubai glaciers are smaller than those in the neighbouring range but equally wild and grand. In the average height of the summit ridge and in the steepness of its escarpments the Stubai range surpasses all other groups in the Central Alps.

Bounded by the Ötztal, the Inn valley and the Wipptal, the Stubai Alps are easily reached from Innsbruck by the Stubaital railway or the Brenner railway up the Wipptal, or on good roads.

This ease of accessibility, combined with the excellent climbing to be had here, has given the Stubai Alps a leading place among the Alpine regions of Austria in terms of accommodation available and paths and access routes. Almost every high valley has a mountain hut, and the network of paths offers endless scope for walkers in summer and ski trekkers in winter.

The highest peaks and finest glaciers in the Stubai Alps are in the main ridge, the **Pfaffengruppe**, with the pointed cone of the *Zuckerhütl (3507 m/11,506 ft), the snow-capped **Wilder Freiger** (3418 m/11,214 ft) and the imposing **Schaufelspitze** (3333 m/10,936 ft). From Neustift in the Stubaital there are several routes leading

Gries im Sellraintal

up into the permanent snow area of the Pfaffengruppe, the most popular being those by way of the Dresdner Hütte (2302 m/ 7553 ft) and the Nürnberger Hütte (2280 m/ 7480 ft). From the Ötztal the best routes are by way of the Hildesheimer Hütte (2899 m/ 9512 ft) near Sölden. The rugged and difficult pyramid of the *Wilde Leck* (3361 m/ 11,027 ft) can be climbed from the Amberger Hütte (2135 m/7005 ft) near Längenfeld in the Ötztal.

The Amberger Hütte is also the starting-point for the ascent of the ***Schrankogel** (3426 m/11,241 ft), the magnificent highest peak in the rugged **Alpeiner Gruppe**, the second large glacier area in the Stubai Alps. From the mighty ***Ruderhofspitze** (3473 m/11,395 ft) heavily fissured glaciers descend towards the Neue Regensburger Hütte (2286 m/7500 ft) and the Franz-Senn-Hütte (2147 m/7044 ft) near Neustift in the Stubaital. The commanding ***Lisenser Fernerkogel** (3299 m/10,824 ft) can be climbed either from here or from Gries in Sellrain by way of the Westfalen-Haus (2273 m/7458 ft). And peak follows peak as the range continues N, sending out numerous lateral spurs.

To the N of the *Gleirschjöchl* (which provides a link between the Guben-Schweinfurter-Hütte (2034 m/6674 ft) near Umhausen in the Ötztal and the Neue Pforzheimer Hütte Adolf-Witzenmann-Haus, 2308 m/7573 ft) near St Sigmund in the Sellraintal, the glaciers feature less prominently.

The **Kühtaier Berge** in this part of the range are one of the most popular skiing areas in Tirol. The Alpenhotel Jagdschloss Kühtai and the nearby Dortmunder Hütte (1948 m/ 6391 ft), which can be reached either from the Sellraintal or the Ötztal, are the most popular bases in this winter paradise, dominated by the *Sulzkogel* (3016 m/9895 ft), with the *Finstertal reservoir* at its foot, and the *Zwieselbacher Rosskogel* (3060 m/ 10,040 ft), from which the only considerable glacier in this area descends to the little *Kraspessee*.

To the NE of the Alpeiner Gruppe are the bizarrely shaped **Kalkkögel**, like a section of the Dolomites transported over the Brenner from Italy. Anyone looking at this wild and jagged range from the Adolf-Pichler-Hütte (1690 m/5545 ft) near Grinzens might be forgiven for supposing that they would be almost impossible to climb; but in fact none of the higher peaks, such as the *Schlicker*

Seespitze (2808 m/9213 ft), present any serious difficulty. The rock walls, buttresses and pinnacles, however, are for experienced rock climbers only.

The Axamer Lizum, on the northern slopes of the Kalkkögel, is a magnificent skiing area.

In another range which branches NE from the Alpeiner Gruppe is the massive ***Habicht** (3277 m/10,752 ft), which attracts many climbers; it can be reached from Fulpmes and Neustift in the Stubaital or from Gschnitz in the Gschnitztal by way of the Innsbrucker Hütte (2379 m/7773 ft). A series of steep and magnificently formed limestone peaks continue the range, ending in the popular and easily climbable ***Serles** group (*Waldrastspitze*, 2719 m/8921 ft), immediately S of Innsbruck.

There are also limestone hills in the eastward continuation of the main Stubai range towards the Brenner. In this area is the **Tribulaun group**, an imposing dolomitic massif with several peaks.

The majestic "Matterhorn of the Stubai Alps", the **Pflerscher Tribulaun** (3096 m/ 10,158 ft), brownish white in colour, can be climbed by tough and experienced climbers from the Tribulaun-Hütte (2064 m/6772 ft), on the Italian frontier.

Below the E side of the *Kleiner Tribulaun* is the *Obernberger See* (1594 m/5230 ft), the most beautiful mountain lake in the Stubai Alps.

There is a ridge path (No. 102) from Sölden in the Ötztal, running N around the Zuckerhütl and then down the Gschnitztal to Steinach or Gries am Brenner.

Stubaital

Land: Tirol (T).

ⓘ **Fremdenverkehrsverband Fulpmes,** Gemeindezentrum 1, A-6166 Fulpmes; tel. (0 52 25) 22 35.
Fremdenverkehrsverband Neustift, A-6167 Neustift, Dorf; tel. (0 52 26) 22 28.

ACCOMMODATION. – IN MIEDERS: *Series*, B, 110 b. – IN FULPMES: *Tirolerhof*, A, 80 b., SB, sauna; *Holzmeister*, B, 60 b.; *Alte Post*, B, 55 b., sauna. – IN TELFES: *Montana*, B, 40 b., sauna; *Leitgeb*, C, 32 b., sauna; *Schöne Aussicht*, C, 19 b. – IN NEUSTIFT: *Jagdhof*, A1, 100 b.; *Sonnenhof*, A, 70 b.; *Neustifterhof*, A, 52 b., SB, sauna; *Wintersport*, B, 130 b., SB, sauna; *Stubaier Hof*, B, 70 b., SB; *Alpenhof*, B, 52 b., sauna.

The *Stubaital is a broad side valley of the Wipptal, flanked by steep hillsides and rocky mountain peaks and watered by the Ruetzbach. Branching off the Brenner Road at Schönberg, it runs SW into the glacier area of the Stubai Alps. The beautiful villages in the valley are popular summer and winter sports resorts.

The first place in the valley is *Mieders* (952 m/3124 ft), a picturesque village from which there is a chair-lift up the *Kopeneck* (1630 m/5348 ft).

Fulpmes (937 m/3074 ft), surrounded by high mountain chains, is the chief place in the valley and a well-known health and skiing resort. To the S is the finely formed *Serles* massif (2719 m/8921 ft). The village has a considerable hardware industry (ice axes, climbing irons, etc.; government training school; ironworking museum) which originally developed out of the medieval mining activity in this area. The parish church (1747) has an interior richly decorated with Rococo stucco-work. Peasant theatre. There is a mineral spring at *Medraz*.

2 km/1¼ miles above Fulpmes is **Telfes** (1002 m/3288 ft), the oldest parish in the valley, first recorded in 1344. From Fulpmes a chair-lift runs up to *Froneben* (1351 m/4433 ft) and the *Kreuzjoch* (2108 m/6916 ft). It is an hour's climb from the Froneben Inn to the *Schlicker Alm* (1616 m/5302 ft; chapel by Clemens Holzmeister, 1959), a good starting-point for climbs in the Kalkkögel; chair-lift to the *Sennjoch* (upper station 2240 m/7350 ft). The *Hoher Burgstall* (2613 m/8573 ft) can also be climbed from Froneben by way of the *Starkenburger Hütte* (2229 m/7313 ft).

Neustift (993 m/3258 ft) is the main tourist place in the valley, and is a popular health and winter sports resort. The handsome parish church, rebuilt in 1768–74, has fine ceiling paintings; in the churchyard is the grave of Franz Senn (1831–84), one of the founders of the Austrian Alpine Club. Ski training school. – A chair-lift runs up to the *Elferkamm* (1800 m/5900 ft), with a great expanse of good walking and skiing country; toboggan-run. The climb from Neustift to the Starkenburger Hütte takes 3½ hours, and from there it is another 1¼ hours to the summit of the Hoher Burgstall.

At Neustift the valley divides into the Oberbergtal and the Unterbergtal. – 10 km/6 miles up the *Unterbergtal* is *Falbeson* (1194 m/3918 ft), from which there is a route up to the Neue Regensburger Hütte (2286 m/7500 ft). A short distance beyond this is *Ranalt* (1260 m/4134 ft), the last hamlet in the valley and a good climbing base. From Ranalt the "Stubaier Gletscherstrasse" (Stubai Glacier Road) continues for another 7·5 km/4½ miles up the Ruetzbach valley to the **Mutterberger Alm** (1728 m/5670 ft; accommodation). From here the *Stubaier Gletscherbahn* (cableway) goes up to the *Dresdner Hütte* (2302 m/7553 ft) and the *Eisgrat* (2900 m/9500 ft; restaurant), with a large skiing facility (ski-lifts, including one to the Eisjoch, 3200 m/10,450 ft; summer skiing on the Daunkogel and Schaufel glaciers).

From the Dresdner Hutte it is an hour's climb to the *Egesengrat* (2635 m/8645 ft; magnificent view of glacier), and from there another 4½–5 hours (with guide) to the summit of the *Zuckerhütl*, the highest peak in the Stubai Alps, commanding superb views. – To the E of the Dresdner Hütte is the *Sulzenauhütte* (2191 m/7189 ft; 3 hours' climb from the Grawa-Alm, 1530 m/5020 ft), another good climbing base.

3 hours' climb S of Ranalt, looking on the beautiful Feuerstein group, is the *Nürnberger Hütte* (2280 m/7480 ft), from which there are a variety of good climbs, for example to the *Mairspitze* (2781 m/9124 ft; 1½ hours). – 3½ hours' climb W of Ranalt is the *Daunbühel* (2456 m/8058 ft).

The road up the *Oberbergtal* from Neustift, running NW, comes in 12 km/7½ miles to the **Bärenbad** (1252 m/4108 ft). From here it is 2 hours' climb (jeep transport available in summer) to the *Oberrisshütte* (1745 m/5725 ft), from which it is another 1½ hours to the *Franz-Senn-Hütte* (2147 m/7044 ft; inn; accommodation), a good climbing and skiing base. The *Ruderhofspitze* (3473 m/11,395 ft) can be climbed in 5–6 hours, the *Hinterer Brunnenkogel* (3325 m/10,909 ft) in 5–6 hours, the *Lisenser Fernerkogel* (3299 m/10,824 ft) in 4½ hours; these climbs should be undertaken only by experienced climbers, preferably with a guide.

Styria

Bundesland: Steiermark (Stm). – Capital: Graz.
Area: 16,387 sq. km/6327 sq. miles.
Population: 1,183,300.
ⓘ **Landesfremdenverkehrsamt Steiermark,**
Landhaus, Herrengasse 16/I, A-8010 Graz;
tel. (03 16) 70 31–22 87.

Krössbach, Stubaital

Styria (Steiermark), the largest of the Austrian provinces after Lower Austria, is bounded on the N by Upper and Lower Austria, on the E by Burgenland and (for short distances) by Hungary and Yugoslavia (Slovenia), on the S by Yugoslavia (Slovenia) and on the W by Carinthia and Salzburg provinces. Extending from the northern Alpine ranges in the Salzkammergut southeastward by way of the main chain of the Alps to the hilly Alpine foreland, Styria displays a great variety of landscape forms – mountains and glaciers, deeply slashed gorges and valleys, great expanses of forest, ranges of gently rounded hills and at the eastern end of the province, merging into the Hungarian plain, great tracts of steppe-like country.

This diversity corresponds to a difference in altitude of no less than 2800 m/9000 ft between the Dachstein massif, at almost 3000 m/9800 ft, and the lowest point of the province in Bad Radkersburg. Between the mountains and glaciers of the high Alps and the vine-clad lowland regions Styria offers a great spectrum of beautiful scenery – the peaks of the Calcareous Alps and the Tauern with their mountain lakes, the upland meadows of the Seetal Alps, the Koralpe and Gleinalpe, the attractive wooded heights of the Fischbach Alps, the sunny and fertile hills of eastern and western Styria. And this variety of landscape produces a corresponding diversity of climate.

Mürzzuschlag (Styria)

In this important area of passage between the Danube region and the Adriatic there were from a very early period traffic routes through the valleys and over the passes, with trading settlements at strategic points. The principal river is the *Mur*, which rises in the Lungau (Salzburg) and flows through the province in a great arc. At first following an easterly course, it runs sharply southward at Bruck an der Mur, where it is joined by the Mürz, flowing down from the Semmering pass. It maintains this N–S direction until just short of the Yugoslav frontier, at Spielfeld, where it turns E again and forms the frontier between Austria and Yugoslavia for some 40 km/25 miles. On the banks of the Mur are the provincial capital, Graz, and the industrial towns of Knittelfeld and Judenburg.

The northern part of Styria is watered by the *Enns*, which rises in the Dachstein area and emerges into the northern Alpine foreland after forcing its way through the wild and romantic Gesäuse gorge beyond Admont.

The eastern part of the province is drained by the *Raab* and its tributaries. The upper reaches of the valleys are mostly narrow and sometimes gorge-like, while below they open out into fertile meadowland.

A major element in the economy of Styria is contributed by ore mining and processing, primarily at Eisenerz with its famous Erzberg ("Ore Mountain", with terraced opencast working), Kapfenberg, Leoben/Donawitz, Bruck an der Mur and Graz. Forestry and upland pastoral farming in the N and wine and fruit production in the S serve mainly to supply local needs. Other sources of revenue are the Altausee salt-mines and the two leading Austrian breweries at Göss (Leoben) and Puntigam (Graz).

A factor of considerable importance to the Styrian economy is now represented by the substantial tourist and holiday trade.

HISTORY. – The oldest evidence of human settlement in Styria is to be found in the numerous caves in the middle Mur valley around Peggau. In one such cave many Palaeolithic implements, probably dating back between 130,000 and 150,000 years, were found in 1947. Finds in the Gleisdorf area point to settlement here about 100,000 years ago. During the Neolithic period men ranged over most of central Styria, and in favourable areas settled down to a sedentary life as farmers. – During the Bronze and Iron Ages the *Norici*, a people apparently of Illyrian origin, settled in Styria. The local deposits of copper were already being worked, although little attention was paid to the iron ore of the region. Rich finds of high artistic quality date from this period, such as the Celtic votive wagon from Strettweg near Judenburg, pieces of armour, helmets and cult objects found in western Styria.

In 113 B.C. there was a great battle at Noreia, near Neumarkt in upper Styria, in which a Roman army was defeated by two Germanic tribes, the Cimbri and the Teutons. It was another hundred years before the *Romans* gained possession by peaceful means of almost the whole of present-day Styria (15 B.C.), and thereafter the region remained Roman until the fall of the Empire in A.D. 476. During this period many towns and other settlements were established, and the province was traversed by roads which are still in use today.

The great migrations wrought havoc in the open landscape of Styria. The *Slavs*, who were subject to the overlordship of the *Avars*, pressed into the plundered territories; then about 750 they appealed for aid against Avar oppression to the Bajuwari (Bavarians), who brought in Christianity from the Salzburg region. In 788 Styria passed under the control of Charlemagne, and thereafter Frankish, Bavarian and Saxon nobles and peasants were established in the region and large grants of ownerless land were made to the Church and to noble families. Styria owed its prosperity during this period to the development of the land for agriculture.

The next major events in the history of Styria were a succession of raids by the *Hungarians* from 895 onwards. It was only after the battle of Augsburg in 955 that the region was regained for Christendom and the great *"Marches"* or frontier lordships were established, strong enough to protect Europe against invasion from the East. A number of such Marches were set up in Styria under the rule of the Traungau family, with their seat at Steyr in Upper Austria and at Enns. The last member of the family was granted the title of duke by the Emperor Frederick I Barbarossa in 1180, and thereafter Styria remained a duchy until 1918, being held successively by the Babenbergs (from 1192), King Ottokar of Bohemia and finally (from 1276) by the Habsburgs. Within a period of a hundred years or so the principal towns and markets of Styria were established and many of them surrounded by defensive walls.

The 11th and 12th c. saw the foundation of the most important Styrian *monasteries*, including Göss (1020), Admont (1072), St Lambrecht (1096–1103), Rein (1128), Seckau (1140), Vorau (1163), Stainz (1230) and many more.

The 14th and 15th c. were marked by struggles for predominance between the great families of the province, which wrought much devastation. Hungarian and Turkish raids, plague and famine, together with plagues of locusts, laid waste great tracts of territory (cf. the "Landplagenbild" on the wall of Graz Cathedral). The Gothic period, which elsewhere was an age of cultural development and flowering, was for Styria a time of bitter struggle against the invaders from the East.

By the beginning of the 16th c. Styria had reached its present boundaries except that Lower Styria remained detached. The Turkish danger and the development of firearms made it necessary to modernise the region's defences, and this brought an influx of Italian architects, who not only constructed new and powerful fortifications around the towns but also built the magnificent noble mansions and the burghers' houses with their fine arcades which still add a picturesque note to many towns. During this period, too, was built the Landhaus in Graz, one of the finest Renaissance buildings outside Italy.

At the *Reformation* Lutheranism made considerable headway in Styria, both among the nobility and the mass of the townspeople; but this was followed towards the end of the 16th c. by the *Counter-Reformation*, in which a leading part was played by the Jesuits, who had established themselves in Graz in 1573. Finally in 1600 all those townspeople who had refused to recant their Protestant faith were banished from the country, and in 1629 the Protestant nobility suffered the same fate.

The Thirty Years War and the continuing Hungarian and Turkish raids impoverished Styria, and although the Turkish danger receded at least temporarily after a Christian victory at St Gotthart-Mogersdorf in 1664 real relief came only after further victories over the Turks at Vienna (1683) and Ofen (1686).

The 18th c. saw a considerable revival of the economy. Factories were established, roads were built and trade began to recover. This resurgence was brought to an end, however, by the Napoleonic wars, when Styria was occupied by the French three times (1797, 1805 and 1809).

During the 19th c. Styria enjoyed a period of economic development as a result of the establishment of new industries and the construction of railways.

The two world wars brought further trials. During the Second World War Graz and the industrial towns of Knittelfeld and Zeltweg were bombed, parts of the province were devastated by the fighting and many places in eastern Styria were partly destroyed. After the war the damage was made good, and since then Styria has shared the destinies of the rest of Austria.

ART. – The earliest finds showing evidence of artistic skill date from the *Celtic period*. They include weapons, various vessels and ornaments. The most famous item is the votive wagon from Strettweg, near Judenburg, but this is probably an Etruscan product imported into Styria. The *Roman period* is represented by a great quantity of sculpture, inscribed stones, implements and ornaments (mostly in the Provincial Museum in Graz), and Roman stones can be seen in many churches, castles and other buildings.

In Graz, Sekau and Rein a number of images of the Virgin dating from the Byzantine period have been preserved. The most splendid example of the *Romanesque style* is the church (a pillared basilica) at Seckau Abbey, but there are other important Romanesque buildings elsewhere in the province, particularly at Pürgg (St John's Church, with notable frescoes). Typical of this period are the charnel-houses (*Karner*), often with chapels for worship. The libraries at Admont and Vorau possess important Romanesque manuscripts.

The *Gothic style* began to develop in Styria only in the second half of the 13th c. One of the earliest Gothic buildings is the parish church of Murau with its stone-roofed steeple, but most Styrian churches date from the late Gothic period. Two of the finest are Graz Cathedral and the pilgrimage church of Maria Strassengel near Graz. The Kornmesserhaus in Bruck an der Mur is a magnificent example of secular Gothic architecture. Styria also boasts some notable items of Gothic painting, sculpture and applied art.

The *Renaissance* is represented in Styria by many magnificent buildings, most notably the Landhaus in Graz and other buildings in that city with beautiful arcaded courtyards. Other fine Renaissance buildings include the Schlösser of Eggenberg, Hollenegg, Tannhausen and Frondsberg.

The principal examples of *Baroque* art are several fine churches in eastern Styria. There is also a great deal of excellent sculpture and painting of this period (Stammel, Hackhofer, Ritter von Mölk, Flurer, Kremser Schmidt; the graphic artist Veit Kauperz).

The 19th and 20th c. can claim only a few major works of architecture, such as the Rathaus and Opera House in Graz, but much painting and sculpture was produced in these centuries. – The Styrian capital, Graz, has developed – particularly since the Second World War – into a major cultural city the influence of which extends beyond the boundaries of the province.

Schloss Eggenberg, Graz

The treasures created by nature and the hand of man in Styria are guarded by a ring of mountain ramparts, traversed by many *passes*. To the S, towards Carinthia, there are the *Turracher Höhe (one of the steepest of the Alpine passes), the Flattnitzer Höhe, the Obdacher Sattel, the *Packsattel* and the little known Radlpass from Eibiswald in southern Styria to the Drava (Drau) valley in Slovenia; to the W towards Salzburg and Upper Austria, the Mandlingpass in the upper Enns valley, the steep road from Obertraun through the Koppental to Bad Aussee, the Pötschenhöhe, the *Pyhrnpass* (with the nearby Hengstpass and Laussapass), and the roads which climb up from Altenmarkt, Grossreifling and Mendling/Palfau in the beautiful valley of the Enns, where the river forces its way through between the Ennstal Alps and the Hochschwabing group; and to the N, towards Upper and Lower Austria, the Zellerrain and Mitterbach roads, the Lahnsattel, the Preiner Gscheid saddle below the Raxalpe and Schneealpe, the *Semmering* and the *Wechsel* passes. Only towards the E is there relatively open country in the Styrian uplands, and it was here that the Styrians of earlier centuries built so many stout castles, the most imposing of which is the *Riegersburg, preserved almost intact.

Many visitors will enter Styria by way of the *Enns valley*. To the N extends the Styrian part of the *Salzkammergut with its numerous lakes (Grundlsee, Altausseer See and the Tauplitzseen, at the foot of the Totes Gebirge). The chief places in the Styrian Salzkammergut are Bad Aussee, Bad Mitterndorf (ski-jump on Kulm, chairlift to Tauplitzalm), Pürgg and Wörschach. The road continues E through Admont and the *Gesäuse and from there along the Salza valley to *Mariazell or past the Leopoldsteiner See to Eisenerz and the *Erzberg.

In the *Mur valley*, between the Tauern and the hills of central Styria (Stubalpe, Gleinalpe, Koralpe), is *Murau* (old-time railway up the Mur valley), with a holiday area on the Stolzalpe. SE of the town is the Benedictine abbey of *St Lambrecht*.

Farther E are the old commercial and industrial towns of *Judenburg* and *Knittelfeld*, to the N of which are the Benedictine abbey of *Seckau, one of the finest monasteries in the country, and the *Österreichring*, a well-known car racing circuit. And, finally, in the SE corner of Styria, is the lively city of **Graz**, the provincial capital, with its many tourist attractions.

Outstanding among the NATURAL FEATURES of Styria are the *Lurgrotten at Peggau and Semriach – beautiful stalactitic caves equipped with electric lighting and paths for the convenience of visitors, and with a passage driven through the rock to link up two cave systems. In the Peggauer Wand and the rock faces of the Röthelstein are other caves in which traces of prehistoric occupation have been found.

Smaller stalactitic caves are the *Grasslhöhle* and *Katerloch* near Weiz and the *Rettenwandhöhle* near Kapfenberg. Also of interest is the Frauenmauerhöhle between Eisenerz and Tragöss, but this should be visited only with a knowledgeable guide. There are other caves, some fully explored, in the limestone mountains, particularly in the Hochschwab area and on the Schöckel.

Styria is also rich in beautiful gorges and waterfalls. The largest and best known of the gorges is the *Gesäuse between Admont and Hieflau, where the Enns has carved a passage through the mountains which is now followed by the road and railway. Near Mixnitz is the *Bärenschutzklamm*, with paths and gangways leading up to the Hochlantsch past a series of beautiful waterfalls. Also well worth seeing are the *Kesselfall* and its gorge, near Semriach.

Near Weiz the River Raab flows between steep rock walls and wooded slopes, with numerous rapids and waterfalls, and in the *Weizbachklamm* the road is crushed up against the foaming mountain stream as it forces its way through between towering cliffs. At the foot of the Totes Gebirge is the *Wörschachklamm*. Other impressive gorges are to be seen near Hieflau and Johnsbach.

Tennengebirge

Land: Salzburg (S).
Altitude: Highest point: Raucheck (2431 m/7976 ft).
(i) **Österreichischer Alpenverein,**
Sektion Werfen,
A-5452 Pfarrwerfen 142.

The Tennengebirge, part of the northern Alpine chain, is a range lying to
the N of the western end of Niedere
Tauern.

The Tennengebirge was originally part of
the same massif as the neighbouring Hagengebirge to the W, but in the course of time the
River *Salzach* carved a passage between
the two – the gloomy defile now known as
the Lueg pass.

On the eastern edge of this great desolate
plateau, varied by rounded heights and
broad depressions, is the Laufener Hütte
(1726 m/5663 ft), and there are other
mountain huts on the steep S face of the
range, with its highest peaks, the **Raucheck**
(2431 m/7976 ft) and the **Bleikogel**
(2412 m/7914 ft).

On the western slope of the plateau, near the
Dr.-Friedrich-Oedl-Haus (1573 m/5161 ft),
is the entrance to the ****Eisriesenwelt**
("World of the Ice Giants"), the largest
known ice cave and one of the great natural
wonders of the Eastern Alps (see under
Werfen).

Gurglertal and runs up by way of the
hotel colony of Hochgurgl, with many
sharp turns, to the summit of the
Timmelsjoch (2497 m/8193 ft; Italian
Passo di Rombo), on the frontier
between Austria and Italy, after
which it descends (with some narrow
stretches) into the Val Passiria. – The
road is usually open only from about
mid May to mid October; on the Italian
side it is suitable only for cars (trailer
caravans prohibited).

At the head of the Gurglertal – the easterly
continuation of the Ötztal – is ***Obergurgl**
(1930 m/6332 ft), Tirol's highest parish,
now a modern resort with excellent skiing
country (several lifts). To the S is the *Grosser
Gurgler Ferner* (Great Gurgl Glacier), on
which Professor Auguste Piccard landed in
his stratospheric balloon in 1931, after
becoming the first man to reach a height of
15,781 m/51,777 ft. A chair-lift runs up to
Gaisberg (2071 m/6795 ft), to the S, and
another lift continues up the **Hohe Mut*
(2659 m/8724 ft), from which there are
breathtaking views of the area around the
Gaisbergferner (20 glaciers). Another chair-
lift runs SE from Obergurgl to the *Festkogel*
(3035 m/9958 ft; upper station 2642 m/
8668 ft). There is an Alpine climbing school
in the village.

Obergurgl is a good climbing base (experienced climbers
only; guide necessary for some climbs). Advice should be
sought locally before undertaking a climb. – To the E are
the peaks of the Gurgler Kamm, including the **Hohe Mut*

Timmelsjoch Road

Land: Tirol (T).
(i) **Verkehrsbüro Obergurgl,**
Haus Kuraten, A-6456 Obergurgl;
tel. (0 52 56) 3 53.
Fremdenverkehrsverband Innerötztal,
Hauptstrasse, Postfach 80, A-6450 Sölden;
tel. (0 52 54) 22 12–0.

ACCOMMODATION. – IN OBERGURGL: *Hochfirst,* A,
180 b., SB, sauna; *Alpina,* A, 133 b., sauna; *Mühle,* in
Poschach, A, 100 b., SB, sauna; *Austria,* A, 70 b., sauna;
Gamper, B, 65 b.; *Bellevue,* B, 55 b.; *Tirol,* B, 42 b.;
Jagdhof, in Untergurgl, C, 40 b. – IN HOCHGURGL:
Hochgurgl, A1, 110 b., SB, sauna; *Angerer Alm,* A, 73 b.,
SB; *Riml,* B, 80 b.; *Wurmkogl,* B, 72 b., sauna; *Laurin,* B,
58 b.

The Timmelsjoch Road (Timmelsjoch-
strasse; toll) crosses the *Timmelsjoch,
a pass almost 2500 m/8200 ft high, to
link the Ötztal with the Val Passiria
(German *Passeiertal*) in Italy. It begins
at Untergurgl (1796 m/5893 ft) in the

Obergurgl

(2659 m/8724 ft; 2½ hours); the *Festkogel* (3035 m/ 9958 ft; 3½ hours), to the SE, affording magnificent panoramic views; and the *Rotmoosjoch* (3155 m/ 10,352 ft; 4–4½ hours), with a beautiful view of the Dolomites. – It is 3½ hours' climb SW to the *Ramolhaus* (3002 m/9850 ft; accommodation), with superb views over the mighty Gurgler Ferner (glacier) to the surrounding peaks, including the *Grosser Ramolkogl* (3551 m/ 11,651 ft; 3 hours N, with guide), the *Hinterer Spiegelkogl* (3426 m/11,241 ft; 1½ hours W), the *Firmisanschneide* (3491 m/11,454 ft; 2½–3 hours SW), the *Schalfkogl* (3540 m/11,615 ft; 3 hours S) and the Gurgler Kamm to the E. – 2½ hours' climb S is the *Langtalereckhütte* (2438 m/7999 ft), near the steep tongue of the Grosser Gurgler Ferner, and 2 hours farther S is the *Hochwildenhaus* (2883 m/9459 ft; luggage lift), magnificently perched on the Steinerner Tisch ("Stone Table") near the old Fidelitashütte. From here there are rewarding climbs (each 3½–4 hours) of the **Hohe Wilde** (3479 m/ 11,415 ft; magnificent views) and the *Karlesspitze* (3465 m/11,369 ft) to the S, on the Italian frontier; and to the W (2½–3 hours, with guide) is the *Schalfkogel* (3540 m/11,615 ft), from which there is a fine panoramic view of the surrounding peaks and glaciers.

To the N of Obergurgl is **Untergurgl** (1796 m/5893 ft; chair-lift to Hochgurgl), at the beginning of the *Timmelsjoch Road* (toll; 11·4 km/7 miles to summit; max. gradient 11%). – The road climbs in four sharp turns to the *Angerer Alm* (2175 m/ 7136 ft), with the hotel colony of **Hochgurgl**. From here there is a chair-lift to the *Grosses Kar* (2410 m/7907 ft) and the *Wurmkogl* (3082 m/10,112 ft). – The road continues up the *Timmelsbachtal* and climbs in seven hairpins to the *Timmelsjoch* (2497 m/8193 ft; Italian *Passo di Rombo*; restaurant), on the Austrian-Italian frontier (closed at night).

The road on the Italian side (trailer caravans prohibited; narrow in places, several tunnels) descends the Val Passiria, passing through *Moso* (1007 m/3304 ft; German *Moos*), and in 27 km/17 miles reaches **S. Leonardo**

(683 m/2241 ft; German *St Leonhard*), which has associations with the Austrian patriot Andreas Hofer (1767–1810). – From here it is another 20 km/12 miles to Merano.

Tirol

Bundesland: Tirol (T). – Capital: Innsbruck.
Area: 12,647 sq. km/4883 sq. miles.
Population: 597,900.

(i) **Tiroler Fremdenverkehrswerbung,**
Bozner Platz 6, A-6010 Innsbruck;
tel. (0 52 22) 2 07 77/59.

The province of Tirol – which takes its name from the ancestral castle of the Counts of Tirol at Merano in Italy – is bounded on the E by Carinthia and Salzburg provinces, on the S by Italy, on the W by Vorarlberg and Switzerland and on the N by Germany (Bavaria). The province is divided into two parts, Northern and Eastern Tirol, separated from one another by the territory ceded to Italy in 1919 which is still known in Austria as South Tirol. A curiosity of geography is the enclave of Jungholz at the NW tip of the province, which is surrounded by Bavarian territory and within the German customs area.

The name of Tirol calls up a whole range of associations – Innsbruck with its backdrop of mountains and its famous Goldenes Dachl; Andreas Hofer, the patriot leader of the Napoleonic period; yodelling, schuhplattler dancing, the old Tirolese costumes; forests and Alpine meadows, rocks and ice; and winter sports.

The political changes after the First World War divided the pre-war territory of Tirol into three parts – Northern Tirol, with the provincial capital of Innsbruck; Eastern Tirol, with Lienz as its principal town; and the former South Tirol which is now part of Italy.

This territory in the heart of the Alps, with its intricate pattern of hills and valleys, is one of Europe's most popular holiday regions both in summer and in winter. For many centuries it was an area of transit between Germany and Italy, its high valleys barely accessible to strangers and inhabited only by a few poor mountain peasants. These valleys still offer the same solitude and tranquillity, but most of them are now

The Timmelsjoch Road

easily accessible on good roads. The more considerable villages and towns grew up in the valleys and on the pass roads.

From the Arlberg in the W, the Zugspitze in the N and the Loferer Steinberge in the E, the province of Tirol extends southward to the main Alpine chain. It is a land of passes – the Thurn pass, the Brenner, the Reschen (Resia) pass, the Timmelsjoch, the Gerlos-pass, the Achenpass, the Zirler Berg and the Arlberg, to name only the most important. The only approach to Tirol which does not go over a pass is the route through the Inn valley via Kufstein, where the river emerges from the mountains into the Alpine foreland; and this is accordingly the route followed by the principal road, motorway and rail connections.

From the Swiss frontier in the SW to the German frontier in the NE the *Inn valley* cuts a swathe through the province, with its side valleys – the Paznauntal, the Kauner Tal, the Pitztal, the Ötztal, the Zillertal, etc. – running up into the grandeur of the mountains.

The rock and névé, the beauty and the sublime solitude of the Zillertal and Ötztal

Alps, the Stubai Alps, the Grossglockner and the Grossvenediger, with peaks rising above 3000 m/10,000 ft and some approaching 4000 m/13,000 ft, exert a magical attraction for climbing and walking enthusiasts. The wild and bizarrely fashioned rock landscapes of the Kaisergebirge, the Karwendel, the Lienz Dolomites and the Kalkkögel near Innsbruck are a paradise for rock-climbers, but hold equal fascination for those who prefer to enjoy their mountain scenery less strenuously from the valley.

Beautiful lakes – deep blue, emerald green or black – mirror in their crystal-clear waters the forms of the rocks, the Alpine meadows and the forests. The largest and best known of the lakes are the Achensee, the Walchsee, the Tristacher See, the warm Schwarzsee at Kitzbühel and the Plansee, but these are only a few of the many lakes which offer excellent bathing in summer.

Almost every kind of sport, but particularly winter, mountain and water sports, can be practised in Tirol; and here, too, visitors can enjoy relaxing and health-giving holidays of a less energetic kind. Walking in the mountains is an experience well calculated to ease away the stresses of everyday life. Health and relaxation are promoted not only by physical activity but by the fresh mountain air and the brilliant sun. And among the many resorts – large and small, modest and fashionable – there are a number with excellent treatment facilities for those who need them.

The natural beauties of Tirol are matched by its treasures of art; for surely few peoples have such a deeply rooted artistic sense as the Tirolese. Evidence of this is provided by the richly stocked Folk Museum in Innsbruck and many local museums. All over Tirol, in busy streets and on remote country roads, the visitor will encounter examples of an innate feeling for form and colour – in secular no less than in religious buildings, and even in objects of everyday use.

Among the finest examples of Tirolese art are the famous over-lifesize bronze statues in the Hofkirche in Innsbruck; but in towns and villages throughout Tirol – in Innsbruck, Bad Hall, Schwaz, Rattenberg and many other places – are to be seen picturesque old houses and irregular lanes, bearing witness to a long architectural and artistic tradition. In some of the finest settings in Tirol are more than a hundred castles and

Pfunds, in the upper Inn valley

castle ruins, medieval strongholds built to command the surrounding territory. And – going even further back – there are many relics of the Roman campaigns in this region and the even earlier Stone Age and Bronze Age inhabitants of Tirol, found casually or by excavation and now carefully preserved in museums.

The people of Tirol are also noted for their cheerful good humour, and their songs, their yodelling and their schuhplattler dances are world-famed. On high days and holidays many country people still wear their colourful traditional costumes. There are numerous festivals featuring costumes, marksmanship and music as well as other picturesque old customs and practices.

HISTORY. – In the Palaeolithic period human groups, still at the hunting and food-gathering stage, moved into the Alps. In Neolithic times (6th–3rd millennia B.C.) stock-rearing and crop-farming developed, and villages of pile-dwellings were established on the lakes of the Pre-Alpine area. The working of minerals began in the Bronze Age (copper-mining on the Kelchalpe and at Mitterberg, salt-working at Hallein). In the early Iron Age (800–400 B.C.) the salt-working industry prospered, as is shown by the rich grave goods found at Hallstatt. The population of the Alps during this period consisted of **Illyrians** (cf. place-names like Wilten, Imst and Vomp).

Between about 400 B.C. and the beginning of the Christian era **Celts** pressed into the region from the W, bringing with them the more highly developed culture of the late Iron Age. From the S the Etruscans advanced into the Alps, but for no great distance. The principal tribes during this period were the *Raeti* within the territory of Tirol and the *Taurisci* to the E. Between 113 and 101 B.C. Germanic tribes (the Cimbri and Teutons) advanced for the first time through the Eastern Alps into the Roman Empire.

From 15 B.C. to A.D. 476 the Eastern Alps were under **Roman** rule, forming part of the provinces of Raetia (the Swiss Grisons and Tirol) and Noricum (Carinthia and Styria).

Roads were built through the principal valleys and over the most important passes, and along these roads many Roman settlements, originally military posts, grew up alongside the older settlements – Veldidena (Wilten, near Innsbruck), Brigantium (Bregenz), Aguntum (near Lienz), etc.

In A.D. 166 the *Marcomanni* ("border people") made a brief incursion through the Eastern Alps to the Adriatic.

Between about 540 and 576 the **Bajuwari** (Bavarians) came in from the N under their hereditary dukes, the Agilolfings, and occupied the Eastern Alps, while the *Alamanni* established themselves in the western part of the region.

About 590 the *Slovenes* began to move into the Alps from the E. In 750 Duke Tassilo III of Bavaria came to the aid of the Slovenes against the Mongol *Avars*, and thereafter retained the overlordship of the region.

In 774 Charlemagne conquered the Lombard kingdom, in 788 the duchy of Bavaria. Between 791 and 796 he defeated the Avars and established an Eastern March (Ostmark). In 876 a Carolingian, Arnulf, became Margrave ("Lord of the March") of Carinthia, and in 950 King Otto I of Germany advanced over the Brenner into Italy, the first German king to do so. After his victory at Augsburg (955) over the Hungarians, who had been pushing W since 900, the Bavarian Eastern March (Austria) was re-established and a new March of Carinthia set up. In 976 the Emperor Otto II elevated Carinthia to an independent duchy.

In 1142 the Count of the Vintschgau (now the Val Venosta in Italy) assumed the title of **Count of Tirol**, after the castle of that name at Merano. In 1248, when the line of the Counts of Andechs died out, Count Albert IV of Tirol inherited their possessions in the Inn valley, the Wipptal and the Pustertal (Val Pusteria), thus uniting extensive territories N and S of the Brenner.

After Albert's death in 1253 his possessions fell to the Counts of Görz (Gorizia), and between 1258 and 1295 Count Meinhard II of Görz-Tirol enlarged and rounded off his domains until he was the only independent lord in Tirol apart from the bishops. In 1286 he became Duke of Carinthia and a Prince of the Empire.

When Count Henry of Görz-Tirol died in 1335 his daughter *Margarete Maultasch* (1318–69) inherited only the county of Tirol, while Carinthia was granted by the Emperor Ludwig the Bavarian to the Habsburgs. Then in 1363, after the death of her only son, Margarete Maultasch made over the county of Tirol to Duke Rudolf of **Habsburg**.

In 1375 Duke Leopold III acquired the county of Feldkirch, but in 1386 he was killed in a battle at Sempach with the Swiss. From 1404 to 1439 the duchy was ruled by Duke Frederick IV, at first in poverty and misfortune but later in increasing prosperity. In 1420 he moved his seat from Merano to Innsbruck. In 1427 he restricted the power of the nobility and established the freedom of the burghers and peasantry.

Under Duke Sigismund (1439–90; from 1453 Archduke) the silver-mines of Schwaz prospered, and the silver coins minted at Hall from 1483 onwards were the forerunners of the more famous thalers (dollars) of Joachimsthal.

In 1500 Maximilian I (1490–1519: from 1493 Emperor), the "last of the knights", reunited the Pustertal (Val Pusteria) and Lienz with Tirol; in 1505 he added Kufstein, Rattenberg and Kitzbühel; and in 1511 the territories of the bishoprics of Brixen and Trient (Bressanone and Trento, now in Italy) were also incorporated in Tirol. A decree of 1511 made provision for the defence of the enlarged territories, instituting universal military service and establishing a militia.

Ferdinand (1519–64; from 1556 Emperor) took action against the advancing tide of *Protestantism*. A peasant rising in Salzburg and Tirol (1525) was repressed, but thereafter certain service obligations and dues were abolished. In 1552 the Elector Moritz of Saxony invaded Tirol. The Hofkirch in Innsbruck was built between 1553 and 1563.

Archduke Ferdinand (Regent of Tirol 1564–95) carried through the *Counter-Reformation* and assembled large art collections in Schloss Amras (Ambras); his wife was the daughter of an Augsburg patrician, Philippine Welser. He caused the Brenner Road to be restored in 1582–84. From 1602 to 1618 Archduke Maximilian was Regent of Tirol, from 1618 to 1632 Archduke Leopold V. From 1632 to 1646 Leopold's widow Claudia de' Medici acted as Regent, and her chancellor Wilhelm Biener sought to curb the pretensions of the nobility. Archduke Ferdinand

Charles (1646–62) was much under the influence of Italian nobles, and in 1651 Biener was beheaded at Rattenberg. – With the death of Sigmund Francis (Archduke 1662–65) the separate Habsburg line in Tirol came to an end, and thereafter the duchy was ruled from Vienna.

In 1677 the Emperor Leopold I founded the University of Innsbruck. During the *War of the Spanish Succession* (1701–14) the Elector Max Emmanuel of Bavaria, then in alliance with Louis XIV of France, advanced as far as the Brenner in 1703, but was turned back by the Tirolese militia under the leadership of Martin Sterzinger and pursued almost all the way back to Munich. The French under Vendôme laid siege to Trient (Trento) but were unable to take the town.

Between 1740 and 1780 the Empress Maria Theresa completely reorganised the administration of the province. In 1765 the Emperor Francis I died at Innsbruck. – In 1772 the Brenner Road and in 1785 the Arlberg Road were made suitable for vehicles.

During the Napoleonic wars, in 1796–97, French forces commanded by Joubert tried to cross the Brenner from the S but were thrown back by the Tirolese militia in the battle of Spinges.

From 1805 to 1813 Tirol was incorporated in Bavaria. In 1809 the Tirolese, led by **Andreas Hofer** (1767–1810), *Joseph Speckbacher* and *Joachim Haspinger*, rose against the French and Bavarians and after a victory at Berg Isel liberated Innsbruck and the territory of Tirol. Under the Treaty of Vienna (14 October 1809), however, the Emperor returned Tirol to Bavaria. Hofer resumed the struggle for freedom but could not match the superior forces of the French viceroy, Eugène de Beauharnais. Betrayed to the French and taken prisoner, he was shot by a firing squad in Mantua, on Napoleon's orders, on 20 February 1810.

In 1813, under the Treaty of Ried, Bavaria ceded Tirol to **Austria** and joined the alliance against Napoleon. – In 1814 Josef Madersperger of Kufstein invented the sewing-machine; in 1864 Peter Mitterhofer developed the first typewriter using type-bars in Innsbruck. The Brenner railway was opened in 1867, the Arlberg in 1884, the Tauern line in 1908. The German and Austrian Alpine Club was founded in 1873.

Under the Treaty of St Germain (1919) Tirolese territory S of the Brenner was ceded to Italy. Northern and Eastern

Tirol then became the province (*Land*) of Tirol. The National Socialist régime incorporated Eastern Tirol in Carinthia and Vorarlberg in Tirol. Since the end of the last war Tirol, restored to its inter-war boundaries, has shared the destinies of the re-established Republic of Austria.

ART. – Tirol has numerous fine buildings and works of art illustrating the development of the arts in this region since the Middle Ages. There are few Romanesque buildings, since almost all of them were altered and rebuilt in later periods, but there are many notable examples of *Gothic*, Renaissance and Baroque architecture. The province's art treasures are particularly numerous in the Inn valley and in the capital, Innsbruck; outstanding buildings in the immediate vicinity of Innsbruck and in the Inn valley are the monastery of Wilten and Stams Abbey.

Secular art and architecture are more richly represented in Tirol than in other Austrian provinces. Here again the Inn valley features prominently with its many castles and country houses. Schloss Ambras, Burg Tratzberg, the castles around Brixlegg and Rattenberg, Kufstein Castle and many more bear witness to Tirolese building activity, particularly during the *Renaissance*; and there is a great range of other buildings – burghers' and merchants' houses, etc. – to be seen at Innsbruck, Bad Hall, Schwaz, Rattenberg, Brixlegg, Kitzbühel and elsewhere.

Religious architecture of the Renaissance period is represented by the Hofkirche in Innsbruck, the interiors of churches at Schwaz and Bad Hall and numbers of funerary monuments and gravestones all over the province.

There are also major examples of *Baroque* art and architecture in Tirol. Many sumptuous buildings were erected during this period in token of the victory over Protestantism. Frequently only the interior of a church was altered, magnificent high altars erected and the walls and ceilings decorated with rich and colourful frescoes. Numerous noble palaces and burghers' houses in the towns also date from this period. The final phase of Baroque art is represented by Rococo (church interiors, house fronts).

A special position in Tirolese architecture is occupied by the peasant house or farmhouse. Particularly notable is the style found in the Inn valley. The typical farmhouse, standing by itself amid orchards, fields and meadows, has a wide overhanging roof, carved wooden gables, balconies and balustrades. In the interior are panelled rooms, magnificent stoves, large chests and presses, tables and well-made benches and chairs, all usually decorated with carving and painting.

The houses are very different in other parts of Tirol, where masonry of undressed stone based on Romanesque models predominates and ornament is almost totally lacking.

The landscape of Northern Tirol is predominantly mountainous; and if nature has not been generous to this region in the provision of mineral resources and fertile soil she has more than made up for this by granting it abundant scenic beauties.

The visitor entering Northern Tirol from Salzburg is greeted first of all by the Kaisergebirge, rearing its crags and pinnacles above St Johann in the valley below, with Kitzbühel a short distance away to the S. S of the Kaisergebirge

Andreas Hofer Monument, Bergisel

are the Kitzbühel Alps with their more rounded forms, their forests and their broad Alpine meadows – fine skiing areas with large winter sports resorts and excellent facilities.

N of the Inn are the Karwendel and the Wettersteingebirge, offering endless scope for rock-climbers and mountain walkers with their boldly shaped limestone massifs and rugged crags, the beautiful Achensee and the meadows which alternate with the rock.

Farther W, ending the chain of the Northern Calcareous Alps, are the Lechtal Alps, with their gentler forms, offering ideal conditions for winter sports.

Between the upper Inn (Reschen-Scheideck) and the Brenner depression are the Ötztal and Stubai Alps with their grand mountain scenery and large glaciers. The imposing forms of the peaks, their magnificent expanses of permanent snow and their valleys reaching up into the world of the glaciers have made these mountains, like the Zillertal Alps to the E of the Brenner, one of the most visited parts of Tirol.

In **Eastern Tirol** (see p. 70) the dominant features are the Venediger group, with its extensive glaciers and its outliers, and the Grossglockner group. To the S of the Drau valley are the Lienz Dolomites, with the jagged forms and beauty of colouring of the Southern Calcareous Alps.

A charming contrast to the glaciers and the rugged rock faces of the mountains is provided by the beautiful wooded slopes and Alpine meadows between the rocky peaks and by the pastureland and fields in the valleys, particularly in the fertile Inn valley with its orchards and cornfields.

At the foot of the glaciers are many lakes, and clear mountain streams surge down the valleys or tumble over waterfalls in the gorges.

*Innsbruck (see p. 92) together with its surrounding area, is the most popular tourist region in Tirol. The town itself attracts visitors and tempts them to stay with its backdrop of mountains, its charming old streets and the treasures of arts and architecture in its

The Pitztal and Ötztal Alps

churches, its museums and its palaces. Within easy reach, too, are other attractions – the Nordkette (the chain of mountains to the N of the town), Schloss Ambras, Bergisel and the Sill gorge, Hall, Igls and the Patscherkofel. The rail trip from Mittenwald in Germany via Seefeld (one of the most important tourist attractions in Tirol) to Innsbruck opens up magnificent prospects of mountain scenery.

A walk through the Karwendel, even without any strenuous climbing, allows the visitor to enjoy the wild unspoiled beauty of the Calcareous Alps. In the Wipptal – busier than the other side valleys of the Inn with the heavy traffic to the Brenner and Italy – there are such popular summer resorts as Matrei, Steinach, St Jodok and Gries. Proximity to Innsbruck and good level walking country are advantages offered by many resorts on the upland terraces – the popular health and winter sports resort of Igls taking pride of place, together with Natters, Mutters and Schönberg and, at the mouth of the Sellraintal, Axams, Grinzens and Oberperfuss.

Access to the beauties of the mountains is facilitated by the many side valleys which branch off on both sides of the Inn. The **Inn valley** itself (see p. 97), with Innsbruck and such focal points of communications and trade as Landeck, Imst, Wörgl and Kufstein, is the principal artery of the province's agriculture, industry and traffic.

To the S of the Inn the **Pitztal** (see p. 153) and **Ötztal** (p. 147) run up into the Ötztal Alps. The resorts of Sölden/Hochsölden and Obergurgl/Hochgurgl in the Ötztal enjoy an international reputation among climbers and skiers.

An attractive E–W connection between the Ötztal and the Inn valley is provided by the *Sellraintal* and Kühtaisattel. The *Timmelsjoch* Road makes an interesting connection between the Ötztal and the Val Passiria in Italy.

From the **Wipptal** (the valley of the Sill), which is followed by the Brenner Road, the *Stubaital* (see p. 184) and the *Gschnitztal* branch off to the SW.

The *Wattental* and the *Zillertal* (p. 247) lead up into the Tuxer Voralpen and the Zillertal Alps, with very beautiful branches to the *Finsinggrund*, the **Tuxer Tal** and the **Gerlostal**.

The eastern part of Northern Tirol, between the Kaisergebirge and the Kitzbühel Alps, offers a variety of tourist attractions in the valleys around **Wörgl** and the resort of **Kitzbühel** (p. 107), world-famous as both a summer and a winter resort – the *Alpbachtal* at Brixlegg, Wildschönau and Kelchsau, the *Spertental* and the roads to St Johann in Tirol, Bad Fieberbrunn and Hochfilzen.

The upper **Lechtal**, on the N side of the Inn between the Allgäu Alps and the Lechtal Alps, is one of the most attractive areas in Tirol. Cars trailing caravans should, however, avoid the Lechtal road.

The **Gurgital** leads from Imst over the Fernpass to Ehrwald or Lermoos and Garmisch-Partenkirchen in Germany, the **Tannheimer Tal** from Weissenbach (near Reutte) over the Gaichtpass and the Oberjoch to Hindelang (Germany). The Lechtal and the *Vilstal* cross the German frontier at Füssen and Pfronten.

The busiest route from Tirol into Bavaria is the road from Innsbruck via Zirl, Seefeld and Scharnitz to Mittenwald, running between the Wettersteingebirge and the Karwendel range.

The **Ausserfern** district to the N of the Fernpass is another favourite holiday area. Ehrwald (starting-point of the Zugspitze cableway), Lermoos and Biberwier lie on the edge of a wide valley basin dominated on the E by the grand W face of the Wetterstein and on the S by the Mieminger Berge.

A beautiful road runs S from the Tegernsee (Bavaria) through the **Achental** and along the E side of the Achensee, Tirol's largest lake, to the road junction of Strass in the Inn valley.

From the Rasthaus Kanzelkehre above Jenbach there is, in good weather, a magnificent panoramic prospect of mountains.

Totes Gebirge

Länder: Salzburg (S) and Upper Austria (OÖ).
Altitude: Highest point: Grosser Priel (2514 m/8248 ft).
ⓘ **Österreichischer Alpenverein,**
  Sektion Bad Aussee,
  A-8992 Altaussee 21.
  Sektion Liezen,
  Rathausplatz 14, A-8940 Liezen.
  Touristenklub Windischgarsten,
  Pichl 76, A-4580 Windischgarsten.

The *Totes Gebirge ("Dead Mountains"), the second of the main massifs
in the Salzkammergut, has the largest
high plateau of any range in the
Calcareous Alps. Bounded on the W
and S by the Traun valley and separated
from the Dachstein group by the Traun
and the wide Mitterndorf basin, this
vast stony waste, furrowed and
swallow-holed, stretches out far to the
E, where its finest peaks, the magnificently rugged Grosser Priel (2514 m/
8248 ft) and the Spitzmauer (2446 m/
8025 ft) slope down to the Stodertal in
sheer rock walls.

Like all the mountains in the Northern Alps,
the Totes Gebirge dates from the Triassic
period. The basis is formed by the Werfen
schists, above these the brittle lower dolomite
and above this again a massive covering of
much fissured Dachstein limestone.

The whole of the eastern plateau consists of
Dachstein limestone, and the great rocky
peaks which rise above it are merely the
remains of a much deeper covering. In beauty
and grandeur the Totes Gebirge is one of
the most imposing ranges in the whole of
the Alps.

The Priel-Schutzhaus (1520 m/4987 ft) near
Hinterstoder is a good rock-climbing base
and the starting-point for walks across the
plateau – to the Pühringer-Hütte (1703 m/
5588 ft) above the *Elmsee* (1670 m/5479 ft) in
the middle of the plateau and from there
either to the two *Lahngangseen* and down to
the Grundlsee below the S face of the range,
or by way of the Appel-Haus (1660 m/
5446 ft) to the lonely *Wildensee* (1554 m/
5099 ft) and from there northward down to
the *Offensee* (651 m/2136 ft), near Ebensee,
in a peaceful forest setting.

The mighty N face of the Totes Gebirge
plunges magnificently down to the *Almsee*
(589 m/1933 ft), a lake of unforgettable
sombre beauty.

In sharp contrast to the bleak grandeur of
the high plateau and its northern face is the
cheerful open landscape on the S side of the
range. Here two considerable valleys cut into
the mountains, with two attractive lakes, the
Altausseer See and the *Grundlsee*.

To the SE of the main plateau is a lower and
narrower terrace, the *Mitterndorfer Seenplatte* (Mitterndorf Lake Plateau), a charming region of beautiful Alpine meadows. In
green hollows nestle several small lakes

The Grundlsee (Styrian Salzkammergut)

(Steirersee, 1451 m/4761 ft; Schwarzensee, 1549 m/5082 ft), mirroring the crags of the Totes Gebirge in their waters, and summer farmsteads and mountain huts are scattered about in the great open expanse, a popular skiing area in winter, when the mountain huts – the Theodor-Karl-Holl-Haus (1650 m/ 5414 ft), the Tauplitzalm-Hütte (1620 m/ 5315 ft) and many more – are the scene of lively activity.

Immediately E of the Totes Gebirge is the **Warscheneck group**, a smaller but still considerable high plateau on the far side of the Stodertal, bounded on the S by the wide Enns valley. Here, too, can be seen, in bewildering variety, the characteristic swallow-holes, furrows and collapsed cavities. The highest peak, the broad rounded summit of the *Warscheneck* (2386 m/ 7828 ft), can be climbed without great difficulty from Windischgarsten or Spital am Phyrn by way of the Dümler-Hütte (1523 m/ 4997 ft) or the Linzer Haus (1385 m/ 4544 ft).

An even finer view is afforded by the *Hochmölbing* (2332 m/7651 ft), the long ridge of which can be reached from the Hochmölbing-Hütte (1702 m/5584 ft), near the spa of Wörschach. This plateau is also a popular skiing area, and the run down the Loigistal, on the N side, is one of the finest descents in the Northern Alps.

There are a few small lakes in the Warscheneck range, perhaps the most beautiful being the *Gleinkersee* (807 m/2648 ft), above Windischgarsten at the foot of the Seestein (1570 m/5151 ft).

To the N of the Warscheneck group is the long, lonely ridge of the *Sengsengebirge*, with the *Hoher Nock* (1961 m/6434 ft), which belongs rather to the broad Pre-Alpine zone to the N than to the Totes Gebirge.

The **Höllengebirge** does not properly belong to the Totes Gebirge. This long narrow plateau stands by itself between the S ends of the two largest Salzkammergut lakes, the Attersee and the Traunsee. The far-ranging views to be had from the summit were one of the main reasons for the construction of the cableway which runs up from Ebensee, on the Traunsee, to the *Feuerkogel* (1594 m/5230 ft), on the eastern rim of the plateau.

From the upper station, where there are a number of houses providing accommoda-tion, the highest peak, the *Grosser Höllen-kogel* (1862 m/6109 ft), can be climbed without difficulty.

Traunsee

Land: Upper Austria (OÖ).

ⓘ **Kurverwaltung Gmunden,**
Am Graben 2, A-4810 Gmunden;
tel. (0 76 12) 43 05.

ACCOMMODATION. – IN GMUNDEN: *Seehotel Schwan*, A, 81 b.; *Schlosshotel Freisitz*, A, 45 b., sauna; *Magerl*, B, 70 b., sauna; *Moosberg*, B, 42 b., SB, sauna; *Goldener Hirsch*, B, 40 b.; *Grünberg*, B, 40 b.; *Ramsau*, B, 30 b.; *Echo am See*, B, 20 b.; *Altmühl*, C, 45 b. – IN ALTMÜNSTER: *Altmünstererhof*, A, 33 b.; *Hocheck*, B, 130 b. – IN TRAUNKIRCHEN: *Post*, A, 100 b.; SP, sauna; *Feichtinger*, B, 76 b.; *Goldener Hirsch*, C, 38 b.; *Berghof*, B, 36 b. – IN EBENSEE: *Seepension Langbathsee*, A, 57 b., SP, sauna; *Post*, A, 50 b.; *Gann*, C, 50 b.

RECREATION and SPORTS. – Water sports – rowing, fishing, water-skiing (at Gmunden); sailing schools (at Gmunden, Altmünster and Traunkirchen).

The *Traunsee (alt. 422 m/1385 ft) is one of the larger lakes in the Salzkam-mergut, 12 km/7½ miles long, up to 3 km/2 miles wide and 191 m/625 ft deep. Above its E side are three peaks – the Erlakogel (1570 m/5151 ft), also known as the "Schlafende Griechin", the "Sleeping Greek Girl", the Hoch-kogel (1483 m/4866 ft) and the Traun-stein (1691 m/5548 ft). Along the W side of the lake, between Gmunden at the N end and Ebensee at the southern tip, runs the Salzkammergut Road, some sections of which, blasted from the rock face, wind their way along high above the lake.

The chief place on the lake, **Gmunden** (440 m/1444 ft; pop. 13,000), at the N end, is a picturesque little town with a number of castles. It has a well-known ceramic manu-factory and attracts many visitors both as a health resort and as a convenient staging point. The *parish church*, on higher ground, dates from the 15th c. but was remodelled in Baroque style in the 18th c.; carved group of the Three Kings (by Thomas Schwanthaler, 1678) on high altar; ceramic "Madonna of the Cloak". The *Rathaus* (16th–17th c.) has a ceramic carillon. The 15th c. Kammerhof houses the interesting *Municipal Museum*.

A little way SW is *Schloss Ort* (17th c.), once the property of Archduke Johann Salvator ("Johann Orth"), who disappeared in South America in 1891; on a peninsula

Traunkirchen

stand the *Kongresshaus* (Villa Toscana and the recently-built congress wing) and the Landschloss (now a Federal School of Forestry), the picturesque Seeschloss (Forestry Office), with a beautiful arcaded courtyard, on a small island in the lake, approached by a wooden bridge 130 m/ 140 yds long. – On the right bank of the Traun, in the district of Traundorf, is *Schloss Cumberland* (1882–86), now a local authority home.

Altmünster (443 m/1453 ft; pop. 7800), on the W side of the lake, has a fine late Gothic church (richly appointed interior) and a children's village. A steep and narow road (6 km/4 miles) ascends the *Gmundner Berg* (822 m/2697 ft; view; mountain hut). – *Schloss Ebenzweier* (17th c.) is now a school.

Traunkirchen (422 m/1385 ft; pop. 1500), situated on a peninsula, is a summer resort with a former Benedictine nunnery. The early Baroque *parish church* has an unusual pulpit in the form of a boat, with figures from the Miraculous Draught of Fishes (1753). Near the church is the little *St Michael's Chapel* (17th c.). On a wooded crag above the village is the old *St John's Church* (1609).

The resort of **Ebensee** (426 m/1398 ft; pop. 10,000) lies at the S end of the lake.

Above the town, to the W, rears the Höllengebirge, with good skiing terrain on its bare rolling plateau. Facing it, on the SE side of the lake, is another little summer resort, *Rindbach*.

SURROUNDINGS. – From Gmunden-Weyer a cableway runs SE up the *Grünberg* (1004 m/3294 ft; guesthouse, restaurant). To the S (2½ hours' climb) is the *Traunstein (1691 m/5548 ft; two huts), which commands extensive views.

15 km/9 miles E of Gmunden, in the wide valley of the Alm, is the resort of *Scharnstein*, with a Schloss (c. 1600) which now houses the Austrian Museum of Criminal Law. 7 km/4½ miles S of Scharnstein is the summer resort of **Grünau** (527 m/1729 ft), a good climbing base, 6 km/4 miles S of which is the *Cumberland Wildlife Park* (brown bears, otters, beavers, etc.; research), with a restaurant and a Forestry Museum. The Alm valley road ends at the *Almsee* (859 m/2818 ft; accommodation), magnificently situated under the sheer N face of the Totes Gebirge (see p. 195); well-known echo.

8 km/5 miles SW of Altmünster, in a forest setting, is the *Hochkreut Wildlife Park*, with red deer, ibexes, bison, moufflons, etc., living in open enclosures.

To the W of Ebensee, between the Traunsee and the Attersee, is the **Höllengebirge**, a long straggling range of steep-sided hills (good skiing on plateau) which reaches its highest point in the *Grosser Höllenkogel (1862 m/6109 ft; Berghotel), to the W.

From Ebensee a road climbs 10 km/6 miles NW up the wooded *Langbathtal* to two lakes, the *Langbathseen (664 m/2179 ft and 753 m/2471 ft). – 15 km/9 miles SE of Ebensee, in a picturesque setting below the N face of the Totes Gebirge, is the little *Offensee* (651 m/2136 ft; restaurant; beautiful nature reserve).

Turracher Höhe

Länder: Styria (Stm) and Carinthia (K).

ⓘ **Gemeindeamt Reichenau,**
Haus Nr. 80, A-9565 Ebene-Reichenau;
tel. (0 42 75) 2 18.
Gemeindeamt Predlitz,
Haus Nr. 107, A-8863 Predlitz;
tel. (0 35 34) 2 62.
Branch, A-8864 Turrach;
tel. (0 35 33) 2 66.

ACCOMMODATION. – ON THE STYRIAN SIDE OF THE PASS
(A-8864): *Seehotel Jägerwirt,* A, 89 b., SB, sauna;
Seewirt, A, 76 b., SB, sauna; *Zemrosser,* B, 30 b., SB,
sauna; *Alpenrose,* B, 24 b., sauna; *Hiebl,* C, 30 b. – ON
THE CARINTHIAN SIDE OF THE PASS (A-9565): *Hochschober,*
A, 120 b., SB, sauna; *Alpengasthof Siegel,* C, 70 b. – IN
TURRACH: *Gasthaus Bergmann,* 22 b. – IN EBENE-
REICHENAU: *Reichenauerhof,* A, 60 b.; *Ski-Sepp,* C, 12 b.

The *Turracher Höhe (1763 m/5784 ft)
lies at the western tip of Styria on
the pass over the Gurktal Alps into
Carinthia. A favourite skiing resort, it
is also popular in summer as a base for
walks in the wooded surrounding area.
On the S side of the pass there are
still stretches of road with gradients
up to 26%.

In the wide high valley round the summit of
the pass are the *Schwarzsee* and the
Turracher See, surrounded by wooded
slopes with good snow in winter which are
now being developed as a skiing area, with
numerous lifts. A chair-lift runs up the
Kornock (2000 m/6560 ft), and there are
good climbs of other peaks in the Nock area.
To the S of the pass is the *Grünsee.*

On the Turracher See

SURROUNDINGS. – To the N the road descends
(gradients of up to 8%) through **Turrach** (1269 m/
4164 ft; pop. 500) to the upper *Mur valley.* – To the S
(gradients of up to 26%), in the uppermost reaches of the
Gurk valley, is the resort of **Ebene-Reichenau** (1062 m/
3484 ft; pop. 2200), with much good walking and skiing
country (several lifts). From here there are good climbs
(each taking several hours) to the *Falkertsee* (1765 m/
5791 ft), the *Kruckenspitze* (1886 m/6188 ft), the
Hochrindhütte (1580 m/5184 ft), etc. – *Bad Kleinkirchheim:* see under Millstätter See.

Upper Austria

Bundesland: Oberösterreich (OÖ). – Capital: Linz.
Area: 11,979 sq. km/4625 sq. miles.
Population: 1,280,000.

ⓘ **Oberösterreichisches
Landesfremdenverkehrsamt,**
Schillerstrasse 50, A-4020 Linz;
tel. (07 32) 66 30 21.
Oberösterreichisches Landesreisebüro,
Hauptplatz 9, A-4020 Linz;
tel. (07 32) 2 71 06 10.

**The province of Upper Austria extends
from the Dachstein massif to the
Bohemian Forest (Böhmerwald) and
from the Inn to the Enns, bounded on
the W by the Federal Republic of
Germany (Bavaria), on the N by
Czechoslovakia, on the E by Lower
Austria, on the S by Styria and on the
SW by Salzburg province. It consists
of the Mühlviertel, the Danube valley,
the Alpine foreland zone and the high
mountain region.**

Upper Austria is drained by the Danube and
its tributaries, the Inn, the Traun and the
Enns on the S and the Mühl, the Rodl, the
Gusen, the Aist and the Naarn on the N.
There are a number of large lakes including
the Attersee, the Traunsee, the Wolfgangsee,
the Mondsee and the Hallstätter See in the
Salzkammergut and many smaller lakes, as
well as a number of moorland lakes in the
upper Innviertel.

The province's main industries are the heavy
industry of Linz (VOEST steelworks, using
Styrian iron ore), the manufacture of commercial vehicles at Steyr, the production of
nitrogen and cellulose at Linz, the Ranshofen
aluminium works, salt-working at Hallstatt,
Bad Ischl and Ebensee, the Danube hydroelectric power station at Jochenstein (run
jointly with Bavaria) and other hydroelectric
schemes on the Danube, the Inn, the Enns
and the Mühl, papermaking, hardware,
textiles and woodworking, and the working
of small reserves of oil in the Innviertel and

natural gas at Wels. Agriculture and forestry are also well developed. And finally tourism makes a major contribution to the economy, particularly in the Salzkammergut, the Traunviertel and the area served by the Pyhrnbahn.

HISTORY. – In prehistoric times Upper Austria was more thinly settled than Lower Austria, although traces of Palaeolithic occupation have been found on the old road northward over the Pyhrn pass, along the Krems valley to Linz and on to České Budějovice in Czechoslovakia. The province became more populous only with the coming of the *Celts*, who began to work the great deposits of salt and created the more advanced Iron Age culture named after *Hallstatt*, then the principal salt-working area (material in the Hallstatt museum).

The *Roman period* brought intensive settlement (place-names in "Walchen") along the Danube and in the fertile upland regions, particularly around Wels. After the battle of Augsburg in 955 the region, which had been converted to Christianity at an early date by missionaries from Passau, was finally secure against invasion from the E. New settlers were now brought in, mainly by the Bishops of Passau and the noble family of Wels-Lambach, later Margraves of Steyr.

Although Upper Austria was now safe from further attacks from the E, it suffered from the conflicts between the Habsburgs and Bavaria which were fought out here. In the first half of the 15th c., too, the territories N of the Danube suffered under Hussite raids; and Upper Austria was also ravaged by the *Peasant Wars* of 1525 and 1625 (stories of the popular hero Fadinger, the Frankenburger Würfelspeil).

During the 17th c. the region saw much fighting between opposing armies. The various wars of succession with Bavaria brought further battles, but also, in 1779, the acquisition of the Innviertel (which was temporarily occupied by the Bavarians during the Napoleonic wars but returned to Austria by the Congress of Vienna in 1815).

The revolutions of 1848 and 1918 passed more quietly in Upper Austria than in other parts of the country. It was largely unscathed by the Second World War, with the exception of Linz and Steyr, which suffered heavy air raids. After the war, in spite of occupation by two Allied powers (the Soviet Union N of the Danube, the United States to the S), its economy recovered relatively rapidly, and since then Upper Austria has shared the destinies of the rest of Austria.

ART. – In addition to rich finds of *prehistoric* (Hallstatt), *Roman* and early Christian material Upper Austria possesses major works of art and architecture from all the main artistic periods of later centuries.

The *Romanesque* period is represented by parts of the monastic churches of Wilhering (near Linz), Lambach, Kremsmünster and Baumgartenberg and the charnel-house at Mauthausen.

There are also numerous examples of *Gothic* art and architecture, such as the parish churches of Steyr, Enns, Braunau and Eferding, the castles of Prandegg, Schaunburg and Ruttenstein, burghers' houses at Steyr, Enns, Wels and Freistadt, fine winged altars at Kefermarkt. St Wolfgang, Hallstatt, Waldburg and Gampern, pictures by Altdorfer at St Florian and frescoes in the church of St Leonhard near Pucking. The *Renaissance* created handsome burghers' houses in Wels, Steyr and Linz, the Schlösser of Aistersheim, Würting, Greinburg and Weinberg, the Landhaus in Linz and the Stadtturm in Enns.

Baroque and *Rococo* buildings, both religious and secular, can be seen at Reichersberg, Schlierbach, Schlägl, Waldhausen, Garsten, Gleink, Suben, Ranshofen, Kremsmünster, Spital am Pyhrn, St Florian, Engelszell, Wilhering, Stadl-Paura, Linz, Steyr and Christkindl. There are also fine Baroque Schlösser at Hohenbrunn, Aurolzmünster, Neuwartenberg and Zell an der Pyhrnbahn. Two families of Baroque artists, the Schwanthalers and the Guggenbichlers, have left much work in Upper Austria.

Schlägl Abbey (Mühlviertel)

There are buildings of the *Empire* and *Biedermeier* periods at Bad Ischl and Ebensee. – Mention should also be made of the ceramics of Gmunden, the carving of Hallstatt and the folk-style woodcarving of Viechtau.

In the N of Upper Austria is the **Mühlviertel** (see p. 141), named after its principal rivers, the Kleine and Grosse *Mühl*. This is a plateau of ancient rocks which rises gradually towards the N and merges into the Bohemian Forest. The valleys are mostly fertile and, particularly in the S, sunny and warm; the slopes of the hills are largely forest-covered. From the summits there are beautiful far-ranging views, particularly towards the S, where the Alps rear up above the plain of the Danube and the Traun like a great wall, grandly marking the boundary of the province with their lofty peaks. A number of hydroelectric projects have been developed in the Mühlviertel, adding a new and attractive note to the landscape with their beautiful artificial lakes. This is a region for quiet and relaxing holidays, with an abundance of good walking.

A very different pattern is presented by the second of the province's main regions, the **Danube valley** (see p. 65). The river, already mighty and navigable when it enters Upper Austria from Bavaria, flows through the province for a distance of some 155 km/ 95 miles. Between Passau and Linz it is constricted within a narrow valley, which opens out beyond Linz. It then continues through the densely populated Strudengau to the boundary of Lower Austria.

Between the Danube and the northern slopes of the Alps, in the **Alpine foreland**, are the most fertile regions of Upper Austria and also its main industrial areas. In this zone is the *Innviertel*, with low ranges of hills rising between beautiful valleys. – Between the Innviertel and the *Traunviertel* is the rather harsher *Hausruckviertel*, in which lignite is mined.

Along the line of an old geological fault lie several spas with mineral springs which are used for curative purposes – Bad Schallerbach (sulphur springs), Bad Hall (brine springs containing iodine and bromine, used in the treatment of eye conditions), Gallspach, Neydharting (peat baths), Weinberg (chalybeate spring) and Gmös (peat baths).

In the heart of the Alpine foreland region is the provincial capital, **Linz** (see p. 124), with its important industrial installations.

To the S of the Pre-Alpine zone is a very attractive *upland region*, with large and beautiful *lakes set amid expanses of forest and green meadowland, under a grandiose mountain world edged by tremendous rock walls. Along the southern edge of this zone, the *Salzkammergut (see p. 173), rise the mighty peaks of the Northern Calcareous Alps, their rugged walls falling sheer down to the plain and the lakes. To the S of the Salzkammergut (named after the salt which has been worked here since time immemorial), on the borders of Styria, the mountain region begins.

The **Dachstein group**, with its limestone peaks rising to 3000 m/9800 ft and its great glaciers, extends into three Austrian provinces – Salzburg and Styria as well as Upper Austria. In its northern foothills are the famous **Dachstein Caves, one of the province's outstanding tourist attractions.

To the W of the deep furrow of the upper Traun valley and the Pötschen pass is the *Totes Gebirge (see p. 195), which extends to the Steyr valley and the Pyhrn pass. This great stone wilderness, ranging between 8 and 12 km/5 and 7½ miles in width and edged by rugged cliffs and steep walls of rock, is well named the Totes Gebirge ("Dead Mountains").

The imposing gorge-like *Stodertal* was opened up to tourist traffic only by the construction of the Pyhrnbahn.

The main traffic routes of Upper Austria run from W to E, like the Salzburg–Linz–Vienna railway line and the motorway which now runs parallel to it. The Danube, too, accompanies the railway from Passau via Linz to Vienna, and an attractive way of seeing Upper Austria is a trip down river on one of the Danube ships (see under Danube Valley). The busiest N–S routes are those leading into the Salzkammergut, over the Pyhrn pass into Styria and up the Enns via Präbichl (Styria) into the Mur valley.

The Pyhrn pass road, from Wels in the N or Liezen in the S, gives access to a tourist region which has become well known as the *Pyhrnbahngebiet* (Pyhrnbahn or Pyhrn Cableway area). Within the triangle formed by the cableways of Spital am Pyhrn, Hinterstoder and Windischgarsten winter visitors, whether skiing enthusiasts or less active vacationers, will find every facility they require; and these facilities are equally well adapted to meet the needs of the walkers and climbers who come to the area in summer.

Upper Austria is rich in interesting NATURAL FEATURES. The most notable among the *caves* of the region are the famous Dachstein Caves (the Giant Ice Cave and the Mammoth Cave). At Ebensee on the Traunsee is the Gassl stalactitic cave, at Carbach the Rötlsee cave. There are also a whole series of picturesque *defiles and gorges*, including the Burgauklamm at the S end of the Attersee, the Gosauzwang near Hallstatt, the Koppenschlucht at Obertraun, the impressive gorge on the Steyr at Klaus, the Trattenbachfall near Spital am Pyhrn, the Traunfall at Gmunden, the Vogelsangklamm at Spital am Pyhrn and the Waldbachstrub near Hallstatt.

Verwall

Länder: Vorarlberg (V) and Tirol (T).
Altitude: Highest point: Kuchenspitze (3170 m/ 10,401 ft).
(i) **Österreichischer Alpenverein,**
Sektion Voralberg,
Langgasse 64, A-6830 Rankwell.
Sektion Landeck,
Ulrichstrasse 39, A-6500 Landeck.

The Verwall or Ferwall group is a range of mountains to the N of the Silvretta between the Klostertal, the Stanzer Tal, the Montafon and the Paznauntal. Consisting of several sub-groups separated by deeply slashed valleys, it is an area of boldly formed peaks flanked by small glaciers, steep rock walls and hollows containing pretty little lakes (the Valschavielsee, the Versailsee, the Blankaseen).

To the N the Arlberg pass provides a link with the Lechtal Alps and the world-famous skiing area on the Arlberg. There are good paths between the various mountain huts, but the higher peaks in the Verwall group call for experience and practice in rock climbing.

The highest peak in the range, the **Kuchenspitze** (3170 m/10,401 ft), with its five dark jagged pinnacles, and the imposing *Patteriol* (3059 m/10,037 ft) can be climbed from St Anton am Arlberg by way of the Konstanzer Hütte (1768 m/5801 ft). The dolomitic peak of the *Seekopf* (3063 m/ 10,050 ft) and the easier *Saumspitze* (3034 m/9955 ft) can be climbed from the Darmstädter Hütte (2426 m/7960 ft).

From the Reutlinger Hütte (2398 m/7868 ft), near Klösterle on the Arlbergbahn (Klostertal), the magnificent *Pflunspitzen* (2916 m/ 9567 ft) and the easy *Eisentaler Spitze*

(2757 m/9046 ft) can be climbed. A superb viewpoint is the *Hoher Riffler** (3168 m/ 10,394 ft), which can be climbed from the Edmund-Graf-Hütte (2408 m/7901 ft) near Pettneu am Arlberg.

One of the finest cross-country routes in the Verwall group is from Stuben am Arlberg by way of the Kaltenberg-Hütte (2100 m/ 6890 ft) up the *Kalter Berg* (2900 m/ 9515 ft).

In the southern part of the range, accessible from St Anton am Arlberg, is the Heilbronner Hütte (2320 m/7612 ft), situated on the *Scheidsee* in an excellent skiing area. This is an important staging point on the popular route through the Verwall to the Silvretta group.

Vienna (Wien)

Land: Wien (W).
Altitude: 170 m/558 ft. – Population: 1,520,000.
Post code: A-1010 (Bezirk I) to A-1230 (Bezirk XXIII).
Telephone code: 02 22.
Before arrival in Vienna (postal enquiries only):
(i) **Wiener Fremdenverkehrsverband,**
Kinderspitalgasse 5, A-1095 Wien.
tel. 43 16 08.

Information
Arrival by car:
Autobahn A1 (Westautobahn)
Exit Wien-Auhof,
April–Oct. 8 a.m.–10 p.m., Nov.–March 10 a.m.–
6 p.m.
Autobahn A2 (Südautobahn)
Exit Zentrum (Triester Strasse),
July–Sep. 8 a.m.–10 p.m., Apr.–Oct. 9 a.m.–7 p.m.
Arrival by rail:
Westbahnhof (upper hall)
Südbahnhof (lower hall)
Arrival by air:
Wien-Schwechat Airport Arrival Hall
Daily 9 a.m.–10 p.m., June–Sep. 9 a.m.–11 p.m.
For boat passengers:
DDSG-Schiffsstation, Wien-Reichsbrücke
May–Sep. 8–9 p.m.
While in Vienna:
Official Tourist Information in the
Opernpassage, daily 9 a.m.–7 p.m.
tel. 43 16 08.
Information on Austria
(*Österreich-Information*),
IV, Margaretenstrasse 1, Mon.–Fri. 9 a.m.–5 p.m.
tel. 57 57 14.

(Roman figures prefixed to addresses in Vienna refer to the Bezirke – districts, wards – of the city. See below, p. 209).

EMBASSIES. – *United Kingdom:* Reisnerstrasse 40, A-1030, tel. 73 15 75–79; consular section Wallnerstrasse 8, A-1010, tel. 63 75 02. – *United States:* Boltzmanngasse 16, A-1091, tel. 31 55 11. – *Canada:* Dr.-Karl-Lueger-Ring 10, A-1010, tel. 63 66 26–28.

HOTELS. – NEAR THE STAATSOPER (Opera House): *Imperial*, A1, I, Kärntner Ring 16, 277 b.; *Sacher*, A1, I, Philharmonikerstr., 4, 203 b.; *Bristol*, A1, I, Kärntner Ring 1, 190 b.; *Ambassador*, A1, I, Neuer Markt 5, 174 b.; *Astoria*, A, I, Kärntner Str. 32, 192 b.; *Europe*, A, I, Neuer Markt 3, 150 b.; *Römischer Kaiser*, A, I, Annargasse 16, 46 b.
NEAR STEPHANSPLATZ: *Royal*, A, I, Singerstr. 3, 143 b.; *Kaiserin Elisabeth*, A, I, Weihburggasse 3, 130 b.; *Am Stephansplatz*, A, I, Stephansplatz 9, 108 b.; *Graben*, A, I, Dorotheergasse 3, 86 b.; *Wandl*, B, I, Petersplatz 9, 223 b.; *Schweizerhof*, B, I, Bauermarkt 22, 150 b.
NEAR THE STADTPARK: *Hilton International Wien*, A1, III, Landstrasser Hauptstr. 2, 1200 b.; *Inter-Continental Vienna*, A1, III, Johannesgasse 28, 990 b.; *Vienna Marriott*, A1, I, Parkring 12a, 560 b.; *Biedermeier im Sünnhof*, A, III, Landstrasser Hauptstr. 28, 420 b.
NEAR DANUBE CANAL: *Stefanie*, A, II, Taborstr. 12, 240 b.; *Capricorno*, A, I, Schwedenplatz 3–4, 79 b.; *Ring*, A, I, Am Gestade 1, 50 b.; *Post*, B, I, Fleischmarkt 24, 200 b.
NEAR RATHAUS: *De France*, A, I, Schottenring 3, 320 b.; *Regina*, A, IX, Roosevelt Platz 16, 232 b.; *Weisser Hahn*, A, VIII, Josefstädter Str. 22, 107 b.; *Academia*, A, VIII, Pfeilgasse 3a, 672 b. (student residence open as a hotel 1 July to 30 September).
S OF KARLSPLATZ: *Erzherzog Rainer*, A, IV, Wiedner Hauptstr. 27, 148 b.; *Kaiserhof*, A, IV, Frankenberggasse 10, 143 b.; *Clima Cityhotel*, A, IV, Theresianumgasse 21a, 78 b.
IN SCHWARZENBERGPLATZ: *Palais Schwarzenberg*, A1, III, Schwarzenbergplatz 9, 80 b.
IN MARIAHILFER STR. AND NEAR WESTBAHNHOF (West Stn.): *Bohemia*, A, XV, Turnergasse 9, 200 b.; *Kummer*, A, VI, Mariahilfer Str. 71a, 165 b.; *President*, A, VI, Wallgasse 23, 160 b.; *Savoy*, A, VII, Lindengasse 12, 82 b.; *Tyrol*, A, VI, Mariahilfer Str. 15, 68 b.; *Wimberger*, B, VII, Neubaugürtel 34, 173 b.; *Münchnerhof*, B, VI, Mariahilfer Str. 81, 160 b.; *Fuchs*, B, XV, Mariahilfer Str. 138, 120 b.
NEAR SÜDBAHNHOF (South Station): *Hungaria*, A, III, Rennweg 51, 310 b.; *Prinz Eugen*, A, IV, Wiedner Gürtel 14, 165 b.; *Kongress*, B, IV, Wiedner Gürtel 34, 80 b.; *Südbahn*, C, IV, Weyringer Gasse 25, 50 b.
AT PRATERSTERN STATION: *Nordbahn*, B, II, Praterstr. 72, 140 b.; *Capri*, B, II, Praterstr. 44–46, 80 b.
NEAR FRANZ-JOSEFS-BAHNHOF: *Madeleine*, A, VII, Geblergasse 21, 150 b.; *Albatross*, A, IX, Liechtensteinstr. 89, 140 b., SB; *Bellevue*, A, IX, Althanstr. 5, 320 b.; *Westminster*, A, IX, Harmoniegasse 5, 120 b.; *Alpha*, A, IX, Boltzmanngasse 8, 112 b.; *Strudlhof*, A, IX, Pasteurgasse 1, 100 b.; *Mozart*, B, IX, Julius-Tandler-Platz 4, 96 b. – *Haus Döbling*, B, XIX, Gymnasiumstr. 85, 948 b. (Student House, open as hotel 1 July to 30 September).
W OF FLORIDSDORFER BRÜCKE: *Panorama*, A, XX, Brigittenauer Lände 224–228, 510 b., and *Haus Dr. Schärf*, C, XX, Lorenz-Müller-Gasse 1, 180 b. (Student residences, open as hotels from 1 July to 30 September).
IN OBERLAA: *Tourotel*, A, X, Kurbadstr. 2 (Spa Centre), 520 b., SB, sauna.
AT SCHÖNBRUNN: *Parkhotel Schönbrunn*, A1, XIII, Hietzinger Hauptstr. 10–14, 776 b., SB; *Novotel Wien-West*, A, XIV, Motorway Service Station Auhof, 228 b., SP; *Jagdschloss*, B, XIII, Jagdschlossgasse 79, 73 b., SP; *Ekazent*, B, XIII, Hietzinger Hauptstr. 22, 50 b.
IN DÖBLING: *Modul*, A1, XIX, Peter-Jordan-Str. 78–80, 83 b.; *Hohe Warte*, A, XIX, Steinfeldgasse 7, 71 b.
ON KAHLENBERG: *Kahlenberg*, A, XIX, Josefsdorf 1, 60 b. (beautiful view of city).
ON NUSSBERG (fine views): *Clima Villenhotel*, A1, XIX, Nussberggasse 2c, 70 b., SB, SP.
AT SCHWECHAT AIRPORT: *Novotel Wien-Airport*, A, 127 b.

GUEST-HOUSES FOR YOUNG and YOUTH HOSTELS. – *Jugendgästehaus Hütteldorf-Hacking*, XIII, Schlossberggasse 8, 300 b.; *Jugendgästehaus Wien-Brigittenau*, XX, Friedrich-Engels-Platz 24, 264 b.; *Jugendherberge Wien*, VII, Myrthengasse 7, 123 b.; *Ruthensteiner Jugendherberge*, XV, Robert-Hamerling-Gasse 24, 77 b.; *Turmherberge Don Bosco*, III, Lechnerstrasse 12, 50 b. (March–November). – Several CAMPING SITES.

RESTAURANTS. – in most hotels; also *Belvedere-Stöckl*, III, Prinz-Eugen-Str. 25 (with garden); *Kervansaray-Hummerbar*, I, Mahlerstr. 9; *Savoyengemächer*, XV, Schweglerstr. 37; *St Stephan im Haas-Haus*, I, Stock-im-Eisen-Platz 4; *Stadtkrug*, I, Weihburggasse 3; *Zum den Drei Husaren*, I, Weihburggasse 4; *Zum König von Ungarn*, I, Schulerstr. 10; *D'Rauchkuchl*, XV, Schweglerstr. 37; *Kupferdachl*, I, Schottengasse 7; *Sailer*, XVIII, Gersthofer Str. 14; *Wagenstein-Weisser Schwan*, IX, Nussdorfer Str. 59 (old-style Viennese restaurant); *Alte Schmiede*, I, Schönlaterngasse 9; *Chez Rainer*, IV, Wiedner Hauptstr. 27–29; *De France*, I, Schottenring 3; *Donauturm*, XXII, Donaupark (view); *Gösser Bierklinik*, I, Steindlgasse 4; *Gösser Bräu*, I, Elisabethstr. 3; *Griechenbeisl*, I, Fleischmarkt, on corner of Griechengasse (a famous and historic old restaurant with a small picture gallery); *Hauswirth*, VI, Otto-Bauer-Gasse 20; *Hubner's Kursalon*, I, Johannesgasse 33; *Thermen-Restaurant*, X, Kurbadstr. 14; *Schöner*, VII, Siebensterngasse 19; *Wiener Rathauskeller*, in New Rathaus; *Zum Laterndl*, I, Landesgerichtsstr. 12; and others. – Vegetarian: *Estakost*, IX, Währinger Str. 57; *Zum Weissen Rauchfangkehrer*, I, Weihburggasse 4; *Siddhartha*, I, Fleischmarkt 16; *Shalimar*, VI, Schmalzhofgasse 11. – Kosher: *Arche Noah*, I, Judengasse; *Orthodox Koscher-Restaurant*, II, Hollandstr. 3.

FOREIGN RESTAURANTS. – FRENCH: *Chez Robert*, XVIII, Gertrudplatz 4; *Salut*, I, Wildpretmarkt 3. – ITALIAN: *Grotta Azzurra*, I, Babenbergerstrasse 5; *Zum Grünen Anker*, I, Grünangergasse 10. – GREEK: *Mykonos*, I, Annagasse 7. – HUNGARIAN: *Mathias Keller*, I, Mayseder-gasse 2; *Ungar-Grill*, VII, Burggasse 97. – YUGOSLAV: *Balkan-Grill*, XVI, Brunnengasse 13, *Dubrovnik*, III, Am Heumarkt 5. – TURKISH: *Kervansaray*, I, Mahlerstrasse 9. – RUSSIAN: *Feuervogel*, IX, Alserbachstrasse 21. – CHINESE: *China-Pavillon*, XV, Winckelmannstr. 38; *Lotus-Haus*, I, Jasomirgottstr. 3. – INDIAN: *Taj Mahal*, Nussdorfer Str. 33.

WINE-CELLARS. – (often serving excellent food). – *Bastei-Keller*, I, Stubenbastei 10; *Melker Stiftskeller*, I,

The Griechenbeisl restaurant

Schottengasse 3; *Piaristenkeller*, VIII, Piaristengasse 45; *Schottenkeller*, I, Freyung 6; *Urbanikeller*, I, Am Hof 12; *Zwölf-Apostel-Keller*, I, Sonnenfelsgasse 3; *Esterházykeller*, I, Haarhof 1.

BEISEL. – (typically Viennese eating places with plain cooking, good beer and local wine). – *Bastei Beisl*, I, Stubenbastei 10; *Beisl-Bar*, I, Himmelpfortgasse 24; *Blauen Steine*, VI, Wallgasse 32; *Figlmüller*, I, Wollzeile 5; *Fröhlich*, III, Erdbergstr. 38; *Glacisbeisl*, VII, in the Messepalast; *Gösserbierhaus*, I, Stubenbastei 2; *Hackerbräustuben*, IV, Rienösslgasse 10; *Jägerstüberl*, XVIII, Gersthofer Str. 70; *Kern*, I, Wallnerstr. 3; *Kleiner Brathauskeller*, I, Rathausstr. 10; *Mathiaskeller-Schwemme*, I, Maysedergasse 2; *Müllerbeisl*, I, Seilerstätte 15; *Ofenloch*, I, Kurrentgasse 8; *Weinhaus Schleimer*, XVI, Brunnengasse 67; *Weissgerberstube*, III, Landstrasser Hauptstr. 28; *Zipfer-Stüberl*, I, Dominikaner Bastei 22; *Zöbinger Weinstube*, I, Drahtgasse 2/Am Hof; *Zum Amalienbad*, X, Buchergasse 64; *Zum alten Deutschmeister*, I, Börsengasse 15; *Zum Hollunderstrauch*, I, Schreyvogelgasse 3; *Zur Post*, XVI, Koppstr. 86; *Zur Stadt Krems*, VII, Zieglergasse 37; etc.

HEURIGENSCHÄNKEN. – "Heuriger" is the most recently made wine, and when wine-producers in the Vienna area are serving this new wine they hang out a bunch of green leaves. The following is a selection of wine-shops (with music) selling "heuriger" throughout the year. – IN THE CENTRAL AREA: *Feuchter Stock*, I, Jasomirgottstrasse 3. – IN GRINZING: *Hengl Karl*, XIX, Himmelstrasse 7; *Weinbottich*, XIX, Cobenzlgasse 28; *Muhr Karl*, XIX, Cobenzlgasse; *Bach-Hengl*, XIX, Sandgasse 9; *Figlmüller*, XIX, Grinzinger Strasse 55; *Rockenbauer Otto*, XIX, Sandgasse 12; *Altes Haus*, XIX, Himmelstrasse 35; *Cobenzl*, XIX, Am Cobenzl 96; *Reinprecht Hugo*, XIX, Cobenzlgasse 22. – IN NUSSDORF: *Spitzbuben*, XIX, Hackhofergasse 13; *Kierlinger Martin*, XIX, Kahlenberger Strasse 20. – IN HEILIGENSTADT: *Pfarrplatz-Mayer*, XI, Pfarrplatz 2. – IN OTTAKRING: *Zehner-Marie*, XVI, Ottakringer Strasse 224.

CAFÉS. – There are numerous cafés (often with tables outside in summer) in Vienna, where coffee has been served since 1683 (*Coffee Museum* of the Jacobs company in the industrial zone of Wien-Auhof, XIV, Jacobsgasse 3). There are also excellent cafés in the outer districts. The following is a selection of cafés in the middle of the city. – *Sacher* (see hotel, famous for "Sachertorte"); *Europa* (see hotel); *Landtmann* (an old-established and famous café), Dr.-Karl-Lueger-Ring 4, opposite the Burgtheater; *Mozart*, Albertinaplatz 2; *Prückel*, Stubenring 24; *Schwarzenberg*, Kärntner Ring 17; *Museum* (with music and art gallery), Friedrichstrasse 6; *Central*, Herrengasse 14; *Hawelka*, Dorotheergasse 6 (frequented by artists); *Imperial*, Kärntner Ring 16; *Dom-Café*, Stephansplatz 9; *Raimund*, Museumstr. 6a; *Volksgarten*, in Volksgarten; etc. – *Imbisstube Trzésniewski*, Dorotheergasse 1 (highly seasoned savoury sandwiches).

KONDITOREIEN. – (cake-shops) in the middle of the city: *Demel*, Kohlmarkt 14 (Old Vienna atmosphere); *Heiner*, Kärntner Strasse 21 and Wollzeile 9; *Lehmann*, Graben 12 and Mariahilfer Str. 137; *Gerstner*, Kärntner Str. 15; *Haag*, Schottengasse 2.

The **Viennese café** is a famous and historic institution. The first café is said to have been established by Frans Georg Kolschitzky, a Pole who is supposed to have brought coffee captured from the Turks to Vienna in 1683 and was granted the right to sell coffee in the city in 1685. (His establishment was at Domgasse 6.) The

A Glossary of Viennese Coffee

The ordering of coffee in a Vienna café is an art in itself: the customer is expected to specify exactly how he wants his coffee to be served. Visitors may find the following vocabulary useful.

The basis of every cup of Viennese coffee is **Mokka** (mocha). If you ask simply for "coffee" (*Kaffee*), you will usually get a "Brauner" (see below). Coffee is always accompanied by a glass of water, and it is perfectly normal to ask for another glass, or even several extra glasses.

Brauner (kleiner, grosser)	"brown" (small or large): with little milk
Dunkel	"dark": with little milk
Einspänner	hot coffee with whipped cream, served in a glass
Eiskaffee	cold coffee, served in a glass, with vanilla ice-cream, whipped cream and a wafer
Espresso (*Es*)	machine-made espresso
Fiaker	a "grosser Schwarzer", served in a glass
Gestreckt	diluted with water
Gold	a golden-brown "Melange"
Kaffee ohne Kaffee	"coffee without coffee" (caffein-free)
Kaffee verkehrt	"coffee the wrong way round": little coffee but plenty of milk
Kaisermelange	"Schwarzer" with yolk of egg
Kapuziner	"Capuchin": dark brown "Melange"
Konsul	"Schwarzer" with a dash of cream
Kurz	"short": very strong
Licht	"licht": with a lot of milk
Mazagran	a glass of cold coffee with maraschino, ice-cubes and a straw
Melange	"mixture": medium dark
Mokka	strong black Viennese coffee
Mokka gespritzt	coffee with a dash of brandy
Nusschwarzer	"nut-black": Mokka
Obers	cream
Obers gespritzt	cream with a dash of coffee
Portion Kaffee	coffee with a jug of milk, to be mixed according to taste
Schale	cup
Schlag(obers)	whipped cream
Schwarzer (kleiner, grosser)	black coffee (small or large)
Schwarzer gespritzt	coffee with a dash of rum
Teeschale	cup of milk
Teeschale Obers gespritzt	cup of cream with some coffee
Türkischer	Turkish coffee boiled in a small copper coffee-pot (along with sugar if taken)
natur	unfiltered
passiert	filtered
Weisser	"white": caffein-free coffee

café soon developed into a regular feature of public and social life, providing newspapers and games as well as coffee. In the Biedermeier period in particular the cafés developed into luxuriously appointed establishments, and later in the 19th c. the elegant cafés on the Ring were built. The café now became the meeting-place of artists, writers, scholars and journalists; and although something of the glory departed with the fall of the Austro-Hungarian monarchy the Viennese café is still a popular meeting-place, with newspapers and magazines always available for the use of customers.

Since the Second World War the modern *espresso bar* has become popular in Vienna. This is usually a small establishment, patronised by those who want a quick cup of coffee and perhaps a snack.

There are also many *Café-Konditoreien* (coffee- and cake-shops), with a tempting assortment of cakes and pastries, and *café-restaurants* with a more substantial bill of fare.

EVENTS. – (see also Museums, etc., below). – Brilliant season of *balls* (Opera Ball); *Shrovetide* celebrations (January to March); *Viennale Film Festival* (March); *Vienna Festival* (*Wiener Festwochen*, mid May to mid June: opera, ballet, drama, concerts, exhibitions); *Floral Procession in the Prater* (June); *Wiener Musik-Sommer* (music festival: July and August); *Schubert Festival* (around 19 November, anniversary of the composer's death); *Antiques Fair* (November); *Christkindlmarkt* (December); **Vienna International Trade Fairs** (*Spring Fair* in March, *Autumn Fair* in November).

Theatres, concerts (Vienna Philharmonic, Vienna Symphony Orchestra, Vienna Boys' Choir), exhibitions, Spanish Riding School, etc.: see monthly programme of events published by the Vienna Tourist Office.

THEATRES. – (closed in summer). – FEDERAL THEATRES: **Staatsoper** (opera, ballet), I, Opernring 2; **Burgtheater** (plays), I, Dr.-Karl-Lueger-Ring 2; **Volksoper** (opera, operettas, musicals), IX, Währinger Strasse 78; **Akademietheater** (plays), III, Lisztstrasse 1.
PRIVATELY OWNED THEATRES: **Theater an der Wien** (musicals, operettas), VI, Léhargasse 5; **Theater in der Josefstadt** (contemporary light plays), VIII, Josephstädter Strasse 26; **Kammerspiele** (comedies, satire), I, Rotenturmstrasse 20; **Volkstheater** (plays, avantgarde pieces), VII, Neustiftgasse 1; **Raimundtheater** (operettas, musicals), VI, Wallgasse 18–20; **Wiener Kammeroper** (operas, singspiels), Fleischmarkt 24 (entrance in Drachengasse); **Kleine Komödie** (light plays), I, Wallfischgasse 4.

Theatre tickets are traditionally obtained through hotel porters. There are also a number of small ticket agencies in the heart of the city.

LITTLE THEATRES: *Arlequin* (puppet theatre) in Café Mozart near the Opera, I, Meysedergasse 5; *Ateliertheater am Naschmarkt*, VI, Linke Wienzeile 4; *Die Komödianten* (theatre in the Künstlerhaus), I, Karlsplatz 5; *Ensemble-Theater* (at the Petersplatz rendezvous), I, Petersplatz 1; *Experiment am Lichtenwerd*, IX, Liechtensteinerstr. 132; *Freie Bühne Wieden*, IV, Wiednerhauptstr. 60b; *Herbert Lederer's Theater am Schwedenplatz*, I, Franz-Josefs-Kai 21; *Intime Bühne*, I, Franz-Josefs-Kai 29; *Kaberett "Der bunte Wagen"* im *Simpl*, I, Wollzeile 36; *Letztes Wiener Stegreiftheater* (open-air stage), VI, Maroltingergasse 43; *Pawlatschen in der Hackhofergasse* ("Spitzbuben" cabaret), XI, Hackhofergasse 13; *Pradltheater Ritterspiele*, I, Bibergasse 2; *Serapionstheater*, XX, Wallensteinplatz 6;

Theater am Belvedere, IV, Mommsengasse 1; *Theater beim Auersperg*, VIII, Auerspergstr. 17; *Theater der Courage*, I, Fleischmarkt 22; *Theater "Die Tribüne"* (Café Landtmann), I, Dr.-Karl-Lueger-Ring 4; *Theater im Kopf*, IX, Porzellangasse 19.

CONCERT HALLS. – **Musikverein** (the home of the Vienna Philharmonic), I, Bösendorferstrasse 12 (entrance Dumbastrasse 3); *Konzerthaus*, III, Lothringer Strasse 20; *Funkhaus des Österreichischen Rundfunks* (Radio House), IV, Argentinierstrasse 30a.

OTHER EVENTS. – **Wiener Stadthalle** (sport, music), XV, Vogelweidplatz; **Messepalast**, VII, Messeplatz 1; *Palais Pálffy* (Austrian Cultural Centre), I, Josefsplatz 6; *Internationales Kulturzentrum*, Palais Erzherzog Karl, I, Annagasse 20 (concerts, readings, lectures); *Alte Schmiede*, I, Schönlaterngasse 9 (readings, discussions, exhibitions); *Hochschule für Musik und Darstellende Kunst* (Academy of Music and Dramatic Art), I, Seilerstätte 26, and III, Lothringer Strasse 18; *Konservatorium* (Conservatoire), I, Johannesgasse 4a.

CINEMAS. – consult daily press.

DANCING. – *Chattanooga*, I, Graben 29a; *Club Take Five*, I, Annagasse 3a; *Fledermaus*, I, Spiegelgasse 2; *Moulin Rouge*, I, Walfischgasse 11; *Scotch Dancing*, I, Parkring 10.

DISCOTHÈQUES. – *Can-Can*, IX, Währinger Gürtel 96; *Capt'n Cook*, I, Franz-Josefs-Kai 23; *King's Club*, I, Plankengasse 6; *Tangente*, I, Augustinerstr. 12; *Queen Anne*, I, Johannesgasse 12.

NIGHT BARS. – *Edenbar*, I, Liliengasse 2; *Eve*, I, Führichgasse 3.

JAZZ. – *Jazzland*, I, Franz-Josefs-Kai 29; *Z-Club*, VII, Kirchengasse 23; *Jazz-Spelunke*, VI, Dürergasse 3.

CASINO. – Cercle Wien (roulette, baccarat, blackjack; daily from 7 p.m.), Palais Esterházy, I, Kärntner Strasse 41.

The famous Viennese **horse-cabs** (*Fiaker*) ply for hire during the summer. There are cab ranks in Heldenplatz, Petersplatz and Kohlmarkt, outside the Albertina and at the Opera House. The fare varies according to the type of cab, route and time of day: a firm price should be agreed with the driver before setting out.

CITY SIGHTSEEING TOURS. – Varied programmes of tours are offered by *Wiener Rundfahrten*, III, Stelzhamergasse 4 (tel. 72 46 83–0) and *Cityrama Sightseeing Rundfahrten*, I, Börsegasse 1 (tel. 63 66 19–0).

TRIPS ON THE DANUBE. – *Round trips* daily (from Schwedenbrücke(by MFS "Vindobona"; *evening trips* with various themes (nostalgia, wine-tasting, disco dancing) from 8.30 p.m.; excursions via Linz to Passau and, from May to October, to the Wachau; from April to October hydrofoils to Bratislava (Czechoslovakia) and Budapest (Hungary); by Soviet ships (cabins) to the Black Sea.

SIGHTSEEING FLIGHTS. – Daily in good weather conditions from 9 a.m. to 5 p.m. (in summer until 6 p.m.) from Wien-Schwechat Airport (tel. 67 94 54).

Best look-out points

Türmerstube in St Stephen's Cathedral
Outlook terraces on Kahlenberg, Leopoldsberg and Höhenstrasse
Donauturm in Donaupark
Upper Belvedere
Giant Wheel (Riesenrad) in Prater
Gloriette in Schönbrunn park

Shopping and Souvenirs

The PRINCIPAL SHOPPING STREETS in the central area (Bezirk I) are the Kärntner Strasse (between the Opera intersection and Stock-im-Eisen-Platz), the Graben (between Stock-im-Eisen-Platz and Kohlmarkt), the Kohlmarkt (between the Graben and Michaelerplatz) and Rotenturmstrasse (between Stephansplatz and Franz-Josefs-Kai); and in Bezirk VI the Mariahilfer Strasse (between the Messepalast and the Westbahnhof).

PEDESTRIAN ZONES: Kohlmarkt – Graben – Kärntner Strasse (between Weihburggasse and Walfischgasse) in the central area and Favoritenstrasse (between Reumann-platz and Columbusplatz) in Bezirk X.

Viennese *craft products*, following old traditions of craftsmanship, are valued for their beauty and quality. Particularly popular are petit point work, hand-painted Augarten porcelain, jewelry and goldsmith's work, hand-made dolls, fine ceramic ware, enamel and wrought-iron, and leather goods of all kinds.

Collectors and art-lovers will find the *antique shops* of Vienna an inexhaustible source of treasure trove; and the city's secondhand bookshops and art dealers offer a tempting range of valuable old books, prints, etchings and pictures.

Art Nouveau (Jugendstil) antiques

Art auctions are held in the State-run Dorotheum (I, Dorotheergasse 17) and in a number of large art galleries and antique dealers. The items to be sold can be viewed before the sale, and the starting prices and auction timetable are indicated.

Viennese fashion, internationally renowned for elegance and chic, is an essential element in the Viennese way of life. The Fashion School in Schloss Hetzendorf provides training for promising young fashion designers.

The *Naschmarkt* is a traditional food market held on weekdays on the covered-over section of the River Wien between the Linke Wienzeile (Bezirk VI) and the Rechte Wienzeile (Bezirk IV).

Flea Market (Flohmarkt): on Naschmarkt on Saturdays (except public holidays) from 9 a.m. to 6 p.m.

RECREATION and SPORTS. – *Stadion* (Stadium) and *Hallenstadion* (Covered Stadium; Krieau); *tenpin bowling* (Prater); *water sports* (Alte Donau, Donaukanal); *trotting races* (Krieau), *flat racing* (Freudenau), *riding*; *gliding* (school in Wiener Neustadt) and *flying* (Schwechat, Aspern); *golf* and *polo* (Freudenau); *tennis* (Kurhalle Oberlaa); *skating*, etc. (Donauparkhalle); *fitness training* (Kurzentrum Oberlaa, Diana-Zentrum).

**Vienna (Wien), capital of the Repub-lic of Austria, lies at the foot of the Wienerwald (Vienna Woods), the north-easterly foothills of the Alps, on the banks of the Danube, which here emerges, up to 285 m/310 yds wide, into the Vienna basin and some 50 km/ 30 miles downstream enters Czecho-slovakia at Bratislava. This situation at the intersection of the old traffic routes from the Baltic to the Adriatic and from the Alpine foreland to the Hungarian plain made Vienna the gate-way for trade between the different provinces which meet here and the natural nucleus of the Habsburg empire with its far-ranging territories, extending from the Alps and the Bohe-mian Forest by way of the Danube valley to the Carpathians.

Although Vienna is the smallest in area of the Austrian provinces it is the most densely populated and the most heavily industrial-ised, and is thus, in spite of its peripheral location in present-day Austria, very much the metropolis and the political, economic, intellectual and cultural hub of the Republic. It is also the see of a Roman Catholic arch-bishop (Cardinal König) and the head-quarters of a number of international organisations.

In recent years Vienna has played some part as a mediator between East and West, and has been the venue of many top-level inter-national meetings and countless conferences and congresses, while continuing to attract hosts of visitors throughout the year with its great tourist sights and its busy programme of entertainments and events. One of the world's great tourist cities of unmistakably cosmopolitan atmosphere, it still retains a distinctive charm and a native flair of which – no less than of the notable elegance of Viennese women – every visitor is at once aware.

HISTORY. – The earliest traces of human settlement in the Vienna basin date from the Neolithic period. In the 3rd millenium B.C. Indo-European peoples moved in from the N. The Illyrian population of the early Iron Age (from about 800 B.C.) was overlaid from about 400 B.C. by *Celts* coming from the W (late Iron Age), and there was probably a Celtic stronghold on the Leopoldsberg. – About A.D. 50 the *Romans* built the fortified military camp of **Vindobona** (from Celtic *Vedunia*, "stream") on their Danube frontier. Its walls enclosed a rectangular area bounded on the W and N by the steeply scarped edge of the Tiefer Graben and the Salzgries, on the E by Rotgasse and Kramergasse and on the S by the Graben and Naglergasse. In the course of the 1st c. a civilian town began to develop on the slopes of the Belvedere, a site occupied since Bronze Age times, lying at the intersection of the route through the valley of the River Wien with the route along the higher W bank of the Danube (the main course of which then followed roughly the line of the present Donaukanal). The Emperor Marcus Aurelius died in Vindobona in the year 180. – The Roman period came to an end in 487, when, on the advice of St Severinus, the remains of the Roman population abandoned the Danube area to the Germanic peoples who had for centuries been pressing in from the N.

In 792, according to tradition, Charlemagne founded St Peter's Church in the course of his campaign against the Avars. In 881 the Bavarians had their first clash with the Hungarians pushing forward from the E at **Wenia**; and a number of Bavarian settlements, identified by the ending *-ing* (Grinzing, Ottakring, Hacking, etc.), had been established by the end of the 9th c. Vienna itself was then only a village huddled in the ruins of the Roman fort. During the Crusades, from 1096 onwards, it acquired some importance as the last German settlement on the road to the East, and by 1137 we find it referred to as a town. In 1156 Duke Henry II Jasomirgott moved his court from the Leopoldsberg to Vienna, which thus became the capital of the Babenberg territories in the Ostmark (Eastern March). In 1158 the Schottenstift was founded, on a site which then lay outside the town walls, to provide accommodation for pilgrims. About 1190 Leopold V established a mint in Vienna. The minnesinger Walther von der Vogelweide lived at the ducal court from 1194 to 1198 and again at some time before 1217. Vienna now rose to prosperity through the production of wine and the trade with the East which passed along the Danube and from 1200 also through Venice. By this period the town had reached the boundaries which remained those of the inner city until 1859. In 1237 the Emperor Frederick II, then locked in conflict with the last Babenberg duke, also called Frederick, granted Vienna the status of *Reichsunmittelbarkeit* (direct subordination to the Emperor), but this grant was not confirmed by Duke Frederick after his return in 1239. After the Duke's death the duchy was ruled from 1251 to 1276 by King Ottokar II of Bohemia, who promoted the development of Vienna.

The ideas of the humanists and the Renaissance gave rise in Vienna, as elsewhere, to a great flowering of intellectual and artistic life. In 1522, however, Ferdinand I executed the burgomaster of Vienna, Siebenbürger, and destroyed the town's aspirations for freedom; and in 1529 he deprived it of its right of self-government. From

22 September to 15 October of that year, under the leadership of Count Niklas Salm, the town held out stoutly against a siege by the *Turks*. In 1551 the first Jesuits arrived in Vienna. From 1559 it was the seat of the government of the Empire and from 1612 the permanent residence of the Imperial court. By the beginning of the 17th c. the town had a population of 25,000.

The *Reformation* was combated by Melchior Khlesl (Bishop from 1598) and completely suppressed by Ferdinand II during the *Thirty Years War*, when Vienna was almost taken by Bohemian, Hungarian and Swedish forces on no less than five occasions. The period of the *Counter-Reformation*, when Vienna was subject to influences from Rome, saw the building of many churches in early Baroque style: between 1620 and 1630 alone eight monasteries were founded in Vienna. In 1679 an epidemic of plague carried off some 12,000 citizens.

From 14 July to 12 September 1683 a force of 200,000 *Turks* under the Grand Vizier Kara Mustafa laid siege to the town, which was heroically defended by 11,000 troops and 5000 members of the citizen militia under the leadership of Count Ernst Rüdiger von Starhemberg. The siege was finally raised by a relieving army of 75,000 men (Imperials, Saxons, Franconians, Bavarians, Swabians and 13,000 Poles) under the leadership of Duke Francis of Lorraine (although nominally commanded by King John Sobieski of Poland), advancing from the Kahlenberg.

After the removal of the Turkish danger Vienna rapidly developed into a brilliant Baroque city, on a scale matching its importance as capital of the Empire. By about 1700 the population had risen to over 100,000. In 1686 the first professional firemen were appointed; in 1688 two thousand street lamps were erected. In order to protect the suburban areas with their numerous noble palaces against attack by the rebellious Hungarians the Linienwall was constructed by the citizens under the direction of Prince Eugene – a rampart which served as a toll barrier until 1893. In 1703 the first daily newspaper appeared. Art and learning flourished under aristocratic patronage. In 1722 the bishopric was raised to the status of an archbishopric.

During the reigns of *Maria Theresa* (1740–80) and *Joseph II* (1780–90) the reform and centralisation of the Imperial administration benefited the capital, though it was deprived of its remaining powers of self-government in 1783. The Viennese love of music and the theatre, however, tied great composers like Gluck, Haydn, Mozart and Beethoven firmly to the capital.

In 1806, during the reign of Francis I, Vienna ceased to be capital of the Holy Roman Empire. About 1800 it had a population of 230,000. In 1805 and again in 1809 it was briefly occupied by the French. During the *Congress of Vienna* (1814–15) and the following decades Metternich made it one of the focal points of European politics and of the reaction against liberal and nationalist aspirations. Music and painting enjoyed a further flowering in the Biedermeier period (roughly 1815–48).

The Danube Shipping Company was founded in 1831; the first railway line from Vienna (the Nordbahn) was built in 1837. Metternich's rule and the tight control exercised by his police were swept away by the ruthlessly suppressed Revolution of March 1848.

During the long reign of the Emperor *Francis Joseph* (1848–1916) Vienna – which recovered its powers of self-government in 1849 – lived through the age of developing technology. In 1850 the suburban districts as far as the Linienwall were incorporated in the city. The vigorous building activity which now followed gave Vienna a handsome new ring road on the line of the old fortifications (pulled down between 1858 and 1868) but also led to a rapid growth of the city without any unified plan. The result was to create very much the Vienna which we see today. In 1865 the first horse-drawn tramway was brought into operation, in 1873 the first water supply scheme from the mountains. In 1851 the population of the city was 431,000, in 1890 (after the incorporation of Districts XI–XIX) 1,364,500, in 1910 2,031,500.

After the First World War Vienna, no longer the nucleus of an empire of 50 million people of twelve different nationalities, became the over-large capital of a small state confined to the Alpine and Danube regions which had to struggle to preserve its great cultural heritage from the past. It faced further difficulties during the Nazi period (1938–45), suffering damage by air attack during the Second World War, and during the post-war occupation by the four victorious Allied powers (division into four occupation zones), but these difficulties were overcome by the vigour and resolution of the people of Vienna, particularly after the signing of the Staatsvertrag and the withdrawal of the occupying forces in 1955.

Vienna is now the headquarters of the International Atomic Energy Authority (IAEA), the United Nations Industrial Development Organisation (UNIDO), the Organisation of Petroleum Exporting Countries (OPEC) and the UNESCO International Music Complex.

The **population** of Vienna, the basic element in which was the Bavarian settlement from the Carolingian period onwards, has shown a powerful capacity to absorb other population groups. Gifted individuals were regularly attracted to Vienna from the Alpine territories and from Bohemia; and from an early period there was a steady influx from Franconia and Swabia. The Slav, Dutch and Italian incomers who were drawn to Vienna by the Babenberg, and particularly the Habsburg, rulers were absorbed into the German cultural sphere and in turn contributed to it. From their manifold contacts with other peoples the citizens of Vienna developed a lively feeling for form and beauty, a natural openness of disposition and curiosity, a cheerful acceptance of life which enabled them to face difficulties with grace and equanimity. The Viennese enjoyment of life encompasses both intellectual and physical pleasures at the same time. Viennese wit is sharp, but is not aimed at destruction. The 19th c. Viennese playwright Nestroy always saw through the externals of comedy to the serious core of things – a Viennese characteristic which lends a touch of melancholy to so many Viennese creations, in music and poetry as in other fields.

The close association between the city and its natural setting is reflected in the down-to-earth naturalness of many aspects of Viennese life. The proverbial Viennese charm turns out on the whole to be somewhat superficial: when occasion arises the local dialect can put things very bluntly. And the people of Vienna are credited with a notable capacity for grumbling when things go wrong.

Intellectual Life. – Vienna's place in German *literature* is ensured by such figures as Walther von der Vogelweide, the 17th c. preacher Abraham a Sancta Clara and the 19th c. dramatists Ferdinand Raimund, Johann Nestroy and Franz Grillparzer. In the field of *education* it came to the fore at a very early period, and it has preserved its attraction for the peoples of SE Europe to the present day. The city has a number of universities and technical

View from Rathaus tower (Burgtheater in foreground)

colleges, and research is catered for by the Academy of Sciences and various important libraries and archives. The public education system is well organised. The *arts* are securely rooted in the gifts and the interest of the population, and fostered by the government and a variety of associations, successors to the princes and nobles who were the patrons of art in earlier centuries. Visitors will find a rich fund of interest and enjoyment in the theatres and concerts, the museums and exhibitions of Vienna.

The city. – With a total area of 404 sq. km/156 sq. miles, the city is divided into 23 Bezirke (districts or wards) numbered I–XXIII. Its layout reflects its long historical development, with some streets still following the pattern of the Roman town.

The *central area* (District I) corresponds to the ducal town of the Middle Ages, cramped within its defensive walls, and the effect of this constriction can still be seen in the height of the buildings and the depth of the cellars of Vienna. Of the medieval structure of the town, however, little is left. There are a few Gothic churches, notably St Stephen's Cathedral which rears up majestically in the old town.

The pattern of the inner city is set by its fine Baroque buildings, in particular the Imperial residence, the Hofburg, which bounds the old town on the W, and numerous palaces of the nobility. Among predominantly Baroque streets and squares are the Josefsplatz, Dr.-Ignaz-Seipel-Platz (formerly Universitätsplatz), Bankgasse and a number of streets opening off the E side of Kärntner Strasse. Neo-classical and Biedermeier buildings are found here and there, particularly in the Hoher Markt and Seilerstätte.

To the N and S of the central area, extending outward to the Ring, are buildings of no great architectural merit dating from the 19th c. development of the area occupied by the former fortifications.

One peculiarity of Vienna, particularly in the inner city, is the large number of passages or lanes (*Durchhäuser*) running through a whole block from one street to another. Some of these alleys are throbbing with life; others afford glimpses of quiet old houses and courtyards.

The central area is surrounded by the monumental buildings and the gardens of the *Ring*, the area developed between 1859 and 1888 on the site of the old fortifications and surrounding glacis which linked up the heart of the medieval town with the older suburbs.

Beyond the Ring and the Donaukanal (Danube Canal) to the NE extends a circuit of *inner suburban districts* (Districts II–IX). In this area many Baroque summer palaces of the nobility were built after the removal of the Turkish threat in 1683, but the pattern of these districts is now largely set by middle-class houses of the Biedermeier period. In the Alsergrund district (Bezirk IX) is a large complex of modern buildings, the General Hospital.

These districts are circled on the N, W and S, at a distance of 1·5–2 km/1–1¼ miles from the Ring, by the broad *Gürtelstrasse* with its gardens and open spaces, an outer ring road laid out from 1893 onwards on the line of the old Linienwall.

Round the Gürtelstrasse are the *outer suburban districts*, which reach up through the valleys to the W and NW (Districts XIII–XIX) to the vineyards and wooded hills of the Wienerwald (Vienna Woods), with the Höhenstrasse to the Kahlenberg. Within these districts can still be found the remains of old villages and numbers of country

houses of the Biedermeier period and late 19th c. The palace of Schönbrunn (District XIII), Maria Theresa's country residence, was completely engulfed by the advancing tide of houses in the 19th c. District XI also preserves something of a country atmosphere; but District X, extending towards the Wiener Berg on the S side of the city, is a predominantly industrial area developed from the middle of the 19th c. One quite recent development, dating only from the 1970s, is the Kurzentrum (health or treatment complex) of Wien-Oberlaa on the Laaer Berg.

The **Danube** now flows through the central area of Vienna only in the form of the *Danube Canal* (Donaukanal), first regulated in 1598. The main river was embanked between 1868 and 1877 and flanked on the E by a flood zone 500 m/550 yds wide; a relieving canal is now under construction. The Danube proper is spanned by two railway bridges (the Nordbahnbrücke and the Stadtlauer Ostbahnbrücke), four road bridges (the Nordbrücke; the Floridsdorfer Brücke, rebuilt 1977–78; the Reichsbrücke, collapsed in 1976, rebuilt by 1980; and the Praterbrücke) and two bridges carrying mains and pipelines; there are also two small ferries.

Below the Reichsbrücke the river is flanked by wide expanses of meadowland, laid out as a park in the *Prater* but still more or less in their natural state in the *Lobau*.

Between the *Alte Donau* (Old Danube), an abandoned arm of the Danube, and the main river is the *Donaupark*, with the Donauturm (Danube Tower) and the modern complex of *UNO-City*.

Below the junction of the Danube Canal with the river is the *Port* of Vienna, still in course of development (to the right the Alberner Hafen, to the left the oil port of Lobau, at the beginning of the still unfinished Danube–Oder Canal).

To the E of the Danube are the industrial suburb of Floridsdorf (District XXI, with some residential areas), which grew up from the 19th c. onwards, incorporating a number of older villages, and Donaustadt (District XXII), reaching eastward to the Marchfeld.

In general the opening times on public holidays are the same as on Sundays.

Most places are closed on 1 January, Good Friday, Easter Day, 1 May, Whit Sunday, Corpus Christi, 1 and 2 November, and 24 and 25 December.

The opening times shown may not apply in the case of special exhibitions. All times are subject to alteration: for up-to-date information apply to the municipal Tourist Information Offices.

Academy of Fine Art (*Akademie der bildenden Künste*),
I, Schillerplatz 3.
Picture Gallery: Tue., Thu. and Fri. 10 a.m.–2 p.m., Wed. 10 a.m.–1 p.m. and 3–6 p.m., Sat. and Sun. 9 a.m.–1 p.m.
Print Cabinet: Mon. and Wed. 10 a.m.–1 p.m., Tue. and Thu. 2–6 p.m., first half of July, second half of Aug. and Sep., Mon.–Fri. 9 a.m.–1 p.m.; closed mid July to mid Aug.
Library: Mon., Wed. and Fri. 9 a.m.–4 p.m., Thu. 9 a.m.–6 p.m. and first half of July, second half of Aug. and Sep. (Mon.–Fri. 9 a.m.–1 p.m.); closed mid July to mid Aug.

Albertina,
I, Augustinerstrasse 1.
Collection of Graphic Art: Mon., Tue. and Thu. 10 a.m.–4 p.m., Wed. 10 a.m.–6 p.m., Fri. 10 a.m.–2 p.m., Sat. and Sun. 10 a.m.–1 p.m.; closed Sun. in July and Aug.

Library: Mon.–Thu. 1–4 p.m.; closed July and Aug.
Goethe Museum: Mon., Tue. and Thu. 10 a.m.–4 p.m.,
Wed. 10 a.m.–6 p.m., Fri. 10 a.m.–2 p.m., Sat. and Sun.
10 a.m.–1 p.m.; closed Sun. in July and Aug.
Austrian Film Museum: Demonstrations Oct.–May,
Mon.–Sat. 6 and 8 p.m.

Alpine Garden: see Oberes Belvedere.

Alte Backstube (*Old Bakehouse*),
VIII, Lange Gasse 34.
Tue.–Sat. 12 noon to midnight, Sun. 3 p.m. to midnight.

Alte Schmiede (*Old Smithy*),
I, Schönlaterngasse 9.
Mon.–Fri. 9 a.m.–3 p.m.

Altes Rathaus (*Old Town Hall*): see Museum of
Austrian Liberation.

Ankeruhr: see Kunstuhr.

Archives of Vienna Philharmonic
(*Archiv der Wiener Philharmoniker*),
I, Bösendorferstrasse 12.
Open to students by appointment (tel. 6 55 09 72).

Arms and Armour Collection: see Neue Hofburg.

Army Museum (*Heeresgeschichtliches Museum*),
Exhibits of Austrian Military History from the 30 Years War
to the First World War.
III, Arsenal, Objekt 18.
Daily except Fri. 10 a.m.–4 p.m.

Augustinerkirche: see Habsburg Vault.

Austrian Gallery: see Unteres Belvedere.

Austrian Gallery of 19th and 20th Century Art: see
Oberes Belvedere.

Hermann Bahr Memorial Room: see National Library.

Baroque Museum: see Unteres Belvedere.

Eduard von Bauernfeld Memorial Room,
The writer (1802–1890), born in Vienna, wrote many
comedies.
Villa Wertheimstein,
XIX, Döblinger Hauptstrasse 96.
Sat. 3.30–6 p.m. and Sun. 10 a.m.–12 noon.

Beethoven Memorial Houses,
VI, Laimgrubengasse 22; May–Sep., Sun. 10 a.m.–
12 noon.
XIX, Probusgasse 6 (Heiligenstädter-Testament-Haus),
also Döblinger Hauptstrasse 92 (Eroica-Haus); Tue.–Fri.
10 a.m.–4 p.m., Sat. 2–6 p.m., Sun. and public holidays
9 a.m.–1 p.m.

Beethoven Memorial Rooms,
I, Mölkerbastei 8 (Pasqualatihaus). Tue.–Fri. 10 a.m.–
4 p.m., Sat. 2–6 p.m., Sun. and public holidays 9 a.m.–
1 p.m.

Beethoven Tomb: see Central Cemetery.

Bell Museum (*Glocken-Museum: Pfundner Collection*),
X, Troststrasse 38.
Seen by appointment (tel. 64 25 43).

Belvedere: see Oberes Belvedere and Unteres Belvedere.

Botanic Garden,
III, Mechelgasse 2 (near Rennweg).
Mid Apr. to mid Oct., daily from 9 a.m. to dusk.

Brahms Tomb: see Central Cemetery.

Burgkapelle: see Hofburg.

Burgtheater,
I, Dr.-Karl-Lueger-Ring 2.
Conducted tours Mon.–Sat. at 9 a.m., 3 and 4 p.m.,
Sun. at 11 a.m., 1, 2 and 3 p.m. (telephone enquiries
54 24–21 80).

Burial Museum (*Bestattungsmuseum*),
IV, Goldeggasse 19.
Mon.–Fri. 12 noon–3 p.m. by appointment
(tel. 65 16 31–2 27).

Cathedral and Diocesan Museum
(*Dom- und Diözesanmuseum*),
I, Stephansplatz 6 (first floor).
Wed.–Sat. 10 a.m.–4 p.m., Sun. and public holidays
10 a.m.–1 p.m.

Central Cemetery (*Zentralfriedhof*),
XI, Simmeringer Hauptstrasse 234.
Tombs of Beethoven, Brahms, Mozart, Schubert, Strauss,
Stolz, etc.
Jan., Feb., Nov. and Dec., 8 a.m.–5 p.m. (admission until
4.30 p.m.); Mar., Apr., Sep. and Oct., 7 a.m.–6 p.m.
(admission until 5.30 p.m.); May–Aug., 7 a.m.–7 p.m.
(admission until 6.30 p.m.).

Circus Museum (*Zirkus- und Clown-Museum*),
II, Karmelitergasse 9.
Wed. 5.30–7 p.m., Sat. 2.30–5 p.m., Sun. 9 a.m.–12 noon.

Clock Museum (*Uhrenmuseum*),
I, Schulhof 2.
Tue., Sun. 9 a.m.–12.15 p.m. and 1–4.30 p.m.

District Museums (*Bezirksmuseen*),
in many Vienna districts.
Information from district authorities.

Heimito von Doderer Memorial Room
(*Heimito-von-Doderer-Gedenkstätte*),
in *Alsergrund District Museum,*
IX, Währinger Strasse 43. Sun. 10 a.m.–12 noon.

Electropathological Museum
(*Elektropathologisches Museum*),
XV, Selzergasse 19.
By appointment (tel. 92 72 72).

Ephesus Museum: see Neue Hofburg.

Esperanto Museum (*International*),
I, Hofburg, Batthyánystiege, Michaelertor.
Mon., Wed. and Fri. 9 a.m.–3.30 p.m.

Fiaker-Museum,
XVII, Veronikagasse 12.
Every first Wed. in month 8 a.m.–1 p.m.

Figaro House: see Mozart Memorial Rooms.

Film Museum: see Albertina.

Fire Brigade Museum (*Feuerwehr-Museum*),
I, Am Hof 10 (Central Fire Station).
Sun. and public holidays 9 a.m.–12 noon.

Folk Museum (*Österreichisches Museum für Volks-
kunde*),
VIII, Laudongasse 15–19.
Tue.–Fri. 9 a.m.–3 p.m., Sat. 9 a.m.–12 noon, Sun. 9 a.m.–
1 p.m.
Library: Tue.–Fri. 9 a.m.–4 p.m.; closed July and Aug.

Sigmund Freud Museum,
IX, Berggasse 19.
Mon.–Fri. 9 a.m.–1 p.m., Sat., Sun. and public holidays
9 a.m.–3 p.m.

Geymüller-Schlössl (*Sobek Collection of clocks*),
XVIII, Pötzleinsdorfer Strasse 102.
Tue.–Fri. 10 a.m.–4 p.m. by appointment (tel. 47 31 39),
Sun. conducted tours at 11 a.m. and 3 p.m.; closed Dec.–
Feb.

Giant Wheel (*Riesenrad*),
II, Prater.
Mar. and Oct. daily 10 a.m.–10 p.m.; Apr.–Sep. 9 a.m.–
11 p.m.

Goethe Museum: see Albertina.

Grillparzer Memorial Room: see Historical Museum.

Grillparzer Memorial Room,
Hofkammerarchiv,
I, Johannesgasse 6.
Mon. 12.30–3.45 p.m., Tue. and Wed. 8.30 a.m.–
12.30 p.m., Thu. and Fri. 8.30 a.m.–3.45 p.m.

Gustinus-Ambrosi-Museum,
II, Augarten/Scherzergasse 1a.
Fri. and Sun. 10 a.m.–4 p.m.

Habsburg Vault (*Herzgruft der Habsburger*),
Augustinerkirche,
I, Augustinerstrasse 3.
Only on request (tel. 52 33 38).

Haus des Meeres (*House of the Sea*),
with *Vivarium Wien,*
VI, Esterházypark.
Daily 9 a.m.–6 p.m.

Haydn Museum (with Brahms Memorial Room),
VI, Haydngasse 19.
Tue.–Sun. 10 a.m.–12.15 p.m. and 1–4.30 p.m.

Historical Museum (*Historisches Museum der Stadt Wien*),
IV, Karlsplatz.
Tue.–Sun. 9 a.m.–4.30 p.m.
Grillparzer Memorial Room. Tue.–Sun. 9 a.m.–4.30 p.m.
Special exhibitions in the Hermesvilla, XIII, Lainzer
Tiergarten; Wed.–Sun. 9 a.m.–4.30 p.m.

Hofburg,
I, Michaelerplatz.
State Apartments: Mon.–Sat. 8.30 a.m.–4.30 p.m., Sun.
8.30 a.m.–1 p.m.
Hoftafel- and Silberkammer: Tue., Wed., Fri. and Sun.
9 a.m.–1 p.m.
Secular and Religious Treasuries: at present closed for
reconstruction. The most important exhibits are in the
Kunsthistorisches Museum.
Burgkapelle (I, Schweizerhof): conducted tours (min.
5 persons) mid Jan. to end June and mid Sep. to mid Dec.
Tue. and Thu. 2.30–3.30 p.m.
Mass in chapel beginning with Vienna Boys' Choir, Jan.
to end June and mid Sep. to end Dec., Sun. and feast days
at 9.15 a.m. (tickets must be obtained in advance).
Spanish Riding School: see entry below.
Neue Hofburg: see entry below.

Holy Trinity Church (*Kirche zur Heiligsten Dreifaltig-
keit*),
(after design by Fritz Wotruba),

XXIII, Mauer, corner of Georgsgasse/Reysergasse.
Open Tue.–Fri. 2–5 p.m., Sat. 2–8 p.m., Sun. 9 a.m.–5 p.m.;
Mass Wed. 8 p.m., Sat. 6.30 p.m., Sun. 9.30 a.m.

House of the Sea: see Haus des Meeres.

Imperial Vault (*Kaisergruft, Kapuzinergruft*),
I, Neuer Markt.
May–Sep., daily 9.30 a.m.–4 p.m., Oct.–Apr. 9.30 a.m.–
12 noon.

Islamic Centre (*Mosque – Islamisches Zentrum*),
XXI, Hubertusdamm 17.
Mon.–Thu. except at prayer times.

Jewish Museum (*Jüdisches Museum*),
XIX, Bauernfeldgasse 4.
Mon.–Thu. 8 a.m.–4 p.m., Fri. 8 a.m.–2 p.m., by
appointment (tel. 36 16 55).

Josephinum: see Museum of the Institute of History of
Medicine.

Emmerich Kálmán Memorial Room: see National
Library.

Kapuzinergruft: see Imperial Vault.

Kunsthistorisches Museum (*Museum of Art*),
I, Maria-Theresien-Platz.
Egyptian and Oriental Collection, Antiquities, Picture
Gallery, Sculpture and Applied Art, Coins and Medals:
Tue.–Fri. 10 a.m.–6 p.m., Sat. and Sun. 9 a.m.–6 p.m.
Special lighting in evening, Tue. and Fri. 6–9 p.m.

Lainzer Tiergarten (*Zoo*).
XIII.
Beginning of Apr. to beginning of Nov., Wed.–Sun. and
public holidays 8 a.m.–6 p.m.; in summer until dusk.
The path around the nearby Hermes Villa is also open in
winter (Wed.–Sun. 10 a.m.–4 or 5 p.m.).

Kunsthistorisches Museum (Museum of Art)

Lehár-Schlössl (*Schikaneder-Schlössl*),
XIX, Hackhofergasse 18.
Parties only by appointment (tel. 3 71 82 13).

Library of Academy of Fine Art: see Academy of Fine Art.

Library of Albertina: see Albertina.

Library of Austrian Folk Museum: see Folk Museum.

Library of Austrian Railways
(*Bibliothek der Österreichischen Bundesbahnen, ÖBB*),
II, Praterstern 3.
Mon.–Thu. 9 a.m.–3 p.m., Fri. 9 a.m.–12 noon.

Library of Federal Geological Institute
(*Bibliothek der Geologischen Bundesanstalt*),
III, Rasumofskygasse 23.
Open to students only, Mon. 1–4 p.m., Tue.–Fri. 8 a.m.–12.30 p.m.

Library of Museum of Applied Art: see Museum of Applied Art.

Library of Museum of Technology: see Museum of Technology.

Library of Parliament: see Parliament.

Library of Society of Music-Lovers
(*Bibliothek der Gesellschaft der Musikfreunde*),
I, Bösendorferstrasse 12.
Mon., Wed. and Fri. 9 a.m.–1 p.m.; closed July–Sep.

Lichtental Museum (*Pfarrmuseum Lichtental*),
IX, Marktgasse 40.
Telephone for appointment (tel. 34 73 01).

Lower Austrian Provincial Museum
(*Niederösterreichisches Landesmuseum*),
I, Herrengasse 9.
Tue.–Fri. 9 a.m.–5 p.m., Sat. 9 a.m.–2 p.m., Sun. 9 a.m.–12 noon.

Mechanical Clock
(*Kunstuhr, Ankeruhr*),
I, Hoher Markt 10–11.
Parade of figures, with music, daily at noon.

Memorial to the Fallen of the Austrian Struggle for Liberation
(*Gedenkstätte für die Opfer des Österreichischen Freiheitskampfes*),
I, Salztorgasse 6.
Mon. 2–5 p.m., Thu. 9 a.m.–12 noon, Sat. 9 a.m.–12 noon and 2–5 p.m.

Mozart Memorial Rooms,
"*Figaro*"-*Haus,*
I, Domgasse 5.
Tue.–Sun. 10 a.m.–12.15 p.m. and 1–4.30 p.m.

Mozart Monument: see St Marx Cemetery.

Mozart Tomb: see Central Cemetery.

Municipal Archives: see Rathaus.

Municipal Library: see Rathaus.

Museum of Applied Art
(*Museum für Angewandte Kunst*),
I, Stubenring 5.

Tue., Wed. and Fri. 10 a.m.–4 p.m., Thu. 10 a.m.–6 p.m., Sun. 10 a.m.–1 p.m.
Library: Tue., Wed. and Fri. 10 a.m.–4 p.m., Thu. 10 a.m.–6 p.m., Sun. 10 a.m.–1 p.m.

Museum of Art: see Kunsthistorisches Museum.

Museum of Austrian Culture: see Neue Hofburg.

Museum of the Austrian Struggle for Liberation
(*Museum des Österreichischen Freiheitskampfes*),
Altes Rathaus,
I, Wipplingerstrasse 8, Staircase 3.
Mon., Wed. and Thu. 8 a.m.–5 p.m.

Museum of Ethnography: see Neue Hofburg.

Museum of Harness
(*Museum für Hufbeschlag, Beschirrung und Besattlung*),
III, Linke Bahngasse 11.
Mon.–Thu. 1.30–3.30 p.m.

Museum of the Institute of History of Medicine
(*Museum des Institutes für Geschichte der Medizin*: *Josephinum*),
IX, Währinger Strasse 25/1.
Mon.–Fri. 9 a.m.–3 p.m.

Museum of Medieval Austrian Art (*Museum mittelalterlichter Österreichischer Kunst*): see Unteres Belvedere.

Museum of Modern Art (*Museum für Moderne Kunst*),
Palais Liechtenstein, IX, Fürstengasse 1.
Daily 10 a.m.–6 p.m. except Tue.

Museum of Technology
(*Technisches Museum für Industrie und Gewerbe*),
with the *Railway Museum* and the *Post and Telegraph Museum.*
XIV, Mariahilfer Strasse 212.
Tue.–Fri. 9 a.m.–4 p.m., Sat. and Sun. 9 a.m.–1 p.m.

Museum of 20th Century (*Museum des 20. Jahrhunderts*),
III, Schweizergarten.
Daily 10 a.m.–6 p.m. except Wed.

Musical Instruments Collection: see Neue Hofburg.

National Archives
(*Österreichisches Staatsarchiv, Haus-, Hof- und Staatsarchiv*),
I, Minoritenplatz 1.
Administrative Archives (I, Wallnerstrasse 6a),
Financial Archives (I, Himmelpfortgasse 8): Mon. and Thu. 8.30 a.m.–12.30 p.m., Tue. and Wed. 12.30–3.45 p.m., Fri. 8.30 a.m.–3.45 p.m.
Archives of Hofkammer (I, Johannesgasse 6): Mon. 12.30–3.45 p.m., Tue. and Wed. 8.30 a.m.–12.30 p.m., Thu. and Fri. 8.30 a.m.–3.45 p.m.
Military Archives (VII, Stiftgasse 2): Mon.–Fri. 8.15 a.m.–3.45 p.m.
Transport Archives (III, Aspangstrasse 33): Mon.–Fri. 8.30 a.m.–3.30 p.m.
Archives of the Republic (under construction; VII, Andreasgasse 7).
Grillparzer Memorial Room: see entry above.

National Library (Österreichische Nationalbibliothek),
I, Josefsplatz (closed in Sep.).
Library Hall: Mon.–Sat. 11 a.m.–12 noon; May–Oct.
exhibition, Mon.–Sat. 10 a.m.–4 p.m.
Printed Books (I, Neue Hofburg).
Manuscripts (I, Josefsplatz 1).
Map and Globe Collection (I, Josefsplatz 1).
Music Collection (I, Augustinerabtei 6).
Papyrus Collection (I, Augustinerabtei 6).
Portrait Collection and Picture Archives (I, Neue Hofburg).
Theatrical Collection (I, Hofburg).
Newspaper Room (I, Neue Hofburg).
Hermann Bahr, Emmerich Kálmán, Caspar Neher, Max Reinhardt, Hugo Thimig, Carl-Michael Ziehrer Memorial Rooms: all Tue. and Thu. 11 a.m.–12 noon after notice by telephone; tel. 52 16 84.

Natural History Museum (*Naturhistorisches Museum*),
I, Maria-Theresien-Platz.
Departments of Mineralogy and Petrography, Botany, Geology and Palaeontology, Zoology, Anthropology and Prehistory, Precious Stones Room and Children's Room: daily except Tue. 9 a.m.–6 p.m.

Caspar Neher Memorial Room: see National Library.

Neidhart Frescoes
Frescoes (*c.* 1400) restored in 20th c.
I, Tuchlauben 19.
Tue.–Sun. 10 a.m.–12.15 p.m. and 1–4.30 p.m.

Neue Galerie,
Stallburg,
I, Reitschulgasse 2.
Mon., Wed. and Thu. 10 a.m.–4 p.m., Sun. 9 a.m.–4 p.m.

Neue Hofburg,
I, Heldenplatz.
Collection of Old Musical Instruments, Collection of Arms and Armour and *Ephesus Museum*: Mon. and Wed.–Fri. 10 a.m.–4 p.m., Sat. and Sun. 9 a.m.–4 p.m.
Museum of Ethnography: Mon. and Thu.–Sat. 10 a.m.–1 p.m., Wed. 10 a.m.–5 p.m., Sun. 9 a.m.–1 p.m.; film shows at 10 a.m. and 12 noon on Sun.

Oberes Belvedere
Austrian Gallery of 19th and 20th Century Art (III, Prinz-Eugen-Strasse 27): Tue.–Sat. 10 a.m.–4 p.m., Sun. 9 a.m.–4 p.m.
Alpine Garden (III, Landstrasser Gürtel 1): Apr.–June 9 a.m.–6 p.m., July–Sep. 9 a.m.–4.30 p.m.

Opera House: see Staatsoper.

Parliament,
I, Dr.-Karl-Renner-Ring.
Conducted tours Mon.–Fri. 11 a.m. except when Parliament is sitting; July and Aug. Mon.–Fri. 11 a.m. and 3 p.m.
Library: Mon.–Fri. 9 a.m.–3.30 p.m.; closed July–Sep. and when Parliament is sitting.

Period Furniture Collection
(*Bundessammlung alter Stilmöbel*),
VII, Mariahilfer Strasse 88.
Tue.–Fri. 8 a.m.–4 p.m., Sat. 9 a.m.–12 noon.

Pfundner Collection: see Bell Museum.

Planetarium,
II, Prater, Hauptallee.
Demonstrations Sat., Sun. and public holidays 3 and 5 p.m.; demonstrations for children Sun. 9.30 a.m.
Special conducted visits by appointment (tel. 72 61 92) on Tue., Wed. and Thu. at 9, 10 and 11 a.m.

Popular Religious Art Collection
(*Sammlung Religiöse Volkskunst*),
I, Johannesgasse 8 (former Ursuline Convent).
Wed. 9 a.m.–3 p.m. and Sun. 9 a.m.–1 p.m.; closed July and Aug.

Postal and Telegraph Museum: see Museum of Technology.

Prater Museum,
II, Prater, Hauptallee.
Sat., Sun. and public holidays 2–6.30 p.m.

Railway Museum: see Museum of Technology.

Rathaus (*Town Hall*),
I, Rathausplatz (Information tel. 4 28 01).
Conducted tours Mon.–Fri. at 1 p.m.
Municipal and Provincial Archives (Staircase VI, first floor, Room 328): Mon.–Fri. 8 a.m.–6 p.m.
Municipal and Provincial Library, Printed Books (Staircase IV, first floor, Room 333): Mon.–Thu. 9 a.m.–6.30 p.m., Fri. 9 a.m.–4.30 p.m.; *Manuscripts and Music*: Mon.–Fri. 9 a.m.–3 p.m.

Max Reinhardt Memorial Room: see National Library.

Roman Remains *Am Hof,*
I, Am Hof 9.
Sat. and Sun. 11 a.m.–1 p.m.

Roman Remains under *Hoher Markt,*
I, Hoher Markt 3.
Tue.–Sun. 10 a.m.–12.15 p.m. and 1–4.30 p.m.

St Marx Cemetery (*Friedhof St Marx*),
(Mozart's gravestone),
XI, Leberstrasse 6–8.
May–Aug., daily 7 a.m.–7 p.m.; Apr. and Sep., 7 a.m.–6 p.m.; Oct.–Mar. 9 a.m.–dusk.

St Stephan's Cathedral (*Stephansdom*),
I, Stephansplatz.
Conducted tours: Mon.–Sat at 10.30 a.m. and 3 p.m., Sun. and public holidays at 3 p.m.
Evening tours: May–Sep., Sat., Sun. at 7 p.m. according to demand.
Catacombs: daily 10–11.30 a.m. and 2–4.30 p.m.
Tower (south tower): 1 Mar.–15 Nov. and 20 Dec.–7 Jan., daily 9 a.m.–4.30 p.m.
Pummerin (Bell in north tower; lift): daily 8 a.m.–5 p.m.

Schikaneder-Schlössl: see Lehár-Schlössl.

Schönbrunn Palace,
XIII, Schönbrunner Schlossstrasse.
State Apartments (conducted tours only): Oct.–Apr.,

daily 9 a.m.–12 noon and 1–4 p.m.; May–Sep., daily
9 a.m.–12 noon and 1–5 p.m.; July and Aug., conducted
tours with concert (beginnig 7.15 p.m.). Information
from the Kulturamt (Friedrich-Schmidt-Platz 5, A-1082
Wien).
Bergl-Zimmer (EG): beginning May to end Sep., daily
9 a.m.–12 noon and 1–5 p.m.
Wagenburg (conducted tours): May–Sep., Tue.–Sun.
10 a.m.–5 p.m.; Oct.–Apr., Tue.–Sun. 10 a.m.–4 p.m.
Historic carriages and sledges are exhibited in the former
Winter Riding School.
Gloriette: beginning May to end Oct., daily 8 a.m.–dusk;
closed beginning Nov.–end Apr.
Park: daily from 6 a.m.–dusk.
Zoo: open throughout the year, daily 9 a.m.–dusk (or
6 p.m. if earlier).

Schubert House (*Schubert-Sterbezimmer*),
The room in which Schubert died.
IV, Kettenbrückengasse 6.
Tue.–Sun. 10 a.m.–12.15 p.m. and 1–4.30 p.m.

Schubert Museum (birthplace),
IX, Nussdorfer Strasse 54.
Tue.–Sun. 10 a.m.–12.15 p.m. and 1–4.30 p.m.

Schubert Tomb: see Central Cemetery.

Sobek Collection: see Geymüller-Schlössl.

Spanish Riding School (*Spanische Reitschule*),
Hofburg,
I, Reitschulgasse 1.
Performances: Mar.–June and Sep.–Nov., Sun.
10.45 a.m. and Wed. 7 p.m., short programme Sat. 9 a.m.
(For departures from this timetable see the daily press or
the monthly programme of events.)
Demonstrations in historical costume: The riders wear
white leather breeches, black top boots, a brown frock
coat and a two-cornered hat with gold braid.
Morning training: Feb., Mon.–Sat. 10 a.m.–12 noon;
Mar.–June and Sep.–mid Dec., Tue.–Sat. 10 a.m.–
12 noon (or as announced in daily press or monthly
programme of events).

Staatsoper (*State Opera House*),
I, Opernring 2.
Conducted tours: July and Aug., daily 9 and 11 a.m.,
1 and 3 p.m.; Sep.–June (on days when there are no
rehearsals: enquiries tel. 53 24–24 80) Mon.–Sat. 2 and
3 p.m., Sun. 11 a.m., 1, 2 and 3 p.m.

Stadthalle (*Municipal Hall*),
XV, Vogelweidplatz 14.
Conducted tours by appointment only (tel. 95 49–0).

Stallburg: see Neue Galerie.

Steinhof Church (*Kirche am Steinhof*),
XIV, Baumgartner Höhe 1.
Guided tours: Sat. 3 p.m.; parties only by appointment
(tel. 94 31 51–23 97).

Adalbert Stifter Museum,
I, Mölkerbastei 8.
Tue.–Fri. 10 a.m.–4 p.m., Sat. 2–6 p.m., Sun. and public
holidays 9 a.m.–1 p.m.

Johann Strauss Museum (residence),
II, Praterstrasse 54.

Theatre Museum (*Österreichisches Theatermuseum*),
I, Hanuschgasse 3 (first floor).
Tue.–Sat. 10 a.m.–5 p.m., Sun. 9 a.m.–1 p.m.

Hugo Thimig Memorial Room: see National Library.

Tobacco Museum (*Tabak-Museum*),
VII, Mariahilferstrasse 2 (Messepalast).
Tue. 10 a.m.–7 p.m., Wed.–Fri. 10 a.m.–3 p.m., Sat. and
Sun. 9 a.m.–1 p.m.

Tramway Museum,
XVI, Maroltingergasse 53.
Mid May–Sep., Sun. 10 a.m.–12 noon.
Trips in old-time trams from Karlsplatz mid May–Sep.,
Sun. 3 p.m. (information tel. 57 31 86).

Treasuries: see Hofburg.

Treasury of Teutonic Order
(*Schatzkammer des Deutschen Ordens*),
I, Singerstrasse 7.
Daily 10 a.m.–12 noon; Tue., Wed., Fri and Sat. also
3–5 p.m.

University Library (*Universitätsbibliothek*),
I, Dr.-Karl-Lueger-Ring 1.
Closed: Sun. and public holidays, 2 Nov., Christmas
holidays, Maundy Thu. to Tue. after Easter, Whit Sat., Whit
Tue., Rector's Day and the month of Aug.

UNO-City: see Vienna International Centre.

Unteres Belvedere (*Lower Belvedere*),
III, Rennweg 6a.
Austrian Gallery, Museum of Medieval Austrian Art in the
Orangery and *Austrian Baroque Museum*: Tue.–Sat.
10 a.m.–4 p.m, Sun. 9 a.m.–4 p.m.

Urania Observatory (*Urania-Sternwarte*),
I, Uraniastrasse 1.
Wed., Fri. and Sat. at 8.30 p.m. and Sun. at 11 a.m.
Conducted visits when sky is clear.

In the Spanish Riding School

Vienna International Centre (*UNO-City*),
XXII, Donaupark.
Entrance Wagramer Strasse 23a.
Guided tours for individuals Apr.–Oct., daily at 11 a.m. and
2 p.m.; for parties previous notice is necessary.
(tel. 26 31–41 93 or 33 28).

Villa Wertheimstein: see Eduard von Bauernfeld
Memorial Room.

Virgil Chapel (*Virgilkapelle*)
and collection of historic Viennese porcelain,
I, Stephansplatz, underground station.

Vivarium Wien: see Haus des Meeres.

Otto Wagner House,
VII, Döblergasse 4.
Tue.–Fri. 10 a.m.–5 p.m.

Water Supply Museum (*Wasserleitungsmuseum der
Stadt Wien*),
In Kaiserbrunn (house no. 53).
May–Oct., Sun. 10 a.m.–12 noon.

Wine Museum (*Weinbaumuseum*),
in *Döblingen District Museum*,
XIX, Döblinger Hauptstrasse 96.
Sat. 3.30–6 p.m. and Sun. 10 a.m.–12 noon.

Carl Michael Ziehrer Memorial Room
(*Carl-Michael-Ziehrer-Erinnerungsraum*):
see National Library.

Some 200 of Vienna's most notable buildings and other
monuments of historical or architectural interest are
identified by plaques giving the essential information
about them. Fuller details are supplied in a helpful
booklet, "Wien: eine Stadt stellt sich vor" ("Introducing
Vienna"), available from bookshops.

CENTRAL AREA (INNERE STADT). –
The central point of the inner city is
the **Stephansplatz** (pedestrian precinct:
Romanesque chapel, brought to light
during construction of Underground), in
which stands ****St Stephen's Cathedral**
(*Stephansdom*), the finest Gothic building
in Austria. It has a High Gothic choir (1304–
40) and a late Gothic nave (1359–c. 1450),
with a steeply pitched roof covered with a
decorative pattern in glazed tiles (coat of
arms). The regularly tapering *S tower
(c. 1350–1433), popularly known as
"Steffl", is Vienna's principal landmark,
137 m/450 ft high to the tip of the spire;
visitors can climb to a height of 96 m/315 ft
(fine panoramic *views). In the unfinished
N tower (1467–1511; completed in Renaissance style 1556–78; elevator) is the great
bell known as the "Pummerin" ("Boomer"),
the largest in Austria (re-cast).

The oldest parts of the W front (the
Riesentor, "Giant's Doorway", and Heiden-
türme, "Heathens' Towers") are relics of an
earlier Romanesque church (13th c.). The N
and S doorways (Bischofstor and Singertor)

have fine High Gothic sculpture (c. 1370).
On the end wall of the choir is a figure
of about 1530 known as the "Zahnweh-
Herrgott" ("Our Lord with Toothache"). The
entrance to the Bishops' Vault (Bischofs-
gruft) and Catacombs (conducted visit
½ hour) is at the Adlertor. The Ducal
Vault (Herzogsgruft) contains the tombs of
Frederick the Handsome (c. 1330) and
Duke Rudolf IV, founder of the Cathedral
(d. 1365).

The oldest identifiable church on the site was a late
Romanesque basilica (13th c.). The choir was built by
Duke *Albrecht II* (1326–58), the nave by *Rudolf IV*
(1358–65), who secured the elevation of Vienna into an
episcopal see. Among the principal architects involved
in the building of the Cathedral were the Bohemian
Hans von Prachatitz (1429–33), who completed the S
tower, and *Hans Puchsbaum* (c. 1440–54), who roofed
the nave.

The spacious *INTERIOR (108 m/355 ft long, 35 m/
115 ft wide, nave 28 m/92 ft high) has more than 100

St Stephen's Cathedral

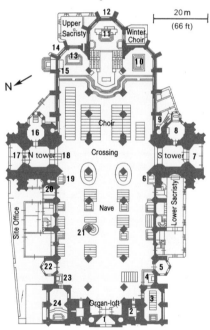

1 Riesentor (Giant's Doorway)	14 Capistranus Pulpit
2 Heidentürme (Heathens' Towers)	15 Monument of Rudolf IV
	16 St Barbara's Chapel
3 Chapel of St Eligius; above, St Bartholomew's Chapel	17 Porch
	18 Entrance to Catacombs
4 Baldachin with Pötschen Madonna	19 Organ-loft by A. Pilgram (with portrait bust of Pilgram)
5 Singertor	20 Lift to "Pummerin"
6 Baldachin by H. Puchsbaum	21 Pulpit by A. Pilgram (with figure of Pilgram looking out of window)
7 Porch	
8 St Catherine's Chapel	
9 Access to tower	22 Bischofstor (Bishop's Doorway)
10 Tomb of Frederick III	
11 High altar (by T. and J. J. Pock)	23 Baldachin by H. Prachatitz
12 "Our Lord with Toothache"	24 Tirna Chapel; above, Treasury Chapel
13 Wiener Neustadt Altar	

statues on the pillars (in N and principal choirs *c.* 1320, in S choir *c.* 1350, in nave 1450–1500), which have preserved their colouring, and numerous *Baroque altars.* In the nave is a magnificent late Gothic sandstone *pulpit (1510–15) by Anton Pilgram. On the pillar bearing the pulpit is the *Dienstbotenmadonna* ("Servants' Madonna"), a Gothic figure of *c.* 1340. On the N side of the nave, near the entrance to the Catacombs, is an organ-loft with a bust of Anton Pilgram (1513). At the W end of the N aisle is a chapel containing the *tomb of Prince Eugene* (d. 1736). In the principal choir is a Baroque high altar of black marble (1640–47); in the N choir are the *Wiener Neustadt Altar* (1447) and many *notable monuments*; and in the S choir is the red marble Gothic *tomb of the Emperor Frederick III (d. 1493), by Nik. Gerh. von Leyden (d. *c.* 1473), completed in 1517. The *organ*, rebuilt (1960) after its destruction during the last war, has 10,000 pipes.

Dimensions. – Length: externally 107 m/350 ft, internally 100 m/330 ft. – Width across transepts (externally) 70 m/230 ft; nave (interior) 35 m/115 ft. – Height: N tower 65 m/215 ft, S tower 137 m/450 ft.

Largest bell: "Pummerin" (19·8 tons), a reproduction of the original bell of 1711, destroyed in 1945.

From Stephansplatz *Rotenturmstrasse* leads NE towards the Danube Canal. At the corner between Stephansplatz and the Wollzeile is the **Archbishop's Palace** (*Erzbischöfliches Palais*), originally the presbytery, which was rebuilt between 1631 and 1641 in restrained Baroque style; it now houses the *Cathedral and Diocesan Museum*. To the SE, at Domgasse 5, is a small *Mozart Museum*.

Adjoining Stephansplatz on the SW is *Stock-im-Eisen-Platz* (pedestrian precinct), at the meeting of three streets, the Graben, Singerstrasse and Kärntner Strasse. In a niche in an office block of 1890 at the corner of Kärntner Strasse is the *Stock im Eisen*, first recorded in 1533, an old fir stump studded with nails hammered in by travelling journeymen.

The Graben, which until the 13th c. marked the SW boundary of the town, is a wide shopping street (pedestrian precinct). In the middle of the street is the **Pestsäule** (*Plague Column*) or *Trinity Column*, of Salzburg marble, 21 m/69 ft high, erected in 1682–94; designed by J. B. Fischer von Erlach the Elder, who also carved the reliefs on the base; clouds by Lodovico Burnacini; rich sculpture decoration of gilded copper representing the plague of 1679 by Paul Strudel, M. Rauchmiller and others. W and E of the column are two fountains with lead figures of SS Joseph and Leopold (by Johann Martin Fischer, 1804).

To the N of the Graben is the square known as Am Hof; from the far end the Kohlmarkt (closed to cars) runs SW to the Michaelerplatz.

Off the Graben to the right **St Peter's Church** (*Peterskirche*), traditionally believed to have been founded by Charlemagne in 792, was rebuilt between 1702 and 1733, probably by J. L. von Hildebrandt, on a centralised plan with a mighty dome; the charming little temple which forms the doorway was added by Andrea Altomonte in 1751. On the E wall is a large marble relief (by Rudolf Weyr, 1906) of Charlemagne as founder of the Ostmark (Eastern March) and of the church. The lofty interior has a painting in the dome by Michael Rottmayr (1714).

N of the Graben by way of Bognergasse is the square called Am Hof, where Roman remains have been excavated under the Fire Brigade headquarters (Fire Brigade Museum at No. 9). On the E side of the square is the **Kirche am Hof** (originally Gothic, 1386–1403; façade of 1662), from the terrace of which the dissolution of the Holy Roman Empire was proclaimed on 6 August 1806. Opposite the choir of the church, at Schulhof 2, is a *Clock Museum* (Uhrenmuseum).

NW of Am Hof is another square known as the *Freyung*, which owes its name to the right of sanctuary enjoyed by the old Schottenkloster, a convent of Scottish-Irish monks. On the NW side of the square is the Baroque **Schottenkirche** (12th c., rebuilt 1638–48), with a vault containing the tombs of Count Rüdiger von Starhemberg (d. 1701), who defended Vienna against the Turks in 1683, and Duke Henry Jasomirgott (d. 1177). Behind the church are the extensive buildings of the monastic house, the *Schottenstift* (Gothic altar by a Viennese artist known as the Schottenmeister; Romanesque chapel; Schottenhof, 1826–32). Opposite the church, to the S, are the *Palais Kinsky*, an elegant Baroque palace by J. L. von Hildebrandt (1713–16), and the *Harrachsches Palais* (*c.* 1690; restored 1948–52).

NE of Am Hof and the Freyung is the busy *Wipplingerstrasse*. On the S side of this street is former *Bohemian Court Chancery* (*Böhmische Hofkanzlei*), a building in High Baroque style (by J. B. Fischer von Erlach the Elder, 1708–14) now occupied by government offices. Opposite it is the **Altes Rathaus** (Old Town Hall), with a richly articulated Baroque façade (*c.* 1700); in the courtyard is the *Andromeda Fountain*, with a masterly piece of high relief sculpture cast in lead by Raphael Donner, the sculptor's last work (1741). To the rear of the building (access from Salvatorgasse) is the Gothic *St Salvator's Church* (Salvatorkirche, 14th and 16th c.; beautiful Renaissance doorway, *c.* 1515), now occupied by the Old Catholics. A little way NW is the Gothic church of *Maria am Gestade (Maria Stiegen*, 14th c.), with a beautiful tower; the church once stood on the high W bank ("Gestade") of the Danube and was the church of the Danube boatmen.

From Stephansplatz the Rotenturmstrasse runs NE to the **Hoher Markt**, once the heart of Roman Vindobona (*Roman remains under the square: entrance at No. 3) and of early medieval Vienna. In the middle of the square is the *Josefsbrunnen*, a fountain erected in 1729–32 by J. E. Fischer von Erlach the Younger. At the E end of the square is the **Ankeruhr** (1914), a mechanical clock which plays a tune at 12 noon, accompanied by a parade of historical figures.

A number of old-world little streets extend between the Hoher Markt and the Danube Canal. At Seitenstettengasse 2 is a house in which the novelist Adalbert Stifter lived in 1842–48; at No. 4 is the *Synagogue*. – A little way N is the little Romanesque **Ruprechtskirche**, traditionally believed to be Vienna's oldest church (12th–13th c.; nave and lower part of tower 11th c.).

S of the Hoher Markt is the Bauernmarkt, No. 10 of which is the *Grillparzerhof*, on the site of the house in which the dramatist Franz Grillparzer (1791–1872) was born; his grave is in the Hietzing cemetery.

From Stephansplatz and Stock-im-Eisen-Platz the *Kärntner Strasse** (pedestrian precinct as far as the Opera House) runs S, cuts across the Ring at the Opera House and continues to the Karlsplatz. This busy

Kärntner Strasse pedestrian precinct

thoroughfare, perhaps the best known street in Vienna, is lined with offices, shops, cafés and hotels. On the E side (No. 35), is the High Gothic *Malteserkirche*, with an Empire façade of 1806.

In Annagasse, SE of the Malteserkirche, is *St Anne's Church* (Annakirche), in restrained Baroque style (renovated 1634, remodelled in 18th c.).

At Himmelpfortgasse 6, N of Johannesgasse, is the long façade of the *Winter Palace of Prince Eugene* (who died here in 1736); it is now occupied by the Ministry of Finance (*Finanzministerium*). This, the finest of Vienna's Baroque palaces, was designed by J. B. Fischer von Erlach the Elder. The central part was built in 1695–98, the wings being added in 1708 and 1723 by Johann Lukas von Hildebrandt; the palace has a magnificent staircase borne by four Atlas figures.

A little way N, at Rauhensteingasse 8, is the *Mozarthof*, built in 1848 on the site of the house in which Mozart died on 5 December 1791. – From here the curving Ballgasse runs E to the quiet Franziskanerplatz, on the E side of which stands the **Franciscan Church** (*Franziskanerkirche*), a Renaissance church (1603–11) with Gothic-type windows containing a richly carved organ of 1642.

From Stock-im-Eisen-Platz *Singerstrasse* runs SE. At No. 7, extending to Stephansplatz, is the High Baroque **Treasury of the Teutonic Order** (*Schatzkammer des Deutschen Ordens*), built in 1667 and remodelled in the 18th c. To the left is the *Elisabethkirche* (originally Gothic), the church of the Order.

In Schülerstrasse, to the E of St Stephen's Cathedral, is the house (No. 8: the rear side is Domgasse 5) in which Mozart lived in 1784–87 and where he wrote "Figaro". – At Domgasse 6 Franz Georg Kolschitzky established the *first coffee-house in Vienna* in 1686.

From Rotenturmstrasse the *Wollzeile* runs E to the Stubenring. Parallel to it on the N is Bäckerstrasse, which leads to Dr.-Ignaz-Seipel-Platz (formerly Universitätsplatz). On the left-hand side is the *Alte Aula*, the most charming Viennese building of the time of Maria Theresa, in Baroque style, originally erected to house the University (by Jean-Nicolas Jadot de Ville-Issey, 1753–55); it has been occupied since 1857 by the **Academy of Sciences** (founded 1847). The N end of the square is taken up by the three-storeyed twin-towered Early Baroque façade of the former **University Church** (*Universitätskirche*), originally built by the Jesuits in 1627–31, with a sumptuous Baroque interior (by Andrea Pozzo, 1703–05) and frescoes on the vaulting (trompe-l'œil dome).

To the E of Universitätsplatz is the **Dominican Church** (*Dominikanerkirche*), remodelled in early Baroque style between 1631 and 1674, with a richly decorated interior. Farther N is the **Head Post Office**.

At Fleischmarkt 13, W of the Post Office, is the *Greek Church*, with a neo-Byzantine façade (1858–61) by Theophil Hansen. Next door (No. 15) is the house in which the painter Moritz von Schwind (1804–71) was born. Griechengasse branches off on the right, and on the right-hand side of this little street, at No. 9, is the well-known Griechenbeisl restaurant.

In the Neuer Markt, to the W of Kärntner Strasse, is the *Donner Fountain* (by Georg Raphael Donner, 1737–39). In the middle is the figure of Providentia, and around the edge of the shallow fountain basin are river gods representing the Danube's tributaries the Enns, the Traun, the Ybbs and the March.

On the W side of the Neuer Markt is the *Capuchin Church* (Kapuzinerkirche), a plain Baroque building of 1622–32 belonging to a Capuchin friary founded by Anna (d. 1618), wife of the Emperor Matthias. On the outside, in an open chapel, is a bronze statue of Marco d'Aviano, a fiery Capuchin preacher who roused the people of Vienna against the Turks in 1683 and who is buried in the church.

In the convent (to the left of the church) is the entrance to the *Imperial Vault* (*Kaisergruft* or *Kapuzinergruft*), the family vault of the Habsburgs since 1633.

A staircase leads down into the Imperial Vault. On the right is the OLD VAULT, with the sarcophagi, often richly decorated, of the Emperors from Matthias to Charles VI (with the exception of Ferdinand II, d. 1637, who is buried in Graz). – *Carolingian Vault:* on right the magnificent sarcophagus (by B. F. Moll, 1735) of Charles VI (d. 1740), on left the richly decorated sarcophagus (by J. L. von Hildebrandt, 1712) of Joseph I (d. 1711). – *Leopoldine Vault:* on the left the Empresses from Anna onwards; on right the Emperor Matthias (d. 1619) and Ferdinand III (d. 1657); on E wall

Countess Fuchs-Mollardt (d. 1754), the teacher and confidante of Maria Theresa. – *Angels' Vault*, the earliest of the vaults, with the sarcophagi of children.

To the left of the staircase is the NEW VAULT, with the sarcophagi of the Habsburg-Lorraine line. We come first to the *Maria Theresa Vault*, a domed chamber built in 1754 by Jean-Nicolas Jadot de Ville-Issey, with the imposing *double sarcophagus of the Empress Maria Theresa* (d. 1780) and her husband **Francis of Lorraine** (d. 1765), a masterpiece of Viennese Rococo by B. F. Moll (1754); on the lid the royal couple are represented just awaking from death. Around this are the sarcophagi (mostly also by Moll) of their children; at the foot is the plain copper sarcophagus of Joseph II (d. 1790). – Next comes the *Francis Vault*, in the middle of which is the neo-classical sarcophagus, by Peter von Nobile, of Francis I (d. 1835); on the right is his daughter Marie Louise (d. 1847), wife of Napoleon I. – To the right is the *Francis Joseph Vault*, in the second chamber of which are the sarcophagi of Francis Joseph I (d. 1916), the Empress Elisabeth (d. 1898) and Crown Prince Rudolf (d. 1889). – On the N side of the Francis Vault is the *Ferdinand Vault:* to the left Maximilian of Mexico (d. 1867), Francis Joseph's brother. – On the W side of the Francis Vault is the long *Tuscany Vault*, with the sarcophagi of Archduke Albrecht (d. 1895) and Archduke Karl (d. 1847).

In the **Albertinaplatz**, the busy square behind the Opera House, stands a *statue of Mozart* by Viktor Tilgner (1896). Facing it, on the Augustinerbastei, is the *Danube Fountain* (1869). Above, on the ramp leading up to the bastion, is a bronze equestrian statue of Archduke Albrecht (1817–95) and behind it a palace in Empire style built by Louis Montoyer for Archduke Karl (1801–04), which now houses the *Albertina collection of graphic art and the *Austrian Film Museum*.

Below the bastion to the W, at the rear entrance to the Burggarten, is a marble statue of the Augustinian Canon and preacher *Abraham a Santa Clara* (Ulrich Mengerle, 1644–1709).

From the Albertinaplatz the Augustinerstrasse, Herrengasse and Schottengasse run NW to the Schottentor. In Augustinerstrasse is the plain E end of the **Augustinian Church** (*Augustinerkirche*), belonging to an Augustinian monastery founded in 1327 and dissolved in 1838, a Gothic hall-church (1330–39) with a new helm-roofed tower built in 1850.

The INTERIOR of the church seems rather bare, following the removal of the Baroque furnishings in 1784 and 1860. Fine Baroque stalls (1725) in nave. Opposite the entrance is the neo-classical marble *monument of Marie Christine* (d. 1798), Duchess of Teschen, Maria Theresa's daughter, by Canova (1805). – On the right is the *Loreto Chapel* (1627), in which, behind the altar, is the "Herzgrüftel" ("Heart Vault"), with urns containing the hearts of the Habsburgs from Matthias (d. 1619) onwards. – To the left of this is the High Gothic (two-aisled) *St

George's Chapel (1341). In the right-hand aisle is the empty marble sarcophagus of the Emperor Leopold II, in neo-classical style (by Franz Zauner, 1799). Set into the floor nearby is the gravestone of Gerard van Swieten (d. 1772), Maria Theresa's personal physician. On the left-hand wall is the Baroque monument, by B. F. Moll, of Field-Marshal Count Leopold Daun (1705–66). – The fiery preacher Abraham a Santa Clara lived in the Augustinian college from 1689 until his death in 1709.

From the Augustinian Church Dorotheer-gasse runs NE to the Graben. On the right-hand side of this street is the **Dorotheum** (1901), a State-run pawnshop and auction house founded in 1707.

In Bräunerstrasse, parallel to Dorotheergasse on the W, is a house (No. 6) in which the dramatist Friedrich Hebbel lived from 1848 to 1860.

To the left of Augustinerstrasse is the *Josefsplatz*, a charming little Baroque square which has been preserved almost unaltered. In the middle of the square stands a neo-classical equestrian statue of the *Emperor Joseph II* (by Franz Anton Zauner, 1806).

On the far side is the ***Austrian National Library** (*Österreichische Nationalbiblio-thek*), built in 1723–26 by J. E. Fischer von Erlach the Younger, a mature work of High Baroque architecture dominated by the projecting central block with its dome.

The Austrian National Library (until 1920 the Court Library) was founded about 1526 by the Emperor Ferdinand I and was originally designed to house the Habsburg collections. Fifty years later, however, in 1579, the first regulations were introduced requiring publishers to deposit copies of their publications. Later acquisitions included the libraries of the Fugger family (1656), Schloss Ambras (1665), Prince Eugene (1737) and the dissolved religious houses (1783). In 1726 Charles VI opened the library to the public. – The National Library now possesses some 2 million volumes and 40,000 manuscripts.

A broad staircase leads up to the **Library Hall** (*Prunksaal*), one of the supreme achievements of Baroque art and architecture. This long hall, occupying the whole length of the building along one side of the Josefsplatz, is articulated by columns and dominated by its oval dome, with paintings by Daniel Gran (1730). Around the walls are the bookcases, with gilt decoration, and a walnut-wood gallery; and the prevailing tone is set by the brown leather bindings and the valuable morocco-bound volumes of Prince Eugene's library in the central section of the hall. Marble statues of Charles VI and other Habsburgs by Paul and Peter Strudel (*c.* 1700).

On the N side of the Josefsplatz are the *Redoutensäle ("Rout Halls") of the Hofburg and the Winter Riding School* (Winterreit-schule, 1729–35: entrance under archway to Michaelerplatz), in which the famous displays of the *Spanish Riding School are given. (The Riding School was founded in 1572. The Lipizzaner stallions, formerly from Lipizza or Lipica, now in Yugoslavia, have since 1918 been bred at a stud in the Styrian village of Piber.)

On the street side of the Josefsplatz is the *Palais Pallavicini* (1784). To the N is the *Stallburg* (1558–70), on the second floor of which is the Neue Galerie (pictures of the 19th and early 20th c.).

The Michaelerplatz lies at the intersection of Augustinerstrasse, Herrengasse, Kohlmarkt and Schauflergasse, coming from Balhaus-platz. On the SW side of the square is the curved façade of the **Michaelertrakt** of the Hofburg, continued to the left by the Winter Riding School. Opposite this, at the corner of Herrengasse and the Kohlmarkt, is the *Loos-Haus*, a block of flats and offices built by Adolf Loos in 1910 in reaction against the Art Nouveau style. Facing it, on the S side of the Kohlmarkt (No. 11), is the large *Michaelerhaus* (*c.* 1720), in which young Haydn lived in a garret in 1750–57.

To the right of this **St Michael's Church** (*Michaelerkirche*) has a neo-classical façade (1792), a porch of 1725 (figure of the Arch-angel Michael by Lorenzo Mattielli) and a slender Gothic tower (1340–44). On the S wall, in the passage leading to Habsburger-gasse, is a large Gothic relief of Christ on the Mount of Olives (1494).

A short distance W of the Michaelerplatz is **Ballhausplatz**. On the W side of the square stands a palace in High Baroque style (by J. L. von Hildebrandt, 1716–21), formerly the Court Chancery, where the Congress of Vienna met in 1814–15, and now the **Federal Chancery** (*Bundeskanzleramt*).

Adjoining it on the N are the **Austrian National Archives** (*Österreichisches Staatsarchiv*), in a building of 1901 – one of the most important collections of documents in Europe, including the archives of the old Holy Roman Empire (exhibition).

Farther N, in Minoritenplatz, surrounded by noble mansions, is the Gothic **Minorite Church** (*Minoritenkirche*: 13th–15th c., main doorway *c.* 1350). To the E, at Herren-gasse 9, is the *Lower Austrian Provincial Museum* (Niederösterreichisches Landes-museum).

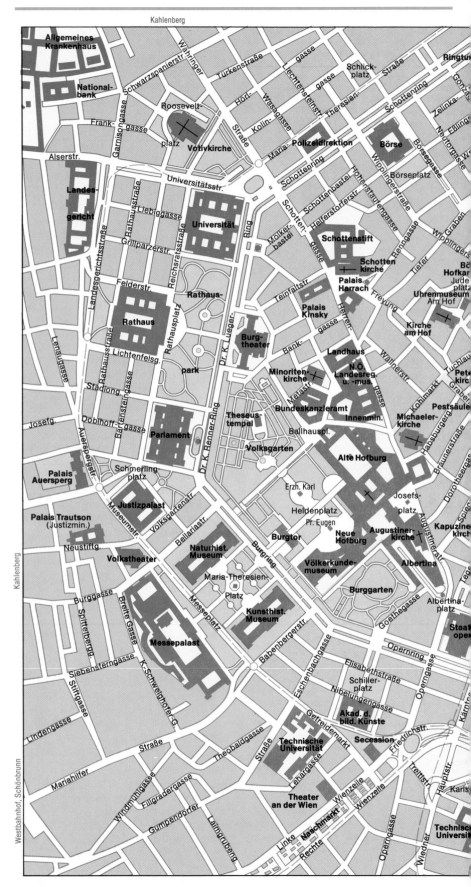

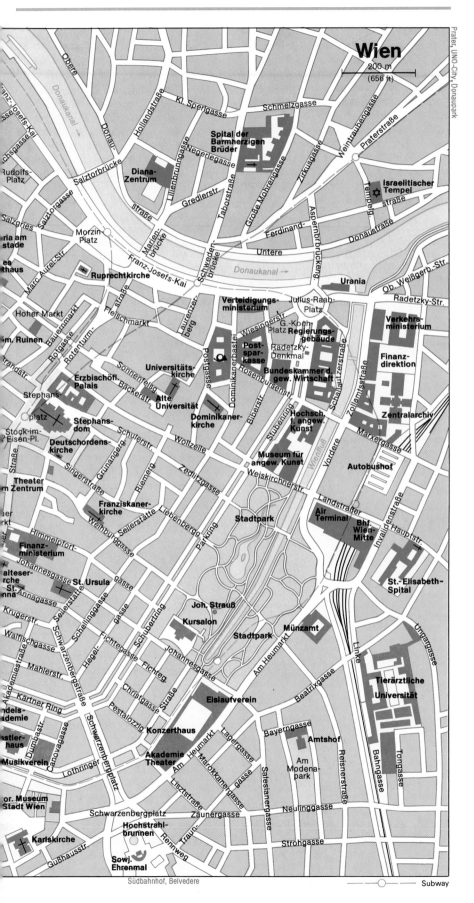

Wien

200 m
(656 ft)

Prater, UNO-City, Donaupark

Donaukanal

Obere

anz-Josefs-Kai

chsgasse

Rudolfs-Platz

Salzgries

ria am
stade

es
haus

Hollandstraße

Kl. Sperlgasse

Schmelzgasse

Donau-

Lilienbrunngasse

Negerlegasse

Spital der
Barmherzigen
Brüder

Weintraubengasse

Praterstraße

straße

Salztorbrücke

Diana-
Zentrum

Gredlerstr.

Taborstraße

Große Mohrengasse

Zirkusgasse

Tempelg

Israelitischer
Tempel

straße

Morzin-
Platz

Marien-
brücke

Schweden-
brücke

Ferdinand-

Aspernbrückeng.

Donaustraße

Marc-Aurel-Str.

Franz-Josefs-Kai

Untere

Donaukanal →

Ruprechtkirche

Urania

Ob. Weißgerb.-Str.

Hoher Markt

Bauernmarkt

Fleischmarkt

Rotenturm-

Laurenzer-
berg

Verteidigungs-
ministerium

Julius-Raab-
Platz

Radetzky-Str.

m. Ruinen

Ropgasse

Wiesingerstr

G.-Koch-
Platz

Regierungs-
gebäude

Verkehrs-
ministerium

randstr

Sonnenfelsg.

Universitäts-
kirche

Postgasse

Dominikanerbastei

Post-
spar-
kasse

Radetzky-
Denkmal

Finanz-
direktion

Erzbischöfl.
Palais

Bäckerstr.

Alte
Universität

Rosenbursenstr.

Bundeskammer d.
gew. Wirtschaft

Zollamtsstraße

Stephans-

Dominikaner-
kirche

Biberstr.

Schaufflerstraße

Zentralarchiv

platz

Stephans-
dom

Schulerstr.

Wollzeile

Stubenring

Hochsch.
f. angew.
Kunst

Marxergasse

Stock-im-
Eisen-Pl.

Deutschordens-
kirche

Grünangerg.

Bienerg.

Zedlitzgasse

Museum für
angew. Kunst

Vordere

Autobushof

Strabe

Singerstraße

Weiskirchnerstr.

Theater
m Zentrum

Franziskaner-
kirche

Liebenberg.

Landstraße

Wienflu

er
rkt

Himmelpfort-

Weihburggasse

Sellerstätte

Parking

Stadtpark

Air
Terminal

Bhf.
Wien-
Mitte

Invalidenstr.

Hauptstr.

Finanz-
ministerium

Johannesgasse

St. Ursula

Sellerstätte

St.-Elisabeth-
Spital

alteser-
rche
St.
nna

Annagasse

gasse

Krugerstr.

Schellinggasse

Schwarzenbergstraße

Fichtegasse

Schubertring

Joh. Strauß

Ungargasse

Walfischgasse

Hegel-

Fichteg.

Kursalon

Münzamt

Linke

Mahlerstr.

Johannesgasse

Stadtpark

Am Heumarkt

Beatrixgasse

Reisnerstraße

Bahngasse

Tongasse

Akademiestraße

Kärtner Ring

Dumbastr.

Canovagasse

Pestalozzig.

Christgasse

Straße

Eislaufverein

Lagergasse

Bayerngasse

Tierärztliche
Universität

ndels-
ademie

stler-
haus

Lothringer-

Schwarzenbergplatz

Konzerthaus

Am Marokkaner

Am
Modena-
park

Amtshof

Musikverein

Akademie
Theater

Marokkanergasse

Salesianergasse

Neulinggasse

or. Museum
Stadt Wien

Schwarzenbergplatz

Zaunergasse

Karlskirche

Gußhausstr.

Hochstrahl-
brunnen

Rennweg

Haupt-

Strohgasse

Sowj.
Ehrenmal

Along the SW side of the Innere Stadt the *Hofburg, an irregular complex of buildings spread over a considerable area which were erected at different times down the centuries. The exteriors are predominantly Renaissance and Baroque, and the influence of these styles can also be seen in the Neue Hofburg, built in the second half of the 19th c. For more than six centuries, until 1918, the Hofburg was the seat of the rulers of Austria, and for two and a half centuries, until 1806, the residence of the German Emperors.

1 Burgtor (Heroes Memorial)
2 Prince Eugene
3 Archduke Charles
4 Burgkapelle (Chapel)
5 Schweizerhof (entrance to treasury)
6 Treasury
7 Michaelertrakt
8 Entrances to State Apartments and Silberkammer
9 Entrance to Spanish Riding School
10 Joseph II
11 Francis II

The Babenberg dukes had their seat from 1156 onwards in what is now the square Am Hof, and the existence of a ducal stronghold to the S of the town is securely attested only from the second half of the 13th c. The Burgkapelle (1449) is one of the oldest surviving parts of the Hofburg. – The Emperor Ferdinand I decided in 1533 to make the Hofburg his regular residence, and between 1536 and 1552 caused the buildings around the Schweizerhof – a name which dates only from the time of Maria Theresa – to be rebuilt. Between 1575 and 1605 the Amalienhof was built, in 1660–69 the Leopoldinischer Trakt, in both cases on earlier foundations. – Of the great buildings of the High Baroque period, designed by J. E. Fischer von Erlach the Younger in the reign of Charles VI, the Court Library (now the National Library) was completed in 1723–26, the Burghof wing of the Imperial Chancery (Reichskanzlei) in 1726–30, the Winter Riding School in 1729–35, the Michaelertrakt only in 1889–93. The Neue Hofburg, the large wing extending to the SW, is only a fragment of a grandiose extension planned by Gottfried Semper and Karl von Hasenauer (1881–1913).

The **Burgtor**, facing on to the Ring, was built in 1821–24 and converted into a memorial to Austrian national heroes in 1934. It stands on the SW side of the Heldenplatz, in which are equestrian statues of *Prince Eugene* and *Archduke Charles* (d. 1847), the victor of Aspern.

To the SE is the **Neue Hofburg**, designed by Hasenauer, Semper and others in the sumptuous neo-Baroque "Ringstrasse style". It now houses part of the collections of the *Kunsthistorisches Museum* (Museum of Art; musical instruments, a unique assemblage of **arms and armour, etc.), the *Ephesus Museum* (statues, reliefs, including some from the old trading town), the *Museum of Ethnography* (bronzes from Benin and a Mexican collection), and the *Portrait Collection* of the National Library (360,000 portraits of all periods).

On the far side of the Heldenplatz is the **Leopoldinischer Trakt** (Leopoldine Range), a plain early Baroque building which, together with the wings round the square In der Burg – the *Amalienhof* (Amalienburg) and the *Reichskanzleitrakt* (Imperial Chancery) – contains the state and private apartments of Maria Theresa (now the Federal Chancellor's residence, not open to the public) and Francis Joseph.

From the Heldenplatz a passage leads into the square known as *In der Burg*, the real heart of the Hofburg, with a bronze statue of the Emperor *Francis I* (d. 1835). Beyond the Reichskanzleitrakt is the **Michaelertrakt**, designed by J. E. Fischer von Erlach the Younger, with an imposing façade and a grand passageway and gateway leading into Michaelerplatz. In the court, to the right, is the entrance to the State Apartments; to the left is the entrance to the *Silberkammer* (porcelain, gold and silver). To the right, on the SE side of In der Burg, is the **Schweizertrakt**, with the oldest parts of the Hofburg.

The *Schweizertor* (1552) leads into the *Schweizerhof*, in which, to the left, is the entrance to the **Treasury** (*Schatzkammer*), with the *jewels and other relics of the Holy Roman Empire and the Austrian Imperial throne, and to the right, the entrance to the *Hofburgkapelle*.

THE RING. – The *Ringstrasse, Vienna's magnificent circular boulevard, was laid out from 1859 onwards on the site of the old medieval fortifications which separated the Innere Stadt from the suburbs, then reaching far out into the countryside. The Ringstrasse, 4 km/2½ miles long and almost 60 m/200 ft wide, surrounds the central area of Vienna on three sides; on the fourth side is the Franz-Josefs-Kai alongside the Danube Canal. With its monumental blocks of offices and flats, principally built between 1861 and 1888, its trees, its parks and gardens and its spacious squares, the Ringstrasse is one of the finest examples of urban development and planning of its day; and moreover it is to this development that we owe the preservation of the older part of the city. It exemplifies the architectural style of the later 19th c., the "Ringstrasse style" (the Austrian equivalent of the Victorian style in Britain), which had no distinctive manner of its own but modelled itself on the architecture of the past.

In the southern part of the Ring is one of the city's busiest traffic intersections, the **Opernkreuzung**, at the junction of the Opernring, the Kärntner Ring and Kärntner Strasse.

Under the intersection is the *Opernpassage*, with various shops and the official Tourist Information Office (underground connection with the Karlsplatzpassage).

The ***Opera House** (*Staatsoper*), built by Eduard van der Nüll and August von Siccardsburg in 1861–69 in a style freely modelled on the early French Renaissance, is a clearly articulated building of powerful effect.

The predecessor of the Staatsoper (which was known until 1918 as the *Hofoper* or Court Opera House) was the *Theater am Kärntner Tor*, built in 1708 and rebuilt in 1763, which in 1849 finally came under the control of the Imperial court. The musical directors included Christoph Willibald Gluck (1754–64), Antonio Salieri (1774–90), Konradin Kreutzer (1822–49), with interruptions) and Otto Nicolai (1837–38 and 1841–47). – In its present house, reopened in 1955 after the repair of war damage, the Vienna Opera has achieved an international reputation.

From the Opera intersection the *Opernring* runs W to the two great museums flanking Maria-Theresien-Platz. Beyond Goethe-gasse, on the right, is the **Burggarten**, laid out in 1818.

Then follows the *Burgring*, on the left of which is Babenbergen Strasse, leading to Mariahilfer Strasse. Beyond this, on the rght, is the *Burgtor*, with the extensive complex of the Hofburg to the rear. *Maria-Theresien-Platz* then opens out on the left, with the ***Maria Theresa Monument** (1887), an impressive and elaborate group almost 20 m/ 65 ft high.

The central figure is the Empress, with the "Pragmatic Sanction" in her left hand. Around the base are four equestrian statues of her generals – to the right Laudon, to the left Daun, to the rear Traun and Khevenhüller; between these figures are four other statues – in front Maria Theresa's chancellor Prince Kaunitz, to the rear General Prince Wenzel Liechtenstein, on left Count Haugwitz, one of the Empress's ministers, and on right her physician, van Swieten; and behind van Swieten is a group depicting Gluck and Haydn with the young Mozart.

Flanking Maria-Theresien-Platz are two handsome and imposing buildings in neo-Renaissance style erected between 1872 and 1890. To the N (right) is the ***Natural History Museum** (*Naturhistorisches Museum*) with splendid collections; particularly notable are the "Venus of Willendorf" (Old Stone Age); material from the graves and mines at Hallstatt and the collection of meteorites; children's room. – To the S is the ***Museum of Art** (*Kunsthistorisches Museum*), with a collection of outstanding richness. Particularly fine are the Museum's collections of sculpture and applied art, the Egyptian Department and the Picture Gallery. The earlier Dutch painters, the 17th c. Flemish masters and the Venetian school are especially well represented. On the 2nd floor is the "Secondary Gallery" (Venetian and Flemish painting of the 16th and 17th c., 17th c. German and Florentine pictures). There is a fine Coin Cabinet. – On the far side of the square is the **Messepalast** (Exhibition Hall), originally the Court Stables (by J. B. and J. E. Fischer von Erlach, *c.* 1723).

To the N of the Burgring is the *Dr.-Karl-Renner-Ring*, with the **Parliament Building**, in Greek classical style (1874–83). Opposite it is the **Volksgarten** (café-restaurant, large discothèque), with the *Temple of Theseus* (Theseustempel, 1823). A little way SW of the Parliament Building is the *Justizpalast* (Law Courts), and beyond this are the *Palais Trautson (now housing the Ministry of Justice), a masterpiece of High Baroque architecture by J. B. Fischer von Erlach the Elder (1710–12), and the *Volkstheater* (1887–89).

A short distance NW of the Justizpalast, in Auerspergstrasse, stretches the long façade of the **Palais Auersperg** (owned by the Auersperg family 1778–1953, thoroughly renovated 1953–54), with fine state apartments and a restaurant.

To the N of the Volksgarten, on the inner side of the Ring, stands the ***Burgtheater** (by Semper and Hasenauer, 1880–86), a massive structure in late Renaissance style, reopened in 1955 after the repair of heavy war damage; it still maintains an old tradition of polished acting and good ensemble playing.

The theatre was founded by Maria Theresa in 1741 as the Komödienhaus, then situated in the Michaelerplatz, and in 1776 was given the status of *Hof- und Nationaltheater* (Court and National Theatre) by Joseph II. It achieved a great reputation between 1814 and 1832 under Josef Schreyvogel, who introduced the simple elegance of the Burgtheater style, and under the direction of Heinrich Laube (1850–67), Franz von Dingelstedt (1870–81) and Adolf Wilbrandt (1881–87) it continued to flourish. From the outset its special quality lay in attention devoted to ensemble playing in a company drawn from all the German-speaking countries.

To the W of the Burgtheater are the *Rathauspark* and *Rathausplatz*. On the W side of the square is the monumental neo-Gothic **Rathaus** (Town Hall, 1872–83), with seven courtyards and a tower 98 m/ 320 ft high, which houses the *Municipal Library*, the *Municipal Archives* and the *Ratskeller* (restaurant).

NW of the Rathaus, at Laudongasse 15–19, is the *Folk Museum*, with collections covering the territory of the old Austro-Hungarian monarchy.

At the end of the *Dr.-Karl-Lueger-Ring*, on left, is the **University**, a massive block 160 m/525 ft long, built by Heinrich Ferstel (1873–84) in the rather ponderous forms of the Italian Renaissance. In the entrance hall is a War Memorial by Josef Müllner (1924).

Around the handsome courtyard, with the Kastaliabrunnen, a marble fountain by E. Hellmer (1910), are arcades containing busts of notable University teachers.

Vienna University, the oldest after Prague (1348) in German-speaking territory, was founded in 1365 by Duke Rudolf IV and reorganised by Gerard van Swieten in the reign of Maria Theresa. From 1755 to 1857 it was housed in the Alte Aula in Dr.-Ignaz-Seipel-Platz.

The **University Library**, in the rear wing, contains more than 1·7 million volumes.

Opposite the University is a relic of the old fortifications, the *Mölkerbastei*, with a number of old Viennese houses. On the 4th floor of No. 8 are a *Beethoven Memorial Room* and a small *Adalbert Stifter Museum*.

N of the University, in the spacious Rooseveltplatz, is the massive neo-Gothic **Votivkirche** (1856–79), of grey Leitha limestone, with two openwork towers 99 m/325 ft high.

From the large intersection known as the Schottentor the *Schottenring* runs NE to the Danube Canal. Half-way along, on the right, is the **Stock Exchange** (*Börse*), built 1872–77 in neo-Renaissance style (destroyed by fire in 1956, reopened 1959). At the corner of the Schottenring and Franz-Josefs-Kai, on right, is the *Ringturm*, an office block with a weather service controlled by the Central Meteorological Institute.

From the Opera intersection the Kärntner Ring, lined with office blocks and hotels, runs SE to the elongated Schwarzenbergplatz, with a bronze equestrian statue of *Prince Karl zu Schwarzenberg*, commander-in-chief of the Allied forces in the battle of Leipzig (1813), an imposing **fountain** (the *Hochstrahlbrunnen*), and the *Monument to the Soviet Army* (1946).

At the S end of the square, on higher ground, is the **Palais Schwarzenberg**, built between 1697 and 1728 by J. L. von Hildebrandt and J. B. and J. E. Fischer von Erlach (state apartments; hotel; gardens).

The final section of the Ring, extending to Julius-Raab-Platz on Franz-Josefs-Kai, consists of the Schubertring, the Parkring and the Stubenring.

SE of the Schubertring, in Lothringer Strasse (corner of Lisztstrasse), is the **Konzerthaus** (1913), with several concert halls and the *Akademietheater*. Adjoining this, to the NE, is the *Vienna Skating Club* (Eislaufverein).

To the SE of the *Parkring* lies the beautiful **Stadtpark**, through which flows the *River*

Johann Strauss Monument, Stadtpark

Wien. In the park are the *Kursalon* (café-restaurant) and numerous monuments, among them a bronze statue of the waltz king *Johann Strauss the Younger* (by E. Helmer, 1921), to the N of the Kursalon; the *Donauweibchen* (Danube Nymph), by Hans Gasser (1865); a bronze bust (by Viktor Tilgner, 1899) of *Anton Bruckner* on the E side of the lake; and marble monuments to *Franz Schubert (by Karl Kundmann, 1872) and *Hans Makart* (by Viktor Tilgner, 1898) on the W side of the lake. On the SW side of the park rises the large *Hotel Intercontinental Vienna*.

At the S end of the *Stubenring* is an important intersection, on the site of the old Stubentor (demolished 1858). To the NW is the Wollzeile, here widened into the Dr.-Karl-Lueger-Platz (monument). To the SE is Weiskirchnerstrasse, the old road to Hungary, which leads to District III; at the near end of this street, on the right, is the *Air Terminal*.

On the right-hand-side of the Stubenring is the *Museum of Applied Art (*Museum für angewandte Kunst*), an ornate brick building in early Renaissance style (by H. Ferstel, 1868–71). – A linking wing connects it with the *Academy of Applied Art* (Hochschule für angewandte Kunst), also by Ferstel (1875–77). – Farther along the Stubenring, also on the right, are the **Regierungsgebäude** (Government Buildings), built by Ludwig Baumann (1909–13) in neo-Baroque style – the last flicker of the "Ringstrasse style". In front of the building, on a high granite base, is an equestrian statue of *Field-Marshal Radetzky* (1766–1858).

Opposite the Radetzky monument is a small square with a monument to *Georg Coch* (1824–90), who introduced the system of postal orders. Behind it is the **Post Office Savings Bank** (*Postsparkassenamt*), an imposing building faced with granite slabs (by Otto Wagner, 1904–06), in the more functional style which displaced the "Ringstrasse style".

The Ring ends in Julius-Raab-Platz, on the S side of the *Danube Canal* (Donaukanal). To the right is the **Urania** building (1910), an establishment of adult education, with an *Observatory*, and conference and lecture halls.

SOUTH OF THE RING. – To the S of the Opernring lies Schillerplatz, on the S side of which is the **Academy of Fine Art** (*Akademie der bildenden Künste*), founded in 1692. The present building, in Italian Renaissance style, with rich terracotta and sculptural decoration, was designed by Theophil Hansen (1872–76).

Behind the Academy is the Getreidemarkt, leading on the right to the Messepalast and on the left to the Wienzeile. In a triangular area of public gardens is the *Secession Building, once the headquarters of a group of artists founded in 1897, the Secession, now used for exhibitions. It is the first and most characteristic example of Art Nouveau ("Jugendstil") architecture in Vienna, a clearly articulated building (by Josef Olbrich, 1898–99) with a gilded iron dome in the form of a laurel tree.

From the Secession the Friedrichstrasse leads (left) to the Operngasse and Karlsplatz. To the right the Wienzeile, a wide street built over the River Wien, runs SW, marking the boundary between Districts IV and VI. Along the middle are the long rows of stalls of the *Naschmarkt* (food market; flea market on Saturdays).

A little way W of the Secession on the Linke Wienzeile is the **Theater an der Wien**, a building in Empire style erected in 1797–1801 for the great theatre director Emanuel Schikaneder which, with later alterations, has continued to play an important part in Viennese theatrical history.

The Theater an der Wien was the successor to the earlier *Freihaustheater* which opened in the Freihaus, in the Naschmarkt, in 1787. Mozart's "Magic Flute" (text by Schikaneder) was first performed in this house on 30 September 1791. Works which have received their first performance in the Theater an der Wien include Beethoven's "Fidelio" (1817) and Johann Strauss's "Die Fledermaus" (1874).

To the S of the Kärntner Ring, between the Secession and Schwarzenbergplatz, is the spacious **Karlsplatz**, completely replanned between 1969 and 1978, under which is the heart of the Vienna Underground system, a complex of stations some 30 m/100 ft deep, on five levels, at the junction of three Underground lines, with the operational headquarters on the system. The main underground concours, the *Karlsplatz-Hauptpassage* (area 4500 sq. m/5380 sq. yds) is connected with the Opernpassage under the Opera intersection by an underground street of shops 100 m/110 yds long and with the Secession by the *Westpassage*, while the *Otto-Wagner-Passage* leads from the Künstlerhaus (Artists' House) to the recently laid out Resselpark. – Two fine Seccesion-style *pavilions* by Otto Wagner (1901) have been renovated and re-erected in Karlsplatz. One is an entrance to the Underground, the other is a cafe.

> Otto Wagner's plans at the turn of the 19th c. provided for a comprehensive urban transport system (tramways). In recent years the most important lines have been replaced by Underground lines, retaining the Secession-style Stadtpark and Schönbrunn stations (which are under statutory protection as national monuments). At present three Underground lines – U1 (Reumannplatz–Karlsplatz–Stephansplatz–Praterstern–Kagran), U2 (Karlsplatz–Schottenring), and U4 (Karlsplatz–Heiligenstadt) – are in operation.

On the S side of the Karlsplatz is the **University of Technology** (*Technische Universität*), founded in 1815 as a Technical College. The original neo-classical building (by Josef Schemerl, 1815–18) has been considerably extended by later additions. The extension to the E (Karlsgasse 4) occupies the site of a house in which Brahms lived from 1872 until his death in 1897.

At the SW corner of the square is the *Karlskirche (St Charles's Church), built by the Emperor Charles VI in fulfilment of a vow made during an epidemic of plague in 1713 and dedicated to St Charles Borromeo. Originally standing by itself on the grassy slopes of the Wien valley outside the town, it is one of the finest churches of the High Baroque period, the masterpiece of *J. B. Fischer von Erlach* (1716–39). It is a richly articulated building on an oval plan, with a mighty dome 72 m/235 ft high. In the middle of the long façade is a temple-like pillared porch, flanked by two columns 33 m/110 ft high modelled on Trajan's Column in Rome, with spiral reliefs depicting scenes from the life of St Charles Borromeo; at each end is a low tower with an arched passage running under it.

Obliquely across from the Karlskirche is the *Historical Museum of Vienna* (Historisches Museum der Stadt Wien).

On the N side of the square are the **Künstlerhaus** (Artists' House, 1868) and the sumptuous **Musikverein** concert hall (1870).

OUTER DISTRICTS. – From the Urania building the *Aspernbrücke* leads over the Danube Canal into Praterstrasse, which runs NE through the LEOPOLDSTADT district to the *Praterstern*, with the entrance to the **Prater**, a large park laid out on the meadowland bordering the Danube. At the near end is the *Volksprater*, an old-established amusement park. – On the bank of the Danube stands the "Peace Pagoda", a Buddhist building with a white and gold dome.

At the entrance to the *Volksprater* is the *Giant Wheel (*Riesenrad*), the very symbol of the Prater, which ranks with St Stephen's Cathedral as one of Vienna's best-known landmarks. Constructed in 1896–97 by an English engineer, Walter B. Basset. The whole mechanism and all the cabins were destroyed by bombing and fire in 1945, but this destruction, like other destruction in Vienna, was soon repaired, and by 1946 the wheel was once again in full working order. From the top of the circuit there is a magnificent panoramic *view of the city.

Giant Wheel, Prater

SOME STATISTICS. – Highest point above ground level: 64·75 m/212 ft. – Diameter of wheel: 61 m/200 ft. – The axle is 10·87 m/36 ft long and 0·50 m/1 ft 8 in. thick and weighs 16·3 tons; the centre of the axle is 34·2 m/112 ft above ground level. – The supporting structure, borne on eight pylons, weighs 165·2 tons. – The wheel, with its 120 spokes, weighs 244·85 tons. – The total weight of iron in the structure is 430·05 tons. – The wheel turns at a speed of 0·75 m/2½ ft per second.

Near the Giant Wheel is the **Planetarium** (1964), with the *Prater Museum* and the *Lipburger Kugelhaus* ("Kugel-Mugel", a curious spherical building). – From the Praterstern the *Hauptallee* (Main Avenue), first laid out in 1537, runs for 4·5 km/2 miles to the *Lusthaus* (restaurant).

To the left of the Hauptallee, on the SE side of the Volksprater, are the **Messegelände** (Fair and Exhibition Grounds), a *trotting track*, a covered *Stadium* and the *Prater Stadium*. – Beyond the Lusthaus are *Freudenau* racecourse and a golf-course.

NE of the Prater on the left bank of the Danube, enclosed by the arms of the *Alte Donau* (Old Danube; bathing, water sports), is the **Donaupark** (area 100 hectares/250 acres), with the 170 m/ 560 ft high *Donauturm (Danube Tower; two express elevators, look-out terrace, revolving restaurant), the *Irissee*, a miniature railway, a chair-lift and the *Donauparkhalle* (ice-rink).

In the southern part of the Donaupark is the conference and office complex (opened 1979), designed by Johann Staber, which is generally known as *UNO-City – officially the *Vienna International Center* – with the offices of the United Nations agencies based in Vienna.

UNO-City, Donaupark

Around the 45 m/150 ft high **central block**, with facilities for international conferences, are four Y-shaped *office blocks*, respectively 120 m/395 ft, 100 m/330 ft, 80 m/260 ft and 60 m/195 ft high, with two towers 58 m/ 190 ft and 54 m/175 ft high housing services. An Austrian conference complex is also planned. Near UNO-City stands a mosque, the gift of Saudi-Arabia.

In the III district, corner of Löwengasse and Kegelgasse, a *residential block has been built (1983–85) to the plans of the artist Friedensreich Hundertwasser (born 1928); this has an irregular brightly painted façade, "onion towers" and windows accommodating trees and shrubs.

To the SE of the Palais Schwarzenberg is the **Belvedere**, the masterpiece of the great architect Johann Lukas von Hildebrandt, built between 1700 and 1723 as a summer palace for Prince Eugene of Savoy. The Unteres Belvedere (Lower Belvedere), on the Rennweg, was designed as the Prince's residence, the Oberes Belvedere (Upper Belvedere), on what is now Prinz-Eugen-Strasse, for great receptions and festive occasions, the two being linked by a narrow strip of rising ground laid out as a terraced garden. In its harmonious union of landscape

and architecture, its lively elegance in spite of its monumental scale, the Belvedere is one of the supreme achievements of the Viennese Baroque. After the death of Prince Eugene, unmarried, in 1736 the furnishings and art treasures were sold; and some years later, in 1752, the buildings and gardens were acquired by the Emperor. The Belvedere now houses a number of museums (*son et lumière* displays).

The **Lower Belvedere** (1714–16) is a long low single-storey building laid out around a grand courtyard with the main entrance; the main front overlooks the gardens. It houses the *Baroque Museum*. In the Orangery, adjoining the main building to the NW, is the *Museum of Medieval Austrian Art*.

The **Belvedere Gardens**, originally laid out by J. L. von Hildebrandt (1693 onwards) and re-designed by the Paris landscape gardener Dominique Girard (1717 onwards), rise symmetrically in three stages for a distance of some 500 m/550 yds, with fountains and statues. The gardens are open to the public all day. From the top there is a beautiful *view of Vienna. To the left (S) is a well-stocked *Alpine Garden*, originally laid out in 1850.

The *Upper Belvedere** (1721–23) stands at the top of the hill above the gardens; the S front, to the rear, is mirrored in a large ornamental pond. It is given a feeling of airy lightness by a carefully contrived distribution of the masses (three central blocks with a third storey, two wings, four corner towers), lavish sculptural decoration and the varied pattern of the roof line. From 1776 to 1890 the Upper Belvedere housed the Imperial picture gallery; from 1904 to 1914 it was the residence of the heir to the throne, Archduke Franz Ferdinand; and since 1924 it has been an art gallery, becoming the *Austrian Gallery of 19th and 20th Century Art* after the Second World War. The Staatsvertrag (see History, p. 28) was signed in the Domed Hall in 1955.

To the E of the Lower Belvedere, on the Rennweg, is the **Salesianerinnenkirche** (Church of the Salesian Nuns), built in 1717–30 together with the convent as a unified ensemble in High Baroque style. Adjoining the church are the **Botanic Garden** and the well-stocked *Botanical Museum*.

The continuation of the Rennweg runs SE to the **Central Cemetery** (*Zentralfriedhof*), with the tombs of leading figures in the spheres of music and art (Gluck, Beethoven,

Schubert, Brahms, Johann Strauss the Younger, Nestroy, Millöcker, Hugo Wolf, Josef Lanner, Anzengruber, Werner Kraus, Hans Moser, Curd Jürgens and many others), and beyond this to **Schwechat Airport**.

To the S of the Belvedere, beyond the Landstrasser Gürtel, is the **Südbahnhof** (South Station). E of the station, in the *Schweizer Garten*, is the **Museum of the 20th Century** (*Museum des 20. Jahrhunderts*), devoted to Austrian and foreign painters and sculptors of the 20th c. (exhibitions).

SE of the Schweizer Garten are the former Arsenal (1849–56), now housing the *Army Museum* (Heeresgeschichtliches Museum), and the Telecommunications Headquarters of the Austrian Post Office, with a *Telecommunications Tower*.

Beyond the Wiener Berg, in the OBERLAA district (8 km/5 miles S of the city), is the **Kurzentrum Wien-Oberlaa**, a spa treatment establishment opened in 1974. Situated at an altitude of 192 m/630 ft, it has one of the strongest and hottest sulphur springs in Austria (53·3 °C/128 °F), indoor and outdoor thermal swimming pools (open in winter as well as in summer), a beautiful *Kurpark* (area over 1,000,000 sq. m/250 acres), numerous outdoor and indoor tennis courts and various other sports facilities, as well as hotels, restaurants and cafés.

In the ALSERGRUND district, to the N of the Votivkirche, are the *Sigmund Freud Museum* (Berggasse 19) and the **Palais Liechtenstein**, in High Baroque style, built between

1691 and 1711 (Fürstengasse 1), with the recently established **Museum of Modern Art** (paintings by Klimt, Schiele, Hausner, Brauer, etc., as well as sculptures).

Farther N is the LICHTENTAL district, in which (Nussdorfer Strasse 54) is *Schubert's Birthplace* (museum, small concert hall).

From the Messepalast the **Mariahilfer Strasse**, a busy shopping street which carries heavy traffic, runs 4 km/2½ miles W, passing close to the **Westbahnhof** (West Station: 750 m/½ mile NW, the modern *Stadthalle*), to Schönbrunn. At the end of the street (No. 212, on right) is the *Museum of Technology* (*Technisches Museum*), displaying the achievements of Austrian technology, with the *Railway Museum* and *Postal Museum*. To the left stands the great Baroque palace of **Schönbrunn**, set in its park.

This large palace, formerly the Emperor's summer residence, lies on the S bank of the River Wien, its beautiful park extending up the hill to the light and elegant Gloriette. The palace and its park, covering an area of more than 2 sq. km/¾ sq. mile, were in open country until engulfed by the advancing city streets in the 19th c. In front of the palace is a large *Grand Courtyard* (Ehrenhof) surrounded by lower buildings.

The main entrance, opposite the Schlossbrücke, has beautiful wrought-iron railings and is flanked by two obelisks bearing gilded eagles. In the courtyard are two fountains (*c.* 1780), the one on the left by Johann Baptist Hagenauer, the one on the right by Franz Anton Zauner. On the near side of

Schönbrunn Palace

the courtyard, to the right, is the *Schloss-theater*, a graceful Rococo building by Ferdinand von Hohenberg (1766).

The **Palace*, a dignified Baroque structure with projecting wings, is not overpoweringly magnificent in spite of its considerable size (façade 200 m/220 yds long). The relatively modest effect is due in part to the traditional yellowish colouring of the walls ("Theresian yellow") and the green window-shutters. The central block has a double external staircase leading up to the first floor, under which is a court with five gateways leading through to the park.

The original house, acquired by the Emperor in 1569, was devastated by the Turks in 1683. In 1694 J. B. Fischer von Erlach the Elder designed a new palace which would have surpassed Versailles in magnificence. His more modest alternative plan, however, was adopted; work began in 1695, and the palace was habitable by 1700, though still unfinished. In 1744–49 it was altered and decorated for **Maria Theresa** by Nicolò Paccassi, who toned down the monumental dignity of the earlier plan into a less pretentious Rococo manner. Thereafter the palace became one of the Empress's favourite residences. In 1805 and 1809 Napoleon stayed in Schönbrunn; he caused the gilded eagles to be set up on the obelisks at the entrance, and in 1809, after the Austrian defeat at Wagram, signed the Treaty of Vienna here. Schönbrunn was also a favourite residence of the Emperor **Francis Joseph** (1830–1916), who was born and died in the palace.

INTERIOR. – The State Apartments on the first floor have sumptuous Rococo decoration (1760–80). The *Blue Staircase* (ceiling paintings of 1701) leads to the *Private Apartments of the Emperor Francis Joseph*, with the iron bedstead in which the Emperor died in 1916. Beyond this are the *Apartments of the Empress Elizabeth* (d. 1898). Farther along the park front are the *Hall of Mirrors* and the three *Rosa Rooms*, with landscape paintings by Josef Rosa or Roos (1760–69). The *Chinese Circular Cabinet*, with lacquer-work and Chinese porcelain, was used by Maria Theresa for private consultations.

The *Little Gallery* in the central area of the palace, with gilded Rococo stucco-work and a ceiling painting by Gregorio Guglielmi (1761), affords a beautiful view of the flowerbeds and the Gloriette; in the *Ceremonial Hall* are a portrait of Maria Theresa by her favourite painter, Martin van Meytens, and five paintings of the wedding of Joseph II (1760). In the *Blue Room* (c. 1750), with Chinese wallpaper, the last Austrian Emperor, Karl, abdicated on 11 November 1918. The *Vieux Laque Room*, with Chinese lacquer-work panels (gold on a black ground), contains portraits by Pompeo Batoni (Francis I, Joseph II and Leopold II, 1771 and 1769). The *Napoleon Room*, with Brussels tapestries (18th c.), was occupied by Napoleon in 1805 and 1809 during the French occupation of Vienna; here, too, his son, the Duke of Reichstadt, died in 1832.

In the E wing is the *"Millions Room"*, with walls panelled in costly rosewood and Indo-Persian miniatures of the 17th and 18th c. The *Tapestry Room* contains three 18th c. Brussels tapestries. The **Grand Gallery*, 43 m/140 ft long, is sumptuously decorated in white and gold (N. Paccassi, 1746), with a ceiling painting by Gregorio Guglielmi.

On the ground floor are the *Chapel* (to the left), with stucco ornament of the first half of the 18th c. and a ceiling painting by Daniel Gran (1744), and a number of rooms with painted wallpaper.

To the W of the grand courtyard, in the English Riding-Stable and the Winter Riding School, is the **Wagenburg** (Coach Museum), with a collection of historic *coaches and harness illustrating the sumptuous equipages of the Imperial court from 1562 to 1918.

*Schönbrunn Park (open to the public throughout the day), with an area of almost 2 sq. km/¾ sq. mile, is one of the finest and best-preserved French-style gardens of the Baroque period. Originally laid out by Jean Trehet in 1706, it was completely re-designed by Ferdinand von Hohenberg and Adrian von Steckhoven from 1765 onwards.

The central feature of the park is a flower garden, on the S side of which, at the foot of the slope leading up to the Gloriette, is the *Neptune Fountain* (by Franz Anton Zauner, 1780). In niches in the carefully clipped hedges on either side are marble statues, mostly by Christian Wilhelm Beyer (1773–81). To the right, immediately outside the W end of the palace, is the *Kammergarten*, formerly the Emperor's private garden. Beyond the clipped hedges footpaths cut across the wooded park, with attractive vistas between the trees. To the left of the main walk are a *Roman ruin* (by Ferdinand von Hohenberg, 1776) and, near this, the "*Beautiful Fountain*" (Schöner Brunnen), built over the spring, said to have been discovered by the Emperor Matthias while out hunting, from which the palace takes its name (pavilion of 1779, with a figure of a nymph by C. W. Beyer). Close by, to the E, is an *obelisk* (1777).

45 m/150 ft above the flower garden, at the top of a grass-covered rise flanked by woodland, is the picturesquely sited *Gloriette, an elegant colonnade 135 m/ 445 ft long (by Ferdinand von Hohenberg, 1775) which affords a superb *view of the park and the city, with the Kahlenberg in the background. – To the S of the Gloriette is the *Pheasant Garden* (Fasangarten), with fine old trees.

On the W side of the park is the **Zoo** (*Tiergarten*), originally established by Archduke Maximilian in 1552. The main features of the Zoo – a series of plain animal houses laid out in star formation around a charming octagonal Baroque pavilion – were built in 1752 by Jean-Nicolas Jadot de Ville-Issey for the Emperor Francis I, who also founded the Natural History Museum. – To the N of the Zoo is the *Palm-House* (Palmenhaus, 1883). To the W is the **Botanic Garden**, founded by Francis I in 1753, with many exotic trees.

To the S, beyond the Tirolese Garden, is the *Hietzing Cemetery*, with the graves of the dramatist Franz Grillparzer (1791–1872), the ballerina Fanny Elssler (1810–84) and the painter Gustav Klimt (1862–1918).

To the W of Schönbrunn Park, on the *Küniglberg* (261 m/856 ft), is the **Radio Headquarters** (*ORF-Zentrum Wien*). – Farther W, extending to the city boundary, is the **Lainzer Tiergarten** (Zoo), an area of some 2320 hectares/9 sq. miles surrounded by a wall, with numerous species of wild animals. Within the grounds is the *Hermesvilla*, a hunting lodge of 1882, with a countryside museum and a bird sanctuary.

SURROUNDINGS. – **On the Höhenstrasse to Klosterneuburg** (37 km/23 miles). The route described is 25 km/15 miles longer than the direct road via Kahlenbergerdorf but scenically much more attractive; the two routes can be combined to make a round trip of 50 km/ 31 miles. Other pleasant round trips can be worked out using the various approach roads from Vienna via Neuwaldegg, Neustift am Walde, Sievering or Grinzing.

The road W from Vienna runs close to **Schönbrunn** and up the *River Wien*. – 11 km/7 miles: *Wien-Hacking* (215 m/705 ft). Bear right over the Wien. Just beyond

this is *Wien-Hütteldorf* (213 m/699 ft). – Then 20 km/ 12½ miles on the *Wiener Höhenstrasse*, which winds its way up through the **Wienerwald** (Vienna Woods), with extensive views. The outskirts of Vienna reach close to the hills in this area. – 6 km/4 miles: *Neuwaldegg* (250 m/820 ft), where we cut across the road from Vienna to Tulln. – 4 km/2½ miles: **Dreimarkstein** (454 m/ 1490 ft; inn; large car park and viewpoint). – 1·5 km/ 1 mile: *Rohrerwiese* (380 m/1247 ft; inn), from which a road (3 km/2 miles SE) runs down to the former vine-growing village of **Sievering** (252 m/827 ft). From Sievering it is 7 km/4¼ miles back to the city. Half an hour's climb N of the Rohrerwiese is the *Hermannskogel* (543 m/1782 ft; inn), with a lookout tower. – 500 m/ 550 yds farther on is the *Fischerhaus*. – 2·5 km/1½ miles: *Meierei Kobenzl* (382 m/1253 ft), a restaurant with a large terrace (view) on the E side of the **Kobenzl** (*Latisberg*, 492 m/1614 ft). – 500 m/550 yds beyond the Meierei a road comes in on the right from Vienna (9 km/ 5½ miles) by way of the old wine village of *Grinzing* (6·5 km/4 miles), famous for its "Heuriger" (new wine). This is a much used road, providing a direct route from the city to the Kahlenberg and Leopoldsberg.

The Höhenstrasse continues in a wide bend round the Wildgrube. – 3·5 km/2 miles beyond the Rohrerwiese junction the road reaches the *Kahlenberg* (483 m/ 1585 ft; car park; large restaurant with terrace, café, hotel), with the *Josefskirche* (rebuilt 1734). From here there is a superb view of the Vienna basin; an even more extensive view is to be had from the *Stephaniewarte* (VHF transmitter), 5 minutes NW. The old Kahlenberg road from *Nussdorf* comes in at the restaurant; and S of Nussdorf is the district of *Heiligenstadt*, where Beethoven used to spend the summer. – 1 km/¾ mile beyond the Kahlenberg car park the road to Klosterneuburg goes off on the left, and 1 km/¾ mile beyond the junction the Höhenstrasse comes to an end on the **Leopoldsberg** (423 m/1388 ft), the most easterly hill in the Wienerwald, rising almost directly up from the Danube 263 m/ 863 ft below. On the Leopoldsberg are an inn, occupying the site of a former Babenberg castle, and a Baroque church. The *view is even finer than from the Kahlenberg. – We now return to the road junction and continue down the N side of the Kahlenberg, with many bends, to (5 km/ 3 miles) **Klosterneuburg** (see p. 113). – Then via *Kahlenbergerdorf* back to **Vienna** (12 km/7½ miles to the city).

Through the Marchfeld (round trip, 108 km/67 miles). – The **Marchfeld**, to the E of Vienna, is a large and fertile plain bounded by the Danube, the River March and the southern edge of the hilly Weinviertel. Although offering no particular scenic attractions (small-scale oil-drilling), it is an area of great historical significance. In the 1st to 4th c. A.D. it was a frontier area which saw much fighting between the Romans and the Germanic Quadi; in the Middle Ages it was the scene of many battles with the Hungarians; in the 17th c. there was fighting with the Turks; and during the Napoleonic wars the battles of Aspern and Deutsch-Wagram were fought here.

Leave Vienna by way of the Praterstern, cross the **Danube** (Reichsbrücke rebuilt 1980) and continue past the imposing new *UNO-City* (on left) in the Donaupark (Donauturm). – 6 km/4 miles: *Kagraner Brücke*, a bridge over the Alte Donau, once the main arm of the river. This was the famous "blue Danube". To the S is the island of Gänsehäufel, a popular bathing place. – 5 km/3 miles: **Aspern**. In front of the parish church is a stone lion commemorating the battle of Aspern (21–22 May 1809), in which Napoleon suffered his first defeat in open battle at the hands of Archduke Charles and was compelled to withdraw across the

Danube. On 5–6 July 1809, however, he won the victory of **Wagram** (10 km/6 miles N of Aspern) and was able to return across the river. To the S of Aspern is the **Lobau**, a charming area of meadowland (nature reserve) traversed by old arms of the Danube.

The road continues past Aspern airfield (flying and parachute-jumping school; car-racing). – 5·5 km/ 3½ miles: *Gross-Enzersdorf* (Hotel Am Sachsengang, A, 110 b.), a little town still partly surrounded by walls, situated at the end of the (unfinished) Danube–Oder Canal. – 14 km/9 miles: *Orth* (145 m/476 ft), a market village on the banks of the Danube. The massive castle (13th and 16th c.), with four towers, contains a fishery museum and a beekeeping collection. – 9 km/5½ miles: *Eckartsau* (153 m/502 ft), with a handsome Baroque Schloss (1722–32), once an Imperial hunting lodge. – 7 km/4½ miles: *Stopfenreuth* (140 m/460 ft). 2 km/ 1¼ miles E is a bridge over the Danube to Bad Deutsch-Altenburg.

The road now turns N towards the March, which flows into the Danube here. – 4 km/2½ miles: *Engelhartstetten*. – 6 km/4 miles: *Schloss Schlosshof*, a massive stronghold on a hill above the March valley, built for Prince Eugene by Johann Lukas von Hildebrandt (1725–29) and enlarged for Maria Theresa in 1760 (restoration in progress). 3 km/2 miles SE is the *Markthof* riding head-quarters. – 8 km/5 miles: **Marchegg** (141 m/463 ft), a little town on the March, which here forms the frontier with Czechoslovakia, and which still preserves its circuit of walls and gates. The Schloss, a former hunting lodge (rebuilt in Baroque style in 1733), now houses the *Lower Austrian Hunting Museum* (all species of game found in Lower Austria). *Marchauen* nature reserve.

The road now turns W. – 15 km/9 miles: *Obersiebenbrunn* (150 m/490 ft), with a large Baroque church (1724) and a Schloss, rebuilt for Prince Eugene in 1730. – 6 km/ 4 miles: *Markgrafneusiedel*, on the Russbach. – 22 km/ 13½ miles: **Vienna**.

36 km/22 miles NE of Vienna, to the S of *Gänserndorf*, is a large **Safari Park** (7 km/4½ miles circuit). – 6 km/ 4 miles from Gänserndorf, near *Prottes*, is an educational walk of the oil and natural gas undertakings.

Villach

Land: Carinthia (K).
Altitude: 499 m/1637 ft. – Population: 53,000.
Post code: A-9500. – Telephone code: 0 42 42.

(i) **Fremdenverkehrsamt der Stadt Villach**,
Europlatz 2;
tel. 2 44 44.

ACCOMMODATION: – IN VILLACH: *Parkhotel Kärnten*, A, 265 b.; *Post*, A, 130 b.; *City*, A, 100 b.; *Europa*, A, 90 b.; *Goldenes Lamm*, B, 80 b.; *Mosser*, B, 60 b.; *Kasino*, C, 65 b.; *Fugger*, C, 40 b. – IN WARMBAD: *Kurhotels Warmbaderhof*, A1, 205 b., SB, SP, sauna; *Kurhotel Josefinenhof*, A, 110 b., SB, sauna; *Nanky*, A, 60 b. – YOUTH HOSTEL.

RECREATION and SPORTS. – Water sports on the nearby lakes; riding; tennis in Warmbad Villach.

Villach, the second town in Carinthia, lies W of Klagenfurt in the wide basin of the Drau, which is joined here by the Gail. The Villacher Alpe to the W and the Karawanken chain to the S, with the jagged Julian Alps to the rear, form a magnificent mountain backdrop. An important traffic junction, the town attracts many visitors on their way to the Carinthian lakes or into Yugoslavia, and the thermal springs of Warmbad Villach draw many people to this popular spa. There was already a bridge and a fortified settlement here in Roman times, under the name of Bilachinum. In 1007 the town passed under the control of the Bishop of Bamberg, and remained under episcopal rule until it was purchased by Maria Theresa in 1759.

Villach from the air

SIGHTS. – The long Hauptplatz, cutting across the middle of the old town, links the bridge over the Drau at its N end with the parish church at its S end. It has a number of fine old burghers' houses, notably the *Alte Post* and the *Paracelsushof* (16th c.) – the latter of which recalls the residence in the town of the scientist and physician Theophrastus Paracelsus (1493–1541). The *Trinity Column* in the square dates from 1739.

The **parish church** (St Jakob), on a terrace above the S end of the square, is a three-aisled Gothic hall-church (14th c.) with a narrow choir and a tower 95 m/312 ft high (view), linked with the church only by an arched gateway. The splendid Baroque canopied altar (1740) has a large Gothic crucifix (1502); in the choir is a huge fresco of St Christopher (c. 1740); stone pulpit of 1555. The baptistery contains a Gothic font and choir-stalls of 1464. The church also has many finely carved gravestones belonging to members of old noble families (16th c.).

Opposite the church, to the SE, is the new *Rathaus* (1952). – In the NW of the town is the parish *church of St Martin* (present church 1962; late Gothic Madonna on high altar).

NW of the Rathaus, at Widmanngasse 38, is the interesting **Municipal Museum** (*Stadtmuseum*), with prehistoric, early historical and medieval material. In the courtyard is a section of the old town walls. – In the Schillerpark, near the secondary school (Peraustrasse), is a large **relief model of Carinthia** (*Kärntner Relief*) on scales of 1:5000 and 1:10,000 (with explanations). – On the left bank of the Drau, to the S of Nikolaigasse, stands the **Kongresshaus** (1971: conference and lecture rooms, stage).

3 km/2 miles S of the town is the spa of **Warmbad Villach** (503 m/1650 ft), with three thermal swimming pools, indoor, outdoor and the "Zillerbad", in the park. The radioactive mineral springs (28–30 °C/82–86 °F) are recommended for the treatment of rheumatism, circulatory disorders and nervous diseases. Many tennis courts.

SURROUNDINGS. – To the SW of the town, above the Gail valley, rises the *Villacher Alpe*, an extensive walking and climbing area, with extensive views. A panoramic road (toll) 17 km/10½ miles long gives access to the area. From the *Rosstratte* car park (1700 m/5580 ft) at the end of the road a chair-lift runs up to almost 2000 m/6560 ft; from the upper station it is 2 hours' climb NW to the summit of the *Dobratsch* (2166 m/7107 ft), the highest peak in the Villacher Alpe, with the Ludwig-Walter-Haus (inn), two chapels and an Alpine garden. – Lower down, to the N (13 km/8 miles by road from Villach), is **Bad Bleiberg** (923 m/3028 ft; Bleibergerhof, A, 160 b., SB, SP; Haus Kärnten, B, 46 b.),

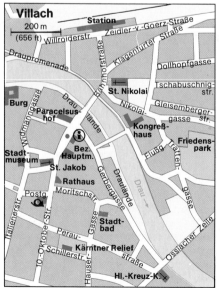
Warmbad Villach

with hot springs (25–30 °C/77–86 °F), an open-air thermal swimming pool and an indoor pool.

3 km/2 miles SE of Villach on the E bank of the Gail is *Maria Gail*, with a fine old church (14th c. frescoes, winged altar of 1520). – 4 km/2½ miles SE is the Faaker See.

The forest-fringed *Faaker See* (alt. 554 m/1818 ft; area 2·4 sq. km/1 sq. mile) is a favourite resort of bathers and water sports enthusiasts, with water temperatures in summer of up to 26 °C/79 °F (several beaches and camping sites). To the S is the Karawanken chain, with the *Mittagskogel* (2143 m/7031 ft). – A road encircles the lake at some distance from its shores. On the N side of the lake is *Drobollach* (490 m/1068 ft; Hübner, A, 80 b., SP); on the SW side *Faak am See* (560 m/1837 ft; Müllneritsch, B, 60 b.; Faakerseehof, B, 35 b.); on the NE side *Egg* (580 m/1903 ft; Karnerhof, A, 130 b.), within the commune of Drobollach, from which there is a road up the hill (viewpoint) of *Tabor* (725 m/237 ft).

At Neu Egg is the *Seeleitn holiday village*, a group of 24 old peasant houses (15th–18th c.) which have been re-erected on this site and equipped with modern facilities and are now let as vacation homes. The "village" has an inn, a mini-golf course, a boccia pitch, a sauna and an open-air swimming pool. Nearby is the holiday village of *Schönleitn*.

Völkermarkt

Land: Carinthia (K).
Altitude: 461 m/1513 ft. – Population: 11,000.
Post code: A-9100. – Telephone code: 0 42 32.
ⓘ **Fremdenverkehrsamt,** Hauptplatz 1;
tel. 25 71 17.

ACCOMMODATION. – *Krone*, A, 53 b.; *Karawanken-blick*, C, 14 b.; *Nagele*, C, 20 b.

RECREATION and SPORTS. – Fishing in the lake; riding.

The old town of Völkermarkt lies on a terrace above the Drau, here dammed to form an artificial lake 21 km/13 miles long. The town ("Volko's market") was founded in 1100 and received its municipal charter in 1253. An important road junction, Völkermarkt was for centuries a place of some consequence as a trading and frontier town; it was several times besieged and occupied.

SIGHTS. – At the N end of the Hauptplatz is the *Rathaus*, in an old castle which the Emperor made over to the town in 1453. The former town hall, the *Altes Rathaus*, on the S side of the square, is a handsome arcaded building of the late 15th c. In the middle of the square, between these two buildings, is an 18th c. *Plague Column*. There is also a monument commemorating the 1960 plebiscite, after which Yugoslavia was obliged to return the town to Austria.

The **parish church** of the Magdalene is Gothic, with a twin-towered Romanesque W front; 15th c. Gothic wall paintings. In front of the church is a Gothic *"lantern of the dead"* (1477). – From the *Bürgerlust* park to the S of the town there is a fine *view over the long artificial lake on the Drau of the Karawanken and the jagged Stein Alps. – To the W of the old town stands the old and frequently rebuilt *church of St Ruprecht*, with a Romanesque tower.

SURROUNDINGS. – 8 km/5 miles NE is *Griffen Abbey*, a Premonstratensian house dissolved in 1786. The abbey church, a late Romanesque pillared basilica with a Baroque façade, is now the parish church. Opposite it is the smaller Old Parish Church (13th c.), with five late Gothic wood reliefs (*c.* 1250) in the choir. Near the village of Griffen is an interesting stalactitic cave. – 14 km/ 9 miles N the mountain village of *Diex* has an old fortified church; the village is at the foot of the *Saualpe* (2081 m/6828 ft). The road passes the ruined castle of *Haimburg*.

20 km/12½ miles SE of Völkermarkt, situated on the River *Feistritz* between two wooded hills, is the little town of **Bleiburg** (479 m/1572 ft; pop. 4000; Altes Brauhaus, A, 56 b.), the name of which (*Blei*, "lead") is derived from the lead-mines which were once worked here. It has a number of churches of the 15th, 16th and 18th c. and a 16th c. castle (above the town to the E).

Another road runs 40 km/25 miles S from Völkermarkt to the **Seebergsattel** (1218 m/3996 ft), on the Yugoslav frontier. The road passes through *Eberndorf* (8 km/ 5 miles: see under Klopeiner See) and comes in 23 km/ 14 miles to **Eisenkappel** (558 m/1831 ft; pop. 1500; Schlosspark, A, 100 b., SB; Sonne, B, 16 b.), the chief place in the Vellach valley and the most southerly market village in Austria, frequented both as a summer and winter sports resort. The name refers to an old chapel and the hammer-drills which once operated here. By the cemetery is the late Gothic pilgrimage church of Maria Dorn (frescoes). 8 km/5 miles SW is the *Trögerner Klamm* (gorge).

Vorarlberg

Bundesland: Vorarlberg (V). – Capital: Bregenz.
Area: 2601 sq. km/1004 sq. miles.
Population: 307,900.

ⓘ **Landesfremdenverkehrsverband Vorarlberg**, Römerstrasse 7/I, A-6900 Bregenz;
tel. (0 55 74) 2 25 25–0.

Vorarlberg is the most westerly province of Austria, the second smallest in area (after Vienna) and the second smallest in population (after Burgenland. It is bounded on the N (in the Bregenzer Wald) by Germany (Bavaria), on the W (along the Alpine Rhine) and S (Rätikon and Silvretta) by Switzerland, on the SW by the Principality of Liechtenstein and on

the E (Verwall group, Arlberg) by Northern Tirol.

As its name indicates, Vorarlberg lies, in relation to the rest of Austria, "in front of the Arlberg", extending from there to the E end of Lake Constance. The scenery ranges from the gardens and orchards, of almost Italian appearance, in the Rhine valley, on the shores of Lake Constance and in the lower parts of the Bregenzer Wald through a forest-covered upland region to the peaks and glaciers of the Silvretta group, rising to more than 3000 m/9800 ft. With its deeply slashed and steep-sided valleys, strikingly shaped peaks, fertile fields and great expanses of meadowland, beautiful mountain lakes, clear rivers and mountain streams, flower-spangled pastures, quiet bays on Lake Constance and attractive old towns and villages, Vorarlberg is a region of particular charm. It is also noted for its industry and love of order of its people.

Vorarlberg is, after Vienna, the most highly industrialised province of Austria and the one with the highest income per head. Since the establishment of the cotton-working industry in Bregenz in the middle of the 18th c. Dornbirn has developed into Austria's principal textile town and Lustenau into a focal point in the production of embroidery. Also of great importance to the economy of Vorarlberg are the hydro-electric installations in the mountains, which are linked to the European grid.

Tourism also contributes to the province's revenue. The principal tourist regions are the **Arlberg** (Lech and Zürs), **Lake Constance and the Rhine valley** (Bregenz, Dornbirn and Hohenems), **Brandnertal/Walgau** (Bludenz, Brand), the **Bregenzer Wald** (Bezau, Damüls, Egg), the **Grosswalsertal** (Fontanella/Faschina), the **Kleinwalsertal** (Mittelberg, Riezlern), the **Klostertal** (Klösterle), the **Montafon** (Gargellen, Gaschurn, Schruns/Tschagguns, Vandans) and the **Oberland** (Feldkirch, Frastanz).

HISTORY. – Finds in various parts of the region have shown that Vorarlberg was inhabited in Stone Age times. It was later occupied by the *Raetians*, probably of Celtic origin, who worked minerals here and farmed the land as high as the upper slopes of the hills.

Place-names such as Schruns, Tschagguns, Gaschurn and Vandans are of Raeto-Romanic origin. – In 13 B.C. the *Romans* sent an army, led by Augustus' son Claudius Drusus, against the Raetians, who were defeated in a battle at Calliano (now in Italy), while another force commanded by Claudius Tiberius marched up the Rhine and almost annihilated the Raetians in a battle at

Nüziders. The Romans then occupied the region, built roads and established garrisons to control the territory. – In A.D. 114 the *Alamanni* made their first incursion into Vorarlberg. After the collapse of the Western Roman Empire, about A.D. 500, the region fell under the control of the *Franks*. In subsequent centuries it was held successively by Carolingian, Ottonian and Hohenstaufen rulers and was frequently rent by strife between various noble families.

At the beginning of the 15th c. large areas of Vorarlberg were devastated during the "Appenzell War" with the Swiss Confederates. The Thirty Years War also wrought havoc in Bregenz and the surrounding area; and in 1635 Vorarlberg was ravaged by a virulent epidemic of plague.

During the War of the Spanish Succession at the beginning of the 18th c. the people of Vorarlberg valiantly defended their land against France, and during the Napoleonic wars the Vorarlberg militia defeated the French at Feldkirch in 1799. After the peace of 1805 Vorarlberg was incorporated in Bavaria; but in 1813 the Bavarians were driven out and the province was reunited with Austria.

The revolutionary events of 1848 passed lightly over Vorarlberg, and the region enjoyed a measure of economic revival.

The First World War did not directly affect Vorarlberg, and in 1918 it was separated from Tirol and given its own provincial government. – Under the National Socialist régime, in 1939, Vorarlberg became part of the "Reichsgau" of Tirol. Although the region saw practically no military activity during the Second World War, its economy suffered severe damage. In the spring of 1945 it was occupied by French forces. Since the end of the war Vorarlberg has shared the fortunes of the rest of Austria, with a notable development of industry and tourism.

ART. – The architectural record of Vorarlberg is relatively modest. Little influenced by the artistic trends which spread from Vienna after the unification of the Habsburg empire, it lacks the sumptuous Baroque creations found elsewhere in Austria. There was, however, a **Vorarlberg school** of architects, emanating from the little town of Au in Bregenzer Wald, which between the end of the Thirty Years War and the closing years of absolutist rule made a notable contribution to the development of Baroque architecture in the Pre-Alpine region. Many churches and religious houses were built by Vorarlberg architects in SW Germany and Switzerland – Weingarten and Einsiedeln by Kaspar Moosbrugger, Birnau and St Gallen by Peter Thumb, etc.

Since Vorarlberg was spared the devastation suffered by the eastern provinces of Austria the various architectural styles succeeded one another here harmoniously, existing structures being retained and new ones added, so that many buildings both religious and secular show a steady development of styles from the early medieval period to modern times. Of special interest, too, are the *castles* of Vorarlberg, which have retained their medieval character and dignity.

An outstanding artistic figure of her time was the woman painter **Angelica Kauffmann** (1741–1807), who can be reckoned a Vorarlberger (though she was born in Chur and died in Rome) since her family home was at

Schoppernau, in the Bregenzer Wald

Schwarzenberg in the Bregenzer Wald. Her portrait appears on the Austrian 100-schilling note.

The *folk poetry* and *folk music* of Vorarlberg, which have produced a substantial body of tales, legends and songs, show a certain dependence on Switzerland and other neighbouring Alemannic territories.

In the NW part of the province the landscape and climatic patterns are set by *Lake Constance* and the wide valley of the Alpine Rhine. In this area are the larger settlements of Vorarlberg, including the provincial capital of **Bregenz** (see p. 55), situated at the foot of the *Pfänder*, a widely celebrated viewpoint. The gateway to the province from the W, Bregenz attracts large numbers of visitors to its historic old town and its summer Festival on the shores of the lake.

The busiest route into the interior of Vorarlberg is the broad and fertile *Rhine valley* with its meadowland and its expanses of reeds (many birds), still largely unspoiled.

In *Lustenau* and particularly in **Dornbirn** (see p. 69), Vorarlberg's largest town, there is a happy mingling of town and countryside, of industry and agriculture. Attractive districts of villas extend into the garden-like landscape, gradually giving place to farming villages.

Above Dornbirn the valley of the Rhine takes on a more imposing aspect, with old castles perched on steep crags rising suddenly out of the plain.

At the old-world town of **Feldkirch** (see p. 74), where the road to the little Principality of *Liechtenstein* branches off, is the beginning of the *III valley*, which runs down from the Silvretta group. The stretch of the valley extending to Bludenz is known as the *Walgau*.

The old town of **Bludenz**, surrounded by pleasant orchards, lies in the geographical heart of the province and is a good base from which to explore the beauties of the surrounding area – the **Grosswalsertal** or the Arlberg and the boldly engineered Flexenstrasse, the Rätikon with its beautifully shaped peaks or the attractive Montafon valley and the ice-capped Silvretta group on the frontier with Switzerland.

The internationally famous winter sports resorts on the *Arlberg* (see p. 50) are equally popular in summer with mountain-lovers; and the resorts in the *Montafon* (p. 139), although primarily concerned with winter sports, are likewise much frequented by walkers and climbers in summer.

The *Silvretta Road* (p. 179) gives access to the two large artificial lakes supplying the Illwerke (hydroelectric power stations) and the many mountain inns and climbing huts in the Silvretta area, with *Piz Buin* (3312 m/10,867 ft) as the highest peak. The Arlberg road through the *Klostertal* and the new Arlberg Tunnel, the longest road tunnel in the world, offer alternative routes into Tirol.

Stuben, in the Klostertal

The area between the upper reaches of the Lech valley, the III valley and the Rhine valley and the German frontier is occupied by the **Bregenzer Wald** (p. 56), a beautiful upland region which takes on an almost mountainous character in the SE, with great variety of scenery. Here visitors will find relatively unspoiled natural beauty, quiet little villages and distinctive local customs and traditions.

The *Kleinwalsertal* (p. 111), although in Vorarlberg, can be reached only from the town of Oberstdorf in Bavaria.

Wachau

Land: Lower Austria (NÖ).

ⓘ **Fremdenverkehrsverband Wachau-Nibelungengau,** Roseggerstr. 10, A-3500 Krems; tel. (0 27 32) 56 20.
Stadtgemeindeamt Dürnstein, Rathaus, Nr. 25, A-3601 Dürnstein; tel. (0 27 11) 2 19.

ACCOMMODATION. – IN AGGSBACH MARKT: *Post*, B, 66 b., sauna; *Lechner*, C, 28 b., sauna; *Kranz*, C, 20 b. – IN AGGSBACH DORF: *Haidn*, C, 30 b. – IN SPITZ: *Mariandl*, B, 93 b.; *Wachauerhof*, B, 55 b.; *Neue Welt*, B, 50 b.; *Goldenes Schiff*, C, 80 b. – IN WEISSENKIRCHEN: *Raffelsbergerhof*, A, 28 b.; *Donauhof*, A, 27 b.; *Salomon*, B, 25 b.; *Donauhof*, C, 21 b. – IN DÜRNSTEIN: *Schloss Dürnstein*, A1, 70 b., SP, sauna; *Richard Löwenherz*, A, 100 b., SP; *Gartenhotel Pfeffel*, B, 60 b., sauna; *Sänger Blondel*, B, 35 b.; *Bohmer*, C, 12 b.

The *Wachau is the 30 km/18 miles stretch of the Danube between Melk and Krems, where the river cuts a narrow rocky valley between the foothills of the Bohemian Forest to the NW and the Dunkelsteiner Wald to the SE. This is surely the most beautiful part of the Danube, with ancient little towns surrounded by vineyards nestling under historic old castles and castle ruins. The best time to visit the Wachau is in spring or autumn, when there are fewer visitors.

5 km/3 miles below Melk, on the right bank of the Danube, is *Schloss Schönbühel*, on a crag rearing 40 m/130 ft above the river. The castle, originally built in the 12th c., dates in its present form from the early 19th c. Also in the village is a Servite convent built in 1668–74.

5 km/3 miles farther on is **Aggsbach Dorf** (250 m/820 ft), also on the right bank. Of a former Carthusian monastery 2·5 km/1½ miles E of the village (1380–1782), now converted into dwelling-houses, there remain part of the Gothic cloister and the abbot's lodging (1592), together with a fine

church. 7 km/4½ miles NE of Aggsbach Dorf is the Servite monastery of *Maria Langegg* (rebuilt in Baroque style 1765–73; old frescoes in church, beautiful library). – From Aggsbach Dorf there is a ferry over the Danube to **Aggsbach Markt**, on the left bank.

7 km/4½ miles W of Aggsbach Markt, high above the Danube valley, stands the late Gothic pilgrimage church of **Maria Laach am Jauerling** (580 m/1903 ft). The church is richly decorated and furnished, with a 16th c. image of the Virgin (six-fingered), a carved altar of 1490 and fine gravestones. 7 km/4½ miles N of Maria Laach is the *Jauerling* (959 m/3146 ft), from which there is a good view of the Danube valley.

A little way downstream are the ruins of *Burg Aggstein, 325 m/1065 ft above the

In the Wachau

Traditional costumes of the Wachau; in the background Dürnstein

river on a high steep-sided crag, with a magnificent view of the valley. The castle, founded in 1231 and several times destroyed and rebuilt, is of imposing bulk; it preserves parts of its towers, kitchen and dining hall, the chapel and its mighty walls. Opposite the castle, on the left bank of the Danube, is the village of *Willendorf*, where the famous "Venus of Willendorf" was found. This Palaeolithic image of a generously proportioned female figure is now in the Natural History Museum in Venice.

Spitz (210 m/689 ft; pop. 1700) is an old market village on the left bank of the Danube, under the vine-clad Tausendeimerberg. Above the village to the SW are the ruins of *Burg Hinterhaus*. The late Gothic parish church of St Maurice, with the choir set at an angle to the nave, has a fine group of Apostles (1380) and an altarpiece by Kremser Schmidt on the high altar. Schloss Erlahof contains a Ship Museum (history of Danube shipping). – 8 km/5 miles NW, on a hill beyond Mühldorf, is the well-preserved *Burg Oberranna* (15th–16th c.). The castle church has a 12th c. crypt (closed).

2 km/1¼ miles below Spitz is the late Gothic fortified *church of St Michael*, with crenellations. Opposite the choir (which is decorated with small figures of animals) is a late 14th c. charnel-house. The church has a richly decorated interior.

6 km/4 miles beyond Spitz, also on the left bank of the Danube, is **Weissenkirchen** (205 m/673 ft; pop. 1800), perhaps the most beautiful of the Wachau vine-growing villages, with old houses and courtyards (16th c.). Particularly fine is the Teisenhofer Hof, with an external staircase, arcades and towers, which now houses the Wachau Museum (many pictures by Kremser Schmidt). A covered flight of steps leads up to the Gothic fortified church of the Assumption, surrounded by a defensive wall and towers. In the square in front of the church is an 18th c. statue of St John Nepomuk.

16 km/10 miles NW, on the plateau, is *Hartenstein* (500 m/1640 ft), below the ruins of an imposing 12th c. castle. At the foot of the crag on which the castle stands is the *Gudenus Cave*, which yielded Palaeolithic material now in the Natural History Museum in Vienna.

***Dürnstein** (209 m/686 ft; pop. 1100) is the most popular tourist attraction in the

Wachau. The little town is enclosed within a triangle of walls and towers, with the walls running up to the ruined castle 150 m/490 ft above the town. The Augustinian convent, founded in 1410 and dissolved in 1788, is a masterpiece of Baroque architecture. The monastic *church*, now the parish church, was built in 1721–25 by J. Munggenast, J. Prandtauer and others; it has one of the finest Baroque towers in Austria, a prominent landmark up and down the Danube valley, and a magnificent main doorway in the courtyard of the convent. The interior (conducted tour) has beautiful stucco reliefs on the ceiling; altarpieces by Kremser Schmidt (1762) in the central side chapels; richly carved pulpit by Kremser Schmidt's father Johann Schmidt; fine choir-stalls. On the W side of the church is a Baroque cloister, with a large Christmas crib (Nativity group) by Johann Schmidt (*c.* 1730). To the S of the church are the ruins of the mid 14th c. *Klarissinnenkirche* (Church of Poor Clares). The Renaissance *Schloss* (1630), directly above the Danube, is now a hotel.

By the *Kremser Tor* (Krems Gate) a short flight of steps leads up to the graveyard, with the remains of the early Gothic *Kunigundenkirche* (13th c.) and a 14th c. charnel-house. – From here another flight of steps leads up the hill (½ hour) to the massive ruins of the 12th c. *Dürnstein Castle* (destroyed by the Swedes in 1645). Here in 1193 Richard Cœur-de-Lion was imprisoned by Duke Leopold VI of Austria, with whom he had fallen out during the Third Crusade; and it is here that the minstrel Blondel is supposed to have discovered his master. There is a magnificent *view from the castle.

Waldviertel

Land: Lower Austria (NÖ).
ⓘ **Fremdenverkehrsverband Waldviertel,**
Dreifaltigkeitsplatz 1, A-3910 Zwettl;
tel. (0 28 22) 22 33.

The Waldviertel lies between the Danube and the Czechoslovak frontier in the NW of Lower Austria. Its name ("forest quarter") refers to the great expanses of forest which once covered this area. It is a rocky plateau of gneiss and granite ranging between 400 m/ 1300 ft and 700 m/2300 ft in height. The western part of the area has a fairly severe climate. In this region, lying off the main tourist routes, there

has been a modest development of textile and glass industries in addition to the traditional agriculture and forestry. The principal rivers are the Grosser and Kleiner Kamp and, to the N, the Thaya. Numerous castles, country houses and religious foundations bear witness to a long and eventful history.

The much eroded granite mountains of the western Waldviertel reach heights of over 1000 m/3300 ft in the Weinsberger Wald, which forms the boundary between the Waldviertel and the Mühlviertel in Upper Austria, and SW of Weitra (Ostrong, 1060 m/ 3478 ft; Weinsberg, 1039 m/3409 ft; Tischberg, 1073 m/3521 ft; Nebelstein, 1015 m/ 3330 ft). They are for the most part covered with coniferous forest. There are numerous small lakes and areas of moorland, particularly in the area around Heidenreichstein.

The eastern Waldviertel is a rolling plateau with gorge-like valleys. The milder climate favours the development of agriculture and stock-farming (particularly sheep).

Visitors who want to get away from the crowds of tourists and enjoy a restful and relaxing holiday will find what they require in the Waldviertel.

The chief place in the Waldviertel is the little town of **Zwettl** (see p. 251), still surrounded by its old walls, with its Cistercian *abbey. Near the town are *Schloss Rosenau* and *Burg Rappottenstein*, set high above the Kleiner Kamp. E of Zwettl are a number of artificial *lakes* created by the damming of the Kamp, with excellent facilities for bathing, boating and fishing. Here, too, are *Burg Ottenstein* and the ruins of Burg Lichtenfels.

The River **Kamp** flows through the Waldviertel from W to E and joins the Danube at Krems. The most beautiful part of the valley is the winding section to the S of Horn. The *Ottenstein* and *Dobra* reservoirs, to the E of Zwettl, form an extensive recreation area with excellent facilities for water sports (sailing, motorboating).

SW of the old town of *Horn* is the Benedictine ****Altenburg Abbey** (see p. 49), which should on no account be missed by visitors to this region. Other places worth visiting in the vicinity of Horn are the pretty

little town of *Eggenburg* and *Schloss Greillenstein*, with a Criminal Law Museum. – From Horn it is well worth while making an excursion into the winding *Unteres Kamptal*, to the S. In this valley are the **Rosenburg*, with its unique tiltyard, and the little resort of *Gars am Kamp* (251 m/824 ft; pop. 4000; peat baths), with a Rathaus of 1593, a ruined castle and an old parish church (originally Romanesque). In the southern part of the valley is the little vine-growing town of *Langenlois* (219 m/719 ft; pop. 5000), with two Gothic churches and handsome houses of the 16th–18th c. (beautiful arcaded courtyards); Wine Museum; Plague Column (1713).

In the north-eastern Weinviertel, near the Czechoslovak frontier, is the old wineproducing town of **Retz** (see p. 156) – which, properly speaking, is in the Weinviertel – with its wine-cellars under the main square. Excursions to *Burg Hardegg, Schloss Riegersburg* and *Geras Abbey*.

Gmünd (507 m/1663 ft; pop. 7000; Hotel Schachner, C, 26 b.) is an old frontier town on the River Lainsitz, in the north-western Waldviertel. In the Stadtplatz are the Old Rathaus (13th c.), with a local museum, and (No. 34) a Glassworking and Stoneworking Museum, devoted to the local glassworks and stone-carving. There are two houses with sgraffito decoration.

NE of Gmünd is the *Blockheide Nature Park*, an open-air geological museum. – 10 km/6 miles SW of Gmünd is *Weitra*, with a parish church of the 14th–15th c. and a Schloss of 1590–1606.

Burg Heidenreichstein, in the Waldviertel

20 km/12½ miles NE of Gmünd the little town of **Heidenreichstein** (561 m/1841 ft; pop. 4500; Hotel Schindl, C, 32 b.; Nöbauer, C, 27 b.; Grossmann, C, 23 b.) has a well-preserved *moated castle (13th–15th c.), a massive stronghold with sturdy round towers. The late Gothic parish church has three pictures by Schnorr von Carolsfeld. – 12 km/7½ miles NW is the little town of **Litschau** (528 m/1732 ft; pop. 2000), picturesquely situated between two small lakes. The parish church (St Michael's) is a Gothic hall-church of the 14th–15th c. The castle (16th–17th c.) has a 13th c. keep. The Neues Schloss dates from the 18th c.

Weinviertel

Land: Lower Austria (NÖ).

ⓘ **Fremdenverkehrsverband Östliches Weinviertel,**
Oserstrasse 12, A-2130 Mistelbach;
tel. (0 25 72) 25 15.
Fremdenverkehrsverband Westliches Weinviertel,
Stadtamt, Hauptplatz, A-2070 Retz;
tel. (0 29 42) 22 23.

The Weinviertel ("Wine Quarter") is a plateau (200–400 m/650–1300 ft high), partly forest-covered, lying N of Vienna between the Danube and the Czechoslovak frontier. It extends to the E of the Waldviertel, from which it is separated by the long ridge of the Manhartsberg. Isolated ranges of hills rise to heights of some 500 m/1600 ft (Leiser Berge, 482 m/1581 ft), dividing the area into an eastern and a western part. It is relatively densely populated. The broad valleys are flanked by fertile hillsides, mainly occupied by vineyards. There are also large fields of sugar-beet and wheat. On the eastern fringe of the Weinviertel are the Zistersdorf and Matzen oilfields.

15 km/9 miles NW of Vienna, on the left bank of the Danube, is **Korneuburg** (167 m/548 ft; pop. 8500; Bauer, B, 100 b.; Sonne, C, 41 b.), the gateway to the western Weinviertel, with a boatbuilding yard. In the Hauptplatz are late Gothic burghers' houses; the large Stadtturm dates from 1447. The imposing Augustinerkirche (mid 18th c.) has a fine Rococo high altar.

3 km/2 miles S is the *Bisamberg* (360 m/1181 ft), with a fine view from the Elisabethhöhe (restaurant). – 6 km/4 miles NW

looms the ***Burg Kreuzenstein** (266 m/873 ft), rebuilt between 1874 and 1915 on the model of the medieval castle which was destroyed by the Swedes in 1645. Both externally and internally the castle gives a good impression of a knightly stronghold of the early 16th c. (many art treasures).

From **Stockerau** (175 m/574 ft; pop. 14,000; Bauer, A, 72 b.; Lenaustuben, B, 30 b.) a road runs N to Hollabrunn. – At *Sierndorf* is a Schloss (1516), set in a park, with an Orangery and the Chapel of St John Nepomuk (figure of the Saint, under a Canopy).

22 km/14 miles NW of Stockerau, near *Kleinwetzdorf*, is the *Heldenberg*, laid out 1848/49 (Hall of Honour, grave of Field Marshal Radetzky, monuments).

Parish church, Hollabrunn

Hollabrunn (237 m/778 ft; pop. 6000; Sporthotel, C, 120 b.; Graf Alfred, C, 33 b.) is the administrative headquarters of the western Weinviertel; it has a Plague Column of 1723 and a local museum. 2 km/1¼ miles SE, at Raschala, is "Mozarts Pinkelstein", recalling an occasion when Mozart satisfied a natural need during his journey to Prague in 1787. – 5 km/3 miles N is *Schöngrabern* (258 m/846 ft), with the late Romanesque *church (13th c.) of Mariä Geburt (Nativity of the Virgin), with a number of remarkable reliefs on the outer wall of the apse.

20 km/12½ miles NE *Mailberg* (217 m/712 ft) has a castle which belonged to the Knights of Malta (rebuilt 1594–1608; Museum; chapel with late Gothic woodcarving).

20 km/12 miles NE of Vienna, in the valley of the Russbach, is the old vine-growing town

of **Wolkersdorf** (176 m/577 ft; pop. 4800; Klaus, A, 100 b.), with an imposing moated castle (rebuilt in 18th c.), a Baroque parish church (Gothic choir) and a Trinity Column. At *Matzen*, 15 km/9 miles E, is a large oilfield. – Off the road to Mistelbach, to the E, is the little spa of *Bad Pirawarth* (174 m/571 ft; peat baths, chalybeate and acidic mineral spring).

Mistelbach (228 m/748 ft; pop. 10,000, Goldene Krone, C, 51 b.; Weisses Rössl, C, 29 b.) is an old town in the heart of the eastern Weinviertel. The parish church of St Martin, on high ground, dates from the 15th c.; it has a massive tower. Adjoining the church is a round Romanesque charnel-house (12th c.). Fine presbytery (1691–1700). The little Baroque Schloss now houses a local museum.

7 km/4½ miles NW stands the massive *Schloss Asparn an der Zaya*, with two towers, which contains a Prehistoric Museum and a Wine Museum, in the park is an open-air museum of prehistory. SW of Asparn is the *Leiser Berge Nature Park* (492 m/1614 ft).

In the northern part of the eastern Weinviertel, 16 km/10 miles N of Mistelbach, is the little wine town of **Poysdorf** (205 m/673 ft; pop. 4000), with an early Baroque parish church (1625–35) and a local museum. – 25 km/ 15 miles NW of Mistelbach, on the Czecho-slovak frontier, is **Laa** *an der Thaya* (186 m/ 610 ft; pop. 7000; Storchennest, C, 37 b.), with remains of its medieval walls and a massive and well-preserved castle (15th– 16th c.) which now contains a Beer Museum (open Sunday mornings only). The early Gothic parish church of St Veit (Vitus) dates from the 13th c. (high altar of 1740).

Weissensee

Land: Carinthia (K).

ⓘ **Verkehrsamt Weissensee,**
Haus Nr. 90, A-9762 Techendorf;
tel. (0 47 13) 22 20 13.

ACCOMMODATION. – IN TECHENDORF: *Moser*, B, 100 b.; *Harrida*, B, 56 b.; *Haus am See*, B, 40 b.; *Forelle*, B, 25 b. – CAMPING SITE. – IN OBERDORF: *Kolbitsch*, B, 55 b. – IN NEUSACH: *Strandhotel*, A, 70 b.; *Neusacherhof*, A, 50 b.; *Bergblick*, B, 45 b. – IN NAGGL: *Sporthotel Alpenhof Weissensee*, B, 60 b.; *Sonnenhof*, B, 54 b.; *Tischler*, B, 24 b.

The *Weissensee, in the Gailtal Alpe SW of Spittal an der Drau, is the highest of the four large Carinthian

lakes (alt. 930 m/3050 ft). It is 11·4 km/ 7 miles long, some 500 m/550 yds wide and up to 98 m/320 ft deep. In warm summers its water reaches a temperature of 25 °C/77 °F. Unlike the Millstätter, Ossiacher and Wörther See, it lies rather off the beaten tourist track and is popular with those who like a quiet and relaxing summer holiday. Much of the shoreline cannot be reached by car because of the steep wooded slopes which rise directly up from the water.

On the NW side of the Weissensee is the chief place on the lake, **Techendorf** (947 m/ 3108 ft; pop. 750), the chief place in the valley with little houses built in old Carinthian style. To the W are *Gatschach*, *Oberdorf*, and *Pradlitz*, all parts of the same commune. – 1·5 km/1 mile E is the village of *Neusach*, where the road along the N shore ends.

From Techendorf a bridge 100 m/110 yds long crosses to the S shore of the lake, from which a double chair-lift ascends to the *Naggler Alm* (1335 m/4380 ft; skiing area), the starting-point of many ridge walks on the hills between the Weissensee and the Gail valley. – 2·5 km/1½ miles E of the bridge is the last place on the S side of the lake, the hamlet of **Naggl**, another little resort. From here there is a pleasant walk round the lake by way of the Laka summit (1851 m/6073 ft) to the E end and then back along the N side to Neusach, keeping about half-way up the steep wooded slopes, with some ups and downs.

There is a motorboat sevice from Techendorf to the E end of the lake, from which a road via Stockenboi and through the Weissenbach valley leads to Feistritz an der Drau (25 km/ 15 miles).

Wels

Land: Upper Austria (OÖ).
Altitude: 317 m/1040 ft. – Population: 54,000.
Post code: A-4600. – Telephone code: 0 72 42.

ⓘ **Tourist-Information**, Stadtplatz 55;
tel. 34 95 and 53 11–708.

ACCOMMODATION. – *Rosenberg*, A, 212 b., sauna; *Stadtkrug*, A, 141 b., sauna; *Greif*, B, 140 b.; *Maxihaid*, B, 36 b.; *Goldenes Kreuz*, B, 32 b.; *Kremsmünstererhof*, C, 100 b.; *Bayerischer Hof*, C, 50 b.

EVENTS. – *Wels International Agricultural Fair*, with folk celebrations (beginning of September in even-numbered years); *Austrian Film Festival* (October).

The old town of Wels lies on the left bank of the Traun in the Alpine foreland region SW of Linz. In Roman times it was the chief town of a district (Ovilava), and is now the industrial and agricultural heart of the fertile Welser Heide area to the N of the town. The long Stadtplatz is one of the finest town squares in Austria.

SIGHTS. – The central axis of the town is the handsome *Stadtplatz* (partly pedestrian zone), which is more like a street than a square. At the W end is the *Ledererturm* (1376), one of the towers on the old town walls.

On the S side of the square are two fine Baroque buildings, the *Kremsmünsterer Hof*, once the town house of Kremsmünster Abbey, and the imposing **Rathaus** (1748), in front of which is the Stadtbrunnen, a reconstruction of the original fountain of 1593. From here a lane runs S to the former *Minorite Church* (1283), one of the earliest Gothic churches in the country, and now occupied by the fire brigade. On the S side of the church, entered from the street called Am Zwinger, is the *Sigmarkapelle* (now a memorial chapel to the dead of the two world wars), which has frescoes of 1480–90.

At the E end of the Stadtplatz is the **parish church** (*Stadtpfarrkirche*), a late Gothic building with a beautiful Romanesque inner doorway and a tall tower with an onion-dome (1732). Notable features of the church are the three fine 14th c. stained-glass windows in the choir and the marble tombs of the lords of Pollheim in the porch under the tower. Opposite the church is the *House of Salome Alt* (1568–1633), mistress of Prince-Bishop Wolfdietrich of Salzburg, who retired to Wels after his downfall. – A little way E the Burggasse runs down to the **Burg**, in the SE corner of the old town, where the Emperor Maximilian I died in 1519. The Burg is now a cultural centre (festival hall and art gallery); in summer concerts and theatrical performances take place in the courtyard. The Burg houses an Agricultural Museum and other collections; *lapidarium* (stones with Roman inscriptions) in the rose-garden.

The old town is bounded on the N by the tree-lined Ringstrasse. At the W end of this street, adjoining No. 2, is a relic of *Schloss Pollheim*, with a tablet commemorating the shoemaker Hans Sachs, who wrote his first poems at the mastersingers' school here in 1513.

Across Pollheimer Strasse from the Schloss (No. 17) is the *Municipal Museum* (Stadtmuseum), with Roman finds and prehistoric exhibits.

To the SW of the old town, beyond the Mühlbach, is the *Volksgarten*, with an animal park. Farther SW, mostly beyond the railway, is the **Messegelände** (the exhibition grounds in which the Wels Fair is held).

SURROUNDINGS. – On the right bank of the Traun is the *Reinberg* (390 m/1280 ft), with the Marienwarte, a popular viewpoint (vista of the Alps). – In *Schmiding*, about 7 km/4 miles NW of the town, is a bird park with an aviary for birds of prey and a tropical house through which visitors may walk. – 15 km/9 miles NW of Wels is **Bad Schallerbach** (303 m/994 ft; hotels: Grünes Törl, A, 54 b.; Post, A, 35 b.), with a hot sulphur spring (37·2 °C/99 °F); open-air and indoor swimming pools. 10 km/6 miles SW of Bad Schallerbach is another little spa, *Gallspach*.

16 km/10 miles SW of Wels is the Benedictine abbey of **Lambach** (see p. 118) and 18 km/11 miles SE the Benedictine abbey of **Kremsmünster** (p. 116).

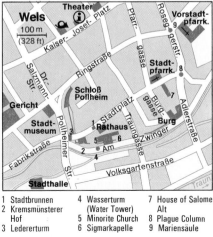

1 Stadtbrunnen
2 Kremsmünsterer Hof
3 Ledererturm
4 Wasserturm (Water Tower)
5 Minorite Church
6 Sigmarkapelle
7 House of Salome Alt
8 Plague Column
9 Mariensäule

Werfen

Land: Salzburg (S).
Altitude: 524 m/1719 ft. – Population: 3000.
Post code: A-5450. – Telephone code: 0 64 68.
ⓘ **Verkehrsverein**, Hauptstrasse; tel. 3 88.

ACCOMMODATION. – *Kärntnerhof*, B, 44 b.; *Erzherzog Eugen*, B, 24 b.; *Eisriesenwelt*, C, 53 b.* *Neuwirt*, C, 37 b.; *Zur Stiege*, C, 17 b. – YOUTH HOSTEL in the castle.

The old market town of Werfen lies in the Salzach valley on the important route from Salzburg to Eastern Tirol, the Grossglockner or Carinthia. Popular with tourists in summer and winter,

Werfen is the starting-point for a visit to the magnificent **ice caves in the Tennengebirge, NE of the town.

SIGHTS. – On the W side of the elongated Hauptplatz is the *parish church* (mid 17th c.). – On a wooded crag above the town to the N is ***Burg Hohenwerfen** (680 m/2230 ft. Originally built in 1077, the castle was strengthened in later periods, and was rebuilt in its present form in the 16th c. It was thoroughly restored and renovated after a fire in 1931, and now houses a youth hostel and a police school.

SURROUNDINGS. – The most rewarding excursion to be made from Werfen is to the ****Eisriesenwelt** ("World of the Ice Giants") on the western edge of the Tennengebirge, the largest known system of ice caves and one of the great sights of the Eastern Alps (open May to October). The caves, carved out of the rock by an underground river in the Tertiary period, were discovered in 1879 but were not opened to the public until 1912. So far 45 km/28 miles of caves have been explored. The conducted tours through the caves (warm clothing and stout footwear essential) takes about 2 hours; the whole trip there and back takes 5 hours.

In the "World of the Ice Giants", Werfen

From the middle of Werfen minibus-taxis run N through the forest to the *Fallstein car park* (903 m/2963 ft). From there it is a half-hour climb to the *Wimmerhütte* (1076 m/ 3530 ft; inn, open in summer), from which a cableway runs up to the commandingly situated *Dr.-Friedrich-Oedl-Haus* (1586 m/5204 ft; inn; accommodation). From this hut a rocky footpath leads up in 20 minutes to the entrance of the caves (1664 m/5460 ft).

During the winter cold air flows into the cave, lowering the temperature of the rock; then in spring the water trickling down the rock freezes. In summer the direction of air movement is reversed and an ice-cold wind blows out of the cave. The outer reaches of the cave are ice-covered for a distance of some 600 m/650 yds. A good footpath leads into the cave, past a frozen waterfall, to the Eistor or "Ice Gate" (1775 m/5824 ft), the highest point in the cave, and then down into the Mörk-Dom, a huge chamber 70 m/ 230 ft long and 40 m/130 ft high, named after the speleologist Alex von Mörk. – The climb to the cave, on foot all the way, takes 3½ hours.

2 km/1¼ miles SE of Werfen, on the right bank of the Salzach, is the little summer resort of **Pfarrwerfen** (553 m/1814 ft; pop. 2000; Sporthotel Eulersberghof, B, 56 b.; Quehenberger, B, 32 b.; Sonneck, C, 42 b.) with a Gothic parish church. From there a narrow mountain road runs 6 km/4 miles E to **Werfenweng** (901 m/2956 ft; pop. 500; Sporthotel Wenghof, A, 110 b.; Alpengasthof, B, 90 b.), a summer and winter resort. Chair-lift to *Strussingalm* (1530 m/5020 ft) and *Bischlinghöhe* (1883 m/6178 ft); several ski-lifts. NE of Werfenweng is the *Dr.-Heinrich-Hackel-Hütte* (1531 m/5023 ft; accommodation), from which numerous peaks can be climbed.

Wetterstein-gebirge

Land: Tirol (T).
Altitude: Highest point: Zugspitze (2963 m/9722 ft).
ⓘ **Österreichischer Alpenverein,**
Sektion Ehrwald,
Spielmannstr. 17, A-6632 Ehrwald.

The Wettersteingebirge, a massive isolated mountain block with long subsidiary ridges, lies on the frontier between Germany (Bavaria) and Austria (the Aussenfern area in Tirol). The highest peak in the range, which is also the highest peak in Germany, is the *Zugspitze (2963 m/9722 ft), with the boldly engineered Tirolese Zugspitzbahn running up to the ridge from Ehrwald-Obermoos – the counterpart of the Bavarian Zugspitzbahn from Garmisch-Partenkirchen.

A difficult climbing route leads to the summit from the Wiener-Neustädter Hütte (2213 m/ 7216 ft), following an almost parallel line to the Zugspitzbahn.

The ***Zugspitzplatt**, a hollow enclosed by the summit ridge, with a small glacier, is a popular skiing area, noted for the assured quality of its snow.

A whole series of peaks in the long Wetterstein ridge to the E offer scope for numerous rock climbs in varying grades of difficulty – for example on the **Hochwanner** (2746 m/9010 ft), with a 1400 m/4600 ft high N face which offers one of the longest climbs in the Calcareous Alps, or the magnificent **Dreitorspitzen** (2674 m/8773 ft, 2633 m/8639 ft and 2606 m/8550 ft).

To the S of the Wettersteingebirge and separated from it by the beautiful Alpine meadows of the *Ehrwalder Alm* (1493 m/ 4899 ft), are the lonelier **Mieminger**

Berge. The best-known peak in this group is the *Hohe Munde* (2661 m/8731 ft), which dominates a long stretch of the Inn valley; the most beautiful is the *Sonnenspitze* (2414 m/7920 ft), which looks down on the lakes on the Fernpass; and the highest is the *Östliche Griesspitze* (2759 m/9052 ft).

In a corrie (hollow) divided into three "steps" are the beautiful *Seebensee* (1650 m/5414 ft) and the dark *Drachensee* (1876 m/6155 ft; Coburger Hütte, 1920 m/6300 ft).

Lermoos, Barwies, Obermieming and Untermieming, Obsteig and Telfs are only a few of the places which make good bases for walks and climbs in the Mieminger Berge and farther N in the Wetterstein area.

Wiener Neustadt

Land: Lower Austria (NÖ).
Altitude: 265 m/869 ft. – Population: 40,000.
Post code: A-2700. – Telephone code: 0 26 22.
ⓘ **Fremdenverkehrsverein,**
Herzog-Leopold-Strasse 17;
tel. 35 31-3 98.

ACCOMMODATION. – *Corvinus*, A, 136 b.; *Central*, B, 90 b.; *Forum*, B, 60 b.; *Bednar*, C, 14 b. – YOUTH HOSTEL: *Jugendgästehaus*, in Europahaus, Promenade 1.

Wiener Neustadt, situated at the southern edge of the Vienna basin, was founded by the Babenbergs in 1194 as a frontier stronghold directed against the Hungarians. It was granted its municipal charter in 1277, and from 1452 to 1493 was an Imperial residence. Later it acquired importance as the seat of a military academy, in which Austrian officers are still trained. Although mainly an industrial town (metal goods, shoes, textiles), Wiener Neustadt also has a number of fine old buildings in the older part of the town.

SIGHTS. – At the SE corner of the old town is the **Burg**, founded in the 13th c. It was enlarged and embellished by King (later Emperor) Frederick III, who made it his principal residence from 1440 to 1493, and Maria Theresa.

The *Theresian Military Academy* was founded by Maria Theresa in 1752; it was closed in 1918 but reopened in 1934, and from 1938 to 1945 was a German military academy, the first commandant of which was the future General Rommel. The building was severely

damaged during the last war but was restored by 1958 and is now once again a training establishment for officers in the Austrian army.

Of the four corner towers of the Burg only one has survived. The W front and the grand courtyard are dominated by ****St George's Church**, the finest late Gothic church interior in Austria. It was built above the vaulted entrance hall in 1440–60 as the burial chapel of Frederick III (though the Emperor is in fact buried in St Stephen's Cathedral in Vienna). On the courtyard side of the church is the famous **Wappenwand** ("Heraldic Wall"), with 14 Habsburg coats of arms and 93 imaginary coats of arms. Below is a statue of the Emperor with the cryptic device A.E.I.O.U., one explanation of which is that it stands for "Austria erit in orbe ultima" ("Austria will last until the end of the world"). The interior of the church is almost square; on the gallery which encircles it are numerous unidentifiable coats of arms, and on the ceiling are the coats of arms of the Habsburg hereditary dominions. Under the steps of the high altar are the remains of the Emperor Maximilian I, the "last of the knights", who was born in the Burg in 1459 and died at Wels in 1519; the famous tomb in Innsbruck which he himself had planned was not completed until 1582 and remained empty. Above the altar and on either side are three superb *stained-glass windows* (15th and 16th c.). On the side walls are the Emperor's and Empress's oratories, with delicate tracery.

In the *Akademiepark* behind the Burg is the large parade-ground used for the passing-out ceremony of the Military Academy in September. Here, too, are monuments to Maria Theresa, Count Kinsky (Master of the Ordnance and director of the Academy from 1779 to 1805) and the Emperor Francis Joseph (1912).

NW of the Burg is the Old Town, in the form of a regular rectangle 600 by 700 m/650 by 760 yds. In the Hauptplatz, surrounded by handsome arcaded buildings, are a Marien-säule (column bearing a figure of the Virgin; 1678) and the *Rathaus* (second half of 16th c.), with a neo-classical façade.

Farther N is the Domplatz, with the imposing **Liebfrauenkirche** (parish church of the Assumption), which was a cathedral until the see was transferred to St Pölten

The Burg, Wiener Neustadt

(1784). The W front and nave are Romanesque (13th c.), the transepts and choir
Gothic (mid 14th c.). On the S side is the
Brauttor (Bride's Doorway) of *c.* 1238.
Inside, on the pillars, are figures of *Apostles
(*c.* 1500) attributed to L. Luchsperger and
his assistants. Above the triumphal arch is a
wall painting of the Last Judgment (1300).
The high altar and choir-stalls are Rococo
(1760–77).

The *Propsthof* to the N of the church is
believed to have originally been a Babenberg
residence, and was later (until 1784) the
bishop's palace; it has a magnificent doorway of 1714. – Farther N, in Petersgasse, is a
former *Dominican friary*, now housing the
Municipal Archives; the church is used as
an exhibition hall.

On the E side of the old town is the
Cistercian house of **Neukloster** (rebuilt in
the 18th c.). The Gothic church (14th c.)
has a rich Baroque interior and contains the
tomb of Eleanor of Portugal (d. 1467), wife
of the Emperor Frederick III and mother of
Maximilian I. Mozart's "Requiem" was
performed for the first time in this church in
1793. – In the SW corner of the old town is
the *Capuchin Church* (Kapuzinerkirche,
15th–17th c.).

To the N of the old town, in a former *Jesuit
College* (1737–43) at Wiener Strasse 63, is
the well-stocked **Municipal Museum**; its

treasures include a copy of the *Corvinus-
becher (*c.* 1480), a gilt goblet bearing the
monograms of King Matthias Corvinus of
Hungary and Frederick III (original in the
town hall). Still farther N is Walther-von-
der-Vogelweide-Platz, with a Gothic monument, the *"Spinnerin am Kreuz"* ("Woman
spinning by the Cross"; 1382–84), 8 m/25 ft
high.

SURROUNDINGS. – On a limestone plateau 15 km/
9 miles W of the town is the **Hohe Wand Nature Park**
(alt. 800–1000 m/2600–3300 ft), reached by a road
(many turns). Many inns and Alpine Club huts provide
good bases for walks on the plateau (from 1 to 6 hours)
– e.g. to the *Grosse Kanzel* (1043 m/3422 ft; extensive
views), *Plackles* (1135 m/3724 ft) or the *Kleine Kanzel*
(1065 m/3494 ft).

40 km/25 miles NW of Wiener Neustadt is the attractive
little market town of **Gutenstein** (482 m/1581 ft), a
pleasant holiday resort, above which loom the ruins of
Burg Gutenstein (580 m/1903 ft), where Frederick the
Handsome died in 1330. 3 km/2 miles SW is the *Mariahilfer Berg* (705 m/2313 ft; extensive views), with a
Baroque pilgrimage church (1668–1724).

35 km/22 miles W of Wiener Neustadt is the market
town of **Puchberg** (578 m/1896 ft; pop. 3300), a
summer and winter resort at the foot of the *Schneeberg*
(2075 m/6808 ft), the highest peak in Lower Austria,
with views extending from the Alps to the puszta. A cog
railway climbs in 1¾ hours to the Hochschneeberg station
(1795 m/5889 ft), from which it is 1¼ hours' climb to the
summit. There is also a chair-lift from Puchberg up the
Himberg (948 m/3110 ft).

17 km/10½ miles S of Wiener Neustadt is **Seebenstein**
(348 m/1142 ft), with a castle (11th and 17th c.), the
finest in the Pittental, which contains a valuable art
collection, including a figure of the Virgin by Tilman
Riemenschneider (20 minutes' climb above the village).

20 km/12½ miles SE of Wiener Neustadt, on a high crag,
is *Burg Forchtenstein* (504 m/1654 ft), enlarged
and fortified by the Esterházy family in 1635–52. It has
a large collection of arms and armour (from the castle
armoury and military trophies), a Hunting Room and a
large number of coaches and carriages. Well 142 m/465 ft
deep. Grillparzer Festival (performances of plays in castle
yard). – 3 km/2 miles SW is the *Rosalienkapelle* (746 m/
2448 ft; view), on the highest point in the wooded
Rosaliengebirge.

Wolfgangsee

Länder: Salzburg (S) and Upper Austria (OÖ).

ⓘ **Verkehrsverein St Gilgen,**
Mozartplatz 1, A-5340 St Gilgen;
tel. (0 62 27) 348.
Kurdirektion St Wolfgang,
A-5360 St Wolfgang;
tel. (0 61 38) 22 39.

ACCOMMODATION. – IN ST GILGEN: *Billroth*, A, 80 b.;
Hollweger, A, 72 b.; *Sporthotel Frisch*, A, 60 b., sauna;
Radetsky-Hof, B, 40 b.; *Zum Goldenen Ochsen*, B, 31 b.,
sauna; *Salzburgerhof*, C, 63 b.; *Am Bach*, C, 55 b. – IN ST
WOLFGANG: *Alphotel Salzkammergut*, A1, 130 b., SB,

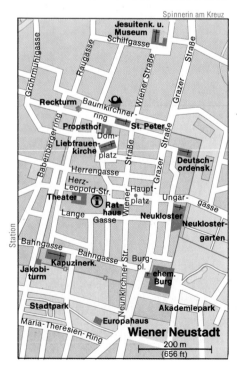

Wiener Neustadt

200 m
(656 ft)

SP; *Weisses Rössl* (famous inn), A, 120 b., sauna; *Strandhotel Margaretha*, A, 90 b., sauna; *Auhof*, A, 69 b., SP, sauna; *Seehotel Cortisen*, A, 52 b., SP; *Eden*, B, 70 b. – IN STROBL: *Parkhotel Seethurn*, A, 96 b., SB, sauna; *Stadt Wien*, A, 88 b.; *Stroblerhof*, A, 66 b., sauna; *Alpenmoorbad Schloss Strobl*, B, 64 b., SB, sauna.

RECREATION and SPORTS. – Rowing, sailing and "electro-boats"; sailing schools in St Gilgen and St Wolfgang; water-skiing and water-ski show in St Gilgen.

The *Wolfgangsee SE of Salzburg – 10 km/6 miles long, 2 km/1¼ miles wide and up to 114 m/375 ft deep – is the best known lake in the Salzkammergut. It is surrounded by wooded slopes and finely shaped hills – to the N the Schafberg, rearing up above the steep Falkensteinwand, above St Gilgen the Zwölferhorn. To the local people it is also known as the Abersee. The road from St Gilgen to Bad Ischl skirts the S side of the lake, with a road to St Wolfgang branching off at Strobl. The NW shores, with their sheer cliffs, are almost inaccessible.**

At the W end of the lake, in a wide meadow-covered valley, is the popular resort of **St Gilgen** (546 m/1791 ft; pop. 3000; bathing beach, indoor swimming pool). Near the Rathaus is the house in which Mozart's mother, Anna Maria Pertl (1720–78), was born. Beautiful Mozart Fountain. – At the E end of the lake is the village of *Strobl*, where the road to St Wolfgang goes off.

St Wolfgang (549 m/1801 ft; pop. 2500) is a very popular health resort on a sunny strip of land on the NE side of the lake, below the Schafberg. The town and its Weisses Rössl hotel, owned by the same family since 1712, became world-famous

as the scene of Ralph Benatzky's operetta "White Horse Inn". On a terrace above the lake is the late Gothic *pilgrimage church* (1470–77; painted in Baroque style (1683–97), with a magnificent **high altar by Michael Pacher (1481), richly decorated with carved figures and panel paintings. The *double altar of St Wolfgang and St John the Baptist is one of Thomas Schwanthaler's major works (1675–76). To the N of the church, in a Baroque fountain-house, is a beautiful bronze *pilgrimage fountain* (1515).

SURROUNDINGS. – The cableway from *St Gilgen* up the *Zwölferhorn* (1522 m/4994 ft) gives access in summer to fine walking country and in winter to a skiing area with several lifts. – There is a pleasant walk of about 1½ hours round the N end of the lake and above the steeply scarped shore to the *Falkensteinwand* (pilgrimage chapel); then another 1½ hours down to St Wolfgang.

From *St Wolfgang* a cog railway operating from May to October runs up in ¾ hour by way of the *Scharbergalpe* (1363 m/4472 ft; inn) to the **Schafberg** (1783 m/5850 ft), to the N of the town. At the upper station is a hotel. From the summit, lying between the Wolfgangsee, the Mondsee and the Attersee, there is one of the finest **views in the Eastern Alps. On foot, the climb from St Wolfgang takes 3½–4 hours. – 15 minutes' walk N of St Wolfgang is the *Kalvarienberg*, with a beautiful view of the lake.

10 km/6 miles NW of the Wolfgangsee, surrounded by forest, is the **Fuschlsee**, 4 km/2½ miles long by 1 km/¾ mile wide. The area around the lake is a nature reserve. At its E end is the summer resort of *Fuschl* (669 m/2195 ft; pop. 800; Parkhotel Waldhof, A, 120 b., SB; Mohrenwirt, A, 115 b., SB; Sporthotel Leitner, B, 96 b.; Seehotel Schlick, B, 80 b.; Jagawirt, B, 50 b.; CAMPING SITE). On a peninsula in the western half of the lake is the little *Schloss Fuschl* (hotel; wildlife park, hunting museum, large collection of tobacco-pipes; conferences). – 10 km/6 miles S of the Fuschlsee is the little *Hintersee* (688 m/2257 ft; bathing). The village of Hintersee (764 m/2507 ft) is a good base for climbers and skiers.

St Wolfgang

Wörther See

Land: Carinthia (K).

ⓘ **Kurverwaltung Velden,**
Am Karawankenplatz 5, A-9220 Velden;
tel. (0 42 74) 21 03 and 21 05.

ACCOMMODATION (some hotels with their own private beach). – IN VELDEN: *Parkhotel*, A1, 180 b., SB, sauna; *Seehotel Europa*, A1, 145 b., sauna; *Schloss Velden*, A, 227 b., SP; *Seehotel Auenhof*, A, 90 b., sauna; *Strandhotel Leopold*, B, 121 b.; *Kärntnerhof*, B, 90 b.; *Carinthia*, B, 85 b.; *Morak*, B, 74 b.; *Michaela*, B, 48 b. – IN PÖRTSCHACH: *Schloss Seefels*, A1, 150 b., SB, SP, sauna; *Parkhotel*, A, 328 b., SB; *Werzer-Astoria*, A, 215 b.; *Dermuth*, A, 103 b.; *Wallerwirt*, A, 100 b., SP; *Ambassador*, A, 95 b.; *Sophia*, A, 50 b.; *Österreichischer Hof*, B, 90 b., SB; *Glocknerhof*, B, 83 b.; *Joainig*, B, 65 b.; *Diana*, B, 36 b. – IN MARIA WORTH: *Linde*, A1, 80 b., and apartments by the lake; *Astoria*, A, 80 b., SB, sauna; *Strandhotel Harrich*, A, 80 b., SB, sauna; *Wörth*, A, 65 b.; *Seehotel Pirker*, A, 64 b., sauna; *Ebner*, B, 110 b.; *Betsch*, B, 32 b., sauna. – IN KRUMPENDORF: *Strandhotel Habich*, A, 82 b., SB; *Solaris*, A, 54 b., sauna; *Egger*, B, 120 b.; *Jerolitsch*, B, 100 b., SB, sauna; *Mozarthof*, B, 43 b.; *Seehotel Koch*, B, 42 b.; *Krumpendorfer Hof*, B, 38 b.

CASINO. – In Velden (roulette, baccarat, blackjack; daily from 4 p.m.).

RECREATION and SPORTS. – Water sports – sailing, rowing, water-skiing, etc.; fishing; tennis; riding; golf-course at Dellach; archery in Velden.

The **Wörther See to the W of Klagenfurt is the largest of the Alpine lakes of Carinthia (16 km/10 miles long, 1–1·5 km/¾–1 mile wide and up to 84 m/ 276 ft deep) and a popular one for water sports. It is surrounded by wooded hills, with the Karawanken range rearing up to the S. The little towns and villages around the lake are easily accessible and are well equipped with facilities for visitors. In July and August the temperature of the water can be as high as 28 °C/82 °F.

Along the N side of the lake, on the main road from Villach to Klagenfurt, are Velden, Pörtschach, Krumpendorf and Klagenfurt-See. The largest place on the quieter S side is the picturesque village of Maria Wörth.

The largest and busiest place on the lake is **Velden** (440 m/1444 ft; pop. 9000), Carinthia's most fashionable resort; the villas and hotels encircle the W end of the lake. The Schloss (16th–17th c.), with four towers and an early Baroque doorway (1603), is now a hotel.

The second largest place on the N side of the lake is the bathing resort of **Pörtschach** (450 m/1476 ft; pop. 2700), with attractive promenades. Part of the little town is charmingly situated on a small peninsula.

The next place, **Krumpendorf** (474 m/ 1555 ft; pop. 2300), has more of a village atmosphere, but here, too, there are excellent facilities for water sports. – At the E end of the lake is **Klagenfurt-See** (see under Klagenfurt).

Half-way along the S side of the lake, obliquely across from Pörtschach, is the resort of **Maria Wörth** (458 m/1503 ft; pop. 2000), with the communes of *Dellach* (golf-courses) and *Reifnitz*. The oldest part of the village occupies a rocky peninsula. High up on the headland, surrounded on

three sides by water, is the late Gothic parish church, a prominent landmark on the lake (Baroque interior; Romanesque crypt; fine 15th–16th c. high altar with a beautiful late Gothic figure of the Virgin). In the churchyard is a round charnel-house of 1278. Close by is the little 12th c. Rosenkranzkirche (Rosary Church) or Winter Church, with well-preserved Romanesque frescoes of the Apostles.

SURROUNDINGS. – NE of *Velden*, beyond the highway in the district of Göriach, is the **Karawankenblick* (660 m/2165 ft), a look-out point with a magnificent prospect over the lake to the rugged Karawanken range. To the W there is a pleasant walk (1¼ hours) to the summit of the *Grosser Sternberg* (726 m/2382 ft), crowned by a conspicuous pilgrimage church. – 1 hour's walk N of Velden is the little *Forstsee* (601 m/1972 ft), a storage reservoir. – 4 km/2½ miles SE of Velden, in a turn on the Drau, is the summer resort of **Rosegg** (483 m/ 1585 ft), with a Schloss belonging to the Princes of Liechtenstein and a wildlife park (deer enclosure). Above the village are the ruins of *Burg Alt-Rosegg* (569 m/ 1867 ft).

3 km/2 miles NE of *Pörtschach* is **Moosburg** (503 m/ 1650 ft), with a 16th c. Schloss and a ruined tower, all that remains of a castle in which the future Emperor Arnulf of Carinthia was born and in which he resided in 887–888. – Other castles near *Krumpendorf* are *Schloss Drasing*, with a large keep (1570), *Schloss Hallegg* (16th c.), with arcades and sgraffito painting, and *Burg Ratzenegg* (14th c.).

SE of *Maria Wörth* is another little summer resort, **Keutschach** (542 m/1778 ft), with a Romanesque parish church and a Baroque Schloss. Below the village to the S is the *Keutschacher See* (506 m/1660 ft). From Keutschach a mountain road runs W up the **Pyramidenkogel* (851 m/2792 ft), with a view of the lake and the surrounding mountains. The summit can be reached from Maria Wörth in 1½ hours.

Zeller See

Land: Salzburg (S).

ⓘ **Kurverwaltung Zell am See,** Brucker Bundesstrasse, A-5700 Zell am See; tel. (0 65 42) 26 00.

ACCOMMODATION. – **Grand Hotel*, A1, 238 b., sauna; **Salzburgerhof*, A1, 110 b., SB, sauna; **Katharina*, A1, 106 b., SB, sauna; **St Georg*, A1, 68 b., SB, sauna; *Latini*, A, 200 b., SB, sauna; *Tirolerhof*, A, 110 b., sauna; *Clima Seehotel*, A, 82 b., sauna; *Alpenblick*, B, 140 b., sauna; *Sporthotel Lebzelter*, B, 100 b. – YOUTH HOSTEL: *Haus der Jugend*. – CAMPING SITE.

RECREATION and SPORTS. – Water sports of all kinds; golf, minigolf, tennis, riding, artificial ice-rink, alpine gliding school and ski school (lower station of the Schmittenhöhebahn).

The *Zeller See lies N of the Grossglockner in the Middle Pinzgau, surrounded by commanding peaks. The

lake is 4 km/2½ miles long, 1·5 km/1 mile wide and up to 69 m/225 ft deep; the temperature of the water in summer can be as high as 20 °C/68 °F. Around the lake and in the little towns and villages reaching up into the valleys are facilities for a variety of sports. To the resorts of Zell am See, Saalbach and Kaprun in the W and S, which are entirely devoted to tourism, was added the so-called "Europa Sport-Region" which offers countless opportunities for various winter sports.

On the W side of the lake is **Zell am See** (758 m/2487 ft; pop. 7500), chief town of the Pinzgau and now one of the principal resorts in Salzburg province. The town was founded by monks from Salzburg about 740, when it was known as "Cella in Bisoncio". It has a *parish church* (originally Romanesque), with two frescoes of Apostles (*c.* 1200) and a very beautiful Gothic carved gallery. Also of interest are the 13th c. *Vogtturm* in the Stadtplatz and *Schloss Rosenberg* (1583), now housing the town hall and museum. To the NW of the town is the *Kur- und Sportzentrum*, with an indoor swimming pool, a sauna and an ice-rink.

On the E side of the lake, reached by boat or by road, is *Thumersbach*, a rather quieter summer resort (bathing beach, Kurpark), from which there is a fine view of Zell and its backdrop of mountains.

There are pleasant walks along the lake, and a footpath from Zell to the bathing station of Seespitz (25 minutes) and then to Thumersbach (1¼ hours), from which the boat can be taken back to Zell. In winter the lake is frequently frozen over, and is then used for various ice sports, – sometimes even as a landing strip for light aircraft.

SURROUNDINGS. – To the W of Zell is the ****Schmittenhöhe** (1965 m/6447 ft), easily accessible by cable-

Saalbach (Glemmtal)

way; on foot the climb takes 3½ hours. The Schmittenhöhe is one of the finest look-out points in the Kitzbühel Alps: to the S can be seen the Grossglockner (with the reservoirs in the Kapruner Tal in front of it) and the Grossvenediger, to the N the Calcareous Alps from the Kaisergebirge to the Dachstein. At the upper station of the cableway are a hotel and St Elisabeth's Chapel. A beautiful ridge path leads in 45 minutes to the *Sonnkogel* (1856 m/6090 ft), from which there is a chair-lift down to the *Sonnenalm* (1382 m/4534 ft; hotel) and from there a cableway to Zell.

The Schmittenhöhe is also the starting-point of the **Pinzgauer Spaziergang* (Pinzgau Walk), a 6–7 hour walk at an altitude of about 2000 m/6500 ft, with superb views all the way, ending at the upper station of the *Schattbergbahn* above Saalbach.

To the E of Thumersbach is the ***Hundstein** (2117 m/6946 ft; Statzerhaus, accommodation), with beautiful panoramic views and good skiing country. The climb by way of the *Rupertihaus* (1654 m/5427 ft; privately owned) takes about 4 hours.

To the N of the Zeller See the **Glemmtal**, through which flows the upper Saalach, turns W. This is an excellent skiing area, with many ski-lifts and mountain huts, which is also popular with walkers in summer. – The chief settlement in the valley is the well-known skiing village of **Saalbach** (1003 m/3291 ft; Alpenhotel, A, 180 b.; SB, sauna; Saalbacherhof, A, 170 b., sauna; Neuhaus, A, 120 b., SB, sauna; Bergers Sporthotel, A, 100 b., SB; Panther, A, 100 b., sauna; Reiterhof, A, 90 b., sauna; Sonne, A, 80 b., sauna. A cableway runs up to the E summit of the *Schattberg* (2021 m/6631 ft) and a chair-lift to the W summit (2095 m/6874 ft); and there are also chair-lifts to the *Kohlmaiskopf* (1794 m/5886 ft) and the *Bernkogel* (upper stations 1224 m/4016 ft and 1389 m/4557 ft). There is also a ski-lift providing a link between Saalbach and Leogang, near Saalfelden.

4 km/2½ miles up the valley from Saalbach is the hamlet of *Hinterglemm*, another place popular for skiing (1074 m/3524 ft; Glemmtalerhof, A, 140 b., SB, sauna; Egger, A, 100 b., SB, sauna; Edelweiss, A, 75 b., sauna; Sporthotel Ellmau, A, 70 b., sauna; Adler, B, 156 b., sauna), with chair-lifts up the Zwölferkogel (1984 m/6510 ft) and to the Hasenau-Alm (1480 m/4856 ft).

Zillertal

Land: Tirol (T).

ⓘ **Verkehrsverband Zell am Ziller,**
Dorfplatz 3, A-6280 Zell am Ziller;
tel. (0 52 82) 22 81.
Fremdenverkehrsverband Mayrhofen,
Postfach 21, A-6290 Mayrhofen;
tel. (0 52 85) 23 05 and 26 35.

ACCOMMODATION. – IN STRASS: *Zillertal*, C, 43 b. – IN SCHLITTERS: *Sepp*, A, 50 b., SB, sauna. – IN FÜGEN: *Post*, A, 100 b., SB, sauna; *Sonne*, A, 80 b.; *Spieljoch*, B, 60 b., sauna; *Annemarie*, B, 42 b. – IN KALTENBACH: *Brückenwirt*, C, 51 b., SB, sauna. – IN STUMM: *Laimboeck*, B, 28 b. – YOUTH HOSTEL in Stummerberg. – IN ZELL: *Zapfenhof*, A, 140 b., SB, sauna; *Tirolerhof*, B, 81 b.; *Zellerhof*, B, 70 b.; *Neuwirt*, B, 50 b. – IN MAYRHOFEN: *Sporthotel Strass*, A, 276 b., SB, sauna; *Neuhaus*, A, 250 b., SB, sauna; *Neue Post*, A, 153 b.; *Kramerwirt*, A, 151 b., sauna; *Elisabeth*, A, 70 b., SB; *Zillertal*, B, 65 b.; *Maria Theresia*, B, 56 b.; *Zillertalerhof*, B, 50 b.

RECREATION and SPORTS. – Trips on the **Zillertalbahn**, an old-time railway (passengers can travel on the footplate); walking. – **Winter sports** (ski-runs and ski trekking), particularly around Fügen (Hochfügen), at the Hochzillertal ski base above Kaltenbach, at Zell (Kreuzjoch area), around Mayrhofen (Penken area) and at Lanersbach and Hintertux. – **Gauderfest** (amusement fair) in Zell am Ziller (May); procession with beerwaggons, music and dancing.

The *Zillertal, now entirely geared to summer holidays and winter sports, is a side valley which opens off the S of the Inn valley to the E of Innsbruck. The lower part of the valley, as far up as Zell, is a wide expanse of meadowland bordered on the W by the Tux Alps and on the E by the Kitzbühel Alps; the upper part narrows into a magnificent high Alpine valley, with side valleys to the S of Mayrhofen running up into the glacier region of the Zillertal Alps. The people of the Zillertal are noted for their love of singing.

The road up the Zillertal turns S off the main road just to the W of *Strass* (522 m/1713 ft; pop. 700), where the Ziller flows into the Inn. – A little way up the valley is the summer resort of **Schlitters** (540 m/1772 ft; pop. 800). On the other bank of the Ziller, to the NW, is *Bruck*, with a fine parish church of 1337 (enlarged in the 17th c.).

Fügen (544 m/1785 ft; pop. 2300), a health resort and winter sports base, has a 17th c. Schloss and a Gothic parish church of 1497 (14th c. wall paintings). Cabin cableway to the *Spieljoch* (1865 m/6119 ft; ski-lifts). A mountain road (12 km/7½ miles) runs up to *Hochfügen* (1475 m/4839 ft; good skiing area with numerous lifts).

Kaltenbach (551 m/1808 ft) has a 15th c. parish church. On the E side of the valley, at the mouth of the Märzengrund, is *Stumm*, with a 16th c. Schloss (privately owned). To the W of Kaltenbach is the **Skizentrum Hochzillertal** (Upper Zillertal ski centre); cabin cableway to the *Forstgartenhöhe* (1730 m/5676 ft) and then chair-lift to 2200 m/7200 ft; numerous ski-lifts; panoramic road (Hochzillertal-Aussichtsstrasse: toll).

Zell *am Ziller* (575 m/1887 ft; pop. 1900), chief town of the lower Zillertal and a popular summer and winter resort, was once a mining village (gold). The parish church (1782) has a large fresco in the dome. On the Hainzenberg is the 18th c. pilgrimage

church of Maria Rast. In the Gerlosbach valley to the E is a hydroelectric station supplied by large pipes bringing down water under pressure. Above Zell to the NE is a large skiing area on the slopes of the *Kreuzjoch*, with a cableway up to 1310 m/4300 ft and then a chair-lift to a large mountain restaurant, near which are several ski-lifts. From Hainzenberg there is a cabin cableway to the *Gerlosteinalm* (1644 m/5394 ft), and from there a chair-lift up the *Arbiskogel* (1830 m/6004 ft).

3 km/2 miles S of Zell is the health and winter sports resort of *Hippach* (hotel: Alpenblick, A, 68 b.), from which there is a chair-lift to the *Grasboden* (1350 m/4430 ft). Hippach is the starting-point for climbs on the *Rastkogel* (2762 m/9062 ft), which can be scaled in 7 hours (passing a number of mountain inns on the way).

Mayrhofen (630 m/2067 ft; pop. 3000) is a well-known holiday resort situated in open meadowland at the head of the valley, surrounded by steep-sided mountains. The parish church, originally dating from the late 16th c., was enlarged in the mid 18th c. Mayrhofen is an excellent base for climbs and ski treks in the Zillertal Alps. The valley divides here into four branches – the Zillergrund to the E, the Stillupptal, the Zemmgrund and the Tuxer Tal.

From Mayrhofen there is an easy and attractive trip to the *Penken (2095 m/6874 ft), to the W of the town – either by cableway and then 1¼ hours' climb to the Gschösswand or on foot all the way (2¾ hours). From the summit there is a ridge walk of 4–4½ hours to the *Rastkogel (2762 m/9062 ft). On the other side of the valley there is a cableway (the Ahornbahn) to the Filzenboden (1960 m/6431 ft), from which it is a 3½ hour climb by way of the Alpenrose inn (open in summer) to the *Ahornspitze (2976 m/9764 ft; view).

To the E of Mayrhofen is the **Zillergrund**, with the upper course of the Zillerbach. A road runs 15 km/9 miles up the valley, but it is open to the public only for the first 5 km/3 miles, as far as Brandberg (1092 m/3583 ft). From there it is a 5–5½ hour climb to the Bärenbad-Alm (1490 m/4889 ft; inn, open in summer; accommodation), at the head of the valley – the starting-point for climbs to the Hundskehljoch (2559 m/8396 ft; 4 hours), on the Italian frontier, or the Plauener Hütte (2362 m/7750 ft; 3 hours; inn, open in summer).

The road up the **Stillupptal** runs through the *Stillupp-klamm, a wooded gorge with several waterfalls, to the Stillupp reservoir and the Kasseler Hütte (2177 m/7143 ft; 6 hours; inn, open in summer). From the hut there is a fine view of the glaciated head of the valley, from which a number of neighbouring peaks can be climbed.

The road up the **Zemmtal** runs SW through the *Dornaubergklamm (gorge) and comes in 10 km/6 miles to Ginzling (999 m/3278 ft), from which the *Dristner (2765 m/9072 ft; 5 hours) and the *Gigelitz (3002 m/

9850 ft; 7 hours) can be climbed. The *Zemmgrund*, which continues S, with several mountain huts providing inn facilities, is the starting-point of a number of climbs (for experienced climbers only) – e.g. the *Hoher Riffler* (3228 m/10,591 ft; about 7 hours) of the *Schwarzensteinalm* (2050 m/6726 ft; 3½ hours). – Some 20 km/12¾ miles from Mayrhofen, at the head of the Zamser Tal (the continuation of the Zemmgrund to the W), lies the *Schlegeis reservoir* (alt. 1782 m/5847 ft; dam 131 m/430 ft high, 722 m/790 yds long). Above the lake to the S is the *Hochfeiler* (3510 m/11,516 ft), the highest peak in the Zillertal Alps.

Hintertux (Tuxer Tal)

The **Tuxer Tal**, which runs W from Mayrhofen (road as far as Hintertux, 20 km/12½ miles, not recommended for trailer caravans), attracts many visitors with its mountain air and its excellent skiing. There are a number of ski-lifts which also give convenient access to the mountains in summer. – From *Lanersbach* (1290 m/4232 ft; hotel: Jägerwirt, B, 84 b., sauna) there are a cableway (not operating at present) to the Schrofenalpe (1690 m/5545 ft) and a chair-lift to the *Eggalm* (1970 m/6464 ft). – **Hintertux** (1494 m/4902 ft; hotels: Badhotel, A, 180 b., SB, sauna; Alpenhof, A, 70 b., SB, sauna) is a much-frequented hotel village, with a thermal spring (22·5 °C/72·5 °F), which is magnificently located near the head of the valley. An hour's walk S are the *Tuxer Wasserfälle*, thundering down into a rock cauldron. A cabin cableway, the Hintertuxer Gletscherbahn, runs up to the *Sommerbergalm* (2080 m/6824 ft) and the *Tuxer-Ferner-Haus* (2660 m/8727 ft), and to the *Gefrorene-Wand-Spitze* (3268 m/10,722 ft) opposite the *Olperer* (3476 m/11,405 ft); on the Tuxer Ferner is a summer ski area.

Zillertal Alps

Länder: Tirol (T) and Salzburg (S).
Altitude: Highest point: Hochfeiler (3510 m/11,516 ft).
ⓘ **Österreichischer Alpenverein,**
    Sektion Zillertal,
    Postamt, A-6290 Mayrhofen.

The ***Zillertal Alps**, with their classically pure lines, their glaciers, many-summited ridges and steep-sided mountain giants, are a range of characteristically Alpine type. This massif of **granitic gneiss and micaceous schists within the Central Alps extends from the Birnlücke in the E to the Brenner in the W and is divided by the Zillertal, Zemmtal and Pfitscher Joch into two sections – the Tuxer Kamm (Tux Ridge) to the N and the main ridge to the S, along which runs the Austrian-Italian frontier.**

The sharp-edged **main ridge** of the Zillertal Alps runs between perfectly shaped glacier basins, the melt-water from which runs down into the deeply slashed branch valleys ("Gründe") which radiate from the Zillertal like a gigantic fan.

The geological structure of the massif is simple, and so, too, are the approaches. From Mayrhofen, the terminus of the Zillertal railway, situated at the meeting of the branch valleys, practically all the Austrian mountain huts can be reached. Among them are the Furtschagl-Haus (2295 m/7530 ft), in the Schlegeisgrund (branch valley) near the *Schlegeis reservoir*, above which rears the highest peak in the Zillertal Alps, the *Hochfeiler (3510 m/11,516 ft) with its steep, permanently snow-covered slopes; the Berliner Hütte (2040 m/6693 ft), in the Zemmgrund, at the junction of three glacier basins running down from the **Grosser Möseler** (3478 m/11,411 ft), the steep-sided **Turnerkamp** (3418 m/11,214 ft) and the broad bulk of the *Schwarzenstein** (3368 m/11,050 ft); the Greizer Hütte (2226 m/7304 ft), at the foot of the sharp-edged pyramid of the **Grosser Löffler** (3376 m/11,077 ft); and the Kasseler Hütte (2177 m/7143 ft), at the mouth of the Stillupptal.

The Schwarzensee and Grosser Möseler

The ridges running NW between the branch valleys have many summits which offer challenging rock climbs. The finest is the **Feldkopf** (3087 m/10,128 ft), a steep and magnificently formed horn. The route to it from the Berliner Hütte runs past the little *Schwarzensee* (2470 m/8104 ft), whose waters mirror the fissured Waxeckkees (glacier).

To the N, running roughly parallel to the main ridge and separated from it by the Zamser Grund, is the **Tuxer Kamm** (Tux Ridge). This also has many large glaciers and commanding peaks. Among them is the bold outline of the *Olperer (3476 m/ 11,405 ft), linked with the steep-sided **Schrammacher** (3410 m/11,188 ft) by a long ridge.

The Hintertuxer Gletscherbahn (cableway) and a chair-lift run up from the Galtalpe (1540 m/5053 ft) to the *Sonnenbergalm* (2080 m/6824 ft), from which other lifts continue up to the *Tuxer Joch* (2340 m/ 7678 ft) or via the Spannagel-Haus (2528 m/8294 ft) to the **Gefrorene Wand** (upper station 3060 m/10,040 ft; summer skiing).

From the Spannagel-Haus the *Hoher Riffler** (3228 m/10,591 ft) can be climbed. A cross-country route affording extensive views runs down to the Friesenberg-Haus (2498 m/8196 ft), on the *Friesenbergsee*, and the Neue Dominikus-Hütte (1810 m/ 5939 ft), on the Schlegeis reservoir. From the **Kraxentrager** (2999 m/9840 ft), the most westerly of the higher peaks in the Tuxer Kamm, there is a view of the sombre little *Brennersee* far below, near the Brenner pass.

The Tuxer Kamm is separated by the Tuxer Tal, the Tuxer Joch and the Schmirntal from the **Tux Pre-Alps** (*Tuxer Voralpen*), a large range between the Wipptal, the lower Inn valley and the Zillertal. Although the Tuxer Kamm and its glaciers are a greater tourist attraction, the Pre-Alps – which rise to heights of over 2800 m/9200 ft – are a popular winter sports area. The interior, between the *Lizumer Reckner* (2886 m/ 9469 ft) and the *Mölser Berg* (2479 m/ 8134 ft), is, however, a closed military area.

The most north-westerly extension of the Tux Pre-Alps is the **Patscherkofel** (2247 m/7372 ft; cableway from Igls), the "weekend mountain" of the citizens of Innsbruck. Its neighbour to the E, the *Glungezer* (2677 m/8783 ft), which can be reached

fairly quickly from the upper station of the Patscherkofel cableway (1945 m/6382 ft), is popular with skiers on account of its long downhill run, with a fall of 2100 m/6900 ft.

To the E of the Zillergrund the **Reichenspitze group** branches northward off the main ridge of the Zillertal Alps, crossing the boundary between Tirol and Salzburg. Here, within a relatively small area, are a number of wild and rugged peaks flanked by much fissured glaciers – among them the jagged horn of the **Reichenspitze** (3303 m/ 10,837 ft) and the twin peaks of the **Wildgerlosspitze** (3282 m/10,768 ft). The Reichenspitze group can be reached either from Mayrhofen, in the Zillertal, by way of the Plauener Hütte (2362 m/7750 ft) or from Krimml, in the upper reaches of the Salzach valley, by way of the Richter-Hütte (2374 m/7789 ft). From the N the *Wildgerlostal* runs up from Gerlos by way of the Durlassboden reservoir to the Zittauer Hütte (2329 m/7641 ft), magnificently set near the *Gerlosseen* at the foot of the Reichspitze.

There are excellent skiing grounds on the northern foothills of the Reichenspitze group, on the gently sloping *Gerlosplatte* near Krimml.

There is a fine ridge walk (Höhenweg 102) from St Jodok, on the Brenner, through the nature reserve around the Hohe Kirche (2634 m/7756 ft) to the Schlegeis reservoir and from there under the main ridge of the Zillertal Alps and down into the Zillergrund.

Zugspitze

Land: Tirol (T).

(i) **Fremdenverkehrsverband Ehrwald,**
A-6632 Ehrwald;
tel. (0 56 73) 23 95.

ACCOMMODATION. – IN EHRWALD: *Schönruh*, A, 90 b.; *Alpenhof*, A, 87 b., sauna; *Spielmann*, A, 69 b., SP; *Grüner Baum*, B, 80 b.; *Stern*, B, 65 b.; *Maria Regina*, C, 63 b. – IN LERMOOS: *Edelweiss*, A, 200 b., SB, sauna; *Post*, A, 115 b., SB, sauna; *Drei Mohren*, B, 103 b.; *Tyrol*, B, 84 b.; *Loisach*, B, 80 b., sauna; *Bellevue*, B, 52 b. – ON ZUGSPITZE: *Zugspitzgipfelhaus*, B, 28 b.; *Schneefernerhaus*, on the German side, 23 b.

The *Zugspitze, part of the Wetterstein range, lies on the frontier between Germany and Austria, surrounded on three sides by deeply slashed valleys. The eastern summit (2963 m/9721 ft), crowned by a gilded cross, lies in Germany.

The summit of the Zugspitze can be reached, on the Austrian side, by cableway (the Tiroler Zugspitzbahn) from Ehrwald-Obermoos, and on the German side by cog railway (the Bayerische Zugspitzbahn) from Garmisch-Partenkirchen or by cableway from the Eibsee.

Visitors going up one way and coming down the other require a passport. – The *Tiroler Zugspitzbahn (cabin cableway) runs by way of an intermediate station at the *Gamskar* (2016 m/6614 ft) to the *Zugspitzkamm* station (2805 m/9203 ft), partly blasted out of the rock, from which a cableway continues up to the *Zugspitzwestgipfel* station (2950 m/9679 ft; large panoramic restaurant) on the western summit. From the Zugspitzkamm station it is possible to walk through a tunnel 800 m/½ mile long, with viewing windows, to the Schneefernerhaus station (2950 m/9679 ft) at the top of the Bavarian cog railway, from which a short cableway runs up to the eastern summit (2963 m/9721 ft; platform on tower 2966 m/9731 ft).

The village of **Ehrwald** (996 m/3268 ft; pop. 2000), now a well-known health and winter sports resort, lies on the eastern edge of the Ehrwald basin, an expanse of Alpine meadows. In the church are 14 modern

Lermoos, with the Zugspitze

Stations of the Cross by H. D. Alberti (b. 1938). – 3 km/2 miles W is **Lermoos** (995 m/3265 ft; pop. 800), which also attracts many visitors in both summer and winter. The parish church (1753) has a beautifully decorated and furnished interior. – Both villages are good bases for walks and climbs in the western Wettersteingebirge.

From Ehrwald there is a chair-lift to the *Ehrwalder Alm* (1493 m/4899 ft; inn), a popular walking and skiing area. From there it is 2½ hours' climb to the **Coburger Hütte** (1920 m/6300 ft; accommodation), magnificently situated above the *Drachensee* (1876 m/6155 ft), a good

base for climbs (experienced climbers only) in the western Mieminger Berge – e.g. to the *Sonnenspitze* (2414 m/7920 ft: 2 hours), the *Grünstein* (2667 m/8750 ft; 5–6 hours) and the *Griesspitzen* (2744 m/9003 ft and 2759 m/9052 ft), the highest peaks in the Mieminger Berge.

From Lermoos a chair-lift runs SW to the *Brettlalm* (1350 m/4429 ft) and the **Grubigstein** (upper station 2035 m/6677 ft), with a superb *view of the Zugspitze massif. There are two other chair-lifts and, around *Biberwier*, many ski-tows.

Zwettl

Land: Lower Austria (NÖ).
Altitude: 535 m/1755 ft. – Population: 13,000.
Post code: A-3910. – Telehone code: 0 28 22.
(i) **Verkehrsverein der Stadt Zwettl,**
   Gartenstrasse 3;
   tel. 24 14 29.

ACCOMMODATION. – *Schön*, A, 22 b.; *Waldesruh*, C, 50 b.; *Deutscher Dichter*, C, 48 b.; *Miedler*, C, 14 b.; *Riedler*, C, 14 b.

The attractive little old-world town of Zwettl, the administrative and communications hub of the western Waldviertel, lies at the junction of the Zwettlbach with the River Kamp. Near the town is the Cistercian abbey of Zwettl, founded by the Count of Kuenringen in 1138, when the town first appears in the records.

SIGHTS. – Considerable stretches of the old *town walls*, with six towers and two gates, have been preserved. In the straggling *Stadtplatz* are 16th and 17th c. burghers' houses, the **Old Town Hall** (*Altes Rathaus*: built 1307, frequently altered in later centuries, well restored 1978), with 15th c. frescoes on the exterior, and a *Plague Column* of 1727. At the SE end of the square is the *parish church*, basically a three-aisled late Romanesque basilica (first half of 13th c.), with a Gothic choir, and octagonal E tower and a W tower.

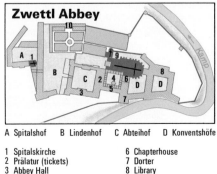

Zwettl Abbey

A Spitalshof   B Lindenhof   C Abteihof   D Konventshöfe

1 Spitalskirche
2 Prälatur (tickets)
3 Abbey Hall
4 Cloister
5 Refectory
6 Chapterhouse
7 Dorter
8 Library
9 Chapel of Holy Sepulchre
10 Abbot's Lodging

The **Propsteikirche** (St John the Evangelist) was built in the 12th c. as the family church of the Counts of Kuenringen; with the churchyard, the round 13th c. charnel-house and the Romanesque *St Michael's Chapel* (frescoes), it forms a handsome group. At Landstrasse 65 is the *Antonturm*, a 13th c. tower on the old town walls, now housing the *Anton-Museum*, a small private museum containing old implements and utensils, weapons and pictures. The late Gothic *St Martin's Church* was originally the church of a hospice just outside the town.

3 km/2 miles NE, in a bend of the River Kamp, is *Zwettl Abbey*, a Cistercian monastery founded in 1138, with monastic buildings dating back to the Romanesque period. The church has a handsome Baroque tower; the choir is a masterpiece of late Gothic architecture. Conducted tours (if number of visitors sufficient).

Passing the Romanesque *Spitalskirche* (1218), we enter the open *Lindenhof*, beyond which is the square enclosed *Abteihof* (17th–18th c.). Then by way of the *Prälatur* into the magnificent *Cloister* (1180–1240), with a variety of features showing the transition from Romanesque to Gothic. On the E side is the even earlier *Chapterhouse* (1159–80), with ribbed vaulting borne on a central granite column. Other early medieval buildings are the *Refectory* (remodelled in Baroque style), the *Warming Room* and the *Dorter*, with the old reredorter (latrines). In the eastern Konventshof is the *Library*, rebuilt in 1730–32 by J. Munggenast, with paintings by Paul Troger; it contains over 400 manuscripts, more than 300 incunabula and some 50,000 volumes. The complex also includes a choir school, a grammar school, a modern house of retreat and a small museum.

The **church** has a magnificent **W tower** 90 m/295 ft high (by J. Munggenast, 1722–27), built of grey granite, with figures, vases and obelisks of lighter coloured stone, and crowned by a gilded figure of Christ. The western part of the nave is also Baroque, but the E end and the transepts are Gothic, and the choir with its radiating chapels is in the noblest style of Gothic (1343–83). The furnishings are Baroque; on the high altar is a carved wooden Assumption (1733). The late Gothic St Bernard's Altar in the N aisle has paintings by Jörg Breu the Elder (*c*. 1500).

SURROUNDINGS. – To the E of Zwettl is the **Ottenstein reservoir** (restaurant; boat hire), a lake 12 km/7½ miles long formed by the damming of the River Kamp. Above the lake, on a peninsula, are the ruins of *Burg Lichtenfels*, and farther E, picturesquely situated on a granite crag, is **Burg Ottenstein**, with a 12th c. keep and other buildings dating from the 16th and 17th c. (restaurant). To the S of the lake lie the villages of *Friedersbach* (Gothic church, with 15th c. stained glass in choir) and *Rastenfeld* (13th c. parish church).

9 km/5½ miles W of Zwettl (3 km/2 miles on road to Weitra, then left), on a hill (620 m/2035 ft), is **Schloss Rosenau** (Schlosshotel, B, 40 b., SB, sauna, tennis; Pension Weissenhofer). The Schloss, well restored and renovated in 1966–71, dates in its present form from 1730 to 1748, when it was rebuilt in Rococo style by Daniel Gran and others. It contains an interesting Museum of Freemasonry.

15 km/9 miles SW of Zwettl, on a wooded crag above the Kleiner Kamp, is *Burg Rappottenstein*. Of the original 12th c. castle there remains the keep and the five-sided tower at the S end. The imposing complex of buildings is laid out around five courtyards. In the first courtyard is the brewhouse (1548–49), in the fifth a two-storey Renaissance loggia; windows with sgraffito painting, late Gothic Squires' Hall, smoke-blackened kitchen. The two-storey chapel (1378) in the keep has 16th c. wall paintings. – 30 km/18 miles farther SW is the old market town of **Königswiesen** (600 m/1970 ft; pop. 3000), now a summer resort. The two-aisled *parish church is a masterpiece of late Gothic architecture, with fine reticulated vaulting.

Abbreviations for the Names of the Austrian Provinces

	Postal	Vehicles
Burgenland	B	B
Kärnten (Carinthia)	K	K
Niederösterreich (Lower Austria)	NÖ	N
Oberösterreich (Upper Austria)	OÖ	O (L: Linz)
Salzburg	S	S
Steiermark (Styria)	Stm	St (G: Graz)
Tirol	T	T
Vorarlberg	V	V
Wien (Vienna)	W	W

Practical Information

The Murtal Railway

Safety on the Road. Some Reminders for the Holiday Traveller

When to Go

The best time of the year for the Pre-Alpine region is from mid May to the beginning of July; in the mountains the best time is July–August, and also September, which usually has settled weather and good visibility. The best months for walking in the upland regions are May, June and September. In the wine-producing areas (Wachau, Burgenland) the spring, when the fruit trees are in blossom, and autumn are particularly attractive. Some of the summer resorts begin to be busy in spring; during the summer the larger resorts tend to be overcrowded and correspondingly expensive. The best times to visit Vienna are the late spring, early summer and the autumn.

Weather

Weather conditions in the Alps are the most unreliable of any in Central Europe, and can present grave dangers for climbers. Signs of *good weather* are a drop of temperature in the evening, when the wind blows down the valley after blowing in the opposite direction during the day, and a fresh fall of snow on the summits. The *föhn*, a warm dry wind blowing down the northern slopes of the Alps, often brings days of magnificent weather, but there is liable to be a sudden change at any time. Warnings of *bad weather* are cirrus clouds travelling from the W and driving snow on the ridges and peaks when the weather is otherwise good. Rain increases the danger of falling rock. *Glaciers* must be avoided after the sun has had time to melt the snow covering over the fissures.

Time

Austria observes Central European Time (1 hour ahead of Greenwich Mean Time). From the beginning of April until the end of September Summer Time is in force (2 hours ahead of GMT).

Travel Documents

Visitors to Austria from the United States, the United Kingdom and Commonwealth countries require only a **passport** to enter the country. No visa is required unless the visit exceeds three months or the visitor proposes to work in Austria.

National **driving licences and car registration documents** from these countries are recognised in Austria. Foreign vehicles must carry an oval *nationality plate*. Third-party insurance is obligatory in Austria, and it is advisable to have an *international insurance certificate* ("green card").

It is advisable to take out adequate *medical insurance* before leaving home. For nationals of the United Kingdom inpatient treatment in public hospitals is usually free (with a small charge for dependants), but other medical services must be paid for.

Customs Regulations

Visitors to Austria can take in, duty-free, for their own use, clothing, toilet articles and jewelry, together with other personal effects, including two cameras and a portable movie-camera, each with 10 films, a portable typewriter, binoculars, a portable radio, a portable television set, a tape-recorder, a record-player and 10 records, musical instruments, camping equipment and sports gear; also 1–2 days' supply of provisions for the journey (including tea and coffee). Visitors may also take in duty-free 200 cigarettes or 50 cigars or 250 grammes of tobacco, 2 litres of wine and 1 litre of spirits.

Currency

The unit of currency is the Austrian **schilling** *(öS)* of 100 *groschen*. There are *banknotes* for 20, 50, 100, 500 and 1000 schillings and *coins* in denominations of 2, 5, 10 and 50 groschen and 1, 5, 10, 20, 25, 50, 100 and 1000 schillings.

Exchange Rates (variable)

1 US dollar=12 öS 1 öS=8·5 cents
£1 sterling =20 öS 1 öS=5 p

There are no limits on the amount of foreign currency that can be taken into Austria or brought out. Austrian currency can be taken in without limit on the amount, but no more than 15,000 schillings may be taken out without special permission. It is advisable to carry money in the form of travellers' cheques or to take an international credit card such as Mastercard, American Express, Visa or Eurocard.

Postal Rates

Letters (up to 20 grammes) within Austria 4·50 öS, to the United Kingdom 6 öS, to the United States or Canada 8 öS. (Airmail supplement 1½ öS.)
Postcards within Austria 3·50 öS, to the United Kingdom 5 öS, to the United States or Canada 7½ öS.

A **telephone call** to the United Kingdom costs 14 öS per minute; to the United States or Canada 40·50 öS per minute.

Getting About in Austria

Driving

Austria has a dense road network, made up of superhighways (motorways) *(Autobahnen)*, expressways *(Schnellstrassen)*, federal highways *(Bundesstrassen)*: blue and yellow number plates), provincial roads *Landesstrassen)* and communal roads *(Gemeindestrassen)*.

The **superhighways** at present open are the *Westautobahn* from Salzburg to Vienna (the continuation of the German superhighway from Munich to Salzburg), the *Inntal autobahn* from Kufstein to Innsbruck and its continuation the *Brennerautobahn* from Innsbruck to the Brenner, and sections of superhighway between Bregenz–Feldkirch–Bludenz. Salzburg–the Lueg Pass–Spittal an der Drau *(Tauernautobahn)*, Klagenfurt–Villach–Arnoldstein,   Vienna–Wiener Neustadt–Grimmenstein, Vienna–Schwechat Airport (East Autobahn), Traboch (SW of Leoben)–Graz–Strass in Steiermark, Graz–Wolfsberg (partly still single lane).

Road signs have been brought into line with international standards throughout practically the whole country. Unless otherwise indicated, traffic coming from the right has priority, even on roundabouts or traffic circles.

Motorcycles must have dipped headlights on at all times.

The general condition of the roads is excellent. **Alpine roads**, particularly minor roads, are sometimes narrow, with many sharp turns. During the busy summer season when there is heavy traffic on these roads (with large numbers of buses), drivers should exercise particular care, especially on blind hills and corners, in tunnels and galleries, etc.; and the distance covered in an hour or a day will be considerably less than on lowland roads. Vehicles going uphill always have priority over those coming down. The **pass roads** are frequently closed in winter, but the most important Alpine crossings – the Brenner, the Fern pass, the Reschen (Resia) pass and the Arlberg pass (recently bypassed by a tunnel) – are usually kept open throughout the year.

Chains should always be carried when travelling in the mountains during the winter, and on certain pass roads are obligatory (rental service is available).

There are also a number of **toll roads**.

The Loibl tunnel

Speed limits: superhighways **130 km/ 80·7 m. per hour)** (towed vehicles 70 km/ 43 m. per hour), other roads **100 km/62 m. per hour** (towed vehicles 60 km/37 m. per hour), built-up areas **50 km/31 m. per hour**. There are stiff fines for exceeding the speed limits.

Seatbelts must be worn.

Alcohol level in blood must not exceed 0·8 per millilitre.

Toll Roads

Figures in brackets refer to altitude

VORARLBERG

Bartholomäberg, Worms–Rellseck or Worms–Weisskopf
(to 1483 m/4867 ft)

Bizau–Schönenbach
(to 1025 m/3364 ft)

Blons–Alpe Hüggen
(to 1500 m/4923 ft)

Hittisau–Reute–Lecknertal
(to 1087 m/3568 ft)

Fontanella–Türtsch–Türtschalpe
(to 1200 m/3938 ft)

Lech, Zug–Spullersee
(to 1800 m/5908 ft)

Mellau–Dosegg-Alm
(to 1000 m/3282 ft)

Raggal, Marul–Grafülla–Laguz
(to 1584 m/5199 ft)

Silvretta–Hochalpenstrasse
(only in summer; to 2032 m/6669 ft)

VORARLBERG/TIROL

Arlberg, Strassentunnel
(to 1300 m/4267 ft)

=A1= **Motorways**

Ⓐ **Traffic Broadcast Areas**

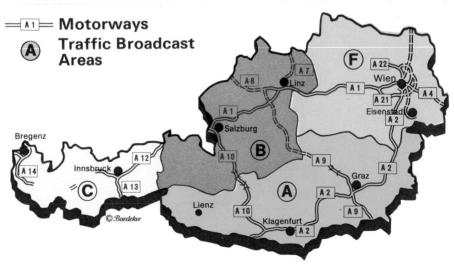

TIROL

Absam–Hall in Tirol, Eichat–Halltal
(to 850 m/2790 ft)

Aschau, Zillertaler Höhenstrasse
(to 1800 m/5908 ft)

Brenner-Autobahn
(to 1374 m/4509 ft)

Thal-Assling (Osttirol)–Bannberger Alpe,
Hochsteinstrasse
(to 2000 m/6564 ft)

Ellmau–Wochenbrunner Alm
(to 1084 m/3558 ft)

Ginzling/Mayrhofen–Breitlahner
Schlegeisstausee
(to 1784 m/5855 ft)

Gnadenwald–Hinterhornalm
(to 1520 m/4989 ft)

Hinterriss–Eng (accessible from W. Germany;
to 1218 m/3997 ft)

Iselsberg (Osttirol)–Zwischenbergen
(to 1460 m/4792 ft)

Iselsberg (Osttirol) – Roaner Alm
(to 1903 m/6246 ft)

Kals am Grossglockner (Osttirol)–Lucknerhaus
(to 1984 m/6511 ft)

Prutz–Weißseeferner, Kaunertal-Gletscherstrasse
(to 2750 m/9026 ft)

Kelchsau–Kurzer und Langer Grund
(to 1100 m/3610 ft)

Kirchdorf–Kaiserbachtal–Griesener Alm
(to 1024 m/3361 ft)

Kitzbühel–Kitzbüheler Horn
(to 1658 m/5442 ft)

Lienz (Osttirol)–Thurn–Zettersfeld
(to 1828 m/6000 ft)

Matrei am Brenner–Maria Waldrast
(to 1636 m/5396 ft)

Matrei (Osttirol)–Matreier Tauernhaus–Innergschössl
(to 1691 m/5550 ft)

Maurach–Achenkirch
(to 930 m/3052 ft)

Mayrhofen–Gasthof Wasserfall
(to 1130 m/3709 ft)

Pertisau–Falzthurnalm–Gramaialm
(950–1261 m/3118–4139 ft)

Pertisau–Pletzachalm–Gernalm
(950–1172 m/3118–3847 ft)

St Jakob in Defereggen, Erlsbach–Oberhausalm
(to 2016 m/6617 ft)

Ötztaler Gletscherstrasse,
Sölden–Rettenbachferner–Tiefenbachferner
(to 2700 m/8861 ft)

Thiersen–Landl–Ackernalm
(to 1383 m/4539 ft)

Tristach (Osttirol)–Kreithof–Dolomitenhütte
(to 1620 m/5317 ft)

Waidring, Höhenstrasse Steinplatte
(to 1378 m/4523 ft)

Weer, Nafingersee–Weidener Hütte
(to 1856 m/6091 ft)

Weer–Saga-Alm
(to 1720 m/5645 ft)

Timmelsjoch–Hochalpenstrasse
(to 2509 m/8235 ft)

SALZBURG PROVINCE

Gasteiner Alpenstrasse
(1083–1588 m/3554–5212 ft)

Filzmoos–Hoferalm
(1057–1268 m/3469–4166 ft)

Krispl–Gaissau–Spielbergalm
(700–1258 m/2297–4128 ft)

Radstadt–Rossbrand–Alpenstrasse
(856–1770 m/2809–5809 ft)

St Koloman/Sommerau–Vordertrattbergalm
(851–1526 m/2793–5008 ft)

St Martin bei Lofer–Kirchental
(634–879 m/2081–2885 ft)

Strobl–Niedergaden, Bleckwandstrasse
(544–1100 m/1785–3610 ft)

Strobl, Postalmstrasse
(544–1282 m/1785–4208 ft)

Pfarrwarfen, Mahdeggstrasse
(538–1202 m/1766–3945 ft)

Tauernautobahn–Scheitelstrecke
(to 1340 m/4398 ft)

Gerlospass-Scheitelstrecke
(to 1507 m/4946 ft)

SALZBURG PROVINCE/EAST TIROL

Felbertauernstrasse
(to 1652 m/5422 ft)

SALZBURG PROVINCE/CARINTHIA

Grossglockner-Hochalpenstrasse
(3 stretches; to 2571 m/8438 ft)

UPPER AUSTRIA

Grünau im Almtal–Kasbergalm
(to 1600 m/5251 ft)

Hinterstoder–Hößstrasse
(to 1400 m/4595 ft)

LOWER AUSTRIA

Göstling an der Ybbs–Hochkar-Alpenstrasse
(to 1491 m/4893 ft)

Bergstrasse Hohe Wand
tolls payable only at weekends in summer
(to 1100 m/3610 ft)

Kleinzell–Ebenwaldhütte–Reisalpe
(to 1400 m/4595 ft)

St Anton an der Jessnitz–Hochberneckstrasse
(to 1000 m/3282 ft)

STYRIA

Admont–Admonter Kaibling
(641–1504 m/2104–4936 ft)

Aflenz-Kurort–Bürgeralm
(to 1510 m/4955 ft)

Aflelnz-Land–Schiesslingalm
(to 1500 m/4923 ft)

Aich-Assach/Ennstal-Gössenberg, Seewigtal-
Bodenseestrasse
(700–1250 m/2297–4103 ft)

Altaussee, Salzkammergut-Panoramastrasse
(850–1600 m/2790–5251 ft)

Bad Mitterndorf–Tauplitzalm
(820–1650 m/2691–5415 ft)

Donnersbach–Planneralp
(800–1650 m/2626–5415 ft)

Gaishorn–Mödlinger Hütte
(to 1521 m/4992 ft)

Gröbming, Stoderzinken-Alpenstrasse
(to 1850 m/6072 ft)

Halltal bei Mariazell–Hubertussee
(785–834 m/2576–2737 ft)

Hohentauern, Scheiblingalm–Edelrautenhütte
(to 1725 m/5661 ft)

Neuberg an der Mürz–Schneealpe
(to 1500 m/4923 ft)

Obdach, Rotheidenstrasse zur Sabathyhütte
(850–1836 m/2790–6026 ft)

Oberzeiring–Klosterneuburger Hütte–Lachtalhaus
(to 1902 m/6242 ft)

Pfaffensattel, Stuhleckstrasse
(to 1368 m/4890 ft)

Pichl an der Enns–Reiteralm
(800–1750 m/2626–5744 ft)

Pichl an der Enns–Ursprungalm
(to 1000 m/3282 ft)

Ramsau, Dachsteinstrasse
(1100–1750 m/3610–5744 ft)

Ratten, Pretulstrasse
(765–1600 m/2511–5251 ft)

Rohrmoos–Untertal, Hochwurzenstrasse
(1250–1850 m/4103–6072 ft)

St Radegund bei Graz, Schöckl-Höhenstrasse
(1100–1446 m/3610–4746 ft)

Schladming–Planai
(to 1300 m/4267 ft)

Waldbach–Breitenbrunn, Hochwechselstrasse
(1100–1738 m/3610/5704 ft)

Pyhrn-Autobahn, Gleinalm and Bosrucktunnel
(to 700 m/2297 ft)

CARINTHIA

Arriach–Gerlitzen
(860–1909 m/2822–6265 ft)

Arriach–Wöllanernock
(860–1960 m/2822–6547 ft)

Bodensdorf–Gerlitzen
500–1800 m/1641–5908 ft)

Feld am See–Wöllanernock
(743–1543 m/2439–5064 ft)

Feld am See–Mirnock
(750–1750 m/2462–5744 ft)

Goldeck-Panoramastrasse Zlan–Stockenboi
(882–1900 m/2895–6236 ft)

Kanzel-Bergstrasse Treffen–Kanzelhöhe
(502–1520 m/1648–4989 ft)

Mallnitz–Jamnigalm
(1200–1700 m/3938–5579 ft)

Maltatal, Falterhütte–Kölnbreinsperre
(to 1920 m/6301 ft)

Millstatt–Lammersdorf–Lammersdorfer Alm
(700–1600 m/2297–5251 ft)

Millstatt–Sappl–Sappler Alm
(700–1300 m/2297–4267 ft)

Nockalmstrasse
(1500–2042 m/4923/6702 ft)

Eisenkappel, Hochobir-Güterweg zur
Eisenkappeler Hütte
(1100–1600 m/3610–5251 ft)

Seeboden–Tschiernock
(800–1680 m/2626–5514 ft)

Villacher Alpenstrasse–Dobratsch
(500–1732 m/1641–5684 ft)

Zell-Pfarre–Koschutahaus
(950–1200 m/3118–3938 ft)

Inexpensive block tickets are available which are valid for the stretches, liable to toll, of the following roads: Pyhrn motorway (Bosrucktunnel), the Brenner and Tauern motorways and the Arlberg and Felbertauern roads.

Buses

Bus services are an important element in the transport system, particulary in the Alpine regions. A distinction is made between the **Kraftpost** (mail bus) and the **Bahnbus** (run by Austrian Federal Railways); and there are also many privately run services.

There are **reduced fares** for frequent travellers (for 6 journeys a reduction of 16¾%; unlimited validity), return tickets on certain routes (25% reduction), and reduced return fares on the Grossglockner Road (mail buses).

Air Travel

Austria is linked with the European network of air services through the Vienna (Schwechat), Linz, Salzburg and Graz airports. There are direct services daily between London and Vienna and less frequently between Manchester and Vienna (British Airways and Austrian Airlines).

Flights from United States
New York–Vienna
Royal Jordanian Airlines (ALIA).
A few flights in each direction.

Romanian Airlines (TAROM).
A few flights in each direction.

Within Austria there are regular services by Austrian Airlines from Vienna to Graz and Salzburg as well as between Salzburg and Linz; *Austrian Air Services* and *Tyrolean Airways* operate from Vienna to Graz, Klagenfurt, Salzburg, Linz and Innsbruck and the routes Salzburg–Linz, Linz–Graz and Graz–Klagenfurt.

Rail Travel

Most of the railway system is run by the **Austrian Federal Railways** (*Österreichische Bundesbahnen*, ÖBB), a State corporation; only a few local lines of tourist importance are privately owned (Achenseebahn, Montafoner Bahn, Stubaitalbahn, etc.).

There are no barriers at the entrances to platforms: tickets are checked on the train. If you want to break your journey this must be certified by the ticket inspector (conductor) before leaving the train. Tickets for distances up to and including 70 km are valid for one day, beyond 70 km for two months. For express trains of all kinds supplements are payable.

Reduced fares: (a passport or identity card bearing a photograph is usually necessary). Local return tickets for journeys not exceeding 70 km, 20%. Kilometric block tickets (2000, 5000 or 10,000 km) are valid for one year; each time they are used the reduction is up to 35%. There are also network and regional tickets. The "Austria" ticket for persons up to 26 years of age is valid for 9 or 16 days and can be used on railway and post buses, ÖBB vessels on the Wolfgangsee and regular services of the DDSG on the Danube between Vienna and Passau.

Other reduced fare tickets are weekly and monthly season tickets, climbers' tickets for members of mountaineering clubs holding a reduced fare permit, and senior citizens' tickets giving a 25% reduction. There are also combined reduced fare tickets with other transport undertakings (e.g. post buses, Danube ships and in winter combination season tickets for use with ski-lifts. Children below the age of 7 are carried free if accompanied by an adult (maximum two children per adult). Children from 7 to 16 pay half fare.

Motorail

There are motorail services from Brussels (Schaerbeek) and 's-Hertogenbosch to Salzburg and Villach. Information from Sealink Travel Ltd, PO Box 29, London SW1V 1JX, British Rail travel offices or appointed travel agents.

Bicycle Rental at Railway Stations

Bicycles can be rented at the following railway stations from the beginning of April to the end of October, for the day or for longer periods on presentation of an official identity document bearing a photograph (e.g. a passport): Admont, Altensteig, Altmünster am Traunsee, Amstetten, Bad Goisern, Bad Hall, Bad Ischl, Bad Schallersbach-Wallern, Baden bei Wien, Berndorf Stadt, Bruck a.d. Leitha, Bruch-Fusch, Dobersberg, Drosendort, Eisenstadt, Faak am See, Feldbach, Fürstenfeld, Gänserndorf, Gars-Thurau, Gmünd, Gmunden, Gemunden-Seebahnhof. Gratwein-Gratkorn, Graz Hbf., Greifenstein/ Altenberg, Grein-Bad Kreuzen, Hall in Tirol, Hallein, Hermagor, Hinterstoder, Hohenems, Hollabrun, Horn, Kammer-Schöfling, Klangenfurt Hbf., Klosterneuburg-Weidling, Korneuburg, Kötschach-Mauthen, Krems a.d. Donau, Kremsmünster Markt, Kufstein, Langenlois, Langenzersdorf, Launsdorf-Hochosterwitz, Ledernitzen, Leibnitz, Lienz (Osttirol), Lochau-Hörbranz, Lunz am See, Mariazell, Martinsberg-Gutenbrunn, Mauthausen, Melk, Mistelbach Hbf., Mittersill, Mödling, Neumarkt-Köstendorf, Neunkirchen, Neusiedl a. See, Oberdrauburg, Ossiach-Bodendorf, Petronell-Carnuntum, Pöchlarn, Puchberg am Schneeberg, Reichraming, Reutte in Tirol, Saalfelden, Salzurg Hbf., Schärding, Schladming, Schlierbach, Schwanenstadt, Seekirchen-Wallersee, Siebenbrunn-Leopoldsdorf, Spittal-Millstättersee, Spitz a.d. Donau, St Andrä-Wördern, St Johann im Pongau, St Paul, St Peter-Seitenstetten, St Pölten Hbf., St Valentin, Stadt Haag, Stockerau, Thal, Traismauer, Tulin, Türnitz, Velden am Wörthersee, Völkermarkt-Kühnsdorf, Waidhofen a.d. Thaya, Waidhofen a.d. Ybbs, Wiener Neustadt, Windischgarsten, Wolkersdorf, Ybbs a.d. Donau, Ybbsitz, Zellerndorf, Zwettl.

The **charge** is 70 öS per calendar day, or 35 öS on presentation of a ticket to the station at which the bicycle is hired, valid on the day on which it is hired. The bicycle can be returned either at the station from which it is hired or at any other station during working hours. Bicycles can be booked in advance. Further information from railway stations.

Mountain Railways, Cableways, Lifts

Austria has large numbers of *Bergbahnen*, a general term which covers mountain railways, cableways, ski-lifts, etc. These enable the older or less strenuously inclined visitor to enjoy the experience of the mountain world, and are also of great assistance to skiers.

Railways
●━━●

Air Services
●━━● Austrian Airlines (all the year round)
●━━● Austrian Air Services
Tyrolean Airways

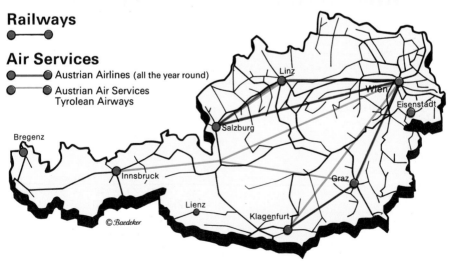

Bregenz · Linz · Wien · Eisenstadt · Salzburg · Innsbruck · Graz · Lienz · Klagenfurt

© *Baedeker*

There are the following types of *Bergbahn*: the **funicular** *(Standseilbahn)*, in which the cars run on rails and are drawn by a cable (e.g. the Hungerburgbahn at Innsbruck); the **cog (rack) railway** *(Zahnradbahn)*, with a cogged middle rail which engages with a pinion on the locomotive (e.g. the line up the Schafberg at St Wolfgang; the **cableway** *(Seilschwebebahn)*, with cabins suspended from a continuous cable (e.g. the Zugspitzbahn, the Galzig-Valluga-Bahn, the Pfänderbahn, the Stubnerkogelbahn, the Nordkettenbahn, the Patscherkofelbahn, the Kanzel-

bahn, the cableway to the Schmittenhöhe); the **chair-lift** *(Sesselbahn, Sessellift)*, with open chairs (sometimes double or treble) suspended from a continuous cable); the **ski-lift** *(Skilift, Schlepplift)*, in which skiers hitch on to a moving cable and are pulled uphill on their skis; and the **sledge-lift** *(Schlittenseilbahn)*, in which sledges are attached to a cable and drawn uphill.

- **Boat Services**
- **Water Sports**

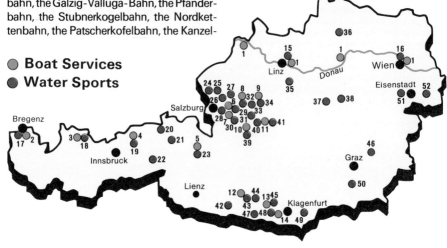

Motorboats

International regulations apply on the Danube and Lake Constance. On all other Austrian waters privately owned motorboats may be permitted only at certain times; in some cases they may be prohibited altogether.

Information can be obtained from local police stations.

Sailing

No special permission is required except on Lake Constance, where it is necessary to have a special licence for sailing boats with a sail area of over 12 sq. m/129 sq. ft. Those in charge of sailing boats must know and observe the accepted rules of seamanship, and the usual safety equipment must be carried (including life-jackets, preferably yellow or red).

Most of the Austrian sailing waters are in Upper Austria, Carinthia and Salzburg provinces, where Alpine influences predominate. Rapid shifts in the

wind and sudden changes in the weather are, therefore, to be expected.

On most Austrian lakes there are sailing clubs and commercial arrangements for the renting of boats. There are frequent regattas, and occasionally European or world championship races.

Information from the *Österreichischer Segel-Verband* (Austrian Sailing Association), Grosse Neugasse 8, A–1040 Wien).

Canoeing

Austrian rivers offer abundant scope for canoeists, ranging from trips down the larger rivers like the Danube, the Drau, the Inn, the Mur and the Salzach to difficult "white water" runs on mountain streams like the Salza, the Steyr, the Möll, the Lieser, the Ziller and the Lech. An international *Wildwasserwoche* (White Water Week) is held annually on the Möll.

Information from the *Österreichischer Paddelsportverband* (Austrian Canoe Club), Berggasse 16, A–1090 Wien.

Boat Services
Water Sports

- **Boat Services**
  (Passenger services)

1 Danube

a *Passau–Linz–Vienna* (can be combined with rail travel) "Donaubus" round trips in Vienna area; special excursions; trips down the Danube to Budapest, Belgrade and the Black Sea.

Erste-Donau-Dampfschiffahrts-Gesellschaft (DDSG)

b *Vienna–Bratislava–Vienna*
Československá Plavba Dunasjská (ČSPD)

c *Vienna–Budapest–Vienna*
"Three Country" trips (Dreiländerfahrten):
Vienna to the Czech-Hungarian frontier and back.
Mahart (Hungarian Shipping Company)

d *Vienna–Bratislava–Budapest–Belgrade–Ismail–Black Sea–Istanbul–Yalta*
Soviet Danube Shipping Co.; Romanian ships

2 Lake Constance (Vorarlberg)
Bregenz–Lindau–Konstanz
Lake cruises; special excursions

3 Plansee (Tirol)
Motorboats
Only in summer

4 Achensee (Tirol)
Motorboats
Only in summer

5 Zeller See (Salzburg province)
Motorboats
Only in summer

6 Mondsee (Upper Austria)
Mondsee–See
Only in summer

7 Wolfgangsee (Upper Austria)
Strobl–St Wolfgang–St Gilgen
Gschwend–St Wolfgang

8 Attersee (Upper Austria)
Kammer–Attersee–Unterach
Only in summer

9 Traunsee (Upper Austria)
Gmunden–Ebensee
Only in summer

10 Hallstätter See (Upper Austria)
Hallstatt-Markt–Lahn–Obertraun
Hallstatt-Markt
Throughout the year

11 Grundlsee (Styria)
Motorboats
Only in summer

12 Millstätter See (Carinthia)
Seeboden–Millstatt–Döbriach
Only in summer

13 Ossiacher See (Carinthia)
St Andrä See–Steindorf
Only in summer

14 Wörther See (Carinthia)
Klagenfurt-See–Velden
Only in summer

● **Water Sports**
(Sailing and windsurfing schools, facilities for water skiing, etc. at many places).

15 Danube
Water sports areas at Krems, Ardagger, Linz-Urfahr, etc.

16 Alte Donau (Vienna)
Area: *c.* 1·6 sq. km/395 acres

17 Lake Constance
Annual regattas

18 Plansee (Tirol)
At Reutte
Area: 5 sq. km/2 sq. miles

19 Achensee (Tirol)
Area: 7·3 sq. km/1800 acres

20 Walchsee (Tirol)
At Kufstein
Area: 1 sq. km/250 acres

21 Schwarzsee (Tirol)
At Kitzbühel

22 Durlassboden reservoir (Tirol)
At Gerlos
Area: 3 sq. km/740 acres

23 Zeller See (Salzburg province)
Area: 4·7 sq. km/1160 acres
Annual regattas

24 Obertrumer See (Salzburg province)
Area: 4·9 sq. km/1210 acres

25 Mattsee (Salzburg province)
Area: 3·6 sq. km/890 acres

26 Wallersee (Salzburg province)
Area: 6·4 sq. km/1580 acres
Annual regattas

27 Zeller See (Upper Austria)
Area: 3·5 sq. km/865 acres

28 Fuschlsee (Salzburg province)
Area: 2·7 sq. km/670 acres

29 Mondsee (Upper Austria)
Area: 14 sq. km/5½ sq. miles
Annual regattas

30 Wolfgangsee (Upper Austria/Salzburg province)
Area: 12.5 sq. km/5 sq. miles

31 Nussensee (Upper Austria)
At Bad Ischl

32 Attersee (Upper Austria/Salzburg province)
Area: 46·7 sq. km/18 sq. miles

33 Langbathseen (Upper Austria)
Accessible from Ebensee

34 Traunsee (Upper Austria)
Area: 25 sq. km/10 sq. miles

35 Steyr reservoir (Upper Austria)
Area: 1·5 sq. km/370 acres

36 Kamp reservoir (Lower Austria)

37 Lunzer See (Lower Austria)
NW of Mariazell
Area: 1·5 sq km/370 acres

38 Erlauf reservior (Lower Austria and Styria)
N of Mariazell
Area: 1·5 sq. km/370 acres

39 Hallstätter See (Upper Austria)
Area: 8·5 sq. km/2100 acres

40 Altausseer See (Styria)
Area: 2·1 sq. km/520 acres

41 Grundlsee (Styria)
Area: 4·2 sq. km/1040 acres

42 Weissensee (Carinthia)
Area: 6·6 sq. km/1630 acres

43 Millstätter See (Carinthia)
Area: 13 sq. km/5 sq. miles
Annual regattas

44 Feldsee or **Brennsee** (Carinthia)
Area: 0·4 sq. km/100 acres

45 Ossiacher See (Carinthia)
Area: 10·3 sq. km/4 sq. miles

46 Stubenbergsee (Styria)
Between Weiz and Hartberg
Area: 0·5 sq. km/125 acres

47 Faaker See (Carinthia)
Area: 2·4 sq. km/595 acres

48 Wörther See (Carinthia)
Area: 22 sq. km/8½ sq. miles

49 Klopeiner See (Carinthia)
Area: 1·4 sq. km/345 acres

50 Waldschacher See (Styria)
S of Graz
Area: 0·5 sq. km/125 acres

51 Neufelder See (Burgenland)
NE of Wiener Neustadt
Area: 0·5 sq. km/125 acres

52 Neusiedler See (Burgenland)
Area: 320 sq. km/125 sq. miles

Language

German, like English, is a Germanic language, and the pronunciation of German usually comes more easily to English-speakers than does a Romance language like French. Much of the basic vocabulary, too, will be familiar to those whose native language is English, though they may have some difficulty with the more complex terms incorporating native Germanic roots rather than the Latin roots used in English. The grammar is not difficult, but has retained a much more elaborate system of conjugations and declensions than English.

Standard German (*Hochdeutsch*) is spoken throughout the country, although many people speak a strong local dialect as well.

Pronunciation. – The *consonants* are for the most part pronounced broadly as in English, but the following points should be noted: *b, d* and *g* at the end of a syllable are pronounced like *p, t* and *k; c* (rare) and *z* are pronounced *ts; j* is pronounced like consonantal *y; qu* is somewhere between the English *qu* and *kv; s* at the beginning of a syllable is pronounced *z; v* is pronounced *f;* and *w* is pronounced *v.* The double letter *ch* is pronounced like the Scottish *ch* in "loch" after *a, o* and *u;* after *ä, e, i* and *ü* it is pronounced somewhere between that sound and *sh. Sch* is pronounced *sh,* and *th* (rare) *t.*

The *vowels* are pronounced without the diphthongisation normal in standard English; before a single consonant they are normally long, before a double consonant short. Note the following: short *a* is like the flat *a* of northern English; *e* may be either closed (roughly as in "pay"), open (roughly as in "pen") or a short unaccented sound like the *e* in 'begin" or in "father"; *ä* is like an open *e; u* is like *oo* in "good" (short) or "food" (long); *ö* is like the French *eu,* a little like the vowel in "fur"; *ü,* like the French *u,* can be approximated by pronouncing *ee* with rounded lips. Diphthongs: *ai* and *ei* similar to *i* in "high"; *au* as in "how"; *eu* and *äu* like *oy; ie* like *ee.*

Numbers

0	null	21	einundzwanzig
1	eins	22	zweiundzwanzig
2	zwei	30	dreissig
3	drei	40	vierzig
4	vier	50	fünfzig
5	fünf	60	sechzig
6	sechs	70	siebzig
7	sieben	80	achtzig
8	acht	90	neunzig
9	neun	100	hundert
10	zehn	101	hundert und eins
11	elf	153	hundertdreiund-
12	zwölf		fünfzig
13	dreizehn	200	zweihundert
14	vierzehn	300	dreihundert
15	fünfzehn	1000	tausend
16	sechzehn	1001	tausend und eins
17	siebzehn	1021	tausend einund-
18	achtzehn		zwanzig
19	neunzehn	2000	zweitausend
20	zwanzig	1,000,000	eine Million

Ordinals

1st	erste
2nd	zweite
3rd	dritte
4th	vierte
5th	fünfte
6th	sechste
7th	siebte
8th	achte
9th	neunte
10th	zehnte
11th	elfte
20th	zwanzigste
100th	hundertste

Fractions

$\frac{1}{2}$	Hälfte
$\frac{1}{3}$	Drittel
$\frac{1}{4}$	Viertel
$\frac{3}{4}$	drei
	Vierteil

Vocabulary

Good morning	Guten Morgen	Loose stones	Rollsplit
Good day	Guten Tag	Town centre	Stadtmitte
Good evening	Guten Abend	Stop	Stop
Good night	Gute Nacht	Road closed	Strasse gesperrt
Goodbye	Auf Wiedersehen	Caution	Vorsicht
Do you speak English?	Sprechen Sie Englisch?	Customs	Zoll
I do not understand	Ich verstehe nicht		
Yes	Ja		
No	Nein		

Rail and air travel

Please	Bitte	Airport	Flughafen
Thank you (very much)	Danke (sehr)	All aboard!	Einsteigen!
Yesterday	Gestern	Arrival	Ankunft
Today	Heute	Baggage	Gepäck
Tomorrow	Morgen	Baggage check	Gepäckschein
Help!	Hilfe!	Bus station	Autobushof
Have you a single room?	Haben Sie ein	Departure	Abfahrt, Abflug (aircraft)
	Einzelzimmer?	Flight	Flug
Have you a double	Haben Sie ein	Halt	Haltestelle
room?	Doppelzimmer?	Information	Auskunft
Have you a room with	Haben Sie ein Zimmer	Lavatory	Toilette(n)
private bath?	mit Bad?	Line	Gleis
What does it cost?	Wieviel kostet das?	Luggage	Gepäck
Please wake me at six	Wollen Sie mich bitte	Non-smoking	Nichtraucher
	um sechs Uhr	Platform	Bahnsteig
	wecken	Porter	Gepäckträger
Where is the lavatory?	Wo is die Toilette?	Restaurant car	Speisewagen
Where is the bathroom?	Wo ist das	Sleeping car	Schlafwagen;
	Badezimmer?		Liegewagen
Where is the chemist's?	Wo ist die Apotheke?		(couchettes)
Where is the post office?	Wo ist das Postamt?	Smoking	Raucher
Where is there a doctor?	Wo gibt es einen Arzt?	Station	Bahnhof
Where is there a dentist?	Wo gibt es einen	Stewardess	Stewardess
	Zahnarzt?	Stop	Haltestelle
Is this the way to the	Ist dies der Weg zum	Ticket	Fahrkarte
station?	Bahnhof?	Ticket collector	Schaffner
		Ticket window	Schalter
		Timetable	Fahrplan, Flugplan (air)
		Train	Zug

Days of the week

Sunday	Sonntag	Waiting room	Wartesaal
Monday	Montag	Window seat	Fensterplatz
Tuesday	Dienstag		
Wednesday	Mittwoch		
Thursday	Donnerstag		

Months

Friday	Freitag	January	Januar
Saturday	Samstag, Sonnabend	February	Februar
Day	Tag	March	März
Public holiday	Feiertag	April	April
		May	Mai
		June	Juni
		July	Juli

Festivals

New Year	Neujahr	August	August
Easter	Ostern	September	September
Ascension	Christi Himmelfahrt	October	Oktober
Whitsun	Pfingsten	November	November
Corpus Christi	Fronleichnam	December	Dezember
Assumption	Mariä Himmelfahrt		
All Saints	Allerheiligen		

At the post office

Christmas	Weihnachten	Address	Adresse
New Year's Eve	Silvester	Express	Eilboten
		Letter	Brief
		Letter-box	Briefkasten

Road and traffic signs

Keeping your distance	Abstand halten!	Parcel	Paket
Caution	Achtung!	Postcard	Postkarte
Road works	Baustelle	Post restante	Postlagernd
No thoroughfare	Durchfahrt verboten	Postman	Briefträger
One-way street	Eibahnstrasse	Registered	Einschreiben
Get into line	Einordnen!	Small packet	Päckchen
Danger	Gefahr	Stamp	Briefmarke
Halt	Halt!	Telegram	Telegramm
Turn	Kurve	Telephone	Telefon
Slow	Langsam	Telex	Fernschreiber

Glossary (mainly of topographical terms)

This glossary is intended as a guide to the meaning of terms which visitors will encounter frequently on maps, plans and signposts. They may occur independently or as part of a compound word.

Abtei	abbey
Ache	mountain stream
Alm, Alp	alpine pasture
Alt	old
Anlage	gardens, park
Anstalt	institution
Au	meadow
Auskunft	information
Austellung	exhibition
Autobahn	motorway, superhighway
Bach	brook, stream
Bad	bath; spa
Bahn	railway; lane (in road)
Bahnhof	railway station
Bau	building
Bauernhaus	peasant's house, farmhouse
Bauernhof	farm, farmstead
Becken	basin, pool
Berg	hill, mountain
Bergbahn	(see p. 181: Mountain Railways, etc.)
Bergbau	mining
Bibliothek	library
Börse	(stock) exchange
Brücke	bridge
Brunnen	fountain
Bühel, Bühl	hill
Bund	federation, league
Bundes-	federal
Burg	(fortified) castle
Damm	causeway
Denkmal	monument, memorial
Dom	cathedral
Dorf	village
Eisenbahn	railway
Engpass	defile
Fähre	ferry
Fall	waterfall
Feld	field
Fels	rock, crag
Ferner	glacier
Fernmeldeturm	telecommunications tower
Fernsehturm	television tower
Feste, Festung	fortress, citadel
Flügel	wing
Flughafen	airport
Fluh	rocky slope
Fluss	river
Forst	forest
Freilichtmuseum	open-air museum
Fremdenverkehrsverein	tourist information office
Friedhof	cemetery, churchyard
Furt	ford
Garten	garden
Gasse	street, lane
Gebäude	building
Gebirge	(range of) hills, mountains
Gemeinde	commune (the smallest administrative unit)
Gericht	court (of law)
Gewerbe	trade, industry, craft
Gipfel	summit, peak
Gletscher	glacier
Grab	tomb, grave
Graben	ditch, moat
Grat	ridge, arête
Gruppe	group

Gut	estate; country house, farm
Hafen	harbour, port
Halbinsel	peninsula
Halle	hall
Hallenbad	indoor swimming pool
Hang	slope, hillside, mountainside
Hauptplatz	main square
Hauptpost	head post office
Hauptstrasse	main street
Haus	house
Heide	heath
Heimatmuseum	local or regional museum
Hochschule	higher eductional establishment, university
Hochtal	high valley
Hof	courtyard; farm; (royal) court
Höhe	hill, eminence
Höhenweg	ridge, path, ridgeway
Höhle	cave, cavern
Holz	wood
Hospital	hospital, hospice
Hügel	hill
Insel	island
Jagdschloss	hunting lodge
Joch	ridge
Jugendherberge	youth hostel
Kai	quay
Kaiser-	imperial
Kamm	ridge
Kammer	chamber, room
Kanzel	pulpit; spur of hill; viewpoint
Kapelle	chapel
Karner	charnel-house, bone-house
Kees	glacier
Keller	cellar
Kirche	church
Klamm	gorge
Klein	small
Klippe	cliff
Kloster	monastery, convent
Kofel, Kogel	rounded mountain-top
Krankenhaus	hospital
Kunst	art
Kur	cure, treatment (at a spa)
Kurhaus	spa establishment
Kurort	spa, health resort
Land	land: specifically, one of the Austrian provinces (*Länder*)
Landes-	provincial; relating or belonging to a *Land*
Laube	arcade, loggia
Luftschwebebahn	aerial cableway
Markt (platz)	market (square)
Marstall	court stables
Matte	alpine meadow
Mauer	wall
Meer	sea
Messe	trade fair
Moor	moor(land)
Moos	moss, bog
Mühle	mill
Münster	minister, monastic church
Naturpark	nature park
Neu	new
Nieder-	lower
Nord	north
Ober-	upper
Oper	opera (house)

Ost	east	Stadseilbahn	funicular
Palais, Palast	palace	Stätte	place, site
Pfad	path, trail	Stausee	lake formed by dam,
Pfarrkirche	parish church		reservoir
Pforte	doorway	Steig	path
Platz	square	Stein	stone
Post	post office	Sternwarte	observatory
Quelle	spring, source	Stiege	staircase
Rathaus	town hall	Stift	religious house; chapter,
Reisebüro	travel agency		college; foundation
Residenz	residence, seat of a ruling	Stiftskirche	monastic church;
	prince; princely capital		collegiate church
Ruine	ruin	Strand	beach
Rundfunk	radio	Strasse	street, road
S-Bahn (Stadtbahn)	urban railway, tramway	Süd	south
Saal	hall, room	Tal	valley
Sattel	saddle	Teich	pond, small lake
Säule	column	Theater	theatre
Schanze	redoubt: ski-jump	Tiergarten, Tierpark	zoo
Schatzkammer	treasury	Tor	gate(way)
Schauspielhaus	theatre	Turm	tower
Schlepplift	ski-lift	U-Bahn (Untergrundbahn)	underground railway
Schleuse	lock, sluice	Ufer	shore
Schloss (pl. Schlösser)	castle, palace, country	Universität	university
	house (usually	Unter-	lower
	designed for show	Verkehr	traffic, transport
	rather than defence)	Verkehrsamt, -büro, -verein	tourist information office
Schlucht	gorge	Viertel	quarter, district
Schnellstrasse	expressway	Vorstadt	suburb, outer district
Schule	school	Wald	wood, forest
See	lake	Wall	rampart
Seilbahn	cableway (aerial/rails)	Wallfahrtskirche	pilgrimage church
Seilschwebebahn	aerial cableway	Wand	wall
Sesselbahn, Sessellift	chair-lift	Wasser	water
Skilift	ski-lift	Wasserburg, -schloss	moated castle
Speicher	reservoir	Wasserfall	waterfall
Sperre	dam, barrage	Weg	way, road
Spielbank	casino	Weiler	hamlet
Spital	hospital	Weinstube	wine-house, wine-bar
Spitze	peak	West	west
Staats-, staatlich	state, national	Wildpark	wildlife park, game park
Stadt	town, city	Zahnradbahn	cog (rack) railway
Städtisch	municipal	Zeughaus	arsenal

Accommodation

Hotels, Inns, Pensions

The **hotels** in the larger Austrian towns and tourist resorts are fully up to the normal international standards of comfort and amenity; but the **inns** (*Gasthöfe*) in the smaller places also offer excellent accommodation and food. There are many *Schlosshotels* (see below, p. 273) in old castles and country houses. And all over the country there are large numbers of **pensions** (*Pensionen*, guest-houses). It is advisable to book accommodation in advance, particularly during the main tourist season and on public holidays.

Hotels, inns and pensions are officially classified in five categories designated by one to five stars, but in this book from A1 to D as follows:

In areas geared to winter sports the hotels are frequently closed in summer, while in the summer resort areas they may be open only from spring to autumn.

Youth Hostels

Youth hostels offering accommodation at reasonable prices are mainly designed for young people: if there is pressure on accommodation those under 30 have preference. The hostels are often in beautiful locations, sometimes in historic old buildings. No more than three nights may be spent in the same hostel (though special arrangements can be made for groups). Foreign visitors must produce a membership card of their national youth hostels association.

Information from the *Österreichischer Jugenher-bergsring*, Schottenring 28, A-1010 Wien, or the *Österreichischer Jugenherbergswerk*, Freyung 6, A-1010 Wien.

	Category		Per person per night
★★★★★	A1	Luxury hotels	600–1500 öS
★★★★	A	First class hotels	300–1000 öS
★★★	B	Excellent middle class hotels, etc.	200–500 öS
★★	C	Good middle class hotels, etc.	170–330 öS
★	D	Modest hotels, inns and pensions	130–200 öS

Rates in Vienna and Salzburg are considerably higher

Holidays on the Farm

Farm holidays have become increasingly popular in Austria in recent years. The movement has been actively promoted by the Hauptverband der Österreichischen Sparkassen (Federation of Austrian Savings Banks), which publishes an annual list of farms (at present almost 4000 in number) offering holiday accommodation.

Holiday Villages
(Erholungsdörfer)

These are villages, still predominantly agricultural, which provide holiday accommodation in quiet and relaxing surroundings, enabling visitors to see something of the local way of life. Frequently they offer shooting and fishing.

Camping

Camping is now a very popular form of holiday in Austria, and there are large numbers of officially recognised camping sites, often in very beautiful settings and equipped with modern facilities, in the mountain regions (particularly in the high valleys with their Alpine meadows and on the passes), on the shores of the warm Carinthian lakes and the lakes of the Salzkammergut, on the banks of the Danube and in many other parts of the country. Members of camping clubs are usually entitled to reductions on the normal charges. In places other than camping sites, that is on roads, car parks and picnic areas, etc., motor and towed caravans are allowed to stop for not more than three nights, unless there is an official camping site available and providing that there are no regulations prohibiting this "free camping", as, for instance, on the Grossglockner Alpine Road.

Winter camping is growing in importance. Since demand exceeds the availability of suitably equipped sites, early booking is essential.

Information can be obtained from the *Camping and Caravaning Club Austria* (Mariahilfer Str. 180, A-1015 Wien).

Holidays for the Handicapped

Numbers of Austrian hotels are equipped with facilities for wheel-chairs.

A list of hotels catering for the handicapped. – "*Hotelführer für Behinderte in Österreich*" – is published regularly. **Information** from the *Verband der Querschnittgelähmten Österreichs* (Brigittenauer Lände 42, A-1200 Wien).

Food and Drink

Austrian **restaurants** and inns are noted for the excellence of their cooking. *Lunch* is served between 12 and 2 in the larger restaurants, but in smaller establishments it is frequently earlier. The afternoon cup of coffee – which, like any other snack between meals, is known as *Jause* – is taken between 4 and 5. *Dinner* is served from 6 onwards. For further information on coffee, see Vienna in A–Z section of this guide.

The Austrian **menu** contains many dialect terms which may be strange even to those who know standard German. The cuisine of southern Germany is represented together with that of Vienna, and many influences from the East have been inherited from the old multi-national empire. The Austrians are particularly fond of meat dishes and sweets.

Soups: Minestra, vegetable soup; *Fischbeuschelsuppe*, pea or vegetable soup with fish roe. Soups may be given body by the addition of dumplings, various kinds of pasta, etc.; *geriebene Gerstl*, crumbled pasta; *gebackene Erbsen*, fried chou pastry; *Schöberl* and *Fridatten*, various forms of pastry-like additions.

Meat: garniertes or *feines Rindfleisch*, boiled beef with various garnishings; *Tafelspitz, Beinfleisch* and *Tellerfleisch*, particular cuts of beef (*Tafelspitz* being the best); *gedämpfter Spitz* and *Lungenbraten*, loin of beef; *Rostbraten*, a cut of beef including ribs, roasted with onions; *Gulasch*, pieces of meat steamed in a paprika sauce; *Paprikahuhn*, chicken steamed in a paprika sauce; *Wiener Schnitzel*, veal cutlet coated with breadcrumbs; *Naturschnitzel*, veal cutlet without breadcrumbs; *Jungfernbraten*, roast loin of pork with kümmel; *Krenfleisch*, stewed pork with horse-radish; *Kaiserfleisch*, slightly

Salzburg Nockerl

cured pork spare rib; *Geselchtes,* salted and smoked meat; *Schöpsernes,* mutton stew; *Beuschl,* a dish made of offal (intestines; usually veal); *Backhendl,* a chicken done like Wiener Schnitzel; *Tiroler Geröstel (Gröstl),* small pieces of boiled meat roasted with potatoes and egg; *Frankfurter,* the typical little Viennese sausage; *Faschiertes,* minced meat; *Grammeln,* crackling (crisp, brown skin of roast pork).

Vegetables: heurige Erdäpfel, new potatoes; *geröstete Erdäpfel,* fried potatoes; *Fisolen,* green beans; *gelbe Rüben,* carrots; *Karfiol,* cauliflower; *Paradeiser,* tomatoes; *Kochsalat,* boiled green salad in flour sauce; *Sprossenkohl,* Brussels sprouts; *Kukuruz,* maize; *Risipisi,* rice with peas; *Häuptlsalat,* lettuce; *Kren,* horse-radish; *Schwammerln,* mushrooms.

Sweets: Strudel, a thin sheet of filled dough rolled up and baked; *Palatschinken,* stuffed pancakes; *Schmarrn,* sweet pancake; *Sterz,* a flour, buckwheat or maize purée fried in fat; *Nockerl,* small flour dumplings; *Salzburger Nockerl,* a kind of pudding made of eggs, sugar, fat and flour; *Germknödel mit Röster,* yeast dumplings with stewed plums; *Marillenknödel,* apricot dumplings; *Tiroler Knödel,* ham dumplings; *Böhmische Dalken,* pancakes of yeast dough with Powidl (plum purée); *Buchteln,* jam-filled yeast dumplings; *Dampfnudeln,* sweet yeast dumplings cooked in milk and sugar; *Gollatschen,* short-crust pastries; *Koch,* a kind of pudding; *Scheiterhaufen,* bread pudding with fruit; *Pofesen* (Bavesen), sweet French toast; *Guglhupf,* ring-shaped poundcake; *Eierspeise,* scrambled eggs; *Ribisl,* red currants; *Ringlotten,* greengages. – *Kipferl,* croissant; *Laberl,* large roll. – *Obers,* cream; *Schlagobers,* whipped cream.

Beer. – Well-known brands are *Schwechater, Gösser, Puntigamer, Stiegl* and *Zipfer. Märzen* is a kind of lager. Bitter beers with a higher hop content, similar to Pilsen, are also popular; little dark beer is drunk. – A *Krügel* is a half-litre (rather less than a pint); a *Seidel* is 35 millilitres (just over a half-pint).

Wine

Wine-making in Austria has a long tradition behind it. Wine was produced here during the Roman period, and there is documentary evidence of wine-production in the 5th c. A.D. The first school of viticulture in Austria was opened at Klosterneuburg in 1860.
There are more then 604 sq. km/233 sq. miles of vineyards in Austria, producing 89%

The Language of the Wine Label

Spätlese: wine made from grapes gathered when fully ripe, after completion of the normal harvest.
Auslese: wine made from grapes picked and pressed separately after all imperfect grapes have been discarded.
Beerenauslese: wine made from over-ripe grapes and grapes with "noble rot" (which concentrates the sugar in the grapes), individually selected.
Trockenbeerenauslese: wine made from grapes which have dried on the vine into a raisin-like state and have been attacked by noble rot.
Naturwein: wine without added sugar.
Reinsortig refers to wines made from a single kind of grape.
Ried is the term applied to a particular vineyard.
White grape: *Grüner Veltliner* vines produce fruity, *spritzig* white wines; *Welschriesling* and *Rheinriesling* delicately aromatic, lively white wines (Rheinriesling being regarded as a nobler vine than Welschriesling); *Müller-Thurgau, Muskat-Ottonel* and *Traminer* slightly fruity, rather sweet wines; *Weissburgunder* and *Zierfandler* full-bodied wines with a fine bouquet.
Red grapes: *Blaufränkisch* and *Blauburgunder* produce fruity ruby-wines; *Blauer Wildbacher* a rosé (Schilcher); *Blauer Portugieser* and *St Laurent* full-bodied dark red wines.
The **Austrian Seal of Quality** (*Österreichischer Weingütesiegel*) is borne only by wine officially classified as of high quality. The designation *Wein aus Österreich* indicates a good table wine.

Since 1 November 1985 new and considerably stricter regulations for wine marketing have come into force. The origin, the type and year of the wine must be stated in absolutely correct terms. There are no longer any blended Austrian wines. In addition, the producer, the level of quality and the alcohol and sugar content must be given. Comprehensive regulations covering designation, compulsory registration and control from the vine to the end product are designed to prevent dishonesty. Improvement of the must by the addition of sugar is permitted only for the less expensive and table wines in small quantities (generally up to 3·5%, but up to 4·5% for table wines). A label of origin can only be used if the wine in question comes exclusively from the stated district.
Tafelwein (table wine), pressed from Austrian grapes, has a must-weight of 13% on the Klosterneuburg scale (KMW). Landwein, similar to Tafelwein, contains a maximum of 11·5% alcohol and a maximum of 6 grams of residual sugar per litre; the grapes must come from a particular district. Tafel and Landwein (with the exception of the Schlicher rosé variety) must not be sold in bottles containing less than one litre.
Qualitätswein is prepared from a registered quality grape variety and comes exclusively from one area. It must be officially tested and the label must bear the test number.
Kabinettwein is a quality wine with at least 17% and not more than 19% must-weight. The must may not be improved and the wine may not contain more than 9 grams of residual sugar per litre.
Prädikatswein (also called Qualitätswein of particular ripeness and method of harvest) is a quality wine which may not be improved and in which the residual sugar may only be obtained by interruption of the fermentation process. The year of production must be stated. Among Qualitätsweine are Spätlese, Auslese, Eiswein, Beerenauslese, Ausbruch and Trockenbeerenauslese.
Sturm is a drink obtained from grape-juice by fermentation which may have more than 1% alcohol content, providing that this is present during the fermentation process. Sturm may not be sold from 1 August to 31 December in the year of production.

white wines and 11% red. The main wine-producing provinces are Lower Austria (62%) and Burgenland (31·7%), together with Styria (4·6%) and Vienna (1·7%). The vineyards of Lower Austria lie around *Krems* (Wachau), in the *Weinviertel*, in the *Danube* region (Klosterneuburg) and to the S of Vienna. In addition to white wines (Vetliner, Weissburgunder, Rheinriesling, etc.) some red wines (Blaufränkisch, Blauer Portugieser) are also produced in the Danube region, at *Gumpoldskirchen*, around *Baden bei Wien* and at *Bad Vöslau*. Burgenland is noted for its substantial white and red wines, the principal wine-producing areas being around the *Neusiedler See*. The *Rust* area produces Spätlese wines of high quality.

The vines most cultivated here are Welschriesling, Muskat, Traminer and Weissburgunder, together with Blauburgunder and Blaufränkisch.
The vineyards of Styria are all on steep hillsides. In addition to white wine (*Spritzig*, with a hint of sparkle) a rosé wine, *Schilcher*, is produced.

The Viennese vineyards extend to the city area and produce well-known white wines. Poplular haunts of the Viennese and visitors to Vienna are the wine-shops selling "Heuriger" (the most recent vintage of wine) which are to be found in Sievering, Grinzing, Nussdorf and other outlying districts of the city.

Spas

Thermal Spas
Medicinal Spas
Peat-Bath Spas

● Thermal Spas

1 Bad Hofgastein (S)
Altitude: 860 m/2800 ft
Radioactive water
Max. 26 °C/116 °F

2 Badgastein (S)
Altitude: 1083 m/3553 ft
Pure water containing radon
Max. 48·3 °C/119 °F

3 Vigaun (S)
Altitude: 468 m/1536 ft
Thermal water containing sodium and calcium chlorides and sulphates
Max. 34 °C/93 °F

4 Bad Mitterndorf-Heilbrunn (Stm)
Altitude: 797 m/2615 ft
Pure water
Max. 26 °C/79 °F

5 Bad Schallerbach (OÖ)
Altitude: 310 m/1017 ft
Pure sulphur water
Max. 37·2 °C/109 °F

6 Bad Kleinkirchheim (K)
Altitude: 1073 m/3521 ft
Pure water
Max. 22·5 °C/72·5 °F

7 Bad Bleiberg *ob Villach* (K)
Altitude: 892 m/2927 ft
Pure water
Max. 30 °C/86 °F

8 Warmbad Villach (K)
Altitude: 503 m/1650 ft
Pure water
Max. 30 °C/86 °F

9 Bad Vöslau (NÖ)
Altitude: 260 m/853 ft
Pure water
Max. 24 °C/74 °F

10 Baden *bei Wien* (NÖ)
Altitude: 228 m/748 ft
Sulphur water
Max. 35·8 °C/96 °F

11 Vienna *(Kurzentrum Oberlaa)*
Altitude: 170 m/558 ft
Sulphur water
Max. 55 °C/131 °F

12 Bad Deutsch-Altenburg (NÖ)
Altitude: 168 m/551 ft
Sulphur water
Max. 28 °C/82 °F

● Medicinal Spas

13 Reuthe (V)
Altitude: 650 m/2133 ft
Chalybeate spring

14 Seefeld (T)
Altitude: 1180 m/3872 ft
Pure water containing calcium and magnesium sulphates and hydrogen carbonate

15 Mehrn/Brixlegg (T)
Altitude: 535 m/1755 ft
Cold spring containing calcium and magnesium sulphates and hydrogen carbonate

16 Bad Häring (T)
Altitude: 594 m/1949 ft
Tepid sulphur water

17 Bad Burgwies/Stuhlfelden (S)
Altitude: 789 m/2589 ft
Pure water containing calcium, magnesium, sodium and hydrogen carbonates and sulphur

18 Dürrnberg *bei Hallein* (S)
Altitude: 800 m/2626 ft
Water containing sodium and calcium chlorides and sulphates

19 **Salzburg** (S)
Altitude: 424 m/1391 ft
Brine; water containing sodium and calcium
chlorides and sulphates

20 **Bad Weinberg** (OÖ)
Altitude: 365 m/1198 ft
Water containing calcium, magnesium and
hydrogen carbonates and sulphates and iron

21 **Zell** *bei Zelldorf* (OÖ)
Altitude: 513 m/1683 ft
Pure radioactive water

22 **Bad Hall** (OÖ)
Altitude: 388 m/1273 ft
Hypertonic water containing sodium chloride and
iodine

23 **Bad Ischl** (OÖ)
Altitude: 469 m/1539 ft
Brine; cold spring containing sodium chloride; cold
spring containing sodium chloride and sulphate and
sulphur

24 **Bad Ausee** (Stm)
Altitude: 659 m/2162 ft
Hypertonic water containing sodium chloride and
sulphate; brine

25 **Bad Goisern** (OÖ)
Altitude: 500 m/1640 ft
Pure water containing sodium chloride, hydrogen
carbonate and sulphur

26 **St Lorenzen** *im Lesachtal* (K)
Altitude: 1128 m/3701 ft
Water containing calcium and magnesium sulphates

27 **Trebesing** (K)
Altitude: 749 m/2457 ft
Acidic water containing calcium and hydrogen
carbonates and sulphates

28 **Wildbad Einöd** (Stm)
Altitude: 740 m/2428 ft
Thermal spring of acidic water containing calcium
and hydrogen carbonates and sulphates

29 **Bad Weissenbach** (K)
Altitude: 461 m/1513 ft
Thermal spring of acidic water containing sodium,
calcium and hydrogen carbonates

30 **Eisenkappel/Vellach** (K)
Altitude: 558 m/1831 ft
Acidic spring containing hydrogen carbonate and
chloride

31 **Bad St Leonhard** *im Lavanttal* (K)
Altitude: 721 m/2366 ft
Cold spring of pure water containing calcium,
sodium and hydrogen carbonates and sulphates and
sulphur

32 **Bad Gams** (Stm)
Altitude: 405 m/1329 ft
Chalybeate spring of particular purity

33 **Bad Gleichenberg** (Stm)
Altitude: 317 m/1040 ft
Acidic water containing sodium and hydrogen
carbonates and chlorides

34 **Bad Radkersburg** (Stm)
Altitude: 209 m/686 ft
Acidic water containing magnesium, calcium and
hydrogen carbonates
New thermal spring (*c.* 70 °C/158 °F) drilled in 1978

35 **Loipersdorf** (Stm)
Altitude: 249 m/817 ft)
Thermal water containing sodium and hydrogen
chlorides and carbonates

36 **Waltersdorf** (Stm)
Altitude: 291 m/955 ft
Thermal hypotonic spring containing sodium and
hydrogen carbonates and chlorides

37 **Bad Tatzmannsdorf** (B)
Altitude: 340 m/1116 ft
Tepid acidic spring containing sodium, calcium and
hydrogen carbonates; tepid acidic chalybeate spring
containing calcium and hydrogen carbonates

38 **Piringsdorf** (B)
Altitude: 306 m/1004 ft
Acidic water containing sodium and calcium
bicarbonates

39 **Bad Schönau** (NÖ)
Altitude: 480 m/1575 ft
Acidic chalybeate spring containing calcium,
magnesium and hydrogen carbonates and sulphates

40 **Sauerbrunn** (B)
Altitude: 290 m/950 ft
Acidic water containing calcium, magnesium,
sodium and hydrogen carbonates and sulphates

41 **Pamhagen** (B)
Altitude: 121 m/397 ft
Acidic drinking water containing sodium and
hydrogen carbonates

42 **Salzerbad** (NÖ)
Altitude: 500 m/1640 ft
Brine spring

● Peat-Bath Spas

43 **Moorbad Reuthe** (V)
Altitude: 650 m/2133 ft

44 **Kitzbühel** (T)
Altitude: 762 m/2500 ft

45 **Hochmoos/St Martin** *bei Lofer* (S)
Altitude: 634 m/2080 ft

46 **Moorbad Schloss Strobl** (S)
Altitude: 544 m/1785 ft

47 **Bad Mitterndorf-Heilbrunn** (Stm)
Altitude: 797 m/2615 ft

48 **Salzburg** (S)
Altitude: 424 m/1391 ft

49 **St Felix/Lamprechtshausen** (S)
Altitude: 457 m/1499 ft

50 **Mattsee** (S)
Altitude: 503 m/1650 ft

51 **Gmös/Laakirchen** (OÖ)
Altitude: 440 m/1444 ft

52 **Bad Wimsbach-Neydharting** (OÖ)
Altitude: 388 m/1273 ft

53 Bad Leonfelden (OÖ)
Altitude: 750 m/2460 ft

54 Grosspertholz (NÖ)
Altitude: 711 m/2333 ft

55 Harbach (NÖ)
Altitude: 631 m/2071 ft

56 Althofen (K)
Altitude: 714 m/2343 ft

57 Moorbad Schwanberg (Stm)
Altitude: 431 m/1414 ft

58 Bad Tatzmannsdorf (B)
Altitude: 340 m/1116 ft

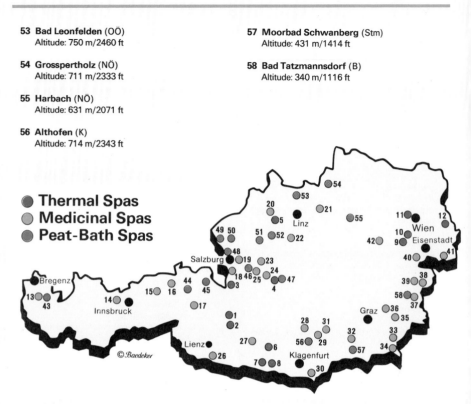

● **Thermal Spas**
○ **Medicinal Spas**
● **Peat-Bath Spas**

Congress Towns, Schlosshotels and Casinos

● **Congress Towns**
Information:
Österreichischer Kongressverband,
Judenplatz 3–4, A-1010 Wien;
tel. (02 22) 63 52 18

1 Bregenz (V)
Festspiel und Kongresshaus, seating c. 2000
Theater am Kornmarkt, seating 800
Sporthalle, seating c. 1200
Gewerkschaftshaus, seating 500
Palais Thurn und Taxis, seating 240
Landesmuseum, seating 150

2 Feldkirch (V)
Stadthalle, seating 1300
Arbeiterkammer, seating 620
Handelskammer, seating 170
Zeughaus, seating 220
Rathaus, seating 80
Palais Liechtenstein, seating 150

3 Innsbruck (T)
Kongresshaus, seating c. 4000
Kongresszentrum at Igls bei Innsbruck
seating c. 420

4 Kössen (T)
Grenzlandhalle, seating 1000

5 Kitzbühel (T)
Kolpingsaal, seating 200
Handelskammer, seating c. 580
Hauptschule, seating 360

6 Saalbach-Hinterglemm (S)
Informationscenter, seating 260
Mehrzweckhalle, seating c. 700

7 Bad Hofgastein (S)
Kurhaus, seating 750
Hotelfachschule, seating 150

8 Badgastein (S)
Kur- und Kongresshaus Gastein, seating 1200
Haus Austria, seating c. 400

9 Salzburg (S)
Kongresshaus, seating over 200
Grosses Festspielhaus, seating c. 2500
Kleines Festspielhaus, seating over c. 1600
Mozarteum, seating over 1000
Universität, seating 750
Wirtschaftsförderungsinstitut, seating 300
Arbeiterkammer, seating 300

10 Linz (OÖ)
Brucknerhaus, seating c. 2000
Sporthalle, seating up to 3500

11 Millstatt (K)
Kongresshaus, seating c. 800
Rathaus, seating 50
Stift, seating 250

12 Villach (K)
Kongresshaus, seating 1600
Rathaus, seating 830
Arbeiterkammer, seating c. 650
Handelskammer, seating 120
Bundesgewerbeschule, seating 200

13 Velden (K)
Gemeindehaus, seating 370

Pfarrheim, seating 150
Kinosaal, seating 250

14 Pörtschach (K)
Kurhaus, seating 680

15 Klagenfurt (K)
Konzerthaus, seating *c.* 1200
Haus der Jugend, seating 150
Stadttheater, seating 880
Arbeiterkammer, seating 800
Wirtschaftsförderungsinstitut, seating *c.* 700
Messehalle 5, seating 400
Universität, seating 200
Stadthaus, seating 720

16 Schladming (Stm)
Dachstein-Tauern-Halle, seating *c.* 1800
Stadtsaal, seating *c.* 330

17 Leoben (Stm)
Montanuniversität, seating *c.* 900
Stadtsaal, seating *c.* 360
Kammersäle, seating *c.* 1160
Barbarasaal, seating 250

18 Graz (Stm)
Kongresszentrum Altstadt, seating *c.* 2000
Arbeiterkammer, seating *c.* 1300
Opernhaus, seating *c.* 1300
Schauspielhaus, seating *c.* 1000
Kongresshalle, seating 500
Universität, seating *c.* 630
Minoritensaal, seating 550
Heimatsaal, seating 200
Stadtwerke, seating 150

19 Krems (NÖ)
Brauhofsaal, seating 1700
Steiner Rathaus, seating 120

20 Vienna
Wiener Hofburg, seating 2400
Osterreichischer Gewerbeverein, seating 270
Palais Palavicini, seating 250
Bundeskammer der Gewerblichen Wirtschaft,
    seating 280
Kursalon der Stadt Wien-Oberlas, seating 2700
Palais Schwarzenberg, seating 250
Sofiensäle, seating 2200
Bohemia, seating 500
Wiener Konzerthaus, seating 1800
Wiener Stadthalle, seating 10,000
Palais Palffy, seating 250
Kongresshaus Wien, seating 800
Palais Auersperg, seating 300
Wienermessepalast, seating 1800

21 Baden bei Wien (NO)
Kongresshaus, seating *c.* 700
Stadttheater, seating *c.* 700
Sommerarena, seating 650
Sparkassensaal, seating 250
Kolpinghaus, seating 200

22 Eisenstadt (B)
Schloss Esterhazy, seating *c.* 1100
Stadthalle, seating 280
Wirtschaftsförderungsinstitut, seating 100
Arbeiterkammer, seating 250
Handelskammer, seating 50
Landwirtschaftskammer, seating 50
Rathaus, seating 40
Bundesgymnasium, seating 400
Georgihalle, seating 1000

● **Schlosshotels**
(Castle and country house hotels)
Information:
*Zentrale reservierungsstelle der Arbeitsgruppe der
    Österreichischen Schlosshotels und Herrenhäuser,*
Hotel Schloss Lebenberg,
A-6379 Kitzbühel;
tel. (0 53 56) 43 01

23 Jagdschloss Kühtai
A-6183 Kühtai;
tel. (0 52 39) 2 25

24 Hotel Fürstenhaus
A-6213 Pertisau am Achensee;
tel. (0 52 43) 54 42

25 Hotel Klosterbräu
A-6100 Seefeld;
tel. (0 52 12) 26 21–0

26 Schlosshotel Igls
A-6080 Igls;
tel. (0 52 22) 72 17

27 Hotel Grünwalderhof
A-6082 Patsch;
tel. (0 52 22) 73 04

28 Jagdschloss Graf Recke
A-5741 Wald im Oberpinzgau;
tel. (0 65 65) 4 17

29 Schloss Lebenberg
A-6370 Kitzbühel;
tel. (0 53 56) 43 01–0

30 Jagdschloss Münichau
A-6370 Kitzbühel;
tel. (0 53 56) 29 62

31 Herrenhaus Tennerhof
A-6370 Kitzbühel;
tel. (0 53 56) 31 81

32 Schloss Haunsperg
A-5411 Oberalm;
tel. (0 62 45) 26 62

33 Schlosshotel Fondachhof
A-5020 Salzburg;
tel. (0 62 22) 2 09 06–07

34 Hotel Schloss Mönchstein
A-5020 Salzburg;
tel. (0 62 22) 4 13 63/66

35 Schlosshotel Sankt Rupert
A-5020 Salzburg;
tel. (0 62 22) 4 32 31

36 Schloss Feyregg
A-4540 Bad Hall;
tel. (0 72 58) 25 91

37 Haus Hubertushof
A-8992 Altaussee;
tel. (0 61 52) 7 12 80

38 Hotel Schloss Pichlarn
A-8952 Irdning;
tel. (0 36 82) 28 41

39 Schloss Leonstein
A-9210 Pörtschach;
tel. (0 42 72) 28 16

40 Hotel Schloss Seefels
A-9210 Pörtschach;
tel. (0 42 72) 23 77

41 Hotel Schloss Velden
A-9220 Velden;
tel. (0 42 74) 26 55

42 Schloss Ernegg
A-3261 Steinakirchen am Forst;
tel. (0 74 88) 2 14

43 Hotel Schloss Dürnstein
A-3601 Dürnstein;
tel. (0 27 11) 2 12

44 Burghotel Kranichberg
A-2640 Gloggnitz;
tel. (0 26 62) 82 42–43

45 Schlosshotel Martinschloss
A-3400 Kloster Neuburg;
tel. (0 22 43) 74 26

46 Hotel im Palais Schwarzenberg
A-1030 Wien;
tel. (02 22) 72 51 25

47 Clubhotel Baden/Schloss Welkersdorf
A-2500 Baden bei Wien;
tel. (0 22 52) 40 71

48 Schloss Drassburg;
A-7021 Drassburg;
tel. (0 26 86) 22 20

49 Hotel Burg Bernstein
A-7434 Bernstein;
tel. (0 33 54) 2 20

Congress Towns
Schlosshotels
Casinos

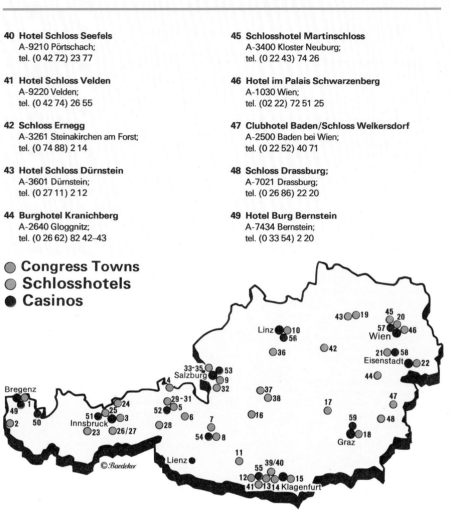

Castles and Country Houses

○ Castles and Country Houses

1 Schloss Hofen (16th c.)
Near Bregenz, Vorarlberg

2 Schloss Hohenems (16th c.)
Near Dornbirn, Vorarlberg

3 Schattenburg (13th c.)
Feldkirch, Vorarlberg

4 Schloss Ambras (16th c.)
Near Innsbruck, Tirol

5 Burg Mariastein (14th c.)
Near Wörgl, Tirol

6 Feste Kufstein (12th/16th c.)
Kufstein, Tirol

7 Schloss Mittersill (16th c.)
Mittersill, Salzburg province

8 Feste Hohenwerfen (11th/16th c.)
Werfen, Salzburg province

Castles and Country Houses

Austria has large numbers of old castles and country houses. These originally served a dual purpose: on the one hand they were designed to provide protection against enemy attack, and on the other they were an assertion of the local baron's or landowner's power and a focal point of government and administration for its territories. During the Middle Ages the defensive function predominated, but later, particularly during the Renaissance, more peaceful purposes prevailed and castles began to be built with an eye to comfort and, indeed, luxury. The term *Burg* implies a fortified castle, as does *Feste*. *Schloss* covers a wide range from a fortified castle to a country house or palace designed for show or comfort rather than protection. Many old castles and country houses are still privately owned.

9 Feste Hohensalzburg (11th and 15th–16th c.)
Salzburg

10 Schloss Sighartstein (12th/18th c.)
Near Neumarkt, Salzburg province

11 Burg Alt-Pernstein (16th c.)
Near Kirchdorf an der Krems,
Upper Austria

12 Burg Freistadt (14th c.)
Freistadt, Upper Austria

13 Burg Clam (12th/17th c.)
Near Grein, Upper Austria

14 Burg Rappottenstein (12th/16th c.)
Near Zwettl, Lower Austria

15 Schloss Rosenau (18th c.)
Near Zwettl, Lower Austria

16 Burg Rastenberg (12th/16th c.)
Near Rastenfeld, Lower Austria

17 Burg Ottenstein (12th and 16th–17th c.)
Near Ottenstein, Lower Austria

18 Burg Heidenreichstein (15th c.)
Heidenreichstein, Lower Austria

19 Schloss Greillenstein (16th–17th c.)
Near Horn, Lower Austria

20 Schloss Rosenburg (16th–17th c.)
Near Altenburg Abbey, Lower Austria

21 Schloss Horn (16th/18th c.)
Horn, Lower Austria

22 Schloss Schallaburg (16th c.)
Near Melk, Lower Austria

23 Schloss Bruck (13th/16th c.)
Near Lienz, East Tirol

24 Burg Mauterndorf (16th c.)
Near Mauterndorf, Salzburg province

25 Schloss Moosham (13th/17th c.)
Near Mauterndorf, Salzburg province

26 Schloss Porcia (16th c.)
Spittal an der Drau, Carinthia

27 Burg Groppenstein (12th/15th c.)
Near Obervellach, Carinthia

28 Schloss Strassburg (12th/17th c.)
Near Strassburg, Carinthia

29 Burg Hochosterwitz (16th c.)
Near St Veit an der Glan, Carinthia

30 Schloss Hollenburg (16th c.)
Near Maria Rain, Carinthia

31 Burg Landsberg (12th/16th c.)
Near Deutschlandsberg, Styria

32 Schloss Eggenberg (16th c.)
Near Graz, Styria

33 Schloss Rabenstein (17th/19th c.)
Near Frohnleiten, Styria

34 Riegersburg (12th/17th c.)
Near Riegersburg, Styria

35 Schloss Festenburg (14th and 17th–18th c.)
Near Vorau, Styria

36 Burg Schlaining (15th/17th c.)
Stadtschlaining, Burgenland

37 Schloss Bernstein (14th/17th c.)
Bernstein, Burgenland

38 Burg Seebenstein (11th/17th c.)
Seebenstein, Lower Austria

39 Burg Forchtenstein (17th c.)
Near Forchtenau, Burgenland

40 Schloss Bruck (18th c.)
Bruck an der Leitha,
Lower Austria

41 Hofburg (15th/19th c.)
Schloss Belvedere (18th c.)
Schloss Schönbrunn (17–18th c.)
Vienna

⬤ Castles and Country Houses

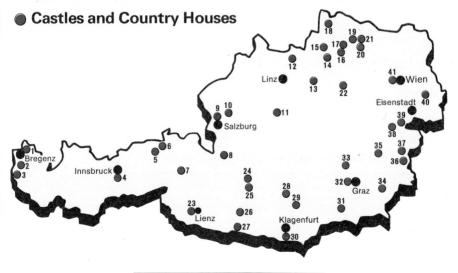

Monasteries and Religious Houses

1 **Mariastern** (Vorarlberg)
Abbey of Cistercian nuns, founded 1856

2 **Mehrerau** (Vorarlberg)
Cistercian abbey, founded by Benedictines 1097

3 **Stams** (Tirol)
Cistercian abbey, founded 1273

4 **Wilten** (Innsbruck)
Premonstratensian House, founded in 12th c.

5 **Fiecht** (Tirol)
Benedictine house, founded 1138

6 **St Peter** (Salzburg)
Benedictine abbey, founded 696

7 **Nonnberg** (Salzburg)
Convent of Benedictine nuns, founded c. 700

8 **Seekirchen** (Salzburg province)
Secular collegiate house, founded 1679

9 **Mattsee** (Salzburg province)
Secular collegiate house, founded 777

10 **Michaelbeuern** (Salzburg province)
Benedictine abbey, probably founded 737

11 **Reichersberg** (Upper Austria)
College of Augustinian Canons, founded 1084

12 **Lambach** (Upper Austria)
Benedictine abbey, founded 1040

13 **Kremsmünster** (Upper Austria)
Benedictine abbey, founded 777

14 **Schlierbach** (Upper Austria)
Founded 1355 as a convent of Cistercian nuns;
since 1620 occupied by Cistercian monks

15 **Engelszell** (Upper Austria)
Trappist abbey, founded 1293

16 **Schlägl** (Upper Austria)
Premonstratensian house, founded 1209

17 **Wilhering** (Upper Austria)
Cistercian abbey, founded 1146

18 **St Florian** (Upper Austria)
College of Augustinian Canons since 1071

19 **Seitenstetten** (Lower Austria)
Benedictine abbey, founded 1109

20 **Melk** (Lower Austria)
Benedictine abbey, founded c. 1000

21 **Lilienfeld** (Lower Austria)
Cistercian abbey, founded 1202

22 **Herzogenburg** (Lower Austria)
College of Augustinian Canons, founded 1112

23 **Göttweig** (Lower Austria)
Benedictine abbey, founded 1070

24 **Zwettl** (Lower Austria)
Cistercian abbey, founded 1138

25 **Altenburg** (Lower Austria)
Benedictine abbey, founded 1144

26 **Geras** (Lower Austria)
Premonstratensian house, founded c. 1150

27 **Admont** (Styria)
Benedictine abbey, founded 1074

28 **St Lambrecht** (Styria)
Benedictine abbey, founded 1076

29 **Gurk** (Carinthia)
Founded 1043 as a convent of Benedictine nuns,
from 1123 a college of Augustinian Canons, now a
Salvatorian house

30 **St Paul im Lavanttal** (Carinthia)
Benedictine abbey, founded 1091

31 **Seckau** (Styria)
Abbey of Benedictine nuns, founded 1140

32 **Rein** (Styria)
Cistercian abbey,
founded 1129

33 **Bertholdstein** (Styria)
Abbey of Benedictine nuns,
founded 1888–89

34 **Vorau** (Styria)
College of Augustinian Canons,
founded 1234

35 **Neukloster** (Wiener Neustadt, Lower Austria)
Cistercian abbey,
founded 1444

36 **Heiligenkreuz** (Lower Austria)
Cistercian abbey,
founded 1133

37 **Schottenstift** (Vienna)
Benedictine abbey,
founded 1155

38 **Klosterneuburg** (Lower Austria)
College of Augustinian Canons,
founded c. 1100

Monasteries and Religious Houses

Austria is rich in old abbeys and other monasteries and religious houses of great historical and artistic interest. Some of them, including Melk, Altenburg and St Florian, are among the country's outstanding tourist attractions.

Many of them are not merely splendid museums of religious art and architecture but continue to serve their original function.

The various orders share the same vows of obedience, celibacy and renunciation of personal possessions. There is a distinction between the orders of canons (who are always ordained priests) and monks (who are usually not ordained). The Augustinians and Premonstratensians are canons, the Benedictines and Cistercians are monks. There are corresponding female houses.

Other Monasteries and Religious Houses (mostly dissolved)

TIROL

Hall
Convent, founded 1566, dissolved 1783;
now occupied by nuns of the Sacred Heart

Sharnitz
Monastery, founded 763,
transferred to Schlehdorf/Kochelsee 772

SALZBURG PROVINCE

Domkloster Salzburg
Augustinian Canons
Founded 1122, dissolved 1519

STYRIA

Göss (Leoben)
Benedictine nuns
Founded c. 1000, dissolved 1782
Part of monastic buildings now
occupied by the well-known Gösser Brewery

Neuberg an der Mürz
Cistercians
Founded 1327, dissolved 1786

Pöllau
Augustinian Canons
Founded 1455, dissolved 1785

Stainz
Augustinian Canons
Founded 1229, dissolved 1785

CARINTHIA

Arnoldstein
Benedictines
Founded 1106, dissolved 1783
Destroyed by fire 1883

Eberndorf
Augustinian Canons
Founded c. 1150, made over
to Jesuits 1603; property conveyed
to St Paul Abbey 1809

Friesach
College of Augustinian Canons
SS Magdalena and Mauritius
Founded 1454, dissolved 1781
Church burned down 1804
Now occupied by Dominican nuns

Secular collegiate house
St Bartholomäus
Founded 1187, still occupied

Propstei Virgilienberg
Founded 1217; great fire 1582;
incorporated in St Bartholomäus 1606
Now in ruins

Griffen
Premonstratensians
Founded 1236, dissolved 1786

Gurnitz
Collegiate house
Founded c. 1240, later dissolved

Kraig
Collegiate house
Founded 1350, later dissolved

Maria Saal
Canons
Created Propstei (provostship) 1116
Secular collegiate house, still occupied

Maria Wörth
Collegiate house
Founded between 1146 and 1156;
to Knights of St George 1529;
to Jesuits 1598;
taken over by St Paul Abbey 1809

Millstatt
Benedictines
Founded between 1060 and 1088,
dissolved 1469

Ossiach
Benedictines
Founded 1024, dissolved 1783

St Andrä im Lavanttal
Augustinian Canons
Founded between 1223 and 1225,
dissolved 1808

St Georgen am Längsee
Benedictine nuns
Founded 1010, dissolved 1783

Strassburg
Secular collegiate house
Founded c. 1330, still occupied

Tanzenberg
Olivetans (a branch of the Benedictines)
Founded 1898, dissolved 1940
Now a seminary

Viktring
Cistercians
Founded 1142, dissolved 1786
Now a textile factory

Völkermarkt
Founded 1231 as Propstei
Secular collegiate house
Still occupied

UPPER AUSTRIA

Altmünster (on Traunsee)
Benedictines
In existence in 9th c.;
dissolved in 10th c.

Baumgartenberg
Cistercians
Founded 1141; by 1784 decayed
Now occupied by a girls' school

Garsten
Benedictines
Founded 1108, dissolved 1787
Now a penal institution

Gleink
Benedictines
Founded 1125, dissolved 1784

Mattighofen
Secular collegiate house
14th–17th c.

Mondsee
Benedictines
Founded 748, dissolved 1791

Ranshofen (on Inn)
Augustinian Canons
Founded 1125, dissolved 1811

Spital am Pyhrn
Secular collegiate house
Founded 1418, dissolved 1807

Suben (on Inn)
Augustinian Canons
Founded 1126, dissolved 1787
Now a penal institution

Traunkirchen
Benedictine nuns
Founded c. 1020, dissolved 1572

Waldhausen
Augustinian Canons
Founded 1147, dissolved 1792

LOWER AUSTRIA

Aggsbach
Carthusians
Founded 1380, dissolved 1782

Ardagger
Secular collegiate house
Founded 1049, dissolved 1784

Dürnstein
Augustinian Canons
Founded 1410, dissolved 1788

Erla
Benedictines
Founded c. 1050, dissolved 1583

Gaming
Carthusians
Founded 1330, dissolved 1782

Gloggnitz
From 12th c. a Propstei of
Formbach Abbey in Bavaria;
dissolved 1803

Kirchberg am Wechsel
Augustinian nuns
Founded before 1236,
dissolved 1782

Klein-Mariazell (in Wienerwald)
Benedictines
Founded 1136, dissolved 1782

Mauerbach (in Wienerwald)
Carthusians
Founded 1316, dissolved 1782

Pernegg
Premonstratensian nuns
Founded c. 1150;
to Premonstratensian Canons 1586;
dissolved 1783

Säusenstein (on Danube)
Augustinian Canons
Founded 1336, dissolved 1789

Schrattenthal
Augustinian Canons
Founded c. 1430, dissolved 1534

St Andrä an der Traisen
Augustinian Canons
Founded 1170, dissolved 1787

St Bernhard (near Horn)
Cistercian nuns
Founded 1263, dissolved 1586

St Pölten
Augustinian Canons
Augustinian rule adopted in 11th c.;
dissolved 1784
Monastic church now Cathedral,
monastic buildings Bishop's Palace

Wiener Neustadt
Augustinian Canons
Founded 1459, dissolved 1551

Ybbs
Cistercian nuns
Founded in 13th c.,
dissolved 1572

Zwettl
Collegiate house
Founded 1483;
incorported in Theresianum 1751
Not to be confused with the great Cistercian abbey

● Monasteries and Religious Houses

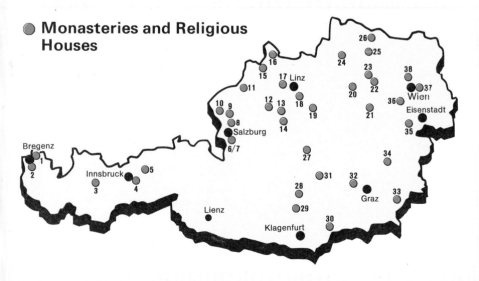

VIENNA

Kahlenberg
Camaldolese (a branch of the Benedictines)
Founded 1628, dissolved 1782
St Joseph's Church still in existence

St Dorothea
Augustinian Canons
Founded 1414, dissolved 1786

There were also many religious houses for females in Vienna

BURGENLAND

Klostermarienberg
Cistercians
Founded 1194, dissolved 1532
Later purchased by Prince Esterházy
and returned to the order;
now held by Lilienfeld Abbey

Marz (near Mattersburg)
Augustinian Canons
Founded in 11th c.,
dissolved in 15th c.

For the Nature-Lover

Climbing

Austria is one of the great climbing countries. Since more than two-thirds of its total area is occupied by the Eastern Alps and their outliers, it offers an almost inexhaustible range of climbs and rock-climbs in all grades of difficulty. Large numbers of cableways and lifts make it easy to reach the climbing areas.

It is essential to be properly clad and equipped. In particular it is important to have sturdy boots, well "broken in", giving support to the ankles. Proper climbing breeches are also to be recommended, together with some protection against rain and covering for the head.

Walkers and climbers who are new to the mountains should remember that the human organism, particularly the vascular system, must adapt itself to a new environment before it recovers its full capacity. Nor should the **dangers** of Alpine country (sudden changes in the weather, mist, falling rock, etc.) be underestimated.

The international Alpine **distress signal**, for climbers who need help, is a series of six signals given at regular intervals over a minute by whatever means are available (blasts on a whistle, shouts, flashes of a torch or a mirror, waves of some easily visible article), followed by a minute's pause, a repetition of the signals, and so on until an answer is received. The answer takes the form of three signals at regular intervals over a minute, followed by a minute's pause and a repetition of the signals.

Many of the climbs referred to in this guide should be undertaken only with a qualified **guide**. Guides can be obtained at all mountain resorts and climbing areas. At many places there are also climbing schools.

The **Austrian Alpine Club** (*Österreichischer Alpenverein*, ÖAV, Wilhelm-Greil-Strasse 15, A-6020 Innsbruck), founded 1862, maintains a large number of mountain huts, which are open to non-members. There are also many huts run by the German Alpine Club.

Nature Parks, Alpine Gardens, Plant Reserves

● **Nature Parks**

1 **Untersberg** (Salzburg province)
Up to more than 1800 m/5900 ft
Area: 27 sq. km/10½ sq. miles

Rocks, Alpine pasture, forest; game preserve, footpaths

2 **Ötscher-Tormäuer** (Lower Austria)
An Alpine nature park on the Ötscher (almost 1900 m/6250 ft high), S of Scheibbs
Area: 90 sq. km/35 sq. miles
Rapids, waterfalls, caves and gorges; nature trail, native animals

3 **Schwarzau im Gebirge** (Lower Austria)
On the W side of the Wiener Schneeberg (2075 m/ 6808 ft)
Area: 0·18 sq. km/44 acres
Rare butterflies, chamois, golden eagles; garden of Alpine plants; caves

4 **Hohe Wand** (Lower Austria)
Altitude: *c.* 1000 m/3300 ft
Area: 20 sq. km/8 sq. miles
Animals free and in enclosures

5 **Sparbach** (Lower Austria)
Near Perchtoldsdorf in the southern Wienerwald
Area: 4 sq. km/1½ sq. miles
Mixed forest; fallow deer and wild pigs free and in enclosures; nature trail

6 **Schlosspark Laxenburg** (Lower Austria)
S of Vienna
English-style landscaped park
8 km/5 miles of paths
Many birds

7 **Blockheide/Eibenstein** (Lower Austria)
Near Gmünd in the northern Waldviertel
Area: 15 sq. km/6 sq. miles
Heath; large weathered granite boulders; look-out tower; open-air geological museum

8 **Geras** (Lower Austria)
In the north-eastern Waldviertel
Area: 1·42 sq. km/350 acres
Game preserve; birds; forest trail

9 **Leiser Berge** (Lower Austria)
In the Weinviertel
Area: 45 sq. km/17½ sq. miles
Forest, vineyards; 35 km/22 miles of footpaths; wine trail and wine-cellars at Falkenstein; wildlife park at Ernstbrunn

10 **Gamstein-Voralpe Hollenstein/Ybbs** (Lower Austria)
50 km S of Amstetten
Area: 33 sq. km/13 sq. miles
Alpine foreland and some of the peaks of the northern chalk alps

11 Jauerling-Wachau (Lower Austria)
On the Jauerling plateau
Area: 114 sq. km/44 sq. miles
Nature trail, fungi museum, herb museum

12 Grebenzen (Styria)
On the border of Carinthia
Area: 70 sq. km/27 sq. miles

13 Pöllauer Tal (Styria)
Area: 124 sq. km/48 sq. miles
Cultivated and natural landscape, sub-Alpine and
Alpine flora

○ Alpine Gardens

14 Schruns (Vorarlberg)
Alpine Garden at the Lindauer Hütte

15 Reutte (Tirol)
Alpine Flower Garden on the Hahnenkamm
Alpine plants with about 1200 m/1313 yds of paths

16 Kühtai (Tirol)
Near Dortmunder Hütte: 500 species of plants
Area: 500 sq. m/600 sq. yds

17 Innsbruck (Tirol)
In University Botanic Garden, with 1200 species of
mountain plants from all over the world;
area on the Patscherkofel (alt. 1900 m/6200 ft)

18 Bad Aussee (Styria)
2 km/1¼ miles NW of town
Area: 11,000 sq. m/13,000 sq. yds
4000 species

19 Linz (Upper Austria)
In Botanic Garden, with 4000 species from all over
the world
Area: 45,000 sq. m/2½ acres

20 Wachau (Lower Austria)
Schönbühel, 5 km/3 miles E of Melk
Area: 4500 sq. m/5400 sq. yds
Some 1500 different Alpine plants

21 Villacher Alpe (Carinthia)
Area: 10,000 sq. m/12,000 sq. yds
Plants of southern Alpine region

22 Klagenfurt (Carinthia)
Botanic Garden
Area: 12,000 sq. m/14,500 sq. yds
Plants of central and southern Alpine regions

23 Gaal-Knittelfeld (Styria)
Area: 4000 sq. m/4800 sq. yds
300 species

24 Frohnleiten (Styria)
Area: 90,000 sq. m/22 acres
10,000 species from all over the world

25 Rannach (Styria)
10 km/6 miles N of Graz
Area: 10,000 sq. m/12,000 sq. yds
Plants from the eastern Alpine region

26 Graz (Styria)
In Botanic Garden
Alpine plants from all over the world

27 Rax (Lower Austria)
At Ottohaus
Area: 1500 sq. m/1800 sq. yds
Plants of NE Alpine region

28 Vienna
Alpine Garden in Belvedere park
Area: 2050 sq. m/2450 sq. yds
Some 4000 species
Alpine Garden in University Botanic Garden, with
some 1000 species from all over the world

○ Protected areas of the World Wildlife Fund

29 Hundsheimer Berge Nature Reserve
(Lower Austria)
Near Deutsch-Altenburg
Plants and insects of the Steppes

30 Marchauen Nature Reserve (Lower Austria)
Near Marchegg
Woodland, former water courses, cranes, white
storks

31 Pürgschachener Moor (Styria)
Near Ardning in the Ennstal Peat bog

● **Nature Parks**
● **Alpine Gardens**
● **Protected Areas of the World Wildlife Fund (WWF)**
● **Plant Reserves**

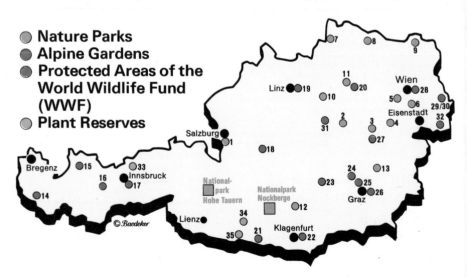

© Baedeker

32 Seewinkel/Lange Lacke Nature Reserve
(Burgenland)
On the E bank of the Neusiedler See
Water fowl breeding area

● Plant Reserves

33 Ahornböden im Karwendel (Tirol)
Alt. 1100–1400 m/3600–4600 ft
Old-established stands of sycamores (very fine in autumn)

34 Lendorf an der Drau (Carinthia)
Yellow rhododendrons

35 Hermagor (Carinthia)
Blue wulfenia (on Nassfeld)

Zoos
Wildlife Parks
Bird Sanctuaries

● Zoos

1 Innsbruck (Tirol)
Alpenzoo (Alpine Zoo) on the slopes of the Nordkette near the Weiherburg
Alpine animals

2 Hellbrunn (Salzburg province)
Tiergarten (Zoo) 5 km/3 miles S of Salzburg in park of Schloss Hellbrunn

3 Klagenfurt (Carinthia)
Reptilienzoo (Reptile Zoo) at the "Minimundus" miniature town on the Wörther See, W of the town
Snakes and other reptiles from all over the world

4 Schönbrunn (Vienna)
Tiergarten (Zoo), founded 1752
More than 4500 animals; 850 species from all over the world

● Wildlife Parks

5 Bregenz/Lochau (Vorarlberg)
On the Pfänder at the upper station of the cableway
Area: 30,000 sq. m/7¼ acres
Red deer, ibex, mufflons, wild boar

6 Feldkirch (Vorarlberg)
On the Ardetzenberg
Area: 90,000 sq. m/22 acres
Native animals; forest trail

7 Telfs (Tirol)
At the Berghof Hieber
Area: 1 sq. km/½ sq. miles
Stags, roebuck

8 Achenkirch (Tirol)
Game compound at the lower station of the Sonnberg chairlift
Stags, roebuck, chamois

9 Fulpmes (Tirol)
Area: 20,000 sq. m/5 acres
Red deer, roe deer, mountain goats, pheasant, partridge, capercaillie

10 Aurach (Tirol)
7 km/4½ miles N of Kitzbühel
Area: 500,000 sq. m/124 acres
Fallow deer, yaks from Tibet, ibex, etc.

11 Kirchberg (Tirol)
Fallow deer compound

12 Assling (Tirol)
More than 20 species including ibex, chamois, red deer, marmots, wild boar, birds of prey

13 Jagdhof Schloss Fuschl (Salzburg province)
20 km/12½ miles E of Salzburg
Area: 180,000 sq. m/44 acres
Red deer, fallow deer, etc.
Hunting and Pipe Museum in Jagdhof

14 Fusch an der Grossglocknerstrasse
(Salzburg province)
Ferleiten Game Park
Red deer, fallow deer, sika deer, moufflons, chamois, ibex, wild boar, lynx, racoons, marmots, etc.

15 Strobl (Salzburg province)
Kleefelderhof Game Park
About 200 animals, bird trail

16 Hochkreut (Upper Austria)
Between the Attersee and Traunsee
Area: 140,000 sq. m/35 acres
Red deer, fallow deer, ibex, bison, etc.

17 Freinberg (Upper Austria)
N of Schärding
Area: 150,000 sq. m/37 acres
Fallow deer, rare sheep, wild boar, lynx, Malayan bear, coati, etc.

● Zoos
○ Wildlife Parks
○ Bird Sanctuaries

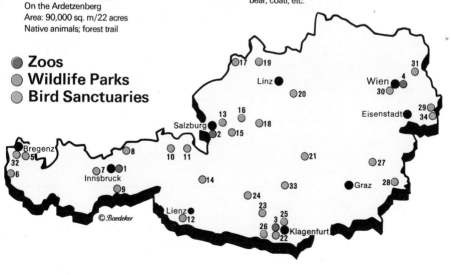

© Baedeker

18 **Cumberland-Wildpark** (Upper Austria)
8 km/5 miles S of Grünau im Almtal
Area: 550,000 sq. m/136 acres
Some 60 species of Austrian animals
Level footpaths

19 **Altenfelden** (Upper Austria)
30 km/19 miles NW of Linz
Area: 820,000 sq. m/203 acres
More than 700 animals, including Indian swamp
deer and thars from the Himalayas; observation post
for watching birds of prey and fish

20 **Haag** (Lower Austria)
SE of Linz in the park of Schloss Salaberg
Area: 330,000 sq. m/82 acres
Enclosure with bison, aurochs, etc.

21 **Mautern** (Styria)
In the foothills of the Niedere Tauern
Area: 500,000 sq. m/124 acres
Red and fallow deer, Père David's deer from China

22 **Maierniggalm Animal Park** (Carinthia)
SW of Klagenfurt
Area: 100,000 sq. m/25 acres
Red deer, fallow deer, pheasant, llamas, ostriches,
etc.

23 **Feld am See** (Carinthia)
Area: 100,000 sq. m/25 acres
Red deer, fallow deer, moufflons, ibex

24 **Diana Game Park Malta** (Carinthia)
In the Maltatal N of Spittal an der Drau
Area: 20,000 sq. m/5 acres
Red deer, black deer, Siberian foxes, lions, tigers,
monkeys

25 **Jägerhof Schloss Mageregg** (Carinthia)
5 km/3 miles N of Klagenfurt
Area: 100,000 sq. m/25 acres
Red and fallow deer

26 **Rosegg** (Carinthia)
10 km/6 miles S of Velden in a turn of the Drau
Area: 350,000 sq. m/86 acres
More than 150 animals, including bison from
America and muntjak from Manchuria;
in summer, bird-watching station (birds of prey)

27 **Herberstein** (Styria)
40 km/25 miles E of Graz
Area: 500,000 sq. m/124 acres
Enclosure with facilities for observing animals

28 **Güssing** (Burgenland)
Area: 3 sq. km/740 acres
Enclosures, indoor and outdoor; observation
platforms
Aurochs, water buffalo, Dybovsky's deer from Korea,
zebus, etc.

29 **Pamhagen Animal Park** (animals of the steppes)
(Burgenland)
E of the Neusiedler See, near the Hungarian Frontier
Water fowl, cattle, wolves, Hungarian woolly sheep,
wild horses

30 **Vienna** (Lainzer Tiergarten)
In a walled park on the western outskirts of the city
Area: 25 sq. km/9½ sq. miles
Deer, roe-deer, aurochs

31 **Safaripark Gänserndorf** (Lower Austria)
30 km/19 miles NE of Vienna
Area: 680,000 sq. m/168 acres
More than 500 animals, including lions and tigers

● **Bird Sanctuaries**

32 **Rheindelta** (Vorarlberg)
On the shores of Lake Constance W of Hard
Area: 20 sq. km/8 sq. miles
Some 300 species of birds

33 **Furtner Teich** (Styria)
NW of Neumarkt
Two reedy ponds
More than 200 species of bird

34 **Andau** (Burgenland)
E of the Neusiedler See, near the Hungarian frontier
Area: 1·4 sq. km/345 acres
Nature reserve (among the protected species being
the great bustard)

Fishing

Austria offers wide scope for anglers, in the
form of both game fishing and coarse fishing,
and the strict government regulation on
pollution ensure that fishing waters are kept
pure.

In the numerous lakes there are trout, char,
pike, catfish and pike-perch, while there is
good fly-fishing in the mountain streams for
brown trout, rainbow trout and grayling.

Permits. – All anglers must have an official fishing permit
(*Amtliche Fischerkarte*), which is issued by the district
local authorities and covers the whole of the particular
province. In addition it is necessary to obtain a permit from
the owner or lessee of the fishing waters. Statutory
minimum sizes and close seasons vary from area to area.
Since the number of visitors' permits for some fishing
grounds is limited, it is advisable to apply in advance.

Sport

Golf-Courses
Gliding Schools
Hang-Gliding Schools

● Golf-Courses

1 Seefeld (Tirol)
Seefeld-Wildmoos, 18 holes

2 Innsbruck (Tirol)
Innsbruck-Rinn, 18 holes
Innsbruck-Lans, 9 holes

3 Pertisau (Tirol)
9 holes

4 Kitzbühel (Tirol)
Two courses, both 9 holes

5 Saalfelden (Salzburg province)
18 holes

6 Zell am See (Salzburg provnce)
18 holes

7 Badgastein (Salzburg province)
9 holes

8 Salzburg
Salzburg-Wals,
Schloss Klessheim, 9 holes

9 Fuschl (Salzburg province)
Hof bei Salzburg, 9 holes

10 Bad Ischl (Upper Austria)
9 holes

11 Irdning (Styria)
18 holes

12 Weissenbach bei Liezen (Styria)
9 holes

13 Bad Kleinkirchheim (Carinthia)
18 holes

14 Dellach (Carinthia)
On the Wörther See, 18 holes

15 15 Weisskirchen/Wels (Upper Austria)
9 holes

16 Linz (Upper Austria)
Linz-Tillysburg, 9 holes

17 Ernegg (Lower Austria)
Schlosshotel, Steinakirchen am Forst,
9 holes

18 Murhof (Styria)
Frohnleiten-Murhof, 18 holes

19 Semmering (Lower Austria)
9 holes

20 Wiener Neustadt (Lower Austria)
18 holes

21 Enzesfeld (Lower Austria)
18 holes

22 Hainburg (Lower Austria)
9 holes

23 Vienna
Freudenau
18 holes

24 Fürstenfeld (Styria)
18 holes

● Gliding Schools

25 Zell am See (Salzburg province)

26 Nieder Öblarn im Ennstal (Styria)

27 Wiener Neustadt West (Lower Austria)

28 Spitzerberg (Lower Austria)

29 Graz-Thalerhof (Styria)

● Golf-Courses
● Gliding Schools
● Hang-Gliding Schools

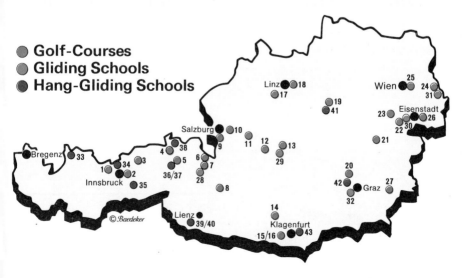

© Baedeker

● **Hang-Gliding Schools**

30 **Tannheim** (Tirol)

31 **Scharnitz** (Tirol)

32 **Hippach** (Tirol)

33 **Kirchberg** (Tirol)

34 **Kirchdorf** (Tirol)

35 **Kössen** (Tirol)

36 **Sillian** (Tirol)

37 **Lienz/Osttirol** (Tirol)

38 **Lackenhof** (Lower Austria)

39 **Bärnbach** (Styria)

40 **Klagenfurt** (Carinthia)

41 **St Radegund** (Styria)

Other Interests

Old-Time Railways
Industrial Archaeology

● **Old-Time Railways**

1 **Montafonerbahn**
   Bludenz–Schruns (Vorarlberg)
   Length: 12·7 km/8 miles
   Gauge 1436 mm/56½ in.
   Steam traction
   At weekends in summer

2 **Achenseebahn**
   Jenbach–Seespitz (Tirol)
   Length: 6·7 km/4 miles
   Gauge: 1000 mm/39½ in.
   Cog railway, steam traction
   May–September

3 **Zillertalbahn**
   Jenbach–Mayrhofen (Tirol)
   Length: 32 km/20 miles
   Gauge: 760 mm/30 in.
   Steam and diesel traction
   Throughout the year

4 **Schafbergbahn**
   St Wolfgang–Schafberg (Salzburg province)
   Length: 5·9 km/3½ miles
   Gauge: 1000 mm/39½ in.
   Steam and diesel traction
   May–October

5 **Linz-Urfahr–Pöstlingberg** (Upper Austria)
   Length: 2·9 km/1¾ miles
   Gauge: 1000 mm/39½ in.
   Electric traction
   Throughout the year

6 **Florianerbahn**
   St Florian-Taunleiten (Upper Austria)
   Length: 8·2 km/5 miles
   Gauge: 900 mm/35½ in.
   Electric traction

7 **Murtalbahn**
   Unzmark–Tamsweg
   (Styria and Salzburg provinces)
   Length: 65 km/40 miles
   Gauge: 760 mm/30 in.
   Diesel and steam traction
   Throughout the year; special trips for steam
   enthusiasts and amateur engine-drivers by
   arrangement with management (Murau)

8 **Gurktalbahn**
   Traibach–Zwischenwässern
   (Carinthia)
   Length: 3·3 km/2 miles
   Gauge: 760 mm/30 in.
   Steam and diesel traction
   Saturdays in summer

9 **Preding–Stainz** (Styria)
   Length: 11·3 km/7 miles
   Gauge: 760 mm/30 in.
   Steam and diesel traction
   According to demand; special trips for steam
   enthusiasts and amateur engine-drivers by
   arrangement (apply to Stainz station)

● **Old-Time Railways**
◐ **Industrial Archaeology**

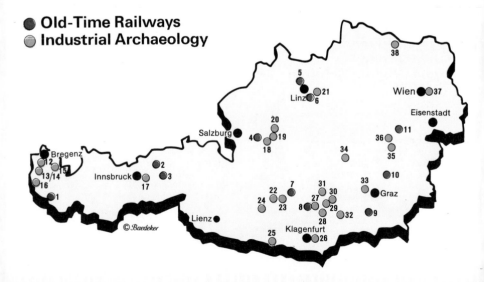

© *Baedeker*

10 Weiz–Birkfeld (Styria)
Length: 23·9 km/15 miles
Gauge: 760 mm/30 in.
Diesel and steam traction
Saturdays, July–September; special steam trips by
arrangement with management (Weiz)

**11 Hochschneebergbahn
Puchberg–Hochschneeberg**
(Styria)
Length: 9·7 km/6 miles
Gauge: 1000 mm/39½ in.
Cog railway, steam traction
Throughout the year if conditions permit

● Industrial Archaelogy

12 Hard (Vorarlberg)
Worsted spinning-mill
Built 1896

13 Dornbirn (Vorarlberg)
Herrburger & Rhomberg Spinning Mill
Built 1896

14 Dornbirn (Vorarlberg)
Fussenegger Textile Works
Drying tower
Built 1897

15 Andelsbuch (Vorarlberg)
Hydroelectric station
Built 1906–08

16 Frastanz (Vorarlberg)
Brewery
Second half of 19th c.

17 Hall (Tirol)
Sudhaus Fürst Lobkowitz
Brine works
Built 1837–40

18 Bad Ischl (Upper Austria)
Kolowrat-Sudhaus
Brine works
Built 1834

19 Stegg (Upper Austria)
Gosauzwang
Aqueduct carrying the brine pipeline from Hallstatt
to Ebensee
Built 1755–58; much altered 1969

20 Ebensee (Upper Austria)
Neues Sudhaus
Brine works
Built 1916–19

21 Mauthausen (Upper Austria)
Salzstadel
Salt warehouse
Built 1806–08

22 Bundschuh (Salzburg province)
Blast furnace
Built 1862

23 Kendlbruck (Salzberg province)
Deutschhammer
Blast furnace
18th c.; in ruins

24 Eisentratten (Carinthia)
Blast furnace
Built 1862

25 Arnoldstein (Carinthia)
Shot-tower
Built 1886

26 Klagenfurt (Carinthia)
Thys'sche Tuchfabrik, Lerchenfelderstrasse 51
Textile factory
Built 1762

27 Hirt (Carinthia)
Ironworks
First half of 19th c.

28 Urtl (Carinthia)
Ironworks
Recorded in 1578

29 Heft (Carinthia)
Ironworks
Built 1857

30 Mosinzgraben (Carinthia)
Fuchsflossofen
Iron foundry
Built 1768

31 Zirbitzkogel (Styria)
Ironworks at an altitude of over 1500 m/4900 ft
18th c.

32 St Gertraud (Carinthia)
Ironworks
Built 1847–48

33 Judendorf-Strassengel (Styria)
Perlmoser Cement Factory
Second half of 19th c.

34 Vordernberg (Styria)
Remains of ironworks machinery
19th c.
Iron refinery
Rebuilt 1840

35 Steinhaus am Semmering (Lower Austria)
Ironworks
Built 1838–40; in ruins

36 Edlach (Lower Austria)
Remains of an iron foundry
Built *c.* 1800

37 Vienna (Semmering district)
Gasholder
Built 1896–99

38 Retz (Lower Austria)
Windmill
19th c.

Caves Open to the Public
Mines Open to the Public
Open-air Museums

● Caves

1 Hundalm-Eishöhle (Tirol)
Near Wörgl
Ice formations, stalactites and stalagmites
Entrance at 1520 m/4985 ft
(3 hours' climb)
Conducted tours on weekends in summer

2 Lamprechtsofenloch (Salzburg province)
Near Weissbach bei Lofer
Underground waterfalls
Entrance on federal highway through Saalach valley
Conducted tours daily throughout the year

3 Eisriesenwelt (Salzburg province)
Near Werfen, Tennengebirge
Ice formations
Entrance at 1656 m/5433 ft
(cableway, then 15 minutes on foot)
Conducted tours daily in summer

4 Entrische Kirche (Salzburg province)
Near Klammstein, Gasteiner Tal
Karstic cavern with stalactites and stalagmites
Entrance from federal highway at Dorfgastein
(30 minutes)
Conducted tours daily in summer

5 Dachstein-Mammuthöhlen (Upper Austria)
Near Obertraun
Large chambers and tunnels
Cableway to 1350 m/4430 ft, then 15 minutes on foot
Conducted tours daily in summer

Dachstein-Rieseneishöhle (Upper Austria)
Near Obertraun
Ice formations
Cableway to 1350 m/4430 ft, then 15 minutes on foot
Conducted tours daily in summer

6 Koppenbrüllerhöhle (Upper Austria)
Near Obertraun
Cavern with stalactites and stalagmites
Reached by footpath (20 minutes)
Conducted tours daily in summer

7 Gassl-Tropfsteinhöhle (Upper Austria)
Near Ebensee
Stalactitic cave (several chambers)
Footpath through forest from Ebensee (2¼ hours)
Conducted tours daily in summer

8 Kraushöhle (Styria)
Near Gams bei Hieflau
First cave in the world open to the public (1882); gypsum crystals
Narrow road from Gams; on foot, ½ hour
Conducted tours daily from spring to end October

9 Tropfsteinhöhle Griffen (Carinthia)
In Griffen
Coloured stalactites and stalagmites
Conducted tours daily in summer, Sat. and Sun. in spring and autumn

10 Hochkarschachthöhle (Lower Austria)
Near Gostling an der Ybbs
Several caverns, stalactites
Near the valley station of the Hochkar chair-lift
Conducted tours Sat. and Sun. throughout the year

11 Ötscher-Tropfsteinhöhle (Lower Austria)
Near Kienberg-Gaming
Stalactites and stalagmites; pools of water
Accessible by car
Conducted tours on Sat. and Sun. in summer, or by appointment

12 Nixhöhle (Lower Austria)
Near Frankenfels
Sinter formations
Footpath (30 minutes)
Conducted tours daily Easter to October

13 Tropfsteinhöhle Alland (Lower Austria)
Near Alland
Stalactitic cave
15 minutes' climb
Conducted tours on Sat. and Sun. Easter to late autumn

14 Einhornhöhle (Lower Austria)
Near Dreistetten
Bones of Ice Age mammals
Footpath (30 minutes)
Conducted tours daily in summer

15 Eisensteinhöhle (Lower Austria)
Near Brunn, on the Schneebergbahn

● Caves Open to the Public
● Mines Open to the Public
○ Open-Air Museums

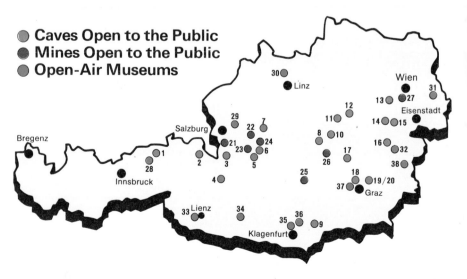

Sinter formations, underground hot spring
20 minutes' climb
Conducted tours on Sat. and Sun. May–October

16 Hermannschöhle (Lower Austria)
Near Kirchberg am Wechsel
Stalactites and stalagmites
Footpath (20 minutes)
Conducted tours daily in summer

17 Rettenwandhöhle (Styria)
Near Kapfenberg
Stalactites and stalagmites
Footpath (15 minutes)
Conducted tours on Sun. and public holidays
April–October

18 Lurgrotte (Styria)
Peggau-Semriach
Water, stalactites and stalagmites
Reached from Peggau or Semriach (10 minutes on foot)
Conducted tours from Peggau daily in summer, from Semriach by appointment

19 Katerloch (Styria)
Near Weiz
Huge stalactites and stalagmites
Accessible by car from Weiz
Conducted tours (strenuous) on Sat. and Sun.
Easter to end October

20 Grasslhöhle (Styria)
In Dürntal bei Weiz
Rich stalactitic and sinter formations
Accessible by car from Weiz
Conducted tours daily throughout the year according to demand

● Mines

21 Salzbergwerk Hallein (Salzburg province)
Near Dürnberg, above Hallein to the S (cableway)
Salt-mine
Conducted tours daily beginning May to end September

22 Salzbergwerk Bad Ischl (Upper Austria)
Entrance at Perneck, 3 km/2 miles S of Bad Ischl
Salt-mine
Conducted tours daily except Sun., mid May to mid September

23 Salzbergwerk Hallstatt (Upper Austria)
Above Hallstatt, to the NW (cableway)
Old salt-mine
Conducted tours daily April–October

24 Salzbergwerk Altaussee (Styria)
Entrance 3 km/2 miles NW of Altaussee
Salt-mine
Conducted tours on weekdays mid May to mid September; June–August also on Sat. and Sun.

25 Silberbergwerk Oberzeiring (Styria)
Silver-mine
Conducted tours daily
Museum at entrance to mine

26 Erzberg bei Eisenerz (Styria)
Iron-mine (opencast working)
Conducted tours daily at 10 a.m. and 2.30 p.m., May to end October, starting from the lower station of the old mine cableway

27 Seegrotte Hinterbrühl (Lower Austria)
Near Mödling
Old gypsum-mine
Conducted tours throughout the year; motorboat trip on underground lake

● Open-Air Museums

28 Kramsach (Tirol)
Museum village, near Kramsach am Inn,
15 km/9 miles SW of Kufstein
Old Tirolese peasant houses

29 Mondsee (Upper Austria)
Mondseer Rauchhaus
Old peasant house

30 Hellmonsödt (Upper Austria)
Mittermayerhof, Pelmberg,
12 km /7½ miles N of Linz

31 Carnuntum (Lower Austria)
Roman site near Petronell,
40 km/25 miles E of Vienna

32 Asparn (Lower Austria)
Museum of Prehistory in Schloss Asparn and its park

33 Oberlienz (East Tirol)
Griftljuden Open-Air Museum
3 km/2 miles NW of Lienz
Village smithy, corn mill, etc.

34 St Peter im Holz (Carinthia)
Teurnia Museum
5 km/3 miles NW of Spittal an der Drau
Early Christian basilica, Roman excavations

35 Magdalensberg (Carinthia)
Roman site
18 km/11 miles NE of Klagenfurt
May–October
Museum

36 Maria Saal (Carinthia)
Carinthian Open-Air Museum
8 km/5 miles NE of Klagenfurt
Peasant houses

37 Stübing bei Graz (Styria)
Austrian Open-Air Museum
15 km/9 miles NW of Graz
Peasant houses and other buildings
Open 1 April–31 October

38 Bad Tatzmannsdorf (Burgenland)
Burgenland Open-Air Museum
Old peasant houses

Winter Sports

Winter Sports Resorts
Summer Skiing Areas

● Winter Sports Resorts

1 Bodensee/Rheintal (Vorarlberg)
Places: Bregenz, Buch, Dornbirn, Eichenberg, Hohenems
Altitude: 400–800 m/1273–2546 ft
Cableways: to 1100 m/3500 ft
Cross-country ski trails: 40 km/25 miles

2 Vorarlberger Oberland (Vorarlberg)
Places: Feldkirch, Frastanz/Bazora, Laterns, Zwischenwasser/Furx
Altitude: 450–900 m/1432–2864 ft
Cableways: to 1800 m/2728 ft
Cross-country ski trails: 35 km/22 miles

3 Brandnertal-Bludenz (Vorarlberg)
Places: Bludenz, Brand, Bürs, Bürserberg
Altitude: 570–1050 m/1814–3341 ft
Cableways: to 1920 m/6109 ft
Cross-country ski trails: 30 km/19 miles

4 Montafon (Vorarlberg)
Places: Gargellen, Gaschurn, Gortipohl, Partenen, St Gallenkirch, Schruns, Silbertal, Tschagguns, Vadans
Altitude: 650–1420 m/2133–4660 ft
Cableways: to 2380 m/7811 ft
Cross-country ski trails: 40 km/25 miles

5 Grosswalsertal (Vorarlberg)
Places: Fontanella/Faschina, Raggal/Marul, Sonntag
Altitude: 900–1150 m/2954–3774 ft
Cableways: to 2000 m/6564 ft
Cross-country ski trails: 25 km/16 miles

6 Bregenzerwald (Vorarlberg)
Places: Alberschwende, Andelsbuch, Au, Bezau, Bizau, Damüls, Egg, Hittisau, Mellau, Schoppernau, Schröcken, Schwarzenberg, Sibratsgfäll, Sulzberg, Warth
Altitude: 600–1500 m/1969–4923 ft
Cableways: to 2050 m/6728 ft
Cross-country ski trails: 320 km/199 miles

7 Kleinwalsertal (Vorarlberg)
Places: Hirschegg, Mittelberg, Riezlern
Altitude: 1100–1200 m/3610–3938 ft
Cableways: to 2400 m/7877 ft
Cross-country ski trails: 40 km/25 miles

8 Klostertal (Vorarlberg)
Places: Braz, Dalaas, Klösterle/Langen, Wald
Altitude: 700–1100 m/2297–3610 ft
Cableways: to 2300 m/7549 ft
Cross-country ski trails: 25 km/16 miles

9 Arlberg (Vorarlberg/Tirol)
Places: Lech, St Anton, St Christoph, Stuben, Zürs
Altitude: 1400–1800 m/4595–5908 ft
Cableways: to 2800 m/9190 ft
Cross-country ski trails: 100 km/62 miles

10 Paznautal (Tirol)
Places: Galtür, Ischgl, Kappl, Pians, See
Altitude: 850–1600 m/2790–5251 ft
Cableways: to 2800 m/9190 ft
Cross-country ski trails: 55 km/34 miles

11 Upper Inn Valley (Tirol)
Places: Fiss, Ladis, Nauders, Pfunds, Ried im Oberinntal, Serfaus, Tösens
Altitude: 800–1400 m/2626–4595 ft
Cableways: to 2700 m/8861 ft
Cross-country ski trails: 170 km/106 miles

12 Kaunertal-Landeck (Tirol)
Places: Feichten, Fliess, Grins, Imsterberg, Kauns, Landeck, Mils, Prutz-Faggen-Fendels, Schönwies, Zams
Altitude: 800–1400 m/2626–4595 ft
Cableways: to 3200 m/10,500 ft
Cross-country ski trails: 90 km/56 miles

13 Pitztal-Imst (Tirol)
Places: Arzl-Wald, Haiming, Imst, Innerpitztal, Jerzens, Nassereith, Roppen, Tarrenz, Wenns-Piller
Altitude: 700–1800 m/2297–5908 ft
Cableways: to 3200 m/10,500 ft
Cross-country ski trails: 210 km/130 miles

14 Lechtal (Tirol)
Places: Bach, Boden-Bschlabs, Elbigenalp, Forchach, Stanzach, Steeg, Vorderhornbach, Weissenbach
Altitude: 900–1400 m/2954–4600 ft
Cableways: to 1800 m/5908 ft
Cross-country ski trails: 130 km/81 miles

15 Tannheim Valley (Tirol)
Places: Grän-Haldensee, Jungholz, Nesselwängle, Schattenwald, Tannheim, Zöblen
Altitude: 1100 m/3610 ft
Cableways: to 1900 m/6236 ft
Cross-country ski trails: 50 km/31 miles

16 Zwischentoren-Reutte (Tirol)
Places: Berwang, Biberwier, Birchlbach, Ehrwald, Heiterwang, Höfen, Lähn-Wengle, Lechaschau,

---

Austria occupies a leading place among the winter sports countries of Europe, and every winter thousands of visitors and skiing enthusiasts flock to its many winter sports resorts.

In addition to the internationally known and fashionable resorts with their lively social life and *après-ski* activities, where people go to be seen as well as to ski, there are many smaller and quieter ones with excellent facilities for winter sports of all kinds.

Everywhere there are good and well-maintained ski-runs, and access to the ski slopes is facilitated by numerous cableways, ski-lifts, etc. Many resorts also have toboggan runs and ice rinks, and there are increasing numbers of enclosed swimming pools and saunas. Everywhere, too, there are trails for those who like cross-country skiing.

Lermoos, Reutte, Wils, Wängle
Cableways: to 2950 m/9682 ft
Cross-country ski trails: 220 km/137 miles

17 Seefeld and Mieming Plateau (Tirol)
Places: Leutasch, Mieming, Mösern, Obsteig,
Reith bei Seefeld, Scharnitz, Seefeld, Telfs,
Wildermieming
Altitude: 650–1250 m/2133–4103 ft
Cableways: to 2100 m/6842 ft
Cross-country ski trails: 370 km/230 miles

18 Inn Valley and Sellrain (Tirol)
Places: Gries im Sellraintal, Hatting, Inzing,
Kematen, Kühtai, Mötz, Oberperfuss, Riez, St
Sigmund-Praxmar, Sellrain, Silz, Stams, Zirl
Altitude: 600–2000 m/1970–6565 ft
Cableways: to 2500 m/8205 ft
Cross-country ski trails: 130 km/81 miles

19 Ötztal (Tirol)
Places: Gries im Ötztal, Längenfeld-Huben,
Niederthai, Obergurgl-Hochgurgl, Ötz, Sautens,
Sölden/Hochsölden, Umhausen, Vent, Zwieselstein
Altitude: 1400–2200 m/4595–7220 ft
Cableways: to 3250 m/10,670 ft
Cross-country ski trails: 160 km/99 miles

20 Wipptal and Stubaital (Tirol)
Places: Fulpmes, Gries am Brenner, Gschnitz, Matrei
am Brenner, Mieders, Navis, Neustift, Obernberg, St
Jodak-Schmirn, Schönberg, Steinach am Brenner,
Telfes, Trins
Altitude: 950–1400 m/3118–4595 ft
Cableways: to 3200 m/10,500 ft
Cross-country ski trails: 460 km/286 miles

21 Innsbruck and district (Tirol)
Places: Aldrans, Axams, Birgitz, Götsens, Grinzens,
Innsbruck-Igls, Lans, Mutters, Natters, Patsch,
Sistrans
Altitude: 750–1000 m/2462–3282 ft

Cableways: to 2340 m/7680 ft
Cross-country ski trails: 170 km/106 miles

22 East of Innsbruck (Tirol)
Places: Absam, Ampass, Baumkirchen, Fritzens,
Gnardenwald, Hall in Tirol, Mils bei Hall, Rinn, Rum,
Tulfes, Volders, Wattens
Altitude: 550–920 m/1805–3020 ft
Cableways: to 2200 m/7220 ft
Cross-country ski trails: 100 km/62 miles

23 Zillertal (Tirol)
Places: Dornauberg-Ginzling, Finkenberg, Fügen,
Gerlos, Hart, Hippach, Kaltenbach, Mayrhofen, Ried,
Schlitters, Strass, Stumm-Stummerberg, Tuxertal,
Uderns, Zell am Ziller
Altitude: 500–1500 m/1640–4923 ft
Cableways: to 3260 m/10,700 ft
Cross-country ski trails: 240 km/150 miles

24 Achental-Schwaz and district (Tirol)
Places: Achenkirch, Jenbach, Maurach-Eben,
Münster, Pertisau, Schwaz-Pill, Stans, Steinberg am
Rofan, Vomp, Weerberg, Weer-Kolsass-Kolsassberg,
Wiesing
Cableways: to 2000 m/6564 ft
Cross-country ski trails: 220 km/125 miles

25 Inn Valley-Wildschönau-Alpbachtal (Tirol)
Places: Alpbach, Angerberg, Brandenberg,
Breitenbach am Inn, Brixlegg, Kramsach, Kundl,
Langkampfen, Mariastein, Rattenberg-Radfeld,
Reith im Alpbachtal, Wildschönau (Oberau,
Niederau Auffach), Wörgl

26 Kitzbühel Alps (Tirol)
Places: Aurach, Brixen im Thale, Ellmau, Hopfgarten
im Brixental, Itter, Jochberg, Keichsau, Kirchberg,
Kitzbühel, Oberndorf, Reith bei Kitzbühel, Söll,
Westendorf
Altitude: 700–860 m/2297–2823 ft
Cableways: to 2000 m/6565 ft
Cross-country ski trails: 250 km/155 miles

Skiing class, Arlberg

27　Kufstein and district (Tirol)
Places: Angath, Bad Häring, Ebbs, Erl,
Hinterthiersee, Kirchbichl, Kufstein, Landl,
Niederndorf, Scheffau, Schwoich, Thiersee
Altitude: 450–870 m/1477–2855 ft
Cableways: to 1700 m/5580 ft
Cross-country ski trails: 240 km/149 miles

28　Kaiserwinkel (Tirol)
Places: Erpfendorf, Fieberbrunn, Going, Hochfilzen,
Kirchdorf, Kössen, St Jakob i.H.,
St Ulrich am Pillensee, Schwendt, Waidring,
Walchsee
Altitude: 630–1000 m/2068–3282 ft
Cableways: to 1870 m/6137 ft
Cross-country ski trails: 470 km/292 miles

29　East Tirol north of Lienz
Places: Hopfgarten im Defereggental, Huben, Kals
am Grossglockner, Matrei in Osttirol, Prägraten, St
Jacob im Defereggental, St Veit im Defereggental,
Virgen
Altitude: 800–1400 m/2626–4595 ft
Cableways: to 2500 m/8205 ft
Cross-country ski trails: 130 km/81 miles

30　Pustertal and Lienz Dolomites (Tirol)
Places: Abfaltersbach, Ainet, Amlach, Anras,
Ausservillgraten, Dölsach, Heinfels, Innervillgraten,
Iselsberg-Stronach, Kartitsch, Lavant, Lienz,
Nikolsdorf, Oberlienz, Obertilliach, Sillian, Strassen,
Thal-Assling, Tristach
Altitude: 650–1450 m/2133–4760 ft
Cableways: to 2400 m/7877 ft
Cross-country ski trails: 220 km/137 miles

31　Salzburg and district (Salzburg province)
Places: Anif, Salzburg
Altitude: about 450 m/1477 ft
Cableways: to 1100 m/3610 ft
Cross-country ski trails: 20 km/12 miles

32　Tennengau and Salzburg Salzkammergut
(Salzburg province)
Places: Abtenau, Annaberg, Bad Dürrnberg,
Faistenau, Hintersee, Krispl-Gaissau, Kuchl,
Lungötz, Russbach, St Gilgen, St Martin am
Tennengebirge, Strobl
Altitude: 500–1000 m/1641–3282 ft
Cableways: to 1600 m/5250 ft
Cross-country ski trails: 250 km/155 miles

33　Hochkönig and Tennengebirge
(Salzburg province)
Places: Bischofshoften, Mühlbach am Hochönig,
Pfarrwerfen, Werfen, Werfenweng
Altitude: 500–1000 m/1641–3283 ft
Cableways: to 1900 m/6236 ft
Cross-country ski trials: 80 km/50 miles

34　Pinzgauer Saalachtal (Salzburg province)
Places: Leogang, Lofer, Maishofen, Maria Alm,
Saalbach-Hinterglemm, Saalfelden, Unken
Altitude: 700–1000 m/2297–3282 ft
Cableways: to 2000 m/6564 ft
Cross-country ski trails: 260 km/162 miles

**35　Unterpinzgau, Europa-Sportregion,
Oberpinzgau** (Salzburg province)
Places: Bruck am Grossglockner, Fusch an der
Grossglocknerstrasse, Kaprun, Königsleiten,
Krimml, Mittersill, Neukirchen am Grossvenediger,
Rauris, Uttendorf/Weissensee, Zell am See
Altitude: 750–1600 m/2462–5250 ft
Cableways: to 3000 m/9846 ft
Cross-country ski trails: 220 km/137 miles

36　Gasteinertal and Grossarltal
(Salzburg province)
Places: Badgastein, Bad Hofgastein, Dorfgastein,
Grossarl, Hüttschlag
Altitude: 800–1100 m/2626–3610 ft
Cableways: to 700 m/8861 ft
Cross-country ski trails: 120 km/75 miles

37　Radstädter Tauern, Sonnenterrasse
(Salzburg province)
Places: Altenmarkt-Zauchensee, Eben im Pongau,
Filzmoos, Flachau, Goldegg, Kleinarl, Obertauern/
Untertauern, Radstadt, St Johann/Alpendorf,
Wagrain
Altitude: 800–1800 m/2626–5908 ft
Cableways: to 2300 m/7550 ft
Cross-country ski trails: 180 km/112 miles

38　Lungau (Salzburg province)
Places: Mariapfarr, Mauterndorf, Obertauern/
Tweng, St Margarethen, St Michael, Tamsweg,
Thomatal-Schönfeld
Altitude: 1000–1800 m/3282–5908 ft
Cableways: to 2400 m/7879 ft
Cross-country ski trails: 250 km/155 miles

39　Goldberg and Mölltal National Park Region
(Carinthia)
Places: Flattach, Grosskirchheim im Mölltal,
Heiligenblut, Kolbnitz-Reisseck, Lurnfeld/
Möllbrücke, Mallnitz, Obervellach, Rangersdorf,
Stall, Winklern
Altitude: 700–1300 m/2297–4267 ft
Cableways: to 2700 m/8861 ft
Cross-country ski trails: 160 km/99 miles

40　Upper Drau Valley (Carinthia)
Places: Berg im Drautal, Dellach im Drautal,
Greifenburg, Irschen, Klebach-Lind, Oberdrauburg,
Steinfeld, Weissensee-Techendorf
Altitude: 600–1000 m/1969–3282 ft
Cableways: to 2200 m/7220 ft
Cross-country ski trails: 100 km/62 miles

41　Carnic ski-region (Carinthia)
Places: Dellach im Gailtal, Hermagor-Nassfeld,
Kirchbach im Gailtal, Kötschach-Mauthen,
Lesachtal, St Stefan im Gailtal, Weissbriach/
Gitschtal
Altitude: 600–1200 m/1969–3938 ft
Cableways: to 2000 m/6564 ft
Cross-country ski trails: 250 km/155 miles

42　Central Drau Valley region (Carinthia)
Places: Paternion, Stockenboi, Weissenstein
Altitude: 500–1000 m/1641–3282 ft
Cableways: to 2100 m/6892 ft
Cross-country ski trails: 80 km/50 miles

43　Millstätter See (Carinthia)
Places: Baldramsdorf, Feld am See, Ferndorf.
Fresach, Lendorf, Millstatt, Radenthein-Döbriach,
Seeboden, Spittal an der Drau
Altitude: 500–800 m/1641–2626 ft
Cableways: to 2100 m/6892 ft
Cross-country ski trails: 230 km/143 miles

44　Bad Kleinkirchheim (Carinthia)
Place: Bad Kleinkirchheim
Altitude: 1100 m/3610 ft
Cableways: to 2000 m/6564 ft
Cross-country ski trails: 20 km/12 miles

45　Lieser and Malta valleys (Carinthia)
Places: Gmünd, Krems in Kärnten, Malta, Rennweg-
Katschberg
Altitude: 700–1200 m/2297–3938 ft

Cableways: to 2200 m/7220 ft
Cross-country ski trails: 50 km/31 miles

46 Turrach, Hochrindl and Simonhöhe region
(Carinthia)
Places: Albeck/Sirnitz, Ebene Reichenau-Turracher Höhe, Feldkirchen, Glanegg, Gnesau, Himmelberg, St Urban am Urbansee, Steuerberg
Altitude: 500–1100 m/1641–3610 ft
Cableways: to 2300 m/7550 ft
Cross-country ski trails: 210 km/1130 miles

47 Villach Winter Sports region (Carinthia)
Places: Arnoldstein, Arriach, Bad Bleiberg, Faaker See-Finkenstein, Hohenthurn, Nötsch im Gailtal, Ossiach, St Jakob, Steindorf, Treffen/Sattendorf, Villach, Warmbad-Villach
Altitude: 500–1000 m/1641–3282 ft
Cableways: to 1900 m/6226 ft
Cross-country ski trails: 250 km/155 miles

48 Wörther See Region (Carinthia)
Places: Klagenfurt, Moosberg, Velden am Wörther See
Altitude: 400–500 m/1313–1641 ft
Cableways: to 600 m/1969 ft
Cross-country ski trails: 260 km/155 miles

49 Rosental region (Carinthia)
Places: Feistritz, Ferlach, Ludmannsdorf, Zeil
Altitude: 500–1000 m/1641–3282 ft
Cableways: to 1100 m/1969 ft
Cross-country ski trails: 70 km/43 miles

50 Völkermarkt region (Carinthia)
Places: Bleiburg, Diex, Eisenkappel-Vellach, Griffen, Neuhaus, Sittersdorf, Völkermarkt
Altitude: 500–1200 m/1641–3936 ft
Cableways: to 2000 m/6564 ft
Cross-country ski trails: 220 km/137 miles

51 St Veit an der Glan region (Carinthia)
Places: Metnitz, St Veit an der Glan, Weitensfeld, Flattnitz
Altitude: 500–1400 m/1641–4595 ft
Cableways: to 1900 m/6236 ft
Cross-country ski trails: 70 km/43 miles

52 Lavanttal region (Carinthia)
Places: Bad St Leonard, Lavamünd, Preitenegg, Reichenfels, St Andrä im Lavanttal, St Paul im

Lavanttal, Wolfsberg
Altitude: 400–1100 m/1313–3610 ft
Cableways: to 2200 m/7220 ft
Cross-country ski trails: 90 km/56 miles

53 Western Styria
Places: Bad Gams, Modriach, Pack, Salla, St Oswald ob Eibiswald, Schwanberg, Soboth, Trahütten
Altitude: 400–1200 m/1312–3938 ft
Cableways: to 1800 m/5908 ft
Cross-country ski trails: 80 km/50 miles

54 Mürztal, Roseggers, Waldheimat, Styrian Semmering, Mürzer Oberland, Upper Feistritztal (Styria)
Places: Falkenstein, Fischbach, Kapellen, an der Mürz, Kindberg, Krieglach/Alpl, Langenzwang, Mürzsteg, Mürzzuschlag, Neuberg an der Mürz, Ratten, Rettenegg, St Kathrein am Hauenstein, Spital/Steinhausn am Semmering
Altitude: 500–1100 m/1641–3610 ft
Cableways: to 1400 m/4595 ft
Cross-country ski trails: 200 km/124 miles

55 Hochschwab alpine region (Styria)
Places: Aflenz-Kurort, Breitenau bei Mixnitz, Etmissl, Gusswerk, Halltal, Mariazell, St Sebastian, Seewiesen, Tragöss, Turnau
Altitude: 600–1000 m/1969–3282 ft
Cableways: to 1800 m/5908 ft
Cross-country ski trails: 110 km/68 miles

56 Gesäuse alpine region (Styria)
Places: Admont, Altenmarkt/St Gallen, Ardning, Hieflau, Johnsbach, St Gallen, Weng bei Admont
Altitude: 500–800 m/1641–2626 ft
Cableways: to 1500 m/4923 ft
Cross-country ski trails: 1120 km/76 miles

57 Liesingtal alpine region (Styria)
Places: Gai, Kalwang, Kammern, Mautern, Traboch, Wald am Schoberpass
Altitude: 600–900 m/1969–2954 ft
Cableways: to 1200 m/3938 ft
Cross-country ski trails: 40 km/25 miles

58 Upper Mur valley (Styria)
Places: Judenburg, Krakaudorf, Murau, Obdach, St Wolfgang am Zirbitz, Oberwölz, Oberzeiring, Predlitz-Turrach, St Georgen-St Lorenzen, St Johann am Tauern, St Lambrecht

● Winter Sports Centres
● Summer Skiing Areas

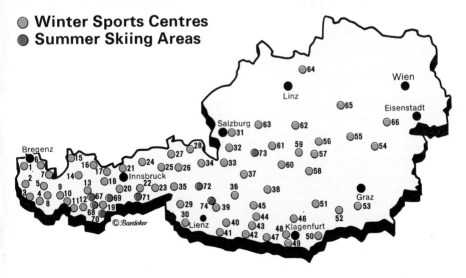

Altitude: 700–1200 m/2297–3938 ft
Cableways: to 2300 m/7550 ft
Cross-country ski trails: 260 km/162 miles

59 Heimat am Grimming (Styria)
Places: Aigen am Putterersee, Donnersbach-
Planneralm, Donnersbachwald-Riesneralm, Irdning,
Liezen-Lassing, Pürgg-Trautenfels, Wörschachwald,
St Martin am Grimming, Weissenbach bei Liezen
Altitude: 600–1000 m/1969–3282 ft
Cableways: to 1600 m/5250 ft
Cross-country ski trails: 120 km/78 miles

60 Dachstein-Tauern region (Styria)
Places: Aich-Assach, Gössenberg, Gröbming, Haus
in Ennstal, Mitterberg, Öblarn, Pruggern, Ramsau
am Dachstein, Rohrmoos-Untertal, Schladming
Altitude: 700–1100 m/2297–3610 ft
Cableways: to 2700 m/8861 ft
Cross-country ski trails: 250 km/155 miles

61 Strian Salzkammergut
Places: Altaussee, Bad Aussee, Bad Mitterndorf
Grundlsee, Pichl/Kainisch, Tauplitz/Tauplitzalm
Altitude: 600–900 m/1969–2954 ft
Cableways: to 2000 m/6564 ft
Cross-country ski trails: 100 km/62 miles

62 Pyhrn-Eisenwurzen (Upper Austria)
Places: Gaflenz-Forsteralm, Hinterstoder, Klaus,
Spital/Pyhrn, Ternberg, Vorderstoder,
Windischgarsten
Altitude: 500–800 m/1691–2626 ft
Cableways: to 1900 m/6263 ft
Cross-country ski trails: 200/124 miles

63 Salzkammergut (Upper Austria)
Places: Altmünster, Bad Goisern, Bad Ischl.
Ebensee, Gmunden, Gosau, Grünau im Almtal,
Hallstatt, Mondsee, Obertraun, St Wolfgang,
Scharnstein, Weyregg am Attersee
Altitude: 400–800 m/1313–2626 ft
Cableways: to 2100 m/6892 ft
Cross-country ski trails: 140 km/87 miles

64 Mühlviertel (Upper Austria)
Places: Bad Leonfelden, Haslach, Hellmonsödt,
Klaffer, Sandl, St Johann am Wimberg,
Schwarzenberg, Ulrichsberg
Altitude: 500–1000 m/1641–3282 ft
Cableways: to 1400 m/4595 ft
Cross-country ski trails: 780 km/485 miles

65 Alpine Foreland (Lower Austria)
Places: Annaberg, Gaming, Göstling an der Ybbs,
Hollenstein an der Ybbs, Lackenhof am Ötscher,
Lilienfeld, Lunz am See, Mitterbach am Erlaufsee,
Puchenstuban St Aegyd am Neuwalde, Türnitz,
Waidhofen an der Ybbs, Ybbsitz
Altitude: 300–1000 m/985–3282 ft
Cableways: to 1800 m/5908 ft
Cross-country ski trails: 150 km/93 miles

66 Niederösterreich alpin (Lower Austria)
Places: Aspangberg-St Peter, Grünbach am
Schneeberg, Mönichkirchen, Puchberg am
Schneeberg, Reichenau an der Rax, Rohr im
Gebirge, St Corona am Wechsel, Schottwien,
Semmering
Altitude: 500–1000 m/1641–3282 ft
Cableways: to 1600 m/5250 ft
Cross-country ski trails: 100 km/62 miles

● **Summer Skiing Areas** (map p. 291)

67 Mittelbergferner (Tirol)
Glacier area: 2730–3240 m/8959–10,634 ft
Reached from St Leonhard-Mittelberg im Pitztal

68 Rettenbachferner and Tiefenbachferner
(Tirol)
Glacier area: 2700–3300 m/8860–10,830 ft
Reached from Sölden in Otztal

69 Stubaier Gletscher and Daunkogelferner
(Tirol)
Glacier area: 2600–3200 m/8533–10,500 ft
Reached from Ranalt im Stubaital

70 Weissenseeferner (Tirol)
Glacier area: 2750–3160 m/9026–10,371 ft
Reached from Feichten im Kaunertal

71 Tuxer Ferner (Tirol)
Glacier area: 2660–3270 m/8736–10,732 ft
Reached from Hintertux

72 Kitzsteinhorn (Salzburg Province)
Glacier area: 2450–3030 m/8040–9944 ft
Reached from Kaprun

73 Dachstein (Steiermark)
Glacier area: 2520–2700 m/8270–8860 ft
Reached from Ramsau

Shopping and Souvenirs

In Austria there are still many small workshops producing a wide range of typical local
craft products. Textiles, pottery, wrought-
iron work and woodcarving are particularly
popular as souvenirs of Austria. Vorarlberg
and Tirol are noted for their fine embroidery,
wooden articles and pottery, Salzburg
province, Styria and Carinthia for wrought-
iron work, traditional costumes and ornaments, pewter and pottery, Lower Austria for
wrought-iron. The *Heimatwerk* shops in the
provincial capitals sell a tempting range of
local craft work. – Shopping in Vienna; see
under Vienna.

In Austria 30% VAT is charged on luxury articles
(jewellery, furs, etc.).
Visitors from other countries can recover this duty if the
value of the goods exceeds 1000 öS and they have not
been used before departure. The appropriate form (U34)
can be obtained in designated tax-free shops.

Calendar of Events

5 January
Salzburg (S), Gmunden (OÖ),   "Glöckerlaufen"
Ebensee (OÖ), Stainach (Stm)

6 January
Many places,   Three Kings
Gmunden (OÖ)   processions

January
Many places in Salzburg   Perchtenlaufen
province
Vienna   Balls
Baden bei Wien (NÖ)   Shrovetide
    celebrations

End January
Salzburg (S)   Mozart Week

January–February
Many places in Salzburg   "Aperschnalzen"
province

February
Many places   Shrovetide
    celebrations

March
Rauris (S)   Cultural Days
Vienna   Vienna Trade Fair

Easter
Salzburg   Easter Festival

April–September
Salzburg (S)   Puppet Theatre

30 April–1 May
Many places   Setting up the
    maypole

May
Many places   Corpus Christi
    processions
Hallstatt (OÖ), Traunkirchen   Corpus Christi
(OÖ)   processions on lake
Stubaital (T)   Tirolean Spring (Arts
    Festival)
Freistritz an der Gail (K)   "Kufenstechen"
    (tilting at a barrel)
Weitensfeld (K)   "Kranzlreiten"
Wiener Neustadt (NÖ)   May Festival

May–June
Forchtenstein (B)   Dramatic
    performances in
    castle
Vienna   Festival

May–September
Egg (V), Schwarzenberg (V),   Bregenzerwald
Reuthe (V)   Cultural Days
Bezau (V), Hittisau (V)
Dürnstein (NÖ)   Concert in convent
Erl (T)   Passion Play (every
    6 years: 1985, etc.)
St Margarethen (B)   Passion Play in
    Roman quarry
Vienna   Son et Lumière,
    Belvedere

May–October
Grafenegg (NÖ)   Concert in castle

Whitsun (Seventh Sunday after Easter)
Melk (NÖ)   Concert in abbey
Salzburg (S)   Whitsun Concerts

Beginning June
Poysdorf (NÖ)   Wine Parade
Salzburg (S)   "Dult"

Mid June
Many mountain villages   Midsummer bonfires

June
Hohenems (V)   Schubert Festival
St Pölten (NÖ)   Summer Festival
Schärding (OÖ)   Traditional Festival
Zederhaus (S)   "Pransgstangentra-
    gen" (procession
    with flower-covered
    poles)

June–July
St Florian (OÖ), Kremsünster   Upper Austria abbey
(OÖ), Garsten (OÖ)   concerts
Forchstenstein (B)   Dramatic
    performances in
    castle
Mauthausen (OÖ)   Theatrical
    performances
Mettmach (OÖ)   Passion play

June–August
Altenburg (NÖ)   Summer music in the
    Waldviertel
Innsbruck (T)   Schloss Ambras
    concerts in the
    Hofburg
Meggenhoften (OÖ)   Farmhouse theatre
Ossiach (K)   Carinthian Summer

June–September
Baden bei Wien (NÖ)   Operetta Festival
Vienna   Musical Summer

July
Many places in Salzburg   "Samson"
province   processions

"Perchtenlauf", St Johann im Pongau

July (cont'd.)

Gmunden am Traunsee (OÖ)	Lake Festival
Grein (OÖ)	Summer Festival in town theatre
Krems (NÖ)	Summer Festival
Mauterndorf, Tamsweg (S)	Samson processions
Laxenburg (NÖ)	Summer Festival
Nötsch in Gailtal (K)	"Kufenstechen" (tilting at barrels)
Perchtoldsdorf (NÖ)	Summer Festival
Schwechat (NÖ)	Nestroy Festival

July–August

Bad Ischl (OÖ)	Opretta Festival
Bregenz (V)	Lake Festival
Friesach (K)	Summer Festival
Gutenstein (NÖ)	Summer Festival
Innsbruck (T)	Tirolean Summer
Klaus (OÖ)	Musical Summer
Melk (NÖ)	Summer Festival
Mörbisch (K)	Summer Festival
Neulengbach (NÖ)	Summer Festival
Petronell (NÖ), Bad Deutsch Altenburg, Reichenau (NÖ)	Carnuntum Festival / Summer Festivals
Salzburg (S)	Festival
Schallaburg (NÖ)	Poets' Morning (Sundays)
Spittal an der Drau (K)	Dramatic performances in Schloss Porcia
Stams (T)	Summer concerts
Vienna	Chamber Opera in Schönbrunn theatre
Wilten (T)	Sacred music in the evening in basilica

July–September

Baden, St Pölten, Carnuntum, Krems, Melk, Reichenau, etc. (NÖ)	Lower Austrian Theatrical Summer
Millstatt (K)	International Organ Weeks

15 August

Throughout Tirol	Hoher Frauentag (Assumption: mass processions)

August

Many places in Burgenland	Vintage Festivals
Many places in Salzburg province and Styria	"Samson" processions
Alpbach (T)	Alpbach Forum

Herzogenburg (NÖ)	International Puppet Theatre Festival
Knittelfeld (Stm)	Austrian Grand Prix (formula one)
Maria Alm am Steinernen Meer (S)	St Bartholomew's Day pilgrimage to the Königssee
Meer (S)	Pilgrimage to the Königssee
Oberndorf aan der Salzach (S)	"Schifferstechen" (tilting on the water)
Obervellach (K)	Cultural Weeks
Rust (B)	Golden Wine Week
St Wolfgang im Salzkammergut (OÖ)	Church Music Weeks
Stockerau (NÖ)	Open-air Festival
Tamsweg (S)	"Preberschiessen"
Many places	Almbtrieb (return from the mountain pastures)

Beginning September

Many places	Harvest Festival

September

Böckstein (S)	Sword dancing by upland people
Vienna	Trade Fair

September–October

Lillenfield, Herzogenburg and St Pölten (NÖ)	Lower Austrian Church Music Days
Linz (OÖ)	International Bruckner Festival
Retz (NÖ)	Vintage Festival
St Veit an der Glan (K)	Wiesenmarkt ("Meadow Market")

October

Vienna	Viennale (Film Festival)

October–November

Graz (Stm)	Styrian Autumm (avant-garde festival)

5/6 November

Many places	"Leonhardiritt" (St Leonard's Ride)

15 November

Klosterneuburg (NÖ)	"Fasslrutschen" (sliding down a large cask)

November

Vienna	Austrian Book Weeks / Schubert Festival / Antiques Fair

November–December

Vienna (W), Salzburg (S)	Christkindlmarkt (Christ Child Market)

December

Many places in Tirol	St Nicholas and "Krampus" processions
Everywhere	Midnight Mass

31 December

Baden bei Wien (NÖ)	New Year Gala
Vienna	New Year's Eve concert by Vienna Philharmonic / Imperial Ball (Kaiserball)

Members of the Riflemen's Club, Navis (Tirol)

Information

Austrian National Tourist Office
(Österreich Information)

Head Office
Margaretenstr. 1,
A-1040 **Wien**;
tel. (02 22) 58 72 000

United States
500 Fifth Avenue,
New York, NY 10110;
tel. (212) 944 6880

500 North Mich. Ave.,
Suite 544,
Chicago, IL 60611,
tel. (312) 644-5556

11601 Wilshire Boulevard, Suite 2480,
Los Angeles, CA 90025,
tel. (213) 477-3332

4800 San Felipe St.,
Suite 500,
Houston, TX 77056;
tel. (713) 850 9999

United Kingdom
30 St George Street,
London, WIR 9FA;
tel. (01) 629 0461

Ireland
4 Ardonyne House,
Pembroke Park, Ballsbridge,
Dublin, 4;
tel. (01) 68 33 21

Canada
2 Bloor Street East, Suite 3330,
Toronto, Ontario M4W 1A8;
tel. (416) 967 3381

1010 Sherbrooke Street West, Suite 1410,
Montreal, P.Q. H3A 2R7;
tel. (514) 849 3709

Suite 1220–1223, Vancouver Block,
736 Granville Street,
Vancouver, B.C. V6Z 1J2;
tel. (604) 683 5808–09

Austrian Automobile and Touring Club
(Österreichischer Automobilund Touring-Club, ÖAMTC)

Schubertring 1–3.
A-1010 **Wien**;
tel. (02 22) 72 99–0

Branch offices in all the larger Austrian towns

Driving, Motoring and Cycling Union of Austria
(Auto-, Motor- und Radfahrerbund Österreichs, ARBÖ)

Mariahilfer Strasse 180,
A-1150 **Wien**;
tel. (02 22) 85 35 35–0

Austrian Alpine Club
(Österreichischer Alpenverein, ÖAV)

Wilhelm–Greil Strasse 15,
A-6010 **Innsbruck**;
tel. (0 52 22) 2 31 71

Branches *(Sektionen)* in many towns and villages

Diplomatic and Consular Offices in Austria

United States
Embassy
Boltzmanngasse 16,
A-1091 **Wien** IX;
tel. (02 22) 31 55 11

Consulate See Embassy

Canada
Embassy
Dr.-Karl-Lueger-Ring 10,
A-1010 **Wien**;
tel. (02 22) 63 66 26–28

United Kingdom
Embassy
Reisnerstrasse 40,
A-1030 **Wien**;
tel. (02 22) 73 15 75–79

Consular Section,
Wallnerstrasse 8,
A-1010 **Wien**;
tel. (02 22) 63 75 02

Consulate
Salurnerstrasse 15/IV,
A-6020 **Innsbruck**;
tel. (0 52 22) 2 83 20

Airlines

Austria Airlines
Kärntner Ring 18,
A-1010 **Wien I;**
tel. (02 22) 65 57 57

608 Fifth Avenue, Suite 507,
New York

50 Conduit Street,
London W1

Trans World Airlines Inc.
Opernring 1/R/742,
A-1010 **Wien**
tel. (02 22) 56 32 00 or (02 22) 56 32 66

TWA General Sales Agents:
Austrian Airlines,
Kärntner Ring 18,
A-1010 **Wien**
tel. Ticket Office (02 22) 56 57 57
    Reservations (02 22) 68 00

Pan American World Airways
Kärntner Ring 5,
A-1010 **Wien;**
tel. (02 22) 52 66 46

Royal Jordanian Airlines
229 Peachtree Street N.E.,
Suite 2415,
Atlanta, GA30303;
tel. (404) 659 2542

104 South Michigan Avenue,
Suite 215,
Chicago, Illinois, 60603;
tel. (312) 236 1702

Tower 14,
Suite 998,
21700 North Western Highway,
Southfield, Mich., 48075;
tel. (313) 424 9233/4/5

Jefferson Chemical Bldg,
3336 Richmond Avenue,
Suite 314,
Houston, Texas, 77098;
tel. (713) 524 3700

510 West 6 Street,
Suite 1132,
Los Angeles, Calif., 90014;
tel. (213) 623 3376/7/8

545 Fifth Avenue,
New York, NY 10017;
tel. (212) 949 0044

1925 K Street North West,
Suite 501,
Washington, DC, 20006;
tel. (202) 857 0401

AM Stadpark
City Air Terminal,
1030 **Wien;**
tel. (02 22) 72 32 42/43 or (02 22) 72 44 21

Romanian Airlines
Tarom Romanian Air Transport,
Wahringerstrasse,
6–8 **Wien;**
tel. (02 22) 34 53 06 or (02 22) 34 31 57

Tarom Romanian Air Transport,
200 East 38th Street,
New York, NY 10016;
tel. (212) 687 6013/6014

British Airways
Kärntner Ring 10,
A-1010 **Wien I;**
tel. (02 22) 65 76 91

Griesgasse 29,
A-5020 **Salzburg;**
tel. (0 62 22) 4 21 09–09

International Telephone Dialling Codes

From the United States or Canada to Austria	**011 43**
From the United Kingdom to Austria	**010 43**
From Austria to the United States or Canada	**01**
From Austria to the United Kingdom	**0 44**

In dialling an international call the zero prefix.d to the local dialling code should be omitted

Emergency calls

The following emergency numbers apply throughout Austria:

Police: dial **133**

First Aid
(Ambulance)   dial **144**

At intervals along motorways there are **emergency telephones which can be used to summon help in case of emergency or breakdown**

(In general, place-names are given in their German form. For the meaning of topographical terms incorporated in place-names – e.g. *Tal, -tal*, "valley", or *Stift, Kloster*, "monastery, abbey, etc.", see the Glossary on p. 264.)

Baedeker's Travel Guides

"The maps and illustrations are lavish. The arrangement of information (alphabetically by city) makes it easy to use the book."
—*San Francisco Examiner-Chronicle*

What's there to do and see in foreign countries? Travelers who rely on Baedeker, one of the oldest names in travel literature, will miss nothing. Baedeker's bright red, internationally recognized covers open up to reveal fascinating A-Z directories of cities, towns, and regions, complete with their sights, museums, monuments, cathedrals, castles, gardens and ancestral homes—an approach that gives the traveler a quick and easy way to plan a vacation itinerary.

And Baedekers are filled with over 200 full colour photos and detailed maps, including a full-size, fold-out roadmap for easy vacation driving. Baedeker—the premier name in travel for over 150 years.

Please send me the books checked below:

☐ **Austria** $16.95
0–13–056127–4

☐ **Caribbean** $16.95
0–13–056143–6

☐ **Costa Brava** $11.95
0–13–055880–X

☐ **Denmark** $16.95
0–13–058124–0

☐ **Egypt** $16.95
0–13–056358–7

☐ **France** $16.95
0–13–055814–1

☐ **Germany** $16.95
0–13–055830–3

☐ **Great Britain** $16.95
0–13–055855–9

☐ **Greece** $16.95
0–13–056002–2

☐ **Greek Islands** $11.95
0–13–058132–1

☐ **Ireland** $16.95
0–13–058140–2

☐ **Israel** $16.95
0–13–056176–2

☐ **Italy** $16.95
0–13–055897–4

☐ **Japan** $16.95
0–13–056382–X

☐ **Loire** $11.95
0–13–056375–7

☐ **Mediterranean Islands** $16.95
0–13–056862–7

☐ **Mexico** $16.95
0–13–056069–3

☐ **Netherlands, Belgium and Luxembourg** $16.95
0–13–056028–6

☐ **Portugal** $16.95
0–13–056135–5

☐ **Provence/Côte d'Azur** $11.95
0–13–056938–0

☐ **Rail Guide to Europe** $16.95
0–13–055971–7

☐ **Rhine** $11.95
0–13–056466–4

☐ **Scandinavia** $16.95
0–13–056085–5

☐ **Spain** $16.95
0–13–055913–X

☐ **Switzerland** $16.95
0–13–056044–8

☐ **Turkish Coast** $11.95
0–13–058173–9

☐ **Tuscany** $11.95
0–13–056482–6

☐ **Yugoslavia** $16.95
0–13–056184–3

Please turn the page for an order form and a list of additional Baedeker Guides.

A series of city guides filled with color photographs and detailed maps and floor plans from one of the oldest names in travel publishing:

Please send me the books checked below:

☐ **Amsterdam**......................$11.95
   0–13–057969–6

☐ **Athens**...........................$11.95
   0–13–057977–7

☐ **Bangkok**.........................$11.95
   0–13–057985–8

☐ **Berlin**...........................$11.95
   0–13–367996–9

☐ **Brussels**.........................$11.95
   0–13–368788–0

☐ **Budapest**........................$11.95
   0–13–058199–2

☐ **Cologne**.........................$11.95
   0–13–058181–X

☐ **Copenhagen**....................$11.95
   0–13–057993–9

☐ **Florence**.........................$11.95
   0–13–369505–0

☐ **Frankfurt**........................$11.95
   0–13–369570–0

☐ **Hamburg**........................$11.95
   0–13–369687–1

☐ **Hong Kong**......................$11.95
   0–13–058009–0

☐ **Istanbul**.........................$11.95
   0–13–058207–7

☐ **Jerusalem**.......................$11.95
   0–13–058017–1

☐ **London**...........................$11.95
   0–13–058025–2

☐ **Madrid**...........................$11.95
   0–13–058033–3

☐ **Moscow**..........................$11.95
   0–13–058041–4

☐ **Munich**...........................$11.95
   0–13–370370–3

☐ **New York**........................$11.95
   0–13–058058–9

☐ **Paris**.............................$11.95
   0–13–058066–X

☐ **Prague**...........................$11.95
   0–13–058215–8

☐ **Rome**.............................$11.95
   0–13058074–0

☐ **San Francisco**..................$11.95
   0–13–058082–1

☐ **Singapore**.......................$11.95
   0–13–058090–2

☐ **Stuttgart**........................$11.95
   0–13–058223–9

☐ **Tokyo**............................$11.95
   0–13–058108–9

☐ **Venice**...........................$11.95
   0–13–058116–X

☐ **Vienna**...........................$11.95
   0–13–371303–2

PRENTICE HALL PRESS
Order Department—Travel Books
200 Old Tappan Road
Old Tappan, New Jersey 07675
In U.S. include $1 postage and handling for 1st book, 25¢ each additional book.
Outside U.S. $2 and 50¢ respectively.

Enclosed is my check or money order for $_____

NAME_____

ADDRESS_____

CITY_____STATE_____ZIP_____